CHRONOLOGY AND FACT BOOK
OF
THE UNITED NATIONS

1941-1991

Annual Review of the United Nations Affairs

Kumiko Matsuura
Joachim W. Müller
Karl P. Sauvant

OCEANA PUBLICATIONS, INC.
DOBBS FERRY, New York

International Standard Book Number (ISBN): 0-379-21200-5

International Standard Serial Number (ISSN): 0066-4340

©Copyright 1992 by Oceana Publications, Inc.

Manufactured in the United States of America

PREFACE

The *Chronology and Fact Book of the United Nations* is a supplement to the series *Annual Review of United Nations Affairs (ARUNA)*. It is the eighth edition of its kind, providing an up-to-date summary of the past 50 years of the United Nations' history.

This edition is issued at an important point of time for the United Nations. The end of the Cold War era and the new, constructive dialogue between North and South have improved dramatically the climate in which the United Nations is operating. This has enabled the organization to become a key player in international affairs. The involvement of the United Nations in Namibia, Central America, Afghanistan, the Iran-Iraq war, Western Sahara, Cambodia, Kuwait and Yugoslavia are recent cases that highlight its new importance. It is therefore appropriate to update the previous edition of the *Chronology and Fact Book of the United Nations* in order to reflect these historic events and the new data of those recent years.

The publication contains three major parts: (i) a *CHRONOLOGY* (chapter I) of events for a period of 50 years, from 1941 to 1991; (ii) a number of *TABLES* (chapter II) containing basic information; and (iii) the main *DOCUMENTS* (chapter III) of the United Nations.

The *CHRONOLOGY* is based on the presentation as shown in the journal *United Nations Chronicle* issued by the United Nations Department for Public Information. When selecting the events for inclusion in the chronology, an attempt was made to strike a balance between the need to be comprehensive and concise, the anticipated interest of readers and, most of all, to reflect adequately the presentation of events as shown in the United Nations publication. As such, the chronology is also a mirror on how the United Nations presents itself to the public through the medium of its journal, the *United Nations Chronicle*. Changes over time in the presentation of the journal are, therefore, reflected in the presentation of the *CHRONOLOGY*. To provide for consistency, a number of general guidelines were followed in the compilation of events: (i) activities of specialized United Nations agencies are, in general, not reported; (ii) in particular during the recent years of the chronology, limited reference is made to decisions of United Nations expert groups, committees or commissions, in order to avoid duplication, since those decisions are in general approved by the General Assembly, at which stage they are reported in the chronology; (iii) prominence is given to the deliberation in the Security Council; (iv) related non-United Nations events and meetings have been recalled in case they are seen as important for United Nations activities; (v) the dates of the sessions of the General Assembly, ECOSOC and Trusteeship Council are noted; (vi) more details on events and the actual contents of decisions have been provided for the most recent years;

and (vii) the identification of individuals has been kept to a minimum, with typically only their function being cited.

Chapter II presents *TABLES* on a wide variety of issues, including a listing of United Nations member states, membership in the United Nations organs, the terms of office of the Secretary-Generals, the Presidents of United Nations organs, information on United Nations peace-keeping operations, the observance of international events, and details on the regular budget of the United Nations. The chapter concludes with a listing of the specialized agencies of the United Nations and the World Bank Group.

Chapter III shows basic *DOCUMENTS*, including the Charter of the United Nations and the Statute of the International Court of Justice. The Rules of Procedure of the United Nations organs are included, followed by the Staff Regulations of the United Nations.

We hope that the *Chronology and Fact Book of the United Nations* provides easy access to basic information on the United Nations and contributes to a better understanding of its activities. Needless to say, this publication does not necessarily reflect the views of the institutions with which the editors are affiliated.

Vienna and New York

Kumiko Matsuura
Joachim W. Müller
Karl P. Sauvant

TABLE OF CONTENTS

LIST OF ABBREVIATIONS

ACC	Administrative Committee on Co-ordination
AIDS	Acquired Immunodeficiency Syndrome
ANC	African National Congress
ANDP	Alliance Nationale Démocratique Populaire
ASEAN	Association of Southeast Asian Nations
CIAV	International Support and Verification Commission
CIS	Commonwealth of Independent States
CNR	National Reconciliation Commission of Guatemala
CPC	Committee for Programme and Co-ordination
CSDHA	Centre for Social Development and Humanitarian Affairs
CSTD	Centre for Science and Technology for Development
DAM	Department of Administrative and Management
DCS	Department of Conference Services
DDA	Department for Disarmament
DIESA	Department of International Economic and Social Affairs
DOMREP	Mission of the Representative of the Secretary-General in the Dominican Republic
DPI	Department of Public Information
DPSCA	Department of Political and Security Council Affairs
DSPQRCDT	Department for Special Political Questions, Regional Co-operation, Decolonization and Trusteeship
DTCD	Department of Technical Co-operation for Development
ECA	Economic Commission for Africa
ECDC	Economic Co-operation among Developing Countries
ECE	Economic Commission for Europe
ECLA	Economic Commission for Latin America
ECLAC	Economic Commission for Latin America and the Caribbean
ECOSOC	Economic and Social Council of the United Nations
ECOWAS	Economic Community of West African States
ECWA	Economic Commission for Western Asia
EEC	European Economic Community
ESCAP	Economic and Social Commission for Asia and the Pacific
ESCWA	Economic and Social Commission for Western Asia
FAO	Food and Agriculture Organization of the United Nations
FMLN	Frente Farabundo Martí para la Liberación Nacional
FNCD	Front National Pour le Changement et la Démocratie
FUNCINPEC	National United Front for an Independent, Neutral, Peaceful and Co-operative Cambodia
GATT	General Agreement on Tariffs and Trade
Habitat	United Nations Centre for Human Settlement
HIV	Human Immune-deficiency Virus
IAEA	International Atomic Energy Agency
IBRD	International Bank for Reconstruction and Development
ICAO	International Civil Aviation Organization
ICC	International Chamber of Commerce
IDA	International Development Association
IDB	Islamic Development Bank
IDB	Inter-American Development Bank
IDDA	Industrial Development Decade for Africa
IDNDR	International Decade for Natural Disaster Reduction
IDS	International Development Strategy
IFAD	International Fund for Agricultural Development
IFC	International Finance Corporation
ILO	International Labour Organization
IMF	International Monetary Fund

IMO	International Maritime Organization
INCB	International Narcotics Control Board
INTERPOL	International Criminal Police Organization
IOC	International Olympic Committee
IPC	Integrated Programme for Commodities
IPU	Inter-Parliamentary Union
ITC	International Trade Centre
ITU	International Telecommunication Union
JIM	Jakarta Informal Meeting
JIU	Joint Inspection Unit
KPNLF	Khmer People's National Liberation Front
LAS	League of Arab States
LDCs	Least Developed Countries
MINURSO	United Nations Mission for the Referendum in Western Sahara
MULPOC	Multinational Programming and Operational Centre
NASA	National Aeronautics and Space Administration (USA)
NGO	Non-Governmental Organization
NNRC	Neutral Nations Repatriation Commission
NNSC	Neutral Nations Supervisory Commission
NPT	Non-Proliferation of Nuclear Weapons Treaty
OAS	Organization of American States
OAU	Organization of African Unity
ODA	Official Development Assistance
OECD	Organization for Economic Co-operation and Development
OEOA	Office of Emergency Operations in Africa
OLADE	Latin American Energy Organization
ONUCA	United Nations Observer Group in Central America
ONUSAL	United Nations Observer Mission in El Salvador
ONUVEH	Observation Mission for the Verification of Elections in Nicaragua
OPEC	Organization of Petroleum Exporting Countries
ORCI	Office for Research and the Collection of Information
OSGAP	Office of the Secretary-General in Afghanistan and Pakistan
OTC	Organization of Trade Co-operation
PAC	Pan-African Congress of Azania
PCC	Paris Conference on Cambodia
PDK	Party of Democratic Kampuchea
PLO	Palestine Liberation Organization
POLISARIO	Frente Popular para la Liberación de Saguia el-Hamra y de Río de Oro
SADCC	Southern African Development Co-ordination Conference
SAP	Structural Adjustment Programme
SELA	Latin American Economic System
SNC	Supreme National Council
SUNFED	Special United Nations Fund for Economic Development
SWAPO	South-West Africa People's Organization
TNC	Transnational Corporation
TPO	Trade Promotion Organization
UAR	United Arab Republic
UK	United Kingdom
UN	United Nations
UN-PAAERD	United Nations Programme of Action for African Economic Recovery and Development
UNAMIC	United Nations Advance Mission in Cambodia
UNAVEM	United Nations Angola Verification Mission
UNCED	United Nations Conference on Environment and Development
UNCHS	United Nations Centre for Human Settlements (Habitat)
UNCND	United Nations Commission on Narcotic Drugs
UNCOK	United Nations Commission on Korea

UNCPCJP	United Nations Crime Prevention and Criminal Justice Programme
UNCPICPUNE	United Nations Conference for the Promotion of International Co-operation in the Peaceful Use of Nuclear Energy
UNCRD	United Nations Centre for Regional Development
UNCTAD	United Nations Conference on Trade and Development
UNCURG	United Nations Commission for the Unification and Rehabilitation of Korea
UNDND	United Nations Division of Narcotic Drugs
UNDOF	United Nations Disengagement Observer Force
UNDP	United Nations Development Programme
UNDRO	United Nations Disaster Relief Organization
UNDTCD	United Nations Department of Technical Co-operation for Development
UNEF	United Nations Emergency Force
UNEP	United Nations Environment Programme
UNEPRO	United Nations Relief Operation in East Pakistan
UNESCO	United Nations Educational, Scientific and Cultural Organization
UNFDAC	United Nations Fund for Drug Abuse Control
UNFICYP	United Nations Peace-keeping Force in Cyprus
UNFPA	United Nations Population Fund
UNGOMAP	United Nations Good Offices Mission in Afghanistan and Pakistan
UNHCR	United Nations High Commissioner for Refugees
UNICEF	United Nations Children's Fund
UNIDO	United Nations Industrial Development Organization
UNIFEM	United Nations Development Fund for Women
UNIFIL	United Nations Interim Force in Lebanon
UNIIMOG	United Nations Iran-Iraq Military Observer Group
UNIKOM	United Nations Iraq-Kuwait Observation Mission
UNIPOM	United Nations India Pakistan Observer Mission
UNITA	Uniao Nacional Para a Independencia Total de Angola
UNITAR	United Nations Institute for Training and Research
UNKRA	United Nations Korean Relief and Reconstruction Agency
UNOGIL	United Nations Observers Group in Lebanon
UNOGIP	United Nations Military Observer Group in India and Pakistan
UNPROFOR	United Nations Protection Force
UNRPR	United Nations Relief for Palestine Refugees
UNRWA	United Nations Relief and Works Agency for Palestine Refugees in the Near East
UNRWAPRNE	United Nations Relief and Works Agency for Palestine Refugees in the Near East
UNSCOB	United Nations Special Committee on the Balkans
UNSCOP	United Nations Special Commission on Palestine
UNSF	United Nations Security Force in West New Guinea (West Irian)
UNTAG	United Nations Transition Assistance Group
UNTCOK	United Nations Temporary Commission on Korea
UNTSO	United Nations Truce Supervision Organization
UNU	United Nations University
UPU	Universal Postal Union
URNG	Unidad Revolucionaria Nacional Guatemalteca
USA	United States of America
USSR	United Soviet Socialist Republics
WFC	World Food Council
WFP	World Food Programme
WHO	World Health Organization
WIPO	World Intellectual Property Organization
WMO	World Meteorological Organization
WTO	World Tourism Organization
WWF	World Wildlife Fund

CHAPTER I
_____

CHRONOLOGY

1941

Aug. 14   ATLANTIC CHARTER: Statement of principles to govern the establishment of a world-wide system of security.

1942

Jan. 1   DECLARATION BY UNITED NATIONS: Atlantic Charter is supported by 26 states.

1943

Oct. 30   MOSCOW DECLARATION: China, UK, USA and USSR agree on the necessity for an international organization.

1944

May 1-17   COMMONWEALTH MEETING: Commonwealth prime ministers reach agreement that UK should discuss plans for an international organization with signers of Moscow Declaration.

Aug. 21-Sept. 29   PREPARATORY MEETING: UK, USA and USSR negotiate modalities of international organization.

Sept. 29-Oct. 7   PREPARATORY MEETING: China, UK and USA negotiate modalities of international organizations.

Oct. 9   DUMBARTON OAKS: Recommendation on the establishment of an international organization is approved.

Nov. 1-6   WELLINGTON CONFERENCE: Australia and New Zealand approve twelve resolutions on an international organization.

1945

Jan. 30-Feb. 2   MALTA CONFERENCE: UK and USA meet prior to Yalta Conference.

Feb. 4-11   SECURITY COUNCIL: UK, USA and USSR agree on Security Council voting formula during the Yalta Conference.

Feb. 21-March 8   INTERAMERICAN CONFERENCE ON PROBLEMS OF WAR AND PEACE: American republics, except Argentina, agree that Dumbarton Oaks proposals constitute basis for an international organization.

April 4-13   COMMONWEALTH MEETING: Agreement is reached that Dumbarton Oaks proposals provide base for an international organization.

April 9-June 25   CHARTER: Conference on international organization is attended by representatives from 50 nations and drafts UN Charter.

1945 (continued)

April 9-20	INTERNATIONAL COURT OF JUSTICE: Committee of jurists, attended by representatives from 44 nations, drafts statute for an International Court of Justice.
June 7	SECURITY COUNCIL: Agreement is reached on Security Council voting procedures.
June 26	CHARTER: 50 nations sign UN Charter.
June 27	PREPARATORY COMMISSION OF THE UN: 1st meeting.
July 6	CHARTER: 1st ratification by Nicaragua.
Aug. 8	CHARTER: USA deposits 1st ratification.
Aug. 16-Nov. 24	PREPARATORY COMMISSION: Executive Committee meets.
Oct. 24	CHARTER: Comes into force with deposit of instrument of ratification by USSR.
Nov. 15	ATOMIC ENERGY: Canada, UK and USA agree on the establishment of a UN commission on atomic energy.
Nov. 24-Dec. 23	PREPARATORY COMMISSION: 2nd session.
Dec. 16-26	ATOMIC ENERGY: Council of foreign ministers of UK, USA and USSR agree on the establishment of a UN commission on atomic energy.

1946

Jan. 10-Feb. 14	GENERAL ASSEMBLY: Part one of 1st regular session.
Jan. 17	SECURITY COUNCIL: 1st meeting.
Jan. 19	IRAN: 1st dispute is brought to Security Council, concerning the presence of USSR troops in Iran.
Jan. 21	GREECE: USSR requests Security Council to consider presence of British troops.
	INDONESIA: Ukraine requests Security Council to consider presence of British troops.
Jan. 23-Feb. 18	ECOSOC: 1st regular session.
Jan. 24	ATOMIC ENERGY: General Assembly establishes the UN Atomic Energy Commission.
Jan. 25	MEMBERSHIP: Albania applies.
Feb. 1	SECRETARY-GENERAL: General Assembly appoints Trygve Lie of Norway as Secretary-General.
Feb. 4	MILITARY STAFF COMMITTEE: 1st meeting.
	SYRIA-LEBANON: Syria and Lebanon requests Security Council to consider presence of French-British troops.
Feb. 6	INTERNATIONAL COURT OF JUSTICE: 1st judge is elected.
Feb. 9	NON-SELF-GOVERNING TERRITORIES: General Assembly requests the Secretary-General to include in his annual report summaries of information received.
Feb. 14	HEADQUARTERS: General Assembly chooses New York as interim headquarters.

1946 (continued)

Feb. 16	COMMISSIONS: ECOSOC establishes Commission on Narcotic Drugs; Economic and Employment Commission; Commission on Human Rights; Temporary Social Commission; Statistical Commission; Temporary Transport and Communication Commission.
	SYRIA-LEBANON: USSR vetoes draft resolution of the Security Council on recommendations to the parties; 1st Security Council veto.
March 21	HEADQUARTERS: Temporary headquarters are established at Hunter College, New York.
April 3	INTERNATIONAL COURT OF JUSTICE: 1st meeting.
April 8-18	LEAGUE OF NATIONS: Dissolved.
April 8	SPAIN: Poland requests Security Council to consider situation.
May 25-June 21	ECOSOC: 2nd regular session.
June 14	ATOMIC ENERGY: USA proposes International Atomic Development Authority to UN Atomic Energy Commission (Baruch plan).
June 18	SPAIN: USSR vetoes draft resolutions of the Security Council on (i) the endorsement of certain principles; (ii) the recommendation to the General Assembly; (iii) the recommendation to the Secretary-General; (iv) the pronouncement on containing substance of matters.
June 19-July 22	HEALTH: UN International Health Conference drafts Constitution for World Health Organization (WHO).
June 19	ATOMIC ENERGY: USSR proposes convention to outlaw production and use of atomic weapons to UN Atomic Energy Commission.
June 21	COMMISSIONS: ECOSOC authorizes Sub-commission on Freedom of Information; Commission on the Status of Women; Sub-commission on Devastated Areas.
	NON-GOVERNMENTAL ORGANIZATIONS: ECOSOC establishes consultative status.
June 24	MEMBERSHIP: Mongolia applies.
June 26	SPAIN: France and USSR veto draft resolution of the Security Council on the simultaneous discussion by the General Assembly.
	SPAIN: USSR vetoes draft resolution of the Security Council on retention of item on agenda.
July 2	MEMBERSHIP: Afghanistan applies.
July 8	MEMBERSHIP: Jordan applies.
July 29-Sep. 13	RECONSTRUCTION: 1st session of the Temporary Sub-commission on the Economic Reconstruction of Devastated Areas.
Aug. 1	LEAGUE OF NATIONS: Property and assets are transferred to UN.
Aug. 2	MEMBERSHIP: Iceland, Ireland, Portugal apply.

1946 (continued)

Aug. 5	MEMBERSHIP: Thailand applies.
Aug. 9	MEMBERSHIP: Sweden applies.
Aug. 16-19	HEADQUARTERS: Moves to Lake Success.
Aug. 24	GREECE: Ukraine requests Security Council to consider situation created by Balkan policy of Greek government.
Aug. 29	MEMBERSHIP: USSR vetoes draft resolution of the Security Council on the applications of Jordan, Ireland and Portugal.
Sept. 11-Oct. 3	ECOSOC: 3rd regular session.
Sept. 20	GREECE: USSR vetoes draft resolution of the Security Council on establishing a commission of investigation.
Sept. 21	SPECIALIZED AGENCIES: Administrative Committee on Co-ordination (ACC) is established.
Sept. 26	ATOMIC ENERGY: Scientific and Technical Committee of the Atomic Energy Commission reports no scientific evidence that effective control was not possible.
Oct. 1	FISCAL: ECOSOC establishes Fiscal Commission.
Oct. 3	COMMISSION: ECOSOC establishes Population Commission.
Oct. 23-Dec. 15	GENERAL ASSEMBLY: 2nd part of 1st regular session.
Nov. 19	MEMBERSHIP: General Assembly admits Afghanistan, Iceland and Sweden as 52nd, 53rd and 54th members.
	DRUGS: General Assembly entrusts UN with functions previously exercised by League of Nations.
Nov. 27-Dec. 13	DRUGS: 1st session of Commission on Narcotic Drugs.
Dec. 3	GREECE: Greece requests Security Council to consider situation on borders.
Dec. 8	UNION OF SOUTH AFRICA: General Assembly makes recommendations concerning Indians in the Union of South Africa.
Dec. 11	CHILDREN: General Assembly establishes UN International Children's Emergency Fund (UNICEF).
	INTERNATIONAL LAW: General Assembly approves principles of Nürnberg.
Dec. 12	SPAIN: General Assembly approves debarment from specialized agencies.
Dec. 13	TRUSTEESHIP: General Assembly approves agreements for New Guinea, Ruanda-Urundi, British and French Togoland, British and French Cameroons, Tanganyika and Western Samoa.
Dec. 14	BUDGET: General Assembly authorizes budget amounting to $47 million ($19 million for 1946 and $28 million for 1947).
	HEADQUARTERS: General Assembly selects New York as permanent headquarters and accepts $8.5 million gift from J.D. Rockefeller, Jr.

1946 (continued)

Dec. 14   SOCIAL DEVELOPMENT: General Assembly decides to continue the social welfare work of the UN Relief and Rehabilitation Administration.

SOUTH WEST AFRICA: General Assembly rejects incorporation by Union of South Africa.

SPECIALIZED AGENCIES: General Assembly approves agreements with the International Labor Organization (ILO), the UN Food and Agriculture Organization (FAO), the UN Educational, Scientific and Cultural Organization (UNESCO) and the International Civil Aviation Organization (ICAO).

Dec. 15   MEMBERSHIP: General Assembly admits Thailand as 55th member.

REFUGEES: General Assembly approves constitution of International Refugee Organization.

Dec. 19   GREECE: Security Council establishes Commission of Investigation (Balkans Commission).

Dec. 31   ATOMIC ENERGY: UN Atomic Energy Commission recommends international system of inspection and control.

1947

Jan. 10   CORFU CHANNEL CASE: UK requests Security Council to consider damage to ships.

TRIESTE: Security Council accepts responsibility.

Jan. 20-Feb. 5   ECONOMIC DEVELOPMENT: 1st session of Economic and Employment Commission.

Jan. 20-Feb. 4   SOCIAL DEVELOPMENT: 1st session of Social Commission.

Jan. 27-Feb. 10   HUMAN RIGHTS: 1st session of Commission on Human Rights.

Jan. 27-Feb. 7   STATISTICS: 1st session of Statistical Commission.

Feb. 4-18   SOCIAL DEVELOPMENT: 1st session of Temporary Social Welfare Committee.

Feb. 6-19   POPULATION: 1st session of Population Commission.

Feb. 6-18   TRANSPORT AND COMMUNICATION: 1st session of Transport and Communications Commission.

Feb. 10-24   WOMEN: 1st session of Commission on the Status of Women.

Feb. 10   FREEDOM OF INFORMATION: Human Rights Commission establishes Sub-commission on Freedom of Information and of the Press.

MINORITIES: Human Rights Commission establishes Sub-commission on Prevention of Discrimination and Protection of Minorities.

Feb. 13   ARMS CONTROL: Security Council establishes Commission for Conventional Armaments.

Feb. 28-March 29   ECOSOC: 4th regular session.

1947 (continued)

March 25	CORFU CHANNEL: USSR vetoes draft resolution of the Security Council on recommendations to the parties.
March 26-April 28	TRUSTEESHIP COUNCIL: 1st regular session.
March 28	REGIONAL COMMISSIONS: ECOSOC establishes Economic Commission for Asia and the Far East (ECAFE) and Economic Commission for Europe (ECE).
April 2	PALESTINE: UK proposes special session of the General Assembly.
	TRUSTEESHIP: Security Council approves Trusteeship Council agreement for the Trust Territory of the Pacific Islands.
April 9	CORFU CHANNEL: Security Council recommends referral to the International Court of Justice.
April 22	MEMBERSHIP: Hungary applies.
April 24	TRUSTEESHIP: Trusteeship Council approves first mission to Western Samoa.
April 28-May 15	PALESTINE: 1st special session of General Assembly on Palestine establishes Special Committee on Palestine (UNSCOP).
April 30	ARMS CONTROL: Military Staff Committee reports on general principles.
May 2-14	ECONOMIC COMMISSION FOR EUROPE: 1st session.
May 7	MEMBERSHIP: Italy applies.
May 12-June 17	INTERNATIONAL LAW: 1st session of the Committee on the Progressive Development of International Law and its Codification.
May 19-June 4	FREEDOM OF INFORMATION: 1st session of Sub-commission on Freedom of Information and of the Press.
May 19-29	FISCAL COMMISSION: 1st session.
June 16-25	ECONOMIC COMMISSION FOR ASIA AND THE FAR EAST: 1st session.
June 25	GREECE: Commission of Investigation (Balkans Commission) reports on situation.
June 26	HEADQUARTERS: UN signs agreement with host country USA.
July 2	MEMBERSHIP: Austria applies.
July 8	EGYPT: Security Council considers presence of British troops.
July 10	MEMBERSHIP: Romania applies.
July 19-Aug. 17	ECOSOC: 5th regular session.
July 24-Aug. 8	DRUGS: 1st session of Commission on Narcotic Drugs.
July 26	MEMBERSHIP: Bulgaria applies.
July 29	GREECE: USSR vetoes draft resolution of the Security Council on establishing investigation commission.
July 30	INDONESIA: Australia and India request Security Council to consider the situation.
Aug. 1	INDONESIA: Security Council calls for cease-fire between the Netherlands and Indonesia.

1947 (continued)

Aug. 8	CHILDREN: ECOSOC approves a UN Appeal for Children.
Aug. 15	MEMBERSHIP: Pakistan applies.
Aug. 18	MEMBERSHIP: USSR vetoes draft resolution of the Security Council on applications of Jordan, Ireland and Portugal.
Aug. 19	GREECE: USSR vetoes draft resolution of the Security Council on the determination of a threat to the peace.
	MEMBERSHIP: USSR vetoes draft resolution of the Security Council, which requests states to cease aid to guerrillas.
Aug. 21	MEMBERSHIP: USSR vetoes draft resolution of the Security Council on applications of Italy and Austria.
Aug. 25	INDONESIA: France and USSR veto draft resolution of the Security Council on the establishment of a commission of investigation; Security Council establishes Good Offices Committee.
Aug. 31	PALESTINE: UNSCOP recommends partition.
Sept. 8-12	STATISTICS: World Statistical Congress.
Sept. 11	ATOMIC ENERGY: UN Atomic Energy Commission reports on principles to govern an international agency.
Sept. 15	GREECE: USSR vetoes draft resolution of the Security Council on proposal for consideration by the General Assembly.
Sept. 16-Nov. 29	GENERAL ASSEMBLY: 2nd regular session.
Sept. 19	MEMBERSHIP: Finland applies.
Sept. 24	TRIESTE: USSR vetoes draft resolution of the Security Council on the nomination of a governor-private meeting.
Sept. 30	MEMBERSHIP: General Assembly admits Pakistan and Yemen as 56th and 57th members.
Oct. 1	MEMBERSHIP: USSR vetoes draft resolution of the Security Council on application of Italy and Finland.
Oct. 20	FLAG: General Assembly adopts UN flag.
Oct. 21	GREECE: General Assembly establishes Special Committee on the Balkans (UNSCOB).
Oct. 30	TRADE: Protocol of Provisional Application of General Agreements on Tariff and Trade (GATT) is signed.
Nov. 1	SOUTH WEST AFRICA: General Assembly again recommends that territory be placed under trusteeship.
	TRUSTEESHIP: General Assembly approves trusteeship for Nauru.
Nov. 14	KOREA: General Assembly establishes Temporary Commission on Korea (UNTCOK).
Nov. 15	SPECIALIZED AGENCIES: General Assembly approves agreements bringing into relationship with the UN the International Bank for Reconstruction and Development (IBRD), the International Monetary Fund (IMF), the Universal Postal Union (UPU) and the International Telecommunication Union (ITU).

1947 (continued)

Nov. 17	EDUCATION: General Assembly recommends that members encourage teaching about the UN in schools.
Nov. 20-Dec. 16	LEGAL: General Assembly establishes International Law Commission.
	TRUSTEESHIP COUNCIL: 1st part of 2nd session.
Nov. 20	BUDGET: General Assembly authorizes $36 million ($1 million for 1947 and $35 million for 1948).
	HEADQUARTERS: General Assembly approves design and $65 million loan from USA for permanent building.
Nov. 21-March 24	TRADE: Conference on Trade and Employment draws up charter for an International Trade Organization (ITO).
Nov. 29	PALESTINE: General Assembly approves partition plan; Jerusalem to be under an international regime.
Dec. 8	TRUSTEESHIP: 1st personal appearance of a petitioner from a trust territory before a principal organ of the UN: Sylvanus E. Olympio from French Togoland before the Trusteeship Council.

1948

Jan. 17	INDONESIA: Netherlands and Indonesia sign Renville.
Jan. 20	KASHMIR: Security Council establishes UN Commission for India-Pakistan.
Feb. 2-March 11	ECOSOC: 6th regular session.
Feb. 18-March 10	TRUSTEESHIP COUNCIL: 2nd part of 2nd regular session.
Feb. 19-March 6	TRANSPORT: UN Maritime Conference drafts convention for an Inter-governmental Maritime Consultative Organization (IMCO).
Feb. 25	REGIONAL COMMISSIONS: ECOSOC establishes Economic Commission for Latin America (ECLA).
March 5	PALESTINE: Security Council appeals to all governments to prevent disorders.
March 23-April 21	FREEDOM OF INFORMATION: UN Conference on Freedom of Information adopts three conventions.
March 23	HEADQUARTERS: $65 million loan agreement with USA.
March 24	TRADE: Charter of an International Trade Organization (ITO) signed.
March 30	ATOMIC ENERGY: Committee 2 (Control) of UN Atomic Energy Commission adjourns because of stalemate.
April 1	PALESTINE: Security Council calls for special session of General Assembly.
April 10	MEMBERSHIP: USSR vetoes draft resolution of the Security Council on application of Italy.
April 16-May 14	GENERAL ASSEMBLY: 2nd special session.
April 16	PALESTINE: Security Council calls for cessation of hostilities.

1948 (continued)

April 19	MEMBERSHIP: General Assembly admits Burma as 58th member.
April 21-May 5	TRUSTEESHIP COUNCIL: 3rd part of 2nd regular session.
April 21	KASHMIR: Security Council recommends plebiscite.
April 23	PALESTINE: Security Council establishes Truce Commission.
May 10	KOREA: UNTCOK observes elections in South Korea.
May 14	ISRAEL: Independent state is proclaimed and recognized by USA.
	PALESTINE: Mandate is terminated; General Assembly establishes mediator for Palestine.
May 15	PALESTINE: Egypt announces entrance of Egyptian troops into Palestine.
May 20	PALESTINE: Count Folke Bernadotte is appointed mediator.
May 22	PALESTINE: Security Council calls upon all states to abstain from hostile military actions.
May 24	CZECHOSLOVAKIA: USSR vetoes draft resolution of the Security Council on the establishment of an investigation commission.
May 28	MEMBERSHIP: Advisory opinion of International Court of Justice.
May 29	PALESTINE: Security Council refuses to order governments to cease military operations, as proposed by USSR with support of USA; calls upon governments to cease-fire.
June 11	PALESTINE: Truce agreement is accepted by all parties.
June 15	PALESTINE: Security Council rejects USSR proposal for military observers from permanent members.
June 16-Aug. 5	TRUSTEESHIP COUNCIL: 3rd regular session.
June 22	ATOMIC ENERGY: USSR vetoes draft resolution of the Security Council on report of the UN Atomic Energy Commission.
June 25	KOREA: UNTCOK resolves that elections in South Korea have expressed free will of people.
July 6	TRUSTEESHIP: 1st regular visiting mission to Tanganyika and Ruanda-Urundi.
July 15	PALESTINE: Security Council orders a cease-fire.
July 19-Aug. 29	ECOSOC: 7th regular session.
July 28	INTERNATIONAL COURT OF JUSTICE: Switzerland becomes a party to the statute.
Aug. 13	KASHMIR: Security Council calls for cease-fire.
Aug. 18	MEMBERSHIP: USSR vetoes draft resolution of the Security Council on application of Ceylon.
Sept. 17	PALESTINE: Count Bernadotte is assassinated.
Sept. 21-Dec. 12	GENERAL ASSEMBLY: 1st part of 3rd regular session.
Oct. 1	CHILDREN: UN Appeal for Children has received $18 million.
Oct. 2	ATOMIC ENERGY: USSR proposes that there be separate conventions on prohibition and control.

1948 (continued)

Oct. 8	DRUGS: Protocol on synthetic drugs.
Oct. 25	BERLIN: USSR vetoes draft resolution of the Security Council on recommendation to the parties.
Nov. 4	ATOMIC ENERGY: General Assembly approves international control and production.
Nov. 18	SPECIALIZED AGENCIES: General Assembly approves agreement with ILO.
	TRUSTEESHIP: General Assembly recommends to increase educational facilities.
Nov. 19	MIDDLE EAST: General Assembly establishes UN Relief for Palestine Refugees (UNRPR) and expects $25 million voluntary contributions.
Nov. 26	SOUTH WEST AFRICA: General Assembly again recommends that the territory be placed under trusteeship.
Nov. 27	GREECE: General Assembly asks for return of all Greek children.
Dec. 3	WOMEN, CHILDREN AND OBSCENE PUBLICATIONS: Functions exercised by French government in connection with traffic in women, children and obscene publications are transferred to UN.
Dec. 4	TECHNICAL ASSISTANCE: Secretary-General authorizes to provide assistance to governments.
Dec. 9	GENOCIDE: General Assembly approves convention.
Dec. 10	HUMAN RIGHTS: General Assembly adopts Universal Declaration.
Dec. 11	BUDGET: General Assembly authorizes $48.0 million ($4.5 million for 1948 and $43.5 million for 1949).
	MIDDLE EAST: General Assembly establishes Conciliation Commission.
Dec. 12	KOREA: General Assembly endorses government of the Republic of Korea and establishes UN Commission on Korea (UNCOK).
Dec. 15	MEMBERSHIP: USSR vetoes draft resolution of the Security Council on application of Ceylon.
Dec. 24	INDONESIA: Security Council calls for cease-fire.

1949

Jan. 1	KASHMIR: Security Council orders cease-fire by India and Pakistan.
Jan. 24-March 25	TRUSTEESHIP COUNCIL: 4th regular session.
Jan. 28	INDONESIA: Security Council orders cease-fire; program of action set forth calling for transfer of sovereignty to Indonesia.
Feb. 7-March 18	ECOSOC: 8th regular session.
Feb. 24	MIDDLE EAST: Egypt-Israel armistice.

1949 (continued)

March 21	KASHMIR: Security Council names Chester W. Nimitz as Plebiscite Administrator.
March 23	MIDDLE EAST: Egypt-Israel armistice.
April 3	MIDDLE EAST: Jordan-Israel armistice.
April 5-May 18	GENERAL ASSEMBLY: 2nd part of 3rd regular session.
April 8	MEMBERSHIP: USSR vetoes draft resolution of the Security Council on application of Republic of Korea.
April 9	CORFU CHANNEL CASE: International Court of Justice rules that Albania is responsible for damage to British ships.
April 11	UN LEGAL CASE: International Court of Justice renders advisory opinion that UN has the capacity to bring an international claim against a government.
April 14	SECURITY COUNCIL VOTING: General Assembly recommends list of 34 items that should not be subject to veto.
April 28	PACIFIC SETTLEMENT OF DISPUTES: General Assembly sets up Panel for Inquiry and Conciliation.
May 4	BERLIN: Four powers approve agreement to lift the blockade on 12 May.
May 7	INDONESIA: Netherlands and Indonesia reach preliminary agreement.
May 11	MEMBERSHIP: General Assembly admits Israel as 59th member.
May 12	BERLIN: Blockade is lifted.
May 14	INDIANS IN UNION OF SOUTH AFRICA: General Assembly invites parties to hold a round-table conference.
June 15-July 22	TRUSTEESHIP COUNCIL: 5th regular session.
July 5-Aug. 15	ECOSOC: 9th regular session.
July 11	SOUTH WEST AFRICA: Union of South Africa announces cessation of reporting.
July 20	MIDDLE EAST: Syria-Israel armistice agreement.
July 29	ATOMIC ENERGY: UN Atomic Energy Commission suspends work.
Aug. 11	MIDDLE EAST: Security Council terminates office of Acting Mediator.
Aug. 15	TECHNICAL ASSISTANCE: ECOSOC recommends expanded program.
Aug. 17-Sept. 6	CONSERVATION: UN Scientific Conference on the Conservation and Utilization of Resources.
Aug. 23-Nov. 2	INDONESIA: Round Table Conference adopts Charter on Transfer of Sovereignty.
Aug. 23-Sept. 19	TRANSPORT: UN Conference on Road and Motor Transport.
Sept. 7	MEMBERSHIP: USSR vetoes draft resolution of the Security Council on application of Nepal.

1949 (continued)

Sept. 13	MEMBERSHIP: USSR vetoes draft resolution of the Security Council on applications of Austria, Ceylon, Finland, Ireland, Italy, Jordan and Portugal.
Sept. 20-Dec. 10	GENERAL ASSEMBLY: 4th regular session.
Sept. 27	TRUSTEESHIP COUNCIL: 1st special session.
Oct. 11	ARMS CONTROL: USSR vetoes draft resolution of the Security Council on the report of Commission on Conventional Armaments.
Oct. 18	ARMS CONTROL: USSR vetoes draft resolution of the Security Council on verification of armaments.
Oct. 21	KOREA: General Assembly continues the UN Commission on Korea (UNCOK).
Oct. 22-Dec. 16	EMPLOYMENT: Expert group meeting on measures for full employment.
Oct. 22	BULGARIA/HUNGARY/ROMANIA CASE: General Assembly requests advisory opinion from the International Court of Justice.
Nov. 15	TRUSTEESHIP: General Assembly adopts seven resolutions concerning welfare of inhabitants.
Nov. 16	TECHNICAL ASSISTANCE: General Assembly approves expanded program.
Nov. 17	SOCIAL DEVELOPMENT: General Assembly places advisory services on a permanent basis.
Nov. 18	GREECE: General Assembly instructs Secretary-General to seek assistance from Red Cross agencies in aiding return of Greek children.
Nov. 21	ERITREA: General Assembly establishes Commission to ascertain the wishes of the people.
	LIBYA: General Assembly decides on independence by 1 January 1952.
	SOMALILAND: General Assembly decides on independence after ten years of Italian administration as a trust territory.
Nov. 22	PANEL OF FIELD OBSERVERS: General Assembly authorizes the Secretary-General to maintain a list of persons qualified to supervise truces and observe plebiscites.
	UN FIELD SERVICE: General Assembly authorizes Field Service.
Nov. 23	ATOMIC ENERGY: General Assembly approves control plan.
Nov. 24	UN ADMINISTRATIVE TRIBUNAL: General Assembly establishes Administrative Tribunal.
Dec. 1	LEGAL PERSONALITY OF THE UN: General Assembly authorizes Secretary-General to bring reparations claims against members or non-members.
	PEACEFUL SETTLEMENT: General Assembly adopts resolution "Essentials of Peace".

1949 (continued)

Dec. 2	TRAFFIC IN PERSONS: General Assembly adopts Convention for the Suppression of the Traffic in Persons and of the Exploitation of the Prostitution of Others.
Dec. 3	REFUGEES: General Assembly establishes Office of the High Commissioner for Refugees (UNHCR).
Dec. 6	SOUTH WEST AFRICA: General Assembly again recommends that territory be placed under trusteeship; urges renewal of reporting by the Union of South Africa; and requests an advisory opinion from the International Court of Justice.
Dec. 8-20	TRUSTEESHIP COUNCIL: 2nd special session.
Dec. 8	MIDDLE EAST: General Assembly establishes UN Relief and Works Agency for Palestine Refugees in the Near East (UNRWAPRNE).
Dec. 9	ADMINISTRATIVE TRIBUNAL: Tribunal appoints members.
	MIDDLE EAST: General Assembly again approves internationalization of Jerusalem.
Dec. 10	BUDGET: General Assembly authorizes $49 million for 1950.
	LIBYA: General Assembly appoints UN Commissioner.
Dec. 13	INDONESIA: USSR vetoes draft resolutions of the Security Council on composition of a commission of investigation and on congratulations to the parties.
Dec. 15	CORFU CHANNEL: International Court of Justice fixes $2.4 million compensation to be paid by Albania.
Dec. 27	INDONESIA: Netherlands transfers sovereignty over whole territory, except New Guinea (West Irian).

1950

Jan. 13	CHINA: USSR withdraws from Security Council on issue of Chinese representation.
Jan. 19-April 4	TRUSTEESHIP COUNCIL: 6th regular session.
Feb. 7-March 6	ECOSOC: 10th regular session.
Feb. 27	NON-GOVERNMENTAL ORGANIZATIONS: ECOSOC clarifies status.
March 1	FIELD SERVICE: Secretary-General establishes Field Service.
March 3	EGYPT/FRANCE CASE: International Court of Justice renders decision.
	MEMBERSHIP: International Court of Justice issues advisory opinion that admission requires a recommendation from the Security Council.
March 14	KASHMIR: Security Council liquidates Commission for India-Pakistan and calls for demilitarization within five months.
March 15-April 6	MISSING PERSONS: UN Conference on Declaration of Death of Missing Persons.
March 29	INTERNATIONAL COURT OF JUSTICE: Liechtenstein becomes a party to the statute.

1950 (continued)

March 30	BULGARIA/HUNGARY/ROMANIA CASE: International Court of Justice issues advisory opinion on peace treaties.
April 12	KASHMIR: Security Council appoints Sir Owen Dixon as UN Representative for India-Pakistan.
June 1-July 21	TRUSTEESHIP COUNCIL: 7th regular session.
June 6	PEACE: Secretary-General circulates Twenty Year Peace Plan.
June 12-14	TECHNICAL ASSISTANCE: Pledging conference results in pledges of $20 million.
June 14	MIDDLE EAST: Israel pays reparations for assassination of Count Bernadotte.
June 25	KOREA: Security Council calls on North Korea to withdraw to 37th parallel, on members to refrain from giving assistance to North Korea, and on members to give every assistance to the UN in carrying out this resolution (USSR absent).
June 27	KOREA: Security Council calls upon members to furnish assistance to the Republic of Korea.
July 3-Aug. 16	ECOSOC: 11th regular session.
July 11	SOUTH WEST AFRICA: International Court of Justice Advisory Opinion notes that there is no obligation to place the territory under trusteeship, but also that the Union of South Africa cannot unilaterally determine the future of the territory.
July 17	KOREA: Security Council establishes unified UN Command.
July 18	BULGARIA/HUNGARY/ROMANIA CASE: International Court of Justice Advisory Opinion notes that Secretary-General is not authorized to appoint a commissioner when parties have not done so.
July 31	KOREA: Security Council requests UN Command to determine relief requirements.
Aug. 1	SECURITY COUNCIL: USSR returns.
Aug. 9	FREEDOM OF INFORMATION: General Assembly appoints committee to draft a convention.
Aug. 21	HEADQUARTERS: 1st units of UN Secretariat move into permanent buildings in New York.
Sept. 6	KOREA: USSR vetoes draft resolution of the Security Council on determination of a breach of the peace.
Sept. 12	CHINA BOMBING: USSR vetoes draft resolution of the Security Council on the establishment of a commission of investigation.
Sept. 15	KASHMIR: UN reports on inability to secure agreement on demilitarization.
Sept. 16	SUEZ: Israel complains to Security Council that Egypt has maintained a blockade of the canal.
Sept. 19-May 18	GENERAL ASSEMBLY: 5th regular session.
Sept. 28	MEMBERSHIP: General Assembly admits Indonesia as 60th member.

1950 (continued)

Oct. 7	KOREA: General Assembly establishes UN Commission for the Unification and Rehabilitation of Korea (UNCURK).
Oct. 12-Dec. 13	ECOSOC: 2nd part of 11th regular session.
Oct. 12	SECRETARY-GENERAL: USSR vetoes draft resolution of the Security Council on the re-appointment of Secretary-General Trygve Lie.
Oct. 25-Nov. 21	COMMODITIES: UN Tin Conference, Geneva.
Nov. 3	PEACE: General Assembly adopts Uniting for Peace resolution.
	PEACE OBSERVATION GROUP: General Assembly establishes Peace Observation Group.
Nov. 4	SPAIN: General Assembly revokes two 1946 resolutions.
Nov. 5	KOREA: UN Command reports presence of Chinese communist troops.
Nov. 8	CHINA: People's Republic is invited to send a representative to the Security Council.
Nov. 16	POSTAL ADMINISTRATION: General Assembly establishes UN Postal Administration.
Nov. 17	DUTIES OF STATES: General Assembly recommends procedure to be followed by states in event of hostilities.
	MIDDLE EAST: Security Council calls upon Egypt, Jordan and Israel to settle their complaints.
Nov. 20	ASYLUM CASE: International Court of Justice issues judgement.
	PEACE PROGRAM: General Assembly commends Secretary-General on twenty year peace program.
Nov. 22	TRUSTEESHIP COUNCIL: 3rd special session.
Nov. 27	ASYLUM CASE: International Court of Justice provides interpretation of 20 November judgement.
Nov. 30	KOREA: USSR vetoes draft resolution of the Security Council on proposal for provisional measures.
Dec. 1	CHILDREN: UNICEF emphasis changes from relief to continuing aid; continuation of fund is approved for three more years.
	GREECE: General Assembly calls for repatriation of members of Greek armed forces; establishes Standing Committee.
	KOREA: General Assembly establishes UN Korean Relief and Reconstruction Agency (UNKRA).
	SOCIAL DEVELOPMENT: General Assembly expands program.
Dec. 2	ERITREA: General Assembly recommends federation with Ethiopia.
	INDIANS IN SOUTH AFRICA: General Assembly recommends a committee to assist the parties and a round-table discussion.
	SOMALILAND: General Assembly approves trusteeship agreement with Italy.

1950 (continued)

Dec. 2   SOUTH AFRICA: General Assembly calls upon South Africa to
              refrain from implementing Group Areas Act (*Apartheid*).
Dec. 4   HUMAN RIGHTS: General Assembly decides to include
              economic, social and cultural rights in one covenant.
Dec. 12   KOREA: General Assembly authorizes service ribbons.
Dec. 13   SOUTH WEST AFRICA: General Assembly establishes
              committee of five to confer with the Union of South Africa
              and considers reports and petitions.
Dec. 14   KOREA: General Assembly establishes four-man group to
              determine basis of a cease-fire.
              MIDDLE EAST: General Assembly expresses concern for
              refugees and directs Conciliation Commission to establish
              office for assessment and payment of compensation.
              PRISONERS: General Assembly establishes *Ad Hoc*
              Commission on Prisoners of War.
              REFUGEES: General Assembly adopts Statute of the Office of
              the High Commissioner for Refugees and elects G.J. van
              Heuven Goedhart.
Dec. 15   BUDGET: General Assembly authorizes $43 million for 1951.
              LIBYA: General Assembly establishes UN Tribunal to assist in
              determining boundaries.
              MIDDLE EAST: General Assembly is unable to agree on a
              resolution on the status of Jerusalem.
              SOMALILAND: General Assembly decides on procedure for
              determining boundaries.
Dec. 23   KOREA: People's Republic of China declares Cease-Fire Group
              illegal and refuses participation.

1951

Jan. 1   REFUGEES: High Commissioner's Office starts operation.
Jan. 12   GENOCIDE: Convention comes into force.
Jan. 30-March 16   TRUSTEESHIP COUNCIL: 8th regular session.
Feb. 1   KOREA: General Assembly declares the People's Republic of
                    China an aggressor; establishes Good Offices Committee and
                    Additional Measures Committee.
Feb. 13   CHINA: General Assembly rejects USSR charges of US
                    aggression.
Feb. 19-May 2   ECONOMIC DEVELOPMENT: Committee of Experts
                    recommends establishment of an International Finance
                    Corporation (IFC) and an international development authority
Feb. 20-March 21   ECOSOC: 12th regular session.
March 5-Oct. 3   COLLECTIVE MEASURES COMMITTEE: Meets.
March 14   INDONESIA: UN Commission for Indonesia decides that
                    military observers are no longer needed.
March 19   FORCED LABOR: ECOSOC establishes *ad hoc* committee.

1951 (continued)

March 28	POSTAL ADMINISTRATION: UN agrees with USA to issue and use its own stamps.
March 29	LIBYA: Provisional government is established.
March 30	KASHMIR: Security Council appoints Frank P. Graham as the UN Representative.
April 3	INDONESIA: UN Commission is adjourned.
May 8	MIDDLE EAST: Security Council instructs Israel to cease work in Huleh marshes.
May 18	KOREA: General Assembly recommends embargo against North Korea and People's Republic of China.
	MIDDLE EAST: Security Council strengthens armistice agreement machinery.
May 28	GENOCIDE CASE: International Court of Justice issues advisory opinion on effect of reservations to Convention.
June 5-July 30	TRUSTEESHIP COUNCIL: 9th regular session.
June 13	ASYLUM CASE: International Court of Justice issues judgement.
June 29	KOREA: UN Command offers to discuss cease-fire.
July 1	KOREA: Communist commander proposes that cease-fire discussions take place near Kaesong.
July 2-25	REFUGEES: UN Conference on the Status of Refugees and Stateless Persons.
July 5	ANGLO-IRANIAN OIL COMPANY CASE: International Court of Justice indicates provisional measures.
July 10	KOREA: Cease-fire talks begin.
July 16	KOREA: Agreement on relationship between UN Command and UNKRA.
July 25	REFUGEES: Convention Relating to the Status of Refugees is signed.
	TRAFFIC IN PERSONS: Convention comes into force.
July 30-Sept. 21	ECOSOC: 1st part of 13th regular session.
Aug. 1-31	CRIMINAL JURISDICTION: 1st session of UN Committee on International Criminal Jurisdiction.
Sept. 1	SUEZ: Security Council calls for termination of Egyptian restrictions on shipping.
Sept. 18	ECONOMIC AND EMPLOYMENT COMMISSION: Commission is terminated.
Oct. 24	POSTAL ADMINISTRATION: 1st UN stamp is issued.
Nov. 5	TECHNICAL ASSISTANCE: 1st major project for training in public administration in Rio de Janeiro, Brazil.
Nov. 6-Feb. 5	GENERAL ASSEMBLY: 6th regular session.
Nov. 10	KASHMIR: Security Council instructs UN Representative to continue efforts to secure agreement on demilitarization.
Nov. 13	CHINA: Question of representation in General Assembly is postponed by a vote of 37 to 11, with 4 abstentions.
Nov. 27	KOREA: Provisional truce.

1951 (continued)

Dec. 14   YUGOSLAVIA: General Assembly recommends that
               communist governments conduct their relations with
               Yugoslavia in the spirit of the Charter.
Dec. 18-20   ECOSOC: 2nd part of 13th regular session.
Dec. 18   TRUSTEESHIP COUNCIL: 4th special session.
               ANGLO-NORWEGIAN FISHERIES CASE: International Court
               of Justice issues judgement.
Dec. 20   GERMANY: General Assembly appoints commission to
               ascertain possibility of free elections.
               SPECIALIZED AGENCIES: General Assembly approves
               agreement with World Meteorological Organization (WMO).
Dec. 21   BUDGET: General Assembly authorizes $54.7 million
               ($1.1 million for 1951 and $53.6 million for 1952 of which
               $5.5 million not authorized until 4 February 1952).
Dec. 24   LIBYA: Becomes independent and applies for membership.

1952

Jan. 11   ARMS CONTROL: General Assembly establishes Disarmament
               Commission to replace Atomic Energy Commission and
               Commission on Conventional Armaments.
Jan. 12   ECONOMIC DEVELOPMENT: General Assembly requests
               ECOSOC to prepare a plan for a fund for economic
               development (later to be called SUNFED).
Jan. 18   TRUSTEESHIP: General Assembly recommends abolition of
               corporal punishment; invites members to provide
               scholarships.
Jan. 19   SOUTH WEST AFRICA: General Assembly establishes *ad hoc*
               committee.
Jan. 23   PEACE OBSERVATION COMMISSION: Establishes Balkans
               Sub-commission.
Jan. 24   MISSING PERSONS: Convention comes into force.
Jan. 26   MIDDLE EAST: General Assembly endorses UNRAWAPRNE
               $50 million program for relief and $200 million program for
               rehabilitation.
Jan. 31   GREECE: Balkans Sub-commission of Peace Observation
               Commission approves military observers for Greek frontiers.
               KASHMIR: Security Council asks UN Representative to
               continue efforts for peaceful settlement.
Feb. 5   HUMAN RIGHTS: General Assembly approves: (i) an article
               on self-determination and (ii) a study of effects of reservations
               to covenants.
Feb. 6-7   TECHNICAL ASSISTANCE: Pledging conference results in
               pledges of $18.8 million.
Feb. 6   MEMBERSHIP: USSR vetoes draft resolution of the Security
               Council on application of Italy.

1952 (continued)

Feb. 27-April 1	TRUSTEESHIP COUNCIL: 10th regular session.
Feb. 27	HEADQUARTERS: New building in New York is formally inaugurated.
March 3-21	FREEDOM OF INFORMATION: Final session of sub-commission.
March 4	ECOSOC: 1st special session.
March 26	TRANSPORT: Convention on Road Traffic comes into force.
April 5	ARMS CONTROL: USA submits proposal to Disarmament Commission for disclosure and verification.
April 14	TUNISIA: Security Council rejects agenda item.
May 20-Aug. 1	ECOSOC: 14th regular session.
May 28	ARMS CONTROL: France, UK and USA propose numerical limitation to Disarmament Commission.
June 3-July 24	TRUSTEESHIP COUNCIL: 1st part of 11th regular session.
June 20	TUNISIA: General Assembly rejects request for special session.
June 23	ECONOMIC DEVELOPMENT: ECOSOC appoints committee to prepare plan for Special UN Fund for Economic Development (SUNFED).
July 1	AMBATIELOS CASE: International Court of Justice issues judgement.
July 3	BACTERIOLOGICAL WARFARE: USSR vetoes draft resolution of the Security Council to establish a commission of investigation.
July 9	BACTERIOLOGICAL WARFARE: USSR vetoes draft resolutions of the Security Council on impartial investigation.
July 22	ANGLO-IRANIAN OIL COMPANY CASE: International Court of Justice denies its own jurisdiction.
Aug. 5	GERMANY: UN Commission to Investigate Conditions for Free Elections in Germany adjourns because of inability to establish contact with authorities in Soviet zone.
Aug. 27	US CITIZENS IN MOROCCO CASE: International Court of Justice issues judgement.
Sept. 11	ERITREA: Federates with Ethiopia.
Sept. 16	MEMBERSHIP: USSR vetoes draft resolution of the Security Council on application of Libya.
Sept. 18	MEMBERSHIP: USSR vetoes draft resolution of the Security Council on application of Japan.
Sept. 19	MEMBERSHIP: USSR vetoes draft resolution of the Security Council on applications of Cambodia, Laos and Viet Nam.
Oct. 1	MISSING PERSONS: International Bureau for the Declaration of Death of Missing Persons opens.
Oct. 14-Dec. 22	GENERAL ASSEMBLY: 1st part of 7th regular session.
Oct. 25	CHINA: Question of representation in General Assembly is postponed by a vote of 42 to 7, with 11 abstentions.
Nov. 1	HYDROGEN BOMB: 1st test by USA.

1952 (continued)

Nov. 6	MIDDLE EAST: General Assembly authorizes UNRWAPRNE budget of $23 million for year ending 30 June 1953.
Nov. 10	SECRETARY-GENERAL: Trygve Lie submits resignation.
Nov. 19-Dec. 3	TRUSTEESHIP COUNCIL: 2nd part of 13th regular session.
Dec. 3	KOREA: General Assembly proposes Repatriation Commission to facilitate return of prisoners.
Dec. 5	UNION OF SOUTH AFRICA: General Assembly establishes Commission on the Racial Situation in the Union of South Africa.
Dec. 10	NON-SELF-GOVERNING TERRITORIES: General Assembly establishes *Ad Hoc* Committee on Factors.
Dec. 16-19	ECOSOC: Resumed 14th regular session.
Dec. 16	FREEDOM OF INFORMATION: General Assembly opens for signature Convention on the International Right of Correction.
Dec. 17	GREECE: General Assembly condemns failure of neighboring states, except Yugoslavia, to repatriate Greek children.
	TUNISIA: General Assembly expresses confidence in negotiations of parties.
Dec. 19	MOROCCO: General Assembly expresses confidence in negotiations of parties.
Dec. 20	WOMEN: General Assembly approves Convention on Political Rights of Women.
Dec. 21	BUDGET: General Assembly authorizes $50.8 million ($2.5 million for 1952 and $48.3 million for 1953).
	TRUSTEESHIP: General Assembly approves greater participation of inhabitants in work of Trusteeship Council.
Dec. 22	KOREA: General Assembly rejects USSR charges of mass murder of prisoners.
Dec. 27	KASHMIR: Security Council urges India and Pakistan to negotiate with UN Representative.

1953

Feb. 24-April 23	GENERAL ASSEMBLY: 2nd part of 7th regular session.
Feb. 26-27	TECHNICAL ASSISTANCE: Pledging conference results in pledges of $22.4 million.
March 13	SECRETARY-GENERAL: USSR vetoes draft resolution of the Security Council on the nomination of Lester Pearson.
March 23	KASHMIR: Report of UN Representative is not discussed.
March 31-Apr. 28	ECOSOC: 15th regular session.
April 8	ARMS CONTROL: General Assembly calls upon Disarmament Commission to continue its work.
April 10	SECRETARY-GENERAL: General Assembly appoints Dag Hammarskjöld from Sweden as Secretary-General.
April 11	KOREA: Agreement is reached on exchange of sick and wounded prisoners.

1953 (continued)

April 23	BACTERIOLOGICAL WARFARE: General Assembly establishes Commission to investigate charges.
	BURMA: General Assembly condemns presence of foreign troops.
	ECONOMIC DEVELOPMENT: Establishment of a Special UN Fund for Economic Development (SUNFED) is proposed.
May 11-June 18	NARCOTIC DRUGS: UN Opium Conference adopts protocol to limit trade in and use of opium.
May 20	AMBATIELOS CASE: International Court of Justice issues judgement.
June 8	KOREA: Agreement on prisoners of war is reached.
June 16-July 21	TRUSTEESHIP COUNCIL: 12th regular session.
June 30-Aug. 5	ECOSOC: 16th regular session.
July 13-Aug. 24	COMMODITIES: UN Sugar Conference adopts International Sugar Convention.
July 27-Aug. 20	CRIMINAL JURISDICTION: Committee on International Criminal Jurisdiction drafts Statute for an International Criminal Court.
July 27	KOREA: Armistice agreement creates Neutral Nations Supervisory Commission and Neutral Nations Repatriation Commission (NNSC and NNRC).
July 30	KOREA: UN troops withdraw from demilitarized zone.
Aug. 5-Sept. 6	KOREA: Exchange of prisoners in "Operation Big Switch".
Aug. 17-28	GENERAL ASSEMBLY: Resumed 7th regular session.
Aug. 28	KOREA: General Assembly recommends that conference is held not later than 28 October.
Sept. 10	KOREA: Neutral Nations Repatriation Commission begins to assume custody of prisoners.
Sept. 15-Dec. 9	GENERAL ASSEMBLY: 1st part of 8th regular session.
Sept. 15	CHINA: Question of representation in General Assembly is postponed by a vote of 44 to 10, with 2 abstentions.
Sept. 24	KOREA: 21,601 prisoners are transferred by UN Command; 359 to Communist Command.
Oct. 6	CHILDREN: General Assembly places UN Children's Fund placed on permanent basis, retaining symbol "UNICEF".
Oct. 23	SLAVERY: League of Nations functions under the Slavery Convention of 1926 are transferred to UN.
Oct. 27	MIDDLE EAST: Security Council approves suspension of work on diversion of Jordan River water by Israel.
Nov. 11	TUNISIA: General Assembly is unable to agree on a resolution.
Nov. 12-13	TECHNICAL ASSISTANCE: Pledging conference results in pledges of $24 million; USSR participates for first time.
Nov. 17	MINQUIERS-ECREHOS ISLANDS CASE: International Court of Justice issues judgement.
Nov. 18	NOTTEBOHM CASE: International Court of Justice issues preliminary judgement.

1953 (continued)

Nov. 24   MIDDLE EAST: Security Council censures Israel for action
                       at Qibya.
Nov. 27   NON-SELF-GOVERNING TERRITORIES: General Assembly
                       adopts list of factors.
                     MIDDLE EAST: General Assembly authorizes UNRWAPRNE
                       budget of $24.8 million for year ending 30 June 1954, and
                       $18.0 million for relief during year ending 30 June 1955.
                     PUERTO-RICO: General Assembly approves cessation of
                       transmission of information by USA.
Nov. 28   ARMS CONTROL: General Assembly suggests to Disarmament
                       Commission the establishment of sub-commission of powers
                       principally concerned.
                     HUMAN RIGHTS: General Assembly considers federal clause
                       and right of petition.
                     SOUTH WEST AFRICA: General Assembly reiterates that
                       territory should be placed under trusteeship.
Nov. 30-Dec. 7   ECOSOC: Resumed 16th regular session.
Dec. 3   KOREA: General Assembly expresses concern over treatment of
                       UN prisoners.
Dec. 7   ECONOMIC DEVELOPMENT: General Assembly appoints
                       Raymond Scheyven to examine replies of Governments
                       concerning SUNFED.
                     FORCED LABOR: General Assembly invites ECOSOC and
                       ILO to consider report of *Ad Hoc* Committee on Forced
                       Labor.
                     KOREA: General Assembly approves UNKRA program to
                       1 July 1955.
                     PRISONERS OF WAR: General Assembly calls upon states
                       holding World War II prisoners to provide an opportunity for
                       repatriation.
Dec. 8   ATOMIC ENERGY: USA proposes to the General Assembly
                       the establishment of an International Atomic Energy Agency.
                     BURMA: General Assembly approves efforts to evacuate
                       foreign troops.
                     UNION OF SOUTH AFRICA: General Assembly expresses
                       concern at report of Commission on Racial Situation in the
                       Union of South Africa.
Dec. 9   BUDGET: General Assembly authorizes $49.4 million
                       ($1.5 million for 1953 and $47.9 million for 1954).
Dec. 20   TRANSPORT: Protocol on Road Signs and Signals comes into
                       force.

1954

Jan. 10   GENERAL ASSEMBLY: General Assembly rejects proposal of
                       India for a reconvened 8th session.

1954 (continued)

Jan. 22	MIDDLE EAST: USSR vetoes draft resolution of the Security Council which calls upon Syria and Israel to co-operate on diversion of waters of River Jordan.
Jan. 23	KOREA: Neutral Nations Repatriation Commission releases all remaining prisoners.
Jan. 28-March 25	TRUSTEESHIP COUNCIL: 13th regular session.
Feb. 18	INTERNATIONAL COURT OF JUSTICE: San Marino becomes a party to the Statute.
March 29	SUEZ: USSR vetoes draft resolution of the Security Council which calls upon Egypt to comply with 1951 resolution of Security Council on restrictions on shipping.
March 30-Apr. 30	ECOSOC: 17th regular session.
April 2	INTERNATIONAL COURT OF JUSTICE: Japan becomes a party to the Statute.
April 9-19	ARMS CONTROL: Disarmament Commission.
April 22	REFUGEES: Convention on Status of Refugees comes into force.
April 26-June 15	KOREA: Foreign ministers fail to agree on peaceful unification.
May 11-June 4	TRANSPORT: UN Conference on Customs Formalities for the Temporary Importation of Road Motor Vehicles and the Tourism adopts two conventions.
May 13-July 22	ARMS CONTROL: Sub-commission of Disarmament Commission.
May 13	ECONOMIC DEVELOPMENT: 1st Scheyven report on SUNFED.
June 2-July 16	TRUSTEESHIP COUNCIL: 14th regular session.
June 15	ALBANIAN GOLD CASE: International Court of Justice issues judgement.
June 18	THAILAND: USSR vetoes draft resolution of the Security Council which requests a Peace Observation Commission.
June 20	GUATEMALA: Security Council calls for termination of action likely to lead to bloodshed; USSR vetoes draft resolution of the Security Council to refer question to Organization of American States.
June 29-Aug. 6	ECOSOC: 18th regular session.
July 7	WOMEN: Convention on the Political Rights of Women comes into force.
July 12	HUNGARY/USA CASE: International Court of Justice finds that Hungary and USSR refused jurisdiction of the Court.
July 13	ADMINISTRATIVE TRIBUNAL AWARDS: International Court of Justice renders advisory opinion.
July 20-29	ARMS CONTROL: Disarmament Commission.
Aug. 1	GREECE: Balkans Sub-commission of Peace Observation Commission discontinues military observers.
Aug. 5	COMMODITIES: ECOSOC establishes Commission on International Commodity Trade.

1954 (continued)

Aug. 5   FISCAL: ECOSOC terminates Fiscal Commission.

Aug. 10   ECONOMIC DEVELOPMENT: 2nd Scheyven report on
                  SUNFED.

Aug. 31-Sept. 10 POPULATION: UN World Population Conference.

Sept. 13-24   STATELESSNESS: UN Conference of Plenipotentiaries on the
                  Status of Stateless Persons approves convention.

Sept. 20   GENERAL ASSEMBLY: Reconvened 8th regular session.

Sept. 21-Dec. 17 GENERAL ASSEMBLY: 9th regular session.

Sept. 21   CHINA: Question of representation in General Assembly is
                  postponed by a vote of 45 to 7, with 5 abstentions.

Oct. 11   SOUTH WEST AFRICA: General Assembly adopts rules
                  concerning reports, petitions and voting.

Oct. 21   REFUGEES: General Assembly approves five year $12 million
                  plan of High Commissioner.

Oct. 29   BURMA: General Assembly approves disarmament and
                  internment of foreign troops.

Nov. 23   SOUTH WEST AFRICA: General Assembly adopts three
                  resolutions, including a request for an advisory opinion from
                  the International Court of Justice, on the applicability of the
                  two-thirds voting rule in the General Assembly.

Nov. 26   TECHNICAL ASSISTANCE: Pledging conference results in
                  pledges of $28 million by 60 nations; General Assembly
                  approves measures for co-ordination of national and
                  international agencies.

Dec. 4   ATOMIC ENERGY: General Assembly approves draft statute
                  of IAEA.
                  HUMAN RIGHTS: General Assembly requests comments on
                  two draft covenants from governments and specialized
                  agencies.

Dec. 10   KOREA: General Assembly requests Secretary-General to assist
                  in securing release of prisoners.
                  WEST IRIAN (NEW GUINEA): General Assembly is unable to
                  agree on a resolution.

Dec. 11   INTERNATIONAL FINANCE CORPORATION: General
                  Assembly asks International Bank for Reconstruction and
                  Development to prepare draft statute.

Dec. 17   BUDGET: General Assembly authorizes $50.7 million
                  ($0.7 million for 1954 and $50.0 million for 1955).
                  TUNISIA: General Assembly expresses confidence in
                  negotiations of parties.

1955

Jan. 5-10   KOREA: Secretary-General negotiates in Peiping for release of
                  prisoners.

Jan. 25-March 28 TRUSTEESHIP COUNCIL: 15th regular session.

1955 (continued)

Feb. 3	CHINA: People's Republic declines Security Council invitation to participate in discussion of offshore islands.
Feb. 15-25	CARTOGRAPHY: UN Regional Cartography Conference for Asia and the Far East.
Feb. 25-May 18	ARMS CONTROL: Sub-committee of Disarmament Commission.
March 7-25	ECONOMIC DEVELOPMENT: Scheyven Committee discusses SUNFED.
March 7	TRADE: GATT proposes Organization of Trade Co-operation.
March 29-April 7	ECOSOC: 19th regular session.
March 29	MIDDLE EAST: Security Council condemns attack by Israeli armed forces in Gaza.
April 6	NOTTEBOHM CASE: International Court of Justice issues judgement.
April 15	INTERNATIONAL FINANCE CORPORATION: International Bank for Reconstruction and Development proposes charter for IFC.
May 9	ARMS CONTROL: USSR submits comprehensive proposal to Sub-committee of Disarmament Commission.
May 16-27	ECOSOC: Resumed 19th regular session.
June 1	ARMS CONTROL: Sub-committee of Disarmament Commission.
June 7	SOUTH WEST AFRICA: International Court of Justice issues advisory opinion.
June 8-July 22	TRUSTEESHIP COUNCIL: 16th regular session.
June 20-26	CHARTER: Commemoration of 10th anniversary.
July 1	ARMS CONTROL: USA proposes aerial photographs.
July 5-Aug. 5	ECOSOC: 20th regular session.
July 23	ARMS CONTROL: Summit meeting of heads of states refers questions to Sub-committee of Disarmament Commission.
Aug. 4	KOREA: Communists release 11 prisoners.
Aug. 8-20	ATOMIC ENERGY: 1st International Conference on the Peaceful Uses of Atomic Energy.
Aug. 29-Oct. 7	ARMS CONTROL: Sub-committee of Disarmament Sub-commission.
Sept. 8	MIDDLE EAST: Security Council calls on Egypt and Israel to co-operate with UN Chief of Staff.
Sept. 13	ARMS CONTROL: UK proposes to Sub-committee of Disarmament Commission a plan for control test area in Europe.
Sept. 20-Dec. 20	GENERAL ASSEMBLY: 10th regular session.
Sept. 20	CHINA: General Assembly postpones question of the representation by a vote of 42 to 12, with 5 abstentions.
Sept. 23	CYPRUS: General Assembly rejects agenda item.
Sept. 30	ALGERIA: Contrary to recommendation of General Committee, item is placed on agenda of General Assembly.

1955 (continued)

Oct. 3-17	COMMODITIES: UN Conference on Olive Oil.
Oct. 21	ARMS CONTROL: Disarmament Commission.
Oct. 24-Dec. 14	TRUSTEESHIP COUNCIL: 5th special session.
Oct. 26-Nov. 16	COMMODITIES: UN Wheat Conference.
Oct. 26	TECHNICAL ASSISTANCE: Pledging conference results in pledges of $29 million by 72 Governments.
Nov. 2	MIDDLE EAST: Secretary-General appeals to the parties.
Nov. 3	INTERNATIONAL FINANCE CORPORATION: General Assembly approves status.
Nov. 21	CHARTER: General Assembly establishes committee to consider time and place for review conference.
Nov. 23	ARMS CONTROL: Disarmament Commission.
Nov. 25	ALGERIA: General Assembly decides not to consider further.
Dec. 2	HUMAN RIGHTS: General Assembly completes tentative approval of preambles and common article 1 of both Covenants.
Dec. 3	ATOMIC ENERGY: General Assembly continues the Advisory Committee on Peaceful use of Atomic Energy.
	MOROCCO: General Assembly hopes for successful negotiations between parties.
	RADIATION: General Assembly establishes UN Scientific Committee on the Effects of Atomic Radiation.
	SOUTH WEST AFRICA: General Assembly adopts 9 resolutions, reiterates that territory should be under trusteeship; requests advisory opinion from International Court of Justice as to right to hear oral petitions; and informs petitioners that territory was still under mandate.
Dec. 5-15	ECOSOC: Resumed 20th regular session.
Dec. 9	ECONOMIC DEVELOPMENT: General Assembly submits eight questions on SUNFED to governments and establishes Committee of Sixteen to examine replies.
Dec. 13	MEMBERSHIP: China vetoes draft resolution of the Security Council on application of Outer Mongolia; USSR vetoes draft resolution of the Security Council on applications of Austria, Cambodia, Ceylon, Finland, Ireland, Italy, Japan, Jordan, Laos, Libya, Nepal, Portugal, Republic of Korea, Spain and Viet Nam.
Dec. 14	MEMBERSHIP: USSR vetoes draft resolution of the Security Council on application of Japan; General Assembly admits Albania, Austria, Bulgaria, Cambodia, Ceylon, Finland, Hungary, Ireland, Italy, Jordan, Laos, Libya, Nepal, Portugal, Romania and Spain as 61st to 76th members.
Dec. 15	GERMANY: Federal Republic of Germany is admitted to Economic Commission for Europe (ECE).
	MEMBERSHIP: USSR vetoes draft resolution of the Security Council on application of Japan.

1955 (continued)

Dec. 15   NON-SELF-GOVERNING TERRITORIES: General Assembly approves cessation of transmission of information from Netherlands Antilles and Surinam.

TRUSTEESHIP: General Assembly appoints Commissioner for British Togoland election.

Dec. 16   BUDGET: General Assembly authorizes $51.8 million ($3.3 million for 1955 and $48.5 million for 1956).

CHARTER: Security Council concurs with the decision of the General Assembly (21 November 1955) to establish a Committee on Review Conference.

TRUSTEESHIP: General Assembly recommends consultation with inhabitants of French Togoland, under UN supervision.

Dec. 19   WEST IRIAN (NEW GUINEA): General Assembly hopes for fruitful negotiations between parties.

Dec. 22   PORTUGAL/INDIA CASE: Portugal requests the International Court of Justice to consider right to passage case.

Dec. 31   KOREA: Contributions to UNKRA total $139.8 million, compared to $226.0 million target.

1956

Feb. 7-April 6   TRUSTEESHIP COUNCIL: 17th regular session.

March 14   AERIAL INCIDENT CASE: International Court of Justice removes USA versus Czechoslovakia case and USA versus USSR case from list.

March 16   ANTARCTICA CASE: International Court of Justice removes UK versus Chile case and UK versus Argentina case from list.

March 19-May 4   ARMS CONTROL: Sub-committee of Disarmament Commission.

April 9   RADIATION: 1st report of UN Scientific Committee on the Effects of Atomic Radiation.

April 17-May 4   ECOSOC: 21st regular session.

April 17   MIDDLE EAST: Secretary-General arrives in Middle East.

April 18   ATOMIC ENERGY: Drafting committee approves draft statute of International Atomic Energy Agency (IAEA).

May 9   TRUSTEESHIP: UN Commissioner supervises British Togoland plebiscite on union with Gold Coast (Ghana).

May 21-June 20   COMMODITIES: 1st session of UN Sugar Conference.

June 1   SOUTH WEST AFRICA CASE: International Court of Justice issues advisory opinion.

June 7-Aug. 14   TRUSTEESHIP COUNCIL: 18th regular session.

June 26   ALGERIA: Security Council rejects agenda item.

July 3-16   ARMS CONTROL: Disarmament Commission.

July 9-Aug. 9   ECOSOC: 22nd regular session.

1956 (continued)

July 24	INTERNATIONAL FINANCE CORPORATION: Starts operation.
Sept. 7	SLAVERY: Convention on the Abolition of Slavery, Slave Trade, and Institutions and Practices similar to Slavery is signed by 33 states.
Sept. 20-Oct. 26	ATOMIC ENERGY: Statute of IAEA is signed by 70 states.
Oct. 4-Nov. 2	COMMODITIES: 2nd session of UN Sugar Conference adopts protocol to 1953 agreement.
Oct. 13	MIDDLE EAST: USSR vetoes draft resolution of the Security Council which calls upon Egypt to cease certain practices.
	SUEZ: Security Council adopts six principles for settlement of Suez question.
Oct. 17	TECHNICAL ASSISTANCE: Pledging conference results in pledges of $30.9 million for 1957.
Oct. 23	TRUSTEESHIP: Plebiscite is held in French Togoland.
Oct. 28	HUNGARY: Situation is placed on agenda of Security Council.
Oct. 29	SUEZ: Israel invades Egypt.
Oct. 30	SUEZ: France and UK veto draft resolutions of the Security Council which call upon France and UK to refrain from use of force and which call upon Israel to refrain from use of force.
Oct. 31	SUEZ: French-UK attack.
Nov. 1-10	SUEZ: 1st emergency special session of General Assembly on Suez urges cease-fire and withdrawal of all forces and that steps be taken to re-open Suez Canal; establishes UN Emergency Force (UNEF); requests France, Israel and UK to withdraw forces.
Nov. 4-10	HUNGARY: 2nd emergency special session of General Assembly on Hungary.
Nov. 4	HUNGARY: USSR vetoes draft resolution of the Security Council which calls upon USSR to desist from use of force.
Nov. 8	SUEZ: Secretary-General appoints first salvage firms to clear canal.
Nov. 10	SUEZ: 1st UNEF contingents arrive in Italy.
Nov. 12	MEMBERSHIP: General Assembly admits Morocco, Sudan and Tunisia as 77th to 79th members.
	SUEZ: Egypt agrees to establishment of UNEF on Egyptian territory.
Nov. 12-March 8	GENERAL ASSEMBLY: 11th regular session.
Nov. 15	SUEZ: 1st UNEF contingents arrive in Ismailia.
Nov. 16	SUEZ: Secretary-General arrives in Egypt.

1956

Nov. 18	CHINA: Question of representation in General Assembly is postponed by a vote of 47 to 24, with 9 abstentions.

1956 (continued)

Nov. 18	SUEZ: Egypt requests UN assistance in clearing Canal.
Nov. 20	SUEZ: Aide-memoire is issued on terms of Secretary-General's agreement with Egypt on UNEF.
Nov. 21	SUEZ: General Assembly agrees to apportion first $10 million of cost of UNEF according to regular assessment formula.
Nov. 24	SUEZ: General Assembly regrets failure of British, French and Israeli troops to withdraw.
Dec. 10-Jan. 31	TRUSTEESHIP COUNCIL: 6th special session.
Dec. 13-26	HUMAN RIGHTS: General Assembly tentatively approves articles 6 to 12 of Covenant on Economic, Social and Cultural Rights.
Dec. 18	MEMBERSHIP: General Assembly admits Japan as 80th member.
Dec. 21	BUDGET: General Assembly authorizes $62.9 million ($2.1 million for 1956, $48.8 million for 1957 and $10.0 million for UNEF).
Dec. 22	SUEZ: Anglo-French withdrawal is completed.
Dec. 28	SUEZ: Clearance of Canal begins.

1957

Jan. 23	SOUTH WEST AFRICA: General Assembly authorizes committee to hear petitioners.
Jan. 24	KASHMIR: Security Council reiterates decision for free plebiscite.
Jan. 30	SOUTH AFRICA: General Assembly deplores policy of *apartheid;* urges negotiations on the question of Indians in South Africa.
Feb. 2	SUEZ: General Assembly calls upon Israel to withdraw.
Feb. 14	ARMS CONTROL: General Assembly recommends that Disarmament Commission considers several proposals.
Feb. 15	ALGERIA: General Assembly hopes for peaceful settlement.
Feb. 20	INTERNATIONAL FINANCE CORPORATION: General Assembly approves agreement bringing IFC into relationship with ECOSOC.
	KASHMIR: USSR vetoes draft resolution of the Security Council which considers the possible use of a UN force.
	WOMEN: General Assembly approves Convention on the Nationality of Married Women.
Feb. 26	CYPRUS: General Assembly hopes for resumption of negotiations.
	ECONOMIC DEVELOPMENT: General Assembly requests *Ad Hoc* Committee to make suggestions.
	SOUTH WEST AFRICA: General Assembly adopts seven resolutions, including request to Committee to study what legal courses of action are open.

1957 (continued)

Feb. 28	WEST IRIAN (NEW GUINEA): General Assembly is unable to agree on a resolution.
March 8	MEMBERSHIP: General Assembly admits Ghana as 81st member.
March 14-May 15	TRUSTEESHIP COUNCIL: 19th regular session.
March 8-Sept. 6	ARMS CONTROL: Sub-committee of Disarmament Commission.
April 8-18	RADIATION: Scientific Committee.
April 16-May 2	ECOSOC: 23rd regular session.
April 16	TRUSTEESHIP: French decree is issued, promulgating statute for the Cameroons.
April 29	KASHMIR: UN reports that it is unable to suggest concrete proposals likely to contribute to a solution.
May 20-July 12	TRUSTEESHIP COUNCIL: 20th regular session.
July 2-Aug. 2	ECOSOC: 24th regular session.
July 6	NORWAY/FRANCE CASE: International Court of Justice declines jurisdiction.
July 29	ATOMIC ENERGY: IAEA comes into being.
Aug. 2	NON-SELF-GOVERNING TERRITORIES: Belgium announces that information would be transmitted to UN Library.
Sept. 9	MEMBERSHIP: USSR vetoes draft resolution of the Security Council on admission of Republic of Korea and Viet Nam.
Sept. 10-14	GENERAL ASSEMBLY: Resumed 11th regular session.
Sept. 12-20	TRUSTEESHIP COUNCIL: 7th special session.
Sept. 17-Dec. 14	GENERAL ASSEMBLY: 12th regular session.
Sept. 17	MEMBERSHIP: General Assembly admits Malaya as 82nd member.
Sept. 24	CHINA: Question of representation in General Assembly is postponed by a vote of 47 to 27, with 7 abstentions.
Oct. 2	INTERHANDEL (SWITZERLAND/USA) CASE: Case is brought to International Court of Justice.
Oct. 10	NETHERLANDS/SWEDEN CASE: Case is brought to International Court of Justice.
	TECHNICAL ASSISTANCE: Pledging conference results in pledges of $32.3 million for 1958.
Oct. 11-Nov. 4	HUMAN RIGHTS: General Assembly tentatively approves articles 14 to 16 of Covenant on Economic Social and Cultural Rights.
Oct. 16	AERIAL INCIDENT CASE: Case Israel, UK and USA versus Bulgaria is brought to International Court of Justice.
Oct. 25	SOUTH WEST AFRICA: General Assembly establishes Good Offices Committee.
Nov. 13-25	HUMAN RIGHTS: General Assembly tentatively approves article 6 of Covenant on Civil and Political Rights.
Nov. 14	RADIATION: General Assembly calls upon all concerned to co-operate with Scientific Committee.

1957 (continued)

Nov. 19   ARMS CONTROL: Membership of Disarmament Commission is increased from 11 to 25.

Nov. 26   KOREA: General Assembly approves termination of UNKRA on 30 June 1958.

NON-SELF-GOVERNING TERRITORIES: General Assembly rejects proposal for study of Charter interpretations.

REFUGEES: General Assembly continues Office of High Commissioner (UNHCR) for 5 years; appeals for activities for Hong Kong refugees.

SOUTH AFRICA: General Assembly deplores failure to change racial policies.

TRADE: General Assembly urges members to approve the establishment of the Organization of Trade Co-operation.

Nov. 27   BELGIUM/NETHERLANDS CASE: Border problem is brought to International Court of Justice.

Nov. 29   KOREA: General Assembly reiterates objective of peaceful unification.

WEST IRIAN: General Assembly is unable to agree on a resolution.

Dec. 2   KASHMIR: Security Council requests UN Representative to make recommendations.

Dec. 9   HUNGARY: Special Representative reports that his negotiations with the USSR and Hungary have been fruitless.

Dec. 10-13   ECOSOC: Resumed 24th regular session.

Dec. 10   ALGERIA: General Assembly wishes that parties enter into pourparler.

Dec. 14   BUDGET: General Assembly authorizes $87.4 million ($2.4 million for 1957, $55.0 million for 1958; and $30.0 million for UNEF).

CYPRUS: General Assembly is unable to agree on a resolution.

ECONOMIC DEVELOPMENT: General Assembly decides to establish a Special Fund for technical assistance instead of SUNFED.

REGIONAL COMMISSION: General Assembly accepts land in Santiago, Chile, for establishing regional offices.

SUEZ: General Assembly approves a 3 per cent surcharge on Canal tolls to pay for $8.4 million cost of clearing the canal.

TRUSTEESHIP: General Assembly recommends establishing an Arbitration Tribunal in connection with Ethiopian boundary; and elects Commissioner to supervise French Togoland elections.

Dec. 16   MIDDLE EAST: Secretary-General names Francisco Uurrutia Holquin as his personal representative to Jordan and Israel.

Dec. 21   HUNGARY: Permanent representative of Hungary refuses to transmit to his government, letter from Special Committee on the Problem of Hungary.

1957 (continued)

Dec. 31   CHILDREN: UNICEF contributions total $17.9 million
for 1957.

1958

Jan. 18   MIDDLE EAST: Secretary-General's representative reports
agreement on Mt. Scopus situation by Israel and Jordan.

Jan. 22   MIDDLE EAST: Security Council calls for suspension of
incidents in Jerusalem.

Jan. 27-Feb. 28   RADIATION: Meeting of Scientific Committee.

Jan. 30-March 26   TRUSTEESHIP COUNCIL: 21st regular session.

Feb. 18   TUNISIA: Security Council hears complaint of French air
attack on Sakiet-Sidi-Yousef; UK-USA offers of good offices.

Feb. 22   SUDAN: Security Council hears complaint against Egyptian
boundary claims.

Feb. 24-April 27   INTERNATIONAL LAW: UN Conference on the Law of the
Sea approves final act, four conventions and a protocol.

Feb. 26-27   NON-GOVERNMENTAL ORGANIZATIONS: Conference on
UN Information.

March 6   UNITED ARAB REPUBLIC: Membership of UN is reduced to
81, as Egypt and Syria join to form the United Arab Republic
(UAR).

March 11-Apr. 15   TECHNICAL ASSISTANCE: Preparatory Committee of the
Special Fund.

March 17   TRANSPORT: IMCO agreement comes into effect with
acceptance by Japan.

March 31   HEADQUARTERS: 4 millionth visitor.

KASHMIR: UN Representative reports to Security Council five
recommendations to parties.

April 15-May 2   ECOSOC: 25th regular session.

April 21   ARMS CONTROL: Security Council hears USSR complaint of
US flight in the Arctic.

April 27   TRUSTEESHIP: UN Commissioner supervises elections in
French Togoland.

April 29   AFRICA: ECOSOC establishes Economic Commission for
Africa (ECA).

April 30   ATOMIC TESTING: USSR announces to UN unilateral
discontinuance of testing.

REFUGEES: ECOSOC establishes Executive Committee of the
Program of the High Commissioner for Refugees.

May 2   ARMS CONTROL: USSR vetoes draft resolution of the
Security Council on plan for an Arctic inspection zone.

May 7-8   ATOMIC ENERGY: Advisory Committee on Peaceful Uses of
Atomic Energy.

May 22   LEBANON: Lebanon complains to Security Council of United
Arab Republic intervention in domestic affairs.

1958 (continued)

June 4	TUNISIA: Security Council adjourns debate until 18 June to permit parties to negotiate.
June 9-Aug. 1	TRUSTEESHIP COUNCIL: 22nd regular session.
June 10	INTERNATIONAL LAW: UN Conference on International Commercial Arbitration adopts Convention on the Recognition and Enforcement of Foreign Arbitral Awards.
June 11	LEBANON: Security Council establishes UN Observers Group in Lebanon (UNOGIL).
June 18	TUNISIA: Agreement for evacuation of French troops is reported to Security Council.
June 21	HUNGARY: Special Committee on the Problem of Hungary deplores executions of Imre Nagy, Pal Maleter and others.
June 30	BUDGET: Available cash balance of UN is sufficient for only three weeks of operations.
July 1-31	ECOSOC: 26th regular session.
July 1	HONDURAS/NICARAGUA CASE: Honduras brings case to International Court of Justice.
July 14	HUNGARY: Special Committee issues report on Problem of Hungary.
	IRAQ: Coup results in change of government.
July 15	LEBANON: Security Council is notified of landing of US troops.
July 16	LEBANON: UNOGIL reports full freedom of access to borders of Lebanon.
July 17	JORDAN: Jordan complains to Security Council of United Arab Republic interference in domestic affairs.
July 18	LEBANON: Security Council defeats USSR proposal for withdrawal of UK and US forces from Jordan and Lebanon and defeats Swedish proposal for suspension of UNOGIL; USSR vetoes draft resolution of the Security Council on additional measures in Lebanon.
July 19	MIDDLE EAST: USSR invites Secretary-General to summit conference on Middle East.
July 21	LEBANON: USSR vetoes draft resolution of the Security Council to strengthen UNOGIL.
Aug. 8-21	MIDDLE EAST: 3rd emergency special session of the General Assembly on the Middle East.
Aug. 10	RADIATION: Scientific Committee issues first comprehensive report on the effects of atomic radiation.
Aug. 11	WOMEN: Convention on Nationality of Married Women comes into effect.
Aug. 13	MIDDLE EAST: President of the USA proposes six point peace program to General Assembly.
Aug. 21	ARMS CONTROL: Eight Powers agree that a workable and effective system for detecting explosions is feasible.

1958 (continued)

Aug. 21	LEBANON-JORDAN: General Assembly calls upon all states to act in accordance with mutual respect and requests Secretary-General to make practical arrangements.
Aug. 22	AERIAL INCIDENT CASE: USA brings case against USSR to the International Court of Justice.
Aug. 26	LEBANON: UNOGIL reports 190 military observers from fifteen countries.
Sept. 1-12	ATOMIC ENERGY: 2nd UN International Conference on the Peaceful Uses of Atomic Energy.
Sept. 8-10	COMMODITIES: UN Exploratory Meeting on Copper.
Sept. 11-13	COMMODITIES: UN Exploratory Meeting on Lead.
Sept. 15	TRUSTEESHIP COUNCIL: 8th special session.
Sept. 16-Dec. 13	GENERAL ASSEMBLY: 13th regular session.
Sept. 20	LEBANON: UNOGIL reports 214 military observers from 21 countries.
Sept. 22-Oct. 24	COMMODITIES: UN Sugar Conference adopts 1958 International Sugar Agreement.
Sept. 23	BARCELONA LIGHT AND POWER CASE: Belgium brings case to International Court of Justice.
	CHINA: Question of representation in the General Assembly is postponed by a vote of 42 to 28, with 11 abstentions.
Sept. 29	LEBANON-JORDAN: Secretary-General reports on practical measures, including UN presence in the area.
Oct. 13-17	TRUSTEESHIP COUNCIL: 8th special session.
Oct. 13	FRENCH TOGOLAND: France informs the Trusteeship Council that French Togoland will become independent in 1960.
Oct. 16-29	HUMAN RIGHTS: General Assembly tentatively adopts articles 7 to 9 of the Draft Covenant on Civil and Political Rights.
Oct. 16	TECHNICAL ASSISTANCE: Pledging conference results in pledges of $27 million for the expanded program and $21 million for the special fund.
Oct. 23-Dec. 11	ECOSOC: Resumed 26th regular session.
Oct. 25	LEBANON: US withdraws troops.
Oct. 27	MIDDLE EAST: $27.5 million pledged by 32 governments for UNRWAPRNE.
	REFUGEES: $3.1 million pledged by 26 governments for the program of the Office of the High Commissioner for Refugees.
Oct. 30	SOUTH AFRICA: General Assembly regrets no change in *apartheid* policy.
	SOUTH WEST AFRICA: General Assembly rejects partition.
Nov. 2	JORDAN: UK withdraws troops.

1958 (continued)

Nov. 4	ARMS CONTROL: General Assembly urges early agreement on testing and on measures against surprise attack; membership of Disarmament Commission is increased from 25 to 81 (full UN membership).
Nov. 6-7	TRUSTEESHIP COUNCIL: 9th special session.
Nov. 14	HUMAN RIGHTS: General Assembly tentatively adopts text of article 10 of the Draft Covenant on Civil and Political Rights.
	KOREA: General Assembly calls on communist authorities to agree to free elections.
Dec. 4	TECHNICAL ASSISTANCE: Paul G. Hoffman is appointed Managing Director of UN Special Fund.
Dec. 5	CYPRUS: General Assembly expresses confidence that parties will reach a solution.
	REFUGEES: General Assembly urges members to co-operate in a Refugee Year.
	TRUSTEESHIP: Trusteeship Council is asked to report to the resumed session of the General Assembly (20 February-13 March 1959), concerning the possibility of independence for both Cameroons; General Assembly invites administering authorities to consider target dates for self-government of trust territories.
Dec. 8	MIDDLE EAST: Security Council hears Israeli complaint against United Arab Republic attack.
Dec. 9	LEBANON: UNOGIL ceases operations.
Dec. 10	INTERNATIONAL LAW: General Assembly decides to convene a 2nd International Conference on the Law of the Sea in 1960.
	LIBYA: General Assembly invites governments to give economic assistance.
Dec. 12	ECONOMIC DEVELOPMENT: General Assembly adopts nine resolutions on improving international commodity trade, stimulating private investment, establishment of a roster for technical personnel, and commodity trade.
	INFORMATION: General Assembly recommends that members open their countries to greater freedom of communication about the UN.
	HUNGARY: General Assembly calls upon USSR and Hungary to desist from repressive measures.
	MEMBERSHIP: General Assembly admits Guinea as 82nd member.
	NATURAL RESOURCES: General Assembly establishes commission to survey rights of peoples to sovereignty over their natural resources.

1958 (continued)

Dec. 12   NON-SELF-GOVERNING TERRITORIES: General Assembly
               urges administering authorities to give constant attention to
               questions of racial discrimination; Committee on Information
               from Non-Self-Governing Territories continues for three
               years.
               MIDDLE EAST: General Assembly reiterates concern for plight
               of refugees and precarious financial position of
               UNRWAPRNE.
Dec. 13   ALGERIA: General Assembly is unable to agree on a
               resolution.
               BUDGET: General Assembly authorizes $91.9 million
               ($6.1 million for 1958, $60.8 million for 1959 and $25.0
               million for UNEF).
               HUNGARY: Credentials Committee of General Assembly takes
               no action on the credentials of the Hungarian delegation.
               OUTER SPACE: General Assembly establishes *Ad Hoc* Study
               Group.
               RADIATION: Scientific Committee.
Dec. 18   ARMS CONTROL: Last meeting of Conference of Experts on
               Surprise Attack.
Dec. 29   ECONOMIC COMMISSION FOR AFRICA: 1st session.

1959

Jan. 26-27   SPECIAL FUND: 1st session of the Governing Council.
Jan. 30-Feb. 18   TRUSTEESHIP COUNCIL: 23rd regular session.
Feb. 13   FRANCE/LEBANON CASE: Case on taxes on French
                   companies is referred to the International Court of Justice.
Feb. 20-March 13   GENERAL ASSEMBLY: Resumed 13th regular session.
March 13   TRUSTEESHIP: General Assembly terminates French
                   trusteeship over Cameroon on 1 January 1960.
March 17-20   TRUSTEESHIP COUNCIL: Resumed 23rd regular session.
March 21   INTERHANDEL CASE: International Court of Justice rejects
                   contention of US domestic jurisdiction and rules that
                   Switzerland has not exhausted all US remedies.
March 25   IMCO CASE: International Court of Justice receives request for
                   advisory opinion on constitutionality of IMCO's Maritime
                   Safety Committee.
April 7-24   ECOSOC: 27th regular session.
May 26-28   SPECIAL FUND: 2nd session of Governing Council authorizes
                   $7.6 million for 13 projects in 16 countries.
May 26   AERIAL INCIDENT CASE: International Court of Justice finds
                   that it is without jurisdiction in the Israel versus Bulgaria
                   case.
June 2-Aug. 6   TRUSTEESHIP COUNCIL: 24th regular session.

1959 (continued)

June 15	RADIATION: UN Scientific Committee of the Effects of Atomic Radiation issues progress report.
June 20	BELGIUM/NETHERLANDS CASE: International Court of Justice rules in favor of Belgian border claim.
June 26	COMMODITIES: International Agreement on Olive Oil enters into force.
June 30-July 31	ECOSOC: 28th regular session.
Sept. 4	LAOS: Security Council considers complaint by Laos, charging North Viet Nam with aiding rebels.
Sept. 7	LAOS: Security Council creates sub-committee of enquiry on the situation in Laos.
Sept. 10	ARMS CONTROL: Disarmament Commission encourages negotiations on disarmament issues outside the UN by the Committee of Ten.
	UNEF: Secretary-General submits 3rd progress report on organization and financing of UNEF.
Sept. 15-Dec. 13	GENERAL ASSEMBLY: 14th regular session.
Sept. 17	ARMS CONTROL: British Foreign Minister proposes three stage disarmament process to General Assembly.
Sept. 18	ARMS CONTROL: USSR calls for general and complete disarmament during General Assembly session.
Sept. 22	CHINA: Question of representation in the General Assembly is postponed by a vote of 44 to 29, with 9 abstentions.
Oct. 6	CAMBODIA/THAILAND CASE: Border dispute on Temple of Preah-Vihear is referred to International Court of Justice.
Oct. 21	TIBET: General Assembly deplores events in Tibet.
Nov. 4	LAOS: Security Council considers report by Sub-committee on Laos.
Nov. 7	TRUSTEESHIP: UN administered plebiscite is held in Northern Section of British Cameroons.
Nov. 17	SOUTH AFRICA: General Assembly regrets failure of South Africa to modify its *apartheid* policy.
Nov. 20	ARMS CONTROL: General Assembly unanimously transmits UK and USSR proposals to Disarmament Commission and to the new Disarmament Committee of Ten outside the UN.
	ATOMIC TESTING: General Assembly asks France to refrain from nuclear tests in the Sahara.
	HUMAN RIGHTS: General Assembly adopts Declaration of Rights of the Child.
Nov. 21	ATOMIC TESTING: General Assembly expresses hope that states will intensify efforts to reach agreement and urges states concerned with negotiations to continue their present voluntary discontinuance of nuclear weapons testing.
Dec. 2-14	TRUSTEESHIP COUNCIL: 10th special session considers plebiscite results in Northern section of British Cameroons.

1959 (continued)

Dec. 5   BUDGET: General Assembly authorizes $84.0 million
              ($0.9 million for 1959, $63.1 million for 1960 and $20.0
              million for UNEF).
              ECONOMIC DEVELOPMENT: General Assembly asks for
              study on establishment of a UN Capital Development Fund.
              TRUSTEESHIP: General Assembly notes 1 July 1960 as
              independence date for Italian administered Somaliland and 27
              April 1960 as independence date for French administered
              Togoland.

Dec. 7   INTERNATIONAL LAW: General Assembly decides to
              convene conference on diplomatic intercourse and immunities.

Dec. 8-10   SPECIAL FUND: 3rd session of Governing Council authorizes
              $23.7 million for 31 projects in 35 countries.

Dec. 9   HUNGARY: General Assembly deplores disregard of its
              resolutions on situation in Hungary by USSR and Hungary.
              KOREA: General Assembly continues work on UNCURK.
              MIDDLE EAST: General Assembly continues work on
              UNRWA.

Dec. 10   REFUGEES: $7 million are pledged at meeting of General
              Assembly in support of the World Refugee Year.
              SOUTH AFRICA: General Assembly appeals to South Africa to
              negotiate with India and Pakistan on treatment of persons of
              Indian origin.

Dec. 12   ALGERIA: General Assembly fails to approve request for
              negotiations between France and Algerian nationalists.
              OUTER SPACE: General Assembly establishes Committee on
              Peaceful Uses of Outer Space.

Dec. 14-15   ECOSOC: Resumed 28th session.

1960

Jan. 1   TRUSTEESHIP: Cameroons, a former French Trust territory,
              becomes independent; first UN trust territory to become a
              sovereign state.

Jan. 25-Feb. 8 TRUSTEESHIP COUNCIL: 25th regular session.

Feb. 18   MIDDLE EAST: Secretary-General warns that Middle Eastern
              situation is deteriorating.

March 15   ATOMIC TESTING: 22 Asian and African States request
              special session of the General Assembly on French nuclear
              tests in the Sahara.

March 17-April 26 INTERNATIONAL LAW: 2nd UN Conference on Law of the
              Sea.

March 30   SOUTH AFRICA: Security Council meets at request of
              29 Asian and African States to consider the situation arising
              from the large-scale killings of unarmed and peaceful
              demonstrators against racial policies of South Africa.

1960 (continued)

April 1	SOUTH AFRICA: Security Council calls upon South Africa to abandon its *apartheid* policies which, if continued, might endanger international peace.
April 5-21	ECOSOC: 29th regular session.
April 12	ECONOMIC DEVELOPMENT: ECOSOC establishes UN Standing Committee for Industrial Development.
	PORTUGAL/INDIA CASE: International Court of Justice renders judgements in Portugal versus India case on right of access of Portugal to its enclaves in India.
April 14-June 30	TRUSTEESHIP COUNCIL: 26th regular session.
April 15	ATOMIC TESTING: Request for special session of the General Assembly on French nuclear tests fails to get majority approval.
April 26	INTERNATIONAL LAW: 2nd UN Conference on Law of the Sea fails to adopt proposals on width of territorial sea and coastal fishing rights.
April 27	TRUSTEESHIP: Togo, a former French administered trust territory, becomes independent.
May 23-June 24	COMMODITIES: UN Tin Conference.
May 25-27	SPECIAL FUND: 4th session of Governing Council approves 30 projects for $58.6 million.
May 26	U-2 INCIDENT: Security Council rejects proposal of USSR condemning incursion by US aircraft.
May 27	SUMMIT TALKS: Security Council urges France, UK, USA and USSR to seek solutions to existing international problems following summit breakdown.
June 6	STATELESS PERSONS: UN Convention guaranteeing basic economic, social and legal rights to the stateless comes into force.
June 8	IMCO CASE: International Court of Justice renders advisory decision.
June 23	EICHMAN INCIDENT: Security Council asks Israel to make "appropriate reparations" for transfer of Adolph Eichman from Argentina to Israel.
June 24	COMMODITIES: 2nd International Tin Agreement is adopted.
June 30	TRUSTEESHIP COUNCIL: Trusteeship Council decides to delay decision on date of 27th session in 1961 until General Assembly acts on the membership problem: too many elected non-administrative members.
July 1	TRUSTEESHIP: Somali, a former Italian administered trust territory, becomes independent.
July 5-Aug. 5	ECOSOC: 30th regular session.
July 12	CONGO: President and Prime Minister of Congo request urgent dispatch of UN military assistance.
July 13	CONGO: Security Council meets at request of Secretary-General to consider situation in Congo.

1960 (continued)

July 14	CONGO: Security Council adopts Tunisian proposal on Congo; calls on Belgium to withdraw troops; authorizes Secretary-General to provide military assistance and technical assistance; begins UN operations in the Congo (ONUC).
July 15	CONGO: 1st troops under ONUC operation arrive in Congo.
July 18-19	CUBA: Security Council decides to adjourn consideration of Cuban complaint against the USA until report is received from Organization of American States.
July 22	CONGO: Security Council calls for rapid withdrawal of Belgium troops.
July 26-Aug. 3	CONGO: Secretary-General visits Congo.
July 26	RB-47 INCIDENT: USSR charges against US plane incident; vetoes draft resolution of the Security Council to refer aerial incident to International Court of Justice; and vetoes draft resolution of the Security Council including a request to the International Red Cross.
August 1	ONUC: Secretary-General announces UN forces of 11,155 in Congo: contingents from Ethiopia, Ghana, Guinea, Ireland, Liberia, Morocco, Sweden and Tunisia.
August 8-19	CRIME: 2nd UN Congress on Prevention of Crime and Treatment of Offenders.
August 9	CONGO: Security Council requests Belgium to withdraw from Katanga Province.
August 11-15	CONGO: Secretary-General makes 2nd visit to help situation.
August 12	SOUTH WEST AFRICA: Committee on South West Africa calls for change in policies and methods in administrative mandated area of South West Africa.
August 13	CONGO: UN forces enter into Katanga.
August 16-18	ARMS CONTROL: Disarmament Commission calls for continued efforts.
August 31	KOREA: UN Korean Reconstruction Agency goes out of existence; carried out $150 million program of aid.
Sept. 8	DOMINICAN REPUBLIC: Security Council considers USSR request to discuss decisions of OAS foreign ministers on the Dominican Republic.
Sept. 12-15	COMMODITIES: International Lead and Zinc Study Group.
Sept. 17	CONGO: Security Council rejects a USSR proposal to have UN command cease interference in internal politics in Congo and calls for an emergency special session of the General Assembly; USSR vetoes draft resolution of the Security Council requesting the Secretary-General to implement previous decisions.
Sept. 17-20	CONGO: 4th emergency special session of the General Assembly on Congo calls for continued assistance to Congo and urges members to refrain from military assistance outside the UN.

1960 (continued)

Sept. 19	KASHMIR: India and Pakistan sign Indus Water Treaty and settle dispute with help of World Bank.
Sept. 20-Dec. 20	GENERAL ASSEMBLY: 15th regular session.
Sept. 20	MEMBERSHIP: General Assembly admits Cameroon, Central African Republic, Chad, Congo (Brazzaville), Congo (Leopoldville), Cyprus, Dahomey, Gabon, Ivory Coast, Madagascar, Niger, Somali, Togo and Upper Volta as 83rd to 96th members.
Sept. 22	AFRICA: US President, speaking before the General Assembly, proposes UN program for independence and development of Africa.
	SECRETARY-GENERAL: Soviet Premier, speaking to the General Assembly, proposes abolition of post of the Secretary-General and replacement by a three man executive body.
Sept. 26	ECONOMIC DEVELOPMENT: International Development Association comes into existence.
Sept. 28	MEMBERSHIP: General Assembly admits Mali and Senegal as 97th and 98th members.
Oct. 3	SECRETARY-GENERAL: Soviet Premier repeats proposal for replacement of post of Secretary-General by executive organ; Secretary-General comments on the USSR proposal for his replacement.
Oct. 7	MEMBERSHIP: General Assembly admits Nigeria as 99th member.
Oct. 8	CHINA: Question of representation in General Assembly is postponed by a vote of 42 to 34, with 22 abstentions.
Oct. 31	SOUTH TYROL: Austria and Italy resume negotiations on the status of South Tyrol urged by the General Assembly.
Nov. 4	SOUTH AFRICA CASES: Ethiopia and Liberia institute proceedings before the International Court of Justice against South Africa: question of violation of treaty obligations on South West Africa.
Nov. 8	ECONOMIC DEVELOPMENT: International Development Association starts operation.
Nov. 18	HONDURAS/NICARAGUA CASE: International Court of Justice renders decision in favor of Honduras.
Nov. 22	CONGO: General Assembly seats representatives named by President Kasavubu.
Dec. 3	MEMBERSHIP: USSR vetoes draft resolution of the Security Council on application of Mauritania.
Dec. 5	REFUGEES: Felix Schnyder is elected to serve as UN High Commissioner for Refugees.
Dec. 13	CONGO: USSR vetoes draft resolution of the Security Council on the proposal of Secretary-General to continue efforts to restore law and order in Congo.

1960 (continued)

Dec. 14   DECOLONIZATION: General Assembly adopts declaration on granting independence to colonial peoples.

Dec. 15   ECONOMIC DEVELOPMENT: General Assembly votes to establish UN Capital Development Fund and approves proposal for concerted action for economic development of developing countries.

Dec. 18   SOUTH WEST AFRICA: General Assembly adopts six resolutions dealing with the problem.

                 TRUSTEESHIP: General Assembly calls for plebiscite for Western Samoa on question of independence in May 1961.

Dec. 19   ALGERIA: General Assembly recognizes right of Algerian people to self determination.

Dec. 20   ARMS CONTROL: General Assembly approves three resolutions on preventing wider dissemination of nuclear weapons and suspension of nuclear tests.

                 BUDGET: General Assembly authorizes $167.1 million ($73.0 million for 1961, $2.6 million for 1960, $19.0 million for UNEF, $48.5 million for ONUC in 1960, and $24.0 million for ONUC for 3 months in 1961).

                 CONGO: General Assembly fails to adopt two resolutions on the Congo and retains issue on agenda.

                 ECOSOC: After inconclusive balloting, General Assembly fails to fill sixth vacancy on ECOSOC and postpones further action until General Assembly resumes in 1961.

                 TRUSTEESHIP: General Assembly creates commission to supervise elections in Ruanda-Urundi and to observe conference on future of the Belgian administered Trust Territory.

Dec. 21-22   ECOSOC: Resumed 30th regular session.

1961

Jan. 3-Feb. 20   CONGO: UN Conciliation Commission for the Congo visits the Congo.

Jan. 4-5   CUBA: Security Council discusses Cuban charges against USA.

Jan. 6-12   SOUTH AFRICA: Secretary-General consults with South African government on its racial policies under Security Council mandate of April 1960.

Jan. 24-Mar. 25 NARCOTICS: UN Conference on Single Convention on Narcotic Drugs.

Feb. 11-12   TRUSTEESHIP: UN supervises plebiscite on future of Cameroons under UK administration.

Feb. 20   CONGO: USSR vetoes draft resolution of the Security Council on atrocities and assassinations in the Congo.

March 2-April 18 INTERNATIONAL LAW: UN Conference on Diplomatic Intercourse and Immunities.

1961 (continued)

March 7-April 22	GENERAL ASSEMBLY: Resumed 15th regular session.
March 10	ANGOLA: Security Council fails to take action on Liberian complaint against Portugal's policies in Angola.
March 16	SOUTH WEST AFRICA: General Assembly appeals to those members "which have particularly close and continuous relations" with South Africa to influence that government to adjust its conduct to UN obligations and to give effect to Assembly resolutions.
March 20	CONGO: UN Conciliation Commission for the Congo reports: stresses need to end foreign interference; advocates federal government; stresses worsening economic situation in Congo.
March 27	ECONOMIC DEVELOPMENT: UN and International Development Association approve agreement.
March 30	DRUGS: General Assembly approves single Convention on World Drug Control: culminates 10 years of codification work.
April 4	ECOSOC: 31st regular session is adjourned after one meeting; constitutional problem of electing 18th member is referred to President of General Assembly.
April 6	MIDDLE EAST: Security Council considers protest of Jordan against Israeli military show in Jerusalem.
April 7	SOUTH WEST AFRICA: General Assembly calls the attention of the Security Council to situation.
April 10	BARCELONA LIGHT AND POWER CASE: Case is removed from International Court of Justice after Belgium announced it would not proceed with the case.
	CAMBODIA/THAILAND CASE: International Court of Justice begins hearings on border dispute.
April 11	TRUSTEESHIP: 11th special session of Trusteeship Council considers report on plebiscite held in UK administered Trust Territory of Cameroons.
April 13	SOUTH AFRICA: General Assembly deplores the disregard of its repeated requests for a revision of *apartheid* policy and urges negotiations with India and Pakistan on the treatment of persons of Indian origin.
April 15	CONGO: General Assembly creates a Commission of Conciliation on the political crisis and establishes a Commission of Investigation on assassinations.
April 18	ECOSOC: General Assembly solves ECOSOC deadlock and elects Italy as 18th member.
April 19-28	ECOSOC: Reconvened 31st regular session.
April 19	MEMBERSHIP: General Assembly supports the admission of Outer Mongolia and Mauritania.
April 20	ANGOLA: General Assembly urges Portugal to make reforms and appoints a sub-committee to study the situation.

1961 (continued)

April 21   BUDGET: General Assembly authorizes $100 million for
                      ONUC from 1 January to 31 October 1961.
                      CUBA: General Assembly urges all members to take peaceful
                      actions to remove tensions.
                      TRUSTEESHIP: General Assembly decides that a referendum
                      and elections be held in Ruanda-Urundi under UN supervision
                      in August 1961; decides that Northern Cameroons would join
                      Nigeria on 1 June 1961 and that Southern Cameroons would
                      join the Republic of Cameroon on 1 October 1961, following
                      February plebiscite; and decides in agreement with UK that
                      Trusteeship Agreement for Tanganyika should end on
                      attainment of independence of Tanganyika on 28 December
                      1961.

May 23-June 1   SPECIAL FUND: 6th session of the Council authorizes
                      $34.6 million for 42 projects in 36 countries.

May 26   CAMBODIA/THAILAND CASE: International Court of Justice
                      unanimously declares it has jurisdiction.

May 30   CAMEROON/UK CASE: Republic of Cameroon institutes
                      proceedings before International Court of Justice on alleged
                      failure of UK to respect obligations of 1946 trusteeship
                      agreement.

June 1-July 19   TRUSTEESHIP COUNCIL: 27th regular session.

June 1   TRUSTEESHIP: Trust territory of British administered
                      Northern Cameroons achieves independence by joining
                      Nigeria.

June 9   ANGOLA: Security Council calls on Portugal "to desist
                      forthwith from repressive measures" in Angola.

July 2-7   KUWAIT: Security Council considers complaint by Kuwait
                      against Iraq, and Iraqi complaint against UK troops in
                      Kuwait.

July 7   KUWAIT: USSR vetoes draft resolution of the Security Council
                      calling on all states to respect independence of Kuwait.

July 4-Aug. 4   ECOSOC: 32nd regular session.

July 21-29   TUNISIA: Security Council considers Tunisian complaint of
                      French "acts of aggression" and adopts interim resolution
                      calling for cease-fire, but fails to resolve question due to
                      French non-participation.

Aug. 10   CONGO: Following prolonged negotiation by ONUC, Secretary
                      General announces receipt of letter from Premier Cyrille
                      Adoula stating that "the Congolese Parliament ... has ended
                      the Congolese constitutional crisis by unanimously placing its
                      confidence in a Government of national unity and political
                      reconciliation".

Aug. 21-31   ECONOMIC DEVELOPMENT: UN Conference on New
                      Sources of Energy.

1961 (continued)

Aug. 21-25	GENERAL ASSEMBLY: 3rd special session considers the situation in Tunisia.
Aug. 25	TUNISIA: General Assembly recognizes the sovereign right of Tunisia to call for the withdrawal of French forces in Tunisia and urges peaceful negotiation for the withdrawal of these forces.
Sept. 18	SECRETARY-GENERAL: Secretary-General Dag Hammarskjöld is killed in plane crash near Ndola, Northern Rhodesia, on his way to meet leader of secessionist province of Katanga of the Congo.
Sept. 19-Dec. 21	GENERAL ASSEMBLY: 16th regular session.
Sept. 21	CONGO: Provisional agreement on cease-fire between ONUC and Katanga authorities comes into effect.
Sept. 27	MEMBERSHIP: Sierra Leone is admitted as 100th member.
Oct. 1	TRUSTEESHIP: Trust territory of British administered Southern Cameroons attains independence by joining Republic of Cameroon.
Oct. 11	SOUTH AFRICA: General Assembly censures South African Foreign Minister for remarks in the General Debate.
Oct. 13	MEMBERSHIP: Following ruling of President of the General Assembly, Syria resumes membership as 101st member.
Oct. 18	TRUSTEESHIP: General Assembly endorses results of plebiscite in Western Samoa whereby the trust area will achieve independence on 1 January 1962.
Oct. 27	ATOMIC TESTS: General Assembly appeals to the USSR to refrain from exploding 50 megaton bomb.
	MEMBERSHIP: General Assembly admits Mauritania and Mongolia as 102nd and 103rd members.
Oct. 30	BUDGET: General Assembly authorizes the expenditure of up to $10 million per month for the ONUC until 31 December 1961.
Nov. 3	SECRETARY-GENERAL: U Thant of Burma is unanimously appointed Acting Secretary-General for a term ending 10 April 1963.
Nov. 8	ATOMIC TESTS: General Assembly calls on all states to consider a treaty to ensure that nuclear weapon tests would be prohibited under effective controls.
Nov. 22-28	DOMINICAN REPUBLIC: Security Council considers Cuban charges that the USA contemplates "armed intervention" in the Dominican Republic.
Nov. 24	ARMS CONTROL: General Assembly calls on all members to consider Africa a denuclearized zone and approves a declaration on the prohibition of the use of nuclear and thermonuclear weapons.

1961 (continued)

Nov. 24   CONGO: Security Council authorizes the Secretary-General to
           "take vigorous action, including the use of ... force" to arrest
           and deport foreign personnel and advisers in Katanga; USSR
           vetoes US amendments to the Security Council resolution.

Nov. 27   CONGO: Acting Secretary-General U Thant and Congolese
           Foreign Minister Justin Bombako sign agreement providing
           for full freedom of movement for ONUC throughout the
           Congo.

           DECOLONIZATION: General Assembly creates special
           committee to encourage the implementation of the 1960
           Declaration on the Granting of Independence to Colonial
           Countries and Peoples.

Nov. 28   SOUTH AFRICA: General Assembly again urges South Africa
           to change its racial policies and calls upon South Africa to
           enter into negotiations on the treatment of people of Indian
           and Indo-Pakistani origin.

           SOUTH TYROL: General Assembly calls upon Italy and
           Austria to find a solution to the problem of the German-
           speaking people in Bolzano.

Dec. 9   TRUSTEESHIP: British Trust Territory of Tanganyika attains
           independence.

Dec. 14   MEMBERSHIP: General Assembly admits Tanganyika as
           104th member.

Dec. 15   CHINA: Question of representation in General Assembly is
           postponed by a vote of 48 to 37, with 19 abstentions.

Dec. 18-19 GOA: Security Council considers Portuguese complaint over
           Indian seizure of Goa, Damao and Lui; USSR vetoes draft
           resolution of the Security Council calling for cessation of
           hostilities and withdrawal of Indian forces.

Dec. 19   SOUTH WEST AFRICA: General Assembly establishes
           committee to seek the independence of South West Africa.

Dec. 20   ALGERIA: General Assembly calls upon France and
           Provisional Government of Algerian people to resume
           negotiations.

           BUDGET: General /Assembly authorizes the Secretary-General
           to issue UN bonds up to $200 million to help ease financial
           crisis; authorizes for the UN regular budget $82.1 million for
           1962 and a decease of $1.3 million for 1961; authorizes $9.8
           million for UNEF for period 1 January to 30 June 1962;
           authorizes $80 million for ONUC for period from 1
           November 1961 to 30 June 1962; and requests an advisory
           opinion from the International Court of Justice as to whether
           expenses for the UNEF and ONUC constitute "expenses of
           the organization" within the meaning of Article 17, paragraph
           2 of the Charter.

1961 (continued)

Dec. 20	DISARMAMENT: General Assembly approves the agreement between the USA and the USSR on the creation of an 18 member negotiating committee on disarmament.
	OUTER SPACE: General Assembly urges international cooperation in the peaceful use of outer space.
	TIBET: General Assembly calls "for the cessation of practices which deprive the Tibetan people" of the right of self-determination.
Dec. 21-22	ECOSOC: Resumed 32nd regular session.

1962

Jan. 1	TRUSTEESHIP: Western Samoa, the former New Zealand Trust Territory, achieves independence.
Jan. 9-15	SPECIAL FUND: 7th session of the Council authorizes $42.8 million for 48 projects in 38 countries.
Jan. 10-11	TRUSTEESHIP COUNCIL: 28th regular session.
Jan. 15-Feb. 23	GENERAL ASSEMBLY: Resumed 16th regular session.
Jan. 30	ANGOLA: General Assembly urges Portugal to undertake reforms to promote the achievement of independence by Angola.
	CONGO: Security Council rejects USSR request for the consideration of the problem of the integration of Katanga.
Jan. 31-Mar. 10	COMMODITIES: UN Wheat Conference negotiates new three year International Wheat Agreement to take effect 31 July 1962.
Feb. 23	SOUTHERN RHODESIA: General Assembly adopts resolution inquiring whether Southern Rhodesia has attained full self-government.
	TRUSTEESHIP: General Assembly creates commission to facilitate negotiations for the independence of the Belgian administered Trust Territory of Ruanda-Urundi.
Feb. 27	CUBA: Security Council decides not to place Cuban complaint against the USA on its agenda.
March 14-23	CUBA: Security Council considers Cuban request for an advisory opinion of the International Court of Justice on legal decision of the Punta del Este Conference of the Organization of American States and rejects Cuban draft resolution.
April 3-18	ECOSOC: 33rd regular session.
April 9	MIDDLE EAST: Security Council declares Israeli attack of 16-17 March on Syrian border a "flagrant" violation of 1956 Security Council resolution and calls upon Israel to refrain from such action in the future.
May 21-29	SPECIAL FUND: 8th session of the Council authorizes $36.9 million for 41 projects in 35 countries.
May 31-July 20	TRUSTEESHIP COUNCIL: 29th regular session.

1962 (continued)

June 7-28	GENERAL ASSEMBLY: Resumed 16th regular session.
June 15	CAMBODIA/THAILAND CASE: International Court of Justice decides by a vote of 9 to 3 that the Temple of Preah Vihear is situated in Cambodia and determines by a vote of 7 to 5 that Thailand is obligated to restore to Cambodia materials that might have been removed from the temple.
June 19	BARCELONA LIGHT AND POWER CASE: Belgium institutes new proceedings against Spain before the International Court of Justice.
June 22	KASHMIR: USSR vetoes draft resolution of the Security Council calling for negotiations between India and Pakistan.
June 28	SOUTHERN RHODESIA: General Assembly deplores the denial of equal political rights and liberties to all people in Southern Rhodesia and urges UK to take corrective steps.
July 1	TRUSTEESHIP: Belgian administered Trust Territory of Ruanda-Urundi becomes independent as the two states of Rwanda and Burundi.
July 3-Aug. 3	ECOSOC: 34th regular session.
July 9-Aug. 25	COMMODITIES: UN Coffee Conference adopts 5 year International Coffee Agreement.
July 20	BUDGET: International Court of Justice decides that expenditure for UNEF and ONUC are "expenses of the organization".
Aug. 6-22	CARTOGRAPHY: UN Technical Conference on the International Map of the World on the Millionth Scale.
Aug. 15	WEST IRIAN: Netherlands and Indonesia sign agreement on transfer of administration of West New Guinea from the Netherlands to UN and then to Indonesia.
Aug. 19	CONGO: UN submits Plan of National Reconciliation to the Central government and the Katanga authorities.
Sept. 18	MEMBERSHIP: General Assembly admits Burundi, Jamaica, Rwanda and Trinidad-Tobago as 105th, 106th, 107th and 108th members.
Sept. 18-Dec. 20	GENERAL ASSEMBLY: 17th regular session.
Oct. 1	WEST IRIAN: Netherlands transfers administration of West New Guinea to the UN Temporary Executive Authority.
Oct. 3-5	WEST IRIAN: UN Special Force arrives in West New Guinea to replace Netherlands naval and land forces (Netherlands forces are withdrawn by 15 November).
Oct. 5	HUMAN RIGHTS: General Assembly adopts Convention on Consent to Marriage, Minimum Age for Marriage and Registration of Marriage.
Oct. 8	MEMBERSHIP: General Assembly admits Algeria as 109th member.
Oct. 12	SOUTHERN RHODESIA: General Assembly urges UK to take steps to release political prisoners.

1962 (continued)

Oct. 22	WEST IRIAN: Dr. Djalal Abdoh of Iran is appointed UN Administrator.
Oct. 23-25	CUBA: Security Council hears complaints by CUBA, USA and USSR on crisis that developed following US disclosure of secret presence of Soviet "missiles and other offensive weapons in Cuba"; and on steps initiated by the USA to "remove the existing threat to the security of the Western Hemisphere": adjourns pending talks between the concerned parties.
Oct. 24	CUBA: Acting Secretary-General U Thant sends message to USA and USSR to take steps to resolve the crisis.
Oct. 25	MEMBERSHIP: General Assembly admits Uganda as 110th member.
Oct. 30	CHINA: Question of representation in General Assembly is postponed by a vote of 56 to 42, with 12 abstentions.
Oct. 31	SOUTHERN RHODESIA: General Assembly urges UK to convene conference with full representation of all political parties to formulate a constitution ensuring rights for the majority of the people.
Nov. 6	ATOMIC TESTING: General Assembly calls for suspension of nuclear weapons tests and asks UK, USA and USSR to try to achieve agreement on cessation of tests by 1 January 1963 at least tests in air, outer space and underwater.
	SOUTH AFRICA: General Assembly deplores *apartheid* policies and urges members to break diplomatic relations with South Africa and to boycott South African goods and ships.
Nov. 26	CONGO: ONUC proposes a planned course of action to take effect in 10 days if Katanga authorities failed to implement the Plan for National Reconciliation.
Nov. 30	SECRETARY-GENERAL: Acting Secretary-General U Thant is elected Secretary-General for a term expiring on 3 November 1966.
Dec. 14	SOUTH WEST AFRICA: General Assembly reaffirms the rights of the people to independence and national sovereignty and condemns South Africa for continual refusal to cooperate with UN.
Dec. 17	DECOLONIZATION: General Assembly supports and encourages steps to promote independence of Zanzibar and Kenya; continues and enlarges the special committee on the implementation of the Declaration on the Granting of Independence to Colonial Countries and Peoples.
Dec. 18-20	ECOSOC: Resumed 34th regular session.
Dec. 18	ANGOLA: General Assembly calls upon Portugal to desist from armed action and repressive measures against people of Angola.

1962 (continued)

Dec. 18	DECOLONIZATION: General Assembly reaffirms the inalienable right of the peoples of Basutoland, Bechuanaland and Swaziland to self-determination and independence and supports constitutional talks on Nyasaland, hoping they will lead to independence.
Dec. 19	BUDGET: General Assembly endorses the advisory opinion of the International Court of Justice that obligations for UNEF and ONUC are expenses of the organization and establishes Working Group to study Administrative and Budgetary procedures.
Dec. 20	BUDGET: General Assembly authorizes for the UN budget $93.9 million for 1963 and an additional $3.7 million for the 1962; authorizes $1.6 million per month for UNEF and $10.0 million per month for ONUC until 30 June 1963.
Dec. 21	SOUTH WEST AFRICA CASES: International Court of Justice rules that it has authority to consider the cases.
Dec. 28	CONGO: ONUC embarks on operation to restore its security and to establish its freedom of movement throughout Katanga.

1963

Jan. 8-9	COMMODITIES: UN Exploratory Meeting on Tungsten.
Jan. 14-21	SPECIAL FUND: 9th session of the Council authorizes $43.7 million for 43 new projects.
Jan. 21	CONGO: ONUC establishes control over all areas previously held by Katanga authorities.
Feb. 4-20	ECONOMIC DEVELOPMENT: UN Conference on the Application of Science and Technology for the Benefit of Less Developed Areas.
April 2-18	ECOSOC: 35th regular session.
April 16-20	COMMODITIES: UN Conference on Olive Oil drafts new International Olive Oil Agreement.
April 24	SENEGAL-PORTUGAL: Security Council deplores violation of Senegalese airspace by Portuguese airplanes on 9th April.
April 29	YEMEN: Secretary-General reports to Security Council steps he has taken since the 1962 revolution in Yemen and good offices meetings with representatives of Yemen, South Arabia and United Arab Republic.
May 1	WEST IRIAN: UN Temporary Executive Authority transfers administration to the Indonesian Government.
May 8-9	HAITI-DOMINICAN REPUBLIC: Security Council considers the Haitian complaint of "repeated threats of aggression and attempts at interference" by Dominican Republic.

1963 (continued)

May 14-June 17 BUDGET: 4th special session of the General Assembly considers the financial problems of the UN and approves general principles as guidelines for sharing costs of future peace-keeping operations involving heavy expenditures; authorizes $9.5 million for UNEF and $33.0 million for ONUC for period 1 July 1963 to 31 December 1963; urges members to pay arrears of assessments for UNEF and ONUC; proposes establishment of a peace fund; continues Working Group of 21 on Administrative and Budgetary Procedures of UN.

May 14 MEMBERSHIP: General Assembly admits Kuwait as 111th member.

May 29-June 26 TRUSTEESHIP COUNCIL: 30th regular session.

June 3-10 SPECIAL FUND: 10th session of Council authorizes $82.7 million for 41 new projects in 35 countries.

June 11 YEMEN: Secretary-General reports to the Security Council on negotiations for a disengagement agreement between United Arab Republic, Saudi Arabia and Yemen; Security Council endorses his plan for the establishment of UN Yemen Observation Mission to assist in withdrawal of forces of United Arab Republic and Saudi Arabia.

July 2-Aug. 3 ECOSOC: 36th regular session.

July 3-4 COMMODITIES: UN Sugar Conference adopts protocol to 1958 International Sugar Agreement.

July 3 YEMEN: Main body of troops of UN Yemen Observation Mission arrive in Yemen.

July 31 PORTUGUESE TERRITORIES: Security Council deprecates the "repeated violations" of Portugal in refusing to implement General Assembly and Security Council resolutions; urges Portugal to recognize the right of inhabitants of these territories to self-determination and independence; asks all nations to prevent the sale and supply of arms for use by Portugal in these territories.

Aug. 6 SOUTH AFRICA: Security Council calls on South Africa to abandon its *apartheid* policies, to release all persons imprisoned for opposing these policies; and calls on all states to stop sale and shipment of arms to South Africa.

Sept. 3 MIDDLE EAST: USSR vetoes draft resolution of the Security Council condemning the "wanton murder" of 2 Israelis by Syrian authorities on 19 August.

Sept. 13 SOUTHERN RHODESIA: UK vetoes draft resolution of the Security Council asking UK not to transfer powers of sovereignty to Southern Rhodesia until fully representative government has been established.

Sept. 17-Dec. 17 GENERAL ASSEMBLY: 18th regular session.

1963 (continued)

Oct. 11   SOUTH AFRICA: General Assembly requests South Africa to abandon trials and release political prisoners who opposed *apartheid* policy.

VIET NAM: General Assembly appoints mission to investigate relations between government of South Viet Nam and the Buddhist Community.

Oct. 14   SOUTHERN RHODESIA: General Assembly urges UK not to transfer sovereignty to Southern Rhodesia until the establishment of a government fully representative of all the peoples, and not to transfer armed forces to Southern Rhodesia.

Oct. 17   ARMS CONTROL: General Assembly calls upon all states to refrain from orbiting or stationing nuclear weapons in outer space.

Oct. 18   BUDGET: General Assembly authorizes $18.2 million for ONUC for the period of 1 January to 30 June 1964.

Oct. 21   CHINA: Question of representation in General Assembly is postponed by a vote of 41 to 57, with 12 abstentions.

Nov. 13   SOUTH WEST AFRICA: General Assembly reaffirms right of the people to self-determination and independence, and considered that any attempt by South Africa to annex a part of the whole of South West Africa "constitutes an act of aggression".

Nov. 20   HUMAN RIGHTS: General Assembly adopts Declaration on the Elimination of All Forms of Racial Discrimination.

Nov. 27   ARMS CONTROL: General Assembly supports studies to create a nuclear-free zone of Latin America and calls upon states to resume negotiations for general and complete disarmament.

ATOMIC TESTING: General Assembly endorses August 1963 Nuclear Weapons Test Ban Treaty.

Dec. 2   CAMEROON/UK CASE: International Court of Justice determines that it cannot adjudicate the merits of the claim of Cameroon.

Dec. 4   SOUTH AFRICA: Security Council requests South Africa to cease its discriminatory policies, condemns South Africa's non-compliance with previous resolutions, and calls upon all states to cease sale and shipment of arms to South Africa.

Dec. 11   BUDGET: General Assembly reduces 1963 budget by $1 million.

DECOLONIZATION: General Assembly continues the special committee on the implementation of the Declaration on the Granting of Independence to Colonial Countries and Peoples; passes resolutions on steps being taken to provide independence for Malta, Northern Rhodesia and Nyasaland;

1963 (continued)

	urges action to promote independence in Aden, Fiji, British Guinea, Basutoland, Bechuanaland and Swaziland.
Dec. 11	OMAN: General Assembly establishes a committee to examine the question of Oman.
	PORTUGUESE TERRITORIES: Security Council regrets the failure of Portugal to abide by previous resolutions and reaffirmed the right of self-determination for these territories.
Dec. 12-20	ECOSOC: Resumed 36th regular session.
Dec. 13	OUTER SPACE: General Assembly adopts declaration of legal principles governing the activities of states in the exploration and use of outer space.
Dec. 16	MEMBERSHIP: General Assembly admits Kenya and Zanzibar as 112th and 113th members.
	SOUTH AFRICA: General Assembly urges states to take measures to "dissuade" South Africa from its *apartheid* policies.
Dec. 17	BUDGET: General Assembly authorizes a UN budget of $101.3 million for 1964 and authorizes $17.5 million for UNEF for 1964.
	CHARTER AMENDMENT: General Assembly proposes that Security Council membership be increased from 11 to 15, and ECOSOC be enlarged from 18 to 25 members.
	SOUTH WEST AFRICA: General Assembly condemns South Africa for its refusal to cooperate to implement the Declaration on the Granting of Independence to Colonial Countries and Peoples.
Dec. 27-28	CYPRUS: Security Council considers complaint of Cyprus against Turkey.
Dec. 27	COMMODITIES: International Coffee Agreement enters into force after receiving the necessary number of ratifications.

1964

Jan. 2	YEMEN: UN Yemen Observation Mission is extended two more months until 4 March 1964.
Jan. 10-11	PANAMA: Security Council considers the complaint of Panama against the USA.
Jan. 13-20	SPECIAL FUND: 11th session of Council authorizes $166 million for 48 new projects.
Jan. 21	ECOSOC: Resumed 36th regular session.
Feb. 3-17	KASHMIR: Security Council gives further consideration to the dispute between India and Pakistan.
Feb. 5	MALAYSIA: Indonesia, Malaysia, and Philippines inform the Secretary-General that they approve in principle a proposal to have Thailand observe a cease-fire between Indonesia and Malaysia on their Borneo frontier.

1964 (continued)

Feb. 5	RWANDA: Secretary-General intervenes to try to end the widespread tribal violence along the frontier of Rwanda and Burundi.
Feb. 17	CYPRUS: Security Council, at request of Cyprus and the UK, again considers the Cyprus problem.
March 4	CYPRUS: Security Council approves a mediator and an international peace-keeping force.
March 11	CYPRUS: UK and USA agree to contribute half the funds to maintain the 7,000 man force in Cyprus for three months (total costs for three months are estimated at $6 million).
March 13	CYPRUS: Security Council, in emergency meeting, reaffirms its appeal to states to refrain from actions that would worsen the situation.
March 14-15	CYPRUS: Canadian advance party of UN force arrives in Cyprus; Finland, Ireland and Sweden confirm that they will contribute troops.
March 23-June 15	ECONOMIC DEVELOPMENT: UN Conference on Trade and Development (UNCTAD) is attended by representatives of 122 governments.
March 27	CYPRUS: UN Cyprus Force (UNFICYP) becomes operational.
April 9	SAUDI ARABIA: Security Council condemns the UK for reprisal air attack against Yemen border attack.
April 20	SOUTH AFRICA: Security Council Group of Experts propose a national convention with participants of all parties in South Africa.
April 23	MEMBERSHIP: Tanganyika and Zanzibar unite to form Tanzania and thereby reduce UN membership from 113 to 112.
May 19-June 4	CAMBODIA-SOUTH VIET NAM: Security Council considers Cambodian charges of US-South Viet Nam aggression.
May 22	SOUTH AFRICA: South Africa informs Security Council that experts report was an invasion of domestic jurisdiction.
May 25	SOUTH AFRICA: General Assembly Special Committee (created in November 1962) asks Security Council to consider the situation in South Africa a threat to peace.
June 4	CAMBODIA-SOUTH VIET NAM: Security Council notes US apology for border violation and appoints three-man commission to explore ways to avoid further violations.
June 15	CYPRUS: Security Council extends mandate of UNFICYP for three months.
June 16	ECONOMIC DEVELOPMENT: Final Act of UN Conference on Trade and Development (UNCTAD) recommends creation of UN Trade and Development Organization to accelerate economic growth in all countries.

1964 (continued)

June 18	SOUTH AFRICA: Security Council condemns *apartheid* policies; appeals for amnesty for political prisoners; and establishes commission to study the feasibility of economic measures by Security Council against South Africa.
June 30	CONGO: Military phase of the UN Operations in the Congo ends; last military forces are withdrawn; technical assistance and civilian operations continues; the cost of UNOC for four years was $276.6 million.
July 13-Aug. 15	ECOSOC: 37th regular session.
July 27	CAMBODIA-SOUTH VIET NAM: Three-man commission of Security Council urges resumption of political relations between the two countries.
Aug. 5-7	GULF OF TONKIN: Security Council meets at US request and considers the situation created by alleged attack of North Vietnam on US naval vessels in international waters on 3 August.
Aug. 8-9	CYPRUS: Security Council asks for cease-fire and for all states to cease activities which will broaden the hostilities.
Aug. 10	CYPRUS: Greece and Turkey accepts Security Council cease-fire appeal.
Sept. 4	YEMEN: UN Observer Mission in Yemen is terminated and peace-keeping forces are withdrawn as neither Saudi Arabia nor the United Arab Republic implemented the disengagement.
Sept. 9-17	MALAYSIA: Security Council considers Malaysia's charges on landings of Indonesian guerrillas in Malaysia: USSR vetoes draft resolution of the Security Council which asks Malaysia and Indonesia to refrain from use of force against each other.
Sept. 25	CYPRUS: Security Council renews mandate of UNFICYP for three more months.
Nov. 10	GENERAL ASSEMBLY: 19th regular session scheduled to open on this date is postponed until 1 December to allow negotiations between USA and USSR over obligations to pay for peace-keeping forces and requirements of Charter Article 19.
Nov. 30	GENERAL ASSEMBLY: USA and USSR accept a proposal of Secretary-General that Assembly will open on 1 December and proceed only on issues in which no formal vote will be required and therefore prevent a possible application of Article 19.
Dec. 1-23	GENERAL ASSEMBLY: 19th regular session (the so-called "no-vote" session); president is elected, but no committees are formed; all business is conducted in plenary session to prevent confrontation between USA and USSR over Article 19.
Dec. 1	MEMBERSHIP: General Assembly admits Malawi, Malta and Zambia as 113th, 114th and 115th members.

1964 (continued)

Dec. 9-30	CONGO: Security Council meets at the request of African states and considers charges that Belgian and US rescue of hostages in Stanleyville is an intervention in internal affairs of the Congo.
Dec. 18	CYPRUS: Security Council extends mandate of UNFICYP for three months.
Dec. 29	BUDGET: General Assembly authorizes Secretary-General to incur expenses necessary until the 1965 budget can be approved by a vote.
Dec. 30	CONGO: Security Council calls for an end of foreign intervention, withdrawal of foreign forces and a cease-fire.
	ECONOMIC DEVELOPMENT: General Assembly establishes the UN Confernce on Trade and Development (UNCTAD) as an "organ" of the UN.
Dec. 31	CAMBODIA-THAILAND: Secretary-General's special representative is withdrawn after he completed his role as intermediary.

1965

Jan. 18-25	GENERAL ASSEMBLY: 19th regular session continues on a "no vote" basis.
Jan. 21	MEMBERSHIP: Indonesia, objecting to Malaysia assuming a non-permanent seat on the Security Council, withdraws from the UN, reducing the membership to 114 member states.
Feb. 1-18	GENERAL ASSEMBLY: 19th regular session continues on a "no vote" basis.
Feb. 16	GENERAL ASSEMBLY: Albania proposes that the General Assembly ceases the consensus operation and returns to regular voting procedures; major procedural debate attempts to offset the Albanian move.
Feb. 18	BUDGET: General Assembly creates special committee to review all aspects of peace-keeping operations, especially the methods of financing as an effort to offset USA-USSR confrontation over Article 19.
	GENERAL ASSEMBLY: USA and USSR agree that the vote forced by Albania is "not a vote" and thereby prevent confrontation over the application of Article 19 for financial arrears.
March 1-8	ECOSOC: Resumed 37th regular session.
March 19	CYPRUS: Security Council extends mandate of UNFICYP for three months.
March 22-26	ECOSOC: 38th regular session.
April 22-June 15	BUDGET: Special Committee on Peace Keeping Operations is unable to break USA-USSR deadlock.

1965 (continued)

April 29	DOMINICAN REPUBLIC: USA notifies the Security Council that it has ordered troops to the Dominican Republic to protect Americans there.
May 3-25	DOMINICAN REPUBLIC: Security Council considers the "armed intervention" of the USA upon request from Cuba and the USSR.
May 6	SOUTHERN RHODESIA: Security Council calls upon UK not to accept any "unilateral declaration of independence by the minority government" of South Rhodesia.
May 14	DOMINICAN REPUBLIC: Security Council calls for a cease-fire and directs the Secretary-General to send a representative to help the situation.
May 19	SENEGAL-PORTUGAL: Security Council deplores incursions by Portuguese military units and asks Portugal to take all necessary steps to prevent further violations of Senegalese border.
May 21	DOMINICAN REPUBLIC: Agreement is reached on 24 hour suspension of hostilities.
May 22	DOMINICAN REPUBLIC: Security Council requests that suspension of hostilities is extended into a cease-fire; parties agree and cease-fire takes effect.
May 28-June 30	TRUSTEESHIP COUNCIL: 32nd regular session.
June 10	CYPRUS: Security Council extends mandate for UNFICYP until 26 December.
June 25-26	TWENTIETH ANNIVERSARY: Commemorative meetings on twentieth anniversary of signing of the Charter is held in San Francisco.
June 30-July 31	ECOSOC: 39th regular session.
Aug. 16	BUDGET: USA informs the Special Committee on Peace-keeping that the USA will not insist on the application of Article 19, thus breaking the deadlock that has prevented the 19th session of the General Assembly from carrying on its normal activities.
Aug. 25	YEMEN: Secretary-General informs Security Council that the United Arabic Republic and Saudi Arabia have signed an agreement on Yemen.
Aug. 31	BUDGET: Special Committee on Peace-keeping Operations reaches consensus that (a) the General Assembly would carry on its work normally in accord with its rules of procedure; (b) the question of the applicability of Article 19 would not be raised with regard to the UNEF and UNOC; (c) the financial difficulties of the UN would be solved through voluntary contributions by member states with the highly developed countries making substantial contributions.

1965 (continued)

Aug. 31   CHARTER AMENDMENTS: Amendments to Articles 23, 27
                   and 61 come into effect after having achieved the necessary
                   number of ratifications; Security Council is enlarged from 11
                   to 15 states and ECOSOC from 18 to 27; voting majority in
                   the Security Council is changed from a majority of seven to
                   nine.

Sept. 1   GENERAL ASSEMBLY: Resumed 19th session adopts the
                   consensus of the Special Committee on Peace-keeping.

Sept. 4   INDIA-PAKISTAN: Security Council meets at the request of
                   the USA after the outbreak of hostilities; Secretary-General
                   reports collapse of the 1949 cease-fire agreement; Security
                   Council calls for a cease-fire and on both countries to
                   withdraw.

Sept. 6   INDIA-PAKISTAN: Security Council again calls for cessation
                   of hostilities.

Sept. 7-16   INDIA-PAKISTAN: Secretary-General visits both India and
                   Pakistan; unable to obtain a cease-fire.

Sept. 20   INDIA-PAKISTAN: Security Council demands that a cease-fire
                   takes effect on 22 September and promises to aid the two
                   parties in arriving at a political settlement.

Sept. 21-Dec. 21   GENERAL ASSEMBLY: 20th regular session.

Sept. 21   INDIA-PAKISTAN: Secretary-General reports on steps to
                   supervise a cease-fire line, including the organization of the
                   UN Observer Mission in India-Pakistan (UNIPOM) with
                   initial size of 100 military observers and supporting staff;
                   India agrees to cease-fire.
                   MEMBERSHIP: General Assembly admits Gambia, Maldive
                   Islands and Singapore as 115th to 117th members.

Sept. 22   INDIA-PAKISTAN: Pakistan agrees to cease-fire; cease-fire
                   takes effect.

Sept. 27   INDIA-PAKISTAN: Security Council expresses concern over
                   violations of cease-fire; again urges states to hold cease-fire
                   and withdraw troops behind the cease-fire lines.

Oct. 4   POPE PAUL: Pope Paul VI visits the UN and pleads for peace
                   before the General Assembly.

Nov. 5   ADEN: General Assembly urges the UK to abolish the state of
                   emergency and cease all repressive acts.
                   INDIA-PAKISTAN: Security Council asks for an unconditional
                   withdrawal of military forces.

Nov. 12   SOUTHERN RHODESIA: Security Council condemns the
                   11 November unilateral declaration of independence and
                   requests that no state "recognize" this "illegal" regime.

Nov. 19   ARMS CONTROL: General Assembly urges Disarmament
                   Committee to give prime attention to a nuclear non-
                   proliferation treaty.

1965 (continued)

Nov. 20	SOUTHERN RHODESIA: Security Council requests all states to cease military arms shipments to the Ian Smith regime and to break economic relations.
Nov. 22-23	ECOSOC: Resumed 39th regular session.
Nov. 22	ECONOMIC DEVELOPMENT: General Assembly establishes the UN Development Program (UNDP) through the consolidation of the Special Fund and the Expanded Program of Technical Assistance to take effect on 1 January 1966.
Dec. 3	ARMS CONTROL: General Assembly urges suspension of all nuclear and thermonuclear tests; reaffirms principle that Africa should be a nuclear-free zone.
Dec. 8	ECONOMIC DEVELOPMENT: General Assembly proposes creation of a UN Capital Development Fund.
Dec. 15	SOUTH AFRICA: General Assembly establishes a voluntary UN trust fund to give assistance to refugees and families of political prisoners in South Africa; again condemns South Africa for its *apartheid* policies.
Dec. 16	HUMAN RIGHTS: General Assembly considers the creation of the post of a UN High Commissioner on Human Rights.
Dec. 17	CYPRUS: Security Council extends mandate of UNFICYP until March 1966.
Dec. 20	CHARTER: General Assembly amends Article 109 of the Charter, changing the majority vote required in the Security Council for Charter amendment from 7 to 9 (necessary as a result of the recent amendment to Article 27 on 31 August).
Dec. 21	BUDGET: General Assembly authorizes $108.5 million for 1965, $121.6 million for 1966, and a Working Capital Fund at $40.0 million.
	ECOSOC: Resumed 39th session.
	HUMAN RIGHTS: General Assembly adopts the Convention on the Elimination of All Forms of Racial Discrimination.

1966

Jan. 1	CHARTER: Amendments to Articles 23, 27 and 61 become effective on 1 January, following the necessary ratifications.
	ECONOMIC DEVELOPMENT: UN Development Program (UNDP) becomes operative.
Feb. 1	SECURITY COUNCIL: First meeting with 15 members instead of 11.
	VIET NAM: Security Council, at the request of the USA, places issue of Viet Nam on the agenda, but then, because of divergence of views between USA, France and USSR, decides not to discuss the issue.
Feb. 23-Mar. 8	ECOSOC: 40th regular session; first session with 27 rather than 18 members on the Council.

1966 (continued)

Feb. 26	INDIA-PAKISTAN: Secretary-General reports to the Security Council that as of 25 February, both countries have withdrawn their troops to the positions held before fighting broke out on 5 August 1965.
March 1	INDIA-PAKISTAN: Task of the UN India-Pakistan Observer Mission is completed.
March 16	CYPRUS: Security Council extends mandate of UNFICYP until June.
March 22	INDIA-PAKISTAN: UNIPOM is disbanded as peace is restored.
April 7	SOUTHERN RHODESIA: UK requests emergency Security Council meeting.
April 9	SOUTHERN RHODESIA: Security Council authorizes UK to use naval force if necessary to prevent oil carrying vessels from arriving at the port of Beira.
May 17-23	SOUTHERN RHODESIA: Security Council considers proposal of African states, requesting all states to break off economic relations with Southern Rhodesia.
May 23-June 23	COMMODITIES: UN Cocoa Conference.
May 27	TRUSTEESHIP COUNCIL: 33rd regular session.
June 16	CYPRUS: Security Council extends mandate of UNFICYP until 26 December 1966.
June 27-July 26	TRUSTEESHIP COUNCIL: Resumed 33rd regular session.
July 5-Aug. 5	ECOSOC: 41st regular session.
July 18	SOUTH WEST AFRICAN CASES: International Court of Justice delivers judgement on the South West African case (Ethiopia versus South Africa and Liberia versus South Africa); court throws out cases arguing neither Ethiopia nor Liberia had established any legal right or interest in South West Africa.
Aug. 4-16	SOUTH ARABIA: Security Council hears UK charges that United Arab Republic planes from Yemen attacked towns in the South Arabian Federation.
Aug. 16	SOUTH ARABIA: Security Council asks all states in the area to relax tensions.
Sept. 20-Dec. 20	GENERAL ASSEMBLY: 21st regular session.
Sept. 20	MEMBERSHIP: General Assembly admits Guyana as 118th member.
Sept. 28	MEMBERSHIP: Indonesia resumes membership; total membership rises to 119 states.
Oct. 14-31	MIDDLE EAST: Security Council considers counter claims from Israel and Syria.
Oct. 14	CONGO: Security Council urges Portugal to allow no mercenaries in Angola and asks all states to refrain from intervention in the Congo.

1966 (continued)

Oct. 17	MEMBERSHIP: General Assembly admits Botswana and Lesotho (formerly Basutoland) as 120th and 121st members.
Oct. 22	SOUTHERN RHODESIA: General Assembly condemns "illegal" regime.
Oct. 24	REFUGEES: UN Day 1966 is dedicated to the cause of refugees and the raising of funds for African refugees.
Oct. 26	HUMAN RIGHTS: General Assembly designates 21 March each year as the International Day for the Elimination of Racial Discrimination.
Oct. 27	SOUTH WEST AFRICA: General Assembly decides by 114 to 2, with 3 abstentions that South Africa has not lived up to the obligations imposed in its mandate from the League of Nations over South West Africa; declares the mandate terminated and places South West Africa under the "direct responsibility of the UN".
Nov. 4	ECONOMIC DEVELOPMENT: General Assembly designates 1967 as the International Tourist Year.
Nov. 16	MIDDLE EAST: Security Council censures Israel for its large scale military operation against Jordan on 13 November.
Nov. 17	ARMS CONTROL: General Assembly decides to convene in 1968 a non-nuclear states conference to consider the non-proliferation of nuclear weapons.
	INDUSTRIAL DEVELOPMENT: General Assembly decides to establish the UN Industrial Development Organization (UNIDO).
	SOUTHERN RHODESIA: General Assembly condemns Portugal and South Africa for aiding the "illegal" regime.
Nov. 29	CHINA: General Assembly reaffirms that the Chinese representation issue requires a two-thirds vote; proposal to seat the Peoples Republic of China fails.
Dec. 2	SECRETARY-GENERAL: U Thant agrees to accept re-election.
Dec. 5	ARMS CONTROL: General Assembly urges all states to strictly observe the 1925 Geneva Protocol on the prohibition of the use of gas and bacteriological weapons.
Dec. 5	INTERNATIONAL LAW: General Assembly decides to convene international conferences in 1968 and 1969 on the law of treaties.
	SOUTHERN RHODESIA: UK requests Security Council meeting.
Dec. 9	MEMBERSHIP: General Assembly admits Barbados as 122nd member.
Dec. 12	ADEN: General Assembly affirms the right of the people of Aden to self-determination.
Dec. 13	ECONOMIC DEVELOPMENT: General Assembly decides to bring the UN Capital Development Fund into operation.

1966 (continued)

Dec. 14   CYPRUS: Security Council extends mandate of the UNFICYP until 26 June 1967.

Dec. 15   SOUTHERN RHODESIA: Security Council evokes Chapter VII of the Charter by voting to impose compulsory economic sanctions against Southern Rhodesia: first such action by the UN.

Dec. 16   BUDGET: General Assembly decreases the 1966 budget to $121.1 million.

                 HUMAN RIGHTS: General Assembly adopts the International Covenant on Economic, Social and Cultural Rights, and the International Covenant on Civil and Political Rights with an Optional Protocol which give individuals the right to appeal beyond their governments to a Human Rights Committee.

                 SOUTH AFRICA: General Assembly condemns the racial policies of South Africa.

                 SOUTHERN RHODESIA: Security Council expresses deep concern over the situation; calls upon all states to not render financial or economic aid to Southern Rhodesia.

Dec. 17   INTERNATIONAL LAW: General Assembly decides to establish as of 1 January 1968 a UN Commission on International Trade Law.

Dec. 19   OUTER SPACE: General Assembly unanimously adopts a treaty declaring that the exploration and use of outer space shall be carried out for the benefit of all mankind.

Dec. 20   BUDGET: General Assembly authorizes $130.3 million for 1967.

1967

Jan. 1   ECONOMIC DEVELOPMENT: Start of the International Tourist Year (1967).

Jan. 10-27   ECONOMIC DEVELOPMENT: UN Development Program approves $186 million for projects in 70 countries.

Jan. 15   MIDDLE EAST: Secretary-General informs Security Council that UNTSO has warned of military build-ups on the Israeli-Syrian border.

April 7   MIDDLE EAST: Syria and Israel bring charges and counter-charges to the Security Council.

April 21-June 13   SOUTH WEST AFRICA: 5th special session of the General Assembly on South West Africa establishes post of UN Commissioner for South West Africa to administer the territory until it becomes independent and the UN Council for South West Africa; elects Chile, Columbia, Guyana, India, Indonesia, Nigeria, Pakistan, Turkey, United Arab Republic, Yugoslavia and Zambia as members of the Council.

May 8-June 8   ECOSOC: 42nd regular session.

1967 (continued)

May 8	MIDDLE EAST: Secretary-General reports deterioration of the situation to the Security Council.
May 16	MIDDLE EAST: United Arab Republic military chief requests that UNEF be withdrawn.
May 17-18	MIDDLE EAST: United Arab Republic troops force UNEF withdrawal from Israeli border posts; United Arab Republic requests immediate withdrawal of UNEF.
May 19	MIDDLE EAST: Secretary-General withdraws UNEF, noting the 1956 arrangement in placing the UNEF in the Unite Arab Republic border with Israel is dependent upon the continued acceptance of the United Arab Republic.
May 22	MIDDLE EAST: Secretary-General flies to Cairo, attempting to reduce tensions in the area.
May 23	PEACE-KEEPING: General Assembly asks Special Committee on Peace-keeping Operations to review the whole question of peace-keeping.
May 24	MIDDLE EAST: Security Council, at the request of Canada and Denmark, considers the threatening situation in the Middle East.
May 27	OUTER SPACE: General Assembly decides to hold a UN Conference on the Peaceful Use of Outer Space in August 1968.
May 29-June 3	MIDDLE EAST: Security Council fails to agree on recommendations to reduce tensions between Israel, Syria and the United Arab Republic.
May 29-June 30	TRUSTEESHIP COUNCIL: 34th regular session.
June 5	MIDDLE EAST: Hostilities break out between Israel, Jordan, Syria and the United Arab Republic; Security Council calls for cease-fire.
June 6-22	ECONOMIC DEVELOPMENT: 4th session of the UNDP approves 54 pre-investment projects in 47 countries costing $129.7 million.
June 6	MIDDLE EAST: Security Council renews call for cease-fire.
June 7	MIDDLE EAST: Hostilities cease along the United Arab Republic and Jordanian borders with Israel, but continue along the Syrian border.
June 9	MIDDLE EAST: Security Council again demands an immediate cease-fire; Israel and Syria comply.
June 11	MIDDLE EAST: Security Council condemns violations along the cease-fire lines.
June 13	CYPRUS: Secretary-General reports some progress, but notes that violence has only been contained because of the presence of UNFICYP.
	MIDDLE EAST: USSR requests an emergency session of the General Assembly to deal with the defiance of Israel of demands of the Security Council for a cease-fire.

1967 (continued)

June 14	MIDDLE EAST: Secretary-General urges humanitarian measures on behalf of prisoners of war and civilians caught in the conflict.
June 17-July 5	MIDDLE EAST: 5th emergency special session of the General Assembly on the Middle East calls for assistance to civilians caught in the war and calls upon Israel to desist from all measures aimed at changing the international status of the city of Jerusalem.
June 19	CYPRUS: Security Council extends the mandate of UNFICYP until 26 December 1967.
July 8	MIDDLE EAST: Fighting occurs along the Suez Canal; cease-fire between the United Arab Republic and Israel.
July 9	MIDDLE EAST: Security Council authorizes the Secretary-General to establish UNTSO military observers along the Suez Canal to help maintain the cease-fire line.
July 10	CONGO: Security Council calls upon all states to ensure that their territory is not used by mercenaries aiming to overthrow the government of the Congo.
July 11-Aug. 4	ECOSOC: 43rd regular session.
July 12-21	MIDDLE EAST: Resumed 5th emergency special of the General Assembly on the Middle East refers its discussions and records to the Security Council.
Aug. 24	DISARMAMENT: USA and USSR present a partial draft of a non-proliferation nuclear weapons treaty to the Disarmament Committee.
Sept. 18	MIDDLE EAST: Resumed 5th emergency special of the General Assembly on the Middle East.
Sept. 19-Dec. 19	GENERAL ASSEMBLY: 22nd regular session.
Sept. 26	SOUTH WEST AFRICA: South Africa rejects role of UN Council for South West Africa.
Oct. 10	ARMS CONTROL: Experts on the effect of the possible use of nuclear weapons submit report to the General Assembly.
Oct. 24-25	MIDDLE EAST: Security Council considers charges from Israel and the United Arab Republic over cease-fire violations along the Suez Canal cease-fire line.
Nov. 1-14	ECOSOC: Resumed 43rd regular session.
Nov. 3	SOUTHERN RHODESIA: General Assembly deplores the failure of economic sanctions to bring down the white minority regime; urges the UK to take all steps necessary to end the regime.
Nov. 7	HUMAN RIGHTS: General Assembly unanimously adopts the Declaration on the Elimination of Discrimination Against Women.
	REFUGEES: General Assembly decides to continue the office of the UN High Commissioner for Refugees for five years beyond 1 January 1969.

1967 (continued)

Nov. 9-22	MIDDLE EAST: Security Council again considers Israel and United Arab Republic complaints.
Nov. 15	CONGO: Security Council calls upon Portugal to end its assistance to mercenaries threatening the Congo government.
	CYPRUS: Fighting breaks out in several places between Greek and Turkish Cypriots; UNFICYP stabilizes the situation.
Nov. 17	PORTUGUESE TERRITORIES: General Assembly condemns Portugal for failing to implement UN resolutions urging steps towards the independence of the Portuguese colonies.
Nov. 22-23	TRUSTEESHIP COUNCIL: 13th special session recommends termination of Trust Agreement for Nauru, and the island's independence by 31 January 1968.
Nov. 22	MIDDLE EAST: Security Council affirms that peace in the Middle East has to include Israeli withdrawal from the occupied territories and the acknowledgement that every state in the area must be secure within its boundaries; also asks the Secretary-General to appoint a Special Representative to promote agreements for peace in the area.
Nov. 25	CYPRUS: Security Council asks all parties to "show the utmost moderation and restraint" in the tension area.
Dec. 3	CYPRUS: Secretary-General appeals to the governments of Cyprus, Greece and Turkey to avoid hasty actions pending permanent solutions to the problems of the area.
Dec. 5	ARMS CONTROL: General Assembly urges all states to sign and ratify the Treaty for the Prohibition of Nuclear Weapons in Latin America.
Dec. 13	ECONOMIC DEVELOPMENT: General Assembly declares 1970 as the International Education Year.
	SOUTH AFRICA: General Assembly again condemns the racial policies of South Africa and condemns states that continue to be major trading parties with South Africa.
Dec. 14	INTERNATIONAL LAW: General Assembly unanimously adopts a Declaration on Territorial Asylum.
	MEMBERSHIP: General Assembly admits South Yemen (formerly the British territories of Aden and South Arabia) as 123rd member.
Dec. 15	ECONOMIC DEVELOPMENT: General Assembly places the administration of the UN Capital Development Fund under UNDP.
Dec. 16	SOUTH WEST AFRICA: General Assembly condemns the refusal of South Africa to comply with UN requests on the area; asks the Security Council to take measure to force South African compliance; condemns the illegal arrest and deportation of South West Africans by South Africa.

1967 (continued)

Dec. 18   SEA BED: General Assembly creates a special committee to
               study the possibility of reserving the ocean floor for peaceful
               purposes.

Dec. 19   BUDGET: General Assembly passes supplementary budget for
               1967, increasing the budget from $130.3 million to $133.1
               million and adopts budget for 1968 of $140.4 million.

               OUTER SPACE: General Assembly adopts agreement on the
               Rescue of Astronauts, the Return of Astronauts, and the
               Return of Objects Launched into Outer Space.

Dec. 22   CYPRUS: Security Council extends the mandate of UNFICYP
               until 26 March 1968.

1968

Jan. 1   HUMAN RIGHTS: Start of the International Year for Human
               Rights (1968).

Jan. 24   ECONOMIC DEVELOPMENT: 5th session of the UNDP
               approves $228 million for 100 projects in 71 countries.

Jan. 25   SOUTH WEST AFRICA: Security Council calls on South
               Africa to discontinue its "illegal" trial of 35 South West
               Africans and to return them to their territory.

Jan. 26   PUEBLO: Security Council begins considerations at the request
               of the USA over the situation caused by the North Korean
               seizure of the USS Pueblo.

Jan. 27   PUEBLO: Security Council adjourns formal discussion of this
               incident to allow consultations outside the UN.

Jan. 31   TRUSTEESHIP: Trust Territory of Nauru achieves
               independence.

               TRUSTEESHIP COUNCIL: Membership of the Council no
               longer conforms to the requirements of the Charter:
               independence of Nauru means that New Zealand ceases to be
               a member and the UK as a permanent member becomes a
               non-administrating member; required balance between
               administrators and non-administrators on the Council does no
               longer exist.

Feb. 1-March 29 ECONOMIC DEVELOPMENT: 2nd UN Conference on Trade
               and Development, New Delhi.

March 1   DRUGS: International Narcotics Control Board is established,
               superseding the Permanent Central Narcotics Board and the
               Drug Supervisory Body.

March 12   SOUTHERN RHODESIA: 36 African states ask the Security
               Council to act against the white minority regime in Southern
               Rhodesia.

March 14   SOUTH WEST AFRICA: Security Council censures South
               Africa for its defiance of previous Council resolutions and
               demands release of South West Africans.

1968 (continued)

March 18	CYPRUS: Security Council extends the mandate of UNFICYP for three months.
March 24	MIDDLE EAST: Security Council condemns Israel for punitive expedition into Jordan in violation of the cease-fire lines.
March 26-May 24	INTERNATIONAL LAW: 1st session of the UN Conference on the Law of Treaties.
April 4	MIDDLE EAST: Security Council expresses its concern over the deteriorating situation.
April 22-May 13	HUMAN RIGHTS: International Conference on Human Rights in Teheran adopts the Proclamation of Teheran on concerns for major human rights problems.
April 24-June 12	GENERAL ASSEMBLY: Resumed 22nd regular session deals with South West Africa and nuclear non-proliferation.
April 24	MEMBERSHIP: General Assembly admits Mauritius as 124th member.
May 6-31	ECOSOC: 44th regular session.
May 21	MIDDLE EAST: Security Council calls upon Israel to rescind all measures designed to change the legal status of Jerusalem.
May 27-June 19	SOUTHERN RHODESIA: Security Council unanimously imposes comprehensive mandatory economic sanctions against Southern Rhodesia (an expansion of the previous list of economic sanctions); establishes committee to examine the implementation of sanctions.
June 11-12	BUDGET: Dominican Republic and Haiti, in arrears in paying budgetary assessments within the scope of Article 19, are omitted in General Assembly voting.
June 12	ARMS CONTROL: General Assembly approves the Treaty on the Non-Proliferation of Nuclear Weapons and urges states to ratify treaty.
	SOUTH WEST AFRICA/NAMIBIA: General Assembly proclaims South West Africa to be known in the future as Namibia; recommends that the Security Council take effective measures to remove South Africa from the area.
June 18	CYPRUS: Security Council extends the mandate of UNFICYP for six more months until 26 December 1968.
June 27	BUDGET: Secretary-General issues urgent appeal to member states for voluntary contributions to UNFICYP.
June 28	ECONOMIC DEVELOPMENT: 6th session of UNDP approves $127 million for 61 pre-investment projects.
July 8-Aug. 2	ECOSOC: 45th regular session.
Aug. 14-27	OUTER SPACE: UN Conference on the Exploration and Peaceful Uses of Outer Space, Vienna.
Aug. 16	MIDDLE EAST: Security Council condemns Israel for launching military attacks across the cease-fire lines.

1968 (continued)

Aug. 21-24	CZECHOSLOVAKIA: Security Council, meeting at the request of Canada, Denmark, France, Paraguay, UK and USA, considers the situation following the USSR intervention in Czechoslovakia.
Aug. 23	CZECHOSLOVAKIA: USSR vetoes draft resolution of the Security Council condemning USSR intervention and asking Warsaw Pact States to remove their troops from Czechoslovakia.
Aug. 27	CZECHOSLOVAKIA: Representative of Czechoslovakia states that his government does not request Security Council consideration of the situation and asks that the item be removed from the agenda because of Czech agreements with the USSR; Security Council ends consideration of the issue.
Sept. 18	MIDDLE EAST: Security Council expresses grave concern over the deteriorating situation.
Sept. 23-Oct. 24	COMMODITIES: UN Sugar Conference drafts new International Sugar Agreement.
Sept. 24-Dec. 21	GENERAL ASSEMBLY: 23rd regular session.
Sept. 24	BUDGET: General Assembly decides to let Haiti cast votes despite being in arrears on contributions, until there is a report from the Committee on Contributions.
	MEMBERSHIP: General Assembly admits Swaziland as 125th member.
Sept. 27	MIDDLE EAST: Security Council asks the Secretary-General to dispatch a special representative to the Arab territories under Israeli military occupation and to report on the treatment of Arabs in those areas.
Sept. 28	ARMS CONTROL: General Assembly recommends ratification of the Latin American nuclear free-zone treaty.
Oct. 14	MIDDLE EAST: Secretary-General reports to the Security Council that the position of Israel precludes his sending the special representative requested on 27 September.
Oct. 17	ECONOMIC DEVELOPMENT: Pledging conference results in pledges of $115 million for UNDP from 97 states.
Oct. 30-Nov. 1	ECOSOC: Resumed 45th regular session.
Nov. 1-4	MIDDLE EAST: Security Council meets a request of Israel and the United Arab Republic to consider most recent cease-fire line incidents.
Nov. 7	SOUTHERN RHODESIA: General Assembly condemns Portugal and South Africa for assistance to the white minority regime in Southern Rhodesia.
Nov. 11	SOUTHERN RHODESIA: Sanctions implementation committee of the Security Council announces that certain states have failed to provide information and specifically asks the UK to give maximum assistance.

1968 (continued)

Nov. 12	MEMBERSHIP: General Assembly admits Equatorial Guinea as 126th member.
Nov. 19-20	ECOSOC: Resumed 45th regular session.
Nov. 19	CHINA: General Assembly again decides to retain the Chinese Nationalists as the representatives of China by a vote of 73 to 47; proposal to seat the People's Republic of China fails.
Nov. 20	BUDGET: Committee on Contribution recommends that Haiti be allowed to vote despite arrears because of serious economic problems; Haiti pays arrears.
Nov. 26	INTERNATIONAL LAW: General Assembly adopts the Convention on the Non-Applicability of Statutory Limitations to War Crimes and Crimes Against Humanity.
Dec. 2	SOUTH AFRICA: General Assembly condemns the "ruthless" persecution of opponents of *apartheid* and expands terms of reference of the trust fund for the persecuted from South Africa to provide legal assistance.
Dec. 3	HUMAN ENVIRONMENT: General Assembly decides to convene a UN Conference on the Human Environment in 1972.
Dec. 5-6	ECOSOC: Resumed 45th regular session.
Dec. 10	CYPRUS: Security Council extends the mandate of UNFICYP until June 1969.
Dec. 16	NAMIBIA: General Assembly again urges Security Council to take effective measures to oust South Africa from the territory.
Dec. 18	IFNI: General Assembly urges that the Spanish territory be transferred in accord with the wishes of the indigenous population of Morocco.
Dec. 19	MIDDLE EAST: General Assembly urges Israel to speed return of refugees who fled in June 1967 war.
Dec. 20	ARMS CONTROL: General Assembly requests report on the consequences of chemical and bacteriological weapons and urges USA and USSR to enter discussions on the limitation of offensive strategic nuclear weapon delivery system.
	SEA BED: General Assembly establishes Committee on the Peaceful Uses of the Sea-bed and the Ocean Floor Beyond the Limits of National Jurisdiction.
Dec. 21	BUDGET: General Assembly approves 1969 budget amounting to $155.2 million.
Dec. 30	COMMODITIES: International Coffee Agreement of 1968 comes into force.
Dec. 31	MIDDLE EAST: Security Council condemns Israeli attack on Beirut Airport.

1969

Jan. 1	COMMODITIES: New International Sugar Agreement provisionally comes into force.
Jan. 4	HUMAN RIGHTS: Convention on the Elimination of All Forms of Racial Discrimination comes into force.
	IFNI: Spain and Morocco sign treaty transferring sovereignty of Ifni to Morocco in accordance with General Assembly resolution.
Jan. 8	BUDGET: Secretary-General issues urgent appeal for voluntary contributions to UNFICYP.
Jan. 9-23	ECONOMIC DEVELOPMENT: 7th session of UNDP approves 107 pre-investment projects costing $340.7 million in 84 countries.
Feb. 20	NORTH SEA CASE: International Court of Justice delivers continental shelf cases (Denmark versus Federal Republic of Germany and Netherlands versus Federal Republic of Germany) in favor of the Federal Republic of Germany.
Feb. 25-March 4	ECONOMIC DEVELOPMENT: 1st meetings of Preparatory Committee for the Second UN Development Decade.
March 3-7	COMMODITIES: UN Olive Oil Conference: adopts Protocol extending 1963 International Olive Oil Agreement to 31 December 1973.
March 7	EQUATORIAL GUINEA: Secretary-General announces that in response to a request, he is sending a personal representative to lend good offices in reducing tensions between Equatorial Guinea and Spain.
March 20	NAMIBIA: Security Council calls upon South Africa to withdraw its administration from the area; declares that South Africa's actions to destroy the national character of Namibia are contrary to the Charter.
March 26-April 3	EQUATORIAL GUINEA: Under UN good offices of Secretary-General's personal representative, Spanish armed forces are withdrawn from Santa Isabel and Fernando Po.
April 1	MIDDLE EAST: Security Council condemns Israel for air attack on Jordanian village on 26 March.
April 5	EQUATORIAL GUINEA: Personal representative of Secretary-General announces the completion of Spanish withdrawal.
April 9-May 22	INTERNATIONAL LAW: 2nd session of the UN Conference on the Law of Treaties adopts an International Convention on the Law of Treaties.
April 21	MIDDLE EAST: Secretary-General submits special report to the Security Council, warning of the almost complete breakdown of the cease-fire line between Israel and the United Arab Republic.
May 12-June 6	ECOSOC: 46th regular session.
May 14	NAMIBIA: Secretary-General reports to the Security Council that South Africa continues to defy resolutions of the Council.

1969 (continued)

May 29-June 19	TRUSTEESHIP COUNCIL: 36th regular session.
June 10	CYPRUS: Security Council extends the mandate of UNFICYP until 15 December 1969.
June 13-24	SOUTHERN RHODESIA: Security Council meets at the request of 60 Asian and African states on the failure of economic sanctions to bring about changes in the area.
June 16-July 3	ECONOMIC DEVELOPMENT: 8th session of UNDP allocates $102 million for 52 new projects in 78 countries.
June 24	SOUTHERN RHODESIA: Security Council fails to adopt draft resolution asking all states to sever relations with Southern Rhodesia.
July 1	ARMS CONTROL: Secretary-General submits report of experts on chemical and biological weapons and the effects of their possible use and escalation.
July 3	MIDDLE EAST: Security Council unanimously censures Israel for measures to change the legal status of Jerusalem.
July 5	MIDDLE EAST: Secretary-General submits report on the almost complete breakdown of the cease-fire line along the Suez Canal between Israel and the United Arab Republic.
July 14-Aug. 8	ECOSOC: 47th regular session.
July 14-Aug. 2	WEST IRIAN: In accordance with the 1962 agreement between Indonesia and the Netherlands and under observation of a representative of the Secretary-General, the eight regional assemblies in West Irian are consulted in an "act of free choice" and the people decide that West Irian would remain with Indonesia.
July 28	ZAMBIA: Security Council censures Portugal for attack on village in Zambia.
Aug. 12	NAMIBIA: Security Council calls upon South Africa to withdraw its administration from Namibia.
Aug. 20	NORTHERN IRELAND: Security Council considers the tension between religious groups in Northern Ireland.
Aug. 26	MIDDLE EAST: Security Council condemns Israeli air attack on villages in Southern Lebanon.
Aug. 29	MICRO-STATES: Security Council establishes a committee of experts to consider the UN relationship with micro-states.
Sept. 15	MIDDLE EAST: Security Council calls upon Israel to desist from violations of UN resolutions on Jerusalem.
Sept. 16-Dec. 17	GENERAL ASSEMBLY: 24th regular session.
Oct. 13-31	ECOSOC: Resumed 47th regular session.
Oct. 31	NAMIBIA: General Assembly again condemns South Africa for its refusal to withdraw its administration from Namibia.
Nov. 11	CHINA: General Assembly again decides to retain the Chinese Nationalists as the representatives of China by a vote of 71 to 48; proposal to seat the People's Republic of China fails.

1969 (continued)

Nov. 19   WEST IRIAN: General Assembly endorses Secretary-General's
report on the successful conclusion of the West Irian situation.

Nov. 21   SOUTHERN RHODESIA: General Assembly urges the Security
Council to take action against the white minority regime of
Southern Rhodesia.

Dec. 1   NAMIBIA: General Assembly urges Security Council action
against South Africa.

Dec. 5   TOURISM: General Assembly recommends the conversion of
the International Union of Official Travel Organization into an
international governmental organization.

Dec. 8   INTERNATIONAL LAW: General Assembly adopts
Convention on Special Missions and Optional Protocol
concerning the compulsory settlement of disputes.

Dec. 9   SENEGAL: Security Council condemns Portugal for shelling
village in Southern Senegal.

Dec. 11   CYPRUS: Security Council extends the mandate of UNFICYP
for six more months.
SOCIAL DEVELOPMENT: General Assembly adopts
Declaration on Social Progress and Development.

Dec. 12   INTERNATIONAL LAW: General Assembly adopts resolution
on the forcible diversion of civil aircraft in flight.

Dec. 15   HUMAN ENVIRONMENT: General Assembly establishes a
Preparatory Committee for the 1972 Conference on the
Human Environment.
SEA-BED: General Assembly requests study of the types of
international machinery to assume international control and
supervision over the sea-bed; declares that pending the
establishment of an international regime no territorial claims
are to be recognized and states and individuals are to refrain
from exploitation of resources of the sea-bed and ocean floor.

Dec. 16   ARMS CONTROL: General Assembly urges the USA and the
USSR to agree to a moratorium of further testing and
developing new offensive and defensive strategic nuclear
weapon systems; declares the use of chemical and biological
weapons is contrary to the rule of international law; declares
the 1970's as the Disarmament Decade.
OUTER SPACE: General Assembly urges the Committee on the
Peaceful Uses of Outer Space to complete a draft covenant on
the liability for damage caused by objects launched into outer
space.

Dec. 17   BUDGET: General Assembly authorizes 1970 regular budget of
$168.4 million.

Dec. 22   GUINEA: Security Council calls upon Portugal to desist from
violations of the territorial integrity of Guinea.

1970

Jan. 1	EDUCATION: Start of the International Education Year (1970).
	RACISM: Start of the International Year to Combat Racism and Racial Discrimination (1970).
Jan. 12-14	ECOSOC: Organization part of 48th regular session.
Jan. 19-27	ECONOMIC DEVELOPMENT: 9th session of UNDP approves $95.5 million for 109 new pre-investment projects.
Jan. 30	NAMIBIA: Security Council establishes *Ad Hoc* Committee to consider steps to take in the face of continued refusal of South Africa to withdraw from the territory.
Feb. 5	BARCELONA TRACTION CASE: International Court of Justice delivers judgement in the 2nd phase of the case between Belgium and Spain, rejecting the Belgian claims, not on the merits, but on lack of *jus standi*.
Feb. 18	ECOSOC: Resumed 48th session.
Feb. 26	SEA-BED: Committee on the Peaceful Uses of the Seabed and Ocean Floor Beyond Nation Jurisdiction begins work.
March 16-26	ECONOMIC DEVELOPMENT: Special Session of UNDP recommends major reforms of the UN development system.
March 17	SOUTHERN RHODESIA: UK and USA veto draft resolution of the Security Council condemning Portugal and South Africa for assistance to Southern Rhodesia.
March 18	SOUTHERN RHODESIA: Security Council condemns regime in Southern Rhodesia and the supporting policies of Portugal and South Africa; calls upon all states to take steps to isolate the illegal regime.
March 23-April 3	ECOSOC: Resumed 48th regular session.
May 11-28	ECOSOC: Resumed 48th regular session.
May 11	BAHRAIN: Security Council endorses report of representative of the Secretary-General, indicating that the majority of the people in Bahrain want full independence.
May 12	MIDDLE EAST: Security Council demands the immediate withdrawal of all Israeli forces from Lebanon.
May 15	COMMODITIES: UN Tin Conference adopts the 4th International Tin Agreement.
May 19	MIDDLE EAST: Security Council condemns Israel for its premeditated military action against Lebanon on 12 May.
May 26-June 19	TRUSTEESHIP COUNCIL: 37th regular session.
June 9-30	ECONOMIC DEVELOPMENT: 10th session of UNDP approves 52 pre-investment projects for $110 million.
June 9	CYPRUS: Security Council extends the mandate for UNFICYP for six months.
June 26	CHARTER: Commemorative meeting on 25th anniversary of signing of the Charter, San Francisco.
July 6-31	ECOSOC: 49th regular session.
July 9-17	YOUTH: World Youth Assembly.

1970 (continued)

July 23	SOUTH AFRICA: Security Council condemns all violations of its arms embargo against South Africa.
July 29	NAMIBIA: Security Council requests all states to refrain from any relations implying recognition of South African authority over Namibia; decides to ask the International Court of Justice for an advisory opinion on the legal consequences for states of the continued presence of South Africa in Namibia.
Sept. 5	MIDDLE EAST: Security Council demands the complete and immediate withdrawal of all Israeli armed forces from Lebanon.
Sept. 9	AIRCRAFT HIJACKING: Security Council appeals to all parties concerned for the immediate release of all passengers and crews without exception and calls upon all states to take steps to prevent further hijackings.
Sept. 15-Dec. 17	GENERAL ASSEMBLY: 25th regular session.
Oct. 9	ECOSOC: Resumed 49th regular session.
Oct. 13	MEMBERSHIP: General Assembly admits Fiji as member.
Oct. 14-24	GENERAL ASSEMBLY: 25th anniversary commemorative meetings is addressed by leading statesmen of 84 states.
Oct. 19	ECOSOC: Resumed 49th regular session.
Oct. 21	SECURITY COUNCIL: 1st periodic meetings as envisioned in Article 28 (2) of the Charter to "review the international situation".
Oct. 24	ECONOMIC DEVELOPMENT: General Assembly adopts International Development Strategy for the 2nd UN Development Decade.
	INTERNATIONAL LAW: General Assembly adopts Declaration on Principles of International Law concerning Friendly Relations and Co-operation among States in Accordance with the Charter of the UN.
Nov. 4	MIDDLE EAST: General Assembly calls for three months extension of stand-still cease-fire and for resumption of peace talks.
Nov. 6-13	ECOSOC: Resumed 49th regular session.
Nov. 10	SOUTHERN RHODESIA: UK vetoes draft resolution of the Security Council calling on the UK not to grant independence to Southern Rhodesia.
Nov. 11	WAR CRIMES: Convention on the Non-Applicability of Statutory Limitations to War Crimes Against Humanity enters into force.
Nov. 17	SOUTHERN RHODESIA: Security Council reaffirms its condemnation of the illegal declaration of independence of Southern Rhodesia and urges the UK to take measures to end the rebellion and enable the people to exert self-determination.

1970 (continued)

Nov. 20	CHINA: General Assembly again decides to retain the Chinese Nationalists as the representatives of China by a vote of 51 to 49, with 25 abstentions: proposal to seat the People's Republic of China fails.
Nov. 22	GUINEA: Security Council demands cessation of the armed attack against Guinea and decides to send special mission to report on the situation.
Dec. 7	ARMS CONTROL: General Assembly recommends Treaty Prohibiting Nuclear Weapons on the Sea-Bed and Ocean Floor.
Dec. 8	GUINEA: Security Council, following a report of its special committee, condemns Portugal for its invasion of Guinea on 22-23 November 1970 and demands from Portugal to pay full compensation for damage to life and property caused by the attack.
	SOUTH AFRICA: General Assembly adopts five resolutions condemning the *apartheid* policies of South Africa.
Dec. 9	INTERNATIONAL LAW: General Assembly adopts Basic Principles for Protection of Civilian Populations in Armed Conflicts.
Dec. 10	CYPRUS: Security Council extends the mandate of UNFICYP for six months.
Dec. 11	ECONOMIC DEVELOPMENT: General Assembly approves a re-structured UNDP.
Dec. 15	WOMEN: General Assembly adopts program of concerted international action for the advancement of women.
Dec. 16	COLLECTIVE SECURITY: General Assembly adopts Declaration on the Strengthening of International Security.
Dec. 17	BUDGET: General Assembly adopts budget of $192.1 million for 1971.
	SEA BED: General Assembly adopts Declaration of Principles Governing the Sea-Bed and Ocean Floor beyond the Limits of National Jurisdiction.

1971

Jan. 11-13	ECOSOC: 50th regular session.
Jan. 14-Feb. 2	ECONOMIC DEVELOPMENT: 11th session of Governing Council of UNDP approves 154 major pre-investment projects costing $130.9 million in assistance to 96 developing states.
Jan. 18-Feb. 20	COMMODITIES: UN Wheat Conference adopts 1971 International Wheat Agreement.
Feb. 19	DRUGS: UN Conference in Vienna adopts the convention on Psychotropic Substances, covering, among others, international control over LSD and mescaline.

1971 (continued)

March 2	COMMODITIES: UN Economic Commission for Asia and the Far East drafts agreement establishing a Pepper Community of the major pepper producing countries.
April 1	DRUGS: UN Fund for Drug Abuse Control is established to help states that do not have sufficient resources to combat the production, consumption and illegal traffic in narcotic drugs.
April 26-May 21	ECOSOC: Resumed 50th regular session.
May 19	EAST PAKISTAN: UN High Commissioner for Refugees begins to act as focal point for coordination of assistance for East Pakistan refugees in India; Secretary-General makes appeal for emergency assistance to refugees from East Pakistan in India.
May 25-June 18	TRUSTEESHIP COUNCIL: 38th regular session.
May 26	CYPRUS: Security Council extends the mandate of UNFICYP for a six months.
June 1-8	INDUSTRIAL DEVELOPMENT: International Conference of UNIDO is held in Vienna to examine long range development strategy.
June 7-23	ECONOMIC DEVELOPMENT: 12th session of the Governing Council of UNDP approves $173 million program.
July 5-30	ECOSOC: 51st regular session.
July 15	SENEGAL: Security Council condemns the acts of violence and destruction by Portuguese forces against Senegal and requests Secretary-General to send special mission to investigate.
July 21	NAMIBIA: International Court of Justice decides in an advisory opinion that South African regime in Namibia is illegal.
Aug. 3	GUINEA: Security Council decides to send special mission to report on the situation threatening its political independence.
Aug. 30	INDIA/ICAO CASE: India institutes proceedings before the International Court of Justice, claiming that the ICAO Council has no jurisdiction in an overflight dispute with Pakistan.
Sept. 21-Dec. 22	GENERAL ASSEMBLY: 26th regular session.
Sept. 21	MEMBERSHIP: General Assembly admits Bhutan, Bahrain and Qatar as members.
Sept. 25	MIDDLE EAST: Security Council calls upon Israel to rescind all previous measures and actions and to take no further steps which might change the status of Jerusalem.
Sept. 27-30	NAMIBIA: Security Council considers report of the *Ad Hoc* Sub-Committee on Namibia, but takes no action.
Sept. 29	GUINEA: Security Council considers report from its special mission.
	SENEGAL: Security Council considers report from its special mission.
Oct. 7	MEMBERSHIP: General Assembly admits Oman as member.
Oct. 12	ZAMBIA: Security Council calls upon South Africa to respect the sovereignty and territorial integrity of Zambia.

1971 (continued)

Oct. 20	NAMIBIA: Security Council calls upon all states to abstain from entering into treaty relationships with South Africa in all cases in which South Africa purports to act on behalf of Namibia.
Oct. 25	CHINA: General Assembly votes 76 to 35, with 17 abstentions, to recognize and seat the representatives of the People's Republic of China in the UN and to "expel" the representative of "Chiang Kai-Shek" from all organs of the UN.
Oct. 27-29	ECOSOC: Resumed 51st regular session.
Nov. 15-16	EAST PAKISTAN: Agreement between Secretary-General and Pakistan is finalized on Conditions for Discharge of Functions of the UN Relief Operation in East Pakistan (UNEPRO).
Nov. 15	CHINA: Representatives of the People's Republic of China make first appearance in the UN.
Nov. 19	MIDDLE EAST: Secretary-General reports to the Security Council that his effort with respect to Jerusalem were unsuccessful because of the "failure" of Israel to comply with the Jerusalem resolution.
Nov. 23	ECOSOC: Resumed 51st regular session.
Nov. 24 & 30	SOUTHERN RHODESIA: Security Council considers the report of its Committee on Sanctions.
Nov. 24	SENEGAL: Security Council calls upon Portugal to take immediately effective measures to respect the sovereignty and territorial integrity of Guinea.
Nov. 29	OUTER SPACE: General Assembly recommends the Convention on International Liability for Damage Caused by Space Objects.
	SOUTH AFRICA: General Assembly adopts 8 resolutions on *apartheid* policies of South Africa.
Nov. 30	ECOSOC: Resumed 51st regular session.
	GUINEA: Security Council approves reports of its special mission, affirming that the territorial integrity of Guinea must be respected.
Dec. 4	EAST PAKISTAN: USSR vetoes draft resolution of the Security Council calling on India and Pakistan for immediate cease-fire and withdrawal of all forces.
Dec. 5	EAST PAKISTAN: USSR vetoes draft resolution of the Security Council calling on India and Pakistan for immediate cease-fire and withdrawal of all forces.
Dec. 6	EAST PAKISTAN: Security Council refers the deteriorating situation that has led to armed clashes between India and Pakistan to the General Assembly (in the face of the Council's inability to get unanimity of its permanent members).
	SOUTH AFRICA: General Assembly directs the Secretary-General to send messages to Heads of States with respect to racist policies of South Africa.

1971 (continued)

Dec. 7   EAST PAKISTAN: General Assembly calls upon India and
            Pakistan to take all measures for an immediate cease-fire and
            withdrawal of their armed forces.

Dec. 9   MEMBERSHIP: General Assembly admits the United Arab
            Emirates as member.

            PERSIAN GULF ISLANDS: Security Council considers Iraqi
            complaint of an Iranian seizure of certain islands in the
            Arabian Gulf.

Dec. 13   CYPRUS: Security Council extends the mandate of UNFICYP
            for six months.

            EAST PAKISTAN: USSR vetoes draft resolution of the
            Security Council calling for immediate cease-fire and
            withdrawal of all forces.

            MIDDLE EAST: General Assembly requests the Secretary-
            General to reactivate the use of a special representative to
            assist efforts to reach peace in the Middle East.

Dec. 14   DISASTER RELIEF: General Assembly decides to establish an
            Office of Disaster Relief Coordinator (UNDRO).

Dec. 16   ARMS CONTROL: General Assembly recommends the
            Convention on the Prohibition of the Development,
            Production and Stockpiling of Bacteriological (Biological) and
            Toxin Weapons and on their Destruction.

Dec. 20   CHARTER: General Assembly recommends amendment to
            Article 61, enlarging ECOSOC from 27 to 54 members.

            ECOSOC: Resumed 51st regular session.

            PROTEIN CRISIS: General Assembly adopts Essential
            Elements of the Strategy Statement on Action to Avert the
            Protein Crisis in the Developing Countries.

Dec. 21   BUDGET: General Assembly passes supplementary budget for
            1971, increasing the budget from $192.1 million to $194.6
            million.

            EAST PAKISTAN: Security Council demands that a durable
            cease-fire and cessation of hostilities be observed in all areas
            of the India/Pakistan sub-continent (including Kashmir).

Dec. 22   BUDGET: General Assembly authorizes a budget of
            $213.1 million for 1972.

            SECRETARY-GENERAL: General Assembly appoints Kurt
            Waldheim of Austria as the UN Secretary-General for a five
            year term beginning 1 January 1972.

Dec. 30   SOUTHERN RHODESIA: UK vetoes draft resolution of the
            Security Council rejecting UK-Ian Smith regime proposals of
            settlement.

1972

Jan. 5-7   ECOSOC: 52nd regular session.

1972 (continued)

Jan. 19	SECURITY COUNCIL: Council decides to hold meetings in Africa (the first away from the UN Headquarters).
Jan. 28-Feb. 4	SECURITY COUNCIL: Council holds meetings in Addis Ababa, Ethiopia.
Jan. 28	ECONOMIC DEVELOPMENT: 13th session of the Governing Council of UNDP approves $302 million in development projects in 90 states.
Feb. 4	NAMIBIA: Security Council calls for consultation to try to enable the people of Namibia to exert their right of self-determination; strongly condemns recent repressive measures against African laborers in Namibia; calls upon South Africa to abolish these measures and to withdraw its police and military forces.
	PORTUGUESE TERRITORIES: Security Council reaffirms the inalienable rights of the peoples of Angola, Mozambique, and Guinea (Bissau) to self-determination and independence.
Feb. 4	SOUTH AFRICA: Security Council condemns the South African government for continuing its policies of *apartheid*; recognizes the legitimacy of the struggle of the oppressed people of South Africa in pursuance of their political rights.
Feb. 28	MIDDLE EAST: Security Council demands from Israel to desist and refrain from any ground and air military action against Lebanon and to withdraw its forces from Lebanon.
	SOUTHERN RHODESIA: Security Council urges all states to fully implement resolutions establishing economic sanctions against Southern Rhodesia; deplores those states that persist in aiding the illegal regime.
March 6-7	COMMODITIES: Organizational meetings of the UN Cocoa Conference.
April 13-May 21	ECONOMIC DEVELOPMENT: 3rd session of the UN Conference of Trade and Development in Santiago, Chile.
April 14	UNITED KINGDOM/ICELAND CASE: UK files proceedings before the International Court of Justice against Iceland with regard to the extend of its jurisdiction.
April 17	INTERNATIONAL LAW: International Court of Justice holds special sitting to commemorate the 50th anniversary of the international judicial system.
April 19	MIDDLE EAST: Security Council increases the number of UN observers on the Israeli-Lebanon boarder.
May 15-June 2	ECOSOC: Resumed 52nd regular session.
May 23-June 16	TRUSTEESHIP COUNCIL: 39th regular session.
June 5-16	HUMAN ENVIRONMENT: UN Conference on the Human Environment, Stockholm; adopts the Declaration on the Human Environment for international action to protect man's habitat on earth.

1972 (continued)

June 6-23	ECONOMIC DEVELOPMENT: 14th session of the Governing Council of UNDP.
June 15	CYPRUS: Security Council extends the mandate of UNFICYP for six months.
June 20	AIRCRAFT HIJACKING: Security Council expresses concern with the threat to lives of passengers and crews arising from hijacking and condemns these acts.
June 26	MIDDLE EAST: Security Council calls upon Israel to refrain from all military action in Lebanon.
July 3-28	ECOSOC: 53rd regular session.
July 3	SECRETARIAT: Committee on Application for Review of Administrative Tribunal Judgements requests advisory opinion of the International Court of Justice as to whether the Administrative Tribunal committed a fundamental error in procedure.
July 21	MIDDLE EAST: Security Council calls upon Israel to return without delay all Syrians and Lebanese military and security personnel abducted by Israeli forces from Lebanese territory.
July 28	SOUTHERN RHODESIA: Security Council approves recommendation to strengthen the sanctions against the illegal regime in Southern Rhodesia.
Aug. 1	NAMIBIA: Security Council invites Secretary-General to continue efforts to contact all parties concerned with the situation.
Aug. 25	MEMBERSHIP: China vetoes draft resolution of the Security Council on admission of Bangladesh for membership.
Aug. 31	COMMODITIES: Pepper Community holds its inaugural meeting under ECAFE in Bangkok.
Sept. 10	MIDDLE EAST: China and USSR veto draft resolution of the Security Council including the phrase "all parties" instead of "the parties"; USA vetoes draft resolution of the Security Council calling on "the parties" concerned to cease military operations.
Sept. 12-15	ECOSOC: Resumed 53rd regular session.
Sept. 19-Dec. 19	GENERAL ASSEMBLY: 27th regular session.
Sept. 20	POPULATION: 1974 is designated the World Population Year.
Sept. 29	SOUTHERN RHODESIA: Security Council calls upon all states to implement sanctions resolutions against Southern Rhodesia.
Oct. 17-18	ECOSOC: Resumed 53rd regular session.
Oct. 21	COMMODITIES: UN Cocoa Conference adopts International Cocoa Agreement.
Oct. 23	SENEGAL: Security Council condemns frontier violations and attack on Senegalese post by Portugal.
Nov. 15	SOUTH AFRICA: General Assembly adopts six resolutions on *apartheid* policies of South Africa.
Nov. 16-17	ECOSOC: Resumed 53rd regular session.

1972 (continued)

Nov. 22	PORTUGUESE TERRITORIES: Security Council calls upon Portugal to cease military operations and all repressive actions against the peoples of Angola, Guinea (Bissau) and Cape Verde.
Dec. 4	SOUTHERN RHODESIA: UK vetoes draft resolution of the Security Council on situation in Southern Rhodesia.
Dec. 6	NAMIBIA: Security Council invites the Secretary-General to continue his efforts to negotiate between the parties.
Dec. 8	BUDGET: General Assembly decreases the 1972 budget from $213.1 million to $208.7 million.
Dec. 1	UN UNIVERSITY: General Assembly decides to establish the UN University (UNU).
Dec. 12	CYPRUS: Security Council extends the mandate of UNFICYP for six months.
Dec. 15	HUMAN ENVIRONMENT: General Assembly recommends establishment of a Governing Council for Environment Programs, an Environment Secretariat (to be located in Nairobi, Kenya) and an Environment Fund.
Dec. 19	BUDGET: General Assembly authorizes a budget of $225.9 million for 1973 and approves the introduction of a biennial budget cycle.

1973

Jan 1	POPULATION: Start of the World Population Year (1973).
Jan. 8-10	ECOSOC: 54th regular session.
Jan. 26	SECURITY COUNCIL: Council decides to hold meetings in Panama.
Feb. 2	ZAMBIA: Security Council condemns all acts of provocation and harassment, including economic blockade, blackmail and military threats against Zambia by the illegal regime of Southern Rhodesia in collusion with South Africa.
Feb. 13	ECONOMIC DEVELOPMENT: 15th session of the Governing Council of UNDP approves $268 million in development assistance.
March 10	ZAMBIA: Security Council appeals to all states for immediate technical, financial and material assistance to Zambia, so that Zambia might maintain its normal flow of trade traffic and enhance its ability to implement fully the mandatory sanction policy against Southern Rhodesia; declares that the only effective solution to the grave situation on the border between Zambia and Rhodesia lies in the exercise of the right of self-determination by the people of Zimbabwe (Southern Rhodesia).
March 19-23	COMMODITIES: UN Conference on Olive Oil extends the International Olive Oil Agreement until 31 December 1978.

1973 (continued)

March 21	LATIN AMERICA: Security Council urges states to adopt appropriate measures to impede the activities of enterprises which deliberately attempt to coerce Latin American countries.
	PANAMA CANAL: USA vetoes a draft resolution of the Security Council urging new treaty on the Panama Canal.
April 17-May 18	ECOSOC: 54th regular session.
April 21	MIDDLE EAST: Security Council condemns all acts of violence and attacks on Lebanon by Israel.
May 9	AUSTRALIA/NEW ZEALAND/FRANCE CASES: Australia and New Zealand file proceedings against France before the International Court of Justice, protesting the atmospheric nuclear tests by France in the South Pacific.
May 11	PAKISTAN/INDIA CASE: Pakistan files proceedings against India before the International Court of Justice with respect to the rights and treatment of Pakistani prisoners of war.
May 22	POPULATION: UNFPA budget funded by voluntary contributions passes the $100 million mark.
	SOUTHERN RHODESIA: Security Council adopts measures to extend and improve the sanctions against Southern Rhodesia.
May 29-June 22	TRUSTEESHIP COUNCIL: 40th regular session.
June 6-29	ECONOMIC DEVELOPMENT: 16th session of the Governing Council of UNDP approves $256.0 million in development assistance.
June 14	MIDDLE EAST: Security Council, after ten meetings, suspends consideration of the situation in the Middle East.
June 15	CYPRUS: Security Council extends the mandate of UNFICYP for six months.
June 22	AUSTRALIA/NEW ZEALAND/FRANCE CASES: International Court of Justice orders France, Australia and New Zealand to take no actions that might aggravate the dispute, and in particular requests France to avoid nuclear tests until the Court reaches its decision in the two cases.
July 4-Aug. 10	ECOSOC: 55th regular session.
July 26	MIDDLE EAST: USA vetoes a draft resolution of the Security Council on the situation in the Middle East.
Aug. 15	MIDDLE EAST: Security Council condemns Israelis for violating Lebanon's sovereignty and territorial integrity, and for the forcible diversion and seizure by the Israeli Air force of a Lebanese airliner from Lebanon's air space.
Sept. 17	ECOSOC: Special Session adopts measures to assist Pakistan following devastating rains and floods.
Sept. 18-Dec. 18	GENERAL ASSEMBLY: 28th regular session.
Sept. 18	CHILE: Security Council considers Cuban complaint about Chilean attacks on Cuba's embassy in Santiago: meeting adjourns without a draft resolution having been tabled.

1973 (continued)

Sept. 18	MEMBERSHIP: General Assembly admits German Democratic Republic, Federal Republic of Germany and Bahamas as members.
Sept. 24	CHARTER: Amendment to Article 61 enlarging ECOSOC from 27 to 54 members comes into force with necessary number of ratifications having been received.
Oct. 2	ENVIRONMENT: Headquarters of the UN Environment Program (UNEP) is opened in Nairobi, Kenya.
Oct. 12	ECOSOC: General Assembly elects 27 additional members to ECOSOC in conformity to the amended Article 61 of the Charter.
Oct. 15	ECOSOC: Resumed 55th session: first meeting of the newly enlarged Council.
Oct. 22	MIDDLE EAST: Security Council calls upon all parties to cease firing and to terminate all military actions immediately.
Oct. 23	MIDDLE EAST: Security Council reaffirms its call for a cease-fire and requests the Secretary-General to take measures for the immediate sending of UN observers to supervise the cease-fire between Israel and Egypt.
Oct. 25	MIDDLE EAST: Security Council requests parties to observe the cease-fire and to return to positions they occupied on 22 October; decides to increase UN military observers and to establish a UN Emergency Force (UNEP).
Oct. 27	MIDDLE EAST: Security Council establishes UNEF for an initial period of six months.
Nov. 2	GUINEA-BISSAU: General Assembly welcomes the independence of Guinea-Bissau and condemns Portugal for its illegal occupation of the area.
	HUMAN RIGHTS: General Assembly approves a program for the Decade of Action to Combat Racism and Racial Discrimination.
	MIDDLE EAST: Security Council agrees on the "geographical" composition of UNEF in the Middle East.
Nov. 20	MIDDLE EAST: Security Council agrees that at least three African states should send contingents to the UNEF in the Middle East.
Nov. 30	HUMAN RIGHTS: General Assembly adopts the International Convention on the Suppression and Punishment of the Crime of *Apartheid*.
Dec. 3-15	LAW OF THE SEA: 1st session of the 3rd UN Conference on the Law of the Sea.
Dec. 11	BUDGET: General Assembly authorizes increase in 1973 budget from $225.9 million to $233.8 million.
	ECOSOC: Resumed 55th regular session.
	NAMIBIA: Security Council decides to discontinue the efforts of the Secretary-General.

1973 (continued)

Dec. 12   INTERNATIONAL LAW: General Assembly proclaims Basic
               Principles of the Legal Status of the Combatants Struggling
               Against Colonial and Alien Domination and Racial Regimes.

Dec. 14   CYPRUS: Security Council extends the mandate of UNFICYP
               for six months.
               INTERNATIONAL LAW: General Assembly adopts the
               Convention on the Prevention and Punishment of Crimes
               Against International Protected Persons, including Diplomatic
               Agents.
               PAKISTAN/INDIA CASE: International Court of Justice
               removes case on treatment of Pakistani prisoners of war from
               the court at the request of Pakistan, because of negotiations
               directly with India.
               SOUTH AFRICA: General Assembly adopts seven resolutions
               against the *apartheid* policies.

Dec. 15   MIDDLE EAST: Security Council expresses hope for full and
               effective role of the Secretary-General at the Peace
               Conference on the Middle East in Geneva.

Dec. 17   ECONOMIC DEVELOPMENT: General Assembly makes its
               first biennial appraisal of progress of the International
               Development Strategy for the Second UN Development
               Decade.

Dec. 18   BUDGET: General Assembly adopts a program budget
               amounting to $540.5 million for the biennium 1974-1975.
               WORKING LANGUAGES: General Assembly includes Chinese
               and Arabic as working languages of the General Assembly
               and the Security Council.

1974

Jan. 1   POPULATION: Start of the World Population Year (1974).
Jan. 7-10   ECOSOC: 56th regular session.
Jan. 14-Feb. 1   ECONOMIC DEVELOPMENT: 17th session of the Governing
                   Council of UNDP approves $202.5 million in development
                   assistance.
Jan. 18   MIDDLE EAST: Egyptian-Israeli agreement on disengagement
                   of forces is signed in presence of UNEF commander on
                   kilometer 101 on the Cairo-Suez road, in pursuance of the
                   Geneva Peace Conference on the Middle East.
Feb. 15-28   IRAN-IRAQ: Security Council discusses incidents on the border
                   between Iran and Iraq.
April 8   MIDDLE EAST: Security Council extends the mandate of
                   UNEF for six months.
April 9-May 1   DEVELOPMENT: 6th special session of the General Assembly
                   on the problems of raw materials and development.
April 22-May 17   ECOSOC: 56th regular session.

1974 (continued)

April 24	MIDDLE EAST: Security Council condemns Israeli violation of Lebanese territory and all acts of violence.
May 1	ECONOMIC DEVELOPMENT: General Assembly adopts the Declaration on the Establishment of a New International Order, and a Program of Action on the Establishment of a New International Economic Order.
May 20-June 12	TRADE: UN Conference on Prescription (Limitation) in the International Sale of Goods adopts Convention on the Limitation Period in the International Sale of Goods.
May 28	IRAN-IRAQ: Security Council endorses a four point agreement between Iran and Iraq aimed at de-escalating the situation on their common border.
May 29	CYPRUS: Security Council extends the mandate of UNFICYP for six months.
May 31	MIDDLE EAST: Security Council welcomes the agreement on disengagement between Israeli and Syrian forces negotiated in implementation of Security Council resolution of 22 October 1973; decides to set up a UN Disengagement Observer Force (UNDOF) for an initial period of six months on the Israeli-Syrian border.
June 3-14	TRUSTEESHIP COUNCIL: 41st regular session.
June 5-24	ECONOMIC DEVELOPMENT: 18th session of the Governing Council of UNDP approves $128.5 million in development assistance.
June 20-Aug. 29	LAW OF THE SEA: 2nd session of 3rd UN Conference on the Law of the Sea, Caracas, Venezuela.
July 3-Aug. 2	ECOSOC: 57th regular session.
July 20	CYPRUS: Security Council calls for cease-fire by all parties in Cyprus and for parties to negotiate.
July 23	CYPRUS: Security Council demands that all parties to the fighting comply immediately with the request for a cease-fire.
July 25	FISHERIES JURISDICTION CASES: International Court of Justice delivers judgement in the two cases concerning fisheries jurisdiction (UK versus Iceland and Federal Republic of Germany versus Iceland) and finds Iceland not entitled to exclude fishing vessels from areas between 12 and 50 miles offshore.
July 31	CYPRUS: Security Council requests the Secretary-General report on the implementation of the cease-fire.
Aug. 14	CYPRUS: Security Council demands fighting cease and calls for resumption of negotiations.
Aug. 15	CYPRUS: Security Council demands that all parties fully respect UNFICYP.
Aug. 16	CYPRUS: Security Council formally disapproves of the Turkish military action in Cyprus and urges a resumption of negotiations.

1974 (continued)

Aug. 19-30   POPULATION: World Population Conference in Bucharest,
                  Romania adopts World Population Plan of Action.
Aug. 30   CYPRUS: Security Council expresses concern over plight of
                  refugees and urges action to provide them with assistance.
Sept. 9-10   REGIONAL COMMISSIONS: 1st special session of the UN
                  Economic Commission for Western Asia (ECWA) decides
                  that Beirut, Lebanon will be its headquarters for five years.
Sept. 16   GENERAL ASSEMBLY: Reconvened 28th regular session.
Sept. 17-Dec. 18 GENERAL ASSEMBLY: 29th regular session.
Sept. 17   MEMBERSHIP: General Assembly admits Bangladesh, Grenada
                  and Guinea-Bissau as members.
Oct. 14   ECOSOC: Resumed 57th regular session.
Oct. 18-23   TRUSTEESHIP COUNCIL: Resumed 41st regular session.
Oct. 23   MIDDLE EAST: Security Council extends the mandate of
                  UNEF for six months.
Oct. 30   SOUTH AFRICA: France, UK and USA veto draft resolution
                  of the Security Council, recommending that the General
                  Assembly expels South Africa from membership in the UN.
Nov. 12   OUTER SPACE: General Assembly recommends Convention
                  on Registration of Objects Launched into Outer Space.
                  SOUTH AFRICA: General Assembly upholds ruling of
                  President who refused to allow South African delegation to
                  participate in work of the General Assembly.
Nov. 13-21   MIDDLE EAST: Chairman on the Palestine Liberation
                  Organization (PLO) addresses General Assembly during
                  debate on the question of Palestine.
Nov. 22   MIDDLE EAST: General Assembly grants observer status to
                  PLO.
Nov. 29   MIDDLE EAST: Security Council extends the mandate of
                  UNDOF for six months.
Dec. 5-16   ECOSOC: Resumed 57th regular session.
Dec. 9   ARMS CONTROL: General Assembly commends the
                  establishment of a Nuclear Weapon Free Zone in the region
                  of the Middle East and endorses in principle the concept of a
                  Nuclear Free Zone in South Asia.
Dec. 12   ECONOMIC DEVELOPMENT: General Assembly adopts the
                  Charter on the Economic Rights and Duties of States.
Dec. 13   CYPRUS: Security Council extends the mandate of UNFICYP
                  for six months and urges the parties to co-operate with the
                  UN force.
Dec. 14   INTERNATIONAL LAW: General Assembly approves a
                  definition of aggression.
Dec. 16   ARMS CONTROL: General Assembly declares the Indian
                  Ocean as Zone of Peace.

1975 (continued)

Dec. 16   ENVIRONMENT: General Assembly decides to establish a UN Habitat and Human Settlements Foundation as of 1 January 1975.

SOUTH AFRICA: General Assembly adopts five resolutions on policies of *apartheid* in South Africa.

Dec. 17   FOOD: General Assembly establishes the UN World Food Council (WFC).

NAMIBIA: Security Council demands that South Africa withdraws its illegal administration from Namibia.

SPECIALIZED AGENCIES: General Assembly approves agreement establishing the World Intellectual Property Organization (WIPO) as a specialized agency.

Dec. 18   BUDGET: General Assembly approves a revised budget appropriation for the 1974-1975 biennium, increasing the budget to $606 million.

GENERAL ASSEMBLY: 28th regular session is suspended instead of adjourned.

SECRETARIAT: General Assembly approves the Statute of the International Civil Service Commission (ICSC).

Dec. 19   CYPRUS: UN High Commissioner for Refugees and the European Community sign agreement covering a gift of $1.1 million worth of food stuffs for UN humanitarian assistance in Cyprus.

Dec. 20   NUCLEAR TEST CASES: International Court of Justice delivers judgement in the two nuclear weapons test cases (Australia versus France and New Zealand versus France) finding that the claims of Australia and New Zealand no longer has an object and that it is therefore not called upon to give a decision.

1975

Jan. 1   WOMEN: Start of the International Women's Year (1975).

Jan. 12-28   ECOSOC: 58th regular session.

Jan. 15-Feb. 3   ECONOMIC DEVELOPMENT: 19th session of the Governing Council of UNDP approves $83.5 million in development assistance.

Jan. 20   UN UNIVERSITY: Inaugurated in Tokyo.

Feb. 4-Mar. 14   INTERNATIONAL LAW: UN Conference on the Representation of States in their Relations with International Organizations in Vienna adopts an international convention governing states and functions of government missions and delegations to international organizations.

Feb. 10-21   ECONOMIC DEVELOPMENT: Commodity Committee initiates action towards development of a program for integrated commodity stabilization.

1975 (continued)

Feb. 20-27   CYPRUS: Security Council considers the situation in Cyprus.

Feb. 23-25   CAPE VERDE: Special UN mission visits the area to propose
                    plans to deal with the prolonged drought.

Feb. 24-28   REFORM: Group of experts meets on proposals for structural
                    changes in the UN to make it fully capable for dealing with
                    international economic co-operation.

March 3-7   ECONOMIC DEVELOPMENT: Preparatory Committee for the
                    special session of the General Assembly on Development and
                    International Economic Co-operation.

March 12-27   INDUSTRIAL DEVELOPMENT: 2nd General Conference of
                    UNIDO Lima, Peru adopts Declaration and Plan of Action on
                    Industrial Development and Cooperation.

March 12   CYPRUS: Security Council requests the Secretary-General to
                    undertake a good offices mission between Greek and Turkish
                    communities.

March 17-May 10   LAW OF THE SEA: Resumed session of 3rd UN Conference
                    on the Law of the Sea, Geneva.

March 17-28   MULTINATIONAL CORPORATIONS: 1st session of the
                    Commission for Transnational Corporations.

March 25   FOOD: Governing body of the World Food Program approves
                    $129 million in food aid.

March 26   ARMS CONTROL: Convention on the Prohibition of the
                    Development, Production, and Stockpiling of Bacteriological
                    (Biological) and Toxic Weapons and on Their Destruction
                    enters into force on the basis of ratifications by UK, USA and
                    USSR.

April 8-May 8   ECOSOC: Resumed 58th regular session.

April 17-May 2   ENVIRONMENT: 3rd session of UNEP.

April 17   MIDDLE EAST: Security Council extends the mandate of
                    UNEF for three months until July.

May 7   LAW OF THE SEA: Chairman of the Committees of the 3rd
                    UN Conference on the Law of the Sea presents informal
                    single negotiating text of proposed convention on Law of the
                    Sea.

May 14   ECONOMIC DEVELOPMENT: 16th session of ECIA adopts
                    the Chaguaramas Declaration appraising the International
                    Development Strategy for the 2nd UN Development Decade.

May 19-30   SECRETARIAT: 1st session of International Civil Service
                    Commission is concerned with development of a unified civil
                    service for UN and the specialized agencies.

May 20-June 21   COMMODITIES: UN Tin Conference in Geneva adopts a new
                    International Tin Agreement.

May 20   REFORM: Group of experts submits report on a new UN
                    structure for global economic cooperation.

May 27-June 7   TRUSTEESHIP COUNCIL: 42nd regular session.

1975 (continued)

May 28	MIDDLE EAST: Security Council extends the mandate of UNDOF for six months until November.
May 30	ARMS CONTROL: 1st Review Conference of the Parties to the Treaty on the Non-Proliferation of Nuclear Weapons adopts a Final Declaration stating that all parties had faithfully observed the treaty provisions prohibiting transfer of nuclear weapons and their technology from nuclear to non-nuclear weapon states.
June 6	NAMIBIA: France, UK and USA veto a draft resolution of the Security Council which determines that "the illegal" occupation of Namibia by South Africa constitutes a threat to international peace and security.
June 11-13	ECONOMIC DEVELOPMENT: 20th session of the Governing Council of UNDP approves $100 million in development assistance.
June 13	CYPRUS: Security Council extends the mandate of UNFICYP for six months.
June 16-20	ECONOMIC DEVELOPMENT: Preparatory Commission for the special session of the General Assembly on Development and International Economic Co-operation.
June 19-July 2	WOMEN: World Conference of International Women's Year in Mexico City adopts World Plan of Action for the Advancement of Women and the Declaration of Mexico on the Equality of Women.
June 23-28	FOOD: Inaugural session of the UN World Food Council in Rome adopts a priority list of action.
July 1	COMMODITIES: New International Tin Agreement comes into effect.
July 2-31	ECOSOC: 59th regular session.
July 24	MIDDLE EAST: Security Council extends the mandate of UNEF for three months.
Aug. 6	MEMBERSHIP: Security Council decides not to include application of the Republic of Korea (South Korea) on its agenda.
Aug. 11	MEMBERSHIP: USA vetoes a draft resolution of the Security Council, recommending that the General Assembly admits the Republic of South Viet Nam and the Democratic Republic of Viet Nam.
Aug. 28-29	TRUSTEESHIP COUNCIL: Resumed 42nd regular session.
Sept. 1-16	ECONOMIC DEVELOPMENT: 7th special session of the General Assembly on Development and International Economic Co-operation adopts measures aimed at accelerating development of the developing countries and narrowing the gap between developed and the developing countries.

1975 (continued)

Sept. 1-12	CRIME: 5th UN Congress on Prevention of Crime and the Treatment of Offenders adopts a draft Declaration on Torture and Other Cruel, Inhuman and Degrading Treatment or Punishment.
Sept. 1	MIDDLE EAST: Egypt and Israel initiate interim agreement of further disengagement in the Sinai.
Sept. 16-Dec. 17	GENERAL ASSEMBLY: 30th regular session.
Sept. 16	MEMBERSHIP: General Assembly admits Cape Verde, Sao Tome and Principe and Mozambique as members.
	TRUSTEESHIP: Australian trust territory of New Guinea becomes independent as Papua New Guinea.
Sept. 22-Oct. 20	COMMODITIES: UN Conference adopts new International Cocoa Agreement.
Sept. 29-Oct. 3	FOOD: Governing body of World Food Program approves $165 million in food aid to 15 countries.
Sept. 30	MEMBERSHIP: USA vetoes a draft resolution of the Security Council recommending that the General Assembly admits the Republic of South Viet Nam and the Democratic Republic of Viet Nam.
Oct. 10	MEMBERSHIP: General Assembly admits Papua New Guinea as member.
Oct. 16	WESTERN SAHARA CASE: International Court of Justice delivers an advisory opinion that no tie of territorial sovereignty has been established between Western Sahara and Morocco or Mauritania in the past.
Oct. 22	WESTERN SAHARA: Security Council requests the Secretary-General to enter into negotiations with Spain, Morocco, Mauritania and Algeria with respect to this issue.
Oct. 23	MIDDLE EAST: Security Council extends the mandate of UNEF for one year.
Oct. 25-28	WESTERN SAHARA: Secretary-General visits Spain, Morocco, Mauritania and Algeria.
Oct. 30	MIDDLE EAST: Secretary-General appeals to all parties in the civil conflict in Lebanon to end their bloodshed.
Nov. 2	WESTERN SAHARA: Security Council urges all parties concerned to avoid any unilateral action that will escalate tension.
Nov. 5	ECONOMIC DEVELOPMENT: UNDP pledging conference results in pledges of $314.6 million from 106 states.
Nov. 6	WESTERN SAHARA: Security Council calls upon Morocco to withdraw its marchers from the area.
Nov. 10	ANGOLA: Secretary-General appeals to the three liberation movements to take urgent steps to end their conflict on the eve of the country's independence.

1975 (continued)

Nov. 10   ZIONISM: General Assembly determines by resolution 3379 (XXX) that "Zionism is a form of racism and racial discrimination" by a vote of 72 to 35, with 32 abstentions (resolution is subsequently revoked on 16 December 1991).

MIDDLE EAST: General Assembly invites the PLO to participate in all discussions on the Middle East to be held under the auspices of the UN.

PEACE: General Assembly adopts Declaration on the Use of Scientific and Technological Progress in the Interests of Peace and for the Benefit of Mankind.

Nov. 12   MEMBERSHIP: General Assembly admits Comoros as member.

WESTERN SAHARA: Secretary-General reports on the announcement of the King of Morocco that he will request the marchers to leave the area.

Nov. 18   KOREA: General Assembly urges continued efforts for the unification of Korea.

PEACE AND SECURITY: General Assembly calls upon all states to extend the process of detente to all regions of the world.

Nov. 19   WESTERN SAHARA: Secretary-General reports that Spain informed him of the agreement with Morocco and Mauritania according to which Spain would terminate its control of the area by February 1976.

Nov. 20   CYPRUS: General Assembly demands withdrawal of all foreign forces from Cyprus.

Nov. 21   SOUTHERN RHODESIA: General Assembly demands an end of all repressive measures against Africans, release of all political prisoners, and termination of the execution of freedom fighters by the "illegal" Smith regime.

Nov. 28   FOOD: General Assembly reconstitutes the UN/FAO Intergovernmental Committee of the World Food Program as a Committee of Food Aid Policies and programs.

Nov. 29   SOUTH AFRICA: General Assembly proclaims that the UN has a special responsibility to the oppressed peoples of South Africa and their liberation movements in their struggle against *apartheid*.

Nov. 30   MIDDLE EAST: Security Council extends the mandate of UNDOF for six months.

Dec. 4   MEMBERSHIP: General Assembly admits Surinam as member.

MIDDLE EAST: Security Council considers the charge of Israeli air attack on refugee camps in Lebanon and invites the representative of the PLO to participate in the discussion.

Dec. 5   MIDDLE EAST: General Assembly condemns Israel's continued occupation of Arab territories.

1975 (continued)

Dec. 8   MIDDLE EAST: USA vetoes draft resolution of the Security
           Council condemning Israel for air attacks against Lebanon.

Dec. 9   CHILE: General Assembly expresses distress at the constant and
           flagrant violation of human rights in Chile.

           HUMAN RIGHTS: General Assembly adopts Declaration on
           the Protection of All Persons from being subjected to Torture
           and Other Cruel, Inhuman or Degrading Treatment or
           Punishment; adopts Declaration on the Rights of Disabled
           Persons.

Dec. 11   ARMS CONTROL: General Assembly defines obligations of
           states towards nuclear-weapon-free zones and recommends
           consideration of the establishment of nuclear-weapon-free
           zones in the Middle East, South Asia and South Pacific.

Dec. 12   TIMOR: General Assembly deplores the military intervention of
           Indonesia in Portuguese Timor.

Dec. 13   CYPRUS: Security Council extends the mandate of UNFICYP
           for six months.

Dec. 15   MIDDLE EAST: General Assembly condemns Israeli policies
           and practices affecting the human rights of the population in
           the occupied Arab territories.

           MULTINATIONAL CORPORATIONS: General Assembly
           condemns all corrupt practices of transnational corporations
           and calls upon states to take measures to prevent such
           practices.

Dec. 16   FISHERIES JURISDICTION: Security Council considers the
           complaint of Iceland against the UK alleging that British
           warships invaded its territorial waters.

Dec. 17   BUDGET: General Assembly approves a revised program
           program budget for the biennium 1974-1975 of $612.6 million
           and a new program budget for the biennium 1976-1977 of
           $745.8 million.

Dec. 22   TIMOR: Security Council calls upon Indonesia to withdraw its
           forces from Eastern Timor, and upon the Portuguese
           administration to facilitate the achievement of self-
           determination; requests the Secretary-General to send a
           special representative to report on the situation.

1976

Jan. 3   HUMAN RIGHTS: International Convention on Economic,
           Social and Cultural Rights (adopted by the General Assembly
           in December 1966) enters into force, having acquired the
           necessary 35 state ratifications.

1976 (continued)

Jan. 5-8   NAMIBIA: International Conference on Namibia and Human
                Rights in Dakar, Senegal adopts a declaration stating that the
                continued occupation of Namibia by South Africa is a threat
                to peace and security.

Jan. 8   HUMAN RIGHTS: 88 states parties to the International
                Convention on the Elimination of all forms of Racial
                Discrimination create the Committee on the Elimination of
                Racial Discrimination.

Jan. 13-15   ECOSOC: Organizational meeting of the 60th regular session.

Jan. 15-Feb. 4 ECONOMIC DEVELOPMENT: 21st session of the Governing
                Council of UNDP approves a five year (1977-1981) plan for
                allocation of $3,426.5 million in program funds.

Jan. 18   LEBANON: Secretary-General calls for end to the fractional
                strife.

Jan. 26   MIDDLE EAST: USA vetoes a draft resolutions of the Security
                Council, affirming that the Palestine people should have a
                right of self-determination.

Jan. 28-Feb. 6 AGRICULTURAL DEVELOPMENT: World Food Council
                approves a draft agreement on the Agricultural Development
                Fund.

Jan. 30   NAMIBIA: Security Council demands that South Africa
                withdraws its illegal administration and transfers power to the
                people of Namibia.

Feb. 6   COMOROS: France vetoes a draft resolution of the Security
                Council requesting France to desist from a referendum in the
                island of Mayotte.

Feb. 16   ENVIRONMENT: 15 Mediterranean coastal states sign Anti-
                Pollution Convention to Protect Mediterranean Sea under
                auspices of UNEP.

Feb. 17-21   CYPRUS: Inter-communal negotiations between Greek and
                Turkish Cypriots are held in Vienna under the good offices of
                the Secretary-General.

Feb. 18   SOMALIA: Security Council discusses border incident arising
                from kidnapping of French children.

Feb. 23   MIDDLE EAST: UNEF transfers the area west of the Giddi
                and Mitla Passes to Egypt and thereby completes
                redeployment of forces in accordance with the Protocol to the
                Agreement between Egypt and Israel.

Feb. 26   LEBANON: Secretary-General appeals for $50 million to assist
                victims of the internal conflict in Lebanon.

March 12-27   INDUSTRIAL DEVELOPMENT: 2nd General Conference of
                UNIDO in Lima, Peru adopts Declaration and Plan of Action
                on Industrial Development and Co-operation (Lima
                Declaration).

1976 (continued)

March 15-May 7	LAW OF THE SEA: 4th session of the 3rd UN Conference on the Law of the Sea continues negotiations on a convention to regulate uses of the ocean.
March 17	SOUTHERN RHODESIA: Security Council commends Mozambique for its decision to sever all economic and trade relations with Southern Rhodesia.
March 23	HUMAN RIGHTS: International Covenant on Civil and Political Rights (adopted by the General Assembly in December 1966) enters into force, having acquired the necessary 35 ratifications.
	MIDDLE EAST: USA vetoes a draft resolution of the Security Council, deploring Israel's policies to change the status of the city of Jerusalem.
March 26	LEBANON: Secretary-General appeals to all factions and leaders in Lebanon to accept an immediate cease-fire.
March 31	ANGOLA: Security Council condemns South Africa's aggression against Angola and requests South Africa to desist from using Namibia to mount aggressive acts against neighboring African states.
April 6	SOUTHERN RHODESIA: Security Council expands the sanctions imposed against Southern Rhodesia to include insurance, trade names and franchises.
April 13- May	ECOSOC: 60th regular session.
April 22	EAST TIMOR: Security Council calls upon Indonesia to withdraw without further delay all its forces from the territory of East Timor.
May 3-28	ECONOMIC DEVELOPMENT: 4th session of UNCTAD in Nairobi, Kenya, adopts an integrated program to increase commodity earnings of developing countries.
May 7	FOOD: Governing body of the World Food Program approves $358 million in food aid for 31 projects in 24 countries.
May 26	MIDDLE EAST: President of the Security Council, in a statement reflecting the opinion of the majority of the members, expresses anxiety at the situation in Arab territories under Israel occupation.
May 28	MIDDLE EAST: Security Council extends the mandate of UNDOF for six months until 30 November.
May 31-June 11	HABITAT: UN Conference on Human Settlements in Vancouver, Canada, adopts a blueprint for national and international action to improve the living places of people throughout the world (Vancouver Declaration on Human Settlements).
June 4-17	EMPLOYMENT: World Employment Conference.

1976 (continued)

June 10-13	AGRICULTURAL DEVELOPMENT: UN Conference in Rome adopts agreement establishing the International Fund for Agricultural Development (IFAD), to be a new UN specialized agency.
June 14-July 5	ECONOMIC DEVELOPMENT: 22nd session of UNDP.
June 14-17	FOOD: 2nd session of World Food Council adopts recommendation on increasing food production in the developing countries, and improving world food security.
June 15	CYPRUS: Security Council extends the mandate of UNFICYP for six months.
June 16	SOUTHERN RHODESIA: Special Committee of 24 on Decolonization urges strong enforcement measures against Southern Rhodesia.
June 19	SOUTH AFRICA: Security Council condemns South Africa for the killing of school children and students at Soweto; recognizes the legitimacy of the struggle against *apartheid*.
June 23	MEMBERSHIP: USA vetoes draft resolution of the Security Council on the admission of Angola to membership.
June 29-July 13	TRUSTEESHIP COUNCIL: 43rd regular session recognizes the June 1975 plebiscite in the Northern Mariana Islands as a free exercise of self-determination in which the majority approved a covenant to establish a commonwealth of Northern Mariana Islands in political union with USA.
June 29	MIDDLE EAST: USA vetoes draft resolution of the Security Council affirming the right of the Palestinian people to self-determination and proposing Israeli withdrawal from the occupied Arab territories by June 1977.
June 30-July 9	ECOSOC: 61st regular session in Abidjan, Ivory Coast, adopts a statement of principles and objectives known as the Declaration of Abidjan.
July 12-Aug. 6	ECOSOC: Resumed 61st regular session, Geneva.
July 14	UGANDA HIJACKING: UK vetoes a draft resolution of the Security Council protesting the Israeli military action at Uganda's Entebbe Airport on the night of 3-4 July, following the hijacking several days earlier of an Air France plane that landed at Entebbe.
July 30	SOUTH AFRICA: Security Council condemns South Africa for an armed attack on a Zambian village on 11 July as a flagrant violation of Zambian sovereignty.
Aug. 2-Sept. 17	LAW OF THE SEA: 5th session of the 3rd UN Conference on the Law of the Sea.
Aug. 10	AEGEAN SEA CASE: Greece institutes proceedings before the International Court of Justice against Turkey in respect of a dispute concerning the Aegean Sea continental shelf.
Aug. 25	AEGEAN SEA: Security Council urges Greece and Turkey to hold direct negotiations on the Aegean Sea dispute.

1976 (continued)

Sept. 11	AEGEAN SEA CASE: International Court of Justice rules against indicating interim measures of protection for Greece in its dispute with Turkey concerning the Aegean Sea continental shelf; refuses Turkey's request that the case be removed from the list.
Sept. 14	MEMBERSHIP: Security Council decides to postpone consideration of Viet Nam's application for membership.
Sept. 15	OUTER SPACE: Convention on Registration of Objects Launched into Outer Space enters into force.
Sept. 20	HUMAN RIGHTS: 38 states parties to the International Covenant on Civil and Political Rights elect 18 members of a new Human Rights Committee to oversee fulfillment of the obligations under the covenant.
Sept. 21-Dec. 22	GENERAL ASSEMBLY: 31st regular session.
Sept. 21	MEMBERSHIP: General Assembly admits the Republic of the Seychelles as 145th member.
Sept. 27-30	AGRICULTURAL DEVELOPMENT: 1st session of the Preparatory Commission of IFAD establishes an interim secretariat as pledges of $966 million neared the agreed target of $1,000 million to bring IFAD into being.
Oct. 1	COMMODITIES: International Cocoa Agreement of 1975 and International Coffee Agreement of 1976 enter provisionally into force.
Oct. 18	ECOSOC: Resumed 61st regular session.
Oct. 19	NAMIBIA: France, UK and USA veto a draft resolution of the Security Council determining that the "illegal" occupation of Namibia and the "war" being waged there by South Africa constituted a threat to international peace and security.
Oct. 21	COMOROS: General Assembly calls upon France to withdraw immediately from the Comorian Island of Mayotte, an integral part of the independent Republic of the Comoros, and to respect its sovereignty.
Oct. 22	MIDDLE EAST: Security Council extends the mandate of UNEF for one year until 24 October 1977.
Oct. 25-27	ECOSOC: Resumed 61st regular session.
Oct. 26	TRANSKEI: General Assembly rejects as invalid a declaration by South Africa that the Transkei, one of its bantustans, has attained independence.
Nov. 2	ECONOMIC DEVELOPMENT: Pledging conference results in pledges of $399.0 million from 102 countries towards UNDP and $13.1 million from 24 countries towards the Capital Development Fund.
Nov. 5	SOUTH AFRICA: General Assembly condemns the collaboration between South Africa and all states continuing to supply that country with nuclear and military equipment and

1976 (continued)

	technology, in particular France, Federal Republic of Germany, Israel, UK and USA.
Nov. 9	SOUTH AFRICA: General Assembly adopts ten resolutions calling for actions against the *apartheid* policies of South Africa.
Nov. 11	MIDDLE EAST: Security Council expresses concern over the "serious situation" in the Israeli occupied Arab Territories
Nov. 12	CYPRUS: General Assembly calls for continued negotiations between Greek and Turkish Communities in Cyprus.
Nov. 15	ECOSOC: Resumed 61st regular session.
	MEMBERSHIP: USA vetoes a draft resolution of the Security Council on the admission of Viet Nam to membership.
Nov. 18	ECOSOC: Resumed 61st regular session decides that the permanent headquarters of the Economic Commission for West Asia (ECWA) be at Baghdad.
Nov. 19	ECONOMIC DEVELOPMENT: General Assembly expresses its deep concern and disappointment at the failure of the Conference on International Economic Cooperation (of 27 industrialized and developed states) to achieve any concrete results and its profound concern at the adverse effect the failure of the conference has on international economic cooperation.
Nov. 23	MIDDLE EAST: General Assembly calls on Israel to "halt further removal of refugees from the Gaza camps".
Nov. 24	CAPE VERDE: General Assembly requests states and the specialized agencies to give urgent aid to Cape Verde to enable it to deal with the catastrophic drought situation and its consequences.
	MIDDLE EAST: General Assembly calls for Israeli withdrawal from occupied Arab lands.
	STATE SUCCESSION: General Assembly decides to hold a UN Conference of Plenipotentiaries on Succession of States in Respect of Treaties in 1977.
Nov. 30	MIDDLE EAST: Security Council extends the mandate of UNDOF for six months until 31 May 1977.
Dec. 1	BELIZE: General Assembly reaffirms the inalienable rights of the people of Belize to self-determination and independence and that the inviolability and territorial integrity of Belize must be preserved (Guatemalan claims part of the area).
	EAST TIMOR: General Assembly declares that the people of East Timor have not been able to exercise freely their right to self-determination and independence; rejects the claim that the territory has been integrated into Indonesia; calls upon Indonesia to withdraw its forces from East Timor.
	MEMBERSHIP: The General Assembly admits the People's Republic of Angola as 146th member.

1976 (continued)

Dec. 8   SECRETARY-GENERAL: General Assembly re-appoints Kurt Waldheim as Secretary-General for a second term from 1 January 1977 to 31 December 1981.

Dec. 9   MIDDLE EAST: General Assembly calls for an early resumption of the Geneva Peace Conference on the Middle East with a participation of all concerned including the PLO.

Dec. 10   ARMS CONTROL: General Assembly adopts the Convention on the Prohibition of Military or any Other Hostile Use of Environmental Modification Technique.

Dec. 14   CYPRUS: Security Council extends the mandate of UNFICYP for six months until 15 June 1977.

Dec. 15   INTERNATIONAL LAW: General Assembly establishes an *Ad Hoc* Committee on the Drafting of an International Convention against the Taking of Hostages.

                 MEMBERSHIP: General Assembly admits Western Samoa as member.

Dec. 16   HUMAN RIGHTS: General Assembly calls upon the Chilean authorities to end the practice of torture and to release immediately those arbitrarily arrested and those detained without charge or imprisoned solely for political reasons.

                 MIDDLE EAST: General Assembly condemns the massive and deliberate destruction of the town of Quneitra during the Israeli occupation, and recognizes that the Syrian Arab Republic is entitled to full and adequate compensation.

Dec. 17   SELF-DETERMINATION: General Assembly decides to hold an International Conference in Support of the Peoples of Zimbabwe (Southern Rhodesia) and Namibia (South West Africa) in 1977 in order to mobilize world support for the efforts of these people to achieve self-determination and independence.

Dec. 21   AGRICULTURAL DEVELOPMENT: Secretary-General announces that the agreement on IFAD was open for signatories as the contribution target of $1,000 million for IFAD has been achieved.

Dec. 22   BUDGET: General Assembly authorizes an increase of the program budget for the biennium 1976-1977 by $38.1 million for a total revised budget of $783.9 million; approves $76.3 million for UNEF from 25 October 1976 to 24 October 1977; $6.2 million for UNDOF from 1 June 1976 to 24 October 1976; and $9.9 million for UNDOF from 25 October 1976 to 31 May 1977.

                 SOUTH AFRICA: Security Council expresses grave concern at the serious situation created by South Africa's closure of certain border posts between South Africa and Lesotho, aimed at coercing Lesotho into according recognition to the

1976 (continued)

bantustan Transkei; calls upon South Africa to reopen these border posts.

1977

Jan. 10-Feb. 4	INTERNATIONAL LAW: UN Conference of Plenipotentiaries on Territorial Asylum urges a further session on the question.
Jan. 11-14	ECOSOC: Organizational meetings of 62nd regular session.
Jan. 14	SOUTHERN RHODESIA: Security Council condemns strongly all acts of provocation and harassment, including military threats and attacks, murder, arson, kidnapping and destruction of property committed against Botswana by the "illegal" regime in Southern Rhodesia; demands the immediate and total cessation of all such acts.
Jan. 18-Feb. 4	ECONOMIC DEVELOPMENT: 23rd session of the Governing Council of UNDP approves $603 million of development assistance for 15 countries.
Jan. 31-Feb. 4	ENVIRONMENT: Mediterranean coastal states recommend action under a "Blue Plan" for the pollution elimination in the region.
Feb. 8	BENIN: Security Council decides to send a special mission to Benin to investigate the attack on 10 January on the city of Cotonou by a commando unit of mercenaries that landed at the airport.
Feb. 28	MIDDLE EAST: Secretary-General reports to the Security Council, after his trip to the area, that the main elements of the Middle East problem remained intractable and extremely difficult.
March 7-April 3	COMMODITIES: UN Negotiating Conference on a Common Fund under the Integrated Program for Commodities reaches a wide consensus that a common fund should be established, but is unable to make formal decision on the issue.
March 14-25	WATER: UN Water Conference in Mar del Plata, Argentina, adopts the Plan of Action of Mar del Plata designed to avert a future water crisis (1st world intergovernmental meeting devoted to the problem of ensuring adequate water supplies for the earth's expanding population).
April 4-May 6	INTERNATIONAL LAW: UN Conference on Succession of States in Respect of Treaties adopts 25 of 39 draft convention articles.
April 12-May 13	ECOSOC: 62nd regular session, Geneva.
April 14-May 11	SPECIALIZED AGENCIES: Committee on Negotiations with Intergovernmental Agencies adopts a draft agreement with IFAD to constitute it as a specialized agency.

1977 (continued)

April 14   BENIN: Security Council strongly condemns the act of armed
                      aggression perpetrated against Benin on 16 January 1977;
                      urges all states to exercise vigilance against the danger posed
                      by mercenaries designed to overthrow governments.

April 18-May 27   COMMODITIES: UN Sugar Conference adjourns without
                      concluding a new international agreement.

April 30   CYPRUS: Secretary-General reports to the Security Council on
                      the intercommunal talks held between the Turkish and Greek
                      Cypriot communities in Vienna, 31 March to 7 April.

May 16-27   FOOD: Committee on Food Aid Policies and Programs of the
                      World Food Program approves $129 million in food aid for
                      19 projects in 16 countries.

May 16-21   SELF-DETERMINATION: International Conference in Support
                      of the Peoples of Zimbabwe and Namibia in Maputo,
                      Mozambique, adopts a Declaration and Program of Action for
                      the Liberation of these territories.

May 18   ARMS CONTROL: Convention on the Prohibition of Military,
                      and any other Hostile Use of Environment Modification
                      Techniques is opened for signature; 34 states sign.

May 23-July 15   LAW OF THE SEA: 6th session of the 3rd UN Conference on
                      the Law of the Sea agrees to a new informal composite
                      negotiating text.

May 25   SOUTH AFRICA: Security Council endorses the assessment
                      and recommendations of the mission which visited Lesotho to
                      study the needs of that country in overcoming economic
                      hardships resulting from South Africa's closure of certain
                      posts on its borders; recommends projects designed to
                      strengthen Lesotho's economy and lessen its dependence on
                      South Africa.

                      SOUTHERN RHODESIA: Security Council endorses the
                      assessment and recommendations of the mission sent to
                      Botswana in February to study the special economic hardship
                      facing that country as a result of the need to defend itself
                      from threats and attack by Southern Rhodesia.

May 26   MIDDLE EAST: Security Council extends the mandate of
                      UNDOF for six months.

May 27   SOUTHERN RHODESIA: Security Council decides to expand
                      the mandatory sanctions imposed against Southern Rhodesia
                      by barring the outflow of funds from the illegal regime of Ian
                      Smith to any office or agency established by that regime in
                      other countries except for those set up exclusively for pension
                      purposes.

                      TRIESTE: Secretary-General is informed by Italy and
                      Yugoslavia that the Treaty of Osimo entered into force and
                      thus terminated the conflict over what had been Free Territory

1977 (continued)

	of Trieste; ends their dispute that first came before the Security Council in 1947.
May 31	SOUTHERN RHODESIA: Secretary-General expresses his deep concern over the gravity and dimension of the latest violation of the territorial integrity of Mozambique by the armed forces of the illegal regime of Southern Rhodesia.
June 6-23	TRUSTEESHIP COUNCIL: 44th regular session.
June 13-July 1	ECONOMIC DEVELOPMENT: Governing Council of UNDP approves measures to raise the effectiveness of the program and to make it more responsive to the needs of developing countries.
June 15	CYPRUS: Security Council extends the mandate of UNFICYP for six months.
June 20-July 1	ARMS CONTROL: 1st Review Conference of the Parties to the 1972 Treaty Prohibiting the Emplacement of Nuclear and Other Weapons of Mass Destruction on the Seabed in Geneva adopts a Final Declaration calling for consideration of further measures to halt the arms race on the seabed.
June 20-24	FOOD: 3rd ministerial session of the World Food Council adopts for the first time an integrated program of action to combat hunger and malnutrition in the world.
June 30	SOUTHERN RHODESIA: Security Council condemns the "illicit racist minority regime" in Southern Rhodesia for its recent acts of aggression against Mozambique, and requests that states give Mozambique material aid to enable it to strengthen its defense.
July 6-Aug. 4	ECOSOC: 63rd regular session.
Aug. 4	REGIONAL COMMISSIONS: ECWA decides to admit Egypt (already a member of the ECA) and the PLO as full members.
Aug. 22-26	SOUTH AFRICA: World Conference for Action Against *Apartheid* sponsored by the UN and OAU in Lagos, Nigeria, adopts a declaration calling on all states to "cease forthwith" all arms supplies to South Africa and any assistance or co-operation enabling South Africa to obtain nuclear capability.
Aug. 29-Sept. 9	DESERT CONDITIONS: UN Conference on Desertification in Nairobi, Kenya, adopts a Plan of Action containing 26 recommendations for national, regional, and international levels aimed at halting the spread of desert conditions through the world, including feasibility studies on the establishment of "green belts".
Sept. 13-19	ECONOMIC DEVELOPMENT: Reconvened 31st regular session of the General Assembly discusses the results of the Paris Conference on International Economic Cooperation and fails to reach agreement.

1977 (continued)

Sept. 15	CYPRUS: Security Council expresses concern over recent developments in Cyprus and warns that unilateral action in Cyprus could endanger any prospects of peaceful settlement.
Sept. 20-Dec. 21	GENERAL ASSEMBLY: 32nd regular session.
Sept. 20	LEBANON: Secretary-General appeals to all concerned to end fighting and to avoid any measures likely to aggravate the situation in Southern Lebanon; UNTSO indicates that Israeli artillery has supported the Christian forces.
	MEMBERSHIP: General Assembly admits Djibouti and Viet Nam as 148th and 149th members.
Sept. 22	ARMS CONTROL: Panel of 13 experts, appointed by the Secretary-General, reports that the arms race is spiralling at an alarming rate and absorbing some $350 billion a year in armaments; warns that the continuation of the arms race is irreconcilable with an acceptable rate of development and the establishment of peace, security and a new world economic order.
Sept. 29	SOUTHERN RHODESIA: Security Council requests the Secretary-General to appoint a representative to enter into discussion with the "British Resident Commissioner designate and with all the parties, concerning the military and associated arrangements that are considered necessary to offset the transition to majority rule in Southern Rhodesia".
Sept. 30	ETHIOPIA-SOMALIA: Secretary-General expresses concern over the growing tension between Ethiopia and Somalia and the extensive hostilities in the Ogaden area of Ethiopia.
Oct. 5 & 17	ECOSOC: Resumed 63rd regular session.
Oct. 21	MIDDLE EAST: Security Council extends the mandate of UNEF for one year until 24 October 1978.
Oct. 28	MIDDLE EAST: General Assembly deplores the establishment of Israeli settlements in the occupied Arab territories and states that they are illegal and an obstacle to Middle East peace.
Oct. 31	ECOSOC: Resumed 63rd regular session.
Nov. 1	COMOROS: General Assembly calls upon the Comoros and France to work out a just and equitable settlement of the problem of the Comorian island of Mayotte which respects the political unity and territorial integrity of the Comoros.
Nov. 3	AERIAL HIJACKING: General Assembly reaffirms its condemnation of acts of aerial hijacking and other similar acts of violence.
Nov. 4	NAMIBIA: General Assembly adopts eight resolutions on Namibia and declares that South Africa is liable to pay reparations to Namibia for the damage caused by its illegal occupation of the territory.

1977 (continued)

Nov. 4   SOUTH AFRICA: Security Council imposes a mandatory arms embargo against South Africa under Chapter VII of the UN Charter, having determined that the policies and actions of the South African government in its acquisition of arms and related materials constitutes a threat to international peace and security (this is the first time the UN takes action under Chapter VI against a member state).

Nov. 7   CYPRUS: General Assembly calls for urgent resumption of negotiations between the Greek and Turkish communities of Cyprus.

Nov. 24   BENIN: Security Council calls on states to assist Benin in repairing the $28 million damage caused by the armed aggression of mercenaries on Benin on 16 January 1977.

Nov. 25   MIDDLE EAST: General Assembly calls again for the early convening of the Geneva Peace Conference on the Middle East under UN auspices, with participation on equal footing of all concerned parties including the PLO.

Nov. 28   EAST TIMOR: General Assembly requests the Secretary-General to send a representative to East Timor to assess the situation.

SOUTH AFRICA: General Assembly strongly condemns all states which collaborated politically, diplomatically, economically and militarily with South Africa in flagrant violation of UN resolutions, particularly the Belgium, Federal Republic of Germany, France, Israel, Italy, Japan, UK and USA.

Nov. 30   MIDDLE EAST: Security Council extends the mandate of UNDOF for six months until 31 May 1978.

Dec. 2   BUDGET: General Assembly appropriates $76.3 million for the operation of UNEF from 25 October 1977 to 24 October 1978 and $18.1 million for UNDOF from 1 June 1977 to 31 May 1978.

Dec. 8   NUCLEAR ENERGY: General Assembly declares that nuclear energy is of great importance for economic and social development.

Dec. 9   SOUTH AFRICA: Security Council establishes a committee of all members to oversee the arms embargo on South Africa.

Dec. 12 & 19   ARMS CONTROL: General Assembly adopts 24 resolutions on disarmament questions and sets the date for a special session cn disarmament of the General Assembly for May-June 1978.

Dec. 13-16   AGRICULTURAL DEVELOPMENT: 1st session of the Governing Council of the newly established 114-nation IFAD.

Dec. 13   ECONOMIC AID: General Assembly recommends specific assistance to 11 developing countries in desperate need.

1977 (continued)

Dec. 14 & 15   SOUTH AFRICA: General Assembly adopts 15 resolutions on the question of the *apartheid* policies of the South African government and urges mandatory economic sanctions against South Africa.

Dec. 15   AGRICULTURAL DEVELOPMENT: General Assembly approves the agreement between the UN and IFAD, establishing it as a specialized agency.

CYPRUS: Security Council extends the mandate of UNFICYP for six months until 15 June 1978.

INDUSTRIAL DEVELOPMENT: General Assembly decides to call a Conference of Plenipotentiaries on the establishment of UNIDO as a specialized agency in February 1978.

Dec. 16   HUMAN RIGHTS: General Assembly decides to convene the World Conference to Combat Racism and Racial Discrimination in August 1978.

WOMEN: General Assembly adopts seven resolutions on the questions of the UN Decade for Women.

Dec. 19   DETENTE: General Assembly adopts the Declaration on the Deepening and Consolidation of International Detente.

ECONOMIC DEVELOPMENT: General Assembly decides to convene a special session in 1980 in order to assess the progress made in the forums of the UN system in the establishment of a New International Economic Order.

MIDDLE EAST: General Assembly states that all measures undertaken by Israel to exploit the human, natural and other resources, wealth and economic activities in the occupied Arab territories are illegal; calls upon Israel to desist such measures immediately.

Dec. 20   REFORM: General Assembly establishes the new post of Director-General for Economic Development to co-ordinate activities of the UN system in the economic and social fields.

Dec. 21   BUDGET: General Assembly approves the program budget for the biennium 1978-1979 amounting to $985.9 million.

Dec. 23   WESTERN SAHARA: Secretary-General achieves the release of eight French nationals being held in the Western Sahara by POLISARIO.

1978

Jan. 1   COMMODITIES: New 1977 International Sugar Agreement comes into force, replacing the 1973 Agreement: this is the first commodity agreement negotiated since the 4th session of UNCTAD, which adopted the Integrated Program for Commodities to secure an international consensus for action on a wide range of products of importance to developing countries.

1978 (continued)

Jan. 9-13	COMMODITIES: 1st Intergovernmental Preparatory Meeting on Tea states that every effort should be made to negotiate an international agreement on tea as soon as possible.
Jan. 10-13	ECOSOC: Organizational meeting of the 64th regular session.
Jan. 16-20	COMMODITIES: Inter-governmental Working Group on Jute drafts international agreement on jute and jute products.
Jan. 17	CHAD-LIBYA: Security Council meets at the request of Chad to hear statements from Chad and Libya regarding charges that troops from Libya entered Chad to aid rebels.
Jan. 18	NAMIBIA: UN Council for Namibia recommends that a special session of the General Assembly be held on Namibia in April.
Jan. 20	ECONOMIC DEVELOPMENT: Governing Council of UNDP approves $270 million for 20 programs.
Jan. 21	CHAD-LIBYA: Security Council is informed by Chad that it withdraws complaint; the two states have resolved their dispute.
Feb. 12-March 11	INDUSTRIAL DEVELOPMENT: Conference on the Establishment of UNIDO as a specialized agency fails to reach agreement on the draft constitution and submits the issue back to the General Assembly.
Feb. 12	ENVIRONMENT: Treaties on Mediterranean pollution, signed in Barcelona in 1976, enter into force.
Feb. 13-March 23	COMMODITIES: UN Wheat Conference fails to reach a new arrangement to replace the extended 1971 International Wheat Agreement and, therefore, by protocol extends the existing arrangement for another year.
March 6-31	MARITIME TRADE: UN Conference on an International Convention on the Carriage of Goods by Sea adopts convention providing for a balanced apportionment of liability for loss, damage and delays in such trade.
March 14	SOUTHERN RHODESIA: Security Council declares "illegal and unacceptable" any internal settlement of the Southern Rhodesian question drawn up under the auspices of the "illegal regime" in that territory and calls upon all states not to accord recognition to such a settlement.
March 17	SOUTHERN RHODESIA: Security Council strongly condemns the recent armed invasion of Zambia by the "illegal racist minority regime in the colony of Southern Rhodesia".
March 19	LEBANON: Security Council calls upon Israel to withdraw its forces from Lebanon and decides to establish an international force to confirm the withdrawal, restore peace and help to ensure the return of Lebanese authority in Southern Lebanon; approves a report by the Secretary-General on arrangements for the United Nations Interim Force in Lebanon (UNIFIL) and establishes the force for an initial period of six months; Secretary-General estimates that UNIFIL would have a

1978 (continued)

	strength of 4,000 and cost $68 million to be borne by all members.
March 23	LEBANON: Secretary-General reports that the cease-fire seems to be holding since 22 March.
March 27	LEBANON: Secretary-General proposes the convening of a special session of the General Assembly on the question of financing UNIFIL; appeals to all parties concerned "strictly to observe the cease-fire, to exercise restraint, and to give the UNIFIL their fullest cooperation".
March 28-May 19	LAW OF THE SEA: 1st part of the 7th session of the 3rd UN Conference on the Law of the Sea.
April 10-21	FOOD: Governing body of the World Food Program approves $130 million in food aid to 13 countries.
April 11-May 8	ECOSOC: 64th regular session.
April 15-24	ENVIRONMENT: Regional conference of UNEP, consisting of representation of eight of the world's major oil producing countries in the Persian Gulf, adopts two anti-pollution treaties to protect and develop their marine environment and coastal area.
April 20-21	LEBANON: 8th special session of the General Assembly on financing the peace-keeping force in Lebanon approves $54 million for UNIFIL for the period from 19 March to 18 September 1978.
April 24-May 3	NAMIBIA: 9th special session of the General Assembly on the question of Namibia adopts the Declaration on Namibia and a Program of Action in support of self-determination and national independence for Namibia; stresses that Namibia was the direct responsibility of the UN; calls for South Africa's complete, immediate and unconditional withdrawal from the entire territory, including Walvis Bay which South Africa has indicated it would annex.
May 3	LEBANON: Security Council approves an increase in the strength of the UNIFIL from 4,000 to 6,000 as requested by the Secretary-General.
May 6	ANGOLA: Security Council demands the immediate and unconditional withdrawal of all South African forces from Angola and condemns South Africa's utilization of the international territory of Namibia as a springboard for the armed invasion of Angola.
May 15-June 8	TRUSTEESHIP COUNCIL: 45th regular session.
May 23-July 1	ARMS CONTROL: 10th special session of the General Assembly on the disarmament question adopts the Final Document which sets forth goals, principles, objectives, and priorities for disarmament and new inter-governmental machinery for disarmament negotiations and deliberations.

1978 (continued)

May 23	LEBANON: Secretary-General expresses satisfaction on learning of the intention of Israel to withdraw its forces from all of Southern Lebanon by 13 June.
May 25	ENVIRONMENT: Governing Council of UNEP approves the establishment within the secretariat of a unit to follow up the Plan of Action to Combat Decertification.
May 31	MIDDLE EAST: Security Council extends the mandate of UNDOF for six months.
June 14	FOOD: 4th ministerial session of the World Food Council calls upon all governments to allocate part of the resources freed by disarmament to development, especially food production.
June 16	CYPRUS: Security Council extends the mandate of UNFICYP for six months.
July 3	ECONOMIC DEVELOPMENT: Governing Council of UNDP approves $400 million for development assistance.
July 5-Aug. 4	ECOSOC: 2nd regular session in 1978, Geneva.
July 27	NAMIBIA: Security Council requests the Secretary-General to appoint a special representative for Namibia in order to ensure its early independence through free elections under UN supervision and control; declares that the territorial integrity and unity of Namibia must be assured through the re-integration of Walvis Bay within its territory.
July 31-Aug. 23	INTERNATIONAL LAW: UN Conference on the Succession of States in Respect of Treaties adopts convention which provides for the freedom of newly independent states from obligations in respect of treaties of their predecessors; decides that South Africa was not a predecessor state of Namibia.
Aug. 14-26	HUMAN RIGHTS: World Conference to Combat Racism and Racial Discrimination adopts a Declaration and a Program of Action recommending comprehensive and mandatory sanctions against racist regimes in Southern Africa, and action to stop multinational corporations and others from investing in territories subject to racism, colonialism and foreign domination.
Aug. 21-Sept. 15	LAW OF THE SEA: Resumed 7th session of the 3rd UN Conference on the Law of the Sea.
Aug. 29	NAMIBIA: Secretary-General submits a report to the Security Council, calling for the establishment of a UN group to assist Namibia in its transition to independence under a plan for the settlement of the situation in the territory, put forward by the five Western members of the Security Council and indicating that the creation of the UN Transition Assistance Group (UNTAG) would cost about $300 million for its one year operation.

1978 (continued)

Aug. 30-Sept. 21   ECONOMIC DEVELOPMENT: UN Conference on Technical
                    Cooperation Among Developing Countries in Buenos Aires
                    approves a wide-ranging series of recommendations for
                    building the national and collective self-reliance of the
                    developing countries, thus reducing North-South dependency
                    relationships.

Sept. 18   LEBANON: Security Council extends the mandate of UNIFIL
                    for four months until January 1979.

Sept. 19-Dec. 21   GENERAL ASSEMBLY: 33rd regular session.

Sept. 19   MEMBERSHIP: General Assembly admits the Solomon Islands
                    as 150th member.

Sept. 29   NAMIBIA: Security Council approves the plan for civilian and
                    military operations in Namibia, designed to pave the way for
                    elections leading to Namibia's independence.

Oct. 6   LEBANON: Security Council calls upon all those involved in
                    the hostilities in Lebanon to end violent acts and to observe
                    scrupulously an immediate and effective cease-fire and
                    cessation of hostilities so that internal peace and national
                    reconciliation can be restored based upon the preservation of
                    Lebanese unity, territorial integrity, independence and
                    national sovereignty.

Oct. 9-13   ARMS CONTROL: Newly established Disarmament
                    Commission (created by the 10th special session of the
                    General Assembly) comes into being.

Oct. 10   SOUTHERN RHODESIA: Security Council notes with regret
                    and concern the decision of the US government to allow the
                    entry of Ian Smith and some members of the illegal Southern
                    Rhodesian regime and calls upon the USA to scrupulously
                    follow the provisions of Security Council resolutions
                    concerning sanctions.

Oct. 16-Nov. 11   ECONOMIC DEVELOPMENT: 1st part of the UN Conference
                    on an International Code of Conduct on the Transfer of
                    Technology in Geneva makes considerable progress in laying
                    down internationally accepted ground rules to ensure access to
                    technology essential to development in fair and reasonable
                    terms.

Oct. 23-Nov. 3   FOOD: Governing body of the World Food Program approves
                    $172 million for 21 projects in 18 countries.

Oct. 23   MIDDLE EAST: Security Council extends the mandate of
                    UNEF for nine months until 24 July 1979.

Nov. 3   BUDGET: General Assembly appropriated $44.6 million for
                    UNIFIL for the period 19 September 1978 to 18 January
                    1979.

1978 (continued)

Nov. 9	CYPRUS: General Assembly demands immediate withdrawal of all foreign armed forces and foreign military presence in Cyprus and calls for a resumption of inter-communal talks on Cyprus.
Nov. 13	NAMIBIA: Security Council calls upon South Africa to immediately cancel the elections planned for December in Namibia and warns that failure to do so would compel the Council to meet to take appropriate action under Chapter VII of the Charter.
Nov. 27	CYPRUS: Security Council calls upon the parties concerned with the situation in Cyprus to comply with UN resolutions on Cyprus "within a specific time-frame".
Nov. 30	MIDDLE EAST: Security Council extends the mandate of UNDOF for six months.
Dec. 7	CONTINENTAL SHELF DISPUTE: Tunisia notifies the International Court of Justice of a special agreement between Tunisia and Libya with respect to determining the delimitation of the continental shelf between Tunisia and Libya.
	MIDDLE EAST: General Assembly declares that a just and lasting settlement in the Middle East must be based on a comprehensive solution under UN auspices; reaffirms that a just and lasting peace in the Middle East cannot be established without the achievement of a just solution of the problem of Palestine.
Dec. 8	BUDGET: General Assembly appropriates $12.2 million for UNDOF for the period 25 October 1978 to 31 May 1979 and $58.1 million for UNEF for the period 25 October 1978 to 24 July 1979.
	LEBANON: Security Council urges a halt to interference with the work of UNIFIL.
Dec. 13	SOUTHERN RHODESIA: General Assembly condemns and rejects the so-called internal settlement reached at Salisbury on 3 March 1978 and states there should be no independence before majority rule in Zimbabwe and that any settlement must involve the full participation of the Patriotic Front.
Dec. 14-16	ARMS CONTROL: General Assembly adopts 41 resolutions on disarmament questions; decides to hold a 2nd special session on disarmament and to convene a meeting of Indian Ocean States; calls for negotiations of treaties prohibiting nuclear and chemical weapons; approves measures to halt military collaboration between Israel and South Africa; considers issues of nuclear weapons and their effect on international security, regional disarmament, and the relationship between security and disarmament.
Dec. 14	CYPRUS: Security Council extends the mandate UNFICYP for six months until 15 June 1979.

1978 (continued)

Dec. 16   HUMAN RIGHTS: General Assembly adopts six resolutions
               aiming to end racism and racial discrimination.

Dec. 18   MEMBERSHIP: General Assembly admits the Commonwealth
               of Dominica as 151st member.

Dec. 19   AEGEAN SEA CASE: International Court of Justice by a vote
               of 12 to 2 finds it is without jurisdiction to entertain the
               application filed by Greece on 10 August 1976 in the case
               concerning the Aegean Sea Continental Shelf (Greece versus
               Turkey).

               ECONOMIC DEVELOPMENT: General Assembly decides to
               suspend the activities of the UN Special Fund for the interim
               because it could not carry out its main function of providing
               assistance to the most seriously affected countries due to the
               lack of voluntary contributions.

Dec. 20   HUMAN RIGHTS: General Assembly endorses the Charter of
               Rights of Migrant Workers in Southern Africa as adopted by
               the Lusaka Conference on Migratory Labor on 7 April 1978.

Dec. 21   NAMIBIA: General Assembly calls for trade, oil and arms
               embargoes against South Africa.

Dec. 22   NAMIBIA: South Africa informs the Secretary-General that it
               has decided to cooperate in carrying out the Namibia
               Independence Plan.

1979

Jan. 15-29   GENERAL ASSEMBLY: Resumed 33rd regular session.

Jan. 15   KAMPUCHEA: USSR vetoes a draft resolution of the Security
               Council, calling on all foreign forces involved in the situation
               in Democratic Kampuchea to observe scrupulously an
               immediate cease-fire, to put an end to hostilities, and to
               withdraw from the country.

Jan. 19   LEBANON: Security Council extends the mandate of UNIFIL
               for five months.

Jan. 23-Feb. 8 LAW OF THE SEA: 3rd UN Conference on the Law of the
               Sea.

Jan. 23   SOUTH AFRICA: General Assembly calls for an end to
               economic and military collaboration with South Africa.

Jan. 29   BUDGET: General Assembly approves an increase in the
               program budget for the biennium 1978-1979 by $93.7 million
               to $1,090.1 million.

Feb. 5-10   ENVIRONMENT: 17 of 18 Mediterranean coastal states meet
               under the auspices of the UNEP and agree to share the
               financial burden of the Mediterranean Action Plan to save
               their sea from pollution and to ensure environmental sound
               development of the coastline.

Feb. 6-9   ECOSOC: Organizational session, New York.

1979 (continued)

Feb. 12-15   TRUSTEESHIP COUNCIL: 14th special session decides to send a visiting mission to observe the referendum in the Marshall Islands.

Feb. 19   CONTINENTAL SHELF CASE: International Court of Justices fixes 30 May 1980 as the time limit for the filling of memorials in the case concerning the delimitation of the continental shelf between Tunisia and Libya, following Libya's special agreement with Tunisia on this matter.

Feb. 26   NAMIBIA: Secretary-General proposes to the Security Council that 15 March be the date for a cease-fire in Namibia and the beginning of the UN transition operation leading to independence.

Feb. 28   SOUTH-EAST ASIA: Security Council considers USSR demands for Chinese withdrawal from Viet Nam and Chinese demands for Vietnamese withdrawal from Kampuchea: meeting adjourns without draft resolution being tabled.

March 8   SOUTHERN RHODESIA: Security Council condemns recent Rhodesian military raids on Angola, Mozambique and Zambia, and declares any elections held under the illegal Ian Smith regime to be "null and void".

March 16   SOUTH-EAST ASIA: USSR vetoes draft resolution of the Security Council which calls on "all parties to conflicts" in South-East Asia to cease hostilities "and withdraw their forces to their own countries".

March 19-29   FOOD: 2nd session of the Committee of the Whole of the General Assembly emphasizes the need for increased food and agricultural production in developing countries and the need for increased external aid in that area.

March 19-April 27   LAW OF THE SEA: 8th session of the 3rd UN Conference on the Law of the Sea.

March 22   COMMODITIES: Negotiating conference of UNCTAD reaches agreement on the fundamental elements of a Common Fund to help stabilize commodity prices after three years of negotiations; Secretary-General hails agreement as an important step in the direction of a New International Economic Order.

     MIDDLE EAST: Security Council decides to establish a commission of three of its members "to examine the situation relating to settlements in the Arab territories occupied since 1967, including Jerusalem".

March 26   MIDDLE EAST: Secretary-General states that the signing of the Egyptian-Israeli peace treaty is a very important and historical development, but that a stable peace in the Middle East would require a just solution to the Palestinian question.

1979 (continued)

March 28	SOUTH AFRICA: Security Council condemns South Africa for invasions of Angola and calls for a report by the Secretary-General on casualties and damage.
April 10-May 11	ECOSOC: 1st regular session, New York.
April 19	LEBANON: Secretary-General reports to the Security Council that a "massive and unprovoked assault" has been carried out on the Naqama headquarters of UNIFIL by the *de facto* forces of Major Haddad in Southern Lebanon.
April 26	LEBANON: Security Council expresses "the deepest concern" about "the significant increase of tension" in Southern Lebanon.
April 30	SOUTHERN RHODESIA: Security Council reaffirms that the "so-called elections" held in Southern Rhodesia were "null and void" and again calls on all states not to recognize any representative or body emerging from them.
May 7-June 1	ECONOMIC DEVELOPMENT: 5th session of UNCTAD, Manila.
May 15-June 8	ARMS CONTROL: 1st session of the new Disarmament Commission (composed of the entire UN membership and established by the special session on Disarmament in 1978).
May 15	LEBANON: Security Council President announces that efforts under the Council's auspices to improve the situation in Southern Lebanon "seem to have produced some results".
May 20-June 1	MIDDLE EAST: Security Council Commission (established to examine the situation relating to settlements by Israel in the Arab territories occupied since 1967, including Jerusalem) visits the Middle East.
May 21-June 15	TRUSTEESHIP COUNCIL: 46th regular session.
May 22	CYPRUS: Secretary-General announces, after meeting with Greek and Turkish Cypriot leaders, that inter-communal talks are to resume on 15 June.
May 23-31	NAMIBIA: Resumed 33rd regular session of the General Assembly considers question of Namibia and demands a trade embargo against South Africa unless it went along with the UN plan for elections in Namibia.
May 24	SOUTH AFRICA: General Assembly rejects South African credentials and thus bares South Africa from participation in the General Assembly: a reaffirmation of the decision in 1974 when the General Assembly decided to suspend South Africa from participation in the work because of its *apartheid* policies.
May 30	MIDDLE EAST: Security Council extends the mandate for UNDOF for six months.

1979 (continued)

June 14	LEBANON: Security Council calls upon Israel "to cease forthwith its acts against the territorial integrity, unity and sovereignty and political independence of Lebanon" and to halt its incursions into Lebanon; extends the mandate of UNIFIL for six months.
June 15	CYPRUS: Security Council extends the mandate of UNFICYP for six months.
June 25	WESTERN SAHARA: Security Council decides to adjourn further consideration of Morocco's complaint of Algerian aggression.
July 4-20	ECOSOC: 2nd regular session, Geneva.
July 12-20	AGRICULTURAL DEVELOPMENT: World Conference on Agrarian Reform and Rural Development in Rome adopts Declaration of Principles and a Program of Action to abolish poverty and hunger.
July 13	INDIAN OCEAN: Meeting of the Littoral and Hinterland States of the Indian Ocean adopts a Final Document calling for a future conference, denuclearization of the area and the strengthening of cooperation in the area.
July 16	ECONOMIC DEVELOPMENT: Governing Council of UNDP approves projects and funding for a wider range of development activities, including $136 million for large scale programs and projects in population activities in 23 countries.
July 19-Aug. 24	LAW OF THE SEA: 2nd part of the 8th session of the 3rd UN Conference on the Law of the Sea.
July 20	MIDDLE EAST: Security Council calls upon the government and people of Israel to cease the establishment of settlements in Arab territories occupied since 1967.
July 25	MIDDLE EAST: Security Council agrees informally not to extend the mandate of UNEF.
Aug. 20-Sept. 1	ECONOMIC DEVELOPMENT: UN Conference on Science and Technology for Development adopts Program of Action designed to put science and technology to work for economic development, particularly in developing countries.
Aug. 30	LEBANON: President of the Security Council appeals to all concerned to make permanent the cease-fire in southern Lebanon.
Sept. 4-7	FOOD: 5th ministerial session of the World Food Council calls upon the UN to give food and agriculture the highest possible priority in the next Development Decade.
Sept. 18-Jan. 7	GENERAL ASSEMBLY: 34th regular session.
Sept. 18	MEMBERSHIP: General Assembly admits Saint Lucia as 152nd member.

1979 (continued)

Sept. 21   SOUTH AFRICA: Security Council condemns the proclamation
            of the so-called "independence" of Venda as action of South
            Africa designed to divide and dispossess the African people
            and establish client states under its domination in order to
            perpetuate *apartheid*.

Sept. 28   NICARAGUA: Committee of the Whole of the UN Economic
            Commission urges governments and international financial
            organizations to lend financial and technical assistance to
            Nicaragua in its rehabilitation, reconstruction and
            development.

Oct. 25   ECOSOC: Resumed 2nd regular session, New York.

Nov. 2   SOUTH AFRICA: Security Council condemns South Africa's
            aggression against Angola and calls on it to cease immediately
            all such acts and to withdraw its armed forces from Angola.

Nov. 5   KAMPUCHEA: Pledging Conference for Emergency
            Humanitarian Relief to the People of Kampuchea results in
            pledges amounting to $210 million from 50 countries.

Nov. 6   ECONOMIC DEVELOPMENT: UN Conference for
            Development Activities results in pledges amounting to
            $660.0 million to 13 UN development activities, including
            $379.3 million from 89 Governments to UNDP.

Nov. 8   ECOSOC: Resumed 2nd regular session, New York.

Nov. 9   IRAN: President of the Security Council, acting on the
            Council's behalf, urgently asks for the release of American
            diplomatic personnel detained in Iran since 4 November.

Nov. 14   KAMPUCHEA: General Assembly calls for the immediate
            withdrawal of all foreign forces from Kampuchea.

Nov. 16   REFUGEES: $114.3 million are pledged to the program of the
            UN High Commissioner for Refugees.

Nov. 20   CYPRUS: General Assembly reiterates its full support for the
            sovereignty and unity of Cyprus and calls again for the
            cessation of all foreign interferences in Cyprus.

Nov. 21   EAST TIMOR: General Assembly reaffirms the inalienable
            right of the people of East Timor to self determination and
            independence.

            WESTERN SAHARA: General Assembly reaffirms the
            inalienable right of the people of Western Sahara to self
            determination and independence and asks Morocco to end its
            occupation of the area.

Nov. 23   SOUTHERN RHODESIA: Security Council calls on the UK to
            act promptly in taking effective measures to ensure the illegal
            regime ceased acts of aggression against Zambia.

Nov. 29   IRAN CASE: USA institutes proceedings before the
            International Court of Justice against Iran regarding the
            situation in the US Embassy in Teheran and requests prompt
            provisional measures to protect US nationals.

1979 (continued)

Nov. 29 REFUGEES: General Assembly calls upon states to increase
their size of intake of Indo-China refugees.

Nov. 30 MIDDLE EAST: Security Council extends mandate of UNDOF
for six months.

Dec. 4 IRAN: Security Council urgently calls on Iran to release
immediately the personnel of the US Embassy being held in
Teheran, to provide them with protection, and to allow them
to leave the country.

Dec. 5 OUTER SPACE: General Assembly approves the Agreement on
the Activities of States on the Moon and Other Celestial
Bodies: treaty is opened for signature and ratification.

Dec. 6 COMOROS: General Assembly reaffirms the sovereignty of the
Comoros over the island of Mayotte and appeals to France to
negotiate with the Comorian government.

MIDDLE EAST: General Assembly declares that a just and
lasting settlement in the Middle East must be based on a
comprehensive solution under UN auspices, which takes into
account all aspects of the Arab-Israeli conflict, including the
inalienable rights of the Palestinian people.

Dec. 11 ARMS CONTROL: General Assembly adopts a Comprehensive
Declaration on International Co-operation for Disarmament
and 38 resolutions on disarmament matters.

Dec. 12 MADAGASCAR: General Assembly invites France to initiate
negotiations with Madagascar for re-integration of the islands
of Glorieuses, Juan de Nova, Europa, and Bassas da India
which were arbitrarily separated from Madagascar.

NAMIBIA: General Assembly adopts seven resolutions on the
question of Namibia and requests the Security Council to
impose mandatory sanctions on South Africa in order to
ensure its compliance with UN resolutions.

Dec. 14 CYPRUS: Security Council extends the mandate of UNFICYP
for six months.

Dec. 15 IRAN CASE: International Court of Justice orders Iran to
release the detained US Embassy personnel and to restore the
seized US premises.

Dec. 17 BUDGET: General Assembly approves $41.6 million for UN
peace-keeping forces in the Middle East (including $10.8
million a month for continued operation of UNIFIL; $18.2
million for repatriation of contingents and liquidation of
UNEF; $12.6 million for operation of UNDOF through 31
May 1980).

HUMAN RIGHTS: General Assembly adopts a Code of Ethics
for Law Enforcement Officials and recommends that it be
used as a body of principles for observance by law
enforcement officials; indicates concern over the violation of

1979 (continued)

	human rights; asks Chile to clarify the fate of persons reported to have disappeared for political reasons.
Dec. 17	INTERNATIONAL LAW: General Assembly adopts the International Convention Against the Taking of Hostages.
	SOUTH AFRICA: General Assembly adopts 18 resolutions opposing various aspects of the *apartheid* policies of South Africa.
Dec. 18	WOMEN: General Assembly adopts an International Convention on the Elimination of All Forms of Discrimination Against Women.
Dec. 19	LEAST DEVELOPED COUNTRIES: General Assembly decides to convene a UN Conference on the least developed countries in 1981.
	LEBANON: Security Council extends mandate of UNIFIL for six months.
Dec. 20	BUDGET: General Assembly reduces the program budget for the biennium 1978-1979 by $5.9 million to $1,090.1 and approves $1,247.8 million for the biennium 1980-1981.
Dec. 21	SOUTHERN RHODESIA: Security Council calls on member states to terminate sanctions instituted against Southern Rhodesia in 1966 and 1968, as a result of assumption of full legislative and executive authority by the British government over Southern Rhodesia and the termination of the state of rebellion in the territory.

1980

Jan. 1-4	IRAN: Secretary-General visits Iran in connection with the detention of US diplomatic personnel in the US Embassy.
Jan. 5-9	AFGHANISTAN: Security Council considers the situation in Afghanistan, resulting from Soviet military intervention in that country in late December 1979; does not adopt a proposed resolution calling for the immediate and unconditional withdrawal of all foreign troops from Afghanistan, but asks for an emergency special session of the General Assembly to examine the question.
Jan. 7	AFGHANISTAN: USSR vetoes a draft resolution of the Security Council, which calls for the withdrawal of all foreign troops from Afghanistan.
	SECURITY COUNCIL: General Assembly elects Mexico as non-permanent member of the Security Council after Cuba and Colombia withdrew their candidacies; neither were able to get the necessary two thirds majority after 155 ballots.

1980 (continued)

Jan. 10-14	AFGHANISTAN: 6th emergency special General Assembly session on the situation in Afghanistan adopts resolution deploring the armed intervention and calling for withdrawal of foreign troops.
Jan. 13	IRAN: USSR vetoes a draft resolution of Security Council which calls for economic sanctions against Iran until all US hostages in Iran are released.
Jan. 15	AFGHANISTAN: General Assembly calls for the immediate withdrawal of foreign troops from Afghanistan.
Feb. 1	ENVIRONMENT: A number of major multilateral development financing institutions and UNEP sign a Declaration of Environmental Policies and Procedures Relating to Economic Development.
Feb. 2	SOUTHERN RHODESIA: Security Council asks the UK to implement the London Agreement fully and impartially.
Feb. 5-6	ECOSOC: Organizational session, New York.
Feb. 9	INDUSTRIAL DEVELOPMENT: 3rd General Conference of UNIDO adopts Declaration and Plan of Action, calling for the creation of a Industrialization Fund.
Feb. 20	IRAN: Secretary-General establishes a UN Commission of Enquiry to undertake a fact-finding mission in Iran to hear that country's grievances, and allow for an early solution to the crisis between Iran and the USA.
Feb. 21	FOOD: 9th Conference of the World Food Program pledges the equivalent of $333 million from 50 countries for 1981-1982.
Feb. 29	COMMODITIES: A new effort by the Committee on Tungsten to reach agreement on international measures to stabilize the tungsten market ends without success.
March 1-April 4	LAW OF THE SEA: 1st part of the 9th session of the 3rd UN Conference on the Law of the Sea.
March 1	MIDDLE EAST: Security Council calls upon Israel to dismantle settlements it has established in the Arab territories occupied since 1967, including Jerusalem, and to cease the establishment and planning of new settlements.
March 10	IRAN: UN Commission of Inquiry, established by the Secretary-General, decides to suspend its activities in Teheran.
March 24	ECONOMIC DEVELOPMENT: UN Conference on International Multi-modal Transport adopts Convention on the Legal Obligations of Multi-modal Transport Operators.
March 26	KAMPUCHEA: Nine countries pledge $24 million for humanitarian assistance for the Kampuchean people.
March 27	ECONOMIC DEVELOPMENT: Pledging Conference for the Interim Fund for Science and Technology for Development results in pledges of $35.8 million from 35 countries for 1980-1981.

1980 (continued)

March 31	NAMIBIA: Secretary-General informs the Security Council that South Africa reaffirms its acceptance of the settlement of the question of Namibia as proposed by the Security Council in 1978.
April 2	CYPRUS: Secretary-General reports that efforts to reopen inter-communal talks between Greek and Turkish Cypriots are not fruitful.
April 3	CHAD: Secretary-General expresses concern regarding the situation between the warring groups in Chad.
April 8-May 2	ECOSOC: 1st regular session, Geneva.
April 11	INTERNATIONAL LAW: UN Conference on Contracts for International Sale of Goods adopts the Convention on Contracts for the International Sale of Goods.
	SOUTH AFRICA: Security Council condemns the "racist regime" of South Africa for its continued, intensified and unprovoked acts against Zambia, and demands that South Africa withdraws forthwith all its military forces from Zambia, ceases all violations of Zambia's airspace, and respects its sovereignty and territorial integrity.
April 14-May 14	COMMODITIES: UN Tin Conference adjourns after having failed to adopt a 6th International Tin Agreement.
April 18	LEBANON: Security Council sharply condemns the cold-blooded murder of two Irish soldiers serving with UNIFIL in Lebanon.
April 21-May 6	ECONOMIC DEVELOPMENT: UN Conference on the International Code of Conduct on the Transfer of Technology fails to reach agreement on the code.
April 24	LEBANON: Security Council condemns acts of hostility against UNIFIL in Lebanon, Israel's military intervention in Lebanon, and acts in violation of the armistice between Israel and Lebanon.
April 30	MIDDLE EAST: USA vetoes a draft resolution of the Security Council on the rights of the Palestinian people.
May 8	MIDDLE EAST: Security Council calls upon Israel to rescind the measures taken against the Palestine mayors of Hebron and Halhoul and the Sharia judge of Hebron.
May 16	ENVIRONMENT: 15 coastal states and the EEC in a conference organized by UNEP adopts a treaty aimed at reducing and controlling the major sources of pollution on the Mediterranean Sea.
May 19-June 12	TRUSTEESHIP COUNCIL: 47th regular session.
May 20	MIDDLE EAST: Security Council again calls upon Israel to rescind the "illegal measures" taken by its military occupation authorities in expelling the mayors of Hebron and Halhoul and the Sharia judge of Hebron, and to facilitate the

1980 (continued)

	immediate return of the expelled Palestine leaders so that they can resume the functions for which they have been elected.
May 24	IRAN: International Court of Justice decides that Iran should immediately release all US diplomatic personnel and other US nationals, and make reparations to the USA for the injury caused by the events of November 1979.
May 26-27	KAMPUCHEA: 20 states and the EEC pledge $116.2 million for relieving the suffering of the Kampuchean refugees.
May 30	MIDDLE EAST: Security Council extends the mandate of UNDOF for six months.
June 5	MIDDLE EAST: Security Council condemns the attempts on the lives of the Palestine mayors of Nablus, Ramalah, and Al-Bireh; calls for the immediate apprehension of the perpetrators; asks Israel to provide compensation for these persons in the Israeli occupied Arab territories.
June 10-14	GENERAL ASSEMBLY: 6th emergency special session.
June 13	CYPRUS: Security Council extends the mandate of UNFICYP for six months.
	SOUTH AFRICA: Security Council strongly condemns the "racial regime" of South Africa for its massive repression of all opponents of *apartheid* and calls for the unconditional amnesty for all political prisoners and a tightening of the arms embargo against South Africa.
June 17	LEBANON: Security Council extends the mandate of UNIFIL for six months.
June 20	ECONOMIC DEVELOPMENT: UNDP approves large scale populations projects totalling approximately $320 million.
June 27	SOUTH AFRICA: Security Council strongly condemns South Africa for its persistent and sustained armed invasion of Angola and demands the withdrawal of all South African forces from Angola.
June 30	MIDDLE EAST: Security Council reaffirms the "overriding necessity" to end the prolonged occupation of Arab territories occupied by Israel since 1967, including Jerusalem.
July 3-25	ECOSOC: 2nd regular session, Geneva.
July 14-30	STATUS OF WOMEN: World Conference of the UN Decade for Women in Copenhagen, Denmark adopts a detailed Program of Action designed to promote the status of women through the second half of the UN Decade for Women (1976-1985).
July 22-29	MIDDLE EAST: 7th emergency special session of the General Assembly on the Palestine question calls upon Israel to withdraw completely and unconditionally from all the Palestinian and other Arab territories occupied since June 1967, including Jerusalem; urges that the withdrawal start before 15 November 1980.

1980 (continued)

July 28-Aug. 29	LAW OF THE SEA: Resumed 9th session of the 3rd UN Conference on the Law of the Sea.
Aug. 20	JERUSALEM: Security Council censures in the strongest terms Israel's enactment of a "basic law" on Jerusalem and its refusal to comply with relevant Council resolutions; calls upon states with diplomatic missions in Jerusalem to withdraw them.
Aug. 25-Sept. 15	ECONOMIC DEVELOPMENT: 11th special session of the General Assembly on global economic matters sends to the 35th regular session of the Assembly all documents before it pertaining to launching within the UN of a new round of global negotiations on international economic cooperation for development.
Aug. 25	MEMBERSHIP: General Assembly admits Zimbabwe (formerly Southern Rhodesia) as 153rd member.
Sept. 4	MALTA-LIBYA: Security Council considers the sea boundary dispute between Malta and Libya.
Sept. 5	CRIME: 6th UN Congress on Crime Prevention and the Treatment of Offenders adopts declaration setting forth principles on the development of criminal policies and criminal justice.
Sept. 16-Dec. 17	GENERAL ASSEMBLY: 35th regular session.
Sept. 16	MEMBERSHIP: General Assembly admits Saint Vincent and the Grenadines as 154th member.
Sept. 28	IRAN-IRAQ: Security Council calls upon Iran and Iraq to refrain immediately from any further use of force and to settle their dispute by peaceful means.
Oct. 5	IRAN-IRAQ: Security Council expresses its concern at the continuing hostilities between Iran and Iraq and urges both parties to be guided by their Charter obligations to settle their disputes peacefully.
Oct. 23	COMMODITIES: International Natural Rubber Agreement enters into force (1st international agreement to be concluded and brought into force since the Integrated Program for Commodities was launched at the 4th session of UNCTAD in 1976).
Oct. 27	KAMPUCHEA: General Assembly decides to convene early in 1981 an international conference on Kampuchea, involving all the parties to the conflict, with the aim to find a comprehensive political settlement.
Nov. 6-7	ECONOMIC DEVELOPMENT: 97 governments pledge $482.2 million to UNDP.
Nov. 7	ECOSOC: Resumed 2nd regular session.
Nov. 10	WATER: General Assembly proclaims 1981-1990 as the International Drinking Water Supply and Sanitation Decade, during which period governments would assume a

1980 (continued)

| | commitment to bring about substantial improvements in standards and levels of services in drinking water supply and sanitation. |

Nov. 11   EAST TIMOR: General Assembly reaffirms the inalienable right of the people of East Timor to self-determination and independence.

SOUTH AFRICA: General Assembly calls on all states, particularly Belgium, Federal Republic of Germany, France, Israel, Italy, Japan, UK and USA, to take urgent effective measures to terminate all collaboration with South Africa in political, diplomatic, economic, trade, military and nuclear fields.

WESTERN SAHARA: General Assembly urges Morocco to join in the peace process and to terminate its occupation of Western Sahara.

Nov. 14   REFUGEES: 45 countries pledge $105 million to the 1981 program of the UNHCR.

Nov. 19   COMMODITIES: UN Cocoa Conference adopts a new International Cocoa Agreement to succeed the 1975 Agreement which expired on 31 March 1980.

Nov. 20   AFGHANISTAN: General Assembly calls for the prompt withdrawal of foreign troops from Afghanistan.

Nov. 24   NAMIBIA: Secretary-General informs the Security Council that South Africa and SWAPO have agreed to convening a UN sponsored meeting in January 1981, with a view to resolving difficulties.

Nov. 26   MIDDLE EAST: Security Council extends the mandate of UNDOF for six months.

Dec. 1   BUDGET: General Assembly appropriates $15 million for UNDOF for the period 1 December 1980 to 31 May 1981.

Dec. 3   ARMS CONTROL: General Assembly declares the 1980's as the 2nd Disarmament Decade; adopts 40 resolutions on disarmament and related matters.

Dec. 5   ECONOMIC DEVELOPMENT: General Assembly proclaims the 3rd UN Development Decade, starting on 1 January 1981, and adopts the International Development Strategy.

Dec. 10   BUDGET: General Assembly authorizes $12.2 million a month for the UNIFIL for the period from 19 December 1980 to 18 December 1981.

Dec. 11   CYPRUS: Security Council extends the mandate of UNFICYP for six months.

DECOLONIZATION: General Assembly adopts three resolutions dealing with the Plan of Action for Full Implementation of the Declaration on Decolonization (1960) and the dissemination of information on decolonization.

1980 (continued)

Dec. 11   MIDDLE EAST: General Assembly adopts six resolutions,
           condemning various aspects of Israeli policies and practices in
           the Israeli occupied Arab territories.
           WOMEN: General Assembly endorses the Program of Action
           designed to promote the status of women that was adopted by
           the World Conference of the UN Decade for Women.

Dec. 15   INTERNATIONAL LAW: General Assembly calls on states to
           accord the delegations of national liberation movements
           recognized by OAU and/or the League of Arab States the
           privileges and immunities necessary for the performance of
           their function in accord with the Vienna Convention on
           Representative of States in their Relations with International
           Organizations of a Universal Character; calls upon member
           states to prohibit acts against the security and safety of
           diplomatic and consular missions in territories under their
           jurisdiction.
           MIDDLE EAST: General Assembly expresses grave concern
           that no just solution of the Palestine problem had been
           achieved, the attainment of which was the indispensable
           condition for a just solution of the Palestine question.

Dec. 16   SOUTH AFRICA: General Assembly adopts 18 resolutions on
           the policies of *apartheid* of South Africa, including a request
           that the Security Council adopts urgently comprehensive and
           mandatory sanctions against South Africa, including an oil
           embargo.

Dec. 17   BUDGET: General Assembly increases the program budget for
           the biennium 1980-1981 by $91.4 million to $1,339.2 million.
           LEBANON: Security Council extends the mandate of UNIFIL
           for six months.

1981

Jan. 7-14   NAMIBIA: UN sponsored conference between South Africa and
             SWAPO ends without agreement being reached on a date for
             a cease-fire in that territory and for the start of the
             implementation of the settlement proposal that would lead to
             independence.

Jan. 15-16   GENERAL ASSEMBLY: Resumed 35th regular session.
Feb. 3-6   ECOSOC: Organizational session, New York.
Feb. 5   SOUTH AFRICA: Security Council expresses grave concern
             over death sentences by the South African Supreme Court on
             three young African men and urges South Africa to pay heed
             to such concern.

1981 (continued)

March 6	NAMIBIA: General Assembly condemns South Africa for its continued illegal occupation of Namibia and calls upon the Security Council to impose comprehensive and mandatory sanctions against South Africa.
March 9-April 6	LAW OF THE SEA: 10th session of the 3rd UN Conference on the Law of the Sea.
March 20	LEBANON: Security Council strongly condemns the "outrageous actions by the so-called *de facto* forces" which have caused the death and injury of personnel of UNIFIL.
April 10	ARMS CONTROL: Convention of Prohibition and Restriction of Certain Conventional Weapons which May be Deemed to be Excessively Injurious or to have Indiscriminate Effects is opened for signature.
	REFUGEES: International Conference for Assistance of Refugees concludes after receiving a total of $560 million in pledges from states for a concerted world-wide effort to alleviate the plight of Africa's 5 million refugees.
April 14-May 8	ECOSOC: 1st regular session, New York.
April 30	NAMIBIA: France, UK and USA veto four draft resolutions of the Security Council on: first draft, determining that the continued illegal occupation of Namibia and repeated armed attacks by South Africa are acts of aggression and imposing comprehensive and mandatory sanctions against South Africa; second draft, calling for severance of all diplomatic, consular and trade relations with South Africa; third draft, imposing an oil embargo; fourth draft, providing for a mandatory arms embargo, more wide ranging than the one in effect.
May 1	LEBANON: Secretary-General appeals to all concerned to preserve and strengthen and cease fire in the northern part of Lebanon, and to support the endeavors of that government to find a peaceful solution to the crisis.
May 2-6 & 11	GENERAL ASSEMBLY: Resumed 35th regular session.
May 13	LEBANON: Secretary-General again appeals to all parties to cooperate fully in efforts to defuse tension in the area and to respect the territorial integrity, unity and independence of Lebanon.
May 18-June 11	TRUSTEESHIP COUNCIL: 48th regular session.
May 22	MIDDLE EAST: Security Council extends the mandate of UNDOF for six months.
May 27	SOUTH AFRICA: Joint UN/OAU International Conference on Sanctions against South Africa affirms that comprehensive and mandatory sanctions, universally applied, are the most appropriate and effective means to ensure South Africa's compliance with the decision of the UN.
June 4	CYPRUS: Security Council extends the mandate of UNFICYP for six months.

1981 (continued)

June 9-29	ECONOMIC DEVELOPMENT: Governing Council of UNDP approves large scale population programs of $135 million for 15 developing countries, and an allocation of $710 million for country programs in 14 states.
June 11	TRUSTEESHIP: Trusteeship Council makes recommendations on the future political status of Micronesia.
June 19	LEBANON: Security Council extends the mandate of UNIFIL for six months.
	MIDDLE EAST: Security Council condemns the air attacks carried out by Israel against Iraqi nuclear installations, which took place on 7 June near Baghdad, and calls upon Israel to refrain from such acts or threats in the future.
June 26	COMMODITIES: UN Tin Conference adopts the text of a new International Tin Agreement.
July 1-24	ECOSOC: 2nd regular session, Geneva.
July 13-17	KAMPUCHEA: International Conference on Kampuchea adopts the Declaration on Kampuchea calling for a comprehensive political settlement in that country and establishes an *ad hoc* committee to assist in such a settlement.
July 21	LEBANON: Security Council calls for "immediate cessation of all armed attacks" that have been taking place in Lebanon.
July 31	MALTA-LIBYA: Security Council resumes consideration of Malta's complaint of "illegal, unwarranted and provocative action" by Libya in connection with Malta's exploratory oil-drilling operations in the Mediterranean Sea.
Aug. 3-28	LAW OF THE SEA: Resumed 10th session of the 3rd UN Conference on the Law of the Sea.
Aug. 10-21	ENERGY: UN Conference on New and Renewable Sources of Energy adopts a wide-ranging Program of Action to deal with the global energy crisis, especially its impact on developing countries.
Aug. 27	SOUTH AFRICA: Security Council members express concern over death sentences imposed by the Supreme Court of South Africa on three members of the African National Congress (ANC) of South Africa.
Aug. 31	SOUTH AFRICA: USA vetoes a draft resolution of the Security Council which strongly condemns South Africa's unprovoked invasion of Angola, and demands the immediate withdrawal of South African troops.
Sept. 1-14	ECONOMIC DEVELOPMENT: UN Conference on the Least Developed Countries adopts wide ranging programs designed to transfer the economies of the world's poorest and weakest countries, and to enable them to provide, at least, internationally accepted minimum standards of nutrition, health, housing and education, as well as job opportunities, for all their citizens, particularly the rural and urban poor.

1981 (continued)

Sept. 3-14	SOUTHERN AFRICA: 8th emergency special session of the General Assembly on Namibia and threats to peace by South Africa calls upon member states and international organizations to give sustained support and material, financial, military and other assistance to SWAPO to enable it to intensify its struggle for the liberation of Namibia; strongly urges the Security Council, in the light of the serious threat to international peace and security posed by South Africa, to respond positively to the overwhelming demand of the international community by immediately imposing comprehensive and mandatory sanctions against South Africa.
Sept. 15-Dec. 18	GENERAL ASSEMBLY: 36th regular session.
Sept. 15	MEMBERSHIP: General Assembly admits Vanuatu as 155th member.
Sept. 25	MEMBERSHIP: General Assembly admits Belize as 156th member.
Oct. 14	REFUGEES: UNHCR receives the 1981 Nobel Peace Prize for its work with million of refugees in the world.
Oct. 21	ECOSOC: Resumed 2nd regular session, Geneva.
	KAMPUCHEA: General Assembly decides to reconvene the International Conference on Kampuchea in order to contribute to a comprehensive political settlement and urges the withdrawal of all foreign forces from Kampuchea.
Oct. 26	SECRETARY-GENERAL: USA vetoes a draft resolution of the Security Council which recommends Salim Ahmed Salim of Tanzania as Secretary-General.
Oct. 27	FOOD: Governing body of the World Food Program approves $211 million for 22 development projects in 19 countries.
	SECRETARY-GENERAL: China vetoes a draft resolution of the Security Council which recommends Kurt Waldheim of Austria for a 3rd term as Secretary-General.
Nov. 2	ECOSOC: Resumed 2nd regular session.
Nov. 4	ECONOMIC DEVELOPMENT: UN Pledging Conference for Development Activities results in pledges of $395 million from 98 governments.
Nov. 9	HUMAN RIGHTS: General Assembly condemns the practice of summary and arbitrary executions and strongly deplores this practice in different parts of the world.
Nov. 11	MEMBERSHIP: General Assembly admits Antigua and Barbuda as 157th member.
	NUCLEAR ENERGY: General Assembly urges all states to continue to support the endeavors of IAEA in furthering the peaceful use of nuclear power, improving the effectiveness of safeguards and promoting nuclear safety.

1981 (continued)

Nov. 13   MIDDLE EAST: General Assembly expresses deep alarm over the unprecedented Israeli act of aggression on the Iraqi nuclear installation on 7 June 1981.

Nov. 16   MIDDLE EAST: Pledging Conference for UNRWA results in pledges of $107 million.

Nov. 18   AFGHANISTAN: General Assembly calls for the immediate withdrawal of foreign troops from Afghanistan and reaffirms the right of the Afghan people to determine their own form of government, free from outside intervention, subversion, coercion or constraint of any kind.

Nov. 20   REFUGEES: Pledging Conference for UNHCR results in pledges of $122 million from 48 countries.

Nov. 23   MIDDLE EAST: Security Council extends the mandate of UNDOF for six months.

Nov. 24   EAST TIMOR: General Assembly reaffirms the inalienable right of the people of East Timor to self-determination and independence.

                   WESTERN SAHARA: General Assembly appeals to Morocco and POLISARIO to observe a cease-fire and to negotiate the Western Sahara question.

Nov. 25   ECOSOC: Resumed 2nd regular session.

                   GULF OF MAINE CASE: Canada and the USA notify the International Court of Justice of a special agreement by which they would submit their continental shelf boundary dispute to a five member chamber of the court.

                   HUMAN RIGHTS: General Assembly adopts the Declaration on the Elimination of All Forms of Intolerance and Discrimination Based on Religion or Belief.

Nov. 27   SEYCHELLES: Secretary-General deplores the attack on the Seychelles carried out by a group of mercenaries on 25 November 1981.

Nov. 30   BUDGET: General Assembly approves $16 million for UNDOF for six months.

Dec. 4   MIDDLE EAST: General Assembly denounces Israel for refusing to allow the Group of Experts on the Social and Economic Impact of the Israeli Occupation on Living Conditions of the Palestinian People in the Occupied Arab Territories to visit the Palestinian territories occupied by Israel.

Dec. 9   ARMS CONTROL: General Assembly adopts 48 resolutions dealing with all aspects of disarmament.

Dec. 10   NAMIBIA: General Assembly adopts 6 resolutions strongly urging the Security Council to act decisively against the dilatory actions of the "illegal South African occupation" in frustrating the self-determination rights of the people of Namibia.

1981 (continued)

Dec. 14   CYPRUS: Security Council extends the mandate of UNFICYP
           for six months.
           HUMAN RIGHTS: General Assembly declares the right to
           development to be an inalienable right.
Dec. 15   SECRETARY-GENERAL: General Assembly appoints Javier
           Pérez de Cuéllar of Peru as the 5th Secretary-General for a
           five year term beginning 1 January 1982.
           SEYCHELLES: Security Council decides to send a commission
           of inquiry to investigate the origin, background and financing
           of the 25 November mercenary aggression against Seychelles,
           as well as to assess and evaluate economic damages.
           SOUTH AFRICA: Security Council condemns "the purported
           proclamation of the independence of Ciskei" as a South
           African Bantustan, and declares it "totally invalid".
Dec. 16   BUDGET: General Assembly approves $73.1 million a month
           for UNIFIL for the next twelve months.
           MIDDLE EAST: General Assembly demands that Israel cease
           forthwith implementation of its canal project linking the
           Mediterranean and the Dead Sea, and requests the Security
           Council to initiate measures to halt the project.
Dec. 17   ECONOMIC DEVELOPMENT: General Assembly expresses
           its deep concern over the fact that over-all voluntary
           contributions from governments have been stagnating and
           falling short in many cases of the targets set by relevant inter-
           governmental bodies.
           MIDDLE EAST: General Assembly condemns Israel's
           continued occupation of the Palestinian and other Arab
           territories, including Jerusalem, "in violation of the UN
           charter"; Security Council declares that the Israeli decision to
           impose its laws, jurisdiction and administration on the
           occupied Syria Golan Heights is "null and void and without
           international legal effect".
           SOUTH AFRICA: General Assembly proclaims 1982 as the
           International Year for Mobilization of Sanctions Against
           South Africa and urges the Security Council to declare the
           apartheid regime in South Africa as a grave threat to
           international peace and security.
Dec. 18   BUDGET: General Assembly approves a program budget of
           $1,506.2 million for the biennium 1982-1983.
           LEBANON: Security Council extends the mandate of UNIFIL
           for six months.

1982

Jan. 20   MIDDLE EAST: USA vetoes a draft resolution of the Security
                   Council which invokes collective sanctions in order to nullify
                   the Israeli annexation of the Syrian Golan Heights.

Jan. 29-Feb. 5   MIDDLE EAST: 9th emergency special session of the General
                   Assembly on the situation in the Israeli occupied Arab
                   territories declares that Israel's decision of 14 December 1981
                   to impose its laws, jurisdiction and administration on the
                   occupied Syrian Golan Heights constituted "an act of
                   aggression" and asks all states to refrain from military and
                   other aid and relationships with Israel.

Feb. 2-5   ECOSOC: Organizational session, New York.

Feb. 11   KAMPUCHEA: Pledging meeting for the Program on
                   Humanitarian Assistance for the Kampuchean people results in
                   pledges of $10 million.

Feb. 24   TUNISIA/LIBYA CONTINENTAL SHELF CASE:
                   International Court of Justice renders a decision delimiting the
                   continental shelf boundary.

Feb. 25   LEBANON: Security Council approves an immediate 1,000
                   man increase in the size of UNIFIL (bringing it up to 7,000),
                   indicating that the existing force is seriously over-strained.

March 2   FOOD: Pledging conference for the World Food Program for
                   1983-1984 results in pledges of $679.9 million, the highest
                   amount ever pledged.

March 8-April 30   LAW OF THE SEA: 11th session of the 3rd UN Conference on
                   the Law of the Sea.

March 16-29   GENERAL ASSEMBLY: Resumed 36th regular session.

April 2   CENTRAL AMERICA: USA vetoes a draft resolution of the
                   Security Council which appeals to all member states to refrain
                   from direct, indirect, overt or covert use of force against any
                   country of Central America and the Caribbean.

                   MIDDLE EAST: USA vetoes a draft resolution of the Security
                   Council which calls on Israel, "the occupying power to
                   rescind its decision to disband the elected municipal council of
                   El Bireh and its decision to remove from their posts the
                   mayors of Nablus and Ramallah".

April 3   FALKLANDS ISLANDS (MALVINAS): Security Council
                   demands immediate withdrawal of all Argentine forces which
                   have invaded the Falklands Islands (Malvinas) and calls for an
                   immediate cessation of hostilities.

April 9   SOUTH AFRICA: Security Council calls upon the South
                   African authorities to commute the death sentences imposed
                   by a Pretoria court in November 1980 on three members of
                   the African National Congress.

April 13-May 7   ECOSOC: 1st regular session, New York.

1982 (continued)

April 20-28	MIDDLE EAST: Reconvened 7th emergency special session of the General Assembly (adjourned on 29 July 1980) on the question of Palestine declares "that Israel's record and actions confirm that it is not a peace-loving Member State and that it has not carried out its obligations under the Charter of its commitment under General Assembly resolution 273 (III) of May 11, 1949" (the resolution by which Israel was admitted Israel to the UN).
April 20	MIDDLE EAST: USA vetoes a draft resolution of the Security Council which notes the "murderous assault" on Moslem worshippers at Jerusalem's Dome of the Rock by an Israeli soldier; and calls on Israel, the occupying power, to observe and apply the provisions of the 4th Geneva Convention and principles of international law, governing military occupation and refrain from causing any hinderance to the discharge of the established functions of the Higher Islamic Council in Jerusalem.
April 29	GENERAL ASSEMBLY: Resumed 36th regular session.
April 30	CHAD: Security Council establishes a voluntary fund to help pay for the Organization of African Unity's peace-keeping force in Chad.
	LAW OF THE SEA: 11th session of the 3rd UN Conference on the Law of the Sea adopts, after nine years of negotiations, a draft Convention on the Law of the Sea by a vote of 130 to 4 (Israel, Turkey, USA, Venezuela), with 17 abstentions.
May 5	FALKLANDS ISLANDS (MALVINAS): Security Council expresses "deep concern" at the deterioration of the situation in the South Atlantic region and strongly supports the Secretary-General in his efforts to bring the parties together.
May 11-June 11	TRUSTEESHIP COUNCIL: 49th regular session.
May 26	FALKLANDS ISLANDS (MALVINAS): Security Council requests the Secretary-General to undertake a renewed mission of good offices and urges the parties to the conflict to co-operate.
	MIDDLE EAST: Security Council extends the mandate of UNDOF for six months.
May 28	SEYCHELLES: Security Council strongly condemns "the mercenary aggression against the Seychelles" which took place in November 1981 and decides to establish a Special Fund for the Seychelles to be supported by voluntary contributions for economic reconstruction.
June 4	FALKLANDS ISLANDS (MALVINAS): UK and USA vetoes a draft resolution of the Security Council which calls for an immediate cease-fire in the conflict.

1982 (continued)

June 5	LEBANON: Security Council calls on all parties "to cease immediately and simultaneously all military activity within Lebanon and across the Lebanese-Israeli border".
June 7-July 10	ARMS CONTROL: 12th special session of the General Assembly on disarmament issues expresses regret that it had not been possible to adopt a document on the Comprehensive Program of Disarmament.
June 8	LEBANON: USA vetoes a draft resolution of the Security Council which condemns Israel for not heeding its previous resolution on hostilities in Lebanon.
June 10	ARMS CONTROL: Secretary-General is presented with a petition signed by 90 million people from around the world calling for disarmament and the abolition of war.
June 15	CYPRUS: Security Council extends the mandate of UNFICYP for six months.
June 16-24	AFGHANISTAN: Afghanistan and Pakistan hold first round of "indirect" talks in Geneva and reach understanding on the possible structure and contents of the settlement.
June 18	LEBANON: Security Council extends the mandate of UNIFIL for two months "as an interim measure" pending an examination of the situation in all its aspects.
June 19	LEBANON: Security Council calls upon all parties to the conflict to respect the rights of the civilian population.
June 25-26	MIDDLE EAST: Resumed 7th emergency special session of the General Assembly on the question of Palestine condemns Israel for not heeding Security Council demands on Palestine.
June 25	ECONOMIC DEVELOPMENT: Governing Council of UNDP approves a record allocation of $2 billion for technical cooperation projects in 1982-1983.
June 26	LEBANON: USA vetoes a draft resolution of the Security Council, calling for the immediate pull-out of Israeli and Palestinian forces from Beirut; General Assembly expresses full support of the Security Council for trying to call for the complete and unconditional withdrawal of Israeli troops from Lebanon.
July 4	LEBANON: Security Council calls for respect for the rights of civilians in Lebanon and reaffirms its previous calls for a cease-fire and unconditional Israeli troop withdrawal from Lebanon.
July 7-30	ECOSOC: 2nd regular session, Geneva.
July 12	IRAN-IRAQ: Security Council calls for a cease-fire, an immediate end of military operations in the conflict between Iran and Iraq, and a troop withdrawal to internationally recognized boundaries.
July 26-Aug. 6	AGING: UN World Assembly on Aging adopts the International Plan of Action containing some 60 specific recommendations.

1982 (continued)

July 26	MALTA/LIBYA CASE: Malta and Libya notify the International Court of Justice of their special agreement requesting the court to decide the boundary delimitation on the continental shelf between them.
July 29	LEBANON: Security Council demands that Israel immediately lifts the blockade of Beirut to allow dispatch of needed supplies to the civilian population.
July 30	INDUSTRIAL DEVELOPMENT: UNIDO's constitution is ratified by the 80th state, thus paving the way for the organization to become a specialized agency.
Aug. 1	LEBANON: Security Council demands cease-fire and authorizes the Secretary-General to deploy observers.
Aug. 3	LEBANON: Security Council expresses serious concern over the state of tension and military action in and around Beirut.
Aug. 4	LEBANON: Security Council expresses shock and alarm at "the deplorable consequences" of the "Israeli invasion of Beirut" and calls for the withdrawal of Israeli troops.
Aug. 6	LEBANON: USA vetoes a draft resolution of the Security Council, calling for a ban on the supply of arms to Israel until it fully withdraws its forces from all Lebanese territory.
Aug. 9-21	OUTER SPACE: 2nd UN Conference on the Exploration and Peaceful Uses of Outer Space expresses the concern of all nations at the possible extension of the arms race into space; calls for the establishment of a UN Space Information System; makes a number of specific technical recommendations on the use of satellites.
Aug. 12	LEBANON: Security Council demands an immediate halt to all military activities in Lebanon and the lifting of restrictions on the city of Beirut in order to permit the entry of supplies to meet the urgent needs of the civilian population.
Aug. 16-19	MIDDLE EAST: Resumed 7th emergency special session of the General Assembly on the question of Palestine calls for the free exercise of the Palestinian right of self-determination and national independence, and rejects all policies at resettlement of the Palestinians outside their homeland.
Aug. 17	LEBANON: Security Council extends the mandate of UNIFIL for two months.
Sept. 19	LEBANON: Security Council condemns the massacre of civilians in Beirut and authorizes the Secretary-General to increase the number of UN observers in the area from 10 to 50; condemns the murder of the President-elect of Lebanon; calls for respect for Lebanese sovereignty.
Sept. 20	GENERAL ASSEMBLY: Resumed 36th regular session.
Sept. 21-Dec. 21	GENERAL ASSEMBLY: 37th regular Session.

1982 (continued)

Sept. 22-25	LAW OF THE SEA: 3rd UN Conference on the Law of the Sea considers technical changes in the final text of the draft convention.
Sept. 24	MIDDLE EAST: Resumed 7th emergency special session of the General Assembly on the question of Palestine condemns the recent massacre of Palestinians and other civilians in Beirut and urges the Security Council to investigate.
Oct. 1	COMMODITIES: UN conference adopts the International Agreement on Jute and Jute Products.
	SOUTH AFRICA: General Assembly and Security Council appeal to South Africa to commute the death sentences imposed in August on three members of the African National Congress.
Oct. 4	IRAN-IRAQ: Security Council deplores the escalation of the conflict between Iran and Iraq and urgently reaffirms its call for a cease-fire and withdrawal of forces.
Oct. 18	LEBANON: Security Council extends the mandate of UNIFIL until 19 January 1983.
Oct. 22	IRAN-IRAQ: General Assembly calls for a cease-fire and withdrawal of troops to internationally recognized boundaries as a preliminary step toward the settlement of the situation.
Oct. 25-27	ECOSOC: Resumed 2nd regular session, New York.
Nov. 4	FALKLANDS ISLANDS (MALVINAS): General Assembly calls for a negotiated solution of the Argentine-UK dispute over these islands.
Nov. 8-9	ECONOMIC DEVELOPMENT: UN Pledging Conference for Development Activities results in pledges of $272.5 million from 95 government.
Nov. 9-10	ECOSOC: Resumed 2nd session, New York.
Nov. 15	CHARTER: General Assembly approves the Manila Declaration on the Peaceful Settlement of International Disputes, stressing the greater uses of the instruments in the UN Charter.
Nov. 19	MIDDLE EAST: General Assembly demands "that Israel withdraws forthwith its officially declared threat to repeat its armed attack against nuclear facilities".
Nov. 23	WESTERN SAHARA: General Assembly reaffirms the right of the people of the Western Sahara to self-determination and independence.
Nov. 29	AFGHANISTAN: General Assembly reaffirms the right of the Afghan people to determine their own form of government and calls for the withdrawal of foreign troops.
Nov. 30	BUDGET: General Assembly authorizes $17.2 million for UNDOF for December to May 1983 and $2.9 million per month for June through November 1983.

1982 (continued)

Dec. 3   WOMEN: General Assembly adopts the Declaration of the Participation of Women in Promoting International Peace and Cooperation.

Dec. 6-10   LAW OF THE SEA: 3rd UN Conference on the Law of the Sea adopts and opens for signature the UN Convention on the Law of the Sea; convention is immediately signed by 119 states and it will come into effect when ratified by 60 states.

Dec. 10   MIDDLE EAST: General Assembly asks the Security Council to recognize Palestinian rights, including the right to establish an independent Arab state in Palestine.

Dec. 14   CYPRUS: Security Council extends the mandate of UNFICYP for six months.

SOUTH AFRICA: Security Council condemns the armed raid by South Africa on Lesotho as a "premeditated aggressive act" and demands that South Africa pays compensation.

Dec. 16-20   TRUSTEESHIP COUNCIL: 15th special session.

Dec. 17   BUDGET: General Assembly approves $15.2 million per month for the UNIFIL for the period of 19 January to 18 December 1983.

Dec. 18   HUMAN RIGHTS: General Assembly declares that "the right to development is an inalienable right" and adopts the Principles of Medical Ethics relevant to the role of health personnel, particularly physicians, in the protection of prisoners and detainees against torture, and other cruel, inhuman or degrading treatment or punishment.

REFUGEES: General Assembly decides to continue UNHCR for a further period of five years.

Dec. 20   TRUST TERRITORIES: Trusteeship Council decides to send a visiting mission to Palau, the Marshall Islands, and the Federal States of Micronesia in order to observe plebiscites in these regions on their political future.

Dec. 21   BUDGET: General Assembly decreases the program budget for the biennium 1982-1983 by $33.3 million to a total of $1,473.0 million.

1983

Jan. 1   DISABLED: Start of the United Nations Decade of Disabled Persons (1983-1992).

RACISM AND RACIAL DISCRIMINATION: Start of the 2nd Decade to Combat Racism and Racial Discrimination (1983-1992).

Jan. 18   LEBANON: Security Council extends the mandate of UNIFIL for six months.

Feb. 1-4   ECOSOC: Organizational session, New York.

1983 (continued)

Feb. 7	AFGHANISTAN: Secretary-General proposes the first outline of a draft comprehensive settlement.
Feb. 14-18	ECONOMIC DEVELOPMENT: Governing Council of UNDP approves $770 million of technical cooperation projects in 25 countries.
Feb. 21	IRAN-IRAQ: Security Council expresses deep concern over the escalating conflict, and again calls for a cease-fire and troop withdrawal.
March 14	COMMODITIES: UN Conference on Tropical Timber.
March 15-April 8	LAW OF THE SEA: 1st session of the Preparation Commission of the International Sea Bed Authority and the International Tribunal for Law of the Sea.
April 4	MIDDLE EAST: Security Council asks the Secretary-General to investigate on the reported "cases of mass poisoning" in the Israeli occupied Arab Territories of the West Bank.
April 6	CHAD: Security Council calls upon Libya and Chad to settle their differences "without undue delay and by peaceful means".
April 11-22	AFGHANISTAN: Afghanistan and Pakistan hold "indirect" talks in Geneva on the situation relating to Afghanistan.
April 29	NAMIBIA: International Conference in Support of the Namibian People for Independence adopts the Declaration on a Program of Action to speed Namibian independence.
May 3-27	ECOSOC: 1st regular session, New York.
May 10-13	GENERAL ASSEMBLY: Resumed 37th regular session.
May 13	CYPRUS: General Assembly calls for immediate withdrawal of all occupation troops from Cyprus and for the pursuit of a mutually acceptable agreement through international negotiations.
May 16-June 28	TRUSTEESHIP COUNCIL: 50th regular session.
May 19	CENTRAL AMERICA: Security Council urges the Contadora Group (Colombia, Mexico, Panama and Venezuela) to continue to pursue peace efforts in Central America.
May 26	MIDDLE EAST: Security Council extends the mandate of UNDOF for six months.
May 31	NAMIBIA: Security Council mandates the Secretary-General to consult with the parties involved in a cease-fire in Namibia to secure speedy implementation of the Council's 1978 guidelines for Namibia's independence.
June 7	SOUTH AFRICA: Security Council issues a new appeal for clemency for three members of the African National Congress.
June 8-July 3	ECONOMIC DEVELOPMENT: 6th session of the UNCTAD states that a trickle-down effect on growth will not activate a growth process in developing countries and stresses that an integrated set of short and long term policies is required.

1983 (continued)

June 12-24	AFGHANISTAN: Afghanistan and Pakistan hold "indirect" talks in Geneva on the situation relating to Afghanistan.
June 15	CYPRUS: Security Council extends the mandate of UNFICYP for six months.
June 24	ECONOMIC DEVELOPMENT: Governing Council of UNDP approves $375 million for technical cooperation in 21 countries for 1984-1985.
June 29	SOUTH AFRICA: Security Council commends Lesotho for its steadfast opposition to *apartheid* and its generosity to South African refugees.
July 9-29	ECOSOC: 2nd regular session, Geneva.
July 18	LEBANON: Security Council extends the mandate of UNIFIL for three months.
Aug. 2	MIDDLE EAST: USA vetoes draft resolution of the Security Council, "determining that the Israeli settlement policy in the occupied Arab territories had no legal validity" and constitutes "a major serious obstruction" to a comprehensive, just and lasting peace in the Middle East.
Aug. 16-27	MIDDLE EAST: UN sponsored International Conference on Palestine adopts declaration reaffirming that the question of Palestine is the core of the Middle East situation and therefore crucial to any settlement.
Sept. 12	KOREAN PLANE INCIDENT: USSR vetoes a draft resolution of the Security Council which deeply deplores the downing of the airliner with the loss of civilian lives and calls for a full investigation by the Secretary-General.
Sept. 19	GENERAL ASSEMBLY: Resumed 37th regular session.
Sept. 20-Dec. 20	GENERAL ASSEMBLY: 38th regular session.
Sept. 23	MEMBERSHIP: General Assembly admits Saint Christopher and Nevis as 158th member.
Oct. 14	UPPER VOLTA/MALI CASE: Upper Volta and Mali notify the International Court of Justice that they have reached a special agreement to submit the question of a boundary frontier delimitation to a chamber of the court.
Oct. 18	LEBANON: Security Council extends the mandate of UNIFIL for six months.
Oct. 27	KAMPUCHEA: General Assembly reiterates its call that all foreign forces be withdrawn from Kampuchea.
Oct. 28	GRENADA: USA vetoes a draft resolution of the Security Council which deeply deplores the armed intervention in Grenada as a flagrant violation of international law and calls for the immediate withdrawal of foreign troops from Grenada.
	NAMIBIA: Security Council declares that the independence of Namibia "cannot be held hostage to the resolution of issues that are alien" to the UN Plan for the independence of Namibia, approved by the Security Council in 1978.

1983 (continued)

Oct. 31   IRAN-IRAQ: Security Council calls upon these two belligerents to cease immediately all hostilities in the Gulf region and calls on all states to respect the rights of free navigation and commerce in international waters.

Nov. 2   GRENADA: General Assembly deeply deplores the armed intervention in Grenada and calls for the immediate withdrawal of foreign troops from that country.

Nov. 10   MIDDLE EAST: General Assembly condemns Israel's refusal to adhere to the 1981 Security Council resolution which called on it to refrain from such acts as its attack on an Iraqi nuclear installation in June 1981 and to place its nuclear facilities under the safeguards of IAEA.

Nov. 11   CENTRAL AMERICA: General Assembly condemns acts of aggression against the states of Central America which have resulted in the loss of human life and irreparable damage to economies, thereby preventing them from meeting the economic and social development needs of their people.

     LEBANON: Security Council expresses "profound concern at the recent and current developments in northern Lebanon which have caused and are still causing widespread suffering and loss of human life".

Nov. 22   CYPRUS: Security Council calls for the withdrawal of the Turkish Cypriot declaration of independence, stating that the declaration was "legally invalid" and will contribute to a worsening of the situation on the island.

Nov. 23   AFGHANISTAN: General Assembly calls for the immediate withdrawal of all foreign troops from Afghanistan.

Nov. 29   MIDDLE EAST: Security Council extends the mandate of UNDOF for six months.

Dec. 1   NAMIBIA: General Assembly calls for the imposition of comprehensive sanctions against South Africa and a rejection of attempts by South Africa and the USA to establish a linkage between the independence of Namibia and withdrawal of Cuban troops from Angola.

Dec. 2   BUDGET: General Assembly approves $17.5 million for UNDOF from 1 December 1983 through 31 May 1984 and $2.9 million per month thereafter until 30 November 1984.

Dec. 5   BUDGET: General Assembly approves $300.2 million for UNIFIL for the period of 19 December 1982 to 18 December 1983, $47.0 million for the period 19 December 1983 to 18 April 1984 and $11.7 million per month from 19 April to 18 December 1984.

Dec. 15   ANTARCTICA: General Assembly asserts that, in the interest of all mankind, Antarctica should continue forever to be used exclusively for peaceful purposes; requests the Secretary-General to prepare a comprehensive, factual and objective

1983 (continued)

study of all aspects of Antarctica, taking into full account the Antarctica Treaty System and other relevant factors.

OUTER SPACE: General Assembly urges effective measures to prevent an arms race in outer space.

Dec. 19   MIDDLE EAST: General Assembly condemns the increasing collaboration between Israel and South Africa, especially in the nuclear field, which, it states, has enabled Israel to subject states of the region to "nuclear blackmail".

Dec. 20   BUDGET: General Assembly approves a program budget of $1,587.2 million for the 1984-1985 biennium.

SOUTH AFRICA: Security Council demands that South Africa withdraws all of its occupation forces from Angola and ceases all violations against that country.

1984

Jan. 6   SOUTH AFRICA: Security Council strongly condemns the latest South African military advances into Angola as a threat to international peace and security.

Feb. 7-10   ECOSOC: Organizational session, New York.

Feb. 29   LEBANON: USSR vetoes a draft resolution of the Security Council on an immediate cease-fire in Lebanon and the deployment of UN forces in the Beirut.

March 8   IRAN-IRAQ: Secretary-General announces that he is sending a group of experts to ascertain the facts regarding allegations of the use of chemical weapons in the Iran-Iraq conflict.

March 24   IRAN-IRAQ: Group of experts to investigate allegations on the use of chemical weapons states that chemical weapons in the form of aerial bombs were used in areas inspected in Iran.

April 6   INTERNATIONAL LAW: USA states that it is temporarily modifying its acceptance of the compulsory jurisdiction of the International Court of Justice in order to rule out cases involving Central America for the next two years.

April 9   NICARAGUA/USA CASE: Nicaragua files a complaint with the International Court of Justice, calling for a halt in the use of US military force against Nicaragua and for a halt to intervention in its internal affairs.

April 19   LEBANON: Security Council extends the mandate of UNIFIL for six months.

May 1-25   ECOSOC: 1st regular session, New York.

May 10   NICARAGUA/USA CASE: International Court of Justice renders a provisional decision calling upon the USA to immediately refrain from any action against Nicaraguan ports, and, in particular, the laying of mines.

May 14-July 18   TRUSTEESHIP COUNCIL: 51st regular session.

1984 (continued)

May 18	CYPRUS: Security Council condemns the exchange of ambassadors between Turkey and the Turkish Cypriot leadership as "illegal and invalid" and calls for the immediate withdrawal of the ambassadors.
May 30	MIDDLE EAST: Security Council extends the mandate of UNDOF for six months.
June 1	IRAN-IRAQ: Security Council asks for respect for the right of free navigation and an end to attacks on commercial ships.
June 10	IRAN-IRAQ: Iran and Iraq accepts the appeal of the Secretary-General to refrain from initiating any deliberate military attack on purely civilian population centers.
June 15	CYPRUS: Security Council extends the mandate of UNFICYP for six months.
	IRAN-IRAQ: Secretary-General, with the agreement of the Security Council, sets up two teams of military observers that will be ready to carry out any on-the-spot inspection requested by Iran or Iraq in connection with their commitment to spare civilian population centers from deliberate attacks.
June 26	GENERAL ASSEMBLY: Resumed 38th regular session.
June 29	COMMODITIES: President of the UN Sugar Conference announces that there was "insufficient will" for a new international sugar agreement with economic provisions and that the Conference will limit itself to concluding an administrative agreement.
July 4-27	ECOSOC: 2nd regular session, Geneva.
July 11	REFUGEES: 2nd International Conference on Assistance to Refugees in Africa adopts a Declaration and Program of Action looking toward long-term solutions.
July 16-Aug. 4	SHIPPING: 1st part of the UN Conference on Conditions for the Registration of Ships.
Aug. 2-20	INDUSTRIAL DEVELOPMENT: 4th General Conference of UNIDO.
Aug. 6-16	POPULATION: UN sponsored International Conference on Population in Mexico City adopts the Mexico City Declaration on Population and Development which updates the World Plan of Action adopted in Bucharest in 1974.
Aug. 17	SOUTH AFRICA: Security Council declares that the new South African constitution is contrary to the principles of the UN Charter, and that enforcement of the constitution will further aggravate the "already explosive situation prevailing inside *apartheid* South Africa".
Aug. 24-30	AFGHANISTAN: Afghanistan and Pakistan hold first round of "proximity" talks in Geneva on the situation relating to Afghanistan and consider a deadlock concerning outstanding substantive provisions and agree that provisions concerning

1984 (continued)

	non-interference and non-intervention be included in a bilateral agreement.
Sept. 6	LEBANON: USA vetoes a draft resolution of the Security Council, calling for the lifting of restrictions and obstacles in the area of Lebanon under Israeli occupation.
Sept. 17	GENERAL ASSEMBLY: Resumed 38th regular session.
Sept. 18-Dec. 18	GENERAL ASSEMBLY: 39th regular session.
Sept. 21	MEMBERSHIP: General Assembly admits Brunei Darussalam as 159th member.
Sept. 28	SOUTH AFRICA: General Assembly rejects the "new constitution in South Africa" and asks the Security Council to avert the resulting tensions in the area.
Oct. 12	GULF OF MAINE CASE: International Court of Justice adjudicates a demarcation line in the Gulf of Maine continental shelf, giving about 2/3's of the Gulf to the USA and the remainder to Canada.
Oct. 18	LEBANON: Security Council extends the mandate of UNIFIL for six months.
Oct. 23	SOUTH AFRICA: Security Council condemns the South African regime for "the continued massacres" of oppressed peoples and demands an "immediate eradication of the policy of *apartheid*".
Oct. 30	KAMPUCHEA: General Assembly calls for the withdrawal of all foreign forces from Kampuchea.
Nov. 1	FALKLANDS ISLANDS (MALVINAS): General Assembly again calls on the UK and Argentina to resume negotiations to find a peaceful solution to their sovereignty dispute.
Nov. 8	ECONOMIC DEVELOPMENT: Pledging conference for UNDP results in pledges of $670 million from 108 governments.
Nov. 12	HUMAN RIGHTS: General Assembly solemnly proclaims that "peoples of our planet have a sacred right to peace" and that its preservation is a fundamental obligation of each country.
Nov. 15	AFGHANISTAN: General Assembly calls for the immediate withdrawal of foreign troops from Afghanistan.
Nov. 26	NICARAGUA/USA CASE: International Court of Justice rules that it has jurisdiction to hear the case brought by Nicaragua against USA, and also rules that the preliminary restraining order against military and paramilitary actions by the USA remains in force.
Nov. 30	BUDGET: General Assembly approves $17.9 million for UNDOF for 1 December 1984 to 31 May 1985 and $3.0 million per month from 1 June to 30 November 1985.
	MIDDLE EAST: Security Council extends the mandate of UNDOF for six months.

1984 (continued)

Dec. 3   AFRICA: General Assembly adopts the Declaration on the
              Critical Economic Situation in Africa, which analyzes the
              causes of the crisis and calls for a wide range of immediate
              and long term measures in an effort to alleviate the economic
              problems affecting the continent.

Dec. 5   SOUTH AFRICA: General Assembly strongly condemns the
              "collusion" of certain Western and other countries with the
              "racist minority regime of South Africa" in the nuclear field,
              and asks all countries not to supply South Africa with nuclear
              supplies and military equipment.

Dec. 9   LAW OF THE SEA: 159 states sign the UN Convention on the
              Law of the Sea by the end of the two year period for
              signatures; it comes into effect one year after 60 states have
              ratify the treaty.

Dec. 10   HUMAN RIGHTS: General Assembly adopts the Convention
              Against Torture and Other Cruel Inhuman or Degrading
              Treatment and Punishment.

Dec. 11   COMOROS: General Assembly again urges France to open
              negotiations with the government of the Comoros over the
              return of the island of Mayotte to that country.
              MIDDLE EAST: General Assembly calls for an international
              conference on the Middle East and asks Israel and USA to
              reconsider their negative position towards such a conference.

Dec. 12   ARMS CONTROL: General Assembly calls for a nuclear test
              ban treaty, a five year freeze on nuclear arms by USA and
              USSR, and efforts to prevent an arms race in outer space.
              NAMIBIA: General Assembly declares that South Africa's
              continued illegal occupation of Namibia is an act of
              "aggression" against the people of Namibia.

Dec. 13   BUDGET: General Assembly approves $50.0 million for
              UNIFIL for the period 19 December 1984 to 18 April 1985
              and $11.7 million per month from 1 April to 18 December
              1985.
              INDUSTRIAL DEVELOPMENT: General Assembly approves
              a resolution instituting transitional arrangements on the
              establishment of UNIDO as specialized agency.

Dec. 14   CYPRUS: Security Council extends the mandate of UNFICYP
              for six months.
              DRUGS: General Assembly proposes a draft Convention
              Against Traffic in Narcotic Drugs and Psychotropic
              Substances and Related Activities, which states that
              "trafficking in narcotic drugs or psychotropic substances is a
              grave international crime against humanity".

1984 (continued)

Dec. 17   AFRICA: Secretary-General announces, during Special Meeting
               on the Crucial Situation in Africa, the creation of the Office
               of Emergency Operations in Africa (OEOA) to coordinate the
               activities of all UN agencies.
               IRAN-IRAQ: Iran and Iraq reach an understanding on the
               sending of a UN mission on the question of prisoners of war
               in the two countries.

Dec. 18   BUDGET: General Assembly revises the program budget for
               the biennium 1984-85 budget from $1,587.2 million to
               $1,611.5 million.

Dec. 19   SOUTH AFRICA: Security Council reaffirms the mandatory
               arms embargo imposed against South Africa in 1977 and
               stresses the continuing need for its strict application.

1985

Jan. 1   TRANSPORT AND COMMUNICATION: Start of the
               Transport and Communications Decade for Asia and the
               Pacific (1985-1994).

Jan. 14   HUNGER: UN Disaster Relief Co-ordinator (UNDRO) reports
               that $312.7 million in cash and kind have been contributed by
               governments, international and non-governmental
               organizations to ease the disastrous starvation situation in
               Ethiopia.

Jan. 18   NICARAGUA/USA CASE: USA informs the International
               Court of Justice that it decided not to participate in further
               court proceedings in the case concerning military and
               paramilitary activities in and against Nicaragua.

Jan. 22   IRAN-IRAQ: Special UN mission examining the situation of
               prisoners of War in Iran and Iraq calls for the release of
               many of the prisoners and for an end to the ill-treatment of
               prisoners held in both countries.

Jan. 28-Feb. 18 SHIPPING: 2nd part of the UN Conference on Conditions for
               the Registration of Ships.

Feb. 4   HUMAN RIGHTS: Convention Against Torture and other
               Cruel, Inhuman or Degrading Treatment or Punishment is
               opened for signature and signed by 21 states; it enters into
               force after 20 ratifications.

Feb. 5-8   ECOSOC: Organizational session, New York.

March 11   LEBANON: USA vetoes a draft resolution of the Security
               Council, condemning "Israeli practices and measures against
               the civilian population in Southern Lebanon, the western
               Bekaa and Rashaya districts which are a violation of
               principles of international law".

1985 (continued)

March 11-12	AFRICA: UN sponsored International Conference on the Emergency Situation in Africa to mobilize international aid to 20 drought stricken states in Africa is attended by 125 states.
April 9-12	GENERAL ASSEMBLY: Resumed 39th regular session.
April 9	STATUS OF WOMEN: General Assembly adopts the Statute of the International Research and Training Institute for the Advancement of Women.
April 12	BURKINO FASO/MALI CASE: International Court of Justice decides to create a special chamber of five to deal with the frontier dispute.
April 17	LEBANON: Security Council extends mandate of UNIFIL for six months.
April 25	IRAN-IRAQ: Security Council declares it is "appalled that chemical weapons have been used against Iranian soldiers during the month of March 1985 in the war between Iran and Iraq".
May 3	NAMIBIA: Security Council declares that the establishment of a "so-called interim government in Namibia" is "null and void", and calls on states to repudiate he South African action and not to recognize it.
May 7-31	ECOSOC: 1st regular session, New York.
May 10	CENTRAL AMERICA: USA vetoes three draft resolutions of the Security Council: first draft with a preambular reference to the US embargo as a source of increased tension in Central America, second draft calling for an immediate end to "trade embargo and other coercive economic measures against Nicaragua" and third draft calling on states to refrain from any action to destabilize and undermine other states, "including the imposition of trade embargoes or restrictions, blockades or other measures incompatible with provisions of the UN Charter"; Security Council reaffirms Nicaragua's right to freely decide its own political, economic and social systems without outside interference, and calls on USA and Nicaragua to resume the dialogue they held in Mexico.
May 13-June 7	TRUSTEESHIP COUNCIL: 52nd regular session.
May 21	MIDDLE EAST: Security Council extends the mandate of UNDOF for six months.
May 24	LEBANON: Security Council expresses serious concern at the heightened violence in certain parts of Lebanon.
May 31	LEBANON: Security Council calls on all concerned "to end acts of violence against civilian population in Lebanon and, in particular, in and around Palestinian refugee camps".
June 14	CYPRUS: Security Council extends the mandate of UNFICYP for six months.

1985 (continued)

June 19	NAMIBIA: Security Council mandates the Secretary-General to resume immediate contact with South Africa in order to implement the UN plan for the independence of Namibia as set out by the Security Council in 1978.
June 20-25	AFGHANISTAN: Afghanistan and Pakistan hold "proximity" talks in Geneva on the situation relating to Afghanistan and (i) formulate two draft bilateral agreements covering the principles of mutual relations, in particular, non-interference and non-intervention, and the voluntary return of the refugees; (ii) complete declaration on international guarantees and convey text to the USA and USSR, previously designated as possible guarantors, for comments.
June 21	SOUTH AFRICA: Security Council condemns the unwarranted attack on the capital of Botswana by South Africa as an act of aggression and requests the Security-General to send a mission to Botswana to assess the damage and recommend proper measures to strengthen Botswana's capacity to receive and assist refugees from South Africa into Botswana.
July 3-26	ECOSOC: 2nd regular session, Geneva.
July 6	SOUTH AFRICA: Security Council strongly condemns South Africa's imposition of a state of emergency in 36 districts and demands that it be lifted immediately.
July 15-27	WOMEN: World Conference to Review and Appraise the Achievement of the UN Decade for Women adopts Forward-Looking Strategy, which outlines action for the advancement of women to the year 2000.
July 26	SOUTH AFRICA: UK and USA veto a draft resolution of the Security Council, condemning South Africa's imposition of a state of emergency and strongly warning that failure to establish a "free, united and democratic society on the basis of universal suffrage" will compel the Security Council to adopt collective measures against South Africa.
July 27-Aug. 2	BOTSWANA: UN mission to assess the damage caused by South African aggression against Botswana visits the area.
Aug. 2	AFRICA: UN Office of Emergency Operations in Africa (OEOA) launches a $30 million appeal to meet the outstanding relief efforts required in the Sudan.
Aug. 21	SOUTH AFRICA: Security Council calls on South Africa to lift the state of emergency and condemns "the continuation of killings and the arbitrary mass arrests and detention carried out by the Pretoria Government"; USA vetoes a draft resolution of the Security Council, which blames the South African government for the burning of the home of Winnie Mandela (the wife of the imprisoned African National Congress leader, Nelson Mandela).

1985 (continued)

Aug. 26-Sept. 6	CRIME: 7th UN Congress on the Prevention of Crime and Treatment of Offenders in Milan, Italy, adopts six draft international instruments on norms and standards of criminal justice.
Aug. 27-30	AFGHANISTAN: Afghanistan and Pakistan hold "proximity" talks in Geneva on the situation relating to Afghanistan.
Sept. 11	BOTSWANA: UN mission to assess property damage inflicted by a South African attack recommends a favorable response of the international community to Botswana's request for $14 million to assist in improving their security capability and its facilities for refugees from South Africa.
Sept. 13	MIDDLE EAST: USA vetoes a draft resolution of the Security Council, which deplores the repressive measures taken by Israel against the civilian Palestinian population in Israeli-occupied territory since 4 August 1985.
Sept. 16	GENERAL ASSEMBLY: Resumed 39th regular session.
Sept. 17-Dec. 18	GENERAL ASSEMBLY: 40th regular session.
Sept. 20	NICARAGUA/USA CASE: Nicaragua files a claim with the International Court of Justice for $375 million in compensation from the USA, "which reflects the minimum direct damage suffered by Nicaragua as a result of US violations of international law".
	SOUTH AFRICA: Security Council condemns South Africa for its military raid into Angola and demands "that South Africa withdraw forthwith and unconditionally all its military forces from the territory of the People's Republic of Angola".
Sept. 24	MEXICO: General Assembly calls for a demonstration of international solidarity and humanitarian concern and asks all nations to contribute to relief and reconstruction efforts after two severe earthquakes in Mexico.
Sept. 25	POPULATION: USA withdraws $10 million originally allocated to UN population projects, arguing that one project in China uses coercive abortion and involuntary sterilization.
Sept. 26	SECURITY COUNCIL: Security Council, meeting at foreign minister level, discusses ways to strengthen the Security Council for the first time since 1970.
Oct. 4	TUNISIA: Security Council condemns Israel's bombing of the PLO headquarters in Tunisia as an act of aggression and upholds Tunisia's right to appropriate reparations as a result of the loss of human life and material damages.
Oct. 14-24	PEACE: Special 40th anniversary commemorative period proclaims 1986 as the International year of Peace, affirms that "promotion of peace is the primary purpose of the United Nations" and calls on all peoples to join in "resolute efforts to safeguard peace and the future of humanity".

1985 (continued)

Oct. 16   DECOLONIZATION: Special commemorative meeting of the
             General Assembly on the 25th anniversary of the adoption of
             the 1960 Declaration on the Granting of Independence to
             Colonial Countries and People.

Nov. 1   NUCLEAR ENERGY: General Assembly asks IAEA to
             consider "additional measures to ensure that Israel undertakes
             not to attack or threaten to attack peaceful nuclear facilities in
             Iraq or elsewhere".

Nov. 5   KAMPUCHEA: General Assembly endorses four principal
             components of a settlement to the situation in Kampuchea: (i)
             withdrawal of all foreign forces from Kampuchea; (ii)
             restoration and preservation of its independence, sovereignty
             and territorial integrity; (iii) right of the Kampuchean people
             to determine their own destiny; and (iv) commitment by all
             states to non-interference and non-intervention in
             Kampuchea's internal affairs.

Nov. 6   SOUTH-EAST ASIA: General Assembly discusses the question
             of peace, stability and co-operation in South-East Asia;
             meeting adjourns without a draft resolution having been
             tabled.

Nov. 8   NUCLEAR ENERGY: General Assembly affirms its confidence
             in the role of the IAEA in the application of nuclear energy
             for peaceful purposes.

Nov. 13-15 & 18   YOUTH: General Assembly convenes as the World Conference
             of International Youth Year (1985) and endorses global
             strategy for youth.

Nov. 13   AFGHANISTAN: General Assembly calls for the immediate
             withdrawal of the foreign troops from Afghanistan and calls
             upon all parties concerned to work for the urgent achievement
             of apolitical solution" and the creation of conditions to
             "enable the Afghan refugees to return voluntarily to their
             homes in safety and honour".

             COLOMBIA: General Assembly urges international support to
             alleviate effects of Colombian volcanic eruption.

Nov. 14-15   DEVELOPMENT ACTIVITIES: Pledging conference for
             development activities results in pledges of $740 million from
             110 countries.

Nov. 15   SOUTH AFRICA: UK and USA veto a draft resolution of the
             Security Council to impose mandatory selective sanctions
             against South Africa under Chapter VII of the Charter.

             USA-USSR SUMMIT: Secretary-General sends identical
             messages to Soviet General-Secretary Mikhail S. Gorbachev
             and US President Ronald Reagan on the eve of their summit.

Nov. 18   USA-USSR SUMMIT: General Assembly expresses its hope
             that the summit between the leaders of the USA and the
             USSR would "give a decisive impetus to their current bilateral

1985 (continued)

	negotiations so that these negotiations produce early and effective agreements on the halting of the nuclear-arms race".
Nov. 21	CULTURAL PROPERTY: General Assembly calls for steps to combat illicit traffic in cultural property.
	MIDDLE EAST: Security Council extends the mandate of UNDOF for six months until 31 May 1986.
Nov. 26	RELIEF EFFORTS: World Hunger Media Awards ceremony is held at UN Headquarters: Irish rock star Bob Geldof, who spearheaded the "Band Aid" and "Live Aid" relief efforts receives a Special Achievement award.
Nov. 27	FALKLANDS ISLANDS (MALVINAS): General Assembly asks Argentina and the UK to initiate negotiations with a view to finding the means "to resolve peacefully and definitively" the problems pending between them, "including all aspects on the future of the Falklands Islands (Malvinas), in accordance with the Charter of the United Nations".
Nov. 29	CRIME: General Assembly adopts the UN Standard Minimum Rules for the Administration of Juvenile Justice (Beijing Rules) and the Declaration of Basic Principles of Justice for Victims of Crime and Abuse of Power emanating from the Seventh UN Congress on the Prevention of Crime and the Treatment of Offenders, held in Milan in August 1985.
Dec. 2	DECOLONIZATION: General Assembly adopts texts on the implementation of the 1960 Declaration on the Granting of Independence to Colonial Countries and Peoples and calls on member states, in particular colonial powers, to take effective steps in order to speedily eradicate all forms of colonialism
	DEVELOPMENT: General Assembly approves a special ministerial-level Assembly session on the critical situation in Africa, May 1986, to focus on solutions to medium- and long-range development challenges facing the African continent.
	SOUTH AFRICA: General Assembly strongly condemns South Africa's continued illegal occupation of Namibia and calls on the States concerned to cease all collaboration with South Africa.
	WESTERN SAHARA: General Assembly asks Morocco and POLISARIO to undertake direct negotiations with a view to bringing about a cease-fire so as to create the necessary conditions for a peaceful and fair referendum for self-determination of the people of Western Sahara.
Dec. 6	SOUTHERN AFRICA: Security Council condemns South Africa "for its continued, intensified and unprovoked acts of aggression" against Angola, and demands that South Africa pay "full and adequate compensation" for the damage to life and property estimated at $36.7 million.

1985 (continued)

Dec. 9   COMOROS: General Assembly reaffirms Comorian sovereignty over the island of Mayotte and urges France to open negotiations with Comoros "with a view to ensuring the effective and prompt return" of that island to the Comoros.

TERRORISM: General Assembly condemns as "criminal" all acts, methods and practices of terrorism "wherever and by whomever committed, including those which jeopardize friendly relations among States and their security", and agrees to co-operate closely in the apprehension and prosecution of those responsible for such acts.

Dec. 10-12   CENTRAL AMERICA: Security Council considers Nicaragua's complaint about "the extremely serious situation created by the escalation of acts of aggression, the repeated threats and the new acts of provocation" directed against Nicaragua "by the current United States Administration": meeting adjourns without a draft resolution having been tabled.

Dec. 10   LAW OF THE SEA: General Assembly calls on all states to become parties to the UN Convention on the Law of the Sea at the earliest "to allow the effective entry into force of the new legal régime for the uses of the sea and its resources".

SOUTH AFRICA: General Assembly adopts nine texts relating to *apartheid*, including a decision to hold in 1986 a world conference on sanctions against South Africa and a International Convention against *Apartheid* in Sports, by which States Parties agree not to permit any sports contact with a country practicing *apartheid*.

TUNISIA/LIBYA CASE: International Court of Justice renders a unanimous decision on the application for revision and interpretation submitted by Tunisia against Libya concerning a 24 February 1982 judgement in the case of the continental shelf (Tunisia/Libya).

Dec. 11   LEGAL: General Assembly acts on a wide variety of legal issues, including those related to protection of children and detained persons, peaceful settlement of disputes, review of the UN Charter, and the Law of Treaties between States and International Organizations.

Dec. 12 & 16   ARMS CONTROL: General Assembly approves resolutions on disarmament matters and including plans for an international conference on the relationship between disarmament and development and for a 3rd special session of the General Assembly on disarmament.

MIDDLE EAST: General Assembly renews call for an international peace conference on the Middle East; asks Israel and the USA to reconsider their views on holding such a peace conference; describes Israel as "not a peace-loving State".

1985 (continued)

Dec. 12   ECOSOC: Resumed 2nd regular session, New York.
                 MIDDLE EAST: Security Council extends the mandate of
                 UNFICYP for six months until 15 June 1986.

Dec. 13   DRUGS: General Assembly approves four resolutions on world
                 drug problems, including the approval of a ministerial-level
                 international conference on drug abuse and illicit trafficking to
                 be held in 1987 in Vienna.
                 HUMAN RIGHTS: General Assembly approves a total of 27
                 resolution and 3 decisions on a wide range of human rights
                 related issues, including the Declaration on the Human Rights
                 of Individuals who are not Nationals of the Country in which
                 They Live which provides for non-citizen's right to life and
                 security of person, right to privacy, right to marry, right to
                 freedom of thought and religion, right to be equal of the
                 courts, right to leave the country and right to own property.
                 NAMIBIA: General Assembly decides to hold in 1986 a special
                 session of the General Assembly on Namibia and an
                 international meeting to be devoted particularly to the
                 attainment of the "immediate independence" of that territory.
                 REFUGEES: General Assembly condemns the "failure to rescue
                 asylum-seekers at sea" and all violations of the rights of
                 refugees and asylum-seekers, particularly those perpetrated by
                 "military or armed attacks" against refugee camps.
                 SOCIAL DEVELOPMENT: General Assembly approves 13
                 resolutions, covering such topics as the world social situation,
                 crime prevention, ageing, the disabled, and national
                 experience in achieving social and economic change; and
                 notes with "deep concern the continuing deterioration of the
                 economic and social situation of the world", particularly in
                 the developing countries and in Africa, where the situation is
                 "critical".
                 WOMEN: General Assembly endorses the results of the World
                 Conference to Review and Appraise the Achievements of the
                 UN Decade for Women (1975-1985); invites governments to
                 set "measurable targets" for overcoming obstacles to the
                 advancement of women; urges UN organizations to ensure
                 implementation of the "Forward-Looking Strategies" with a
                 view to achieving "a substantial improvement in the status of
                 women by the year 2000".

Dec. 16-19   AFGHANISTAN: Afghanistan and Pakistan hold "proximity"
                 talks in Geneva on the situation relating to Afghanistan: a
                 problem relating to the format of discussion prevents
                 consideration of the draft instrument on interrelationships.

Dec. 16   ANTARCTICA: General Assembly reviews question of
                 Antarctica for the third time and adopts three texts concerning
                 (i) the updating and expansion of a 1984 UN study on

1985 (continued)

Antarctica; (ii) the invitation to the Antarctic Treaty
Consultative Parties to inform the Secretary-General of their
negotiations to set up a minerals régime; and (iii) exclusion of
South Africa from participation in the meetings of the
Consultative Parties.

Dec. 16   INDIAN OCEAN: General Assembly calls for convening the
Conference on the Indian Ocean "not later than 1988".

INFORMATION: General Assembly asks for continuing efforts
to promote the establishment of a new, more just and
effective world information and communication order.

MIDDLE EAST: General Assembly appeals to all governments
to make "most generous efforts to meet the anticipated needs"
of UNRWA and declares that Israel's "grave breaches" of the
1949 Geneva Convention relative to the Protection of Civilian
Persons in Time of War are "war crimes and an affront to
humanity".

OUTER SPACE: General Assembly urges all states to
"contribute actively to the goal of preventing an arms race in
outer space as an essential condition for the promotion of
international co-operation in the exploration and uses of outer
space for peaceful purposes".

Dec. 17   DEVELOPMENT: General Assembly decides to reconvene the
Second Committee for one week immediately prior to the 1st
regular 1986 session of ECOSOC to discuss the continuing
global economic and financial crisis; invites Governments to
observe annually, on 5 December, an International Volunteer
Day for Economic and Social Development.

Dec. 18   BUDGET: General Assembly approves a program budget of
$1,663 billion and a real growth rate of 0.1 per cent for the
1986-1987 biennium by a vote of 127 to 19, with 11
abstentions.

CENTRAL AMERICA: General Assembly decides to defer
consideration of the situation in Central America until the
resumption of its 40th session in 1986.

REFORM: General Assembly establishes the "Group of 18", an
18-member high level group of experts to review the
administrative and financial affairs of the UN, to improve its
functioning in areas "which would contribute to strengthening
the effectiveness of the United Nations in dealing with
political, economic and social issues".

TERRORISM: Security Council condemns "all acts of hostage-
taking and abduction" and calls for the immediate safe release
of all hostages and abducted persons "wherever and by
whomever they are being held".

1985 (continued)

Dec. 30   SOUTHERN AFRICA: Security Council condemns South Africa's "aggressive act" against Lesotho on 20 December 1985 and demands that South Africa pays "full and adequate compensation" to Lesotho for the resulting damage and loss of life.

TERRORISM: Security Council condemns the "unjustifiable and criminal terrorist attacks" at the Rome and Vienna airports on 27 December "which caused the taking of innocent human lives".

1986

Jan. 1   DEVELOPMENT: Start of the UN Program of Action for African Economic Recovery and Development (1986-1990).

PEACE: Start of the International Year of Peace (1986).

Jan. 10   BURKINA FASO/MALI CASE: International Court of Justice issues provisional measures calling on the two countries to ensure that no action of any kind is taken that might "aggravate or extend" the frontier dispute.

Jan. 17   MIDDLE EAST: USA vetoes a draft resolution of the Security Council which deplores "Israeli acts of violence as well as abusive practices and measures against the civilian population in southern Lebanon".

Jan. 21   CYPRUS: USSR makes comprehensive proposals.

Jan. 30   MIDDLE EAST: USA vetoes a draft resolution of the Security Council which strongly deplores "provocative acts" by Israelis, including Knesset members violating the "sanctity of the sanctuary of the Haram Al-Sharif in Jerusalem" (Al-Aqsa Mosque).

Jan. 31   SECRETARIAT: Under-Secretary-General for Special Affairs Brian E. Urquart leaves office: Mr. Urquart began his UN career in July 1945 and was involved in organizing and directing peace-keeping forces in the Middle East, Congo and Cyprus, and in negotiations for an independent Namibia.

Feb. 4-April 25   ARMS CONTROL: 1st part of 1986 Disarmament Conference.

Feb. 4-7   ECOSOC: Organizational session, New York.

Feb. 4-6   ISRAEL-LIBYA: Security Council meets on interception by Israel of Libyan aircraft.

TRUSTEESHIP COUNCIL: 16th special session.

Feb. 6   LIBYA-ISRAEL: USA vetoes a draft resolution of the Security Council which condemns Israel "for its forcible interception and diversion" of a Libyan civilian aircraft in international airspace, and its subsequent detention of the aircraft.

1986 (continued)

Feb. 7	SHIPS: UN Convention on Conditions for Registration of Ships adopts which aims to strengthen the links between a state and ships flying its flag by enabling states to exercise their jurisdiction and control over such ships.
Feb. 13-26	TRUSTEESHIP: Visiting mission to Palau to observe the plebiscite on the Compact of Free Association with the USA.
Feb. 13	SOUTHERN AFRICA: Security Council strongly condemns "racist South Africa" for "recent threats to perpetrate acts of aggression against the front-line States and other States in southern Africa", and warns that country against committing any acts of "aggression, terrorism and destabilization" against independent African States and using mercenaries.
Feb. 24	IRAN-IRAQ: Security Council calls upon Iran and Iraq to observe an "immediate cease-fire, a cessation of all hostilities on land, at sea and in the air and withdrawal of all forces to the internationally recognized boundaries without delay".
Feb. 25	REFORM: "Group of 18" on UN efficiency and financing convenes.
March 7-18	AFGHANISTAN: Impasse is resolved on format of talks on situation relating to Afghanistan.
March 20	LEGAL: UN Conference on the Law of Treaties between States and International Organizations or between International Organizations adopts Vienna Convention on the law of treaties, to which international organizations are party.
March 21	IRAN-IRAQ: Security Council issues statement on UN mission to investigate use of chemical weapons in Iran-Iraq war.
March 26-31	SOUTHERN MEDITERRANEAN: Security Council considers US armed attack against Libya.
April 9-15	WESTERN SAHARA: Talks on Western Sahara, New York.
April 12-24	SOUTHERN MEDITERRANEAN: USA vetoes a draft resolution of the Security Council condemning the USA for an armed attack against Libya.
April 16-18	DISARMAMENT AND DEVELOPMENT: Panel of Eminent Personalities on Relationship between Disarmament and Development.
April 18	MIDDLE EAST: Security Council extends the mandate of UNIFIL for three months until 19 July.
April 21	USA-LIBYA: France, UK and US veto a draft resolution of the Security Council which condemns "armed attack" by the US against the Libyan cities of Tripoli and Benghazi "in violation of the Charter of the United Nations and the norms of international conduct".
April 28-May 23	ECOSOC: 1st regular session, New York.
April 28-May 9	GENERAL ASSEMBLY: Resumed 40th regular session.
April 28-May 2	DEVELOPMENT: UN Nickel Conference in Geneva adopts the terms of reference of the International Nickel Study Group.

1986 (continued)

April 29	INTERNATIONAL COURT OF JUSTICE: 40th anniversary.
May 5-23	AFGHANISTAN: Afghanistan and Pakistan hold "proximity" talks in Geneva on the situation in Afghanistan and discuss for the first time instrument on interrelationships; reach agreement on most provisions with only two outstanding issues remaining, first, the arrangements to ensure implementation and second, the time-frame for withdrawal troops.
May 5-8	WESTERN SAHARA: Talks on Western Sahara, New York.
May 9	FINANCIAL CRISIS: Resumed 40th regular session of the General Assembly agrees to economy measures for UN in 1986.
May 12-June 30	TRUSTEESHIP COUNCIL: 53rd regular session.
May 16	SOUTH AFRICA: International Convention against *Apartheid* in Sports is signed by 43 States at a ceremonial meeting of the Special Committee against *Apartheid*.
May 23	SOUTHERN AFRICA: UK and US veto a draft resolution of the Security Council which calls for condemnation of and sanctions against South Africa for "military raids" into Botswana, Zambia and Zimbabwe.
May 27-June 1	AFRICAN RECOVERY: 13th special session of the General Assembly on critical African economic situation adopts five-year program of action for economic recovery of Africa which full implementation is expected to require $128.1 billion over the five-year period, with African nations to provide $82.5 billion and $46.1 billion coming from "external resources".
May 28	TRUSTEESHIP: Trusteeship Council notes that in the Marshall Islands, Micronesia and Palau have chosen free association with the USA and that the Northern Mariana Islands have chosen commonwealth status; considers that the USA, as administering authority of the trust territory of the Pacific Islands, had "satisfactory discharged its obligations under the terms of the Trusteeship Agreement".
May 29	MIDDLE EAST: Security Council extends the mandate of UNDOF for six months until 30 November 1986.
June 10-Aug. 29	ARMS CONTROL: 2nd part of 1986 Conference on Disarmament concludes with its President reporting "positive and substantive developments" during the year.
June 12	NAMIBIA: Secretary-General urges decisive action to implement UN plan for Namibian independence by 1 August.
June 13	CYPRUS: Security Council extends the mandate of UNFICYP for six months until 15 December 1986.
	SOUTH AFRICA: Security Council calls for the immediate lifting of the state of emergency imposed in South Africa on 12 June to permit the observance of the 10th anniversary of

1986 (continued)

	the Soveto massacre on 16 June without "any provocative interference or intimidation on the part of the police and military forces".
June 16-20	SOUTH AFRICA: World Conference on Sanctions against South Africa in Paris calls for universal system of mandatory economic sanctions against South Africa.
June 18	SOUTH AFRICA: UK and US veto a draft resolution of the Security Council calling for condemnation of and sanctions against South Africa for a "premeditated and unprovoked attack" on the port of Namibe in Angola as well as the continuing occupation of the territory of that state.
June 20	DISARMAMENT AND DEVELOPMENT: Resumed 40th session of the General Assembly decides to postpone to 1987 the International Conference on Disarmament and Development, originally scheduled to be held in Paris from 15 July to 2 August 1986.
	ECONOMIC DEVELOPMENT: Resumed 40th regular session of General Assembly is unable to agree on economic issues: transmits them to 41st session.
	SOUTH AFRICA: World Conference on Sanctions against South Africa adopts declaration calling for world-wide comprehensive sanctions against South Africa.
June 27	USA/NICARAGUA CASE: International Court of Justice decides that the USA by activities "in and against Nicaragua" has acted in breach of "customary international law" not to use force, not to violate the sovereignty of another state and not to intervene in the affairs of another state.
June 30	TRUSTEESHIP: Council considers termination of Micronesia Agreement "appropriate".
July 1-3	US-NICARAGUA: Security Council considers a complaint by Nicaragua regarding what is termed "the escalation of the United States Government's policy of aggression against Nicaragua, which threatens international peace and security": meeting adjourns without a draft resolution having been tabled.
July 1	TRADE: UN Conference on Olive Oil adopts a new International Agreement on Olive Oil.
July 2-23	ECOSOC: 2nd regular session, Geneva.
July 6	FRANCE-NEW ZEALAND: Secretary-General issues ruling on settlement of problems between France and New Zealand arising from the "Rainbow Warrior" affair and rules that France should formally apologize to New Zealand for the attack, pay reparations of $7 million and agree not to place obstacles to trade between New Zealand and the EEC.

1986 (continued)

July 7-11   NAMIBIA: International Conference for the Immediate
                 Independence of Namibia calls for implementation of UN plan
                 for Namibia independence and sanctions against South Africa.

July 16   WESTERN SAHARA: Secretary-General and King Hassan II
                 hold talks in Rabat, Morocco.

July 18   MIDDLE EAST: Security Council extends the mandate of
                 UNIFIL until 19 January 1987.

July 25   TRADE: UN Cocoa Conference adopts a new International
                 Cocoa Agreement.

July 28   NICARAGUA-COSTA RICA/HONDURAS CASE: Nicaragua
                 asks the International Court of Justice to institute separate
                 proceedings against Costa Rica and against Honduras in
                 connection with frontier incidents and armed attacks which
                 Nicaragua alleged have organized by "contra" and anti-
                 Nicaraguan forces.

July 31-Aug. 8   AFGHANISTAN: Afghanistan and Pakistan hold "proximity
                 talks" in Geneva on the situation relating to Afghanistan.

July 31   CENTRAL AMERICA: USA vetoes a draft resolution of the
                 Security Council which makes "an urgent and solemn call"
                 for full compliance with the Judgement of the International
                 Court of Justice of 27 June 1986 in the case of "Military and
                 Paramilitary Activities in and against Nicaragua".

Aug. 11-Sept. 13 MIDDLE EAST: Five UNIFIL soldiers die as a result of armed
                 confrontations in the area.

Aug. 14   IRAN-IRAQ: Secretary-General calls on Iran and Iraq to "bring
                 a moratorium into effect" on attacks on civilian areas "from
                 the day of Eid-al-Adha, a commemoration of special
                 significance to all Muslims".

Aug. 18   REFORM: "Group of 18" on UN efficiency and financing
                 presents report to Secretary-General which includes 71
                 recommendations on UN's functioning.

Sept. 5   MIDDLE EAST: Security Council members call for urgent
                 measures to reinforce the security of the UN peace-keeping
                 force in Lebanon, after attacks resulted in deaths and injuries
                 among troops.

Sept. 8-26   ARMS CONTROL: 2nd Review Conference of State Parties to
                 the Convention on the Prohibition of the Development,
                 Production and Stockpiling of Bacteriological (Biological) and
                 Toxin Weapons and on Their Destruction in Geneva
                 concludes with call for measures to strengthen biological
                 weapons ban.

Sept. 9   FINANCIAL CRISIS: Secretary-General makes observations on
                 what he calls "the most severe financial crisis" in UN history.

Sept. 15   GENERAL ASSEMBLY: Resumed 40th regular session.

Sept. 16-Dec. 19 GENERAL ASSEMBLY: 41st regular session.

1986 (continued)

Sept. 17-20	NAMIBIA: 14th special session of the General Assembly, its 2nd devoted to Namibia, calls for implementation of UN plan for Namibian independence and sanctions against South Africa.
Sept. 18	RELIEF: UN Office for Emergency Operations for Africa (OEOA) reports that acute emergency conditions continue to afflict more than 14 million Africans, particularly in the strife-affected countries of Angola, Ethiopia, Mozambique and Sudan.
Sept. 23	MIDDLE EAST: Security Council adopts resolution condemning "in the strongest terms" the attacks against UNIFIL and expressing "indignation at the support which such criminal actions may receive".
Oct. 1	CENTRAL AMERICA: Secretary-General meets with members of the "Contadora Group" and its Support Group which presents him with a joint declaration entitled "Peace is still possible in Central America".
Oct. 6	SETTLEMENT: Observation of the 1st World HABITAT Day.
Oct. 8	IRAN-IRAQ: Security Council calls for immediate cease-fire in conflict, cessation of all hostilities and withdrawal of forces to international boundaries without delay.
Oct. 10	SECRETARY-GENERAL: General Assembly appoints Secretary-General Javier Pérez de Cuéllar to a 2nd term for the period 1 January 1987 to 31 December 1991.
Oct. 14	RELIEF: General Assembly asks states to provide emergency assistance to El Salvador after devastating earthquake.
Oct. 21	DECOLONIZATION: General Assembly adopts 20 texts on decolonization issues and reviews the status of 14 territories.
	KAMPUCHEA: General Assembly endorses four principal components of settlement of situation in Kampuchean.
Oct. 27	SOUTH ATLANTIC: General Assembly declares the Atlantic Ocean, in the region between Africa and South America, a "Zone of Peace and Co-operation of the South Atlantic".
Oct. 28	CENTRAL AMERICA: USA vetoes a draft resolution of the Security Council urging full and immediate compliance with ruling of the International Court of Justice regarding case the brought by Nicaragua.
Oct. 29	NUCLEAR ENERGY: General Assembly calls on Israel to urgently place all its nuclear facilities under IAEA safeguards; appeals for high safety standards in nuclear plants; decides to convene a UN Conference for the Promotion of International Co-operation in the Peaceful Uses of Nuclear Energy, scheduled for 23 March-10 April 1987.
Oct. 31	MIDDLE EAST: Security Council approves security measures and financial arrangements for UNIFIL.

1986 (continued)

Oct. 31   RELIEF: General Assembly appeals for urgent and intensified
                international efforts to meet Africa's emergency needs.

Nov. 3   COMOROS: General Assembly reaffirms the sovereignty of the
                Comoros over the island of Mayotte, and urges France to
                accelerate the process of negotiations with the Comoros "with
                a view to ensuring the effective and prompt return" of that
                island to the Comoros.

Nov. 5   AFGHANISTAN: General Assembly calls for the immediate
                withdrawal of the foreign troops from Afghanistan, calling
                upon all parties concerned to work for the urgent achievement
                of a political solution.

                LAW OF THE SEA: General Assembly calls on all states that
                have not yet done so to consider ratifying or acceding to the
                UN Convention on the Law of the Sea at the earliest date "to
                allow the effective entry into force of the new legal régime
                for the uses of the sea and its resources".

Nov. 10 & 20   SOUTH AFRICA: General Assembly urges Security Council to
                impose a mandatory oil embargo against South Africa; creates
                11-member monitoring group; adopts 13 texts on *apartheid*
                and Namibia issues.

Nov. 11   NUCLEAR ENERGY: General Assembly urges all states to co-
                operate with IAEA to promote peaceful use of nuclear
                energy.

Nov. 18   CENTRAL AMERICA: General Assembly urges support for
                efforts of the Contadora Group (Colombia, Mexico, Panama,
                Venezuela) towards a negotiated settlement in Central
                America.

Nov. 19   LIBYA-CHAD: Security Council considers a complaint from
                Chad regarding the "serious" situation prevailing in that
                country the "northern part of which has been occupied by
                neighbouring Libya": meeting adjourns without a draft
                resolution having been tabled.

Nov. 20-26   TRUSTEESHIP COUNCIL: 17th special session.

Nov. 20   US-LIBYA: General Assembly condemns April 1986 attack of
                USA against Libya.

Nov. 25   FALKLANDS ISLANDS (MALVINAS): General Assembly
                reiterates its request to Argentina and the UK to initiate
                negotiations with a view to finding the means "to resolve
                peacefully and definitively" the problems pending between
                them, "including all aspects of the future of the Falklands
                Islands (Malvinas)".

Nov. 26   MIDDLE EAST: Security Council extends the mandate of
                UNDOF for six months until 31 May 1987.

Nov. 28   SOUTH AFRICA: Security Council urges states to implement
                strictly the 1977 mandatory arms embargo against South
                Africa.

1986 (continued)

Nov. 28	TRUSTEESHIP: Trusteeship Council dispatches mission to observe a plebiscite in Palau on a revised Compact of Free Association with the US, since "several citizens" of Palau have challenged the results of a plebiscite held in February 1986, which has been upheld by the US Supreme Court.
Dec. 2 & 4	MIDDLE EAST: General Assembly adopts seven resolutions on Middle East and Palestine issues, calling for comprehensive settlement under UN auspices and endorsing calls for setting up a preparatory committee to act on convening a peace conference.
Dec. 2	DECOLONIZATION: General Assembly decides that New Caledonia is a Non-Self-Governing Territory and affirmed the right of the people of New Caledonia to self-determination and independence.
Dec. 3 & 4	ARMS CONTROL: General Assembly adopts 65 resolutions and 2 decisions relating to various disarmament matters, including more than 20 dealing with nuclear issues.
Dec. 3	INFORMATION: General Assembly calls for co-operation in a new world information and communication order, seen as "an evolving and continuous process".
	LEGAL: General Assembly adopts 15 resolutions and 3 decisions covering a wide variety of legal issues, including diplomates' safety, host country relations and the Declaration on Social and Legal Principles Relating to the Protection and Welfare of Children.
	MIDDLE EAST: General Assembly declares that Israel's "grave breaches" of the 1949 Geneva Convention relative to the Protection of Civilian Persons in Time of War are "war crimes and an affront to humanity".
	RELIEF: General Assembly adopts 11 resolutions relating to the situation of Palestine refugees; asks governments to make "most generous efforts" to meet needs of UNRWA; extends the mandate of UNRWA until 1990.
	REMOTE SENSING: General Assembly adopts a set of 15 principles relating to remote sensing of the earth from space.
Dec. 4	ANTARCTICA: General Assembly reviews question of Antarctica for the fourth time and adopts three texts.
	DRUGS: General Assembly adopts 3 texts on 1987 international conference and on issues to combat drug abuse and illicit trafficking.
	HUMAN RIGHTS: General Assembly acts on a wide range of human rights issues, adopting more than 40 texts, including the adoption of a 10-article Declaration on the Right to Development.

1986 (continued)

Dec. 4   PEACE AND SECURITY: General Assembly calls on states to
              "democratize international relations" and ensure security "on
              an equal basis for all States and in all spheres of international
              relations".
              REFUGEES: General Assembly adopts 9 resolutions relating to
              refugees and calls for world-wide aid for refugees.
              SOCIAL DEVELOPMENT: General Assembly adopts
              resolutions relating to self-determination, *apartheid*, racism,
              racial discrimination and to a wide range of social concerns
              including youth, crime prevention and criminal justice,
              ageing, and the disabled; condemns increased use of
              mercenaries.
              WOMEN: General Assembly calls on member states to
              approve, as a matter of priority, effective measures to
              implement the Forward-looking Strategies for the
              Advancement of Women, adopted in July 1985.

Dec. 5 & 8   DEVELOPMENT: General Assembly adopts 36 resolutions and
              23 decisions on key issues relating to trade, food, housing and
              other development matters; proclaims the period 1988-1997
              the World Decade for Cultural Development.

Dec. 5   VOLUNTEER: Observation of 1st International Volunteer Day
              for Economic and Social Development.

Dec. 8   DEVELOPMENT: General Assembly reaches consensus on
              strengthened international co-operation to resolve external
              debt problems of developing countries.
              MIDDLE EAST: Security Council reaffirms that 1949 Geneva
              Convention applies to territories occupied by Israel.

Dec. 10   CENTRAL AMERICA: Security Council considers a complaint
              by Nicaragua about the serious incidents occurring at present
              in the Central American region which endanger international
              peace and security: meeting adjourns without a draft
              resolution having been tabled.

Dec. 11   FINANCIAL CRISIS: General Assembly agrees that the
              Secretary-General should proceed with economy measures to
              counteract predicted budgetary shortfall.
              MIDDLE EAST: Security Council extends the mandate of
              UNFICYP for six months until 15 June 1987.

Dec. 17   SOUTH AFRICA: Secretary-General calls on South Africa to
              end the state of emergency and to release the large numbers
              of children detained under the emergency regulations as well
              as other political detainees.

Dec. 19   REFORM: General Assembly approves reforms to improve UN
              functioning and efficiency, based on the recommendation of
              the "Group of 18".

1986 (continued)

Dec. 22   IRAN-IRAQ: Security Council expresses "profound concern at the serious situation which continues to exist between Iran and Iraq".

MALI/BURKINA FASO CASE: International Court of Justice delivers its judgement in the case unanimously adopting the line of the frontier in the disputed area between the two states.

1987

Jan. 1   HOMELESS: Start of the International Year of Shelter for the Homeless (1987).

Jan. 13   IRAN-IRAQ: Secretary-General suggests Security Council ministerial-level meeting on Iran-Iraq.

Jan. 15   MIDDLE EAST: Security Council extends the mandate of UNIFIL for a period of six months and 12 days until 31 July 1987.

Jan. 18-21   CENTRAL AMERICA: Secretary-General undertakes peace mission to five Central American nations and reaffirms his support for Contadora efforts.

Feb. 3-April 30   ARM CONTROL: 1st part of 1987 Conference on Disarmament.

Feb. 3-6   ECOSOC: Organizational session, New York.

Feb. 6   ITALY/USA CASE: USA institutes proceedings with the International Court of Justice against Italy alleging violation of the Treaty of Friendship, Commerce and Navigation.

Feb. 10-13   MOTHERHOOD: Safe Motherhood Conference, Nairobi.

Feb. 13   MIDDLE EAST: Security Council expresses profound concern over continued suffering within Palestinian refugee camps in southern Lebanon and calls on parties concerned to permit access to them for humanitarian purposes.

Feb. 20   SOUTH AFRICA: UK and US veto a draft resolution of Security Council, calling for selective mandatory sanctions against South Africa.

Feb. 25-March 9   AFGHANISTAN: Afghanistan and Pakistan hold "proximity" talks in Geneva on situation relating to Afghanistan and discuss two proposals on time-frame for troop withdrawal, the last remaining issue; reduce the gap between proposed time-frames from 45 months to 11 months.

March 23-April 10 NUCLEAR ENERGY: UN Conference for the Promotion of International Co-operation in the Peaceful Uses of Nuclear Energy is unable to agree on a set of "universally acceptable" principle for international co-operation in the field and means to promote such co-operation.

March 24   SOUTH AFRICA: 1st meeting of new 11-member group to monitor oil embargo against South Africa.

1987 (continued)

April 9	SOUTH AFRICA: UK and US veto a draft resolution of the Security Council, calling for comprehensive mandatory sanctions against South Africa.
May 4-29	ECOSOC: 1st regular session, New York.
May 7	MIDDLE EAST: Secretary-General reports on Middle East peace conference.
May 11-28	TRUSTEESHIP COUNCIL: 44th regular session.
May 14	IRAN-IRAQ: Security Council strongly condemns the repeated use of chemical weapons in the continuing conflict between Iran and Iraq in open violation of the Geneva Protocol of 1925.
May 27	SECRETARIAT: International Court of Justice issues judgment on former staff member situation.
May 28	TRUSTEESHIP: Trusteeship Council recommends early completion of process of approval of Compact of Free Association between Palau and the USA.
May 29	MIDDLE EAST: Security Council extends the mandate of UNDOF for six months until 30 November 1987.
June 1-5	ENVIRONMENT: World Environment Festival, New York.
June 9-Aug. 28	ARMS CONTROL: 2nd part of 1987 Conference on Disarmament reports considerable progress in negotiations on a multilateral convention on the complete and effective prohibition of the development, production and stockpiling of chemical weapons and on their destruction.
June 12	CYPRUS: Security Council extends the mandate of UNFICYP for six months until 15 December.
June 15-19	AFRICAN RECOVERY: Meeting on Africa Recovery Program, Nigeria.
June 16	SOUTH AFRICA: Soweto Day is observed.
June 17-26	DRUGS: International Conference on Drug Abuse and Illicit Trafficking in Vienna adopts declaration which expressed commitment for "vigorous action" and co-operation towards the goal of an international society free of drug abuse.
June 23-July 9	ECOSOC: 2nd regular session, Geneva.
June 26	TORTURE: Convention against Torture enters into force.
July 9-Aug. 3	TRADE AND DEVELOPMENT: 7th session of UNCTAD in Geneva adopts by consensus a Final Act in which industrialized and developing countries agree on a common approach to development through economic growth.
July 11	POPULATION: Day of the Five Billion is observed: new-born baby in Yugoslavia is proclaimed five billionth person on Earth.
July 20	IRAN-IRAQ: Security Council calls for a cease-fire, an end to all military actions in the region, withdrawal of forces to internationally recognized boundaries, dispatch of a team of UN observers to supervise those actions, consideration of the

1987 (continued)

	question of entrusting an impartial body to inquire into responsibility for the conflict and the release and repatriation of prisoners of war.
July 29	KAMPUCHEA: Ho Chiu Minh City Understanding.
July 31	MIDDLE EAST: Security Council extends the mandate of UNIFIL for six months until 31 January 1988.
Aug. 7	CENTRAL AMERICA: Presidents of Costa Rica, El Salvador, Guatemala, Honduras and Nicaragua sign the Guatemala Agreement (also known as Esquipulas II) for the establishment of peace in Central America, which calls for national reconciliation, dialogue and amnesty, an end to hostilities, democratization, free elections, termination of aid to "irregular forces and insurrectionist movements", non-use of territory to attack other States, negotiations on security, verification and control and limitation of weapons, and assistance to refugees and displaced persons.
Aug. 13	TRUSTEESHIP COUNCIL: 18th special session.
Aug. 24-Sept. 11	DISARMAMENT AND DEVELOPMENT: International Conference on the Relationship between Disarmament and Development in New York adopts by consensus Final Document reaffirming the international commitment to allocate a portion of the resources released through disarmament for socio-economic development, so as to bridge the gap between developed and developing countries.
Sept. 7-10	AFGHANISTAN: Afghanistan and Pakistan hold "proximity" talks in Geneva on the situation relating to Afghanistan and reduce gap between the two positions on the time-frames for troop withdrawal to 8 months.
Sept. 11-15	IRAN-IRAQ: Secretary-General meets with leaders of Iran and Iraq in visits to capitals of those nations.
Sept. 14	GENERAL ASSEMBLY: Resumed 41st regular session.
Sept. 15-Dec. 21	GENERAL ASSEMBLY: 42nd regular session.
Oct. 7	CENTRAL AMERICA: General Assembly expresses "firmest support" for the Guatemala Agreement for the establishment of peace in Central America.
Oct. 10	ECOSOC: Resumed 2nd regular session, New York.
Oct. 12	HUMAN SETTLEMENT: General Assembly observes International Year of Shelter for the Homeless and endorses a Global Strategy for Shelter to the Year 2000.
Oct. 14	KAMPUCHEA: General Assembly reiterates its conviction regarding the four principal components of any just and lasting resolution of the Kampuchean problem: (i) withdrawal of all foreign forces from Kampuchea; (ii) restoration and preservation of its independence, sovereignty and territorial integrity; (iii) the right of the Kampuchean people to determine their own destiny; and (iv) commitment by all

1987 (continued)

	States to non-interference and non-intervention in Kampuchea's internal affairs.
Oct. 19	ENVIRONMENT: Prime Minister Gro Harlem Brundtland of Norway introduces the report of the World Commission on Environment and Development to the General Assembly.
Oct. 20	AIDS: General Assembly pledges support for war against AIDS during special meeting.
	ATOMIC ENERGY: General Assembly urges all states to co-operate with IAEA to promote the use of nuclear energy and enhance the safety of nuclear installations, to strengthen technical assistance to developing countries and to ensure the effectiveness of the IAEA safeguards system.
	ECOSOC: Resumed 2nd regular session, New York.
	NAMIBIA: Council for Namibia, at its 1st ministerial-level meeting, calls for "unconditional and speedy" implementation of the UN plan for the independence of Namibia.
Oct. 22	WOMEN: 10th anniversary of the UN Development Fund for Women (UNIFEM).
Oct. 30	NAMIBIA: Security Council authorizes the Secretary-General to arrange a cease-fire between South Africa and SWAPO as the next step towards the independence of Namibia.
Nov. 5-7	SOUTH AFRICA: International Conference against *Apartheid* Sport in Harare, Zimbabwe, asks the International Olympic Committee (IOC) to adopt a code of conduct with respect to sports contact with South Africa and asks governments and concerned organizations to make maximum use of the UN Register of Sports Contacts with South Africa in acting against "collaborators with *apartheid*".
Nov. 6	NAMIBIA: General Assembly adopts five resolutions, including a rejection of attempts by Pretoria and its allies to establish a "linkage" between Namibian independence and the presence of Cuban forces in Angola.
Nov. 10	AFGHANISTAN: General Assembly calls again for an immediate withdrawal of the foreign troops from Afghanistan and asks all parties concerned to work for the "urgent achievement of a political solution" and the creation of conditions to enable the Afghan refugees to return voluntarily to their homes "in safety and honour".
	SOUTH ATLANTIC: General Assembly commends efforts by the states of the South Atlantic to promote peace and co-operation in the region and urges them to continue their actions aimed at fulfilling the goals of the 1986 Declaration of the "Zone of peace and co-operation of the South Atlantic".
Nov. 11	MAYOTTE: General Assembly reaffirms the sovereignty of the Comoros over the island of Mayotte, located in the Indian Ocean, and urges France to accelerate the process of

1987 (continued)

negotiations to ensure the "effective and prompt return" of that island to the Comoros.

Nov. 12   LEGAL: General Assembly calls for full and immediate compliance with the judgement of the International Court of Justice of 27 June 1986 concerning military and paramilitary activities in and against Nicaragua.

Nov. 17   FALKLANDS ISLANDS (MALVINAS): General Assembly asks Argentina and the UK to initiate negotiations to resolve problems pending between them regarding the future of the Falklands Islands (Malvinas).

Nov. 18   LAW OF THE SEA: General Assembly calls on all states that have not done so to ratify or accede to the UN Convention on the Law of the Sea to allow the entry into force of the new legal régime for the uses of the sea and its resources and expresses satisfaction at the registration in 1987 of the first pioneer investors - India, France, Japan and USSR.

LEGAL: General Assembly adopts 15 texts on legal issues, condemning, among other things, as criminal acts, methods and practices of terrorism and adopting a declaration on the non-use of force in international relations.

Nov. 20   SOUTH AFRICA: General Assembly adopts eight resolutions, including an urgent appeal to the Security Council to impose comprehensive mandatory sanctions against South Africa.

Nov. 25   ECOSOC: Resumed 2nd regular session, New York.

MIDDLE EAST: Security Council extends the mandate of UNDOF for six months until 31 May 1988.

SOUTH AFRICA: Security Council strongly condemns South Africa for what it calls its continuing aggression and occupation of Angola and calls for withdrawal of South African troops from that front-line state.

Nov. 30   ARMS CONTROL: General Assembly approves 62 resolutions on disarmament, of which a record number of 26 are adopted by consensus, and decides to hold the 3rd special session devoted to disarmament in 1988.

Dec. 4   DECOLONIZATION: General Assembly adopts 25 resolutions on a wide range of issues, including those on Namibia, Falklands Islands (Malvinas), New Caledonia, Western Sahara, St. Helena and 12 other small territories; activities of foreign economic and other interests; military activities by colonial powers; and implementation of the declaration on decolonization by the specialized agencies.

ECOSOC: Resumed 2nd regular session, New York.

Dec. 7   HUMAN RIGHTS: General Assembly adopts 34 texts on human right issues, including genocide and torture.

1987 (continued)

Dec. 7   REFUGEES: General Assembly adopts 13 resolutions,
              addressing, among other things, international procedures for
              the protection of refugees, the need for aid to specific
              countries handling refugee situations and support for
              scholarships for refugees from countries in southern Africa.
Dec. 8   DEVELOPMENT: General Assembly calls on the international
              community to increase monetary aid and non-concessional
              loans, stabilize commodity prices, extend more humanitarian
              aid, and enact debt-relief measures, including writing off
              some loans.
              INFORMATION: General Assembly calls for co-operation in
              establishing a new world information and communication
              order, seen as an evolving process and based, among other
              things, on the free circulation and wider and better balanced
              dissemination of information.
              MIDDLE EAST: General Assembly considers the "grave
              breaches" by Israel of the 1949 Geneva Convention relative to
              the Protection of Civilian Persons in Time of War "war
              crimes and an affront to humanity".
Dec. 10   HUMAN RIGHTS: 40th anniversary of the Human Rights Day.
Dec. 11   DEVELOPMENT: General Assembly calls on developed
              countries to refrain from using economic measures as a means
              of political and economic coercion against developing
              countries, including blockades, embargoes, and other
              economic sanctions; recommends a constructive,
              comprehensive dialogue within the UN system to develop
              improvements in the international economic system through
              reform and strengthening of principles and rules governing
              trade, monetary and financial relations within which countries
              operate; calls for innovative approaches to reduce the debt
              burden of developing countries; and stresses intensified efforts
              to help African countries, least developed and poorest
              developing countries.
              ENVIRONMENT: General Assembly adopts the major
              document "Environmental Perspective to the Year 2000 and
              Beyond" to guide governments in helping to achieve
              environment-sound development in the area of population,
              food and agriculture, energy, industry, health and human
              settlement, and international economic relations.
              MIDDLE EAST: General Assembly approves four resolutions,
              again endorsing an international peace conference under UN
              auspices.
Dec. 14-16   TRUSTEESHIP COUNCIL: Resumed 44th regular session.
Dec. 14   CYPRUS: Security Council extends the mandate of UNFICYP
              for six months until 15 June 1988.

1987 (continued)

Dec. 20   BUDGET: General Assembly approves a program budget of
            $1,770.0 billion for the biennium 1988-1989.

Dec. 22   MIDDLE EAST: Security Council strongly deplores the
            "opening of fire by the Israeli army, resulting in the killing
            and wounding of defenceless Palestinian civilians" and calls
            for the exercise of "maximum restraint" to contribute towards
            the establishment of peace.

Dec. 23   SOUTH AFRICA: Security Council condemns the delay in
            withdrawal of South African troops from Angola and asks the
            Secretary-General to continue monitoring the withdrawal.

Dec. 24   IRAN-IRAQ: Security Council expresses "grave concern" over
            slow pace and lack of real progress on Iran-Iraq talks.

1988

Jan. 1   DEVELOPMENT: Start of the World Decade for Cultural
            Development (1988-1997).

Jan. 5   MIDDLE EAST: Security Council strongly requests Israel, as
            the occupying Power, to abide by its obligations arising from
            the 1949 4th Geneva Convention relative to the Protection of
            Civilian Persons in Time of War.

Jan. 14   MIDDLE EAST: Security Council expresses "deep regret" at
            continued deportations and calls on Israel to ensure the safe
            and immediate return of the already deported individuals to
            those territories.

Jan. 16   CENTRAL AMERICA: Five Central American countries sign
            the Alajuela Joint Declaration in Alajuela, Costa Rica, and
            ratify the Guatemala Agreement of 7 August 1987.

Feb. 2-April 29   ARMS CONTROL: 1st part of the 1988 Conference on
            Disarmament.

Feb. 2-5   ECOSOC: Organizational meeting, New York.

Feb. 16-17 TERRORISM: Security Council considers at the requests of the
            Republic of Korea and Japan, allegations that two North
            Korean "special agents" planted a timebomb on a Korean Air
            Lines plane in November 1987, causing it to explode in mid-
            air off the coast of Burma: meeting adjourns without a draft
            resolution having been tabled.

Feb. 17   TERRORISM: Lt.-Col. William Higgins, a US national who
            heads UNTSO, is abducted in Lebanon.

Feb. 18   MIDDLE EAST: USA vetoes draft resolution of the Security
            Council which asks Israel to "cease all acts of encroachment
            of land, construction of roads and setting up of fences that
            violate the border, and any attempts to occupy or change the
            status of Lebanese territory or to impede the return of the
            effective authority of the Government of Lebanon in
            sovereign Lebanese territory".

1988 (continued)

Feb. 29-March 2 HOST COUNTRY AGREEMENT: Resumed 42nd regular session of the General Assembly considers the question of the closing of the PLO Observer Mission to the UN and asks the International Court of Justice for an advisory opinion as to whether the USA is under obligation to enter into arbitration in accordance with the 1947 Headquarters Agreement.

Feb. 29 MIDDLE EAST: Security Council extends the mandate of UNIFIL for a period of six months until 31 July 1988.

March 1 MIDDLE EAST: USA vetoes a draft resolution of the Security Council which deplores Israeli policies and practices "which violate the human rights of the Palestinian people" and calls on Israel, as the occupying Power and as a High Contracting Party to the 1949 4th Geneva Convention on Protecting Civilians in Time of War, to accept the convention's *de jure* applicability to comply with its obligations under that convention.

March 2-April 8 AFGHANISTAN: Afghanistan and Pakistan hold last round of "proximity" in Geneva on the situation in Afghanistan and complete and open for signature all instruments comprising the settlement.

March 8 SOUTH AFRICA: UK and USA veto a draft resolution of the Security Council requiring an end to further investment in and financial loans to South Africa; all forms of military, police, or intelligence co-operation with that country, in particular the sale of computer equipment; the export and sale of oil to Pretoria; all promotion of and support for trade with South Africa; importation of iron and steel; and the sale of Krugerrands and all other coins minted in South Africa.

March 11 HOST COUNTRY AGREEMENT: USA informs the Secretary-General that its 1987 Anti-Terrorism Act requires the closing of the PLO office in New York, "irrespective of any obligations the United States may have under the Agreement between the United Nations and the United States regarding the Headquarters of the United Nations".

March 16 IRAN-IRAQ: Security Council strongly deplores the escalation of hostilities between Iran and Iraq, particularly attacks against civilian targets and cities that have taken a heavy toll in human lives and have caused vast material destruction, in spite of the belligerent parties' declared readiness to cease such attacks.

SOUTH AFRICA: Security Council calls for commutation of the death sentences against six young South Africans known as the "Sharpeville Six".

March 17 FALKLANDS ISLANDS (MALVINAS): Security Council considers a complaint by Argentina about the situation created in the South Atlantic by the UK government's decision to

1988 (continued)

conduct military manoeuvres in the Falklands Islands (Malvinas) from 7 to 31 March: meeting adjourns without a draft resolution having been tabled.

March 18-23   HOST COUNTRY AGREEMENT: Resumed 42nd regular session of the General Assembly considers the question of the closing of the PLO Observer Mission to the UN and determines that the US legislation by which the PLO Mission is to be closed is "inconsistent with provisions of the Agreement and was contrary to the international legal obligations of the Host Country under the Agreement"; deplores the host country's failure to comply with those obligations; and urges it "to desist from taking any action inconsistent with the functioning of the PLO Mission".

March 18 & 22   CENTRAL AMERICA: Security Council considers what Nicaragua calls the "serious situation created by the escalation of threats and aggression" against it and by the US decision to send American troops to Honduras: meeting adjourns without a draft resolution having been tabled.

April 14   AFGHANISTAN: Afghanistan agreement is signed in the Salle du Grand Conseil of the Palais des Nations in Geneva by representatives of Afghanistan, Pakistan, USA and USSR, calling for troop withdrawal, from 15 May to 15 February 1989; voluntary return of refugees; non-interference and non-intervention by both Afghanistan and Pakistan; and international guarantees by USA and USSR.

April 15   MIDDLE EAST: USA vetoes a draft resolution of the Security Council which condemns Israeli policies and practices violating the human rights of Palestinians in the occupied territories, in particular the "killing and wounding of defenceless Palestinian civilians".

April 25   TUNISIA: Security Council condemns "aggression" against the sovereignty and territorial integrity of Tunisia, after a top leader of the PLO was assassinated at his home in a Tunis suburb.

April 26   HOST COUNTRY AGREEMENT CASE: International Court of Justice rules that the USA must submit to international arbitration regarding its decision to close the PLO Observer Mission to the UN.

April 27   AID: Pledging conference in Maputo for aid to Mozambique results in pledges of $272 million .

May 3-27   ECOSOC: 1st regular session, New York.

May 3-4   SOUTHWESTERN AFRICA: Four-nation conference (Angola, Cuba, South Africa, USA) on southwestern Africa in London results in hopeful signs on ending the war in Angola and bringing independence to Namibia.

1988 (continued)

May 9
: IRAN-IRAQ: Security Council vigorously condemns the continued use of chemical weapons in the conflict between Iran and Iraq, contrary to obligations under the 1925 Geneva Protocol prohibiting the use in war of asphyxiating, poisonous and other gases and of bacteriological methods of warfare.

May 10-June 3
: TRUSTEESHIP COUNCIL: 55th regular session.

May 10
: MIDDLE EAST: USA vetoes a draft resolution of the Security Council which condemns the "recent invasion" by Israeli forces of southern Lebanon and asks for the "cessation of all acts that violate the sovereignty of Lebanon and the security of its civilian population".

May 11-12
: CENTRAL AMERICA: Resumed 42nd regular session of the General Assembly urges the international community to increase technical, economic and financial co-operation with Central American countries.

May 13
: HOST COUNTRY AGREEMENT: Resumed 42nd regular session of the General Assembly calls on the USA to submit to international arbitration its dispute with the UN over the status of the PLO Observer Mission, in accordance with the procedure laid down in the Headquarters Agreement.

May 16
: LAW OF THE SEA: France, Japan and the USSR become pioneer investors in the International Sea-Bed Area which is considered a significant step towards putting into practice the 1982 UN Convention on the Law of the Sea.

May 17
: AID: Pledging conference for help to Angola results in pledges of $75 million.

May 27
: TRUSTEESHIP: Trusteeship Council recommends that the process of approval of the compact of Free Association for Palau - one of the four administrative entities which make up the Trust Territory of the Pacific Islands or Micronesia - be completed at the earliest possible date and notes assurance of the USA to fulfil obligations under the Charter and the Trusteeship Agreement.

May 31-June 26
: ARMS CONTROL: 3rd special session of the General Assembly on disarmament is unable to reach consensus on a Concluding Document, covering new aims and priorities in the field of disarmament, prevention of an arms race in outer space, relationship between disarmament and development, nuclear-weapon-free zones, zones of peace, South Africa's acquisition of nuclear arms, and Israel's acquisition of nuclear arms.

May 31
: MIDDLE EAST: Security Council extends the mandate of UNDOF for six months until 30 November 1988.

June 15
: CYPRUS: Security Council extends the mandate of UNFICYP for six months until 15 December 1988.

1988 (continued)

June 23	FINANCIAL CRISIS: Secretary-General tells representatives of 21 member states, including the major contributors, that the UN could face "insolvency" in late October or November unless a solution to its severe financial crisis is found.
June 24-25	SOUTHWESTERN AFRICA: Four-nation conference (Angola, Cuba, South Africa, USA) on southwestern Africa, Cairo.
June 24	SOUTHERN AFRICA: Security Council condemns "aggressive acts" by South Africa against Botswana.
June 26	DRUG: 1st observation of International Day against Drug Abuse.
June 30	HOST COUNTRY AGREEMENT: US District Court judge rules that the 1987 Anti-Terrorism Act does not require the closing of the PLO office and the USA should "refrain from impairing the function" of the PLO Mission.
July 6-29	ECOSOC: 2nd regular session, Geneva.
July 7-Sept. 20	ARMS CONTROL: 2nd part of the 1988 Conference on Disarmament ends without tangible progress on major disarmament issues, including such top-priority issues as a chemical weapons ban and a nuclear-test ban.
July 11-13	SOUTHWESTERN AFRICA: Four-nation (Angola, Cuba, South Africa, USA) conference on southwestern Africa in New York initials an agreement, which is subsequently approved by their governments, stipulating 14 "essential principles" to establish the basis for peace in the region are recognized as "indispensable to a comprehensive settlement".
July 20	USA-IRAN: Security Council expresses its "deep distress at the downing of an Iranian civil aircraft" on 3 July "by a missile fired from a United States warship" and its "profound regret over the tragic loss of innocent lives" and also expresses its "sincere condolences to the families of the victims of the tragic incident and to the peoples and Governments of their countries of origin".
July 25-28	KAMPUCHEA: 1st Jakarta Informal Meeting (JIM) between the four Kampuchean parties, the ASEAN countries, Viet Nam and Laos, Jakarta, Indonesia.
July 29	HOSTAGES: Security Council demands the immediate release of Lieutenant-Colonel William R. Higgins, Chief of the UN observer group in Lebanon, who was kidnapped while on duty on 17 February.
	MIDDLE EAST: Security Council extends the mandate of UNIFIL for six months until 31 January 1989.
July 30	DEVELOPMENT: Common Fund for Commodities enters into force, providing for a new financial institution with capital from both developing and developed countries to help finance buffer stocks of commodities in price stabilization schemes.

1988 (continued)

Aug. 2-5   SOUTHWESTERN AFRICA: Four-nation (Angola, Cuba,
                South Africa, USA) conference on southwestern Africa in
                Geneva reaches tripartite agreement between Angola, Cuba
                and South Africa, which commits South Africa to relinquish
                control of Namibia and to carry out the independence plan
                approved by the UN more than 10 years ago (Geneva
                Protocol).

Aug. 8   SOUTHWESTERN AFRICA: Angola, Cuba, South Africa and
                the USA announce in Geneva that a *de facto* cease-fire is in
                effect as a result of their approval of a number of steps aimed
                to prepare the way for the independence of Namibia in
                accordance with resolution 435; recommends to the Secretary-
                General a target date of 1 November 1988 for the beginning
                of implementation of that resolution.

Aug. 9   IRAN-IRAQ: Security Council establishes the UN Iran-Iraq
                Military Observer Group (UNIIMOG) for an initial period of
                six months to observe the 740-mile border between the two
                states.

Aug. 12   SOUTHWESTERN AFRICA: SWAPO informs the Secretary-
                General that it would comply with the cease-fire announced in
                Geneva on 8 August.

Aug. 16-17   GENERAL ASSEMBLY: Resumed 42nd regular session.

Aug. 16   DENMARK/NORWAY CASE: Denmark institutes proceedings
                with the International Court of Justice an application
                instituting proceedings against Norway regarding a dispute
                over delimitation of Denmark's and Norway's fishing zones
                and continental shelf areas in the waters between the east
                coast of Greenland and the Norwegian island of Jan Mayen.

Aug. 20   IRAN-IRAQ: UN-sponsored cease-fire between Iran and Iraq
                takes effect to end the eight-year-long conflict.

Aug. 22-24   REFUGEES: International Conference on the Plight of
                Refugees, Returnees and Displaced Persons in Southern
                Africa in Oslo adopts Declaration and Plan of Action to help
                millions of refugees in southern Africa.

Aug. 24-26   SOUTHWESTERN AFRICA: Four-nation (Angola, Cuba,
                South Africa, USA) conference on southwestern Africa,
                Brazzaville.

Aug. 24   CYPRUS: Leaders of the Greek Cypriot and Turkish Cypriot
                announce their willingness to meet without pre-conditions and
                to attempt to achieve by 1 June 1989 a negotiated settlement
                of all aspects of the Cyprus problem.

Aug. 25   IRAN-IRAQ: Iran and Iraq start direct peace in Geneva with the
                aim to achieve a comprehensive, just and honorable settlement
                of all outstanding issues.

1988 (continued)

Aug. 26	IRAN-IRAQ: Security Council asks for continued prompt investigations of future charges of possible use of chemical and bacteriological (biological) or toxin weapons that might violate the Geneva Protocol or other relevant rules of customary international law.
Aug. 30	SOUTHWESTERN AFRICA: South Africa informs the Secretary-General that it has completed withdrawal of its troops from Angola in accordance with the agreement reached in Geneva on 8 August.
	WESTERN SAHARA: Morocco and POLISARIO agree to the peace plan submitted jointly by the UN Secretary-General and the OAU Chairman.
Sept. 7-9	SOUTHWESTERN AFRICA: Four-nation (Angola, Cuba, South Africa, USA) conference on southwestern Africa, Brazzaville.
Sept. 19	GENERAL ASSEMBLY: Resumed 42nd regular session.
Sept. 20-Dec. 22	GENERAL ASSEMBLY: 43rd regular session.
Sept. 20	WESTERN SAHARA: Security Council calls on the Secretary-General to appoint a Special Representative for Western Sahara and to report on the holding of the referendum and on ways to ensure its organization and supervision by the UN in co-operation with the OAU.
Sept. 22	ENVIRONMENT: Convention for the Protection of the Ozone Layer enters into force.
Sept. 26-29	SOUTHWESTERN AFRICA: Four-nation (Angola, Cuba, South Africa, USA) conference on southwestern Africa, Brazzaville.
Sept. 28	PEACE AND SECURITY: Foreign ministers of the five permanent members of the Security Council stress their continuing confidence in the UN which, they believe, has an increasingly significant role to play in the achievement of international peace and security and note with satisfaction the "marked improvement in international relations at the global level and the general trend towards dialogue and peaceful settlement of disputes" over the last year, and welcome the active involvement of the UN in that process.
Sept. 29	NOBEL PEACE PRIZE: Nobel Committee awards the 1988 Nobel Peace Prize to the UN peace-keepers.
Oct. 3	NAMIBIA: Security Council meets on 10th anniversary of resolution 435 and supports "the resolute action led by the Secretary-General" to achieve Namibian independence, noting the recent efforts, involving Angola, Cuba, South Africa and the USA, to find a peaceful solution to the conflict in southwestern Africa.

1988 (continued)

Oct. 12	AFGHANISTAN: Secretary-General launches "Operation Salam" for humanitarian and economic assistance to Afghanistan; voluntary contributions are pledged amounting to $897 million.
Oct. 14	AFGHANISTAN: Secretary-General reports that signatories to the Afghanistan peace settlement of 14 April 1988 have reported serious violations by the other side; expresses deep concern that fighting continues in Afghanistan.
Oct. 17	ECOSOC: Resumed 2nd regular session, New York.
Oct. 18-19	KOREA: North and South Korea present proposals in General Assembly on reunification.
Oct. 31	AFGHANISTAN: Security Council formalizes arrangements for 50 officers from UN peace-keeping operations to assist in monitoring implementation of the Afghanistan peace settlement of 14 April 1988.
Nov. 1-2	DEVELOPMENT: UN pledging conference for development activities results in pledges and contributions of nearly $1 billion for UNDP, $264 million for UNICEF and $114.5 million for UNFPA.
Nov. 1	LAW OF THE SEA: General Assembly calls on states that have not done so to consider ratifying or acceding to the 1982 UN Convention on the Law of the Sea at the earliest, and to "safeguard the unified character of the Convention and related resolutions".
Nov. 2	MIDDLE EAST: General Assembly adopts resolution entitled "the uprising (intifadah) of the Palestinian people" and condemns what it termed Israel's "persistent policies and practices violating the human rights" of Palestinians in the occupied territories.
Nov. 3	AFGHANISTAN: General Assembly calls on all parties concerned to scrupulously respect and faithfully implement the Afghanistan peace settlement, signed in Geneva on 14 April 1988.
	KAMPUCHEA: General Assembly enumerates the principal components of a "just and lasting resolution of the problem", which include: withdrawal of all foreign forces form Kampuchea "under effective international supervision and control"; creation of an "interim administering authority"; promotion of national reconciliation among all Kampucheans under the leadership of Prince Norodom Sihanouk; and the "non-return to the universally condemned policies and practices of a recent past".
Nov. 10	IRAN-IRAQ: Iran and Iraq sign memorandums of understanding with the International Committee of the Red Cross (ICRC) in Geneva, concerning the first large-scale repatriation of sick and wounded prisoners of war.

1988 (continued)

Nov. 15   CENTRAL AMERICA: General Assembly expresses its strongest support for the August 1987 Guatemala Agreement for the establishment of peace in Central America and for the San José Joint Declaration, signed in Costa Rica in January 1988.

                 MIDDLE EAST: Special session of the General Assembly on the "intifadah" in the occupied territories acknowledges the proclamation of the state of Palestine by the Palestine National Council (PNC) and decides that the UN system should refer to the PLO as "Palestine".

Nov. 18   AFRICAN RECOVERY: General Assembly calls for steps to halt African economic slide and declares that African governments have the central role to play in the design and implementation of their economic adjustment programs.

Nov. 22   DECOLONIZATION: General Assembly declares the 1990s as the International Decade for the Eradication of Colonialism; asks the Secretary-General to provide the basis for an action plan aimed at ushering in the twenty-first century a world free from colonialism.

                 WESTERN SAHARA: General Assembly welcomes the efforts of the Secretary-General and the Chairman of the OAU to promote a just and definitive solution; welcomes the agreement of 30 August 1988 between the two parties to the conflict (Morocco and POLISARIO).

Nov. 25-Dec. 20   DRUGS: Plenipotentiary conference in Vienna adopts the UN Convention against Illicit Traffic in Narcotic Drugs and Psychotropic Substances, which supplements existing international instruments aiming to control the production, distribution and use of drugs worldwide.

Nov. 27   HEADQUARTER AGREEMENT: USA announces it would not grant a visa to Mr. Arafat, PLO Chairman, to address the General Assembly in New York, stating it has "convincing evidence" that PLO elements has engaged in terrorism against Americans and others.

Nov. 30   HEADQUARTER AGREEMENT: General Assembly deplores the failure to grant a visa to Mr. Arafat and urges the USA to reconsider and reverse its decision which violates the Headquarters Agreement.

Dec. 2   HEADQUARTER AGREEMENT: General Assembly deplores the failure of the USA to respond favorably to its 30 November request and decides "in the present compelling circumstances and without prejudice to normal practice" to transfer its debate on the question of Palestine to Geneva.

Dec. 5 & 9   LEGAL: General Assembly adopts three new legal instruments: (i) Declaration on the Prevention and Removal of Disputes and Situations which May Threaten International Peace and

1988 (continued)

Security and on the Role of the United Nations in this Field;
(ii) Body of Principles for the Protection of All Persons under
Any Form of Detention or Imprisonment; and (iii) Convention
on International Bills of Exchange and International
Promissory Notes.

Dec. 5   SOUTH AFRICA: General Assembly decides to convene a
          special session on *apartheid* and "its destructive consequences
          in southern Africa".

Dec. 6   ENVIRONMENT: General Assembly states that climate change
          is "a common concern of mankind", worried by the potential
          disastrous effects of the global warming and the depletion of
          the ozone layer.

Dec. 7   ARMS CONTROL: General Assembly declares the 1990s as the
          3rd Disarmament Decade and adopts a record number of
          resolutions and decision on the subject of disarmament.

          PEACE AND SECURITY: General Assembly encourages
          member states to contribute to international dialogue, in order
          to find universally acceptable ways and means of
          strengthening on a comprehensive basis the security system
          laid down in the Charter and enhance the role of the UN in
          maintaining international peace and security.

Dec. 8   HUMAN RIGHTS: General Assembly marks the 40th
          anniversary of the adoption of the Universal Declaration of
          Human Rights and mandates the UN to do more to prevent
          people from being tortured, detained in mental institutions and
          "disappearing" for political reasons, and to help them enjoy
          the right to own property as much as the right to eat, be
          housed and get an education.

Dec. 10   HUMAN RIGHTS: 40th anniversary of adoption of Universal
          Declaration of Human Rights.

          NOBEL PEACE PRIZE: Secretary-General accepts the 1988
          Noble Peace Prize to the UN peace-keeping forces in Oslo,
          stating that the prize recognized an idea of "striking
          originality and power".

Dec. 13-15 MIDDLE EAST: General Assembly debates the question of
          Palestine in Geneva in accordance with its decision of 2
          December; USA announces that it will enter into a direct
          dialogue with the PLO.

Dec. 13   SOUTHERN AFRICA: Bilateral agreement is reached between
          Angola and Cuba on a detailed timetable for the withdrawal
          of approximately 50,000 Cuban troops from Angola, in
          stages, over 27 months beginning 1 April 1989 (Protocol of
          Brazzaville).

Dec. 15   CYPRUS: Security Council extends mandate of UNFICYP for
          six months until 15 June 1989.

1988 (continued)

Dec. 15   MIDDLE EAST: General Assembly declares that the question
             of Palestine is "the core of the conflict in the Middle East";
             renews its call for an international peace conference on the
             Middle East and for Israeli withdrawal from occupied
             territories and other territories, including Jerusalem.

Dec. 20   DEVELOPMENT: General Assembly states that the negative
             effects of structural adjustment in the developing countries has
             "exacerbated poverty" and urges the establishment of a
             "supportive international economic environment for growth
             and development"; urges attack on problem of external debt
             of developing countries estimated at $1.3 trillion and
             proclaims a Second Transport and Communications Decade in
             Africa (1991-2000).

             HABITAT: General Assembly adopts the Global Strategy for
             Shelter to the Year 2000 in an effort to solve the world-wide
             housing crisis.

Dec. 21   FINANCIAL CRISIS: General Assembly urges members states
             to meet their financial obligations to the UN on time and in
             full, following a statement by the Secretary-General that the
             organization will "continue to face the very real risk of
             defaulting on its day-to-day financial commitments".

             TERRORISM: Pan Am fight 103 is destroyed by explosives
             over Lockerbie, Scotland, killing 270 people, including the
             UN Commissioner for Namibia Bernt Carlsson.

Dec. 22   ANGOLA: Security Council establishes the UN Angola
             Verification Mission (UNAVEM) for a period of 31 months
             (1 April 1989 to 1 August 1991) to monitor the withdrawal of
             Cuban troops from Angola.

             SOUTHERN AFRICA: Signing ceremony at UN Headquarters
             of Geneva Protocol of 5 August and Protocol of Brazzaville
             of 13 December; Angola and South Africa pledge co-
             operation with the UN in bringing Namibia to independence;
             Cuba pledges to withdraw all its forces from Angola, with the
             UN verifying the pullout; US Secretary of State George
             Shultz, who presides over the ceremony, states that the
             regional settlement is "a momentous turning point in the
             history of southern Africa"; Secretary-General states that all
             the signatories have committed themselves to "a sequence of
             steps necessary to achieve peace in south-western Africa and
             to open the way to the independence of Namibia".

1989

Jan. 1   ENVIRONMENT: 1987 Montreal Protocol on Substances that
             Deplete the Ozone Layer enters into force.

1989 (continued)

Jan. 3   ANGOLA: UNAVEM arrives in Angola to monitor the
                  withdrawal of the first 3,000 Cuban troops.

Jan. 7-11   ARMS CONTROL: Conference of States Parties to the 1925
                  Geneva Protocol and Other Interested States on the
                  Prohibition of Chemical Weapons in Paris reaffirms the
                  validity of the 1925 Protocol; calls for complete ban on
                  chemical weapons; stresses the need to conclude, at an early
                  date, a convention on the prohibition of the development,
                  production, stockpiling and use of all chemical weapons, and
                  on their destruction.

Jan. 11   LIBYA: France, UK and USA veto a draft resolution of the
                  Security Council which deplores the downing on 4 January of
                  two Libyan reconnaissance planes by the armed forces of the
                  USA and calls upon the USA to "suspend its military
                  manoeuvres off the Libyan coast in order to contribute to the
                  reduction of tension in the area".

Jan. 16   NAMIBIA: Security Council officially declares 1 April 1989 as
                  the day for the start of Namibia's transition to independence;
                  authorizes sending the UN Transition Assistance Group
                  (UNTAG) to Namibia; calls for a reevaluation of the needs
                  for UNTAG: subsequent controversy over whether and how
                  to scale down the operation delayed approval of plan by the
                  Security Council to 16 February.

Jan. 23   NAMIBIA: Security Council confirms that the "principles
                  concerning the Constituent Assembly and the Constitution for
                  an independent Namibia", approved by the Security Council
                  in 1982, remains binding on the parties.

Jan. 30   MIDDLE EAST: Security Council extends mandate of UNIFIL
                  for a period of six months until 31 July 1989.

Feb. 7-April 27   ARMS CONTROL: 1st part of 1989 Conference on
                  Disarmament, Geneva.

Feb. 8   IRAN-IRAQ: Security Council extends mandate of UNIIMOG
                  until 30 September 1989.

Feb. 9-10   ECOSOC: Organizational session, New York.

Feb. 14-March 7   ECONOMIC DEVELOPMENT: Resumed 43rd regular session
                  of the General Assembly approves special session on
                  international economic co-operation from 23 to 27 April
                  1990.
                  PEACE-KEEPING: Resumed 43rd regular session of the
                  General Assembly approves $416 million for UNTAG and
                  another $9.2 million for UNAVEM.

Feb. 14   CENTRAL AMERICA: Central American Presidents sign Costa
                  Del Sol Joint Declaration in Costa del Sol, El Salvador,
                  entrusting the UN with the tasks of verification of elements of
                  the peace agreement signed in Esquipulas, Guatemala, in
                  August 1987, monitoring the 1990 election in Nicaragua and

1989 (continued)

	helping with the demobilization and voluntary repatriation or relocation of members of the Nicaraguan resistance and their families currently in Honduras.
Feb. 15	AFGHANISTAN: USSR troops are completely withdrawn from Afghanistan.
Feb. 16	NAMIBIA: Security Council gives the go-ahead to the Namibia independence plan and UNTAG operation, setting the starting date of 1 April 1989 and including: release of political prisoners, repeal of discriminatory laws, withdrawal of South African soldiers, return of refugees, registration drive and electoral campaign around 1 July, election to Constituent Assembly around 1 to 8 November 1989, independence day and end of UNTAG mission by April 1990.
	SOUTHERN AFRICA: Security Council welcomes and fully supports the tripartite and bilateral agreements between Angola, Cuba and South Africa; calls on all parties to co-operate in their implementation.
Feb. 17	MIDDLE EAST: USA vetoes a draft resolution of the Security Council which strongly deplores Israel's "persistent policies and practices" against Palestinians in the occupied territories, "especially the violation of human rights, and in particular the opening of fire that has resulted in injuries and deaths of Palestinian civilians, including children".
	NAMIBIA: UN advance party arrives in Windhoek.
Feb. 19-21	KAMPUCHEA: 2nd Jakarta Informal Meeting (JIM) between the four Kampuchean parties, the ASEAN countries, Viet Nam and Laos in Jakarta, Indonesia, concurs that a cease-fire will take effect on the date of entry into force of an agreement on the solution of Kampuchea question and that immediately afterwards, all Vietnamese troops, military advisers and personnel, armaments and other materials will be withdrawn by a target date of 30 September 1989.
March 5-7	ENVIRONMENT: Conference on the Saving the Ozone Layer, London.
March 16-17	TRUSTEESHIP COUNCIL: 19th special session approves a two-member visiting mission to observe current conditions in Palau, one of four administrative entities of the Trust Territory of the Pacific Islands (Micronesia).
March 20-22	ENVIRONMENT: Conference at Basel adopts Convention on the Control of Transboundary Movements of Hazardous Waste and Their Disposal.
March 28	NAMIBIA: UN Council for Namibia decides that until the UN independence plan for Namibia is implemented, its own mandate remains unfulfilled.

1989 (continued)

March 31   CENTRAL AMERICA: Five Central American governments
               formally request the UN to set up an observer force, known
               as UN Observer Group in Central America (ONUCA), to
               verify the end of assistance to irregular forces and
               insurrectionist movements operating in the region and the
               non-use of the territory of one country for the purpose of
               attacking or destabilizing others; Honduras signs on the
               condition that Nicaragua drops its case against Honduras
               before the International Court of Justice.

April 1   NAMIBIA: Start of transition process; official cease-fire takes
               effect; reports of armed incursions and clashes between
               SWAPO and local police in northern Namibia are received.
               RELIEF: UN launches "Operation Lifeline Sudan", a massive
               humanitarian effort to deliver food and emergency supplies
               before the onset of the rainy season to at least 2.2 million
               citizens of a country beset by continuing civil strife and
               natural calamities.

April 2   NAMIBIA: South Africa informs Secretary-General of SWAPO
               border crossings into northern Namibia, stating that a grave
               situation has arisen as a result of "continued and escalating
               violation" by SWAPO of the tripartite agreements signed in
               December 1988; SWAPO states that its members have been
               strictly ordered to observe the cease-fire and have only
               responded in self-defence when attacked inside Namibia by
               South African soldiers.

April 4   NAMIBIA: African Group of UN member countries asks the
               Secretary-General to ensure that South African troops are
               confined to base; South Africa states that unless active and
               effective measures are taken to stem the rapid deterioration of
               the situation, the whole peace process in Namibia "is in
               danger of collapse".

April 5   KAMPUCHEA: Viet Nam states that it would withdraw all its
               forces from Kampuchea by the end of September 1989, by
               which time foreign interference in Kampuchea's internal
               affairs and all foreign military aid to all Kampuchean parties
               must cease.

April 8   NAMIBIA: SWAPO announces that its leadership has ordered
               its troops inside Namibia "to stop fighting, regroup and report
               to Angola within 72 hours under the escort of UNTAG".

April 9   NAMIBIA: Joint Commission composed of representatives of
               Angola, Cuba and South Africa, with the USA and USSR as
               observers adopt the "Mt. Etjo Declaration", calling for
               "restoration of the situation in existence on 31 March", with
               SWAPO forces leaving Namibia at specified border assembly

1989 (continued)

	points under UNTAG supervision, to be transferred to bases north of the 16th parallel in Angola.
April 10-17	TRUSTEESHIP: Two-member mission visits Palau to observe the current conditions.
April 11-26	AFGHANISTAN: Security Council considers Afghan complaint against Pakistan: meeting adjourns without a draft resolution having been tabled.
April 13-23	IRAN-IRAQ: Iran and Iraq hold direct talks in Geneva, aiming at achieving a final peace.
April 20	MIDDLE EAST: Resumed 43rd session of the General Assembly condemns "the killing and wounding of defenceless Palestinian civilians, and specifically the latest action of members of the Israeli armed forces against the defenceless civilians in the Palestinian town of Nahhalin" and asks the Security Council to urgently consider international measures to protect Palestinian civilians in the Palestinian territory occupied by Israel, including Jerusalem.
April 24	LEBANON: Security Council urges all parties to the conflict "to respond favorably" to cease-fire appeals and reiterates full support for action by a ministerial committee of the League of Arab States "to put an end to the loss of human lives, to alleviate the sufferings of the Lebanese people and to achieve an effective cease-fire indispensable for a settlement of the Lebanese crisis".
April 26	REFORM: Secretary-General reports that despite unfavorable circumstances resulting from the financial crisis of the UN, progress has been made in the UN reform process set in motion in 1985 by the "Group of 18".
April 28	PANAMA: Panama complains before the Security Council that the USA was "meddling" in its elections, scheduled for 7 May.
May 2-26	ECOSOC: 1st regular session, New York.
May 2	ENVIRONMENT: 81 nations and the European Community agree in Helsinki, Finland, to a total banning of certain ozone-killing chemicals by the year 2000 or sooner.
May 6	ENVIRONMENT: Eight Amazonian countries declare that international concern about the environment in that part of the world should be translated into financial and technological aid; promise to give "full political impetus" to the sustainable development of the Amazon region.
May 7	PANAMA: USA states that the Noriega régime has "nullified the election and resorted to violence and bloodshed" after trying to steal it "through massive fraud and intimidation".
May 9	EAST TIMOR: Indonesia and Portugal resume talks on the question of East Timor under the auspices of the Secretary-General.

1989 (continued)

May 15-Aug. 1   TRUSTEESHIP COUNCIL: 56th regular session notes report
                  that the "overwhelming majority" of the citizens of Palau
                  preferred free association with the USA as its future political
                  status and expresses its hope that a recent agreement on
                  economic and social assistance for Palau with its
                  administering authority, the USA, would expedite the
                  approval process for the proposed Compact of Free
                  Association.

May 24   NAMIBIA: Security Council expresses satisfaction that the
                  situation in Namibia "now seemed to be returning to normal"
                  and that the way has been cleared for the independence
                  process.

May 29-31   REFUGEES: International Conference on Central American
                  Refugees in Guatemala City adopts declaration which
                  recognizes that solutions to the refugee problem are an
                  integral part of the effort for peace, democracy and
                  development in the region; adopts Concerted Plan of Action
                  which links aid to affected populations to the region's
                  economic and social development objective.

May 30   MIDDLE EAST: Security Council extends mandate of UNDOF
                  for six months until 30 November 1990.

May 31   CYPRUS: Secretary-General reports that the talks between the
                  two sides, which begun in August 1988, have "progressed to
                  the point where the contours of an overall agreement are
                  discernible" and have "brought out a number of specific ideas
                  that could go a long way in resolving major issues".

June 8   MIDDLE EAST: USA vetoes a draft resolution of the Security
                  Council, strongly deploring Israeli policies and practices
                  "which violate the human rights of the Palestinian people in
                  the occupied territory".

June 9   CYPRUS: Security Council extends mandate of UNFICYP for
                  six months.

June 13-Aug. 31   ARMS CONTROL: 2nd part of 1989 Conference on
                  Disarmament in Geneva reports only limited progress on a
                  chemical weapons ban.

June 13-14   REFUGEES: International Conference on Indochinese Refugees
                  adopts comprehensive Plan of Action and calls for a lasting
                  multilateral solution to the continuing problem of refugees and
                  asylum-seekers form Viet Nam and Laos.

June 14   TERRORISM: Security Council calls upon all states to co-
                  operate in devising and implementing measures to prevent all
                  acts of terrorism, including those involving explosives and
                  urges all states, in particular the producers of plastic or sheet
                  explosives, to intensify research into means of making such
                  explosives more easily detectable.

1989 (continued)

June 19	ECONOMIC DEVELOPMENT: UN agreement setting up a Common Fund for Commodities comes into force (Common Fund aims to establish a mechanism to financing buffer stocks, in order to contain price fluctuations in the trade in basic commodities).
June 26	CENTRAL AMERICA: Secretary-General reports to the Security Council that plans to send a UN observer force to Central America are "in suspense", indicating that the political climate in the region has deteriorated and, in some cases, there has been a resurgence of violence; reports that the UN is taking the first steps to monitor the 1990 elections in Nicaragua, as requested by the Costa del Sol summit in 14 February.
July 3-23	NAMIBIA: Registration of voters as part of the UN-supervised independence process.
July 5-28	ECOSOC: 2nd regular session, Geneva.
July 18	NAURU/AUSTRALIA CASE: International Court of Justice fixes time-limits for written proceedings in the case brought by Nauru in May 1989 against Australia, regarding a dispute over rehabilitation of phosphate lands mined under Australian administration before Nauruan independence.
July 19	NAMIBIA: Secretary-General arrives in Windhoek, Namibia, promising to do everything in his power to help Namibia achieve independence "in conditions of peace and security for all".
July 20	USA/ITALY CASE: International Court of Justice rejects allegations by the USA that Italian authorities, through their acts and omissions in respect of the company ELSI, have violated provisions of a 1948 Treaty of Friendship, Commerce and Navigation; reparation claims are rejected (the French company ELSI, is wholly owned by two US corporations).
July 27	CENTRAL AMERICA: Security Council establishes the UN Observer Mission for the Verification of Elections in Nicaragua (ONUVEN) to verify that political parties in Nicaragua enjoy complete freedom of organization and mobilization without hindrance or intimidation and that the electoral rolls are properly drawn.
July 30-Aug. 30	CAMBODIA: International Conference on Peace in Cambodia in Paris reaches no agreement on a global settlement, but clears the way towards peace in that country.
July 31	LEBANON: Security Council extends mandate of UNIFIL for six months until 31 January 1990; condemns hostage-taking and abductions.

1989 (continued)

July 31   TERRORISM: Secretary-General expresses "outrage and revulsion" at the murder of Lt.-Col. William Higgins, a US national who headed UNTSO, and was abducted in Lebanon on 17 February 1988.

Aug. 3   AFGHANISTAN: Secretary-General expresses grave concern over the latest escalation of fighting in Afghanistan, the danger of its spreading and the continued suffering of the Afghan people.

Aug. 7   CENTRAL AMERICA: Five Central American Presidents sign the Tela Declaration in Tela, Honduras, ratifying the Guatemala Agreement (7 August 1987), the Alajuela Declaration (16 January 1988) and the Costa del Sol Joint Declaration (14 February 1989); endorsing Joint Plan for the voluntary demobilization, repatriation or relocation "of the members of the Nicaraguan resistance and their families" and for assistance "in the voluntary demobilization of the members of the FMLN" (El Salvador); providing for the creation by the UN and OAS of the International Support and Verification Commission (CIAV).

Aug. 11   PANAMA: Panama complains to the Security Council that recent "hostile acts" by the USA have worsened the crisis between the two countries: meeting adjourns without a draft resolution having been tabled.

Aug. 14   CENTRAL AMERICA: Five Central American countries ask the UN and the OAS to set up the International Support and Verification Commission (CIAV).

Aug. 15   LEBANON: Security Council urgently appeals for a cease-fire by all parties in Lebanon and supports the peace efforts of the Arab Tripartite Committee (Algeria, Morocco, Saudi Arabia).

Aug. 23   GUINEA-BISSAU/SENEGAL CASE: Guinea-Bissau begins proceedings against Senegal at the International Court for Justice regarding a dispute over the maritime delimitation between the two countries.

Aug. 25   CENTRAL AMERICA: International Support and Verification Commission (CIAV) is established; the joint UN/OAS operation is asked to collect the "weapons, *matériel* and military equipment of members of the Nicaraguan resistance and to keep them in its custody".

Aug. 29   NAMIBIA: Security Council demands the disbandment of all paramilitary and ethnic forces in Namibia, in particular the counter-insurgency unit Koevoet, and the dismantling of their command structures, as required by the UN independence plan.

1989 (continued)

Aug. 30	MIDDLE EAST: Security Council deeply regrets the continuing deportation by Israel of Palestinian civilians from occupied Palestinian territories and calls for the safe and immediate return of those deported.
Sept. 8	FINANCIAL CRISIS: Secretary-General announces that the UN financial crisis continues with outstanding contributions to the regular budget exceeding $688 million and to peace-keeping operations exceeding $661 million.
Sept. 15	NAMIBIA: Members of the Security Council strongly condemn the assassination in Windhoek of SWAPO official Anton Lubowski.
Sept. 18	GENERAL ASSEMBLY: Resumed 43rd regular session.
Sept. 19-Dec. 29	GENERAL ASSEMBLY: 44th regular session.
Sept. 19-29	ARMS CONTROL: 3rd Review Conference of the Parties to the Treaty on the Prohibition of the Emplacement of Nuclear Weapons and Other Weapons of Mass Destruction on the Sea-Bed and the Ocean Floor and in the Subsoil Thereof, Geneva.
Sept. 19-28	SEA-BED: 3rd Review Conference on Operation of Sea-Bed Treaty in Geneva adopts declaration, asking the Conference on Disarmament to "proceed promptly" with consideration of further disarmament measures "to prevent an arms race on the sea-bed, the ocean floor and the subsoil thereof".
Sept. 19	IRAN-IRAQ: Secretary-General announces that Iran and Iraq have agreed to a round of "shuttle negotiations" between the two sides; says that he was optimistic because both countries wanted and needed peace.
Sept. 21-26	KAMPUCHEA: According to Viet Nam, all troops are withdrawn.
Sept. 23	LEBANON: USA and USSR issue a joint statement expressing their "deep concern" over the absence of peace and a settlement in Lebanon and urging a continued search for a political solution.
Sept. 29	IRAN-IRAQ: Security Council extends mandate of UNIIMOG until 31 March 1990.
	POLITICAL CLIMATE: Permanent members of the Security Council state that the UN has an important role to play "at the present time of positive change in the international political climate from confrontation to relaxation and interaction among States".
Oct. 18	MAYOTTE: General Assembly urges France to accelerate the process of negotiations to ensure the "effective and prompt" return of the island of Mayotte to the Comoros.
Oct. 19	FALKLANDS ISLANDS (MALVINAS): Argentina and UK state that all hostilities between them have ceased and that neither will pursue claims against the other.

1989 (continued)

Oct. 23   CENTRAL AMERICA: General Assembly expresses strongest support for the peace process in Central America and fully supports the Secretary-General's efforts in that regard.

Oct. 24   KAMPUCHEA: Secretary-General reports "unprecedented momentum" in the process of dialogue and negotiations.

Oct. 31   NAMIBIA: Security Council reiterates its demand for the complete disbandment of "all remaining paramilitary and ethnic forces and commando units, in particular the Koevoet and the South West Africa Territorial Forces".

Nov. 1   AFGHANISTAN: General Assembly calls for "scrupulous respect" for and faithful implementation of the Geneva Accords concluded on 14 April 1988 by all parties concerned.

CENTRAL AMERICA: Nicaragua unilaterally suspends the cease-fire in place since March 1988, after denouncing what it described as attacks and massive border infiltrations by Nicaraguan resistance forces.

DRUGS: General Assembly calls for a special session to spearhead the international fight against drug abuse and narcotics trafficking to rally international efforts to counter the drug scourge as a matter of urgency.

FALKLANDS ISLANDS (MALVINAS): General Assembly defers question, following the agreement between Argentina and the UK to resume a dialogue.

Nov. 3   NAMIBIA: Security Council expresses "profound concern" over the potential implications for the elections of what the Secretary-General calls "fraudulent" an alleged UNTAG reports regarding an imminent invasion into Namibia from Angola by SWAPO.

Nov. 7-11   NAMIBIA: UNTAG monitors elections; 97 per cent voter turnout; elections are declared "free and fair".

Nov. 7   CENTRAL AMERICA: Security Council establishes a 260-strong military UN Observer Group in Central America (ONUCA, after its Spanish acronym) to verify the cessation of aid to irregular forces and the non-use of the territory of one state for attacks on other states for an initial period of six months.

MIDDLE EAST: USA vetoes a draft resolution of the Security Council, strongly deploring Israeli policies and practices "which violate the human rights of the Palestinian people in the occupied territory"; calling upon Israel to "desist from committing such practices and actions and lift its siege", and urging that Israel returns the "illegally and arbitrarily confiscated property to its owners".

Nov. 11   NAMIBIA: In response to allegations that SWAPO detained Namibians in camps in Angola and Zambia, the UN, following a mission to the area, reports that it has found no

1989 (continued)

detainees there and that it could not account for 315 of the more than 1,100 individuals originally reported missing or detained.

Nov. 13 CENTRAL AMERICA: Secretary-General states that the situation in El Salvador has "seriously deteriorated" and talks between the government and the FMLN in which a UN representative has been involved "seemed to be in jeopardy".

Nov. 14 SOUTH ATLANTIC: General Assembly calls on all states to help promote the objectives of the 1986 Declaration of the Zone of Peace and Co-operation of the South Atlantic and to refrain from any action which might create or aggravate situations of tension and potential conflict in the region.

Nov. 15 PEACE AND SECURITY: General Assembly calls for a strengthening of the UN role in maintaining international peace and security; in a powerful symbol of the end of the cold war, the USA and USSR, for the first time in history, jointly propose a political resolution.

Nov. 16 KAMPUCHEA: General Assembly enumerates the principal components of a "just, lasting and comprehensive political settlement" of the problem, including (i) withdrawal of all foreign forces, under supervision and control of the UN; (ii) creation of an interim administering authority; (iii) promotion of national reconciliation among all Kampucheans under the leadership of Prince Norodom Sihanouk; and (iv) the non-return to the universally condemned policies and practices of a recent past.

MIDDLE EAST: Secretary-General reports that "sufficient agreement does not exist, either within the Security Council or among the parties to the conflict, to permit the convening" of an international peace conference on the Middle East.

Nov. 17 LEGAL: General Assembly declares the period 1990-1999 as the UN Decade of International Law, thus heeding a growing world-wide recognition of the need to strengthen the rule of law in international relations.

Nov. 20 CHILDREN: General Assembly adopts the Convention on the Rights of the Child, a universal standard against which children's basic rights will be measured throughout the world.

LAW OF THE SEA: General Assembly calls on all states to safeguard the unified character of the 1982 UN Convention on the Law of the Sea and invites all states to make "renewed efforts to facilitate universal participation in the Convention".

NAMIBIA: Security Council congratulates the people of Namibia on the elections held and reaffirms that the UN will continue to play an important role in supervising the transition to independence.

1989 (continued)

Nov. 22   MIDDLE EAST: Secretary-General reports that "valuable time is passing" in the Middle East and the "willingness to negotiate that exists today may be eroded by bitterness resulting from events on the ground".

SOUTH AFRICA: General Assembly adopts 12 resolutions on the policies of *apartheid*, urging a mandatory oil embargo, and deploring rescheduling of South African debt and continued collaboration with South Africa in the military, nuclear intelligence and technology fields.

Nov. 29   MIDDLE EAST: Security Council extends the mandate of UNDOF for six months until 31 May 1990.

Dec. 4 & 6   MIDDLE EAST: General Assembly calls once again for the convening of an international peace conference on the Middle East; reaffirms its conviction that the question of Palestine is the core of the conflict in the region and condemns what it terms Israeli "persistent policies and practices" violating the human rights of Palestinians in the occupied territories.

Dec. 4   TERRORISM: General Assembly condemns as criminal and not justifiable "all acts, methods and practices of terrorism wherever and by whomever committed" and calls on all states to refrain from organizing, instigating, assisting or participating in terrorist acts in other states.

Dec. 5   CENTRAL AMERICA: Secretary-Generals of UN and OAS inform the Central American presidents that "much to their regret and for reasons beyond their control" they have been unable to set in motion the Joint Plan to demobilize the Nicaraguan resistance, adopted by the presidents at Tela, Honduras, on 7 August 1989.

Dec. 6   LITERACY: General Assembly launches the 1990 International Literacy Year to eliminate illiteracy and functional illiteracy, targeting in particular rural areas and urban slums, women and girls and populations with special educational needs.

Dec. 7   CYPRUS: Secretary-General states that a basis exists for "effective negotiations" leading to an overall agreement on Cyprus, provided the leaders of the Greek Cypriot and Turkish Cypriot sides "manifest the necessary goodwill and recognize that a viable solution must satisfy the legitimate interests of both communities".

Dec. 8   FAMILY: General Assembly proclaims 1994 as International Year of the Family to highlight global awareness of family issues and the improvement of national mechanisms directed at tackling serious family-related problems.

FINANCIAL CRISIS: Secretary-General reports that throughout 1989 the possibility of imminent bankruptcy has been a source of grave concern to him.

1989 (continued)

Dec. 8   MIDDLE EAST: General Assembly adopts 11 resolutions,
concerning Palestine refugees; calling for guarantees of the
legal and human rights of refugees; covering issues such as
resettlement and housing, compensation for lost property,
education; and extending the mandate of UNRWA until 30
June 1993.

SOCIAL DEVELOPMENT: General Assembly commemorates
the 20th anniversary of the proclamation in 1969 of the
Declaration on Social Progress and Development.

SPACE: General Assembly proclaims 1992 the International
Space Year, with international co-operation for the benefit
and in the interests of all states.

Dec. 10-12   CENTRAL AMERICA: Summit of five Central American
presidents in San Isidro de Coronado, Costa Rica, adopts a
declaration, requesting an expansion of the mandate of
ONUCA to give it direct responsibility for demobilizing
irregular forces in the region in order to prevent the supply of
weapons both to the Nicaraguan resistance and to FMLN in
El Salvador and to verify any cease-fire.

Dec. 11   DECOLONIZATION: General Assembly states that colonialism
in all its forms poses a serious threat to international peace
and security and is incompatible with the UN Charter, the
Universal Declaration of Human Rights and the 1960
Declaration on Decolonization.

WESTERN SAHARA: General Assembly welcomes the efforts
of the Secretary-General of the UN and the Chairman of the
OAU to promote a just and lasting solution to the question of
Western Sahara; stresses the importance of the agreement in
principle by the two parties to the conflict (Morocco and
POLISARIO).

Dec. 12-14   SOUTH AFRICA: 16th special session of the General Assembly
adopts Declaration on *Apartheid* and its Destructive
Consequences in Southern Africa.

Dec. 14   CYPRUS: Security Council extends mandate of UNFICYP for
six months until 15 June 1990.

Dec. 15   ARMS CONTROL: General Assembly recommends that a
conference of states parties to the 1963 partial test-ban treaty
be convened in two sessions, in 1990 and 1991, to convert
that agreement into a comprehensive ban on all nuclear-
weapon testing, including underground explosions; adopts
three texts on the subject of developments in USSR-USA
bilateral disarmament negotiations; asks that high priority be
given to work on a convention to ban development,
production, stockpiling and use of chemical weapons.

1989 (continued)

Dec. 15   CENTRAL AMERICA: General Assembly condemns the
           murder of Father Ignacio Ellacuria, Rector of the Central
           American University, as well as other Jesuit priests in El
           Salvador as a "brutal assassination".
           DEATH PENALTY: General Assembly adopts 2nd Optional
           Protocol to the International Covenant on Civil and Political
           Rights, which calls for states parties to commit themselves to
           take measures to abolish the death penalty within their
           jurisdictions.
           REFUGEES: General Assembly condemns violations of the
           rights and safety of refugees and asylum-seekers, in particular
           those perpetrated by military or armed attacks against refugee
           camps and settlements, forced recruitment into armed forces
           and other forms of violence.

Dec. 18   WOMEN: General Assembly commemorates the 10th
           anniversary of the adoption of the Convention on the
           Elimination of All Forms of Discrimination against Women.

Dec. 20   PANAMA: USA informs the Security Council that its
           intervention in Panama was an act of self-defence to protect
           American lives and the integrity of the Panama Canal
           Treaties.

Dec. 21   BUDGET: General Assembly approves by consensus program
           budget of $1,974.6 million for the biennium 1990-1991.
           CENTRAL AMERICA: Secretary-General expresses hope that
           the cycle of great expectations and deep disappointments that
           which has characterized the peace process in the region will
           finally be broken.

Dec. 22   DEVELOPMENT: General Assembly proclaims the 2nd
           Industrial Development Decade for Africa (1991-2000), notes
           the "serious social consequences" and "unsatisfactory rates of
           growth of output and development" that accompany the debt
           burden and calls for "a durable solution to the debt problems"
           in developing countries.
           ENVIRONMENT: General Assembly agrees to convene a world
           conference in Brazil in 1992 ("Earth Summit") on ways to
           encourage environmentally sound development and agrees to
           draft as soon as possible a convention to protect the Earth's
           climate for adoption at the conference in Brazil.
           NATURAL DISASTER: General Assembly designates the
           1990s as the International Decade for Natural Disaster
           Reduction (1990-1999) and agrees to observe the first
           Wednesday of October as the International Day for Natural
           Disaster Reduction.
           TRADE AND DEVELOPMENT: General Assembly adopts
           seven resolution on the needs and problems of land-locked
           developing countries, eliminating the use of coercive

1989 (continued)

	economic measures, an international code of conduct on transfer of technology and the trade embargo against Nicaragua.
Dec. 23	PANAMA: France, UK and USA veto a draft resolution of the Security Council which demands the immediate cessation of the UN intervention in Panama and the withdrawal of its armed forces.
Dec. 29	PANAMA: General Assembly demands "the immediate cessation of the intervention and the withdrawal from Panama of the armed invasion forces of the United States", it also strongly deplores the intervention, calling it "a flagrant violation of international law and of the independence, sovereignty and territorial integrity of States".

1990

Jan. 1	DECOLONIZATION: Start of the International Decade for the Eradication of Colonialism (1990-1999).
	DISASTER: Start of the International Decade for Natural Disaster Reduction (1990-1999).
	LAW: Start of the UN Decade of International Law 1990-1999).
	LITERACY: Start of the International Literacy Year (1990).
Jan. 8	TRUSTEESHIP COUNCIL: 20th special session.
Jan. 9	MIDDLE EAST: Secretary-General calls for a "fully concerted and well co-ordinated" international effort to help parties to the Arab-Israeli conflict to enter into an effective negotiating process aimed at securing a comprehensive, just and lasting peace in the Middle East.
Jan. 11	AFGHANISTAN: Security Council extends the mandate of UNGOMAP for two months until 15 March.
Jan. 15-16	KAMBODIA: Permanent members of the Security Council (China, France, UK, USA, USSR) in Paris set out 17 principles to guide their work towards a resolution of the problem of Kambodia, including a UN-verified withdrawal of foreign forces, a cease-fire and cessation of outside military assistance.
Jan. 17	ECOSOC: Organizational session, New York.
	NICARAGUA: USA vetoes a draft resolution of the Security Council which declares the search by US military forces of the residence of the Ambassador of Nicaragua in Panama as "a violation of the privileges and immunities recognized under international law".
Jan. 26	CHILDREN: 59 governments sign the Convention on the Rights of the Child at a ceremony held at UN Headquarters.

1990 (continued)

Jan. 31-Feb. 10   TRUSTEESHIP: UN visiting mission to observe a plebiscite in Palau reports that 60.8 per cent voted favor of the Compact of Free Association with the USA, that the referendum was conducted freely, fairly and in accordance with the rules, and that its results reflected "the freely expressed wishes of the people of Palau".

Jan. 31   MIDDLE EAST: Security Council extends the mandate of UNIFIL for six months until 31 July 1990; reiterates strong support for the territorial integrity, sovereignty and independence of Lebanon within its internationally recognized boundaries.

Feb. 6-April 24   ARMS CONTROL: 1st part of 1990 session of the Conference on Disarmament devotes work on a nuclear-test ban and on elaboration of a multi-lateral convention on chemical weapons.

Feb. 6-8   ECOSOC: Organizational session, New York.

Feb. 9   CUBA: Security Council considers a complaint by Cuba about an "armed attack" by the USA on 31 January on a Panama-registered merchant ship manned by Cuban nationals: meeting adjourns without a draft resolution having been tabled.

Feb. 11-12   CAMBODIA: Permanent members of the Security Council (China, France, UK, USA, USSR) discuss the modalities of peace-keeping, including military aspects, and an administrative structure during the interim period.

Feb. 11   SOUTH AFRICA: Black South African political leader Nelson Mandela is released from prison.

Feb. 14-15   FALKLANDS ISLANDS (MALVINAS): Argentina and UK in Madrid decide to re-establish diplomatic relations and agree on a set of confidence-building measures.

Feb. 15   DRUGS: Presidents of Bolivia, Colombia, Peru and USA in Cartagena de Indias, Colombia, agree that the war against drugs has to be simultaneously waged on three equally important fronts - demand reduction, consumption and supply; USA commits itself to financially support alternative development, designed to replace the coca economy in Peru and Bolivia and illicit drug trafficking in all three Andean countries.

Feb. 20-23   DRUGS: 17th special session of the General Assembly on drugs proclaims a UN Decade against Drug Abuse (1991-2000) and adopts a Political Declaration and a Global Program of Action against the drug scourge, emphasizing the need to prevent the diversion of precursor chemicals and equipment used in the manufacture of narcotic drugs and the need to aide transit countries in controlling illicit trafficking.

1990 (continued)

Feb. 25	NICARAGUA: UN-monitored election take place "without intimidation or violence"; election are declared as "free and fair".
Feb. 25-March 1	CAMBODIA: Informal Meeting on Cambodia in Jakarta reaches common understanding among all concerned, notably the Cambodian parties, regarding the establishment of a Supreme National Council and the UN role in the settlement process.
Feb. 27	IRAN-IRAQ: Security Council expresses full support for the Secretary-General's efforts to hold "appropriately structured direct talks" between Iran and Iraq under this auspices.
March 2	GUINEA-BISSAU/SENEGAL CASE: International Court of Justice dismisses the request of Guinea-Bissau for the indication of provisional measures in its dispute with Senegal; the case, instituted by Guinea-Bissau on 23 August 1989, concerns the status of a decision given by an arbitral tribunal in a dispute over the maritime delimitation between the two countries.
March 12-13	CAMBODIA: Permanent members of the Security Council (China, France, UK, USA, USSR) in Paris call for comprehensive political settlement leading to an early restoration of peace and a neutral political environment for elections; suggest that during the period leading to the election, a Supreme National Council, agreed on by the four Cambodian parties, be established as a unique legitimate body in which "national sovereignty and unity should be enshrined"; agree in principle on an "enhanced United Nations role in the resolution of the Cambodian problem", including the creation of a UN Transition Authority in Cambodia (UNTAC), given the need for a neutral administration in the country during the transitional period.
March 12	CYPRUS: Security Council calls on the leaders of the two communities in Cyprus to pursue their efforts to reach freely a mutually acceptable solution of the problem, providing for a bi-communal, bi-zonal federation, in line with their 1977 and 1979 high-level agreement.
	GENERAL ASSEMBLY: Resumed 44th regular session.
March 15-29	MIDDLE EAST: Security Council reviews the situation in the occupied Arab territories, focusing on reports that recent immigrants to Israel from the USSR were being settled in those territories.
March 15	AFGHANISTAN: Secretary-General establishes the Office of the Secretary-General in Afghanistan and Pakistan (OSGAP), following the termination of the mandate of UNGOMAP, so as to continue with his good offices mission.
	HAITI: Haiti's president requests UN assistance to help organize elections, including the sending of observers.

1990 (continued)

March 21   NAMIBIA: Country becomes independent; Secretary-General
            swears in Namibia's first President.
March 23   NICARAGUA: President-elect Chamorro's incoming
            administration and the Nicaraguan resistance reach a cease-
            fire and demobilization arrangement (Toncontín Agreement).
March 26   GENERAL ASSEMBLY: Resumed 44th regular session.
March 27   CENTRAL AMERICA: Security Council widens the mandate of
            ONUCA so that it can "play a part in the voluntary
            demobilization of the members of the Nicaraguan resistance";
            new mandate includes taking delivery of and destroying
            weapons, *matériel* and military equipment, including military
            uniforms, of the Nicaraguan resistance; original mandate
            included the verification of "cessation of aid to irregular
            forces and insurrectionist movements operating in the region
            and the non-use of the territory of one State for attacks on
            other States".
March 29   IRAN-IRAQ: Security Council extends the mandate of
            UNIIMOG until 30 September 1990.
March 30   CENTRAL AMERICA: Unidad Revolucionaria Nacional
            Guatemalteca (URNG) and the National Reconciliation
            Commission of Guatemala (CNR) sign Basic Agreement for
            the Search for Peace by Political Means in Oslo, Norway.
April 2   GENERAL ASSEMBLY: Resumed 44th regular session.
April 3   CENTRAL AMERICA: Five Central American Presidents in
            Montelimar, Nicaragua, accept the Secretary-General's
            proposal for destruction of weapons received by ONUCA.
April 4   CENTRAL AMERICA: Government of El Salvador and FMLN
            hold first round of direct peace talks and sign an accord to
            quickly end the armed conflict, "promote the democratization
            of the country, guarantee unrestricted respect for human
            rights and reunify Salvadoran society", to be "verified by the
            UN, subject to Security Council approval".
April 9-11 DRUGS: World Ministerial Summit to Reduce the Demand for
            Drugs and to Combat the Cocaine Threat in London adopts
            Declaration by which 124 countries, both developed and
            developing, commit themselves to give higher priority to
            prevention and reduction of illicit drug demand at the national
            and international levels.
April 17   MEMBERSHIP: Security Council recommends to the General
            Assembly Namibia's admission to the UN.
April 19   CENTRAL AMERICA: Government of Nicaraguan, the
            Resistance and Cardinal Obando y Bravo sign a series of
            agreements, calling for a cease-fire as of 12 noon that day,
            security zones and a timetable for demobilization.

1990 (continued)

April 20	CENTRAL AMERICA: Security Council expands mandate of ONUCA so that it can monitor the cease-fire agreed on 19 April.
April 23-May 1	ECONOMIC DEVELOPMENT: 18th special session of the General Assembly on international economic co-operation adopts a Declaration on International Economic Co-operation, in particular the Revitalization of Economic Growth and Development of the Developing Countries.
April 23	MEMBERSHIP: Namibia, the newly independent southern African nation, becomes the 160th UN member state.
May 1-25	ECOSOC: 1st regular session, New York.
May 2-5	ENVIRONMENT: International conference to examine the impact of climate change on African countries in Nairobi urges appropriate national policy responses.
May 3	MIDDLE EAST: Security Council considers the settlement of recent immigrants to Israel from the Soviet Union in the occupied Arab territories: meeting adjourns without a draft resolution having been tabled.
May 4	CENTRAL AMERICA: Security Council extends mandate of ONUCA for six months until 7 November 1990 and sets target date for concluding the demobilization process.
May 16-21	CENTRAL AMERICA: Government of El Salvador and FMLN hold second round of direct peace talks.
May 17	GENERAL ASSEMBLY: Resumed 44th regular session.
May 21-June 1	TRUSTEESHIP COUNCIL: 57th regular session.
May 22	MEMBERSHIP: Democratic Yemen and Yemen merge to form a single state known as Republic of Yemen; membership of the UN is thereby reduced from 160 to 159.
May 25-26	CAMBODIA: Permanent members of the Security Council (China, France, UK, USA, USSR) review their efforts to bring about a comprehensive political settlement of the Cambodian problem.
May 30	PEACE-KEEPING: Security Council members state that they are encouraged by recent achievements of UN peace-keeping and are ready to consider launching new peace-keeping operations "as and when necessary in the interest of international peace and security".
May 31	MIDDLE EAST: USA vetoes a draft resolution of the Security Council, sending a three-member commission to the occupied Palestinian territories to examine the "situation relating to the policies and practices of Israel" and reaffirming that the 1949 Geneva Convention relative to the Protection of Civilian Persons in Time of War is applicable to the "Palestinian and other Arab territories occupied by Israel since 1967, including Jerusalem"; Security Council extends the mandate of UNDOF for a six month period until 30 November 1990.

1990 (continued)

June 1   CENTRAL AMERICA: Guatemalan political parties and
                Unidad Revolucionaria Nacional Guatemalteca (URNG) sign
                agreement in Madrid (El Escorial Agreement), which ratifies
                the Basic Agreement for the Search for Peace by Political
                Means, singed in Oslo, Norway, on 30 March by URNG and
                the National Reconciliation Commission of Guatemala (CNR).

                TRUSTEESHIP: Trusteeship Council notes with satisfaction
                assurances given by the USA as administering authority of the
                Trust Territory of the Pacific Islands (Micronesia) that it will
                continue to fulfil its responsibilities under the Trusteeship
                Agreement.

June 12-Aug. 24 ARMS CONTROL: 2nd part of 1990 session of the Conference
                on Disarmament devotes work on a nuclear-test ban and on
                elaboration of a multi-lateral convention on chemical
                weapons.

June 12   CENTRAL AMERICA: UNDP reports that two years after its
                inception, the UN Special Plan of Economic Co-operation for
                Central America is achieving remarkable results, with over
                $400 million in resource mobilized so far to help support
                social, political and economic development for the region.

June 15-17   CENTRAL AMERICA: 1st economic summit of the five
                Central American presidents in Antigua, Guatemala, declares
                "that peace is inseparable from social justice and that full
                democracy cannot be consolidated in Central America so long
                as hunger and poverty exists".

June 15   CYPRUS: Security Council extends mandate of UNFICYP for
                six months until 15 December 1990.

June 19   NAMIBIA: Council of Namibia recommends to the General
                Assembly to dissolve itself and the UN Fund for Namibia.

June 21-22   NAMIBIA: Donor conference for the reconstruction and
                development of the newly-independent country of Namibia
                results in pledges for a $697 million.

June 21   CENTRAL AMERICA: Government of El Salvador and FMLN
                hold second round of direct peace talks in San José, Costa
                Rica, and agree to improve the human rights situation in
                wartorn El Salvador.

June 22   SOUTH AFRICA: Nelson Mandela, deputy president of ANC,
                speaks from the rostrum of the General Assembly, thanking
                the UN for its efforts to secure his release and that of other
                South African prisoners and urges the UN and individual
                governments to continue the sanctions which they had
                imposed on South Africa.

June 25   CENTRAL AMERICA: Government of El Salvador and FMLN
                hold third round of direct peace talks in Mexico City.

1990 (continued)

June 27   WESTERN SAHARA: Security Council approves a plan for a
              settlement of the Western Sahara question under which the
              UN would supervise a cease-fire between Morocco and
              POLISARIO and conduct a referendum in which the Western
              Saharan people would choose between independence and
              integration with Morocco.

June 28   GENERAL ASSEMBLY: Resumed 44th regular session.

June 29   CENTRAL AMERICA: ONUCA completes demobilization of
              21,863 members of the Nicaraguan Resistance forces in
              accordance with the deadline set by the Security Council.

July 4-27   ECOSOC: 2nd regular session, Geneva.

July 5-9   WESTERN SAHARA: Secretary-General, Morocco and
              POLISARIO in Geneva discuss on how best to implement the
              peace plan for Western Sahara as approved by the Security
              Council on 27 June; Secretary-General reports on progress
              towards a just and honorable solution of the question of
              Western Sahara through a credible referendum.

July 19   CYPRUS: Security Council expresses full support for Secretary-
              General's effort to assist the Greek and Turkish Cypriot
              communities to reach a just and lasting solution to the Cyprus
              problem.

July 26   CENTRAL AMERICA: Secretary-General states that "for the
              first time, the parties have reached agreement on a substantive
              issue, human rights, which is of central importance to the
              negotiation and to the solution of the decade-long Salvadoran
              conflict", and foresees a broad monitoring role for the United
              Nations "once a cease-fire is in place - also under United
              Nations verification".

July 31   MIDDLE EAST: Security Council extends the mandate of
              UNIFIL for six months until 31 January 1991.

Aug. 2   IRAQ-KUWAIT: Iraq invades, occupies and annexes Kuwait;
              Security Council condemns Iraq's invasion of Kuwait,
              demands an immediate and unconditional Iraqi withdrawal,
              and calls for immediate and intensive negotiations between
              Iraq and Kuwait to resolve their differences.

Aug. 3   IRAQ-KUWAIT: USA and USSR call for an "international cut-
              off of all arms supplies to Iraq" in a joint statement.

Aug. 6   IRAQ-KUWAIT: Security Council (i) imposes comprehensive
              economic sanctions against Iraq which oblige states to prevent
              the import into their territories of all commodities and
              products exported from Iraq or Kuwait, and to keep their
              national and others operating in their territories from selling
              or supplying to Iraq or Kuwait any commodities or products,
              including weapons or any other military equipment, except for
              supplies intended strictly for medical purposes and, in
              humanitarian circumstances, foodstuffs; (ii) establishes a

1990 (continued)

	Sanction Committee, consisting of all Security Council members, to examine reports on the progress of implementing the resolution; and (iii) asks for an end to Iraqi occupation of Kuwait and the restoration of Kuwait's sovereignty, independence and territorial integrity.
Aug. 9	IRAQ-KUWAIT: Security Council declares Iraq's annexation of Kuwait as "null and void"; Sanction Committee meets.
	IRAQ-KUWAIT: USA reports to the Security Council of its deployment of military forces to the Persian Gulf region "in exercise of the inherent right of individual and collective self-defence" and in response to requests from governments in the region, including Kuwait and Saudi Arabia.
Aug. 10	IRAQ-KUWAIT: Extraordinary Arab Summit Conference in Cairo calls upon Iraq to withdraw its forces immediately from Kuwait and insists on the restoration of the legitimate government existing in Kuwait before the Iraqi invasion; Saudi Arabia and other Arab States in the Gulf take support measures for self-defence.
Aug. 12	IRAQ-KUWAIT: Iraq calls for simultaneous elaboration of provisions for "the immediate and unconditional withdrawal of Israel from the occupied Arab territories in Palestine, Syria and Lebanon, as well as the withdrawal of Syria from Lebanon and the withdrawal of Iraq from Iran, and the formulation of provisions relating to the situation in Kuwait".
Aug. 16	IRAQ-KUWAIT: USA informs the Security Council that it has, at Kuwait's request, joined Kuwait in intercepting vessels seeking to trade with Iraq or Kuwait in violation of UN mandatory sanctions.
Aug. 17-22	CENTRAL AMERICA: Government of El Salvador and FMLN hold fourth round of direct peace talks.
Aug. 18	IRAQ-KUWAIT: Security Council demands that Iraq permit and facilitate the immediate departure from Iraq and Kuwait of third-country nationals and that no action be taken to jeopardize their safety, security or health; and demands that Iraq rescind its orders to close diplomatic and consular missions in Kuwait and withdraw immunity of their personnel.
Aug. 19	PERSIAN GULF: Iraq proposes that the Security Council to ensure that the USA withdraws its forces from the region; and to give assurance to Saudi Arabia that it would take a collective military stand against Iraq if Iraq attempted any aggression against Saudi Arabia.
Aug. 20-Sept. 15	ARMS CONTROL: 4th Review Conference of Parties to the Treaty on the Non-Proliferation of Nuclear Weapons (NPT) in Geneva is unable to reach a consensus on a final declaration.

1990 (continued)

Aug. 25   IRAQ-KUWAIT: Security Council endorses a naval blockade of Iraq, calling on those states "co-operating with the Government of Kuwait, which are deploying maritime forces to the area", to use "such measures commensurate to the specific circumstances" as might be necessary under the Council's authority "to halt all inward and outward maritime shipping in order to inspect and verify their cargoes and destinations" and ensure strict implementation of the sanctions imposed; and asks states concerned to use the Council's long-inactive Military Staff Committee to co-ordinate their actions.

Aug. 27-Sept. 7   CRIME: 8th UN Crime Congress on the Prevention of Crime and the Treatment of Offenders in Havana, Cuba, adopts draft model treaties on extradition, mutual assistance in criminal matters, transfer of proceedings, supervision of offenders and prevention of crimes against cultural property.

Aug. 27-28   CAMBODIA: Permanent members of the Security Council (China, France, UK, USA, USSR) reach a final agreement on a framework for a comprehensive settlement of the Cambodian problem.

Aug. 29   CENTRAL AMERICA: Secretary-General asks the Security Council to consider establishing a preparatory office in El Salvador for the UN verification mission.

Sept. 3-14   DEVELOPMENT: 2nd Conference on the Least Developed Countries in Paris adopts new Program of Action aimed at advancing the world's poorest countries; offers a "menu approach" for donors to increase their official aid to the least developed countries; stresses bilateral assistance in the form of grants or highly concessional loans; and calls on donors to help reduce LDC debt.

Sept. 9-10   CAMBODIA: Cambodian parties hold "informal meeting" and accept the framework document as the basis for settling the Cambodia conflict, which was approved by the five permanent members of the Security Council during their meeting on 27-28 August.

Sept. 11-17   GENERAL ASSEMBLY: Resumed 44th regular session.

Sept. 11   NAMIBIA: General Assembly officially dissolves the UN Council for Namibia, stating that the Council had fulfilled its mandate.

Sept. 13-18   CENTRAL AMERICA: Government of El Salvador and FMLN hold fifth round of direct peace talks.

Sept. 13   IRAQ-KUWAIT: Security Council requests the Secretary-General to obtain information with regard to the humanitarian needs arising from the imposition of sanctions, particularly as to children under 15 years of age, expectant mothers, maternity cases, the sick and the elderly, and asks Iraq to ensure the safety of "third-State nationals".

1990 (continued)

Sept. 13   MONROVIA: Secretary-General expresses deep concern over the intensity of fighting in Monrovia, capital of Liberia, which made it impossible for the UN to resume its "much needed relief operations".

Sept. 16   FINANCE: Secretary-General reports that the UN is currently owed more than $1 billion from its members and states that this "is a bleak picture at a time when many hopes and expectations are being placed in the work of the United Nations".

IRAQ-KUWAIT: Security Council strongly condemns "aggressive acts" by Iraq against diplomatic premises and personnel in Kuwait and demands the immediate release of foreign nationals.

Sept. 17-18   CAMBODIA: 1st meeting of the Supreme National Council (SNC) in Bangkok, including the National United Front for an Independent, Neutral, Peaceful and Co-operative Cambodia (FUNCINPEC), headed by Prince Norodom Sihanouk, the Khmer People's National Liberation Front (KPNLF), led by Son Sann, the Party of Democratic Kampuchea (PDK), led by Khieu Samphan, and the Kampuchean People's Revolutionary Party, led by Heng Samrin.

Sept. 17   SOUTH AFRICA: General Assembly calls on South Africa to establish a climate fully conducive to negotiations by taking steps stipulated in the Declaration on *Apartheid* and its Destructive Consequences in Southern Africa and by implementing its commitment to repeal all South African legislation designed to circumscribe political activity, such as the Internal Security Act.

Sept. 18-Dec. 21   GENERAL ASSEMBLY: 45th regular session.

Sept. 18   IRAQ-KUWAIT: Sanction Committee appeals to states, on an urgent basis, to provide immediate assistance to Jordan to mitigate the consequences of the difficulties faced by that country as a result of the Persian Gulf crisis.

MEMBERSHIP: General Assembly admits Liechtenstein as the 160th member.

Sept. 20   CAMBODIA: Security Council welcomes the formation by the parties to the Cambodia conflict of a Supreme National Council (SNC) and urges SNC members to elect a chairman as soon as possible.

Sept. 24   IRAQ-KUWAIT: Secretary-General states that Iraq's invasion and purported annexation of Kuwait has "evoked a historic response" from the Security Council which has "established that such actions, which are in direct contravention of the principles of the Charter and international law, cannot be committed with impunity"; Security Council deals with an increasing number of requests for assistance to countries

1990 (continued)

	affected by the sanctions process and entrusts the Sanctions Committee to act on those requests.
Sept. 25	IRAQ-KUWAIT: Security Council reiterates its call for strict and complete compliance with sanctions and confirms that sanctions applied to all means of transport, including aircraft, and spelled out specific exceptions.
Sept. 27	IRAN-IRAQ: Security Council extends the mandate of UNIIMOG until 30 November, asks the Secretary-General to report before that date on his consultations with the parties involved about UNIIMOG's future and his recommendations on that matter.
Sept. 28	IRAQ-KUWAIT: Permanent members of the Security Council (China, France, UK, USA, USSR), following a meeting with the Secretary-General, welcome the "firm and decisive" role played by the UN and the good offices of the Secretary-General.
Sept. 29-30	CHILDREN: World Summit for Children in New York brings together 71 heads of states and government and urges the international community to throw its weight behind the summit's Declaration and Plan of Action: a moral and practical commitment to save and improve the lives of children everywhere.
Oct. 3	MEMBERSHIP: General Assembly recognizes the unification of the Federal Republic of Germany and the German Democratic Republic to be known as Germany; in a declaration issued on the eve of unification, the Secretary-General says that 3 October was a day of truly historic significance; merger of the two Germanys reduces membership to 159.
	PEACE AND SECURITY: USA and USSR, in a joint statement entitled "Responsibility for Peace and Security in the Changing World", declare that "the confrontational nature of relations between East and West is giving way to a co-operative relationship and partnership".
Oct. 10	DECOLONIZATION: 30th anniversary of the Declaration on the Granting of Independence to Colonial Countries and Peoples.
	HAITI: General Assembly approves a plan for electoral assistance to Haiti at a cost of up to $6.5 million.
Oct. 12	MIDDLE EAST: Security Council expresses alarm at the violence which took place on 8 October at "the Al Haram Al Shareef and other Holy Places of Jerusalem" and condemns acts of violence by the Israeli security forces "resulting in injuries and loss of human life".
Oct. 15	CAMBODIA: General Assembly urges all parties to the conflict to exercise maximum self-restraint to create the peaceful climate needed for a comprehensive political settlement.

1990 (continued)

Oct. 24   MIDDLE EAST: Security Council deplores Israel's refusal to receive the Secretary-General's mission to the region, urging it to reconsider that decision.

Oct. 29   IRAQ-KUWAIT: Security Council demands that Iraq ceases to take third-state nationals in Iraq and Kuwait hostage; stops mistreating and oppressing nationals of Kuwait and third States; and ensures their immediate access to food, water and basic services.

Nov. 1   MAYOTTE ISLAND: General Assembly reaffirms the sovereignty of the Comoros over the island of Mayotte and urges France to accelerate the process of negotiations with Comoros to ensure the "effective and prompt return of the island to the Comoros".

Nov. 2   DEVELOPMENT: Pledging Conferences for Development Activities results in pledges of $1.8 billion, a significant increase in comparison to past years.

Nov. 5   CENTRAL AMERICA: Security Council extends the mandate of ONUCA for six months until 7 May 1991.

Nov. 7   AFGHANISTAN: General Assembly asks to work urgently for the achievement of a solution, the cessation of hostilities and the creation of conditions of peace and normalcy to enable Afghan refugees to return voluntarily to their homeland in safety and honour.

Nov. 9   CYPRUS: Security Council stresses the "urgent need" to arrive at a negotiated settlement of the Cyprus problem and calls for renewed political will and commitment by all parties to facilitate a process of negotiations.

                    ECOSOC: Resumed 2nd regular session, New York.

Nov. 11   DRUGS: UN Convention against Illicit Traffic in Narcotic Drugs and Psychotropic Substances enters into force.

Nov. 15   PEACE AND SECURITY: General Assembly reaffirms its previous call to strengthen the UN role in maintaining international peace and security; for the first time the resolution was jointly proposed by USA and USSR.

Nov. 20   CENTRAL AMERICA: General Assembly expresses its "strongest support" for continuing negotiations to reach a firm and lasting peace in Central America and cites as the basis for the search for peace the agreement reached by the presidents of the five Central American countries at the Esquipulas II summit meeting, 7 August 1987.

                    WESTERN SAHARA: General Assembly urges the Secretary-General and the Chairman of OAU to intensify efforts for holding a UN-organized and supervised self-determination referendum in the territory, in co-operation with OAU.

1990 (continued)

Nov. 23-26	CAMBODIA: Paris Conference on Cambodia (PCC), including the permanent members of the Security Council (China, France, UK, USA, USSR), reaches consensus on a political settlement covering the mandate for a UN Transitional Authority in Cambodia (UNTAC); withdrawal, cease-fire and related measures; elections; repatriation of refugees an displaced persons; and principles for a new constitution: consensus paves the way for reconvening the Paris Conference on Cambodia at ministerial level.
Nov. 26-Dec. 7	DEVELOPMENT: 2nd UN Conference to Review All Aspects of the Set of Multilaterally Agreed Equitable Principles and Rules for the Control of Restrictive Business Practices, Geneva.
Nov. 28	IRAN-IRAQ: Security Council extends mandate of UNIIMOG for two months until 31 January 1991; asks Secretary-General to make recommendations after consultations with both parties on the future of UNIIMOG; condemns Iraq's attempts to alter the demographic composition and destroy the civil records of Kuwait, and mandates the Secretary-General to take custody of a copy of Kuwait's population register and to establish rules and regulations governing access to and use of that register.
	INTERNATIONAL LAW: General Assembly adopts program of activities for the UN Decade of International Law (1990-1999), focusing on the first three-year period of the decade, ending in 1992.
Nov. 29	IRAQ-KUWAIT: Security Council authorizes the use of "all necessary means to uphold and implement" all relevant Council resolutions and "to restore international peace and security in the area" if Iraq did not fully implement those resolutions on or before 15 January 1991; demands that Iraq comply fully with those resolutions and decides, "while maintaining all its decisions, to allow Iraq one final opportunity, as a pause of goodwill, to do so".
Nov. 30	MIDDLE EAST: Security Council extends the mandate of UNDOF for a six-month period, until 31 May 1991.
Dec. 4	DISARMAMENT: General Assembly adopts a declaration on disarmament and declares the 1990s the Third Disarmament Decade.
Dec. 5	IRAQ-KUWAIT: Four non-aligned members of the Security Council (Colombia, Cuba, Malaysia, Yemen) submit a "peace plan", proposing a UN peace-keeping force to oversee withdrawal of Iraqi troops from Kuwait.

1990 (continued)

Dec. 6 & 13   MIDDLE EAST: General Assembly calls once again for the convening of an international peace conference on the Middle East, reaffirming its conviction that the core of the conflict is the question of Palestine.

Dec. 14   CYPRUS: Security Council extends the mandate of the UNFICYP for six months until 15 June 1991.

LAW OF THE SEA: General Assembly invites states to make renewed efforts to facilitate universal participation in the UN Convention on the Law of the Sea and asks states to ratify or accede to the Convention at the earliest date to allow the effective entry into force of the new legal régime for the uses of the sea and its resources.

WOMEN: General Assembly endorses plans to hold a 4th international conference on women in 1995.

Dec. 15-17   CENTRAL AMERICA: Five Central American Presidents in Puntarenas, Costa Rica, commit themselves "to the establishment of a new model of regional security" and review progress in Central America.

Dec. 16   HAITI: UN Observer Group for the Verification of the Election in Haiti (ONUVEH) monitors the presidential election.

HUMAN RIGHTS: General Assembly commemorates the 25th anniversary of the two International Covenants on Human Rights: (i) the International Covenant on Economic, Social and Cultural Rights and (ii) the International Covenant on Civil and Political Rights.

Dec. 18   EL SALVADOR: General Assembly expresses "its deep concern about the persistence of politically motivated violations of human rights in El Salvador, such as summary executions, torture, abductions and enforced disappearances, and about the atmosphere of intimidation in which certain sectors of the population live".

HUMAN RIGHTS: General Assembly approves, following ten years of negotiations, the International Convention on the Protection of the Rights of All Migrant Workers and Members of Their Families, a new multilateral human rights instrument; decides to convene a high-level World Conference on Human Rights in 1993.

SOCIAL DEVELOPMENT: General Assembly proclaims 1993 as International Year for the World's Indigenous People with the goal to strengthening international co-operation "for the solution of problems faced by indigenous communities in such areas as human rights, the environment, development, eduction, health and so on".

1990 (continued)

Dec. 19   SOUTH AFRICA: General Assembly calls on all governments
            and intergovernmental organizations to adhere strictly to the
            Program of Action contained in the Declaration on *Apartheid*
            and its Destructive Consequences in Southern Africa.

Dec. 20   MIDDLE EAST: Security Council requests the Secretary-
            General to make new efforts on an "urgent basis" to monitor
            and observe the situation of Palestinian civilians under Israeli
            occupation; deplores Israel's decision to resume deportation of
            Palestinian civilians in the occupied territories, and urges it to
            accept *de jure* applicability of the 1949 4th Geneva
            Convention relative to the Protection of Civilian Persons in
            Time of War to "all the territories occupied by Israel since
            1967" and to abide scrupulously by the Convention's
            provisions.

Dec. 21   CHERNOBYL: General Assembly proposes the creation of a
            task force to stimulate and monitor UN technical and other
            assistance to the region affected by the 1986 accident at the
            Chernobyl nuclear power plant in the Ukraine.

            DEBT: General Assembly calls for immediate action to find a
            "durable, equitable and mutually agreed growth and
            development-oriented solution" to the debt crisis of
            developing countries: reaches consensus on this issue for the
            first time since 1986.

            DEVELOPMENT: General Assembly launches the International
            Development Strategy for the Fourth UN Development
            Decade (1991-2000), a plan for accelerated economic and
            social progress and strengthened international co-operation
            which aims to reverse the slow growth, poverty and declining
            living standards experienced by much of the developing world
            during the 1980s; requests a special meeting of ECOSOC at a
            ministerial level during 1991 to examine the impact of new
            East-West relations on the world economy, reflecting
            widespread concern that resources earmarked for developing
            countries will be diverted to Eastern European countries as
            they joint the international market.

            ENVIRONMENT: General Assembly launches negotiations on a
            climate convention.

Dec. 22   TRUSTEESHIP: Security Council votes to terminate the
            trusteeship agreement for three of the four entities comprising
            the Trust Territory of the Pacific Islands, administered by the
            UN since 1947.

1991

Jan. 1	DEVELOPMENT: Start of the 4th UN Development Decade (1991-2000), 2nd Transport and Communication Decade in Africa (1991-2000) and 2nd Industrial Development Decade for Africa (1991-2000).
	DRUGS: Start of the UN Decade against Drug Abuse (1991-2000).
Jan. 12-13	IRAQ-KUWAIT: Secretary-General undertakes mission to Iraq, meeting with Iraqi's president to urge him to comply with Security Council resolutions: upon return the Secretary-General reports sadly that the talks were "polite but, unfortunately, unsuccessful" and that "the world stands between peace and war".
Jan. 16	IRAQ-KUWAIT: Seven-week war breaks out to oust Iraq from Kuwait and waged by a coalition of troops representing 34 nationalities; Kuwait informs the Security Council that it is "exercising its right to self-defence and to the restoration of its rights", and in so doing is "cooperating with the forces of fraternal and friendly States which are equally determined to end the obdurate Iraqi occupation".
Jan. 18	NUCLEAR WEAPONS: Amendment Conference of the States Parties to the 1963 Treaty Banning Nuclear Weapon Tests in the Atmosphere, in Outer Space and under Water decides that further work is needed before a proposed amendment converting it into a comprehensive test-ban treaty can be adopted.
Jan. 20	HAITI: UN Observer Group for the Verification of the Election in Haiti (ONUVEH) monitors the election of senators, deputies and local officers.
Jan. 22-March 28	DISARMAMENT: 1st part of 1991 Conference on Disarmament.
Jan. 22	LIBERIA: Security Council calls on the parties in the conflict to continue to respect the cease-fire agreement which they have signed on 24 October 1990 and to cooperate fully with the Economic Community of West African States (ECOWAS) to restore peace and normalcy in that country.
Jan. 28	IRAQ-ISRAEL: Israel reports to the Security Council that "destructive and unprovoked" missile attacks by Iraq have caused civilian deaths, injuries and damage to homes and property.
Jan. 30	ECOSOC: Organizational session, New York.
	MIDDLE EAST: Security Council extends mandate of UNIFIL for six months until 31 July 1991.
Feb. 1	PERSIAN GULF: Secretary-General appeals for humanitarian assistance for refugees, displaced persons and civilians in the area; International Committee of the Red Cross reports that

1991 (continued)

	millions of civilians have been caught up in the violence, without shelter or protection against occupation and bombing.
Feb. 7-8	ECOSOC: Organizational session, New York.
Feb. 18	ENVIRONMENT: A tough amendment to the 1973 International Convention for the Prevention of Pollution from Ships enters into force, absolutely banning the dumping of plastics, glass, metal, dunnage and other refuse from ships everywhere in the North Sea.
Feb. 23	IRAQ-KUWAIT: Coalition forces launch ground operations, moving hundreds of tanks and tens of thousands of troops from positions in Saudi Arabia into Iraq and Kuwait.
Feb. 27	IRAQ-KUWAIT: Kuwait City is liberated; Iraq informs Security Council that it has decided to comply with all relevant Security Council resolution; Iraq reports that all of its armed forces have withdrawn from Kuwait and promises to release all prisoners of war immediately after the cease-fire; Security Council accepts the Secretary-General's recommendation to let the mandate of UNIIMOG expire.
Feb. 28	IRAQ-KUWAIT: Coalition forces suspend offensive combat operation; Secretary-General calls the oil slick in the Persian Gulf "an ecological catastrophe of major proportions".
March 2	IRAQ-KUWAIT: Security Council affirms, following initial post-war consultation, that all 12 resolutions concerning the Iraq-Kuwait situation continue to "have full force and effect".
March 6	KUWAIT: Kuwait informs the Secretary-General that its government is resuming the functions of state and "directing the affairs of the nation from Kuwait".
March 22	IRAQ: Countries most severely affected as a result of their compliance with Council-ordered sanctions against Iraq appeal for help to the Security Council, saying they had lost more than $30 billion; Sanctions Committee decides to lift the embargo on civilian and humanitarian imports to Iraq.
March 25	ECOSOC: Resumed organizational session, New York.
March 28	CYPRUS: Security Council urges all those concerned with the situation in Cyprus to cooperate fully with the Secretary-General and to continue discussions that took place over the past few months in order to resolve the outstanding issues without delay.
April 3	PERSIAN GULF: Security Council establishes detailed conditions for the formal cease-fire ending the hostilities resulting from Iraq's occupation of Kuwait; calls on Iraq to accept a 1963 border agreement with Kuwait, to compensate Kuwait and other countries for damage arising from the seven-month occupation and to relinquish or destroy weapons of mass destruction, including chemical, biological and

1991 (continued)

	nuclear arms under the auspices of the Special Commission on Iraqi Disarmament.
April 5	PERSIAN GULF: Security Council calls the massive flow of refugees across international frontiers and cross-border incursions a threat to international peace and security in the region; demands that Iraq immediately ends the repression of its civilian population, including those in Kurdish-populated areas; insists that it allow international humanitarian organizations immediate access to all those in need of assistance.
April 6	PERSIAN GULF: Iraq officially accepts the conditions for the formal cease-fire as established by the Security Council.
April 9	IRAQ-KUWAIT: Security Council establishes the UN observer mission to monitor the Iraq-Kuwait border (UNIKOM).
April 19	WESTERN SAHARA: Secretary-General outlines his plan to implement the settlement proposals as accepted by Morocco and POLISARIO on 30 August 1988, which provides for UN supervision of a cease-fire between Morocco and POLISARIO and details how a referendum on the future of Western Sahara should be organized by which the people of the Territory will chose between independence and integration with Morocco.
April 23	GENERAL ASSEMBLY: Resumed 45th regular session.
April 29	WESTERN SAHARA: Security Council establishes the UN Mission for the Referendum in Western Sahara (MINURSO) to implement the Secretary-General's plan for the settlement of the question of Western Sahara.
May 3-31	TRUSTEESHIP COUNCIL: 58th regular session expresses hope that the people of Palau will be able to complete the process of exercising freely their right to self-determination and notes with satisfaction assurances given by the USA, which is the administering authority of Palau, that it is prepared to assist in any appropriate endeavor leading to the final determination of a political status of Palau, in accordance with the free choice of its people.
May 3	PEACE-KEEPING: Resumed 45th regular session of the General Assembly approves $61 million for UNIKOM's first six months, from 9 April to 8 October 1991.
May 6	CENTRAL AMERICA: Security Council extends the mandate of ONUCA for six months until 7 November 1991.
May 13-31	ECOSOC: 1st regular session, New York.
May 13	REFORM: Resumed 45th regular session of the General Assembly asks ECOSOC to streamline its work program, to hold one substantive annual session instead of two, to abolish the traditional "general debate" and introduce a new "high-level segment" attended by ministers and agency heads.
May 14-22	IRAQ: 1st nuclear inspection team.

1991 (continued)

May 16-June 27	DISARMAMENT: 2nd part of 1991 Conference on Disarmament.
May 17	FINLAND/DENMARK CASE: Finland institutes proceedings with the International Court of Justice against Denmark, citing that the projected construction by Denmark of a "high-level bridge, 65 metres above main sea level" would violate Finland's rights in respect of free passage through the Great Belt, linking the Baltic to the North Sea, as established in the relevant conventions and customary international law.
	GENERAL ASSEMBLY: Resumed 45th regular session.
	IRAQ-KUWAIT: Iraq-Kuwait Boundary Demarcation Commission is established.
	WESTERN SAHARA: General Assembly approves, in principle, an allocation of some $180 million to finance MINURSO for the nine-month period and asks member states for voluntary contributions to finance a repatriation program for Western Saharans.
May 20	CENTRAL AMERICA: Security Council establishes the UN Observer Mission in El Salvador (ONUSAL) to verify compliance with a human rights accord signed by the Government of El Salvador and FMLN.
	IRAQ-KUWAIT: Security Council establishes a compensation fund for claims against Iraq resulting from its 2 August 1990 invasion and occupation of Kuwait.
May 21	AFGHANISTAN: Secretary-General proposes five elements to serve as a basis for a political settlement which could be acceptable to the vast majority of Afghans.
May 22	AFGHANISTAN: Afghan government states that the Secretary-General's proposals of 21 May could lead to an end of the war and bloodshed in Afghanistan and could be a firm foundation for ensuring peace in the country.
May 23	AFGHANISTAN: Pakistan welcomes the five elements presented by the Secretary-General on 21 May to serve as a basis for a political settlement in Afghanistan.
May 24	MIDDLE EAST: Security Council deplores the deportation by Israel of four Palestinians on 18 May from the occupied territories and calls for their safe and immediate return.
May 30	ANGOLA: Security Council establishes a new mandate for the UN Angola Verification Mission (UNAVEM), created in 1988 to oversee withdrawal of Cuban troops from that nation: UNAVEM II is to carry out new verification tasks arising from the Angola Peace Accords until general elections in that country are completed.
	MIDDLE EAST: Security Council extends the mandate of UNDOF for six month until 30 November 1991.

1991 (continued)

May 31	ANGOLA: Government of Angola and UNITA sign agreement for the cessation of hostilities and peaceful transition in Angola, known as the Peace Accords for Angola, which calls for a *de facto* cease-fire from 15 May 1991 and the holding of elections to be completed by 30 November 1992.
June 9-15	IRAQ: 1st chemical weapons inspection mission.
June 10	GENERAL ASSEMBLY: Resumed 45th regular session.
June 14	CYPRUS: Security Council extends the mandate of UNFICYP for six months until 15 December 1991.
	SOUTH-EAST ASIA: Comprehensive Plan of Action (CPA) for Indo-Chinese refugees is adopted, establishing a legal framework to address the problem of refugees and asylum seekers from Viet Nam and Laos.
June 17-21	ECOSOC: Resumed 1st regular session, New York.
June 17	IRAQ: Security Council decides that the full cost of the destruction of proscribed weapons within Iraq should be borne by Iraq and approves a set of guidelines to facilitate full international implementation of the arms embargo provisions.
	SOUTH AFRICA: South African Parliament repeals the law, more than four decades after it was enacted, that laid the legal foundation for *apartheid*, classifying all South Africans by race from birth.
June 21	GENERAL ASSEMBLY: Resumed 45th regular session.
June 23-July 3	IRAQ: 2nd nuclear inspection team reports that Iraqi military have twice denied or restricted access to a designated site.
June 25-27	SOUTH AFRICA: International Conference on the Educational Needs of the Victims of *Apartheid* in South Africa calls for support for efforts to restructure South Africa's educational system to provide appropriate opportunities for black South Africans and help to facilitate the transition to a non-racial and democratic South Africa.
June 26	CAMBODIA: Secretary-General expresses gratification at the decision of members of the Supreme National Council (SNC) of Cambodia to implement an unlimited cease-fire and to stop receiving foreign military assistance.
June 28	CYPRUS: Security Council regrets that despite the Secretary-General's efforts, necessary progress has not yet been made in achieving an outline for an agreement on a settlement for Cyprus.
	GENERAL ASSEMBLY: Resumed 45th regular session.
	IRAQ: Security Council asks Iraq to grant a nuclear inspection team "immediate and unimpeded access" to a site it has attempted to inspect on 28 June, as well as to any other site deemed necessary, stating that "any recurrence of non-compliance would have serious consequences".

1991 (continued)

June 30-July 7	IRAQ: 1st ballistic missile capabilities mission begins with the destruction of ballistic missiles.
June 30	IRAQ: UN conveys to Iraq the Security Council's "urgent demand for unequivocal assurances that the Government will take all necessary measures to ensure that no hindrances are placed in the way of the discharge of the Special Commission's mandate".
July 1-12	IRAQ-KUWAIT: Iraq-Kuwait Boundary Demarcation Commission, Geneva.
July 3-26	ECOSOC: 2nd regular session in Geneva devotes a special two-day high-level discussion of the impact of changing East-West relations on the global economy.
July 3	IRAQ: UN mission to southern Iraq to look into the situation of displaced groups in the marshlands of that region reports a substantial military presence and activity directed against the people of the area.
July 6-19	IRAQ: 3rd nuclear inspection mission reports that it has placed under IAEA seals "a considerable amount of nuclear material and a number of equipment items".
July 8	QATAR/BAHRAIN CASE: Qatar institutes proceedings with the International Court of Justice against Bahrain, contesting the latter's sovereignty over "the Hawar islands and the shoals of Dibal and Qit'at Jaradah".
July 10	IRAQ: Iraq complains that the Security Council is not fulfilling its mandate, which provides for a review, every 60 days, of the list of articles covered by the embargo; states that the humanitarian situation has gone beyond legally acceptable limits.
July 15-17	CENTRAL AMERICA: 10th summit of Central American Presidents (Costa Rica, El Salvador, Guatemala, Honduras, Nicaragua, Panama) in San Salvador, El Salvador, adopts the Declaration of El Salvador on the establishment of appropriate institutional machinery for the effective attainment of Central American integration in the political, economic, social and cultural domains.
July 17-18	CAMBODIA: Permanent members of the Security Council (China, France, UK, USA, USSR) and the two Co-Chairmen of the Paris Conference on Cambodia (PCC) meet in Pattaya, Thailand.
July 18-20	IRAQ: 2nd ballistic missile capabilities mission.
July 18	IRAQ: Clashes take place between Kurds and the Iraqi military in Suleimaniya and Arbil, with estimated casualties ranging up to 500; IAEA condemns Iraq for non-compliance with its safeguards agreement: this is the first time a state party to the Non-Proliferation Treaty is condemned for concealing a nuclear program.

1991 (continued)

July 19   IRAQ: FAO issues a "special alert" to donors to meet the
                 immediate food needs of Iraq.

July 22-26   GUATEMALA: Government of Guatemala and URNG hold
                 talks with the participation of a UN observer, aimed at ending
                 the internal armed conflict in Guatemala and bringing about
                 national reconciliation; talks deal with the first general agenda
                 item on democratization and human rights.

July 23-Sept. 4 ARMS CONTROL: 3rd part of Conference on Disarmament,
                 Geneva.

July 23   IRAQ: Iraq states that IAEA's condemnation is based on
                 "predetermined political concepts and motives, the intention
                 being to bestow technical legitimacy through a specialized
                 agency in preparation for a fresh act of military aggression
                 against Iraq, following the full revelation by Iraq of its
                 nuclear program".

July 25   WESTERN SAHARA: Identification Commission, entrusted to
                 identify and register all Western Saharans eligible to vote in
                 the referendum, announces the completion of the first step of
                 its work with the revision of the census list containing 70,204
                 names.

July 26   EL SALVADOR: ONUSAL is launched in San Salvador to
                 verify fulfillment of the commitments undertaken by the
                 Government of El Salvador and FMLN to respect and
                 promote human rights in El Salvador; launch takes place
                 exactly one year after the signing of the Agreement on
                 Human Rights in San José, Costa Rica.

July 27-Aug. 10 IRAQ: 4th nuclear inspection mission.

July 29   IRAQ: IAEA informs the Secretary-General that "the possibility
                 exists that there are still undeclared locations with sensitive
                 equipment and material".

July 30   AFGHANISTAN: Iran, Pakistan and the Afghan Mujahideen
                 state, after a meeting in Pakistan, that there are "positive
                 elements" in the 21 May statement of the Secretary-General
                 which could be considered for a comprehensive solution
                 acceptable to Afghans "after necessary clarifications";
                 "Operation Salam", a program of emergency relief and
                 rehabilitation in Afghanistan implemented by UN agencies,
                 announces that the 1991 budget is cut by $31 million to $105
                 million, because of lack of resources.

                 IRAQ: IAEA reports to the Security Council that the full extent
                 of Iraq's enrichment program has not yet been disclosed.

July 31   MIDDLE EAST: Security Council extends the mandate of
                 UNIFIL for a six-months period until 31 January 1992.

1991 (continued)

Aug. 1	EL SALVADOR: USA and USSR submit to the Secretary-General a joint communiqué, supporting his efforts and suggesting that he personally gets involved in the negotiations.
Aug. 2-8	IRAQ: 1st biological weapons inspection mission.
Aug. 2	KUWAIT: Kuwait states that Iraq has not abandoned its expansionist and hostile policies towards Kuwait and requests the Security Council to maintain its determination and resolve to oblige Iraq fully and scrupulously to abide by international decisions.
Aug. 4	IRAQ: Secretary-General recommends to the Security Council the basic structure and measures for the sale of Iraqi oil, aimed at meeting the country's humanitarian requirements.
Aug. 5	IRAQ-KUWAIT: Iraq turns over 3,216 gold bricks to Kuwait at the Iraqi-Saudi border, through a special UN team.
Aug. 6	HONDURAS: Honduras asks ONUCA to urgently establish observation posts along its border with Nicaragua to prevent the entry of armed elements "which are seeking to destabilize that country's Government".
Aug. 8-15	IRAQ: 3rd ballistic missile capabilities mission.
Aug. 8	HOSTAGES: John McCarthy, a British Journalist detained for five years, is released in Lebanon.
	IRAQ-KUWAIT: Kuwait reports that Iraq still holds 2,479 Kuwaiti and non-Kuwaiti citizens who are either imprisoned or detained.
Aug. 9	WESTERN SAHARA: Secretary-General expresses concern over reports of renewed military action in Western Sahara.
Aug. 11	HOSTAGES: Edward Tracy, a US citizen held for nearly five years, is released in Lebanon; former hostage John McCarthy delivers a letter to the Secretary-General from the "Islamic Jihad", which promises to release all detainees within 24 hours if the Secretary-General would make "a personal endeavour, within a comprehensive solution" to secure the release of all detainees throughout the world.
Aug. 12-Sept. 4	ENVIRONMENT: 3rd session of the Preparatory Committee for the UN Conference on Environment and Development (UNCED), known as "Earth Summit", agrees on (i) a framework for "Agenda 21", which is to be adopted in Rio de Janeiro, as a comprehensive blueprint for action into the twenty-first century, and (ii) an "Earth Charter" or "Rio Declaration on Sustainable Development" that will form the basis for commitment by states to conference goals.
Aug. 12-16	IRAQ-KUWAIT: Iraq-Kuwait Boundary Demarcation Commission in Geneva authorizes an independent survey and mapping of the entire border.

1991 (continued)

Aug. 12	IRAQ: UN announces that the Special Commission will have to undertake its own direct high-altitude aerial surveys to determine further designations of Iraqi sites for inspection: operations begins during first half of August, using an American U-2 high-altitude one seater aircraft.
Aug. 15-23	IRAQ: 2nd chemical weapons inspection mission.
Aug. 15	IRAQ: Security Council condemns what it terms "serious violations" by Iraq of its disarmament obligations after several incidents in which Iraq blocked UN inspection teams access to facilities and documents; partially lifts a ban on the sale of Iraqi oil not exceeding $1.6 billion; sets compensation payments for damage inflicted on Kuwait during the war at 3C per cent of Iraq's annual oil exports.
Aug. 16	SOUTH AFRICA: UNHCR and South Africa sign agreement on voluntary repatriation of South African refugees and political exiles: this landmark agreement formally establishes first UN presence in South Africa.
Aug. 19-Sept. 4	CAMBODIA: Survey mission visits the region in connection with military matters and the establishment of a mine-awareness program in Cambodia.
Aug. 23	IRAQ: Iraq charges that "the massive destruction brought by the United States and its allies on Iraq's civilian facilities and infrastructure in the course of their military operations" clearly demonstrated the US' "unlawful use" of the "cover of international legitimacy and Security Council resolution in order to destroy an entire people".
Aug. 24	HOSTAGES: Jack Mann, a British citizen held for 28 months, is released in Lebanon.
Aug. 25-29	DISASTER PREVENTION: 4th International Conference on Seismic Zonation at Stanford University, USA: reviews zonation-related advances in earth sciences, engineering, urban planning, social sciences and public policy.
Aug. 26-29	CYPRUS: Representatives of the Secretary-General hold separate meetings with the leaders of the two communities.
Aug. 27	ANGOLA: Resumed 45th regular session of the General Assembly approves a budget of $49.5 million for the United Nations Verification Mission (UNAVEM II) to cover its operations from 1 June to 31 December.
	IRAQ: Security Council discusses a long-term plan to monitor and verify Iraq's weapons of mass destruction: meeting adjourns without a draft resolution having been tabled.
	WESTERN SAHARA: Secretary-General, after meeting in Geneva with a POLISARIO representative, expresses confidence that the situation would "calm down".

1991 (continued)

Aug. 28	IRAQ-KUWAIT: Kuwait alleges that Iraqi forces, in a premeditated and planned action, have attacked the Kuwaiti island of Bubiyan with heavy weapons (the island is three kilometers outside the demilitarized zone); states that 43 attackers have been taken prisoner and seven Iraqi boats have been destroyed.
Aug. 29-30	CAMBODIA: Permanent members of the Security Council (China, France, UK, USA, USSR) and the two Co-Chairmen of the Paris Conference on Cambodia (PCC) in Pattaya, Thailand, achieve significant progress on national reconciliation efforts for Cambodia.
Aug. 29	CAMBODIA: 1st joint meeting between the permanent members of the Security Council (China, France, UK, USA, USSR), the two Co-Chairmen of the Paris Conference on Cambodia (PCC) and the Supreme National Council (SNC) of Cambodia.
	IRAQ-KUWAIT: Iraq states that Kuwait's claim of infiltration is "a fabrication without any foundation", intended to "perpetuate the blockade of Iraq, to secure a stranglehold on its people and to create confusion" as to Iraq's full compliance with Security Council resolutions; Iraq informs the Secretary-General that since March it has repatriated 6,328 Kuwaitis and five non-Kuwaiti nationals under the supervision of the International Committee of the Red Cross and that Kuwait impedes the return of other Kuwaitis on the pretext that verification procedures have not been completed.
Aug. 31-Sept. 4	IRAQ: 3rd chemical weapons inspection mission.
Aug. 31-Sept. 8	IRAQ: 4th chemical weapons inspection mission.
Sept. 1	FINANCE: Unpaid assessments to the regular budget total $809.5 million; on the peace-keeping side outstanding contribution amount to $486.9 million; the USA as the largest debtor owes some $700 million ($531 million to the regular budget and $172 million to the peace-keeping operations).
Sept. 3	IRAQ-KUWAIT: Secretary-General reports that UNIKOM, after investigating the Bubiyan incidents (see 28 and 29 August), neither found evidence of firing at the location nor was shown evidence that there had been weapons on the Iraqi boats.
Sept. 4	DISARMAMENT: Conference on Disarmament concludes seven-month session in Geneva and predicts a final agreement in 1992 on an international convention banning chemical weapons.
	SOUTH AFRICA: Secretary-General states that "over the last 12 months, the process towards the end of *apartheid* in South Africa, although halting, remained on course" and emphasizes that the "wave of violence that has engulfed the country" has

1991 (continued)

	become a "severe test of confidence" and a "serious obstacle to the evolving political dialogue".
Sept. 6-12	IRAQ: 4th ballistic missile capabilities mission.
Sept. 6	WESTERN SAHARA: UN settlement plan is launched with a formal cease-fire between the forces of Morocco and POLISARIO and the stationing of UN military observers at 10 observation posts.
Sept. 7-14	CYPRUS: Representatives of the Secretary-General hold separate meetings with the leaders of the two communities; both leaders agree to proceed directly to completing an overall framework agreement.
Sept. 9-27	DISARMAMENT: 3rd Review Conference of the States Parties to the Convention on the Prohibition of the Development, Production and Stockpiling of Bacteriological (Biological) and Toxin Weapons and on their Destruction in Geneva discusses verification, confidence-building and technology transfer issues and adopts Final Declaration, in which participants state that the use of biological weapons is "repugnant to the conscience of mankind".
Sept. 9-20	ENVIRONMENT: 3rd session of the Intergovernmental Convention on Climate Change in Nairobi, Kenya, achieves progress on the drafting of an international treaty to counteract the global warming trend to be signed at the UN Conference on Environment and Development in Rio de Janeiro in June 1992.
Sept. 9	IRAQ: UN representative expresses concern over more serious clashes in northern Iraq between government and non-government forces which threatens to impede "any meaningful humanitarian endeavour".
Sept. 10	IRAQ-KUWAIT: Iraq begins returning valuable items removed from Kuwait's national library and Kuwait's National Museum.
Sept. 11-13	NON-GOVERNMENTAL ORGANIZATIONS: Annual Conference for Non-governmental Organizations (NGOS) discusses questions related to the environment, world trade, the search for peace, promoting economic and social justice through development and the interrelationship between peace, justice and development in the work of the UN.
Sept. 13-16	GENERAL ASSEMBLY: Resumed 45th regular session.
Sept. 13	AFGHANISTAN: Secretary-General welcomes the announcement by the USSR and the USA in Moscow of their intention to discontinue weapons deliveries to all Afghan sides, effective 1 January 1992.
	IRAQ: Security Council consults on Iraq's reported refusal to allow an inspection team of the Special Commission to fly UN helicopters over Iraqi weapons sites.

1991 (continued)

Sept. 14-20	IRAQ: 5th nuclear inspection mission.
Sept. 16	EL SALVADOR: Secretary-General, government of El Salvador and FMLN begin a series of meetings at UN Headquarters.
	EMERGENCY RELIEF: Pledging Conference for the Special Emergency Program for the Horn of Africa advances one third of the way towards its $400 million funding goal.
	IRAQ: Iraq calls for the establishment of a fact-finding commission to investigate reports that Iraqi soldiers have been buried alive by US forces during the military operations.
Sept. 17-Dec. 20	GENERAL ASSEMBLY: 46th regular session.
Sept. 17	MEMBERSHIP: General Assembly admits the Democratic People's Republic of Korea, the Republic of Korea, the Federated States of Micronesia, the Marshall Islands, Estonia, Latvia and Lithuania as 160th to 166th member.
Sept. 19-21	GUATEMALA: Government of Guatemala and URNG hold talks with the participation of a UN observer on issues of human rights, aimed at ending the internal armed conflict in Guatemala and bringing about national reconciliation.
Sept. 19	IRAQ: Security Council confirms the ceiling on the sale of Iraqi oil of $1.6 billion and authorizes the immediate release by the Secretary-General of the first one third of that amount to meet Iraq's essential civilian needs.
Sept. 20-Oct. 3	IRAQ: 2nd biological weapons inspection mission.
Sept. 20-21	CAMBODIA: Permanent members of the Security Council (China, France, UK, USA, USSR) and the two Co-Chairmen of the Paris Conference on Cambodia (PCC) meet in Pattaya, Thailand: after consultations with the participants of the meeting, the Secretary-General states that an advance mission could be envisaged as the first stage of the good offices mechanism foreseen in the draft agreements.
Sept. 22-30	IRAQ: 6th nuclear inspection team is detained for four days by Iraqi authorities in a Baghdad parking lot outside a nuclear facility, after having obtained what is described as "top secret" documentation on Iraq's nuclear-weapons program; some of the materials is returned, but the "most sensitive" is confiscated.
Sept. 23	IRAQ: Security Council considers Iraq's refusal to let UN inspection teams overfly Iraqi weapon sites with its own helicopters and asks for a formal, written commitment by Iraq on this matter.
Sept. 24	IRAQ: Iraq protests to the Security Council on how the inspection team has "exceeded its original mandate" by photocopying personal files of industrial and metallurgical personnel; Iraq complies with the Security Council request to allow for the use of the UN helicopters during the

1991 (continued)

inspections; Security Council expresses its "strong condemnation" of how Iraqi authorities have repeatedly prevented the inspectors from carrying out their duties and states that it is "unacceptable" that the inspectors could not freely leave the premises they have inspected.

Sept. 25   EL SALVADOR: Government of El Salvador and FMLN sign a "broad agreement on conditions and guarantees for the reintegration into society of members of the FMLN", known as the New York Agreement.

IRAQ: Secretary-General appeals to Iraq for the release of the inspection team.

YUGOSLAVIA: Security Council strongly urges the parties to the conflict in Yugoslavia to abide strictly by the cease-fire agreements of 17 and 22 September; appeals urgently to all parties to settle their disputes peacefully through negotiation at the Conference on Yugoslavia, to be sponsored by the European Community; and decides that all states should immediately implement a general and complete embargo on all deliveries of weapons and military equipment to Yugoslavia.

Sept. 27   REFORM: Foreign Ministers of the permanent members of the Security Council (China, France, UK, USA, USSR) pledge to make preventive diplomacy a top priority and to work to reinforce the Organization's role in peace-keeping and peacemaking; reaffirms that a revitalized UN has a central and increasingly important part to play in international affairs, in keeping with its Charter principles and in creating a new international order.

Sept. 30   EL SALVADOR: Security Council reaffirms its strong support for the urgent completion of the peace process in El Salvador and expresses its readiness to support the implementation of a settlement; urges the government of El Salvador and FMLN to proceed urgently in reaching a cease-fire and an overall settlement of the armed conflict during the next round of negotiations.

IRAQ: Iraq states that the UN inspection teams' "contrived and biased mode of behaviour" is being used to "give currency to allegations against the Iraqi nuclear program dedicated to peaceful purposes within the framework of the concerted campaign of animosity against Iraq".

Oct. 1   SOCIAL DEVELOPMENT: 1st International Day for the Elderly is observed.

Oct. 2   IRAQ: Iraq charges that the chief inspector of the UN nuclear inspection team has "private links with foreign intelligence circles" and attempts to "insinuate spurious documents that

1991 (continued)

	had nothing to do with us" in order to provide a rationale for "false accusations".
Oct. 3	HAITI: Security Council calls for restoration of the legitimate government following the October coup.
	IRAQ: IAEA reports that there is evidence of a broad-based effort on an implosive-type nuclear weapon, success in machining nuclear-weapons components from natural uranium and parallel developments of a nuclear missile delivery system.
Oct. 6-Nov. 9	IRAQ: 5th chemical weapons inspection mission.
Oct. 7	IRAQ-KUWAIT: Security Council extends the mandate of UNIKIOM for six-month period until 9 April 1992.
Oct. 10	CYPRUS: Security Council endorses the Secretary-General's intentions to resume discussions in early November with the two parties in Cyprus and with Greece and Turkey to complete a set of ideas of an overall framework agreement on Cyprus.
	IRAQ: Security Council approves two new plans to better monitor and verify Iraq's compliance with UN demands for disarmament measures, as specified in the cease-fire agreement.
Oct. 11	HAITI: General Assembly strongly condemns the October coup in Haiti, including the "illegal replacement" of the constitutionally-elected President, Jean-Bertrand Aristide.
Oct. 16	CAMBODIA: Security Council establishes a UN Advance Mission in Cambodia (UNAMIC) to assist the Cambodian parties to maintain a cease-fire and help them address and resolve any cease-fire violations.
Oct. 21	HOSTAGES: Jesse Turner, an American professor detained in Lebanon for almost five years, is released.
Oct. 23	CAMBODIA: Peace treaty is signed at the Paris Conference on Cambodia (PCC) to end the 13-year conflict, including (i) an agreement on a comprehensive political settlement of the Cambodian conflict, the mandate for the UN Transitional Authority in Cambodia (UNTAC), military matters, elections, repatriation of Cambodian refugees and displaced persons, and the principles of a new Cambodian constitution; (ii) an agreement concerning the sovereignty, independence, territorial integrity and inviolability, neutrality and national unity of Cambodia; and (iii) a declaration on the rehabilitation and reconstruction of the country.
Oct. 28	DEBT: Special day devoted to African debt relief is observed by General Assembly.

1991 (continued)

Oct. 31   CAMBODIA: Security Council calls on all Cambodian parties
           to comply fully with the new cease-fire arrangements and asks
           the Secretary-General to submit his implementation plan,
           including a detailed cost estimate for UNTAC.

Nov. 6   CENTRAL AMERICA: Security Council extends the mandate
           of ONUCA until 30 April 1992 (on 16 January, the Council
           decides to terminate ONUCA's mandate effective 17
           January).

Nov. 9   CAMBODIA: UNAMIC with headquarters in Phnom Penh,
           officially begins operations.

Nov. 13   CUBA: General Assembly defers to 1992 consideration of the
           question of a US economic embargo against Cuba.

Nov. 18   HOSTAGES: Terry Waite, a British hostage since 20 January
           1987, and Thomas Sutherland, an American kidnapped on 9
           June 1985, are released in Lebanon.

Nov. 20   CAMBODIA: General Assembly fully supports the Paris
           Agreements on Cambodia and urges all parties to implement
           fully the accord in close cooperation with UNTAC.

Nov. 21   SECRETARY-GENERAL: Boutros Boutros-Ghali, former
           Deputy Prime Minister of Egypt, is recommended by the
           Security Council for the post of Secretary-General for a five-
           year term beginning 1 January 1992.

Nov. 26   YUGOSLAVIA: Security Council receives a request from
           Yugoslavia, asking for a peace-keeping operation in that
           country.

Nov. 27   YUGOSLAVIA: Security Council strongly urges the parties to
           the conflict to comply with the 23 November cease-fire
           agreement.

Nov. 29   MIDDLE EAST: Security Council extends the mandate of
           UNDOF for six month until 31 May 1992.

Dec. 2-4   HOSTAGES: Americans Joseph Cicippio, kidnapped on 12
           September 1986, Alann Steen kidnapped on 24 January 1987,
           and Terry Anderson kidnapped on 16 March 1985, are
           released in Lebanon.

Dec. 3   SECRETARY-GENERAL: General Assembly appoints Boutros
           Boutros-Ghali as Secretary-General for a five-year term
           beginning 1 January 1992.

Dec. 5   AFGHANISTAN: General Assembly calls for faithful
           implementation of the 1988 Geneva Agreements on
           Afghanistan and calls on all parties concerned to promote
           actively a search for ways towards a political solution
           acceptable to Afghans.

Dec. 6   ANTARCTICA: General Assembly, while welcoming the recent
           signing in Madrid of the Protocol on Environmental
           Protection by the Antarctic Treaty Parties, expresses

1991 (continued)

disappointment that the Protocol was not negotiated with the full participation of the international community.

Dec. 9   ARMS CONTROL: General Assembly calls for the creation of a universal and non-discriminatory register of conventional arms as of 1 January 1992.

IRAN-IRAQ: Secretary General sets out in his report to the Security Council that Iraq's "attack of 22 September 1980" against Iran "entails the responsibility for the conflict" between the two neighbouring countries.

PEACE AND SECURITY: General Assembly urges the Secretary-General to continue monitoring the security situation of small states and to consider bringing to the attention of the Security Council any threats to their security; adopts a Declaration on Fact-finding by the United Nations in the Field of the Maintenance of International Peace and Security which states that fact-finding should be "comprehensive, objective, impartial and timely" and that the dispatch of fact-finding missions could "signal the concern" of the UN and should aim to build confidence and defuse the dispute or situation "while avoiding any aggravation of it".

Dec. 11   DECOLONIZATION: General Assembly states that geographical location, size of population or area, limited natural resources and other such factors should not delay the speedy exercise of the right to self-determination of any non-self-governing territories.

MIDDLE EAST: General Assembly welcomes the convening, under the co-sponsorship of USA and USSR, of the peace conference on the Middle East in Madrid on 30 October 1991; terms peace conference "a significant step towards the establishment of a comprehensive, just and lasting peace in the region"; also states that the convening of an international peace conference on the Middle East under UN auspices would contribute to the promotion of peace in the region.

Dec. 12   CYPRUS: Security Council extends the mandate of UNFICYP for six months until 15 June 1992.

Dec. 13   SOUTHERN AFRICA: General Assembly acknowledges progress made in overcoming obstacles to negotiations towards a new constitutions and arrangements on the transition to a democratic order in South Africa and welcomes the signing of the 14 September National Peace Accord.

Dec. 15   YUGOSLAVIA: Security Council agrees with the Secretary-General's assessment that "conditions for establishing a peace-keeping operation in Yugoslavia still do not exist".

Dec. 16   SOCIAL DEVELOPMENT: General Assembly adopts a set of 18 "Principles for Older Persons" designed "to add life to the years that have been added to life".

1991 (continued)

ZIONISM: General Assembly revokes resolution 3379 (XXX) of 10 November 1975, which had determined that "zionism is a form of racism and racial discrimination".

Dec. 17   CENTRAL AMERICA: General Assembly endorses the Secretary-General's efforts to bring about a firm and lasting peace in Central America.

HUMAN RIGHTS: General Assembly adopts 32 resolutions and decisions relating to human rights, including a new set of international standards for the protection of the mentally ill.

POVERTY: General Assembly calls for international cooperation for the eradication of poverty in developing countries.

Dec. 18   AFRICAN RECOVERY: General Assembly adopts a New Agenda for Africa recovery, containing recommendations for sustained and sustainable growth and development beyond 1991.

CRIME: General Assembly calls for the creation of a new commission on crime prevention and criminal justice as a functional body of ECOSOC.

DEBT: General Assembly expresses its concern that the debt burden constitutes a major obstacle to the "acceleration of growth and development and eradication of poverty" in many countries, despite the countries' often strenuous stabilization and structural adjustment programs.

Dec. 19   DEVELOPMENT: General Assembly urges the international community to implement commitments to the UN program of Action for the Least Developed Countries (LDCs) for the 1990s as "a matter of urgency".

ENTREPRENEURSHIP: General Assembly asks the UN system to improve the efficiency of its activities for promoting entrepreneurship, including the provision of technical assistance to interested countries.

RELIEF: General Assembly establishes the position of a UN Emergency Relief Coordinator to be appointed by the Secretary-General in order to ensure "rapid response" to disasters.

WESTERN SAHARA: Secretary-General reports that there will be a delay of some months before the "necessary conditions" are established for implementing the settlement plan for Western Sahara.

Dec. 20   AIDS: General Assembly urges member states to give the AIDS pandemic top priority by developing strong national AIDS programs to prevent transmission of the virus.

BUDGET: General Assembly approves a program budget of $2.3 billion for the biennium 1992-1993.

1991 (continued)

Dec. 20   CAMBODIA: General Assembly approves $14 million for UNAMIC for the period 1 November 1991 to 30 April 1992.

DEVELOPMENT: General Assembly notes the assurances by developed countries and multilateral financial institutions that resources allocated to Central and Eastern Europe "would not reduce or divert the resources", including development assistance and food aid allocated to the developing countries.

ENVIRONMENT: General Assembly urgently appeals to assist in the study and mitigation of the environmental consequences of the Gulf war.

FISHING: General Assembly makes an unanimous call for an absolute ban on large-scale pelagic drift-net fishing by the end of 1992 "notwithstanding that it will create adverse socio-economic effects on the communities involved in high seas pelagic drift-net fishing operations".

Dec. 23   CYPRUS: Security Council asks the leaders of the two communities in Cyprus and of Greece and Turkey to cooperate fully with the Secretary-General in urgently completing the set of ideas on an overall framework agreement on Cyprus.

HOSTAGES: Body of Lieutenant-Colonel William Higgins, an American national who had served with UNIFIL, abducted on 17 February 1988 and according to his captors executed on 31 July 1989, is handed over to the US Embassy in Lebanon.

Dec. 24   MEMBERSHIP: Russian President Boris Yeltsin informs the Secretary-General that the membership of the USSR in the UN, including the Security Council, will be continued by the Russian Federation (RSFSR), with the support of the countries of the Commonwealth of Independent States (CIS).

Dec. 31   CENTRAL AMERICA: Government of El Salvador and FMLN reach an agreement at UN Headquarters in New York, setting terms for a cease-fire and an end to El Salvador's 12-year civil war.

CHAPTER II

_____

TABLES

TABLE 1
UNITED NATIONS MEMBER STATES, DATE OF ADMISSION
AND SCALE OF ASSESSMENTS

As of 22 May 1992, there are 178 members states of the UN. The dates on which they joined the organization are listed below:

Member	*Date of Admission*	*Assessment in Per Cent*
Afghanistan	19 November 1946	0.01
Albania	14 December 1955	0.01
Algeria	8 October 1962	0.16
Angola	1 December 1976	0.01
Antigua and Barbuda	11 November 1981	0.01
Argentina	24 October 1945	0.57
Armenia	2 March 1992	0.13
Australia	1 November 1945	1.51
Austria	14 December 1955	0.75
Azerbaijan	2 March 1992	0.22
Bahamas	18 September 1973	0.02
Bahrain	21 September 1971	0.03
Bangladesh	17 September 1974	0.01
Barbados	9 December 1966	0.01
Belarus*	24 October 1945	0.48
Belgium	27 December 1945	1.06
Belize	25 September 1981	0.01
Benin	20 September 1960	0.01
Bhutan	21 September 1971	0.01
Bosnia and Herzegovina	22 May 1992	0.04
Bolivia	14 November 1945	0.01
Botswana	17 October 1966	0.01
Brazil	24 October 1945	1.59
Brunei Darussalam	21 September 1984	0.03
Bulgaria	14 December 1955	0.13
Burkina Faso	20 September 1960	0.01
Burundi	18 September 1962	0.01
Cambodia	14 December 1955	0.01
Cameroon	20 September 1960	0.01
Canada	9 November 1945	3.11
Cape Verde	16 September 1975	0.01
Central African Republic	20 September 1960	0.01
Chad	20 September 1960	0.01

*On 19 September 1991, Byelorussia informed the UN that it had changed its name to Belarus.

Member	Date of Admission	Assessment in Per Cent
Chile	24 October 1945	0.08
China	24 October 1945	0.77
Colombia	12 November 1975	0.13
Comoros	20 September 1960	0.01
Congo	2 November 1945	0.01
Costa Rica	20 September 1960	0.01
Côte d'Ivoire	20 September 1960	0.01
Croatia	22 May 1992	0.13
Cuba	24 October 1945	0.09
Cyprus	20 September 1960	0.02
Czechoslovakia	24 October 1945	0.55
Democratic People's Republic of Korea	17 September 1991	0.05
Denmark	24 October 1945	0.65
Djibouti	20 September 1977	0.01
Dominica	18 December 1978	0.01
Dominican Republic	24 October 1945	0.02
Ecuador	21 December 1945	0.03
Egypt*	24 October 1945	0.07
El Salvador	24 October 1945	0.01
Equatorial Guinea	12 November 1968	0.01
Estonia	17 September 1991	0.07
Ethiopia	13 November 1945	0.01
Fiji	13 October 1970	0.01
Finland	14 December 1945	0.57
France	24 October 1945	6.00
Gabon	20 September 1960	0.02
Gambia	21 September 1965	0.01
Georgia	31 July 1992	0.21
Germany**	18 September 1973	8.93
Ghana	8 March 1957	0.01
Greece	25 October 1945	0.35
Grenada	17 September 1974	0.01

---

*Egypt and Syria were original Members of the UN from 24 October 1945. allowing a plebiscite on 21 February 1958, the United Arab Republic was established by a union of Egypt and Syria and continued as a single member. On 13 October 1961, Syria, having resumed its status as an independent state, resumed its separate membership in the UN. On 2 September 1971, the United Arab Republic changed its name to the Arab Republic of Egypt.

**The Federal Republic of Germany and the German Democratic Republic were admitted to membership in the UN on 18 September 1973. Through the accession of the German Democratic Republic to the Federal Republic of Germany, effective from 3 October 1990, the two German states have united to form one sovereign state.

Member	Date of Admission	Assessment in Per Cent
Guatemala	21 November 1945	0.02
Guinea	12 December 1958	0.01
Guinea-Bissau	17 September 1974	0.01
Guyana	20 September 1966	0.01
Haiti	24 October 1945	0.01
Honduras	17 December 1945	0.01
Hungary	14 December 1955	0.18
Iceland	19 November 1946	0.03
India	30 October 1945	0.36
Indonesia*	28 September 1950	0.16
Iran (Islamic Republic of)	24 October 1945	0.77
Iraq	21 December 1945	0.13
Ireland	14 December 1945	0.18
Israel	11 May 1949	0.23
Italy	14 December 1955	4.29
Jamaica	18 September 1962	0.01
Japan	18 December 1956	12.45
Jordan	14 December 1955	0.01
Kazakhstan	2 March 1992	0.35
Kenya	16 December 1963	0.01
Kuwait	14 May 1963	0.25
Kyrgyzstan	2 March 1992	0.06
Lao People's Democratic Republic	14 December 1955	0.01
Latvia	17 September 1991	0.13
Lebanon	24 October 1945	0.01
Lesotho	17 October 1966	0.01
Liberia	2 November 1945	0.01
Libya Arab Jamahiriya	14 December 1955	0.24
Liechtenstein	18 September 1990	0.01
Lithuania	17 September 1991	0.15
Luxembourg	24 October 1945	0.06
Madagascar	20 September 1960	0.01
Malawi	1 December 1964	0.01
Malaysia**	17 September 1957	0.12

*By letter of 20 January 1965, Indonesia announced its decision to withdraw from the UN "at this stage and under the present circumstances". By telegram of 19 September 1966, it announced its decision "to resume full cooperation with the United Nations and to resume participation in its activities". On 28 September 1966, the General Assembly took note of this decision and the President invited representatives of Indonesia to take seats in the Assembly.

**The Federation of Malaya joined the UN on 17 September 1957. On 16 September 1963, its name was changed to Malaysia, following the admission to the new federation of Singapore, Sabah (North Borneo) and Sarawak. Singapore became an independent state on 9 August 1965 and a member of the UN on 21 September 1965.

Member	Date of Admission	Assessment in Per Cent
Maldives	21 September 1965	0.01
Mali	28 September 1960	0.01
Malta	1 December 1964	0.01
Marshall Islands	17 September 1991	0.01
Mauritania	27 October 1961	0.01
Mauritius	24 April 1968	0.01
Mexico	7 November 1945	0.88
Micronesia, Federated States of	17 September 1991	0.01
Moldova	2 March 1992	0.15
Mongolia	27 October 1961	0.01
Morocco	12 November 1956	0.03
Mozambique	16 September 1975	0.01
Myanmar	19 April 1948	0.01
Namibia	23 April 1990	0.01
Nepal	14 December 1955	0.01
Netherlands	10 December 1945	1.50
New Zealand	24 October 1945	0.24
Nicaragua	24 October 1945	0.01
Niger	20 September 1960	0.01
Nigeria	7 October 1960	0.20
Norway	27 November 1945	0.55
Oman	7 October 1971	0.03
Pakistan	30 September 1947	0.06
Panama	13 November 1945	0.02
Papua New Guinea	10 October 1975	0.01
Paraguay	24 October 1945	0.02
Peru	31 October 1945	0.06
Philippines	24 October 1945	0.07
Poland	24 October 1945	0.47
Portugal	14 December 1955	0.20
Qatar	21 September 1971	0.05
Republic of Korea	17 September 1991	0.69
Romania	14 December 1955	0.17
Russian Federation*	24 October 1945	6.71
Rwanda	18 September 1962	0.01

*The Union of Soviet Socialist Republics was an original member of the UN from 24 October 1945. In a letter dated 24 December 1991, Boris Yeltsin, President of the Russian Federation, informed the Secretary-General that the membership of the Soviet Union in the Security Council and all other UN organs was being continued by the Russian Federation with the support of the 11 member countries of the Commonwealth of Independent States.

Member	Date of Admission	Assessment in Per Cent
Saint Kitts and Nevis	23 September 1983	0.01
Saint Lucia	18 September 1979	0.01
Saint Vincent and the Grenadines	16 September 1980	0.01
Samoa	15 December 1976	0.01
San Marino	2 March 1992	0.01
Sao Tome and Principe	16 September 1975	0.01
Saudi Arabia	24 October 1945	0.96
Senegal	28 September 1960	0.01
Seychelles	21 September 1976	0.01
Sierra Leone	27 September 1961	0.01
Singapore	21 September 1965	0.12
Slovenia	22 May 1992	0.09
Solomon Islands	19 September 1978	0.01
Somalia	20 September 1960	0.01
South Africa	7 November 1945	0.41
Spain	14 December 1955	1.98
Sri Lanka	14 December 1955	0.01
Sudan	12 November 1956	0.01
Suriname	4 December 1975	0.01
Swaziland	24 September 1968	0.01
Sweden	19 November 1946	1.11
Syria Arab Republic*	24 October 1945	0.04
Tajikistan	2 March 1992	0.05
Thailand	16 December 1946	0.11
Togo	20 September 1960	0.01
Trinidad and Tobago	18 September 1962	0.05
Tunisia	12 November 1956	0.03
Turkey	24 October 1962	0.27
Turkmenistan	2 March 1992	0.06
Uganda	25 October 1962	0.01
Ukraine	24 October 1945	1.87
United Arab Emirates	9 December 1971	0.21
United Kingdom of Great Britain and Northern Ireland	24 October 1945	5.02
United Republic of Tanzania**	14 December 1961	0.01

---

*Egypt and Syria were original members of the UN from 24 October 1945. Following a plebiscite on 21 February 1958, the United Arab Republic was established by a union of Egypt and Syria and continued as a single member. On 13 October 1961, Syria, having resumed its status as an independent state, resumed its separate membership in the UN.

**Tanganyika was a member of the UN from 14 December 1961 and Zanzibar was a member from 16 December 1963. Following the ratification on 26 April 1964 of Articles of Union between Tanganyika and Zanzibar, the United Republic of Tanganyika and Zanzibar continued as a single member, changing its name to the United Republic of Tanzania on 1 November 1964.

Member	*Date of Admission*	*Assessment in Per Cent*
United States	24 October 1945	25.00
Uruguay	18 December 1945	0.04
Uzbekistan	2 March 1992	0.26
Vanuatu	15 September 1981	0.01
Venezuela	15 November 1945	0.49
Viet Nam	20 September 1977	0.01
Yemen*	30 September 1947	0.01
Yugoslavia	24 October 1945	0.16
Zaire	20 September 1960	0.01
Zambia	1 December 1964	0.01
Zimbabwe	25 August 1980	0.01
	Total	100.02

---

*Yemen was admitted to membership in the UN on 30 September 1947 and Democratic Yemen on 14 December 1967. On 22 May 1990, the two countries merged and have since been represented as one member with the name "Yemen".

TABLE 2
SECURITY COUNCIL MEMBERSHIP

The permanent members are: China, France, UK, USSR (Russian Federation as of 24 December 1991) and USA. In addition to the permanent members, the non-permanent are shown below.

Year	Non-permanent members
1946	Australia, Poland, Brazil, Mexico, Egypt, Netherlands
1947	Australia, Poland, Brazil, Colombia, Syria, Belgium
1948	Canada, Ukraine, Argentina, Colombia, Syria, Belgium
1949	Canada, Ukraine, Argentina, Cuba, Egypt, Norway
1950	India, Yugoslavia, Ecuador, Cuba, Egypt, Norway
1951	India, Yugoslavia, Ecuador, Brazil, Turkey, Netherlands
1952	Pakistan, Greece, Chile, Brazil, Turkey, Netherlands
1953	Pakistan, Greece, Chile, Colombia, Lebanon, Denmark
1954	New Zealand, Turkey, Brazil, Colombia, Lebanon, Denmark
1955	New Zealand, Turkey, Brazil, Peru, Iran, Belgium
1956	Australia, Yugoslavia, Cuba, Peru, Iran, Belgium
1957	Australia, Philippines, Cuba, Colombia, Iraq, Sweden
1958	Canada, Japan, Panama, Colombia, Iraq, Sweden
1959	Canada, Japan, Panama, Argentina, Tunisia, Italy
1960	Ceylon, Poland, Ecuador, Argentina, Tunisia, Italy
1961	Ceylon, Poland, Ecuador, Chile, United Arab Republic, Liberia
1962	Ghana, Romania, Venezuela, Chile, United Arab Republic, Liberia
1963	Ghana, Philippines, Venezuela, Brazil, Morocco, Norway
1964	Ivory Coast, Czechoslovakia, Bolivia, Brazil, Morocco, Norway

Year	*Non-permanent members*
1965	Ivory Coast, Czechoslovakia, Bolivia, Uruguay, Jordan, Netherlands
1966*	Mali, Nigeria, Bulgaria, Japan, Argentina, Uruguay, Jordan, Netherlands, Uganda, New Zealand
1967	Mali, Nigeria, Bulgaria, Japan, Argentina, Brazil, Canada, Denmark, Ethiopia, India
1968	Algeria, Hungary, Pakistan, Paraguay, Senegal, Brazil, Canada, Denmark, Ethiopia, India
1969	Algeria, Hungary, Pakistan, Paraguay, Senegal, Colombia, Finland, Nepal, Spain, Zambia
1970	Burundi, Colombia, Finland, Nepal, Nicaragua, Poland, Sierra Leone, Somalia, Syria
1971	Argentina, Belgium, Burundi, Italy, Japan, Nicaragua, Poland, Sierra Leone, Somalia, Syria
1972	Argentina, Belgium, Guinea, India, Italy, Japan, Panama, Somalia, Sudan, Yugoslavia
1973	Australia, Austria, Guinea, India, Indonesia, Kenya, Panama, Peru, Sudan, Yugoslavia
1974	Australia, Austria, Byelorussia, Cameroon, Costa Rica, Indonesia, Iraq, Kenya, Mauritania, Peru
1975	Byelorussia, Costa Rica, Guyana, Iraq, Italy, Japan, Mauritania, Sweden, Cameroon, Tanzania
1976	Benin, Guyana, Italy, Japan, Libya, Panama, Pakistan, Romania, Sweden, Tanzania
1977	Benin, Canada, Germany (Federal Republic of), India, Libya, Mauritius, Pakistan, Panama, Romania, Venezuela
1978	Bolivia, Canada, Czechoslovakia, Gabon, Germany (Federal Republic of), India, Kuwait, Mauritius, Nigeria, Venezuela

---

*As a result of an amendment to Article 23 of the Charter, the number of non-permanent members of the Security Council increased from 6 to 10.

Year	Non-permanent members
1979	Bangladesh, Bolivia, Czechoslovakia, Gabon, Jamaica, Kuwait, Nigeria, Norway, Portugal, Zambia
1980	Bangladesh, German Democratic Republic, Jamaica, Mexico, Niger, Norway, Philippines, Portugal, Tunisia, Zambia
1981	German Democratic Republic, Ireland, Japan, Mexico, Niger, Panama, Philippines, Spain, Tunisia, Uganda
1982	Guyana, Ireland, Japan, Jordan, Panama, Poland, Spain, Togo, Uganda, Zaire
1983	Guyana, Jordan, Malta, Netherlands, Nicaragua, Pakistan, Poland, Togo, Zaire, Zimbabwe
1984	Egypt, India, Malta, Netherlands, Nicaragua, Pakistan, Peru, Ukraine, Upper Volta, Zimbabwe
1985	Australia, Burkina Faso, Denmark, Egypt, India, Madagascar, Peru, Thailand, Trinidad and Tobago, Ukrainian Soviet Socialist Republic
1986	Australia, Bulgaria, Congo, Denmark, Ghana, Madagascar, Thailand, Trinidad and Tobago, United Arab Emirates, Venezuela
1987	Argentina, Bulgaria, Congo, Germany (Federal Republic of), Ghana, Italy, Japan, United Arab Emirates, Venezuela, Zambia
1988	Algeria, Argentina, Brazil, Germany (Federal Republic of), Italy, Japan, Nepal, Senegal, Yugoslavia, Zambia
1989	Algeria, Brazil, Canada, Colombia, Ethiopia, Finland, Malaysia, Nepal, Senegal, Yugoslavia
1990	Canada, Colombia, Côte d'Ivoire, Cuba, Ethiopia, Finland, Malaysia, Romania, Yemen*, Zaire
1991	Austria, Belgium, China, Côte d'Ivoire, Cuba, Ecuador, India, Romania, Yemen, Zaire, Zimbabwe

---

*Democratic Yemen was elected for a term of office beginning on 1 January 1990. On 22 May 1990, Democratic Yemen and Yemen merged and have since that date been represented as one member with the name "Yemen".

TABLE 3
ECONOMIC AND SOCIAL COUNCIL MEMBERSHIP

Year	Members
1946	Belgium, Canada, Chile, China, Colombia, Cuba, Czechoslovakia, France, Greece, India, Lebanon, Norway, Peru, UK, USA, USSR, Ukraine, Yugoslavia
1947	Byelorussia, Canada, Chile, China, Cuba, Czechoslovakia, France, India, Lebanon, Netherlands, New Zealand, Norway, Peru, Turkey, UK, USA, USSR, Venezuela
1948	Australia, Brazil, Byelorussia, Canada, Chile, China, Denmark, France, Lebanon, Netherlands, New Zealand, Peru, Poland, Turkey, UK, USA, USSR, Venezuela
1949	Australia, Belgium, Brazil, Byelorussia, Chile, China, Denmark, France, India, Lebanon, New Zealand, Peru, Poland, Turkey, UK, USA, USSR, Venezuela
1950	Australia, Belgium, Brazil, Canada, Chile, China, Czechoslovakia, Denmark, France, India, Iran, Mexico, Pakistan, Peru, Poland, UK, USA, USSR
1951	Belgium, Canada, Chile, China, Czechoslovakia, France, India, Iran, Mexico, Pakistan, Peru, Philippines, Poland, Sweden, UK, USA, USSR, Uruguay
1952	Argentina, Belgium, Canada, China, Cuba, Czechoslovakia, Egypt, France, Iran, Mexico, Pakistan, Philippines, Poland, Sweden, UK, USA, USSR, Uruguay
1953	Argentina, Australia, Belgium, China, Cuba, Egypt, France, India, Philippines, Poland, Turkey, Sweden, UK, USA, USSR, Uruguay, Venezuela, Yugoslavia
1954	Argentina, Australia, Belgium, China, Cuba, Czechoslovakia, Denmark, Ecuador, Egypt, France, India, Norway, Pakistan, Turkey, UK, USA, USSR, Venezuela, Yugoslavia
1955	Argentina, Australia, China, Czechoslovakia, Dominican Republic, Ecuador, Egypt, France, India, Netherlands, Norway, Pakistan, Turkey, UK, USA, USSR, Venezuela, Yugoslavia

Year	*Members*
1956	Argentina, Brazil, Canada, China, Czechoslovakia, Dominican Republic, Ecuador, Egypt, France, Greece, Indonesia, Norway, Pakistan, UK, USA, USSR, Yugoslavia
1957	Argentina, Brazil, Canada, China, Dominican Republic, Egypt, Finland, France, Greece, Indonesia, Mexico, Netherlands, Pakistan, Poland, UK, USA, USSR, Yugoslavia
1958	Brazil, Canada, Chile, China, Costa Rica, Finland, France, Greece, Indonesia, Mexico, Netherlands, Pakistan, Poland, Sudan, UK, USA, USSR, Yugoslavia
1959	Afghanistan, Bulgaria, Chile, China, Costa Rica, Finland, France, Mexico, Netherlands, New Zealand, Pakistan, Poland, Spain, Sudan, UK, USA, USSR, Venezuela
1960	Afghanistan, Brazil, Bulgaria, Chile, China, Costa Rica, Denmark, France, Japan, Mexico, Netherlands, New Zealand, Poland, Spain, Sudan, UK, USA, USSR, Venezuela
1961	Afghanistan, Brazil, Bulgaria, Denmark, El Salvador, Ethiopia, France, Italy, Japan, Jordan, New Zealand, Poland, Spain, UK, USA, USSR, Uruguay, Venezuela
1962	Australia, Brazil, Colombia, Denmark, El Salvador, Ethiopia, India, Italy, Japan, Jordan, Senegal, UK, USA, USSR, Uruguay, Yugoslavia
1963	Argentina, Australia, Austria, Colombia, Czechoslovakia, El Salvador, Ethiopia, France, India, Italy, Japan, Jordan, Senegal, UK, USA, USSR, Uruguay, Yugoslavia
1964	Algeria, Argentina, Australia, Austria, Chile, Colombia, Czechoslovakia, Ecuador, France, India, Iraq, Japan, Luxembourg, Senegal, UK, USA, USSR, Yugoslavia
1965	Algeria, Argentina, Austria, Canada, Chile, Czechoslovakia, Ecuador, France, Gabon, Iraq, Japan, Luxembourg, Pakistan, Peru, Romania, UK, USA, USSR
1966*	Algeria, Cameroon, Canada, Chile, Czechoslovakia, Dahomey, Ecuador, France, Gabon, Greece, India, Iran, Iraq, Luxembourg, Morocco, Pakistan,

---

*As a result of an amendment to Article 61 of the Charter, the number of members of ECOSOC was increased from 18 to 27.

Year   *Members*

Panama, Peru, Philippines, Romania, Sierra Leone, Tanzania, UK, USA, USSR, Venezuela

1967   Belgium, Cameroon, Canada, Czechoslovakia, Dahomey, France, Gabon, Guatemala, India, Iran, Kuwait, Libya, Mexico, Morocco, Pakistan, Panama, Peru, Philippines, Romania, Sierra Leone, Sweden, Tanzania, Turkey, UK, USA, USSR, Venezuela

1968   Argentina, Belgium, Bulgaria, Chad, Congo (Brazzaville), Czechoslovakia, France, Guatemala, India, Iran, Ireland, Japan, Kuwait, Libya, Mexico, Morocco, Panama, Philippines, Sierra Leone, Sweden, Tanzania, Turkey, UK, USA, USSR, Upper Volta, Venezuela

1969   Argentina, Belgium, Bulgaria, Chad, Congo (Brazzaville), France, Guatemala, India, Indonesia, Ireland, Jamaica, Japan, Kuwait, Libya, Mexico, Norway, Pakistan, Sierra Leone, Sudan, Tanzania, Turkey, UK, USA, USSR, Upper Volta, Uruguay, Venezuela

1970   Argentina, Brazil, Bulgaria, Ceylon, Chad, Congo (Brazzaville), France, Ghana, Greece, India, Indonesia, Ireland, Italy, Jamaica, Japan, Kenya, Norway, Pakistan, Peru, Sudan, Tunisia, UK, USA, USSR, Upper Volta, Uruguay, Yugoslavia

1971   Brazil, Ceylon, Congo (Democratic Republic of), France, Ghana, Greece, Haiti, Hungary, Indonesia, Italy, Jamaica, Kenya, Lebanon, Madagascar, Malaysia, New Zealand, Niger, Norway, Pakistan, Peru, Sudan, Tunisia, UK, USA, USSR, Uruguay, Yugoslavia

1972   Bolivia, Brazil, Burundi, Ceylon, Chile, China, Finland, France, Ghana, Greece, Haiti, Hungary, Italy, Japan, Kenya, Lebanon, Madagascar, Malaysia, New Zealand, Niger, Peru, Poland, Tunisia, UK, USA, USSR, Zaire

1973   Algeria, Bolivia, Brazil, Burundi, Chile, China, Finland, France, Haiti, Hungary, Japan, Lebanon, Madagascar, Malaysia, Mali, Mongolia, Netherlands, New Zealand, Niger, Poland, Spain, Trinidad and Tobago, Uganda, UK, USA, USSR, Zaire

Following the ratification of an amendment to Article 61 of the Charter, the General Assembly on 12 October 1973, elected 27 additional members to the Council. Therefore, from 12 October to 31 December 1973 the membership of the Council was enlarged to 54. The 27 additional members were:

Argentina, Barbados, Belgium, Canada, Denmark, Egypt, Ghana, Guinea, India, Indonesia, Italy, Kenya, Pakistan, Peru, Philippines, Romania,

Year	*Members*

Senegal, Sudan, Sri Lanka, Sweden, Tunisia, Turkey, Ukraine, Yemen, Yugoslavia

1974   Algeria, Argentina, Australia, Belgium, Bolivia, Brazil, Burundi, Canada, Chile, China, Colombia, Congo, Czechoslovakia, Democratic Yemen, Egypt, Ethiopia, Fiji, Finland, France, German Democratic Republic, Germany (Federal Republic of), Guatemala, Guinea, India, Indonesia, Iran, Italy, Ivory Coast, Jamaica, Japan, Jordan, Kenya, Liberia, Mali, Mexico, Mongolia, Netherlands, Pakistan, Poland, Romania, Senegal, Spain, Sweden, Thailand, Trinidad and Tobago, Turkey, Uganda, UK, USA, USSR, Venezuela, Yugoslavia, Zaire, Zambia

1975   Algeria, Argentina, Australia, Belgium, Brazil, Bulgaria, Canada, China, Colombia, Congo, Czechoslovakia, Democratic Yemen, Denmark, Ecuador, Egypt, Ethiopia, Fiji, France, Gabon, German Democratic Republic, Germany (Federal Republic of), Guatemala, Guinea, Indonesia, Iran, Italy, Ivory Coast, Jamaica, Japan, Jordan, Kenya, Liberia, Mali, Mexico, Mongolia, Netherlands, Norway, Pakistan, Peru, Romania, Senegal, Spain, Thailand, Trinidad and Tobago, Turkey, Uganda, UK, USA, USSR, Venezuela, Yemen, Yugoslavia, Zaire, Zambia

1976   Afghanistan, Algeria, Argentina, Australia, Austria, Bangladesh, Belgium, Bolivia, Brazil, Bulgaria, Canada, China, Colombia, Congo, Cuba, Czechoslovakia, Democratic Yemen, Denmark, Ecuador, Egypt, Ethiopia, France, Gabon, German Democratic Republic, Germany (Federal Republic of), Greece, Iran, Italy, Ivory Coast, Jamaica, Japan, Jordan, Kenya, Liberia, Malaysia, Mexico, Nigeria, Norway, Pakistan, Peru, Portugal, Romania, Thailand, Togo, Tunisia, Uganda, UK, USA, USSR, Venezuela, Yemen, Yugoslavia, Zaire, Zambia

1977   Afghanistan, Algeria, Argentina, Australia, Austria, Bangladesh, Bolivia, Brazil, Bulgaria, Canada, China, Colombia, Cuba, Czechoslovakia, Denmark, Ecuador, Ethiopia, France, Gabon, Germany (Federal Republic of), Greece, Iran, Iraq, Italy, Jamaica, Japan, Kenya, Malaysia, Mauritania, Mexico, Netherlands, New Zealand, Nigeria, Norway, Pakistan, Peru, Philippines, Poland, Portugal, Rwanda, Somalia, Sudan, Syria, Togo, Trinidad and Tobago, Tunisia, Uganda, UK, USA, USSR, Ukraine, United Arab Emirates, United Republic of Cameroon, United Republic of Tanzania, Upper Volta, Venezuela, Yugoslavia

1978   Afghanistan, Algeria, Argentina, Austria, Bangladesh, Bolivia, Brazil, Central African Empire, China, Colombia, Cuba, Dominican Republic, Finland, France, Germany (Federal Republic of), Greece, Hungary, India, Iran, Iraq, Italy, Jamaica, Japan, Lesotho, Malaysia, Malta, Mauritania, Mexico, Netherlands, New Zealand, Nigeria, Philippines, Poland, Portugal, Romania, Rwanda, Somalia, Sudan, Sweden, Syria, Togo, Trinidad and

Year   *Members*

Tobago, Tunisia, Uganda, UK, USA, USSR, Ukraine, United Arab
Emirates, United Republic of Cameroon, United Republic of Tanzania,
Upper Volta, Venezuela, Yugoslavia, Zambia

1979   Algeria, Argentina, Barbados, Brazil, Central African Empire, China,
Colombia, Cyprus, Dominican Republic, Ecuador, Finland, France, German
Democratic Republic, Germany (Federal Republic of), Ghana, Hungary,
India, Indonesia, Iran, Iraq, Ireland, Italy, Jamaica, Japan, Lesotho, Malta,
Mauritania, Mexico, Morocco, Netherlands, New Zealand, Pakistan,
Philippines, Poland, Romania, Rwanda, Senegal, Somalia, Spain, Sudan,
Sweden, Syria, Trinidad and Tobago, Turkey, UK, USA, USSR, Ukraine,
United Arab Emirates, United Republic of Cameroon, United Republic of
Tanzania, Upper Volta, Venezuela, Zambia

1980   Algeria, Argentina, Australia, Bahamas, Barbados, Belgium, Brazil,
Bulgaria, Central African Republic, China, Cyprus, Dominican Republic,
Ecuador, Ethiopia, Finland, France, German Democratic Republic, Germany
(Federal Republic of), Ghana, Hungary, India, Indonesia, Iraq, Ireland,
Italy, Japan, Jordan, Lesotho, Libya, Malawi, Malta, Mexico, Morocco,
Nepal, Nigeria, Pakistan, Romania, Senegal, Spain, Sweden, Thailand,
Trinidad and Tobago, Turkey, UK, USA, USSR, United Arab Emirates,
United Republic of Cameroon, United Republic of Tanzania, Venezuela,
Yugoslavia, Zaire, Zambia

1981   Algeria, Argentina, Australia, Bahamas, Bangladesh, Barbados, Belgium,
Brazil, Bulgaria, Burundi, Byelorussia, Canada, Chile, China, Cyprus,
Denmark, Ecuador, Ethiopia, Fiji, France, German Democratic Republic,
Germany (Federal Republic of), Ghana, India, Indonesia, Iraq, Ireland, Italy,
Jordan, Kenya, Libya, Malawi, Mexico, Morocco, Nepal, Nicaragua,
Nigeria, Norway, Pakistan, Peru, Poland, Senegal, Spain, Sudan, Thailand,
Turkey, UK, USA, USSR, United Republic of Cameroon, Venezuela,
Yugoslavia, Zaire, Zambia

1982   Argentina, Australia, Austria, Bahamas, Bangladesh, Belgium, Benin, Brazil,
Bulgaria, Burundi, Byelorussia, Canada, Chile, China, Colombia, Denmark,
Ethiopia, Fiji, France, Germany (Federal Republic of), Greece, India, Iraq,
Italy, Japan, Jordan, Kenya, Liberia, Libya, Malawi, Mali, Mexico, Nepal,
Nicaragua, Nigeria, Norway, Pakistan, Peru, Poland, Portugal, Qatar,
Romania, Saint Lucia, Sudan, Swaziland, Thailand, Tunisia, UK, USA,
USSR, United Republic of Cameroon, Venezuela, Yugoslavia, Zaire

1983   Algeria, Argentina, Austria, Bangladesh, Benin, Botswana, Brazil, Bulgaria,
Burundi, Byelorussia, Canada, China, Colombia, Congo, Denmark, Djibouti,
Ecuador, Fiji, France, German Democratic Republic, Germany (Federal
Republic of), Greece, India, Japan, Kenya, Lebanon, Liberia, Luxembourg,
Malaysia, Mali, Mexico, Netherlands, New Zealand, Nicaragua, Norway,

Year *Members*

Pakistan, Peru, Poland, Portugal, Qatar, Romania, Saint Lucia, Saudi Arabia, Sierra Leone, Sudan, Suriname, Swaziland, Thailand, Tunisia, UK, USA, USSR, United Republic of Cameroon, Venezuela

1984 Algeria, Argentina, Austria, Benin, Botswana, Brazil, Bulgaria, Canada, China, Colombia, Congo, Costa Rica, Djibouti, Ecuador, Finland, France, German Democratic Republic, Germany (Federal Republic of), Greece, Indonesia, Japan, Lebanon, Liberia, Luxembourg, Malaysia, Mali, Mexico, Netherlands, New Zealand, Pakistan, Papua New Guinea, Poland, Portugal, Qatar, Romania, Saint Lucia, Saudi Arabia, Sierra Leone, Somalia, Sri Lanka, Suriname, Sweden, Thailand, Tunisia, Uganda, UK, USA, USSR, Venezuela, Yugoslavia, Zaire

1985 Algeria, Argentina, Bangladesh, Botswana, Brazil, Bulgaria, Canada, China, Colombia, Congo, Costa Rica, Djibouti, Ecuador, Finland, France, German Democratic Republic, Germany (Federal Republic of), Guinea, Guyana, Haiti, Iceland, India, Indonesia, Japan, Lebanon, Luxembourg, Malaysia, Mexico, Morocco, Netherlands, New Zealand, Nigeria, Papua New Guinea, Poland, Romania, Rwanda, Saudi Arabia, Senegal, Sierra Leone, Somalia, Spain, Sri Lanka, Suriname, Sweden, Thailand, Turkey, Uganda, UK, USA, USSR, Venezuela, Yugoslavia, Zaire, Zimbabwe

1986 Argentina, Australia, Bangladesh, Belgium, Brazil, Byelorussia Soviet Socialist Republic, Canada, China, Colombia, Costa Rica, Djibouti, Egypt, Finland, France, Gabon, German Democratic Republic, Germany (Federal Republic of), Guinea, Guyana, Haiti, Iceland, India, Indonesia, Iraq, Italy, Jamaica, Japan, Morocco, Mozambique, Nigeria, Pakistan, Panama, Papua New Guinea, Peru, Philippines, Poland, Romania, Rwanda, Senegal, Sierra Leone, Somalia, Spain, Sri Lanka, Sweden, Syrian Arab Republic, Turkey, Uganda, UK, USA, USSR, Venezuela, Yugoslavia, Zaire, Zimbabwe

1987 Australia, Bangladesh, Belgium, Belize, Bolivia, Brazil, Bulgaria, Byelorussia Soviet Socialist Republic, Canada, China, Colombia, Denmark, Djibouti, Egypt, France, Gabon, German Democratic Republic, Germany (Federal Republic of), Guinea, Haiti, Iceland, India, Iran (Islamic Republic of), Iraq, Italy, Jamaica, Japan, Morocco, Mozambique, Nigeria, Norway, Oman, Pakistan, Panama, Peru, Philippines, Poland, Romania, Rwanda, Senegal, Sierra Leone, Somalia, Spain, Sri Lanka, Sudan, Syrian Arab Republic, Turkey, UK, USA, USSR, Uruguay, Venezuela, Zaire, Zimbabwe

1988 Australia, Belgium, Belize, Bolivia, Bulgaria, Byelorussian SSR, Canada, China, Colombia, Cuba, Denmark, Djibouti, Egypt, France, Gabon, German Democratic Republic, Germany (Federal Republic of), Ghana, Greece, Guinea, India, Iran (Islamic Republic of), Iraq, Ireland, Italy, Jamaica, Japan, Lesotho, Liberia, Libya, Mozambique, Norway, Oman, Pakistan, Panama, Peru, Philippines, Poland, Portugal, Rwanda, Saudi Arabia, Sierra

Year   *Members*

Leone, Somalia, Sri Lanka, Sudan, Syrian Arab Republic, Trinidad and
Tobago, UK, Uruguay, USA, USSR, Venezuela, Yugoslavia, Zaire

1989   Bahamas, Belize, Bolivia, Brazil, Bulgaria, Cameroon, Canada, China,
Colombia, Cuba, Czechoslovakia, Denmark, France, Germany (Federal
Republic of), Ghana, Greece, Guinea, India, Indonesia, Iran (Islamic
Republic of), Iraq, Ireland, Italy, Japan, Jordan, Kenya, Lesotho, Liberia,
Libya, Netherlands, New Zealand, Nicaragua, Niger, Norway, Oman,
Poland, Portugal, Rwanda, Saudi Arabia, Somalia, Sri Lanka, Sudan,
Thailand, Trinidad and Tobago, Tunisia, UK, Ukrainian Soviet Socialist
Republic, Uruguay, USA, USSR, Venezuela, Yugoslavia, Zaire, Zambia

1990   Algeria, Bahamas, Bahrain, Brazil, Bulgaria, Burkina Faso, Cameroon,
Canada, China, Colombia, Cuba, Czechoslovakia, Ecuador, Finland, France,
German Democratic Republic*, Germany (Federal Republic of), Ghana,
Greece, Guinea, India, Indonesia, Iran (Islamic Republic of), Iraq, Ireland,
Italy, Jamaica, Japan, Jordan, Kenya, Lesotho, Liberia, Libya, Mexico,
Netherlands, New Zealand, Nicaragua, Niger, Pakistan, Romania**,
Rwanda, Saudi Arabia, Sweden, Thailand, Trinidad and Tobago, Tunisia,
UK, Ukrainian Soviet Socialist Republic, Uruguay, USA, USSR, Venezuela,
Yugoslavia, Zaire, Zambia

1991   Algeria, Argentina, Austria, Bahamas, Bahrain, Botswana, Brazil, Bulgaria,
Burkina Faso, Cameroon, Canada, Chile, China, Czechoslovakia, Ecuador,
Finland, France, Germany, Guinea, Indonesia, Iran (Islamic Republic of),
Iraq, Italy, Jamaica, Japan, Jordan, Kenya, Malaysia, Mexico, Morocco,
Netherlands, New Zealand, Nicaragua, Niger, Pakistan, Peru, Romania,
Rwanda, Somalia, Spain, Sweden, Syrian Arab Republic, Thailand, Togo,
Trinidad and Tobago, Tunisia, Turkey, UK, Ukrainian Soviet Socialist
Republic, USA, USSR, Yugoslavia, Zaire, Zambia

---

*Member until 3 October 1990.
**As of 16 November 1990 to fill the seat vacated by the German Democratic Republic as a
result of its accession to the Federal Republic of Germany on 3 October 1990.

TABLE 4
TRUSTEESHIP COUNCIL MEMBERSHIP

According to Article 86 of the Charter the Trusteeship Council is composed of three categories of: a) members administering trust territories; b) members mentioned by name in Article 23 as are not administering trust territories; c) members elected for three-year terms by the General Assembly as may be necessary to ensure that the total number of members of the Trusteeship Council is equally divided between those members of the UN which administer trust territories and those which do not.

Year   *Members according to categories*

1947	a)	Australia, Belgium, France, New Zealand, UK
	b)	China, USA, USSR
	c)	Iraq, Mexico

1948	a)	Australia, Belgium, France, New Zealand, UK, USA
	b)	China, USSR
	c)	Costa Rica, Iraq, Mexico, Philippines

1949	a)	Australia, Belgium, France, New Zealand, UK, USA
	b)	China, USSR
	c)	Costa Rica, Iraq, Mexico, Philippines

1950	a)	Australia, Belgium, France, New Zealand, UK, USA
	b)	China, USSR
	c)	Argentina, Dominican Republic, Iraq, Philippines

1951	a)	Australia, Belgium, France, New Zealand, UK, USA
	b)	China, USSR
	c)	Argentina, Dominican Republic, Iraq, Thailand

1952	a)	Australia, Belgium, France, New Zealand, UK, USA
	b)	China, USSR
	c)	Dominican Republic, El Salvador, Iraq, Thailand

1953	a)	Australia, Belgium, France, New Zealand, UK, USA
	b)	China, USSR
	c)	Dominican Republic, El Salvador, Syria, Thailand

1954	a)	Australia, Belgium, France, New Zealand, UK, USA
	b)	China, USSR
	c)	El Salvador, Haiti, India, Syria

Year	*Members according to categories*

1955 a) Australia, Belgium, France, New Zealand, UK, USA
      b) China, USSR
      c) El Salvador, Haiti, India, Syria

1956 a) Australia, Belgium, France, Italy*, New Zealand, UK, USA
      b) China, USSR
      c) Burma, Guatemala, Haiti, India, Syria

1957 a) Australia, Belgium, France, Italy, New Zealand, UK, USA
      b) China, USSR
      c) Burma, Guatemala, Haiti, India, Syria

1958 a) Australia, Belgium, France, Italy, New Zealand, UK, USA
      b) China, USSR
      c) Burma, Guatemala, Haiti, India, United Arab Republic

1959 a) Australia, Belgium, France, Italy, New Zealand, UK, USA
      b) China, USSR
      c) Burma, Haiti, India, Paraguay, United Arab Republic

1960 a) Australia, Belgium, France, Italy, New Zealand, UK, USA
      b) China, USSR
      c) Bolivia, Burma, India, Paraguay, United Arab Republic

1961 a) Australia, Belgium, New Zealand, UK, USA
      b) China, France, USSR
      c) Bolivia, Burma, India, United Arab Republic

1962 a) Australia, Belgium, New Zealand, UK, USA
      b) China, France, USSR
      c) Bolivia, India

1963 a) Australia, New Zealand, UK, USA
      b) China, France, USSR
      c) Liberia

1964 a) Australia, New Zealand, UK, USA
      b) China, France, USSR
      c) Liberia

1965 a) Australia, New Zealand, UK, USA
      b) China, France, USSR
      c) Liberia

---

*Italy officially became a member of 14 December 1955.

Year	Members according to categories

1966 a) Australia, New Zealand, UK, USA
      b) China, France, USSR
      c) Liberia

1967 a) Australia, New Zealand, UK, USA
      b) China, France, USSR
      c) Liberia

1968 1 January to 31 January:
      a) Australia, New Zealand, UK, USA
      b) China, France, USSR
      c) Liberia
      1 February to 31 December:
      a) Australia, USA
      b) China, France, UK, USSR

1969/ a) Australia, USA
 1976 b) China, France, UK, USSR

1977/ a) USA
 1991 b) China, France, UK, USSR

TABLE 5
INTERNATIONAL COURT OF JUSTICE MEMBERSHIP*

The Court consists of 15 judges. The following persons have served as judges on the court for the term indicated (terms expire on 5th February of the year noted).

Year	Member	Country
1946-1955	Alvarez, A.	Chile
1946-1951	Alzevedo, Ph. (died in office)	Brazil
1946-1965	Badawi Pashi, Ahdel Hamid (died in office)	Egypt - UAR
1946-1964	Basdevant, Jules	France
1946-1952 ·	Fabela Alfaro, Isodor	Mexico
1946-1959	Guerrero, J.G. (died in office)	El Salvador
1946-1961	Hackworth, Green H.	USA
1946-1957	Hsu Mo (died in office)	China
1946-1961	Klaestad, Helge	Norway
1946-1952	Krylov, Sergei Borisovich	USSR
1946-1955	McNair, Sir Arnold Duncan	UK
1946-1958	Reed, John E.	Canada
1946-1967	Winiarski, Bohdan	Poland
1946-1958	Zoricic, Milovan	Yugoslavia
1951-1964	Carneiro, Levi Fernandez	Brazil
1952-1953	Golunski, Sergei Aleksandrovich (resigned)	USSR
1952-1953	Rau, Sir Benegal (died in office)	India
1952-1961	Ugon, Enrique C. Armand	Uruguay
1953-1961	Kojeunikov, Feodor Ivanovick	USSR
1954-1973	Khan, Mohammad Zafrulla	Pakistan
1955-1964	Cordova, Roberto	Mexico
1955-1960	Lauterpacht, Hersch (died in office)	UK
1955-1964	Quintana, Lucio M. Moreno	Argentina
1957-1967	Koo, V.K. Wellington	China
1958-1967	Spender, Sir Percy	Australia
1958-1967	Spiropoulos, Jean	Greece
1959-1963	Alfaro, Ricardo J.	Panama
1960-1973	Fitzmaurice, Sir Gerald	UK
1961-1970	Rivero, Jose Luis Bustamante y	Peru
1961-1970	Jessup, Philip C.	USA
1961-1970	Koretsky, Vladimir M.	USSR
1961-1970	Morelli, Gaetano	Italy

---

*Current members of the Court in bold.

Year	*Member*	*Country*
1961-1970	Tanaka, Kotaro	Japan
1964-1982	Forster, Isaac	Senegal
1964-1982	Gros, Andre	France
1967-1976	Ammoun, Fouad	Lebanon
1967-1976	Bengzon, Cesar	Philippines
1967-1976	Onyeama, Charles D.	Nigeria
1967-1976	Petrén, Sture	Sweden
1967-1985	**Lachs, Manfred**	Poland
1970-1979	de Castro, Federico	Spain
1970-1979	Dillard, Hardy C.	USA
1970-1979	Ignacio-Pinto, Louis	Benin
1970-1979	Jimenez de Aréchaga, Eduardo	Uruguay
1973-1985	Morozov, Planton D. (resigned)	USSR
1973-1981	Waldock, Sir Humphrey (died in office)	UK
1973-1988	Singh, Nagendra (died in office)	India
1973-1991	Ruda, Jose Maria	Argentina
1976-1994	**Elis, Taslim Olawale**	Nigeria
1976-1985	Mosler, Herman	Germany (F.R.)
1976-1994	**Oda, Shigeru**	Japan
1976-1980	Tarazi, Salah El Dine (died in office)	Syria
1979-1997	**Ago, Robert**	Italy
1979-1980	Baxter, Richard R. (died in office)	USA
1979-1982	El-Erian, Abdullah Ali (died in office)	Egypt
1979-1988	Camara, Jose Sette	Brazil
1981-1985	El-Khani, Abdallah Fikri	Syria
1981-1997	**Schwebel, Stephen M.**	USA
1982-1987	de Lacharrière, Guy Ladreit (died in office)	France
1982-2000	**Jennings, Sir Robert Yewdall**	UK
1982-1991	Mbaye, Kéba	Senegal
1982-1997	**Bedjaoui, Mohammed**	Algeria
1985-1994	**Evensen, Jens**	Norway
1985-1994	**Zhengyu, Ni**	China
1985-1997	**Tarassov, Nikolai K.**	USSR
1987-2000	**Guillaume, Gilbert**	France
1988-1997	**Shahabuddeen, Mohamed**	Guyana
1989-1991	Pathak, Raghunandan Swarup	India
1991-2000	**Mawdsley, Andrés Aguilar**	Venezuela
1991-2000	**Ranjeva, Ranjeva**	Sri Lanka
1991-2000	**Weeramantry, Christopher G.**	Madagascar

TABLE 6
SECRETARY-GENERAL: TERMS OF OFFICE

Period	Secretary-General	Country
1946, Feb. 1 - 1953, April 10	Trygve Lie	Norway
1953, April 10 - 1961, Sept. 18	Dag Hammarskjöld	Sweden
1961, Nov. 3 - 1971, Dec. 31	U Thant*	Burma
1972, Jan. 1 - 1981, Dec. 31	Kurt Waldheim	Austria
1982, Jan. 1 - 1991, Dec. 31	Javier Pérez de Cuéllar	Peru
1992, Jan. 1 - 1996, Dec. 31	Boutros Boutros-Ghali	Egypt

*Acting Secretary-General from 1961, Nov. 3 to 1962, Nov. 30.

TABLE 7
PRESIDENTS OF THE GENERAL ASSEMBLY*

Year	President	Country
1946	Mr. Paul-Henri Spaak	Belgium
1947	Mr. Oswaldo Aranha	Brazil
1948	Mr. H.V. Evatt	Australia
1949	Mr. Carlos P. Romulo	Philippines
1950	Mr. Nasrollah Entezam	Iran
1951	Mr. Luis Pdilla Nervo	Mexico
1952	Mr. Lester B. Pearson	Canada
1953	Mr. Vijaya Lalshmi Pandit	India
1954	Mr. Eelco N. van Kleffens	Netherlands
1955	Mr. José Maza	Chile
1956	Prince Wan Waithayakon	Thailand
1957	Sir Leslie Munro	New Zealand
1958	Mr. Charles Malik	Lebanon
1959	Mr. Víctor Andrés Belaúnde	Peru
1960	Mr. Frederick H. Boland	Ireland
1961	Mr. Mongi Slim	Tunisia
1962	Sir Muhammad Zafrulla Khan	Pakistan
1963	Mr. Carlos Sosa Rodríguez	Venezuela
1964	Mr. Alex Quaison-Sackey	Ghana
1965	Mr. Amintore Fanfani	Italy
1966	Mr. Abdul Rahman Pazhwak	Afghanistan
1967	Mr. Corneliu Manescu	Romania
1968	Mr. Emilio Arenales Catalán	Guatemala
1969	Mr. Angie E. Brooks	Liberia
1970	Mr. Edvard Hambro	Norway
1971	Mr. Adam Malik	Indonesia
1972	Mr. Stanislaw Trepczynski	Poland
1973	Mr. Leopoldo Benites	Ecuador

---

*General Assembly Presidents normally preside over special and emergency special sessions of the United Nations during their tenure. The exceptions were: Mr. José Arce of Argentina, who presided over the second special session in 1948, and Mr. Rudecindo Ortega of Chile, who presided over the first and second emergency special sessions held in 1956.

Year	*President*	*Country*
1974	Mr. Abdelaziz Bouteflika	Algeria
1975	Mr. Gaston Thorn	Luxembourg
1976	Mr. H.S. Amerasinghe	Sri Lanka
1977	Mr. Lazar Mojsov	Yugoslavia
1978	Mr. Indalecio Liévano	Colombia
1979	Mr. Salim A. Salim	United Republic of Tanzania
1980	Mr. Rüdiger von Wechmar	Federal Republic of Germany
1981	Mr. Ismat T. Kittani	Iraq
1982	Mr. Imre Hollai	Hungary
1983	Mr. Jorge E. Illueca	Panama
1984	Mr. Paul J.F. Lusaka	Zambia
1985	Mr. Jaime de Piniés	Spain
1986	Mr. Humayun Rasheed Choudhury	Bangladesh
1987	Mr. Peter Florin	German Democratic Republic
1988	Mr. Dante M. Caputo	Argentina
1989	Mr. Joseph Nanven Garba	Nigeria
1990	Mr. Guido de Marco	Malta
1991	Mr. Samir S. Shihabi	Saudi Arabia

TABLE 8
PRESIDENTS OF THE ECONOMIC AND SOCIAL COUNCIL

Year	Session	President	Country
1946	I	Sir A. Ramaswami Mudaliar	India
	II	Sir A. Ramaswami Mudaliar	India
	III	Sir A. Ramaswami Mudaliar	India
1947	IV	Andrija Stampar	Yugoslavia
	V	Sir A. Ramaswami Mudaliar	India
1948	VI	Charles Malik	Lebanon
	VII	Charles Malik	Lebanon
1949	VIII	James Thorn	New Zealand
	IX	James Thorn	New Zealand
1950	X	Heran Santa Cruz	Chile
	XI	Heran Santa Cruz	Chile
	X resumed	Heran Santa Cruz	Chile
	XII	Heran Santa Cruz	Chile
1951	XIII	Heran Santa Cruz	Chile
	XIII resumed	Heran Santa Cruz	Chile
1952	1st special	Jiri Nosek	Czechoslovakia
	XIV	Sayed Amjad Ali	Pakistan
	XIV resumed	Sayed Amjad Ali	Pakistan
1953	XV	Raymond Scheyven	Belgium
	XVI	Raymond Scheyven	Belgium
	XVI resumed	Raymond Scheyven	Belgium
1954	XVII	Juan I. Cooke	Argentina
	XVIII	Juan I. Cooke	Argentina
	XVIII resumed	Juan I. Cooke	Argentina
1955	XIX	Douglas Copland	Australia
	XIX resumed	Douglas Copland	Australia
	XX	Douglas Copland	Australia
	XX resumed	Douglas Copland	Australia
1956	XXI	Hans Engen	Norway
	XXII	Hans Engen	Norway
	XXII resumed	Hans Engen	Norway
1957	XXIII	Mohammad Mir Khan	Pakistan
	XXIV	Mohammad Mir Khan	Pakistan
	XXIV resumed	Mohammad Mir Khan	Pakistan
1958	XXV	George F. Davidson	Canada
	XXVI	George F. Davidson	Canada
	XXVI resumed	George F. Davidson	Canada

Year	*Session*	*President*	*Country*
1959	XXVII	Daniel Cosio Villegas	Mexico
	XXVIII	Daniel Cosio Villegas	Mexico
	XXVIII resumed	Daniel Cosio Villegas	Mexico
1960	XXIX	C.W.A. Schurmann	Netherlands
	XXX	C.W.A. Schurmann	Netherlands
	XXX resumed	C.W.A. Schurmann	Netherlands
1961	XXXI	Foss Shanahan	New Zealand
	XXXII	Foss Shanahan	New Zealand
	XXXII resumed	Foss Shanahan	New Zealand
1962	XXXIII	Jerzy Michalowski	Poland
	XXXIV	Jerzy Michalowski	Poland
	XXXIV resumed	Jerzy Michalowski	Poland
1963	XXXV	Alfonso Patino	Colombia
	XXXVI	Alfonso Patino	Colombia
	XXXVI resumed	Alfonso Patino	Colombia
1964	XXXVI resumed	J. Hajek	Czechoslovakia
	XXXVII	Sir Ronald Walker	Australia
1965	XXXVII resumed	Sir Ronald Walker	Australia
	XXXVIII	Akira Matsui	Japan
	XXXIX	Akira Matsui	Japan
	XXXIX resumed	Akira Matsui	Japan
1966	XL	Twefik Bouattoura	Algeria
	XLI	Twefik Bouattoura	Algeria
1967	XLII	Milan Klusak	Czechoslovakia
	XLIII	Milan Klusak	Czechoslovakia
	XLIII resumed	Milan Klusak	Czechoslovakia
1968	XLIV	Manuel Perez-Guerrero	Venezuela
	XLV	Manuel Perez-Guerrero	Venezuela
	XLV resumed	Manuel Perez-Guerrero	Venezuela
1969	XLVI	R. Scheyven	Belgium
	XLVII	R. Scheyven	Belgium
	XLVII resumed	R. Scheyven	Belgium
1970	XLVIII	J.B.P. Maramis	Indonesia
	XLVIII resumed	J.B.P. Maramis	Indonesia
	XLIX	J.B.P. Maramis	Indonesia
	XLIX resumed	J.B.P. Maramis	Indonesia
1971	L	Rachid Driss	Tunisia
	L resumed	Rachid Driss	Tunisia
	LI	Rachid Driss	Tunisia
	LI resumed	Rachid Driss	Tunisia

Year	Session	President	Country
1972	LII	Karoly Szarda	Hungary
	LII resumed	Karoly Szarda	Hungary
	LIII	Karoly Szarda	Hungary
	LIII resumed	Karoly Szarda	Hungary
1973	LIV	Sergio Armando Frazao	Brazil
	LIV resumed	Sergio Armando Frazao	Brazil
	LV	Sergio Armando Frazao	Brazil
	2nd special	Sergio Armando Frazao	Brazil
	LV resumed	Sergio Armando Frazao	Brazil
1974	LVI	Aprno Kartulo	Finland
	LVII	Aprno Kartulo	Finland
	LVII resumed	Aprno Kartulo	Finland
1975	LVIII	Iqbal A. Akhund	Pakistan
	LVIII resumed	Iqbal A. Akhund	Pakistan
	LIX	Iqbal A. Akhund	Pakistan
1976	LX	Siméon Ake	Ivory Coast
	LXI	Siméon Ake	Ivory Coast
	LXI resumed	Siméon Ake	Ivory Coast
1977	LXII	Ladislav Smid	Czechoslovakia
	LXIII	Ladislav Smid	Czechoslovakia
1978	*	Donald O. Mills	Jamaica
1979		Hugo Scheltema	Netherlands
1980		Andreas V. Mavromattis	Cyprus
1981		Paul V.F. Lusaka	Zambia
1982		Miljan Komatina	Yugoslavia
1983		Sergio Correáà da Costa	Brazil
1984		Karl Fischer	Austria
1985		Kohayashi Tomohiko	Japan
1986		Manuel dos Santos	Mozambique
1987		Eugeniusz Noworyta	Poland
1988		Andrés Aguilar	Venezuela
1989		Kjeld Wilhelm Mortensen	Denmark
1990		Chinmaya R. Gharekhan	India
1991		Hocine Djoudi	Algeria

---

*Since 1978, rather than number the session by Roman numerals, the yearly meetings of the Economic and Social Council have been yearly sessions, divided into an Organizational Part, a First Part, a Second Part and a Resumed Second Part. The same individual serves as Council President for ll the meetings in the given year.

TABLE 9
PRESIDENTS OF THE TRUSTEESHIP COUNCIL

Year	Session	President	Country
1947	I	Francis B. Sayre	USA
1947-8	II	Francis B. Sayre	USA
1948	III	Liu Chieh	China
1949	IV	Liu Chieh	China
	V	Roger Garreau	France
	1st special	Roger Garreau	France
	2nd special	Roger Garreau	France
1950	VI ·	Roger Garreau	France
	VII	Henriquez-Urena	Dominican Republic
	3rd special	Henriquez-Urena	Dominican Republic
1951	VIII	Henriquez-Urena	Dominican Republic
	IX	Sir Alan Burns	UK
	4th special	Sir Alan Burns	UK
1952	X	Sir Alan Burns	UK
	XI	Awni Khalidy	Iraq
1953	XII	L.K. Munro	New Zealand
1954	XIII	L.K. Munro	New Zealand
	XIV	M.R. Urquia	El Salvador
1955	XV	M.R. Urquia	El Salvador
	XVI	Mason Sears	USA
	5th special	M. R. Urquia	El Salvador
1956	XVII	Mason Sears	USA
	XVIII	Rafik Asha	Syria
1956-7	6th special	Rafik Asha	Syria
1957	XIX	Rafik Asha	Syria
	XX	John Douglas Lloyd Hood	Australia
	7th special	John Douglas Lloyd Hood	Australia
1958	XXI	Emilio Arenales Catalan	Guatemala
	XXII	Claeys Bouuaert	Belgium
	8th special	Claeys Bouuaert	Belgium
	9th special	Claeys Bouuaert	Belgium
1959	XXIII	Max H. Dorsinville	Haiti
	XXIV	Max H. Dorsinville	Haiti
	10th special	Max H. Dorsinville	Haiti
1960	XXV	Girolamo Vitelli	Italy
	XXVI	Girolamo Vitelli	Italy
1961	11th special	U Tin Maung	Burma
	XXVII	U Tin Maung	Burma

Year	Session	President	Country
1962	XXVIII	Jonathan B. Bingham	USA
	XXIX	Jonathan B. Bingham	USA
1963	XXX	Nathan Barnes	Liberia
1964	XXXI	Frank Corner	New Zealand
1965	12th special	Frank Corner	New Zealand
	XXXII	Andre Naudy	France
1966	XXXIII	Francis D.W. Brown	UK
1967	XXXIV	Miss Angie Brooks	Liberia
	13th special	Miss Angie Brooks	Liberia
1968	XXXV	Mrs. Eugenie M. Anderson	USA
1969	XXXVI	Paul Gaschignard	France
1970	XXXVII	Sir Laurence McIntyre	Australia
1971	XXXVIII	David Neil Lane	UK
1972	XXXIX	W. Tapley Bennet Jr.	USA
1973	XL	Bertrand de Guilhem de Lataillade	France
1974	XLI	Sir Laurence McIntyre	Australia
	XLI resumed	Sir Laurence McIntyre	Australia
1975	XLII	James Murray	UK
1976	XLIII	Guy Scalabre	France
1977	XLIV	Robin A.C. Byatt	UK
1978	XLV	Jean-Claude Borchenn	France
1979	14th special	Jean-Claude Brochenn	France
	XLVI	Sheila E. Harden	UK
1980	XLVII	Albert Turot	France
1981	XLVIII	Marrack Goulding	UK
1982	XLIX	Paul Poudade	France
	15th special	Paul Poudade	France
1983	L	John W.D. Margetson	UK
	L resumed	John W.D. Margetson	UK
1984	LI	Laurent Rapin	France
1985	LII	Peter M. Maxey	UK
1986	16th special	Peter M. Maxey	UK
	LIII	Laurent Rapin	France
	17th special	Laurent Rapin	France
1987	LIV	John A. Birch	UK
	18th special	John A. Birch	UK
1988	LV	Jean-Michel Gaussot	France
	19th special	Jean-Michel Gaussot	France
1989	LVI	John A. Birch	UK
1990	20th special	Thomas L. Richardson	UK
	LVII	Anne Gazeau-Secret	France
1991	LVIII	Thomas L. Richardson	UK

TABLE 10

UNITED NATIONS PEACE-KEEPING OPERATIONS

1. United Nations Truce Supervision Organization (UNTSO)

Headquarters:	Jerusalem.
Location:	Observer groups are stationed in Beirut and in Sinai.
Duration:	1949 - to present.
Function:	To assist, initially, the Mediator and the Truce Commission in supervising the observance of the truce in Palestine called for by the Security Council; subsequently to supervise the General Armistice Agreements of 1949 and the observation of the cease-fire in the Suez Canal area and the Golan Heights following the Arab-Israeli war of June 1967; currently to assist and co-operates with UNDOF and UNIFIL in the performance of their tasks.

2. United Nations Military Observer Group in India and Pakistan (UNMOGIP)

Headquarters:	Rawalpindi and Srinagar.
Location:	Cease-fire line between India and Pakistan in the State of Jammu and Kashmir.
Duration:	1949 - to present.
Function:	To supervise the cease-fire between India and Pakistan.

3. First United Nations Emergency Force (UNEF I)

Headquarters:	Gaza
Location:	Initially the Suez Canal sector and the Sinai peninsula, later along the Armistice Demarcation Line in the Gaza area and the international frontier in the Sinai peninsula (on the Egyptian side).
Duration:	November 1956 - June 1967.
Function:	To secure and to supervise the cessation of hostilities, including the withdrawal of the armed forces in France, Israel and the UK from Egyptian territory, and further the withdrawal to serve as a buffer between the Egyptian and Israeli forces.

4.   United Nations Observation Group in Lebanon (UNOGIL)

    Headquarters: Beirut.
    Location: Lebanese-Syrian border areas and vicinity of zones held by opposing forces.
    Duration: June 1958 - December 1958.
    Function: To ensure that there was no illegal infiltration of personnel or supply of arms or other *matérial* across the Lebanese borders.

5.   United Nations Operation in the Congo (ONUC)

    Headquarters: Leopoldville (now Kinshasa).
    Location: Republic of the Congo (now Zaire).
    Duration: July 1960 - June 1964.
    Function: Initially, to ensure withdrawal of Belgian forces, to assist the government in maintaining law and order and to provide technical assistance; later to maintain the territorial integrity and the political independence of the Congo, to prevent the occurrence of civil war, and to secure the removal from the Congo of all foreign military, paramilitary and advisory personnel not under the UN Command, and all mercenaries.

6.   United Nations Security Force in West New Guinea (West Irian) (UNSF)

    Headquarters: Hollandia (now Jayaphra).
    Location: West Irian (now Indonesia).
    Duration: October 1962 - April 1963.
    Function: To maintain peace and security in the territory under the UN Temporary Executive Authority (UNTEA) established by agreement between Indonesia and the Netherlands.

7.   United Nations Yemen Observation Mission (UNYOM)

    Headquarters: San'a.
    Location: Yemen.
    Duration: July 1963 - September 1964.
    Function: To observe and certify the implementation of the disengagement agreement between Saudi Arabia and the United Arab Republic.

8.   United Nations Peace-keeping Force in Cyprus (UNFICYP)

    Headquarters: Nicosia.
    Location: Cyprus.
    Duration: March 1964 - to present.
    Function: To prevent the recurrence of fighting and, as necessary, to
                       contribute to the maintenance and restoration of law and order
                       and a return to normal conditions, including, since the hostilities
                       of 1974, the supervision of the cease-fire and the maintenance of
                       a buffer zone between the lines of the Cyprus National Guard
                       and the Turkish and Turkish Cypriot forces.

9.   Mission of the Representative of the Secretary-General in the Dominican
     Republic (DOMREP)

    Headquarters: Santo Domingo.
    Location: Dominican Republic.
    Duration: May 1965 - October 1966
    Function: To observe the situation and to report on breaches of the cease-
                       fire between the two *de facto* authorities.

10.   United Nations India-Pakistan Observation Mission (UNIPOM)

    Headquarters: Lahore and Amritsar.
    Location: Along the India/Pakistan border between Kashmir and the
                       Arabian Sea.
    Duration: September 1965 - March 1966.
    Function: To supervise the cease-fire along the India/Pakistan border
                       except the State of Jammu and Kashmir where UNMOGIP
                       operated, and the withdrawal of all armed personnel to the
                       positions held by them before 5 August 1965.

11.   Second United Nations Emergency Force (UNEF II)

    Headquarters: Ismailia
    Location: Suez Canal sector and later the Sinai peninsula.
    Duration: October 1973 - July 1979.
    Function: To supervise the cease-fire between Egyptian and Israeli forces
                       and, following the conclusion of the agreements of 18 January
                       1974 and 4 September 1975, to supervise the redeployment of
                       Egyptian and Israeli forces and to man and control the buffer
                       zones established under those agreements.

12. United Nations Disengagement Observer Force (UNDOF)

Headquarters:	Damascus.
Location:	Syrian Golan Heights.
Duration:	June 1974 - to present.
Function:	To supervise the cease-fire between Israel and Syria; to supervise the redeployment of Syrian and Israeli forces; and to establish a buffer zone, as provided in the Agreement on Disengagement between Israeli and Syrian Forces of 31 May 1974.

13. United Nations Interim Force in Lebanon (UNIFIL)

Headquarters:	Naquoura.
Location:	Southern Lebanon.
Duration:	March 1978 - to present.
Functions:	To confirm the withdrawal of Israeli forces from southern Lebanon, to restore international peace and security and to assist the Government of Lebanon in ensuring the return of its effective authority in the area.

14. United Nations Good Offices Mission in Afghanistan and Pakistan (UNGOMAP)

Headquarters:	Kabul and Islamabad.
Location:	Afghanistan and Pakistan.
Duration:	April 1988 - March 1990.
Function:	To assist in monitoring the implementation of the Afghanistan peace settlement between Afghanistan and Pakistan of 14 April 1988.

15. United Nations Iran-Iraq Military Observer Group (UNIIMOG)

Headquarters:	Baghdad and Teheran.
Location:	Along the 740-mile border between Iran and Iraq.
Duration:	August 1988 - February 1991.
Function:	To verify, confirm and supervise the cease-fire and withdrawal of troops.

16. United Nations Angola Verification Mission I (UNAVEM I)

Headquarters:	Luanda.
Location:	Angola.
Duration:	January 1989 - June 1991.
Function:	To monitor the withdrawal of Cuban troops.

17. United Nations Transition Assistance Group (UNTAG)

Headquarters: Windhoek.
Location: Namibia.
Duration: April 1989 - March 1990.
Function: To monitor and supervise the Namibia independence plan
                including the release of political prisoners, repeal of
                discriminatory laws, withdrawal of South African soldiers, return
                of refugees, registration drive and electoral campaign, election to
                Constituent Assembly, declaration of independence.

18. United Nations Observer Group in Central America (ONUCA)

Headquarters: Tegucigalpa.
Location: Costa Rica, El Salvador, Guatemala, Honduras and Nicaragua.
Duration: November 1989 - to present.
Function: To verify the compliance of the five Central American countries
                with their security undertakings, in the Esquipulas II Agreement
                of 1987, to cease aid to irregular forces and insurrectionist
                movements in the region and not to allow their territory to be
                used for attacks on other states; mandate was subsequently
                enlarged to monitor the demobilization of the Nicaraguan
                resistance as well as the cease-fire and the separation of forces
                agreed by the Nicaraguan parties as part of the demobilization
                process.

19. United Nations Iraq-Kuwait Observation Mission (UNIKOM)

Headquarters: Umm Qasr.
Location: Khawr Abd Allah waterway between Iraq and Kuwait and the
                demilitarized zone based on the border established by the two
                countries under a 1963 agreement.
Duration: April 1991 - to present.
Function: To monitor and deter violations of the boundary through its
                presence in and surveillance of the demilitarized zone; and to
                observe any hostile action mounted from the territory of one
                state to the other.

20. United Nations Angola Verification Mission II (UNAVEM II)

Headquarters: Luanda.
Location   Angola.
Duration: June 1991 - to present.
Function: To verify the arrangements agreed by the Angolan parties for the monitoring of the cease-fire and for the monitoring of the Angolan police during the cease-fire period, as set out in the Peace Accords for Angola, until after the general elections to be held in Angola in the fall of 1992.

21. United Nations Observer Mission in El Salvador (ONUSAL)

Headquarters: San Salvador.
Location: El Salvador.
Duration: July 1991 - to present.
Function: To monitor all agreements concluded between the government of El Salvador and FMLN, including during the initial phase the monitoring of the human rights situation in El Salvador and, during a second phase, investigate cases and situations involving human rights violations.

22. United Nations Mission for the Referendum in Western Sahara (MINURSO)

Headquarters: Laayoune.
Location: Western Sahara.
Duration: September 1991 - to present.
Function: To supervise a cease-fire between Morocco and POLISARIO, organize and implement a referendum on the future of Western Sahara by which the people of the Territory will chose between independence and integration with Morocco.

23. United Nations Advance Mission in Cambodia (UNAMIC)

Headquarters: Phnom Penh.
Location: Cambodia.
Duration: October 1991 - March 1992.
Function: To assist the Cambodian parties to maintain their cease-fire and help the parties address and resolve any violations or alleged violations of the cease-fire, to provide training in mine-clearance and to initiate a mine-clearance program.

24. United Nations Transitional Authority in Cambodia (UNTAC)

Headquarters:	Phnom Penh.
Location:	Cambodia.
Duration:	March 1992 - present.
Function:	To organize free and fair general elections, verify withdrawal of foreign forces, supervise cease-fire, assist in mine-clearance, ensure weapons control, provide civil administration, maintain law and order, foster an environment in which respect for human rights is ensured, repatriate and resettle Cambodian refugees and displaced persons, rehabilitate essential Cambodian infrastructures during the transitional period.

25. United Nations Protection Force (UNPROFOR)

Headquarters:	Sarajevo.
Location:	Yugoslavia.
Location:	Mainly in the three UN Protected Areas (UNPA) in Croatia - Eastern Slavonia, Western Slavonia, Krajina - and in certain parts of Bosnia-Hercegovina.
Duration:	March 1992 - to present
Function:	To create the conditions of peace and security required for the negotiation of an overall settlement of the Yugoslav crisis within the framework of the European Community's Conference on Yugoslavia.

TABLE 11
CURRENT INTERNATIONAL DECADES AND YEARS

Period	*Decades and Years*
1983-1992	United Nations Decade of Disabled Persons
1983-1993	Second Decade to Combat Racism and Racial Discrimination
1985-1994	Transport and Communication Decade for Asia and the Pacific
1988-1997	World Decade of Cultural Development
1990s	International Decade for Natural Disaster Reduction
1990s	Second Industrial Development Decade for Africa
1990s	Third Disarmament Decade
1990-1999	United Nations Decade of International Law
1990-2000	International Decade for the Eradication of Colonialism
1991-2000	Fourth United Nations Development Decade
1991-2000	Second Transport and Communications Decade in Africa
1991-2000	United Nations Decade against Drug Abuse
1992	International Space Year
1993	International Year for the World's Indigenous People
1994	International Year of the Family

TABLE 12
ANNUAL DAYS AND WEEKS

Period	Annual Days and Weeks
Mar. 8	International Women's Day
Mar. 21	International Day for the Elimination of Racial Discrimination
Mar. 21-27	Week of Solidarity with the Peoples Struggling against Racism and Racial Discrimination
Mar. 23	World Meteorological Day
April 7	World Health Day
May 17	World Telecommunication Day
May 25-31	Week of Solidarity with the People of All Colonial Territories, as well as Those in South Africa, Fighting for Freedom, Independence and Human Rights
May 31	World No-Tobacco Day
June 4	International Day of Innocent Children Victims of Aggression
June 5	World Environment Day
June 16	International Day of Solidarity with the Struggling People of South Africa
June 26	International Day against Drug Abuse and Illicit Trafficking
July 11	World Population Day
Aug. 9	International Day of Solidarity with the Struggle of Women in South Africa
Sept. 8	International Literacy Day
Sept. (3rd Tuesday)	International Day of Peace
Sept. (during last week)	World Maritime Day
Oct. 1	International Day for the Elderly

Period	*Annual Days and Weeks*
Oct. 9	World Post Day
Oct. 11	Day of Solidarity with South African Political Prisoners
Oct. 16	World Food Day
Oct. 24	World Development Information Day
Oct. 24	United Nations Day
Oct. 24-30	Disarmament Week
Oct. (1st Monday)	Universal Children's Day
Oct. (1st Monday)	World Habitat Day
Oct. (2nd Wednesday)	International Day for Natural Disaster Reduction
Nov. 20	Africa Industrialization Day
Nov. 29	International Day of Solidarity with the Palestinian People
Nov. 11 (week of)	International Week of Science and Peace
Dec. 1	World AIDS Day
Dec. 5	International Volunteer Day for Economic and Social Development
Dec. 10	Human Rights Day

TABLE 13
REGULAR BUDGET OF THE UNITED NATIONS*

Year	Budget (in OOOs of US$)
1946	19,390
1947	28,617
1948	39,825
1949	43,204
1950	44,521
1951	48,926
1952	50,548
1953	49,869
1954	48,529
1955	50,228
1956	50,683
1957	53,175
1958	61,122
1959	61,657
1960	65,735
1961	71,649
1962	85,818
1963	92,877
1964	102,949
1965	108,473
1966	121,081
1967	133,084
1968	141,788
1969	156,967
1970	168,957
1971	194,628
1972	208,650
1973	233,820
1974-75**	612,550
1976-77	745,814
1978-79	1,084,186
1980-81	1,339,151
1982-83	1,472,962
1984-85	1,611,551
1986-87	1,711,801
1988-89	1,788,746
1990-91	2,134,072
1992-93	2,389,235

*Excluding peace-keeping operations.
**Start of biennium budgets.

TABLE 14
SPECIALIZED AGENCIES OF THE UNITED NATIONS
AND THE WORLD BANK GROUP

1. Food and Agriculture Organization (FAO)

    Headquarters: Rome, Italy

    Creation: The FAO was established on 16 October 1945 when twenty
                    governments accepted the constitution adopted by an interim
                    commission. The function and assets of the former International
                    Institute of Agriculture (Rome) were transferred to the FAO.

    Purpose: According to the Preamble of the FAO Constitution, the
                    organization is "to promote the common welfare by furthering
                    separate and collective action ... for the purposes of raising levels
                    of nutrition and standards of living of the peoples under their
                    respective jurisdictions, securing improvements in the efficiency
                    of the production and distribution of all food and agricultural
                    products, bettering the condition of rural populations, and thus
                    contributing towards an expanding world economy".

2. International Bank for Reconstruction and Development (IBRD)

    Headquarters: Washington, D.C., USA

    Creation: The Articles of the IBRD were adopted at the 1944 Bretton
                    Woods Conference. The Bank began operation in 1946-1947.

    Purposes: The IBRD was established to promote the international flow of
                    capital for productive purposes and to assist in financing the
                    rebuilding of nations devastated by the Second World War. Its
                    objectives include the promotion of private foreign investments
                    and the balanced growth of international trade.

3. International Civil Aviation Organization (ICAO)

    Headquarters: Montreal, Canada

    Creation: The Chicago Conference of 52 states drafted the Convention to
                    establish the ICAO on 7 December 1944. ICAO formally came
                    into existence on 4 April 1947 after the Convention had been
                    ratified by 26 states.

Purposes: According to Article 44 of the ICAO the functions of the organization are "developing the principles and techniques of international air navigation and fostering the planning and development of international air transport so as to ensure the safe and orderly growth of international civil aviation throughout the world."

4.   International Development Association (IDA)

Headquarters: Washington, D.C., USA

Creation: The annual meeting of the IMF and the IBRD in 1959 approved proposals for the establishment of the IDA which was then formally established in September 1960, and began operation in November 1960.

Purposes: The purpose of IDA is to promote economic development by providing finance to the less developed areas of the world on easier and more flexible terms than those of conventional loans. It is designed particularly to finance projects which do not attract private investment in countries which are not able to service loans from IBRD.

5.   International Fund for Agricultural Development (IFAD)

Headquarters: Rome, Italy

Creation: Established as a Specialized Agency of the United Nations by an Agreement adopted in June 1976. The Agreement was opened for signature and ratification in December 1976, when the target of $1,000 million in pledges was reached. It entered into force in November 1977 when instruments of ratification were deposited with the Secretary-General of the United Nations by at least 36 member countries of the three constituent categories of IFAD: six countries from Category I (OECD group) and six countries from Category II (OPEC group) for a total of $750 million, as well as 24 countries from Category III (other developing nations).

Purposes: The Agreement establishing the IFAD sets out the objectives as to "mobilize additional resources to be made available in concessional terms for agricultural development in developing member states." The projects and programs to be financed will be primarily those "designed to introduce, expand or improve food production systems and to strengthen related policies and institutions within the framework of national priorities and strategies". IFAD takes into account "the need to increase food production in the poorest food deficit countries, the potential for increasing food production in other developing countries and the importance of improving the nutritional level of the poorest populations in developing countries and the conditions of their lives". The Fund's major target group, irrespective of the stage of economic development of the country, is the small and landless farmers. It is the major objective of IFAD to ensure that the benefits of its projects go to the poorer sections.

6. International Finance Corporation (IFC)

Headquarters: Washington, D.C., USA

Creation: The IFC was established in July 1956. Although affiliated with the IBRD, it is a separate legal entity, and its funds are entirely separate from those of the IBRD.

Purposes: The IFC is empowered to invest in productive private enterprises in association with private investors, and without government guarantee of repayment in cases where sufficient private capital is not available on reasonable terms, and to serve as a clearing house to bring together investment opportunities, private capital, and experienced management.

7. International Labour Organization (ILO)

Headquarters: Geneva, Switzerland

Creation: The ILO was established in the Treaty of Versailles, and came into being on 11 April 1919. Its constitution was amended to allow its current relationship with the United Nations, and these provisions came into effect on 26 September 1946.

Purposes: The objectives of the ILO were set out in the Preamble of its revised Constitution and the so-called "Philadelphia Declaration" adopted in 1944. The ILO seeks to improve working and living conditions through the adoption of ILO conventions and recommendations setting minimum standards in such fields as wages, hours or work and conditions of employment, and social security.

8. International Maritime Organization (IMO)

Headquarters: London, England

Creation: The Convention of IMO was concluded at Geneva in 1948 and came into force on 17 March 1958.

Purposes: IMO's objective is to facilitate cooperation among governments in
                technical matters of all kinds affecting shipping, in order to
                achieve the highest practicable standards of maritime safety and
                efficiency in navigation. IMO has a special responsibility for
                safety of life at sea; and the organization also provides for a wide
                exchange of information between nations on all technical maritime
                subjects, as well as promoting cooperation on these matters.

9.   International Monetary Fund (IMF)

Headquarters: Washington, D.C., USA

Creation: The Articles of the IMF were drafted at the Bretton Woods
                Conference in 1944.

Purposes: The principle aims of the IMF are to promote international
                monetary cooperation, to facilitate the balanced growth of
                international trade, to promote exchange stability and to assist in
                the establishment of a multilateral system of payments. To assist
                it in achieving these aims, the IMF has resources in gold and
                members' currencies which may be made available to assist
                members in dealing with temporary balance of payments
                difficulties without their being compelled to resort to measures
                which would, if adopted, be inimical to national or international
                prosperity.

10. International Telecommunication Union (ITU)

Headquarters: Geneva, Switzerland

Creation: The International Telegraph Union which was created under the
                Paris Convention of 1865, became the ITU by virtue of the ITU
                Convention which came into force in 1934. Various
                modifications have been made of the ITU Convention, and the
                most recent of which is the Montreux Convention of 1965 which
                entered into force on 1 January 1967.

Purposes: The purposes of ITU as indicated under Article 4 of the Montreux
                Convention are "(a) to maintain and extend international
                cooperation for the improvement and rational use of
                telecommunications of all kinds; (b) to promote the development
                of technical facilities and their most efficient operation with a
                view to improving the efficiency of telecommunications services,
                increasing their usefulness and making them, so far as possible,
                generally available to the public; and (c) to harmonize the actions
                of nations in the attainment of those common ends."

11. United Nations Educational, Scientific and Cultural Organization (UNESCO)

    Headquarters: Paris, France

    Creation: Established following a conference in London in November 1945.

    Purposes: According to Article 1 of the UNESCO Constitution its purpose is "to contribute to peace and security by promoting collaboration among the nations through education, science, and culture in order to further universal respect for justice, for the rule of law, and for the human rights and fundamental freedoms which are affirmed for the peoples of the world, without distinction of race, sex, language, or religion, by the Charter of the United Nations."

12. United Nations Industrial Development Organization (UNIDO)

    Headquarters: Vienna, Austria

    Creation: UNIDO was established in 1966 as an autonomous organization within the UN secretariat. The transformation to a specialized agency was started in 1975, when the Second General Conference of UNIDO called for a substantial strengthening of the organization. A plenipotentiary conference in 1979 agreed on a constitution for UNIDO as a specialized agency which entered into force in 1985.

    Purposes: UNIDO aims to promote and accelerate industrial development in the developing countries with a view to assisting in the establishment of a new international economic order and to promote industrial development and co-operation on global, regional and national as well as on sectoral levels. To do so, UNIDO acts as a middleman in bringing together the industrial players in a development project by preparing industrial studies and conducting research by industry sector as well as by country; encouraging the development and transfer of technology; providing technical assistance to developing countries; maintaining an industrial and technical information bank; maintaining industrial statistics and carrying out empirical studies used in the industrialization process.

13. Universal Postal Union (UPU)

    Headquarters: Berne, Switzerland

    Creation: The first International Postal Congress meeting in Berne, Switzerland, in 1974, established by the Convention the General Postal Union. This was renamed the Universal Postal Union in

1878. In 1947, the UPU was made a specialized agency of the United Nations and a fundamental revision of the UPU Constitution was made in Vienna in 1964.

Purposes: The aim of the UPU according to Article 1 of the Vienna Constitution is to secure the organization and improvement of the postal services and to promote in this sphere the development of international collaboration and undertake, as far as possible, technical assistance in postal matters requested by members countries." To this end the countries who have adopted the UPU Convention constitute a single postal territory.

14. World Health Organization (WHO)

Headquarters: Geneva, Switzerland

Creation: The Constitution of the WHO was approved by representatives of 61 states on 22 July 1946 at a conference convened for that purpose; the WHO formally came into existence on 7 April 1948.

Purposes: According to Article 1 of the WHO Constitution, the objective of WHO is "the attainment by all people of the highest possible level of health".

15. World Intellectual Property Organization (WIPO)

Headquarters: Geneva, Switzerland

Creation: WIPO was established by a convention signed at Stockholm on 14 July 1967. This convention entered into force on 1 January 1974. On 17 December 1974, WIPO became the 14th specialized agency, by a decision of the UN General Assembly.

Purposes: WIPO was established to promote the protection of intellectual property throughout the world through co-operation among states and, where appropriate, in collaboration with any other international organization; and to ensure administrative co-operation among the unions previously established to afford protection to intellectual property. The principal unions so established are those of Paris and Berne: (a) The Paris Union, officially the International Union for the Protection of Industrial Property, is composed of states party to a convention concluded at Paris in 1883 and last revised in 1967; (b) the Berne Union, officially the International Union for the Protection of Literary and Artistic Works, is composed of states party to a convention concluded at Berne in 1886 and last revised in 1971.

16. World Meteorological Organization (WMO)

Headquarters: Geneva, Switzerland

Creation: The International Meteorological Organization was established in Utrecht, the Netherlands, in 1978. This organization was transformed into the WMO at a Conference in Washington, D.C., in 1947 which adopted the World Meteorological Convention which came into effect as WMO on 23 March 1950.

Purposes: The WMO was created (a) to facilitate international cooperation in the establishment of networks of stations and centers to provide meteorological services and observations; (b) to promote the establishment and maintenance of systems for the rapid exchange of meteorological information, (c) to promote standardization of meteorological observations and to ensure the uniform publication of observation and statistics; (d) to further the application of meteorology to aviation, shipping, agriculture, and other human activities; and (e) to encourage research and training in meteorology.

17. General Agreement of Tariffs and Trade (GATT)

Headquarters: Geneva, Switzerland

Creation: Following a resolution by the UN General Assembly in 1946 a Preparatory Committee for an International Conference on International Trade and Employment was created. In October 1947 this Preparatory Committee drafted a General Agreement on Tariffs and Trade, as well as a draft Charter for an International Trade Organization (ITO) both of which were considered at the Havana Conference in 1948 which adopted the ITO Charter. The Charter of the ITO failed to come into being because certain governments, particularly the USA failed to ratify the document. As a result of the BATT has since been administered by the secretariat of what was to have been the Interim Commission of the International Trade Organization. The Parties to the GATT made a major review of the General Agreement in 1955 and 1967, and with amendments the GATT continues operative.

Purposes: The General Agreement is a multilateral treaty containing reciprocal rights and obligations. It embodies four essential elements: (1) Trade is to be conducted on the basis of non-discrimination. In particular, all the contracting parties are bound by the most-favored clause in the application of import and export duties and charges and in their administration; (2) Protection is provided to domestic industries exclusively through the customs tariff and not through other measures; (3) Inherent in the

Agreement is the concept of consultation aimed at avoiding damage to the trading interests of the member states; (4) GATT provides a framework within which negotiations can be held for the reduction of tariffs and other barriers to trade and a structure for embodying the results of such negotiations in a legal instrument.

18. International Atomic Energy Agency (IAEA)

Headquarters: Vienna, Austria

Creation: An international conference in September 1956 drafted the Statute of the IAEA which entered into force on 29 July 1957.

Purposes: The purpose of the IAEA is "to seek to accelerate and enlarge the contribution of atomic energy to peace, health, and prosperity throughout the world." The IAEA is charged with ensuring that assistance provided by it is in no way used to further any military purposes. More specifically the IAEA is concerned with: (a) encouraging and assisting research on atomic energy for peaceful purposes throughout the world; (b) acting as an intermediary in the supply of materials, services, equipment and facilities; (c) fostering the exchange of scientific and technical information; (d) encouraging the exchange and training of scientists and experts; and (f) establishing safety standards.

CHAPTER III

DOCUMENTS

1. CHARTER OF THE UNITED NATIONS[1]

Contents

---

[1]*Charter of the United Nations and Statute of the International Court of Justice*, United Nations, Office of Public Information (DPI/511), New York, pp. 1-57.

WE THE PEOPLES OF THE UNITED NATIONS DETERMINED

to save succeeding generations from the scourge of war, which twice in our lifetime has brought untold sorrow to mankind, and

to reaffirm faith in fundamental human rights, in the dignity and worth of the human person, in the equal rights of men and women and of nations large and small, and

to establish conditions under which justice and respect for the obligations arising from treaties and other sources of international law can be maintained, and

to promote social progress and better standards of life in larger freedom,

AND FOR THESE ENDS

to practice tolerance and live together in peace with one another as good neighbours, and

to unite our strength to maintain international peace and security, and

to ensure, by the acceptance of principles and the institution of methods, that armed force shall not be used, save in the common interest, and

to employ international machinery for the promotion of the economic and social advancement of all peoples,

HAVE RESOLVED TO COMBINE OUR EFFORTS TO ACCOMPLISH THESE AIMS

Accordingly, our respective Governments, through representatives assembled in the city of San Francisco, who have exhibited their full powers found to be in good and due form, have agreed to the present Charter of the United Nations and do hereby establish an international organization to be known as the United Nations.

CHAPTER I
PURPOSES AND PRINCIPLES
Article 1

The Purposes of the United Nations are:

1. To maintain international peace and security, and to that end: to take effective collective measures for the prevention and removal of threats to the peace, and for the suppression of acts of aggression or other breaches of the peace, and to bring about by peaceful means, and in conformity with the principles of justice and international law, adjustment or settlement of international disputes or situations which might lead to a breach of the peace;

2. To develop friendly relations among nations based on respect for the principle of equal rights and self-determination of peoples, and to take other appropriate measures to strengthen universal peace;

3. To achieve international co-operation in solving international problems of an economic, social, cultural, or humanitarian character, and in promoting and encouraging

respect for human rights and for fundamental freedoms for all without distinction as to race, sex, language, or religion; and

4.   To be a centre for harmonizing the actions of nations in the attainment of these common ends.

Article 2

The Organization and its Members, in pursuit of the Purposes stated in Article 1, shall act in accordance with the following Principles.

1.   The Organization is based on the principle of the sovereign equality of all its Members.

2.   All Members, in order to ensure to all of them the rights and benefits resulting from membership, shall fulfil in good faith the obligations assumed by them in accordance with the present Charter.

3.   All Members shall settle their international disputes by peaceful means in such a manner that international peace and security, and justice, are not endangered.

4.   All Members shall refrain in their international relations from the threat or use of force against the territorial integrity or political independence of any state, or in any other manner inconsistent with the Purposes of the United Nations.

5.   All Members shall give the United Nations every assistance in any action it takes in accordance with the present Charter, and shall refrain from giving assistance to any state against which the United Nations is taking preventive or enforcement action.

6.   The Organization shall ensure that states which are not Members of the United Nations act in accordance with these Principles so far as may be necessary for the maintenance of international peace and security.

7.   Nothing contained in the present Charter shall authorize the United Nations to intervene in matters which are essentially within the domestic jurisdiction of any state or shall require the Members to submit such matters to settlement under the present Charter; but this principle shall not prejudice the application of enforcement measures under Chapter VII.

CHAPTER II
MEMBERSHIP
Article 3

The original Members of the United Nations shall be the states which, having participated in the United Nations Conference on International Organization at San Francisco, or having previously signed the Declaration by United Nations of 1 January 1942, sign the present Charter and ratify it in accordance with Article 110.

Article 4

1. Membership in the United Nations is open to all other peace-loving states which accept the obligations contained in the present Charter and, in the judgment of the Organization, are able and willing to carry out these obligations.

2. The admission of any such state to membership in the United Nations will be effected by a decision of the General Assembly upon the recommendation of the Security Council.

Article 5

A Member of the United Nations against which preventive or enforcement action has been taken by the Security Council may be suspended from the exercise of the rights and privileges of membership by the General Assembly upon the recommendation of the Security Council. The exercise of these rights and privileges may be restored by the Security Council.

Article 6

A Member of the United Nations which has persistently violated the Principles contained in the present Charter may be expelled from the Organization by the General Assembly upon the recommendation of the Security Council.

CHAPTER III
ORGANS
Article 7

1. There are established as the principal organs of the United Nations: a General Assembly, a Security Council, an Economic and Social Council, a Trusteeship Council, an International Court of Justice, and a Secretariat.

2. Such subsidiary organs as may be found necessary may be established in accordance with the present Charter.

Article 8

The United Nations shall place no restrictions on the eligibility of men and women to participate in any capacity and under conditions of equality in its principal and subsidiary organs.

CHAPTER IV
THE GENERAL ASSEMBLY
Composition
Article 9

1. The General Assembly shall consist of all the Members of the United Nations.

2. Each Member shall have not more than five representatives in the General Assembly.

Functions and Powers
Article 10

The General Assembly may discuss any questions or any matters within the scope of the present Charter or relating to the powers and functions of any organs provided for in the present Charter, and, except as provided in Article 12, may make recommendations to the Members of the United Nations or to the Security Council or to both on any such questions or matters.

Article 11

1. The General Assembly may consider the general principles of co-operation in the maintenance of international peace and security, including the principles governing disarmament and the regulation of armaments, and may make recommendations with regard to such principles to the Members or to the Security Council or to both.

2. The General Assembly may discuss any questions relating to the maintenance of international peace and security brought before it by any Member of the United Nations, or by the Security Council, or by a state which is not a Member of the United Nations in accordance with Article 35, paragraph 2, and, except as provided in Article 12, may make recommendations with regard to any such questions to the state or states concerned or to the Security Council or to both. Any such question on which action is necessary shall be referred to the Security Council by the General Assembly either before or after discussion.

3. The General Assembly may call the attention of the Security Council to situations which are likely to endanger international peace and security.

4. The powers of the General Assembly set forth in this Article shall not limit the general scope of Article 10.

Article 12

1.   While the Security Council is exercising in respect of any dispute or situation the functions assigned to it in the present Charter, the General Assembly shall not make any recommendation with regard to that dispute or situation unless the Security Council so requests.

2.   The Secretary-General, with the consent of the Security Council, shall notify the General Assembly at each session of any matters relative to the maintenance of international peace and security which are being deal with by the Security Council and shall similarly notify the General Assembly, or the Members of the United Nations if the General Assembly is not in session, immediately the Security Council ceases to deal with such matters.

Article 13

1.   The General Assembly shall initiate studies and make recommendations for the purpose of:

a. promoting international co-operation in the political field and encouraging the progressive development of international law and its codification;

b. promoting international co-operation in the economic, social, cultural, educational, and health fields, and assisting in the realization of human rights and fundamental freedoms for all without distinction as to race, sex, language, or religion.

2.   The further responsibilities, functions and powers of the General Assembly with respect to matters mentioned in paragraph 1(b) above are set forth in Chapters IX and X.

Article 14

Subject to the provisions of Article 12, the General Assembly may recommend measures for the peaceful adjustment of any situation, regardless of origin, which it deems likely to impair the general welfare or friendly relations among nations, including situations resulting from a violation of the provisions of the present Charter setting forth the Purposes and Principles of the United Nations.

Article 15

1.   The General Assembly shall receive and consider annual and special reports from the Security Council; these reports shall include an account of the measures that the Security Council has decided upon or taken to maintain international peace and security.

2.   The General Assembly shall receive and consider reports from the other organs of the United Nations.

Article 16

The General Assembly shall perform such functions with respect to the international trusteeship system as are assigned to it under Chapters XII and XIII, including the approval of the trusteeship agreements for areas not designated as strategic.

Article 17

1.   The General Assembly shall consider and approve the budget of the Organization.

2.   The expenses of the Organization shall be borne by the Members as apportioned by the General Assembly.

3.   The General Assembly shall consider and approve any financial and budgetary arrangements with specialized agencies referred to in Article 57 and shall examine the administrative budgets of such specialized agencies with a view to making recommendations to the agencies concerned.

Voting

Article 18

1.   Each member of the General Assembly shall have one vote.

2.   Decisions of the General Assembly on important questions shall be made by a two-thirds majority of the members present and voting. These questions shall include: recommendations with respect to the maintenance of international peace and security, the election of the non-permanent members of the Security Council, the election of members of the Economic and Social Council, the election of members of the Trusteeship Council in accordance with paragraph 1(c) of Article 86, the admission of new Members to the United Nations, the suspension of the rights and privileges of membership, the expulsion of Members, questions relating to the operation of the trusteeship system, and budgetary questions.

3. Decisions on other questions, including the determination of additional categories of questions to be decided by a two-thirds majority, shall be made by a majority of the members present and voting.

Article 19

A Member of the United Nations which is in arrears in the payment of its financial contributions to the Organization shall have no vote in the General Assembly if the amount of its arrears equals or exceeds the amount of the contributions due from it for the preceding two full years. The General Assembly may, nevertheless, permit such a Member to vote if it is satisfied that the failure to pay is due to conditions beyond the control of the Member.

Procedure
Article 20

The General Assembly shall meet in regular annual sessions and in such special sessions as occasion may require. Special sessions shall be convoked by the Secretary-General at the request of the Security Council or of a majority of the Members of the United Nations.

Article 21

The General Assembly shall adopt its own rules of procedure. It shall elect its President for each session.

Article 22

The General Assembly may establish such subsidiary organs as it deems necessary for the performance of its functions.

CHAPTER V
THE SECURITY COUNCIL
Composition
Article 23

1. The Security Council shall consist of fifteen Members of the United Nations. The Republic of China, France, the Union of Soviet Socialist Republics, the United Kingdom of Great Britain and Northern Ireland, and the United States of America shall be

permanent members of the Security Council. The General Assembly shall elect ten other Members of the United Nations to be non-permanent members of the Security Council, due regard being specially paid, in the first instance to the contribution of Members of the United Nations to the maintenance of international peace and security and to the other purposes of the Organization, and also to equitable geographical distribution.

2.   The non-permanent members of the Security Council shall be elected for a term of two years. In the first election of the non-permanent members after the increase of the membership of the Security Council from eleven to fifteen, two of the four additional members shall be chosen for a term of one year. A retiring member shall not be eligible for immediate re-election.

3.   Each member of the Security Council shall have one representative.

Functions and Powers
Article 24

1.   In order to ensure prompt and effective action by the United Nations, its Members confer on the Security Council primary responsibility for the maintenance of international peace and security, and agree that in carrying out its duties under this responsibility the Security Council acts on their behalf.

2.   In discharging these duties the Security Council shall act in accordance with the Purposes and Principles of the United Nations. The specific powers granted to the Security Council for the discharge of these duties are laid down in Chapters VI, VII, VIII, and XII.

3.   The Security Council shall submit annual and, when necessary, special reports to the General Assembly for its consideration.

Article 25

The Members of the United Nations agree to accept and carry out the decisions of the Security Council in accordance with the present Charter.

Article 26

In order to promote the establishment and maintenance of international peace and security with the least diversion for armaments of the world's human and economic resources, the Security Council shall be responsible for formulating, with the assistance of the Military Staff Committee referred to in Article 47, plans to be submitted to the Members of the United Nations for the establishment of a system for the regulation of armaments.

Voting

Article 27

1.   Each member of the Security Council shall have one vote.

2.   Decisions of the Security Council on procedural matters shall be made by an affirmative vote of nine members including the concurring votes of the permanent members; provided that, in decisions under Chapter VI, and under paragraph 3 of Article 52, a party to a dispute shall abstain from voting.

Procedure

Article 28

1.   The Security Council shall be so organized as to be able to function continuously. Each member of the Security Council shall for this purpose be represented at all times at the seat of the Organization.

2.   The Security Council shall hold periodic meetings at which each of its members may, if it so desires, be represented by a member of the government or by some other specially designated representative.

3.   The Security Council may hold meetings at such places other than the seat of the Organization as in its judgment will best facilitate its work.

Article 29

The Security Council may establish such subsidiary organs as it deems necessary for the performance of its functions.

Article 30

The Security Council shall adopt its own rules of procedure, including the method of selecting its President.

Article 31

Any Member of the United Nations which is not a member of the Security Council may participate, without vote, in the discussion of any question brought before the Security Council whenever the latter considers that the interests of that Member are specially affected.

Article 32

Any Member of the United Nations which is not a member of the Security Council or any state which is not a Member of the United Nations, if it is a party to a dispute under consideration by the Security Council, shall be invited to participate, without vote, in the discussion relating to the dispute. The Security Council shall lay down such conditions as it deems just for the participation of a state which is not a Member of the United Nations.

CHAPTER VI
PACIFIC SETTLEMENT OF DISPUTES
Article 33

1.   The parties to any dispute, the continuance of which is likely to endanger the maintenance of international peace and security, shall, first of all, seek a solution by negotiation, enquiry, mediation, conciliation, arbitration, judicial settlement, resort to regional agencies or arrangements, or other peaceful means of their own choice.

2.   The Security Council shall, when it deems necessary, call upon the parties to settle their dispute by such means.

Article 34

The Security Council may investigate any dispute, or any situation which might lead to international friction or give rise to a dispute, in order to determine whether the continuance of the dispute or situation is likely to endanger the maintenance of international peace and security.

Article 35

1.   Any Member of the United Nations may bring any dispute, or any situation of the nature referred to in Article 34, to the attention of the Security Council or of the General Assembly.

2.   A state which is not a Member of the United Nations may bring to the attention of the Security Council or of the General Assembly any dispute to which it is a party if it accepts in advance, for the purposes of the dispute, the obligations of pacific settlement provided in the present Charter.

3.   The proceedings of the General Assembly in respect of matters brought to its attention under this Article will be subject to the provisions of Articles 11 and 12.

Article 36

1. The Security Council may, at any stage of a dispute of the nature referred to in Article 33 or of a situation of like nature, recommend appropriate procedures or methods of adjustment.

2. The Security Council should take into consideration any procedures for the settlement of the dispute which have already been adopted by the parties.

3. In making recommendations under this Article the Security Council should also take into consideration that legal disputes should as a general rule be referred by the parties to the International Court of Justice in accordance with the provisions of the Statute of the Court.

Article 37

1. Should the parties to a dispute of the nature referred to in Article 33 fail to settle it by the means indicated in that Article, they shall refer it to the Security Council.

2. If the Security Council deems that the continuance of the dispute is in fact likely to endanger the maintenance of international peace and security, it shall decide whether to take action under Article 36 or to recommend such terms of settlement as it may consider appropriate.

Article 38

Without prejudice to the provisions of Articles 33 to 37, the Security Council may, if all the parties to any dispute so request, make recommendations to the parties with a view to a pacific settlement of the dispute.

CHAPTER VII
ACTION WITH RESPECT TO THREATS TO THE PEACE, BREACHES OF THE PEACE, AND ACTS OF AGGRESSION
Article 39

The Security Council shall determine the existence of any threat to the peace, breach of the peace, or act of aggression and shall make recommendations, or decide what measures shall be taken in accordance with Articles 41 and 42, to maintain or restore international peace and security.

Article 40

In order to prevent an aggravation of the situation, the Security Council may, before making the recommendations or deciding upon the measures provided for in Article 39, call upon the parties concerned to comply with such provisional measures at its deems necessary or desirable. Such provisional measures shall be without prejudice to the rights, claims, or position of the parties concerned. The Security Council shall duly take account of failure to comply with such provisional measures.

Article 41

The Security Council may decide what measures not involving the use of armed force are to be employed to give effect to its decisions, and it may call upon the Members of the United Nations to apply such measures. These may include complete or partial interruption of economic relations and of rail, sea, air, postal, telegraphic, radio, and other means of communication, and the severance of diplomatic relations.

Article 42

Should the Security Council consider that measures provided for in Article 41 would be inadequate or have proved to be inadequate, it may take such action by air, sea, or land forces as may be necessary to maintain or restore international peace and security. Such action may include demonstrations, blockade, and other operations by air, sea, or land forces of Members of the United Nations.

Article 43

1.   All Members of the United Nations, in order to contribute to the maintenance of international peace and security, undertake to make available to the Security Council, on its call and in accordance with a special agreement or agreements, armed forces, assistance, and facilities, including rights of passage, necessary for the purpose of maintaining international peace and security.

2.   Such agreement or agreements shall govern the numbers and types of forces, their degree of readiness and general location, and the nature of the facilities and assistance to be provided.

3.   The agreement or agreements shall be negotiated as soon as possible on the initiative of the Security Council. They shall be concluded between the Security Council and Members or between the Security Council and groups of Members and shall be

subject to ratification by the signatory states in accordance with their respective constitutional processes.

Article 44

When the Security Council has decided to use force it shall, before calling upon a Member not represented on it to provide armed forces in fulfilment of the obligations assumed under Article 43, invite that Member, if the Member so desires, to participate in the decisions of the Security Council concerning the employment of contingents of that Member's armed forces.

Article 45

In order to enable the United Nations to take urgent military measures, Members shall hold immediately available national air-force contingents for combined international enforcement action. The strength and degree of readiness of these contingents and plans for their combined action shall be determined, within the limits laid down in the special agreement or agreements referred to in Article 43, by the Security Council with the assistance of the Military Staff Committee.

Article 46

Plans for the application of armed force shall be made by the Security Council with the assistance of the Military Staff Committee.

Article 47

1.   There shall be established a Military Staff Committee to advise and assist the Security Council on all questions relating to the Security Council's military requirements for the maintenance of international peace and security, the employment and command of forces placed at its disposal, the regulation of armament, and possible disarmament.

2.   The Military Staff Committee shall consist of the Chiefs of Staff of the permanent members of the Security Council or their representatives. Any member of the United Nations not permanently represented on the Committee shall be invited by the Committee to be associated with it when the efficient discharge of the Committee's responsibilities requires the participation of that Member in its work.

3.   The Military Staff Committee shall be responsible under the Security Council for the strategic direction of any armed forces placed at the disposal of the Security Council. Questions relating to the command of such forces shall be worked out subsequently.

4.   The Military Staff Committee, with the authorization of the Security Council and after consultation with appropriate regional agencies, may establish regional sub-committees.

Article 48

1.   The action required to carry out the decisions of the Security Council for the maintenance of international peace and security shall be taken by all the Members of the United Nations or by some of them, as the Security Council may determine.

2.   Such decisions shall be carried out by the Members of the United Nations directly and through their action in the appropriate international agencies of which they are members.

Article 49

The Members of the United Nations shall join in affording mutual assistance in carrying out the measures decided upon by the Security Council.

Article 50

If preventive or enforcement measures against any state are taken by the Security Council, any other state, whether a Member of the United Nations or not, which finds itself confronted with special economic problems arising from the carrying out of those measures shall have the right to consult the Security Council with regard to a solution of those problems.

Article 51

Nothing in the present Charter shall impair the inherent right of individual or collective self-defense if an armed attack occurs against a Member of the United Nations, until the Security Council has taken measures necessary to maintain international peace and security. Measures taken by Members in the exercise of this right of self-defense shall be immediately reported to the Security Council and shall not in any way affect the authority and responsibility of the Security Council under the present Charter to take at any time such action as it deems necessary in order to maintain or restore international peace and security.

CHAPTER VIII
REGIONAL ARRANGEMENTS
Article 52

1.   Nothing in the present Charter precludes the existence of regional arrangements or agencies for dealing with such matters relating to the maintenance of international peace and security as are appropriate for regional action, provided that such arrangements or agencies and their activities are consistent with the Purposes and Principles of the United Nations.

2.   The Members of the United Nations entering into such arrangements or constituting such agencies shall make every effort to achieve pacific settlement of local disputes through such regional arrangements or by such regional agencies before referring them to the Security Council.

3.   The Security Council shall encourage the development of pacific settlement of local disputes through such regional arrangements or by such regional agencies either on the initiative of the states concerned or by reference from the Security Council.

4.   This Article in no way impairs the application of Articles 34 and 35.

Article 53

1.   The Security Council shall, where appropriate, utilize such regional arrangements or agencies for enforcement action under its authority. But no enforcement action shall be taken under regional arrangements or by regional agencies without the authorization of the Security Council, with the exception of measures against any enemy state, as defined in paragraph 2 of this Article, provided for pursuant to Article 107 or in regional arrangements directed against renewal of aggressive policy on the part of any such state, until such time as the Organization may, on request of the Governments concerned, be charged with the responsibility for preventing further aggression by such a state.

2.   The term enemy state as used in paragraph 1 of this Article applies to any state which during the Second World War has been an enemy of any signatory of the present Charter.

Article 54

The Security Council shall at all times be kept fully informed of activities undertaken or in contemplation under regional arrangements or by regional agencies for the maintenance of international peace and security.

CHAPTER IX
INTERNATIONAL ECONOMIC AND SOCIAL CO-OPERATION
Article 55

With a view to the creation of conditions of stability and well-being which are necessary for peaceful and friendly relations among nations based on respect for the principle of equal rights and self-determination of people, the United Nations shall promote:

a. higher standards of living, full employment, and conditions of economic and social progress and development;

b. solutions of international economic, social, health, and related problems; and international cultural and educational co-operation; and

c. universal respect for; and observance of, human rights and fundamental freedoms for all without distinction as to race, sex, language, or religion.

Article 56

All members pledge themselves to take joint and separate action in co-operation with the Organization for the achievement of the purposes set forth in Article 55.

Article 57

1. The various specialized agencies, established by inter-governmental agreement and having wide international responsibilities, as defined in their basic instruments, in economic, social, cultural, educational, health, and related fields, shall be brought into relationship with the United Nations in accordance with the provisions of Article 63.

2. Such agencies thus brought into relationship with the United Nations are hereinafter referred to as specialized agencies.

Article 58

The Organization shall make recommendations for the coordination of the policies and activities of the specialized agencies.

Article 59

The Organization shall, where appropriate, initiate negotiations among the states concerned for the creation of any new specialized agencies required for the accomplishment of the purposes set forth in Article 55.

Article 60

Responsibility for the discharge of the functions of the Organization set forth in this Chapter shall be vested in the General Assembly and, under the authority of the General Assembly, in the Economic and Social Council, which shall have for this purpose the powers set forth in Chapter X.

CHAPTER X
THE ECONOMIC AND SOCIAL COUNCIL
Composition
Article 61

1. The Economic and Social Council shall consist of fifty-four Members of the United Nations elected by the General Assembly.

2. Subject to the provisions of paragraph 3, eighteen members of the Economic and Social Council shall be elected each year for a term of three years. A retiring member shall be eligible for immediate re-election.

3. At the first election after the increase in the membership of the Economic and Social Council from twenty-seven to fifty-four members, in addition to the members elected in place of the nine members whose term of office expires at the end of that year, twenty-seven additional members shall be elected. Of these twenty-seven additional members, the term of office of nine members so elected shall expire at the end of one year, and of nine other members at the end of two years, in accordance with arrangements made by the General Assembly.

4. Each member of the Economic and Social Council shall have one representative.

Functions and Powers
Article 62

1. The Economic and Social Council may make or initiate studies and reports with respect to international economic, social, cultural, educational, health, and related matters and may make recommendations with respect to any such matters to the General Assembly, to the Members of the United Nations, and to the specialized agencies concerned.

2. It may make recommendations for the purpose of promoting respect for, and observance of, human rights and fundamental freedoms for all.

3. It may prepare draft conventions for submission to the General Assembly, with respect to matters falling within its competence.

4. It may call, in accordance with the rules prescribed by the United Nations, international conferences on matters falling within its competence.

Article 63

1. The Economic and Social Council may enter into agreements with any of the agencies referred to in Article 57, defining the terms on which the agency concerned shall be brought into relationship with the United Nations. Such agreements shall be subject to approval by the General Assembly.

2. It may co-ordinate the activities of the specialized agencies through consultation with and recommendations to such agencies and through recommendations to the General Assembly and to the Members of the United Nations.

Article 64

1. The Economic and Social Council may take appropriate steps to obtain regular reports from the specialized agencies. It may make arrangements with the Members of the United Nations and with the specialized agencies to obtain reports on the steps taken to give effect to its own recommendations and to recommendations on matters falling within its competence made by the General Assembly.

2. It may communicate its observations on these reports to the General Assembly.

Article 65

The Economic and Social Council may furnish information to the Security Council and shall assist the Security Council upon its request.

Article 66

1. The Economic and Social Council shall perform such functions as fall within its competence in connexion with the carrying out of the recommendations of the General Assembly.

2. It may, with the approval of the General Assembly, perform services at the request of Members of the United Nations and at the request of specialized agencies.

3. It shall perform such other functions as are specified elsewhere in the present Charter or as may be assigned to it by the General Assembly.

Voting

Article 67

1.   Each member of the Economic and Social Council shall have one vote.

2.   Decisions of the Economic and Social Council shall be made by a majority of the members present and voting.

Procedure

Article 68

The Economic and Social Council shall set up commissions in economic and social fields and for the promotion of human rights, and such other commissions as may be required for the performance of its functions.

Article 69

The Economic and Social Council shall invite any Member of the United Nations to participate, without vote, in its deliberations on any matter of particular concern to that Member.

Article 70

The Economic and Social Council may make arrangements for representatives of the specialized agencies to participate, without vote, in its deliberations and in those of the commissions established by it, and for its representatives to participate in the deliberations of the specialized agencies.

Article 71

The Economic and Social Council may make suitable arrangements for consultation with non-governmental organizations which are concerned with matters within its competence. Such arrangements may be made with international organizations and, where appropriate, with national organizations after consultation with the Member of the United Nations concerned.

Article 72

1.   The Economic and Social Council shall adopt its own rules of procedure, including the method of selecting its President.

2.   The Economic and Social Council shall meet as required in accordance with its rules, which shall include provision for the convening of meetings on the request of a majority of its members.

CHAPTER XI
DECLARATION REGARDING NON-SELF-GOVERNING TERRITORIES
Article 73

Members of the United Nations which have or assume responsibilities for the administration of territories whose peoples have not yet attained a full measure of self-government recognize the principle that the interests of the inhabitants of these territories are paramount, and accept as a sacred trust the obligation to promote to the utmost, within the system of international peace and security established by the present Charter, the well-being of the inhabitants of these territories, and, to this end:

a. to ensure, with due respect for the culture of the peoples concerned, their political, economic, social, and educational advancement, their just treatment, and their protection against abuses;

b. to develop self-government, to take due account of the political aspirations of the peoples, and to assist them in the progressive development of their free political institutions, according to the particular circumstances of each territory and its peoples and their varying stages of advancement;

c. to further international peace and security;

d. to promote constructive measures of development, to encourage research, and to co-operate with one another and, when and where appropriate, with specialized international bodies with a view to the practical achievement of the social, economic, and scientific purposes set forth in this Article; and

e. to transmit regularly to the Secretary-General for information purposes, subject to such limitation as security and constitutional considerations may require, statistical and other information of a technical nature relating to economic, social, and educational conditions in the territories for which they are respectively responsible other than those territories to which Chapters XII and XIII apply.

Article 74

Members of the United Nations also agree that their policy in respect of the territories to which this Chapter applies, no less than in respect of their metropolitan areas, must be based on the general principle of good-neighbourliness, due account being taken of the interests and well-being of the rest of the world, in social, economic, and commercial matters.

CHAPTER XII
INTERNATIONAL TRUSTEESHIP SYSTEM
Article 75

The United Nations shall establish under its authority an international trusteeship system for the administration and supervision of such territories as may be placed thereunder by subsequent individual agreements. These territories are hereinafter referred to as trust territories.

Article 76

The basic objectives of the trusteeship system, in accordance with the Purposes of the United Nations laid down in Article 1 of the present Charter, shall be:

a. to further international peace and security;

b. to promote the political, economic, social, and educational advancement of the inhabitants of the trust territories, and their progressive development towards self-government or independence as may be appropriate to the particular circumstances of each territory and its peoples and the freely expressed wishes of the peoples concerned, and as may be provided by the terms of each trusteeship agreement;

c. to encourage respect for human rights and for fundamental freedoms for all without distinction as to race, sex, language, or religion, and to encourage recognition of the interdependence of the peoples of the world; and

d. to ensure equal treatment in social, economic, and commercial matters for all Members of the United Nations and their nationals, and also equal treatment for the latter in the administration of justice, without prejudice to the attainment of the foregoing objectives and subject to the provisions of Article 80.

Article 77

1. The trusteeship system shall apply to such territories in the following categories as may be placed thereunder by means of trusteeship agreements:

a. territories now held under mandate;

b. territories which may be detached from enemy states as a result of the Second World War; and

c. territories voluntarily placed under the system by states responsible for their administration.

2. It will be a matter for subsequent agreement as to which territories in the foregoing categories will be brought under the trusteeship system and upon what terms.

Article 78

The trusteeship system shall not apply to territories which have become Members of the United Nations, relationship among which shall be based on respect for the principle of sovereign equality.

Article 79

The terms of trusteeship for each territory to be placed under the trusteeship system, including any alteration or amendment, shall be agreed upon by the states directly concerned, including the mandatory power in the case of territories held under mandate by a Member of the United Nations, and shall be approved as provided for in Articles 83 and 85.

Article 80

1. Except as may be agreed upon in individual trusteeship agreements, made under Articles 77, 79, and 81, placing each territory under the trusteeship system, and until such agreements have been concluded, nothing in this Chapter shall be construed in or of itself to alter in any manner the rights whatsoever of any states or any peoples or the terms of existing international instruments to which Members of the United Nations may respectively be parties.

2. Paragraph 1 of this Article shall not be interpreted as giving grounds for delay or postponement of the negotiation and conclusion of agreements for placing mandated and other territories under the trusteeship system as provided for in Article 77.

Article 81

The trusteeship agreement shall in each case include the terms under which the trust territory will be administered and designate the authority which will exercise the administration of the trust territory. Such authority, hereinafter called the administering authority, may be one or more states or the Organization itself.

Article 82

There may be designated, in any trusteeship agreement, a strategic area or areas which may include part or all of the trust territory to which the agreement applies, without prejudice to any special agreement or agreements made under Article 43.

Article 83

1. All functions of the United Nations relating to strategic areas, including the approval of the terms of the trusteeship agreements and of their alteration or amendment, shall be exercised by the Security Council.

2. The basic objectives set forth in Article 76 shall be applicable to the people of each strategic area.

3. The Security Council shall, subject to the provisions of the trusteeship agreements and without prejudice to security considerations, avail itself of the assistance of the Trusteeship Council to perform those functions of the United Nations under the trusteeship system relating to political, economic, social, and educational matters in the strategic areas.

Article 84

It shall be the duty of the administering authority to ensure that the trust territory shall play its part in the maintenance of international peace and security. To this end the administering authority may make use of volunteer forces, facilities, and assistance from the trust territory in carrying out the obligations towards the Security Council undertaken in this regard by the administering authority, as well as for local defence and the maintenance of law and order within the trust territory.

Article 85

1. The functions of the United Nations with regard to trusteeship agreements for all areas not designated as strategic, including the approval of the terms of the trusteeship agreements and of their alteration or amendment, shall be exercised by the General Assembly.

2. The Trusteeship Council, operating under the authority of the General Assembly, shall assist the General Assembly in carrying out these functions.

CHAPTER XIII
THE TRUSTEESHIP COUNCIL
Composition
Article 86

1. The Trusteeship Council shall consist of the following Members of the United Nations:

a. those Members administering trust territories;

b. such of those Members mentioned by name in Article 23 as are not administering trust territories; and

c. as many other Members elected for three-year terms by the General Assembly as may be necessary to ensure that the total number of members of the Trusteeship Council is equally divided between those Members of the United Nations which administer trust territories and those which do not.

2. Each member of the Trusteeship Council shall designate one specially qualified person to represent it therein.

Functions and Powers
Article 87

The General Assembly and, under its authority, the Trusteeship Council, in carrying out their functions, may:

a. consider reports submitted by the administering authority;

b. accept petitions and examine them in consultation with the administering authority;

c. provide for periodic visits to the respective trust territories at times agreed upon with the administering authority; and

d. take these and other actions in conformity with the terms of the trusteeship agreements.

Article 88

The Trusteeship Council shall formulate a questionnaire on the political, economic, social, and educational advancement of the inhabitants of each trust territory, and the administering authority for each trust territory, and the administering authority for each trust territory within the competence of the General Assembly shall make an annual report to the General Assembly upon the basis of such questionnaire.

Voting
Article 89

1. Each member of the Trusteeship Council shall have one vote.

2. Decisions of the Trusteeship Council shall be made by a majority of the members present and voting.

Procedure
Article 90

1. The Trusteeship Council shall adopt its own rules of procedure, including the method of selecting its President.

2. The Trusteeship Council shall meet as required in accordance with its rules, which shall include provision for the convening of meetings on the request of a majority of its members.

Article 91

The Trusteeship Council shall, when appropriate, avail itself of the assistance of the Economic and Social Council and of the specialized agencies in regard to matters with which they are respectively concerned.

CHAPTER XIV
THE INTERNATIONAL COURT OF JUSTICE
Article 92

The International Court of Justice shall be the principal judicial organ of the United Nations. It shall function in accordance with the annexed Statute, which is based upon the Statute of the Permanent Court of International Justice and forms an integral part of the present Charter.

Article 93

1. All Members of the United Nations are *ipso facto* parties to the Statute of the International Court of Justice.

2. A state which is not a Member of the United Nations may become a party to the Statute of the International Court of Justice on conditions to be determined in each case by the General Assembly upon the recommendation of the Security Council.

Article 94

1. Each Member of the United Nations undertakes to comply with the decision of the International Court of Justice in any case to which it is a party.

2. If any party to a case fails to perform the obligations incumbent upon it under a judgment rendered by the Court, the other party may have recourse to the Security

Council, which may, if it deems necessary, make recommendations or decide upon measures to be taken to give effect to the judgment.

Article 95

Nothing in the present Charter shall prevent Members of the United Nations from entrusting the solution of their differences to other tribunals by virtue of agreements already in existence or which may be concluded in the future.

Article 96

1.   The General Assembly or the Security Council may request the International Court of Justice to give an advisory opinion on any legal question.

2.   Other organs of the United Nations and specialized agencies, which may at any time be so authorized by the General Assembly, may also request advisory opinions of the Court on legal questions arising within the scope of their activities.

CHAPTER XV
THE SECRETARIAT
Article 97

The Secretariat shall comprise a Secretary-General and such staff as the Organization may require. The Secretary-General shall be appointed by the General Assembly upon the recommendation of the Security Council. He shall be the chief administrative officer of the Organization.

Article 98

The Secretary-General shall act in that capacity in all meetings of the General Assembly, of the Security Council, of the Economic and Social Council, and of the Trusteeship Council, and shall perform such other functions as are entrusted to him by these organs. The Secretary-General shall make an annual report to the General Assembly on the work of the Organization.

Article 99

The Secretary-General may bring to the attention of the Security Council any matter which in his opinion may threaten the maintenance of international peace and security.

Article 100

1. In the performance of their duties the Secretary-General and the staff shall not seek or receive instructions from any government or from any other authority external to the Organization. They shall refrain from any action which might reflect on their position as international officials responsible only to the Organization.

2. Each Member of the United Nations undertakes to respect the exclusively international character of the responsibilities of the Secretary-General and the staff and not to seek to influence them in the discharge of their responsibilities.

Article 101

1. The staff shall be appointed by the Secretary-General under regulations established by the General Assembly.

2. Appropriate staffs shall be permanently assigned to the Economic and Social Council, the Trusteeship Council, and, as required, to other organs of the United Nations. These staffs shall form a part of the Secretariat.

3. The paramount consideration in the employment of the staff and in the determination of the conditions of service shall be the necessity of securing the highest standards of efficiency, competence, and integrity. Due regard shall be paid to the importance of recruiting the staff on as wide a geographical basis as possible.

CHAPTER XVI
MISCELLANEOUS PROVISIONS
Article 102

1. Every treaty and every international agreement entered into by any Member of the United Nations after the present Charter comes into force shall as soon as possible be registered with the Secretariat and published by it.

2. No party to any such treaty or international agreement which has not been registered in accordance with the provisions of paragraph 1 of this Article may invoke that treaty or agreement before any organ of the United Nations.

Article 103

In the event of a conflict between the obligations of the Members of the United Nations under the present Charter and their obligations under any other international agreement, their obligations under the present Charter shall prevail.

Article 104

The Organization shall enjoy in the territory of each of its Members such legal capacity as may be necessary for the exercise of its functions and the fulfilment of its purposes.

Article 105

1.   The Organization shall enjoy in the territory of each of its Members such privileges and immunities as are necessary for the fulfilment of its purposes.

2.   Representatives of the Members of the United Nations and officials of the Organization shall similarly enjoy such privileges and immunities as are necessary for the independent exercise of their functions in connexion with the Organization.

3.   The General Assembly may make recommendations with a view to determining the details of the application of paragraphs 1 and 2 of this Article or may propose conventions to the Members of the United Nations for this purpose.

CHAPTER XVII

TRANSITIONAL SECURITY ARRANGEMENTS

Article 106

Pending the coming into force of such special agreements referred to in Article 43 as in the opinion of the Security Council enable it to begin the exercise of its responsibilities under Article 42, the parties to the Four-Nation Declaration, signed at Moscow, 30 October 1943, and France, shall, in accordance with the provisions of paragraph 5 of that Declaration, consult with one another and as occasion requires with other Members of the United Nations with a view to such joint action on behalf of the Organization as may be necessary for the purpose of maintaining international peace and security.

Article 107

Nothing in the present Charter shall invalidate or preclude action, in relation to any state which during the Second World War has been an enemy of any signatory to the present Charter, taken or authorized as a result of that war by the Governments having responsibility for such action.

CHAPTER XVIII
AMENDMENTS
Article 108

Amendments to the present Charter shall come into force for all Members of the United Nations when they have been adopted by a vote of two thirds of the members of the General Assembly and ratified in accordance with their respective constitutional processes by two thirds of the Members of the United Nations, including all the permanent members of the Security Council.

Article 109

1. A General Conference of the Members of the United Nations for the purpose of reviewing the present Charter may be held at a date and place to be fixed by a two-thirds vote of the members of the General Assembly and by a vote of any nine members of the Security Council. Each Member of the United Nations shall have one vote in the conference.

2. Any alteration of the present Charter recommended by a two-thirds vote of the conference shall take effect when ratified in accordance with their respective constitutional processes by two thirds of the Members of the United Nations including all the permanent members of the Security Council.

3. If such a conference has not been held before the tenth annual session of the General Assembly following the coming into force of the present Charter, the proposal to call such a conference shall be placed on the agenda of that session of the General Assembly, and the conference shall be held if so decided by a majority vote of the members of the General Assembly and by a vote of any seven members of the Security Council.

CHAPTER XIX
RATIFICATION AND SIGNATURE
Article 110

1. The present Charter shall be ratified by the signatory states in accordance with their respective constitutional processes.

2. The ratifications shall be deposited with the Government of the United States of America, which shall notify all the signatory states of each deposit as well as the Secretary-General of the Organization when he has been appointed.

3. The present Charter shall come into force upon the deposit of ratifications by the Republic of China, France, the Union of Soviet Socialist Republics, the United Kingdom

of Great Britain and Northern Ireland, and the United States of America, and by a majority of the other signatory states. A protocol of the ratifications deposited shall thereupon be drawn up by the Government of the United States of America which shall communicate copies thereof to all the signatory states.

4.   The states signatory to the present Charter which ratify it after it has come into force will become original Members of the United Nations on the date of the deposit of their respective ratifications.

Article 111

The present Charter, of which the Chinese, French, Russian, English, and Spanish texts are equally authentic, shall remain deposited in the archives of the Government of the United States of America. Duly certified copies thereof shall be transmitted by that Government to the Governments of the other signatory states.

IN FAITH WHEREOF the representatives of the Governments of the United Nations have signed the present Charter.

DONE at the city of San Francisco the twenty-sixth day of June, one thousand nine hundred and forty-five.

2. STATUTE OF THE INTERNATIONAL COURT OF JUSTICE[1]

Contents

Chapter		*Page*
I.	Organization of the Court	310
II.	Competence of the Court	317
III.	Procedure	319
IV.	Advisory opinions	324
V.	Amendment	325

---

[1]*Charter of the United Nations and Statute of the International Court of Justice*, United Nations, Office of Public Information (DPI/511), New York, pp. 58-77.

Article 1

The International Court of Justice established by the Charter of the United Nations as the principal judicial organ of the United Nations shall be constituted and shall function in accordance with the provisions of the present Statute.

CHAPTER I
ORGANIZATION OF THE COURT
Article 2

The Court shall be composed of a body of independent judges, elected regardless of their nationality from among persons of high moral character, who possess the qualifications required in their respective countries for appointment to the highest judicial offices, or are jurisconsults of recognized competence in international law.

Article 3

1.   The Court shall consist of fifteen members, no two of whom may be nationals of the same state.

2.   A person who for the purposes of membership in the Court could be regarded as a national of more than one state shall be deemed to be a national of the one in which he ordinarily exercises civil and political rights.

Article 4

1.   The members of the Court shall be elected by the General Assembly and by the Security Council from a list of persons nominated by the national groups in the Permanent Court of Arbitration, in accordance with the following provisions.

2.   In the case of Members of the United Nations not represented in the Permanent Court of Arbitration, candidates shall be nominated by national groups appointed for this purpose by their governments under the same conditions as those prescribed for members of the Permanent Court of Arbitration by Article 44 of the Convention of The Hague of 1907 for the pacific settlement of international disputes.

3.   The conditions under which a state which is a party to the present Statute but is not a Member of the United Nations may participate in electing the members of the Court shall, in the absence of a special agreement, be laid down by the General Assembly upon recommendation of the Security Council.

Article 5

1.   At least three months before the date of the election, the Secretary-General of the United Nations shall address a written request to the members of the Permanent Court of Arbitration belonging to the states which are parties to the present Statute, and to the members of the national groups appointed under Article 4, paragraph 2, inviting them to undertake, within a given time, by national groups, the nomination of persons in a position to accept the duties of a member of the Court.

2.   No group may nominate more than four persons, not more than two of whom shall be of their own nationality. In no case may the number of candidates nominated by a group be more than double the number of seats to be filled.

Article 6

Before making these nominations, each national group is recommended to consult its highest court of justice, its legal faculties and schools of law, and its national academies and national sections of international academies devoted to the study of law.

Article 7

1.   The Secretary-General shall prepare a list in alphabetical order of all the persons thus nominated. Save as provided in Article 12, paragraph 2, these shall be the only persons eligible.

2.   The Secretary-General shall submit this list to the General Assembly and to the Security Council.

Article 8

The General Assembly and the Security Council shall proceed independently of one another to elect the members of the Court.

Article 9

At every election, the electors shall bear in mind not only that the persons to be elected should individually possess the qualifications required, but also that in the body as a whole the representation of the main forms of civilization and of the principal legal systems of the world should be assured.

Article 10

1.   Those candidates who obtain an absolute majority of votes in the General Assembly and in the Security Council shall be considered as elected.

2.   Any vote of the Security Council, whether for the election of judges or for the appointment of members of the conference envisaged in Article 12, shall be taken without any distinction between permanent and non-permanent members of the Security Council.

3.   In the event of more than one national of the same state obtaining an absolute majority of the votes both of the General Assembly and of the Security Council, the eldest of these only shall be considered as elected.

Article 11

If, after the first meeting held for the purpose of the election, one or more seats remain to be filled, a second and, if necessary, a third meeting shall take place.

Article 12

1.   If, after the third meeting, one or more seats still remain unfilled, a joint conference consisting of six members, three appointed by the General Assembly and, three by the Security Council, may be formed at any time at the request of either the General Assembly or the Security Council, for the purpose of choosing by the vote of an absolute majority one name for each seat still vacant, to submit to the General Assembly and the Security Council for their respective acceptance.

2.   If the joint conference is unanimously agreed upon any person who fulfils the required conditions, he may be included in its list, even though he was not included in the list of nominations referred to in Article 7.

3.   If the joint conference is satisfied that it will not be successful in procuring an election, those members of the Court who have already been elected shall, within a period to be fixed by the Security Council, proceed to fill the vacant seats by selection from among those candidates who have obtained votes either in the General Assembly or in the Security Council.

4.   In the event of an equality of votes among the judges, the eldest judge shall have a casting vote.

Article 13

1.   The members of the Court shall be elected for nine years and may be re-elected; provided, however, that of the judges elected at the first election, the terms of five judges

shall expire at the end of three years and the terms of five more judges shall expire at the end of six years.

2. The judges whose terms are to expire at the end of the above-mentioned initial periods of three and six years shall be chosen by lot to be drawn by the Secretary-General immediately after the first election has been completed.

3. The members of the Court shall continue to discharge their duties until their places have been filled. Though replaced, they shall finish any cases which they may have begun.

4. In the case of the resignation of a member of the Court, the resignation shall be addressed to the President of the Court for transmission to the Secretary-General. This last notification makes the place vacant.

Article 14

Vacancies shall be filled by the same method as that laid down for the first election, subject to the following provision: the Secretary-General shall, within one month of the occurrence of the vacancy, proceed to issue the invitations provided for in Article 5, and the date of the election shall be fixed by the Security Council.

Article 15

A member of the Court elected to replace a member whose term of office has not expired shall hold office for the remainder of his predecessor's term.

Article 16

1. No member of the Court may exercise any political or administrative function, or engage in any other occupation of a professional nature.

2. Any doubt on this point shall be settled by the decision of the Court.

Article 17

1. No member of the Court may act as agent, counsel, or advocate in any case.

2. No member may participate in the decision of any case in which he has previously taken part as agent, counsel, or advocate for one of the parties, or as a member of a national or international court, or of a commission of enquiry, or in any other capacity.

3. Any doubt on this point shall be settled by the decision of the Court.

Article 18

1.   No member of the Court can be dismissed unless, in the unanimous opinion of the other members, he has ceased to fulfil the required conditions.

2.   Formal notification thereof shall be made to the Secretary-General by the Registrar.

3.   This notification makes the place vacant.

Article 19

The members of the Court, when engaged on the business of the Court, shall enjoy diplomatic privileges and immunities.

Article 20

Every member of the Court shall, before taking up his duties, make a solemn declaration in open court that he will exercise his powers impartially and conscientiously.

Article 21

1.   The Court shall elect its President and Vice-President for three years; they may be re-elected.

2.   The Court shall appoint its Registrar and may provide for the appointment of such other officers as may be necessary.

Article 22

1.   The seat of the Court shall be established at The Hague. This, however, shall not prevent the Court from sitting and exercising its functions elsewhere whenever the Court considers it desirable.

2.   The President and the Registrar shall reside at the seat of the Court.

Article 23

1.   The Court shall remain permanently in session, except during the judicial vacations, the dates and duration of which shall be fixed by the Court.

2.   Members of the Court are entitled to periodic leave, the dates and duration of which shall be fixed by the Court, having in mind the distance between The Hague and the home of each judge.

3. Members of the Court shall be bound, unless they are on leave or prevented from attending by illness or other serious reasons duly explained to the President, to hold themselves permanently at the disposal of the Court.

Article 24

1. If, for some special reason, a member of the Court considers that he should not take part in the decision of a particular case, he shall so inform the President.

2. If the President considers that for some special reason one of the members of the Court should not sit in a particular case, he shall give him notice accordingly.

3. If in any such case the member of the Court and the President disagree, the matter shall be settled by the decision of the Court.

Article 25

1. The full Court shall sit except when it is expressly provided otherwise in the present Statute.

2. Subject to the condition that the number of judges available to constitute the Court is not thereby reduced below eleven, the Rules of the Court may provide for allowing one or more judges, according to circumstances and in rotation, to be dispensed from sitting.

3. A quorum of nine judges shall suffice to constitute the Court.

Article 26

1. The Court may from time to time from one or more chambers, composed of three or more judges as the Court may determine, for dealing with particular categories of cases; for example, labor cases and cases relating to transit and communications.

2. The Court may at any time form a chamber for dealing with a particular case. The number of judges to constitute such a chamber shall be determined by the Court with the approval of the parties.

3. Cases shall be heard and determined by the chambers provided for in this Article if the parties so request.

Article 27

A judgement given by any of the chambers provided for in Articles 26 and 29 shall be considered as rendered by the Court.

Article 28

The chambers provided for in Articles 26 and 29 may, with the consent of the parties, sit and exercise their functions elsewhere than at The Hague.

Article 29

With a view to the speedy dispatch of business, the Court shall form annually a chamber composed of five judges which, at the request of the parties, may hear and determine cases by summary procedure. In addition, two judges shall be selected for the purpose of replacing judges who find it impossible to sit.

Article 30

1. The Court shall frame rules for carrying out its functions. In particular, it shall lay down rules of procedure.

2. The Rules of the Court may provide for assessors to sit with the Court or with any of its chambers, without the right to vote.

Article 31

1. Judges of the nationality of each of the parties shall retain their right to sit in the case before the Court.

2. If the Court includes upon the Bench a judge of the nationality of one of the parties, any other party may choose a person to sit as judge. Such person shall be chosen preferably from among those persons who have been nominated as candidates as provided in Articles 4 and 5.

3. If the Court includes upon the Bench no judge of the nationality of the parties, each of these parties may proceed to choose a judge as provided in paragraph 2 of this Article.

4. The provisions of this Article shall apply to the case of Articles 26 and 29. In such cases, the President shall request one or, if necessary, two of the members of the Court forming the chamber to give place to the members of the Court of the nationality of the parties concerned, and failing such, or if they are unable to be present, to the judges specially chosen by the parties.

5. Should there be several parties in the same interest, they shall, for the purpose of the preceding provisions, be reckoned as one party only. Any doubt upon this point shall be settled by the decision of the Court.

6.   Judges chosen as laid down in paragraphs 2, 3, and 4 of this Article shall fulfil the conditions required by Articles 2, 17 (paragraph 2), 20, and 24 of the present Statute. They shall take part in the decision on terms of complete equality with their colleagues.

Article 32

1.   Each member of the Court shall receive an annual salary.

2.   The President shall receive a special annual allowance.

3.   The Vice-President shall receive a special allowance for every day on which he acts as President.

4.   The judges chosen under Article 31, other than members of the Court, shall receive compensation for each day on which they exercise their functions.

5.   These salaries, allowances, and compensation shall be fixed by the General Assembly. They may not be decreased during the term of office.

6.   The salary of the Registrar shall be fixed by the General Assembly on the proposal of the Court.

7.   Regulations made by the General Assembly shall fix the conditions under which retirement pensions may be given to members of the Court and to the Registrar, and the conditions under which members of the Court and the Registrar shall have their travelling expenses refunded.

8.   The above salaries, allowances, and compensation shall be free of all taxation.

Article 33

The expenses of the Court shall be borne by the United Nations in such a manner as shall be decided by the General Assembly.

CHAPTER II
COMPETENCE OF THE COURT
Article 34

1.   Only states may be parties in cases before the Court.

2.   The Court, subject to and in conformity with its Rules, may request of public international organizations information relevant to cases before it, and shall receive such information presented by such organizations on their own initiative.

3.   Whenever the construction of the constituent instrument of a public international organization or of an international convention adopted thereunder is in question in a case before the Court, the Registrar shall so notify the public international organization concerned and shall communicate to it copies of all the written proceedings.

Article 35

1. The Court shall be open to the states parties to the present Statute.

2. The conditions under which the Court shall be open to other states shall, subject to the special provisions contained in treaties in force, be laid down by the Security Council, but in no case shall such conditions place the parties in a position of inequality before the Court.

3. When a state which is not a Member of the United Nations is a party to a case, the Court shall fix the amount which that party is to contribute towards the expenses of the Court. This provision shall not apply if such state is bearing a share of the expenses of the Court.

Article 36

1. The jurisdiction of the Court comprises all cases which the parties refer to it and all matters specially provided for in the Charter of the United Nations or in treaties and conventions in force.

2. The states parties to the present Statute may at any time declare that they recognize as compulsory ipso facto and without special agreement, in relation to any other state accepting the same obligation, the jurisdiction of the Court in all legal disputes concerning:

a. the interpretation of a treaty;

b. any question of international law;

c. the existence of any fact which, if established, would constitute a breach of an international obligation;

d. the nature or extent of the reparation to be made for the breach of an international obligation.

3. The declarations referred to above may be made unconditionally or on condition of reciprocity on the part of several or certain states, or for a certain time.

4. Such declarations shall be deposited with the Secretary-General of the United Nations, who shall transmit copies thereof to the parties to the Statute and to the Registrar of the Court.

5. Declarations made under Article 36 of the Statute of the Permanent Court of International Justice and which are still in force shall be deemed, as between the parties to the present Statute, to be acceptances of the compulsory jurisdiction of the International Court of Justice for the period which they still have to run and in accordance with their terms.

6. In the event of a dispute as to whether the Court has jurisdiction, the matter shall be settled by the decision of the Court.

Article 37

Whenever a treaty or convention in force provides for reference of a matter to a tribunal to have been instituted by the League of Nations, or to the Permanent Court of International Justice, the matter shall, as between the parties to the present Statute, be referred to the International Court of Justice.

Article 38

1.   The Court, whose function is to decide in accordance with international law such disputes as are submitted to it, shall apply:

a. international conventions, whether general or particular, establishing rules expressly recognized by the contesting states;

b. international custom, as evidence of a general practice accepted as law;

c. the general principles of law recognized by civilized nations;

d. subject to the provisions of Article 59, judicial decisions and the teachings of the most highly qualified publicists of the various nations, as subsidiary means for the determination of rules of law.

2.   This provision shall not prejudice the power of the Court to decide a case *ex aeqno et bono*, if the parties agree thereto.

CHAPTER III
PROCEDURE
Article 39

1.   The official languages of the Court shall be French and English. If the parties agree that the case shall be conducted in French, the judgement shall be delivered in French. If the parties agree that the case shall be conducted in English, the judgement shall be delivered in English.

2.   In the absence of an agreement as to which language shall be employed, each party may, in the pleadings, use the language which it prefers; the decision of the Court shall be given in French and English. In this case the Court shall at the same time determine which of the two tests shall be considered as authoritative.

3.   The Court shall, at the request of any party, authorize a language other than French or English to be used by that party.

Article 40

1.   Cases are brought before the Court, as the case may be, either by the notification of the special agreement or by a written application addressed to the Registrar. In either case the subject of the dispute and the parties shall be indicated.

2.   The Registrar shall forthwith communicate the application to all concerned.

3.   He shall also notify the Members of the United Nations through the Secretary-General, and also any other states entitled to appear before the Court.

Article 41

1.   The Court shall have the power to indicate, if it considers that circumstances so require, any provisional measures which ought to be taken to preserve the respective rights of either party.

2.   Pending the final decision, notice of the measures suggested shall forthwith be given to the parties and to the Security Council.

Article 42

1.   The parties shall be represented by agents.

2.   They may have the assistance of counsel or advocates before the Court.

3.   The agents, counsel, and advocates of parties before the Court shall enjoy the privileges and immunities necessary to the independent exercise of their duties.

Article 43

1.   The procedure shall consist of two parts: written and oral.

2.   The written proceedings shall consist of the communication to the Court and to the parties of memorials, counter-memorials and, if necessary, replies; also all papers and documents in support.

3.   These communications shall be made through the Registrar, in the order and within the time fixed by the Court.

4.   A certified copy of every document produced by one party shall be communicated to the other party.

5.   The oral proceedings shall consist of the hearing by the Court of witnesses, experts, agents, counsel, and advocates.

Article 44

1. For the service of all notices upon persons other than the agents, counsel, and advocates, the Court shall apply direct to the government of the state upon whose territory the notice has to be served.

2. The same provision shall apply whenever steps are to be taken to procure evidence on the spot.

Article 45

The hearing shall be under the control of the President or, if he is unable to preside, of the Vice-President; if neither is able to preside, the senior judge present shall preside.

Article 46

The hearing in Court shall be public, unless the Court shall decide otherwise, or unless the parties demand that the public be not admitted.

Article 47

1. Minutes shall be made at each hearing and signed by the Registrar and the President

2. These minutes alone shall be authentic.

Article 48

The Court shall make orders for the conduct of the case, shall decide the form and time in which each party must conclude its arguments, and make all arrangements connected with the taking of evidence.

Article 49

The Court may, even before the hearing begins, call upon the agents to produce any document or to supply any explanations. Formal note shall be taken of any refusal.

Article 50

The Court may, at any time, entrust any individual, body, bureau, commission, or other organization that it may select, with the task of carrying out an enquiry or giving an expert opinion.

Article 51

During the hearing any relevant questions are to be put to the witness and experts under the conditions laid down by the Court in the rules of procedure referred to in Article 30.

Article 52

After the Court has received the proofs and evidence within the time specified for the purpose, it may refuse to accept any further oral or written evidence that one party may desire to present unless the other side consents.

Article 53

1. Whenever one of the parties does not appear before the Court, or fails to defend its case, the other party may call upon the Court to decide in favour of its claim.

2. The Court must, before doing so, satisfy itself, not only that it has jurisdiction in accordance with Articles 36 and 37, but also that the claim is well founded in fact and law.

Article 54

1. When, subject to the control of the Court, the agents, counsel, and advocates have completed their presentation of the case, the President shall declare the hearing closed.

2. The Court shall withdraw to consider the judgment.

3. The deliberations of the Court shall take place in private and remain secret.

Article 55

1. All questions shall be decided by a majority of the judges present.

2. In the event of an equality of votes, the President or the judge who acts in his place shall have a casting vote.

Article 56

1. The judgment shall state the reasons on which it is based.
2. It shall contain the names of the judges who have taken part in the decision.

Article 57

If the judgment does not represent in whole or in part the unanimous opinion of the judges, any judge shall be entitled to deliver a separate opinion.

Article 58

The judgment shall be signed by the President and by the Registrar. It shall be read in open court, due notice having been given to the agents.

Article 59

The decision of the Court has no binding force except between the parties and in respect of that particular case.

Article 60

The judgment is final and without appeal. In the event of dispute as to the meaning or scope of the judgment, the Court shall construe it upon the request of any party.

Article 61

1. An application for revision of a judgment may be made only when it is based upon the discovery of some fact of such a nature as to be a decisive factor, which fact was, when the judgment was given, unknown to the Court and also to the party claiming revision, always provided that such ignorance was not due to negligence.
2. The proceedings for revision shall be opened by a judgment of the Court expressly recording the existence of the new fact, recognizing that it has such a character as to lay the case open to revision, and declaring the application admissible on this ground.
3. The Court may require previous compliance with the terms of the judgment before it admits proceedings in revision.
4. The application for revision must be made at latest within six months of the discovery of the new fact.

5. No application for revision may be made after the lapse of ten years from the date of the judgment.

Article 62

1. Should a state consider that it has an interest of a legal nature which may be affected by the decision in the case, it may submit a request to the Court to be permitted to intervene.

2. It shall be for the Court to decide upon this request.

Article 63

1. Whenever the construction of a convention to which states other than those concerned in the case are parties is in question, the Registrar shall notify all such states forthwith.

2. Every state so notified has the right to intervene in the proceedings; but if it uses this right, the construction given by the judgment will be equally binding upon it.

Article 64

Unless otherwise decided by the Court, each party shall bear its own costs.

CHAPTER IV
ADVISORY OPINIONS
Article 65

1. The Court may give an advisory opinion on any legal question at the request of whatever body may be authorized by or in accordance with the Charter of the United Nations to make such a request.

2. Questions upon which the advisory opinion of the Court is asked shall be laid before the Court by means of a written request containing an exact statement of the question upon which an opinion is required, and accompanied by all documents likely to throw light upon the question.

Article 66

1. The Registrar shall forthwith give notice of the request for an advisory opinion to all states entitled to appear before the Court.

2.   The Registrar shall also, by means of a special and direct communication, notify any state entitled to appear before the Court or international organization considered by the Court, or, should it not be sitting, by the President, as likely to be able to furnish information on the question, that the Court will be prepared to receive, within a time limit to be fixed by the President, written statements, or to hear, at a public sitting to be held for the purpose, oral statements relating to the question.

3.   Should any such state entitled to appear before the Court have failed to receive the special communication referred to in paragraph 2 of this Article, such state may express a desire to submit a written statement or to be heard; and the Court will decide.

4.   States and organizations having presented written or oral statements or both shall be permitted to comment on the statements made by other states or organizations in the form, to the extent, and within the time limits which the Court, or, should it not be sitting, the President, shall decide in each particular case. Accordingly, the Registrar shall in due time communicate any such written statements to states and organizations having submitted similar statements.

Article 67

The Court shall deliver its advisory opinions in open court, notice having been given to the Secretary-General and to the representatives of Members of the United Nations, of other states and of international organizations immediately concerned.

Article 68

In the exercise of its advisory functions the Court shall further be guided by the provisions of the present Statute which apply in contentious cases to the extent to which it recognizes them to be applicable.

CHAPTER V
AMENDMENT
Article 69

Amendments to the present Statute shall be effected by the same procedure as is provided by the Charter of the United Nations for amendments to that Charter, subject however to any provisions which the General Assembly upon recommendation of the Security Council may adopt concerning the participation of states which are parties to the present Statute but are not Members of the United Nations.

Article 70

The Court shall have power to propose such amendments to the present Statute as it may deem necessary, through written communications to the Secretary-General, for consideration in conformity with the provisions of Article 69.

3. RULES OF THE PROCEDURE OF THE GENERAL ASSEMBLY[1]

Contents

Page

RULES OF PROCEDURE

Rule

I. SESSIONS
Regular Sessions

Special sessions

Regular and special sessions

---

[1]*Rules of Procedure of the General Assembly* (A/520/Rev. 15), United Nations, New York, 1985, pp. iii-xix and 1-70.

IX. RECORDS

X. PUBLIC AND PRIVATE MEETINGS OF THE
GENERAL ASSEMBLY, ITS COMMITTEES AND ITS SUBCOMMITTES

XI. MINUTE OF SILENT PRAYER OR MEDITATION

XII. PLENARY MEETINGS
Conduct of business

Voting

XIII. COMMITTEES

Establishment, officers, organization of work

INTRODUCTION

1.   At its first regular session, the General Assembly adopted provisional rules of procedure (A/71/Rev.1) based on a text contained in the report of the Preparatory Commission of the United Nations.[1]

2.   At the same session, the General Assembly, by resolution 102 (I) of 15 December 1946, established the Committee on Procedures and Organization, consisting of 15 Member States.

3.   At its second session, the General Assembly considered the report of the Committee on Procedures and Organization,[2] which contained draft rules of procedure proposed by the Committee,[3] and, by resolution 173 (II) of 17 November 1947, adopted its rules of procedure. These rules entered into force on 1 January 1948.

4.   At the same session, the General Assembly, by resolution 116 (III) of 21 November 1947, decided to add new rules 113, 114, 116 and 117,[4] relating to the admission of new Members.

5.   At its third session, the General Assembly, by resolution 262 (III) of 11 December 1948, decided to include Spanish among its working languages and to amend accordingly rules 44 to 48.[5]

6.   At the same session, the General Assembly, by resolution 271 (III) of 29 April 1949, established the Special Committee on Methods and Procedures of the General Assembly, consisting of 15 Member States.

7.   At its fourth session, the General Assembly considered the recommendations contained in the report of the Special Committee on Methods and Procedures of the General Assembly[6] and, by resolution 362 (IV) of 22 October 1949, decided:

(a) To amend rules 14, 31, 33, 35, 59, 64, 65, 67, 68, 69, 72, 80, 81, 82, 97, 98, 102, 103, 105, 106, 107, 110, 117, 118 and 119;[7]

(b) To add new rules 1A, 19, 19B, 19C, 31A, 35A, 35B, 56A, 89A, and 97A.[8]

By the same resolution, the General Assembly adopted several of the recommendations and suggestions of the Special Committee and requested the Secretary-General to prepare a document embodying these recommendations and suggestions in a convenient form for

---

[1]PC/20, chap. I, sect. 3.

[2]*Official Records of the General Assembly, Second Session, Plenary Meetings*, vol. II, annex IV, document A/388.

[3]*Ibid.*, document A/388, part III.

[4]Rules 134, 135, 137 and 138 of the present rules of procedure.

[5]Rules 51 to 55 of the present rules of procedure.

[6]*Official Records of the General Assembly, Fourth Session, Supplement No.12* (A/937).

[7]Rules 15, 35, 38, 40, 66, 71, 72, 74, 75, 76, 79, 88, 89, 90, 106, 108, 113, 114, 116, 117, 118, 121, 128, 129 and 130 of the present rules of procedure.

[8]Rules 2, 20, 22, 23, 36, 41, 42, 62, 99 and 107 of the present rules of procedure.

use by the General Committee and delegations of Member States in the Assembly. The text of these recommendations and suggestions is reproduced in annex I.

8. At the same session, the General Assembly, by resolution 366 (IV) of 3 December 1949, adopted rules for the calling by the Economic and Social Council, under Article 62, paragraph 4, of the Charter, of international conferences of States.

9. At its fifth session, the General Assembly, by resolution 377 A (V) of 3 November 1950, adopted several amendments and additions to its rules of procedure relating to the holding of emergency special sessions; by that resolution, the Assembly decided:

(a) To add a paragraph (b) to rule 8;

(b) To add a paragraph (b) to rule 9;

(c) To insert a new sentence at the end of rule 10;

(d) To insert a new sentence at the end of rule 16;

(e) To insert a new sentence at the end of rule 19;

(f) To insert a new rule 65.[9]

10. At the same session, the General Assembly, by resolution 475 (V) of 1 November 1950, adopted a new rule 84 A[10] concerning the majority required for decisions of the Assembly on amendments to proposals relating to important questions and on parts of such proposals put to the vote separately.

11. At the same session, the General Assembly, by resolution 479 (V) of 12 December 1950, adopted rules for the calling by the Economic and Social Council, under Article 62, paragraph 4, of the Charter, of non-governmental conferences.

12. At its sixth session, the General Assembly, by resolution 597 (VI) of 20 December 1951, established the Special Committee for the Consideration of the Methods and Procedures of the General Assembly for Dealing with Legal and Drafting Questions, consisting of 15 Member States.

13. At its seventh session, the General Assembly considered the report of the Special Committee for the Consideration of the Methods and Procedures of the General Assembly for Dealing with Legal and Drafting Questions[11] and, by resolution 684 (VII) of 6 November 1952, adopted certain recommendations contained in that report; the resolution also provided that:

(a) The terms of these recommendations should be embodied as an annex to the rules of procedure;

---

[9]Rule 63 of the present rules of procedure.

[10]Rule 84 of the present rules of procedure.

[11]*Official Records of the General Assembly, Seventh Session, Annexes*, agenda item 53, document A/2174.

(b) The said annex should also reproduce paragraphs 19, 20, 29, 30 and 35 to 39 of the report of the Special Committee.

The texts of the recommendations and the specified parts of the report of the Special Committee are reproduced in annex II.

14. At the same session, the General Assembly, by resolution 689 A (VII) of 21 December 1952, established the Special Committee on Measures to Limit the Duration of Regular Sessions of the General Assembly, consisting of 15 Member States. By resolution 689 B (VII) of the same date, the General Assembly adopted an amendment to rule 2 whereby the Assembly would, at the beginning of each session, fix "a closing date for the session" rather than "a target date for the closing of the session".

15. At its eighth session, the General Assembly considered the report of the Special Committee on Measures to Limit the Duration of Regular Sessions of the General Assembly[12] and, by resolution 791 (VIII) of 23 October 1953, decided:

(a) To amend rules 38 and 39, relating to the composition of the General Committee;

(b) To amend rule 98,[13] relating to priorities in the consideration of items in the Main Committees.

16. At its ninth session, the General Assembly, by resolution 844 (IX) of 11 October 1954, adopted six special rules designed to govern its procedure for the examination of reports and petitions relating to the Territory of South West Africa.[14] The text of these special rules is reproduced in annex III.

17. At its eleventh session, the General Assembly, at the 577th plenary meeting on 15 November 1956, decided:

(a) To establish an eighth vice-presidency of the Assembly;

(b) To change the name of the "*Ad Hoc* Political Committee" to "Special Political Committee" and to confer a permanent character on that Committee.

At the same session, the General Assembly, by resolution 1104 (XI) of 18 December 1956, adopted consequential amendments to rules 31, 38, 39 and 101.[15]

18. At its twelfth session, the General Assembly, by resolution 1192 (XII) of 12 December 1957, decided to increase the number of Vice-Presidents of the Assembly from 8 to 13 and adopted consequential amendments to rules 31 and 38. In an annex to the resolution, the General Assembly approved the pattern according to which the Vice-Presidents should be elected.

---

[12]*Ibid., Eighth Session, Annexes*, agenda item 54, document A/2402.

[13]Rule 99 of the present rules of procedure.

[14]By resolution 2372 (XXII) of 12 June 1968, the General Assembly decided that "South West Africa" would be known as "Namibia".

[15]Rule 98 of the present rules of procedure.

19. At its sixteenth session, the General Assembly, by resolution 1659 (XVI) of 28 November 1961, decided to increase the membership of the Advisory Committee on Administrative and Budgetary Questions from 9 to 12 and adopted consequential amendments to rules 156 and 157.[16]

20. At its seventeenth session, the General Assembly, at the 1162nd plenary meeting on 30 October 1962, established the *Ad Hoc* Committee on the Improvement of the Methods of Work of the General Assembly. By resolution 1845 (XVII) of 19 December 1962, the General Assembly decided to continue the *Ad Hoc* Committee.

21. At its eighteenth session, the General Assembly considered the report of the *Ad Hoc* Committee on the Improvement of the Methods of Work of the General Assembly[17] and, by resolution 1898 (XVIII) of 11 November 1963, took note of the observations contained in that report and approved the recommendations submitted by the Committee. The text of the resolution is reproduced in annex IV.

22. At the same session, the General Assembly, by resolution 1990 (XVIII) of 17 December 1963, decided to increase the number of Vice-Presidents of the Assembly from 13 to 17 and adopted consequential amendments to rules 31 and 38. In annex to the resolution, the General Assembly approved the pattern according to which the President of the Assembly, the 17 Vice-Presidents of the Assembly and 7 Chairmen of the Main Committees should be elected.

23. At its twentieth session, the General Assembly, by resolution 2046 (XX) of 8 December 1965, following the entry into forces of the amendments to Articles 23, 27 and 61 of the Charter, amended its rules of procedure as follows:

(a) In rule 8 (b), the word "seven" was replaced by the word "nine";

(b) In rule 143,[18] the word "three" was replaced by the word "five";

(c) In rule 146,[19] the word "six" was replaced by the word "nine".

The pattern for the election of the non-permanent members of the Security Council is reproduced in a foot-note to rule 142.

24. At its twenty-second session, the General Assembly, by resolution 2323 (XXII) of 16 December 1967, decided to amend rules 89 and 128[20] by adding to each of these rules a new paragraph (b) to take into account the installation of mechanical means of voting.

---

[16]Rules 155 and 156 of the present rules of procedure.

[17]*Official Records of the General Assembly, Eighteenth Session, Annexes*, agenda item 25, document A/5423.

[18]Rule 142 of the present rules of procedure.

[19]Rule 145 of the present rules of procedure.

[20]Rules 87 and 127 of the present rules of procedure.

25. At the same session, the General Assembly, at the 1629th plenary meeting on 13 December 1967, took note of a correction to the French version of rule 15[21] whereby the words *"caractère d'importance ou d'urgence"* in the first sentence of that rule were replaced by the words *"caractère d'importance et d'urgence"*.

26. At its twenty-third session, the General Assembly by resolution 2390 (XXII) of 25 November 1968, decided to increase the membership of the Committee on Contributions from 10 to 12 and adopted a consequential amendment to rule 159.[22]

27. At the same session, the General Assembly, by resolution 2479 (XXIII) of 21 December 1968, decided to include Russian among its working languages and to amend accordingly rule 51.

28. At its twenty-fourth session, the General Assembly, by resolution 2553 (XXIV) of 12 December 1969, adopted amendments to rules 52, 53 and 55[23] consequent upon the amendment to rule 51 adopted at the twenty-third session.

29. At its twenty-fifth session, the General Assembly, by resolution 2632 (XXV) of 9 November 1970, established the Special Committee on the Rationalization of the Procedures and Organization of the General Assembly, consisting of 31 Member States.

30. At its twenty-sixth session, the General Assembly considered the report of the Special Committee on the Rationalization of the Procedures and Organization of the General Assembly[24] and, by resolution 2837 (XXVI) of 17 December 1971, decided:

(a) To amend rule 60[25] to reflect the practice of the General Assembly and its committees regarding the records and sound recordings of meetings;

(b) To amend rules 69 and 110[26] to authorize the presiding officer to declare a meeting open and permit the debate to proceed when at least one third of the members of the General Assembly or one quarter of the members of a committee are present;

(c) To amend rules 74 and 116[27] to permit no more than two representatives to speak in favour, and to against, a proposal to limit the time to be allowed to each speaker or the number of times each representative may speak on any question;

(d) To amend rule 100 to include in it more detailed provisions relating to the organization of work of the Main Committees, and to renumber it rule 101[28] (former rule 101 became rule 100[29]);

---

[21]*Official Records of the General Assembly, Twenty-second Session, Annexes*, agenda item 8, document A/BUR/169.

[22]Rule 158 of the present rules of procedure.

[23]See introduction para. 34.

[24]*Official Records of the General Assembly, Twenty-sixth Session, Supplement No. 26* (A/8426).

[25]Rule 58 of the present rules of procedure.

[26]Rules 67 and 108 if the present rules of procedure.

[27]Rules 72 and 114 of the present rules of procedure.

[28]Rule 99 of the present rules of procedure.

[29]Rule 98 of the present rules of procedure.

(e) To amend rule 105[30] to provide that:

(i)   Each Main Committee shall elect a Chairman, two Vice-Chairmen and a Rapporteur;

(ii)   Each other committee shall elect a Chairman, one or more Vice-Chairmen and a Rapporteur;

(iii)   Elections shall be held by secret ballot unless the committee decides otherwise in an election where only one candidate is standing;

(iv)   The nomination of each candidate shall be limited to one speaker, after which the committee shall immediately proceed to the election,

and to adopt consequential amendments to rules 39 and 107,[31]

(f) To insert a new rule 122,[32] relating to congratulations to the officers of Main Committees, and to renumber accordingly the existing rules 112 to 164.[33]

By resolution 2837 (XXVI), the General Assembly also approved the conclusions of the Special Committee and decided that they should be annexed to the rules of procedure; these conclusions are reproduced in annex V. In one of the recommendations,[34] the Secretary-General was requested to undertake a comparative study of the versions of the rules of procedure in the various official languages in order to ensure their concordance; this request was complied with and the relevant editing changes were incorporated in the rules.

31. At the same session, the General Assembly, by resolution 2798 (XXVI) of 13 December 1971, decided to increase the membership of the Advisory Committee on Administrative and Budgetary Questions from 12 to 13 and adopted a consequential amendment to rule 157.[35]

32. At the same session, the General Assembly, by resolution 2847 (XXVI) of 20 December 1971, decided to amend Article 61 of the Charter to increase from 27 to 54 the number of members of the Economic and Social Council. By that resolution, the General Assembly also decided that, upon the entry into force of the amendment to the Charter, the word "nine" in rule 147[36] would be replaced by the word "eighteen". The amendment to the Charter entered into force on 24 September 1973. The pattern for the election of the members of the Economic and Social Council, as set forth in resolution 2847 (XXVI), is reproduced in a footnote to rule 145.

---

[30]Rule 103 of present rules of procedure.
[31]Rule 105 of the present rules of procedure.
[32]Rule 110 of the present rules of procedure.
[33]Rules 111 to 163 of the present rules of procedure.
[34]Resolution 2837 (XXVI), annex II, para. 128.
[35]Rule 155 of the present rules of procedure.
[36]Rule 145 of the present rules of procedure.

33. At its twenty-seventh session, the General Assembly, by resolution 2913 (XXVII) of 9 November 1972, decided to increase the membership of the Committee on Contributions from 12 to 13 and adopted a consequential amendment to rule 160.[37]

34. At its twenty-eighth session, the General Assembly, by resolutions 3189 (XXVIII) and 3190 (XXVIII) of 18 December 1973, decided:

(a) To include Chinese among the working languages of the General Assembly, its committees and its subcommittees;

(b) To include Arabic among the official and the working languages of the General Assembly and its Main Committees.

By resolution 3191 (XXVIII) of 18 December 1973, the General Assembly adopted consequential amendments to its rules of procedure, as follows:

(a) Rules 51 to 59 were replaced by new rules 51 to 57;

(b) Rules 60 to 165 were renumbered accordingly.

35. At its thirty-first session, the General Assembly, by resolution 31/95 A of 14 December 1976, decided to increase the membership of the Committee on Contributions from 13 to 18, by resolution 31/96 of the same date, adopted a consequential amendment to rule 158.

36. At its thirty-second session, the General Assembly, by resolution 32/103 of 14 December 1977, decided to increase the membership of the Advisory Committee on Administrative and Budgetary Questions from 13 to 16 and adopted a consequential amendment to rule 155. By the same resolution, the General Assembly also decided:

(a) To adopt an amendment to rule 156 whereby the members of the Advisory Committee would serve for a period of three years corresponding to "three calendar years" rather than "three financial years, as defined in the Financial Regulations of the United Nations";

(b) To amend rule 157 to take into account, *inter alia*, the biennial presentation of the budget.

37. At its thirty-third session, the General Assembly, by resolution 33/12 of 3 November 1978, adopted an amendment to rule 159 whereby the members of the Committee on Contribution would serve for a period of three years corresponding to "three calendar years" rather than "three financial years, as defined in the Financial Regulation of the United Nations".

38. At the same session, the General Assembly, by resolution 33/138 of 19 December 1978, decided to increase the number of Vice-Presidents of the Assembly from 17 to 21 and adopted consequential amendments to rules 31 and 38. In an annex to the resolution, which replaced the annex to resolution 1990 (XVIII),[38] the General Assembly

---

[37]Rule 158 of the present rules of procedure.
[38]See introduction, para. 22.

approved the pattern according to which the president of the Assembly, the 21 Vice-Presidents of the Assembly and the 7 Chairmen of the Main Committees should be elected; the text of that annex is reproduced in a footnote to rule 31.

39. At its thirty-fourth session, the General Assembly, by decision 34/401 of 21 September, 25 October, 29 November and 12 December 1979, adopted a number of provisions concerning the rationalization of the procedures and organizations of the Assembly. Sections I to V of the decision are reproduced in annex VI.

40. At its thirty-fifth session, the General Assembly, by resolutions 35/219 A and B of 17 December 1980, decided to include Arabic among the official and working languages of the subsidiary organs of the Assembly, not later than 1 January 1982, and adopted consequential amendments to rules 51, 52, 54 and 56.

41. At its thirty-ninth session, the General Assembly, by resolution 39/88 B of 13 December 1984, approved the conclusions of the Special Committee on the Charter of the United Nations and on the Strengthening of the Role of the Organization concerning the rationalization of the procedures of the General Assembly and decided that they should be annexed to the rules of procedure; these conclusions are reproduced in annex VII.

42. The present revised edition of the rules of procedure embodies all the amendments adopted by the General Assembly up to and including its thirty-ninth session.

43. The previous versions of the rules of procedure and of the amendments and corrigenda thereto have been issued under the following symbols:

December 1947 . . . A/520

June 1948 . . . . . . A/520/Corr.1 (French only)

January 1950 . . . . A/520/Rev.1

January 1951 . . . . A/520/Rev.2

July 1954 . . . . . . A/520/Rev.3

March 1956 . . . . . A/520/Rev.4

September 1957 . . . A/520/Rev.5 (formerly A/3660)

January 1958 . . . . A/520/Rev.5/Corr.1 (formerly A/3660/Corr.1)

February 1961 . . . A/520/Rev.6 (formerly A/4700)

February 1962 . . . A/520/Rev.6/Corr.1 (formerly A/4700/Corr.1)

June 1964 . . . . . . A/5200/Rev.7

March 1966 . . . . . A/520/Rev.8

January 1968 . . . . A/520/Rev.9

April 1969 . . . . . . A/520/Rev.9/Corr.1

July 1970 . . . . . . A/520/Rev.10

May 1972 . . . . . . A/520/Rev.11

November 1973 . . .   A/520/Rev.11/Amend.1
February 1974   . . .   A/520/Rev.12
January 1977   . . . .   A/520/Rev.12/Amend.1
March 1978 . . . . .   A/520/Rev.12/Amend.1
March 1979 . . . . .   A/520/Rev.13
March 1982 . . . . .   A/520/Rev.14

May 1985

EXPLANATORY NOTE

Rules 49, 83, 83, 85, 144, 146 and 161, which reproduce textually provisions of the Charter, are printed in bold type and are, in addition, provided with a foot-note. A foot-note has also been added to other rules which, while based directly on provisions of the Charter, do not reproduce those provisions textually.

Figures indicated between square brackets in sections dealing with rules for plenary meetings refer to identical or corresponding rules for committee meetings, and vice versa.

Attention is drawn to rule 162, which provides that the italicized headings of the rules, which were inserted for reference purposes only, shall be disregarded in the interpretation of the rules.

RULES OF PROCEDURE

I. SESSIONS
REGULAR SESSIONS

Opening date

Rule 1[1]

The General Assembly shall meet every year in regular session commencing on the third Tuesday in September.

Closing date

Rule 2[2]

On the recommendation of the General Committee, the General Assembly, at the beginning of each session, fix a closing date for the session.

Place of meeting

Rule 3

The General Assembly shall meet at the Headquarter of the United Nations unless convened elsewhere in pursuance of a decision taken at a previous session or at the request of a majority of the Members of the United Nations.

Rule 4

Any Member of the United Nations may, at least one hundred and twenty days before the date fixed for the opening of a regular session, request that the session be held elsewhere than at the Headquarters of the United Nations. The Secretary-General shall immediately communicate the request, together with his recommendations, to the other Members of the United Nations. If within thirty days of the date of this communication a majority of the Members concur in the request, the session shall be held accordingly.

---

[1]Rule based directly on a provision of the Charter (Art. 20).
[2]See introduction, paras. 7 and 14; see also annex V, para. 4.

Notification session

Rule 5

The Secretary-General shall notify the Members of the United Nations, at least sixty days in advance, of the opening of a regular session.

Temporary adjournment of session.

Rule 6

The General Assembly may decide at any session to adjourn temporarily and resume its meetings at a later date.

SPECIAL SESSIONS

Summoning by the General Assembly

Rule 7[3]

The General Assembly may fix a date for a special session.

Summoning at the request of the Security Council or Members

Rule 8[4]

(a) Special sessions of the General Assembly shall be convened within fifteen days of the receipt by the Secretary-General of a request for such a session from the Security Council or from a majority of the Members of the United Nations or of the concurrence of a majority of Members as provided in rule 9.

(b) Emergency special sessions pursuant to General Assembly resolution 377 A (V) shall be convened within twenty-four hours of the receipt by the Secretary-General of a request for such a session from the Security Council, on the vote of any nine members thereof, or of a request from a majority of the Members of the United Nations expressed by vote in the Interim Committee or otherwise, or of the concurrence of a majority of Members as provided in rule 9.

---

[3]Rule based directly on a provision of the Charter (Art. 20).
[4]See introduction, paras. 9 and 23.

Request by Members

Rule 9[5]

(a) Any Member of the United Nations may request the Secretary-General to convene a special session of the General Assembly. The Secretary-General shall immediately inform the other Members of the request and inquire whether they concur in it. If within thirty days if the date of the communications of the Secretary-General a majority of the members concur in the request, a special session of the General Assembly shall be convened in accordance with rule 8.

(b) This rule shall apply also to a request by any Members of the United Nations for an emergency special session pursuant to resolution 377 A (V). In such a case, the Secretary-General shall communicate with the other Members by the most expeditious means of communication available.

Rule 10[5]

The Secretary-General shall notify the Members of the United Nations, at least fourteen days in advance, of the opening of a special session convened at the request of the Security Council, and at least ten days in advance in the case of a session convened at the request of a majority of the members or upon the concurrence of a majority in the request of any Member. In the case of an emergency special session convened pursuant to rule 8 (b), the Secretary-General shall notify members at least twelve hours before the opening of the session.

REGULAR AND SPECIAL SESSIONS

Notification to other bodies

Rule 11

Copies of the notice convening each session of the General Assembly shall be addressed to all other principal organs of the United Nations and to the specialized agencies referred to in Article 57, paragraph 2, of the Charter.

---

[5]See introduction, para. 9.

II. AGENDA
REGULAR SESSIONS

Provisional Agenda

Rule 12

The provisional agenda for a regular session shall be drawn up by the Secretary-General and communicated to the Members of the United Nations at least sixty days before the opening of the session.

Rule 13

The provisional agenda of a regular session shall include:

(a) The report of the Secretary-General on the work of the Organization;

(b) Reports from the Security Council, the Economic and Social Council, the Trusteeship Council, the International Court of Justice, the subsidiary organs of the General Assembly and the specialized agencies (where such reports are called for under agreements entered into);

(c) All items the inclusion of which has been ordered by the General Assembly at a previous session;

(d) All items proposed by the other principal organs of the United Nations;

(e) All items proposed by any Member of the United Nations;[6]

(f) All items pertaining to the budget for the next financial year and the report on the accounts for the last financial year;

(g) All items which the Secretary-General deems it necessary to put before the General Assembly;

(h) All items proposed under Article 35, paragraph 2, of the Charter by States not Members of the United Nations.

Supplementary items

Rule 14

Any Member or principal organ of the United Nations or the Secretary-General may, at least thirty days before the date fixed for the opening of a regular session, request the inclusion of supplementary items in the agenda. Such items shall be placed on a supplementary list, which shall be communicated to members at least twenty days before the opening of the session.

---

[6]See annex V, para. 18, and annex VII, para. 2.

Additional items

Rule 15[7]

Additional items of an important and urgent character, proposed for inclusion in the agenda less than thirty days before the opening of a regular session or during a regular session, may be placed on the agenda if the General Assembly so decides by a majority of the members present and voting. No additional item may, unless the General Assembly decides otherwise by a two-thirds majority of the members present and voting, be considered until seven days have elapsed since it was placed on the agenda and until a committee has reported upon the question concerned.

SPECIAL SESSIONS

Provisional agenda

Rule 16[8]

The provisional agenda of a special session convened at the request of the Security Council shall be communicated to the Members of the United Nations at least fourteen days before the opening of the session. The provisional agenda of a special session convened at the request of a majority of the Members, or upon the concurrence of a majority in the request of any Member, shall be communicated at least ten days before the opening of the session. The provisional agenda of a emergency special session shall be communicated to Members simultaneously with the communication convening the session.

Rule 17

The provisional agenda for a special session shall consist only of those items proposed for consideration in the request for the holding of the session.

Supplementary items.

Rule 18

Any member or principal organ of the United Nations or the Secretary-General may, at least four days before the date fixed for the opening of a special session, request the inclusion of supplementary items in the agenda. Such items shall be placed on a supplementary list, which shall be communicated to Members as soon as possible.

---

[7]See introduction, paras. 7 and 25; see also annex V, paras. 18 and 24.
[8]See introduction, para. 9.

Additional items

Rule 19

During a special session, items on the supplementary list and additional items may be added to the agenda by a two-thirds majority of the members present and voting. During an emergency special session, additional items concerning the matters dealt with in resolution 377 A (V) may be added to the agenda by a two-thirds majority of the members present and voting.

REGULAR AND SPECIAL SESSIONS

Explanatory memorandum

Rule 20[9]

Any item proposed for inclusion in the agenda shall be accompanied by an explanatory memorandum and, if possible, by basic documents or by a draft resolution.

Adoption of the agenda

Rule 21[10]

At each session the provisional agenda and the supplementary list, together with the report of the General Committee thereon, shall be submitted to the General Assembly for approval as soon as possible after the opening of the session.

Amendment and deletion of items

Rule 22[11]

Items on the agenda may be amended or deleted by the General Assembly by a majority of the members present and voting.

Debate on inclusion of items

Rule 23

Debate on the inclusion of an item in the agenda, when that item has been recommended for inclusion by the General Committee, shall be limited to three speakers

---

[9]See introduction, para. 7; see also annex V, para. 18.
[10]See annex V, paras. 19-23, and annex VII, paras. 1 and 2.
[11]See introduction, para. 7.

in favour of, and three against, the inclusion. The President may limit the time to be allowed to speaker under this rule.

Modification of the allocation of expenses

Rule 24

No proposal for a modification of the allocation of expenses for the time being in force shall be placed on the agenda unless it has been communicated to the Members of the United Nations at least ninety days before the opening of the session.

III. DELEGATIONS

Composition

Rule 25[12]

The delegation of a Member shall consist of not more than five representatives and five alternate representatives and as many advisers, technical advisers, experts and persons of similar status as may be required by the delegation.

Alternates

Rule 26

An alternate representative may act as a representative upon designation by the chairman of the delegation.

IV. CREDENTIALS

Submission of credentials

Rule 27

The credentials of representatives and the names of members of a delegation shall be submitted to the Secretary-General if possible not less than one week before the opening of the session. The credentials shall be issued either by the Head of the State or Government or by the Minister for Foreign Affairs.

---

[12]Rule based directly on a provision of the Charter (Art. 9, para. 2). See annex V, para. 44.

Credentials Committee

Rule 28

A Credentials Committee shall be appointed at the beginning of each session. It shall consist of nine members, who shall be appointed by the General Assembly on the proposal of the President. The Committee shall elect its own officers. It shall examine the credentials of representatives and report without delay.

Provisional admission to a session

Rule 29

Any representative to whose admission a Member has made objection shall be seated provisionally with the same rights as other representatives until the Credentials Committee has reported and the General Assembly has given its decision.

V. PRESIDENT AND VICE-PRESIDENTS

Temporary President

Rule 30

At the opening of each session of the General Assembly, the chairman of that delegation from which the President of the previous session was elected shall preside until the Assembly has elected a President for the session.

Elections

Rule 31[13]

The General Assembly shall elect a President and twenty-one Vice-Presidents,[14] who

---

[13]See introduction, paras. 17, 18, 22 and 38.

[14]In the annex to resolution 33/138 of 19 December 1978, the General Assembly decided as follows:

"1. In the election of the President of the General Assembly, regard shall be had for equitable geographical rotation of this office among the regions mentioned in paragraph 4 below.

"2. The twenty-one Vice-Presidents of the General Assembly shall be elected according to the following pattern, subject to paragraph 3 below:

"(a) Six representatives from African States;

"(b) Five representatives from Asian States;

"(c) One representative from an Eastern European State;

"(d) Three representatives from Latin American States;

"(e) Two representatives from Eastern European or other States;

"(f) Five representatives from the permanent members of the Security Council.

shall hold office until the close of the session at which they are elected.[15] The Vice-Presidents shall be elected, after the election of the Chairmen of the seven Main Committees referred to in rule 98, in such a way as to ensure the representative character of the General Committee.

Acting President

Rule 32 [105]

If the President finds it necessary to be absent during a meeting or any part thereof, he shall designate one of the Vice-Presidents to take his place.

Rule 33 [105]

A Vice-President acting as President shall have the same powers and duties as the President.

Replacement of the President

Rule 34 [105]

If the President is unable to perform his functions, a new President shall be elected for the unexpired term.

"3. The election of the President of the General Assembly will, however, have the effect of reducing by one number of vice-presidencies allocated to the region from which the president is elected.

"4. The seven Chairmen of the Main Committees shall be elected according to the following pattern:

"(a) Two representatives from African States;

"(b) One representative from an Asian State;

"(c) One representative from an Eastern European State;

"(d) One representative from a Latin American State;

"(e) One representative from a Western European or other State;

"(f) The Seventh chairmanship shall rotate every alternate year among representatives of States mentioned subparagraphs (b) and (d) above."

[15]Rule based directly on a provision of the Charter (Art. 21, second sentence).

General Powers of the President

Rule 35[16] [106]

In addition to exercising the powers conferred upon him elsewhere by these rules, the president shall declare the opening and closing of each plenary meeting, ensure observance of these rules, accord the right to speak, put questions and announce decisions. He shall rule on points of order and, subject to these rules, shall have complete control of the proceedings at any meeting and over the maintenance of order thereat. The President may, in the course of the discussion of an item, propose to the General Assembly the limitation of the time to be allowed to speakers, the limitation of the number of times each representative may speak, the closure of the list of speakers or closure of the debate. He may also propose the suspension or adjournment of the meeting or the adjournment of the debate on the item under discussion.

Rule 36[16] [107]

The President in the exercise of this functions, remains under the authority of the General Assembly.

The President shall not vote

Rule 37 [104]

The President, or a Vice-President acting as President, shall not vote but shall designate another member of his delegation to vote in his place.

VI. GENERAL COMMITTEE

Composition

Rule 38[17]

The General Committee shall comprise the President of the General Assembly, who shall preside, the twenty-one Vice-Presidents and the Chairmen of the seven Main Committees. No two members of the General Committee shall be members of the same delegation, and it shall be so constituted as to ensure its representative character. Chairmen of other committees upon which all Members have the right to be represented and which are established by the General Assembly to meet during the session shall be

---

[16]See introduction, para. 7; see also annex I, para. 39, annex IV, para. (g), annex V, paras. 39 and 67, annex VI, para. 3, and annex VII, para 7.
[17]See introduction, paras. 7, 15, 17, 18, 22 and 38.

entitled to attend meetings of the General Committee and may participate without vote in the discussions.

Substitute members

Rule 39[18]

If a Vice-President of the General Assembly finds it necessary to be absent during a meeting of the General Committee, he may designate a member of his delegation to take his place. The Chairman of a Main Committee shall, in case of absence, designate one of the Vice-Chairmen if the Committee to take his place. A Vice-Chairman shall not have the right to vote if he is of the same delegation as another member of the General Committee.

Functions

Rule 40[19]

The General Committee shall, at the beginning of each session, consider the provisional agenda, together with the supplementary list, and shall make recommendations to the General Assembly, with regard to each item proposed, concerning its inclusion in the agenda, the rejection of the request for inclusion or the inclusion of the item in the provisional agenda of a future session. It shall, in the same manner, examine requests for the inclusion of additional items in the agenda and shall make recommendations thereon to the General Assembly. In considering matters relating to the agenda of the General Assembly, the General Committee shall not discuss the substance of any item except in so far as this bears upon the question whether the General Committee should recommend the inclusion of the item in the agenda, the rejection of the request for inclusion or the inclusion of the item in the provisional agenda of a future session, and what priority should be accorded to an item the inclusion of which has been recommended.

Rule 41[19]

The General Committee shall make recommendations to the General Assembly concerning the closing date of the session. It shall assist the President and the General Assembly in drawing up the agenda for each plenary meeting, in determining the priority

---

[18]See introduction, paras. 15, 17 and 30; see also annex V, para. 10.

[19]See introduction, para. 7; see also annex IV, para. (f), annex V, paras. 11-14, annex VI, para. 1, and annex VII, para. 4.

of its items and in co-ordinating the proceedings of all committees of the Assembly. It shall assist the President in the general conduct of the work of the General Assembly which falls within the competence of the President. It shall not, however, decide any political question.

Rule 42[20]

The General Committee shall meet periodically throughout each session to review the progress of the General Assembly and its committees and to make recommendations for furthering such progress. It shall also meet at such other times as the President deems necessary or upon the request of any other of its members.

Participation by members requesting the inclusion of items in the agenda
Rule 43

A member of the General Assembly which has no representative on the General Committee and which has requested the inclusion of an item in the agenda shall be entitled to attend any meeting of the General Committee at which its request is discussed and may participate, without vote, in the discussion of that item.

Revision of the form of resolutions
Rule 44

The General Committee may revise the resolutions adopted by the General Assembly, changing their form but not their substance. Any such changes shall be reported to the General Assembly for its consideration.

Duties of the Secretary-General
Rule 45

The Secretary-General shall act in that capacity in all meetings of the General Assembly,[21] its committees and its subcommittees. He may designate a member of the Secretariat to act in his place at these meetings.

---

[20]See introduction, para. 7; see also annex I, para. 20, annex IV, para. (f), annex V, paras. 13 and 14, annex VI, para. 2, and annex VII, para. 4.

[21]Rule based directly on a provision of the Charter (Art. 98).

Rule 46

The Secretary-General shall provide and direct the staff required by the General Assembly and any committees or subsidiary organs which it may establish.

Duties of the Secretariat

Rule 47

The Secretariat shall receive, translate, print and distribute documents, reports and resolution of the General Assembly, its committees and its organs;[22] interpret speeches made at the meetings; prepare, print and circulate the records of the session,[23] have the custody and proper preservation of the documents in the archives of the General Assembly; distribute all documents of the Assembly to the Members of the United Nations, and, generally, perform all other work which the Assembly may require.

Report of the Secretary-General on the work of the organization

Rule 48

The Secretary-General shall make an annual report, and such supplementary reports as are required, to the General Assembly on the work of the Organization.[21] He shall communicate the annual report to the Members of the United Nations at least forty-five days before the opening of the session.

Notification under Article 12 of the Charter

Rule 49[24]

The Secretary-General, with the consent of the Security Council, shall notify the General Assembly at each session of any matters relative to the maintenance of international peace and security which are being dealt with by the Security Council, and shall similarly notify the General Assembly, or the Members of the United Nations if the General Assembly is not in session, immediately the Security Council ceases to deal with such matters.

---

[22]See annex V, para. 107, and annex VI, paras. 25, 26 and 28-30.
[23]See annex V, para. 108.
[24]Rule reproducing textually a provision of the Charter (Art. 12, para. 2).

Rule 50[25]

The General Assembly shall establish regulations concerning the staff of the Secretariat.[26]

VIII. LANGUAGES

Official and working languages

Rule 51[27]

Arabic, Chinese, English, French, Russian and Spanish shall be both the official and the working languages of the General Assembly, its committees and its subcommittees.

Interpretation

Rule 52[27]

Speeches made in any of the six languages of the General Assembly shall be interpreted into the other five languages.

Rule 53

Any representative may make a speech in a language other than the languages of the General Assembly. In this case, he shall himself provide for interpretation into one of the languages of the General Assembly or of the committee concerned. Interpretation into the other languages of the General Assembly or of the committee concerned by the interpreters of the Secretariat may be based on the interpretation given in the first such language.

Languages of verbatim and summary records

Rule 54[27]

Verbatim or summary records shall be drawn up as soon as possible in the languages of the General Assembly.

---

[25]Rule based directly on a provision of the Charter (Art. 101, para. 1).
[26]For the Staff Regulations of the United Nations, see ST/SGB/Staff Regulations/Rev. 16.
[27]See introduction, paras. 5, 27, 28, 34, 40.

Languages of the Journal of United Nations
Rule 55[27]

Documents of the General Assembly, *the Journal of the United Nations* shall be published in the languages of the Assembly.

Languages of resolutions and other documents
Rule 56[27]

All resolutions and other documents shall be published in the languages of the General Assembly.

Publications in languages other than the languages of the General Assembly
Rule 57[27]

Documents of the General Assembly, its committees and its subcommittees shall, if the Assembly so decides, be published in any language other than the languages of the Assembly or of the committee concerned.

IX. RECORDS

Records and sound recordings of meetings
Rule 58[28]

(a) Verbatim records of the meetings of the General Assembly and of the Political and Security Committee (First Committee) shall be drawn up by the Secretariat and submitted to those organs after approval by the presiding officer. The General Assembly shall decide upon the form of the records of the meetings of the other Main Committees and, if any, of the subsidiary organs and of special meetings and conferences. No organs of the General Assembly shall have both verbatim and summary records.

(b) Sound recordings of the meetings of the General Assembly and of the main Committees shall be made by the Secretariat. Such recordings shall also be made of the proceedings of subsidiary organs and special meetings and conferences when they so decide.

---

[28]See introduction, para. 30; see also annex V, para. 108, and annex VI, para, 27.

Resolutions

Rule 59

Resolutions adopted by the General Assembly shall be communicated by the Secretary-General to the Members of the United Nations within fifteen days after the close of the session.

X. PUBLIC AND PRIVATE MEETINGS OF THE GENERAL ASSEMBLY, ITS COMMITTEES AND ITS SUBCOMMITTEES

General principles

Rule 60

The meetings of the General Assembly and its Main Committees shall be held in public unless the organ concerned decides that exceptional circumstances require that the meeting be held in private. Meetings of other committees and subcommittees shall also be held in public unless the organ concerned decides otherwise.

Private meetings

Rule 61

All decisions of the General Assembly taken at a private meeting shall be announced at an early public meeting of the Assembly. At the close of each private meeting of the Main Committees, other committees and subcommittees, the Chairman may issue a *communiqué* through the Secretary-General.

XI. MINUTE OF SILENT PRAYER OR MEDITATION

Invitation to silent prayer or meditation

Rule 62[29]

Immediately after the opening of the first plenary meeting and immediately preceding the closing of the final plenary meeting of each session of the General Assembly, the President shall invite the representatives to observe one minute of silence dedicated to prayer or meditation.

---

[29]See introduction, para. 7.

XII. PLENARY MEETINGS
CONDUCT OF BUSINESS

Emergency special sessions

Rule 63[30]

Notwithstanding the provisions of any other rule and unless the General Assembly decides otherwise, the Assembly, in case of an emergency special session, shall convene in plenary meeting only and proceed directly to consider the item proposed for consideration in the request for the holding of the session, without previous reference to the General Committee or to any other committee; the President and Vice-Presidents for such emergency special sessions shall be, respectively, the chairmen of those delegations from which were elected the President and Vice-Presidents of the previous session.

Report of the Secretary-General

Rule 64

Proposals to refer any portion of the report of the Secretary-General to one of the Main Committees without debate shall be decided upon by the General Assembly without previous references to the General Committee.

Reference to committees

Rule 65

The General Assembly shall not, unless it decides otherwise, make a final decision upon any item on the agenda until it has received the report of a committee on that item.

Discussion of reports of Main Committees

Rule 66[31]

Discussion of a report of a Main Committee in a plenary meeting of the General Assembly shall take place if at least one third of the members present and voting at the plenary meeting consider such a discussion to be necessary. Any proposal to this effect shall not be debated but shall be immediately put to the vote.

---

[30]See introduction, para. 9.
[31]See introduction , para. 7; see also annex VI, para. 15.

Quorum

Rule 67[32] [108]

The President may declare a meeting open and permit the debate to proceed when at least one third of the members of the General Assembly are present. The presence of a majority of the members shall be required for any decision to be taken.

Speeches

Rule 68[33] [109]

No representative may address the General Assembly without having previously obtained the permission of the President. The President shall call upon speakers in the order in which they signify their desire to speak. The President may call a speaker to order if his remarks are not relevant to the subject under discussion.

Precedence

Rule 69 [111]

The Chairman and the Rapporteur of a committee may be accorded precedence for the purpose of explaining the conclusions arrived at by their committee.

Statements by the Secretariat

Rule 70 [112]

The Secretary-General, or a member of the Secretariat designated by him as his representative, may at any time make either oral or written statements to the General Assembly concerning any question under consideration by it.

Points of order

Rule 71[34] [113]

During the discussion of any matter, a representative may rise to a point of order, and the point of order shall be immediately decided by the President in accordance with the rules of procedure. A representative may appeal against the ruling of the President.

---

[32]See introduction, para. 30; see also annex IV, para. (g) (i), annex V, para. 67, and annex VII, para. 7.

[33]See annex IV, para. (g) (ii), annex V, paras. 69-71, and annex VI, para. 17.

[34]See introduction, para. 7; see also annex V, para. 79.

The appeal shall be immediately put to the vote, and the President's ruling shall stand unless overruled by a majority of the members present and voting. A representative rising to a point of order may not speak on the substance of the matter under discussion.

Time-limit on speeches

Rule 72[35] [114]

The General Assembly may limit the time to be allowed to each speaker and the number of items each representative may speak on any question. Before a decision is taken, two representatives may speak in favour of, and two against, a proposal to set such limits. When the debate is limited and a representative exceeds his allowed time, the President shall call him to order without delay.

Closing of list of speakers, right of reply

Rule 73[36] [115]

During the course of a debate, the president may announce the list of speakers and, with the consent of the General Assembly, declare the list closed. He may, however, accord the right of reply to any member if a speech delivered after he has declared the list closed makes this desirable.

Adjournment of debate.

Rule 74[37] [116]

During the discussion of any matter, a representative may move the adjournment of the debate on the item under discussion. In addition to the proposer of the motion, two representatives may speak in favour of, and two against, after which the motion shall be immediately put to the vote. The President may limit the time to be allowed to speakers under this rule.

Closure of debate.

Rule 75[37] [117]

A representative may at any time move the closure of the debate on under discussion, whether or not any other representative has signified his wish to speak. Permission on

---

[35]See introduction, paras. 7 and 30.
[36]See annex V, paras. 46, 69, 77 and 78, and annex VI, paras. 8-11.
[37]See introduction, para. 7.

the closure of the debate shall be accorded only to two speak. Permission to speak on the closure of the debate shall be accorded only to two speaker opposing the closure, after which the motion shall be immediately put to the vote. If the General Assembly is in favour of the closure, the President shall declare the closure of the debate. The President may limit the time to be allowed to speakers under this rule.

Suspension or adjournment of the meeting
Rule 76[37] [118]

During the discussion of any matter, a representative may move the suspension or the adjournment of the meeting. Such motions shall not be debated but shall be immediately put to the vote. The President may limit the time to be allowed to the speaker moving the suspension or adjournment of the meeting.

Order of procedural motions
Rule 77 [119]

Subject to rule 71, the motions indicated below shall have precedence in the following order over all other proposals or motions before the meeting:
    (a) To suspend the meeting;
    (b) To adjourn the meeting;
    (c) To adjourn the debate on the item under discussion;
    (d) To close the debate on the item under discussion.

Proposal and amendments
Rule 78[38] [120]

Proposals and amendments shall normally be submitted in writing to the Secretary-General, who shall circulate copies to the delegations. As a general rule, no proposal shall be discussed or put to the vote at any meeting of the General Assembly unless copies of it have been circulated to all delegations not later than the day preceding the meeting. The President may, however, permit the discussion and consideration of amendments, or of motions as to procedure, even though such amendments and motions have not been circulated or have only been circulate the same day.

---

[38]See annex V, paras. 87 and 88.

Decisions on competence

Rule 79[37] [121]

Subject to rule 77, any motion calling for a decision on the competence of the General Assembly to adopt a proposal submitted to it shall be pout to the vote before a vote is taken on the proposal in question.

Withdrawal of motions

Rule 80 [122]

A motion may be withdrawn by its proposer at any time before voting on it has commenced, provided that the motion has not been amended. A motion thus withdrawn may be reintroduced by any member.

Reconsideration of proposals

Rule 81 [123]

When a proposal has been adopted or rejected, it may not be reconsidered at the same session unless the General Assembly, by a two-thirds majority of the members present and voting, so decides. Permission to speak on a motion to reconsider shall be accorder only to two speakers opposing the motion, after which it shall be immediately put to the vote.

VOTING

Voting rights

Rule 82[39] [124]

Each member of the General Assembly shall have one vote.

Two-thirds majority

Rule 83[39]

Decision of the General Assembly on important question shall be made by a two-thirds majority of the members present and voting. These questions shall include: recommendations with respect to the maintenance of international peace and security, the election of the non-permanent members of the Security Council, the

---

[39]Rules 82, 83, and 85 reproduce the three paragraphs of Article 18 of the Charter.

election of the members of the Economic and Social Council, the election of members of the Trusteeship Council in accordance with paragraph 1 c of article 86 of the Charter, the admission of new Members to the United Nations, the suspension of the rights and privileges of membership, the expulsion of Members, questions relating to the operation of the trusteeship system, and budgetary questions.

Rule 84[40]

Decisions of the General Assembly on amendments to proposals relating to important questions, and on parts of such proposals put to the vote separately, shall be made by a two-thirds majority of the members present and voting.

Simple majority
Rule 85[39] [125]

Decisions of the General Assembly on questions other than those provided for in rule 83, including the determination of additional categories of questions to be decided by a two-thirds majority, shall be made by a majority of the members present and voting.

Meaning of the phrase "members present and voting"
Rule 86 [126]

For the purposes of these rules, the phrase "members present and voting" means members casting an affirmative or negative vote. Members which abstain from voting are considered as not voting.

Method of voting
Rule 87[41] [127]

(a) The General Assembly shall normally vote by show of hands or by standing, but any representative may request a roll-call. The roll-call shall be taken in the English alphabetical order of the names of the members, beginning with the member whose name is drawn by lot by the President. The name of each member shall be called in any roll-call, and one of its representatives shall reply "yes", "no" or "abstention". The result of

---

[40]See introduction, para. 10; see also annex III, special rule F.
[41]See introduction, para. 24; see also annex V, para. 84.

the voting shall be inserted in the record in the English alphabetical order of the names of the members.

(b) When the General Assembly votes by mechanical means, a non-recorded vote shall replace a vote by show of hands or by standing and a recorded vote shall replace a roll-call vote. Any representative may request a recorded vote. In the case of a recorded vote, the General Assembly shall, unless a representative requests otherwise, dispense with the procedure of calling out the names of the members; nevertheless, the result of the voting shall be inserted in the record in the same manner as that of a roll-call vote.

Conduct during voting

Rule 88[42] [128]

After the President has announced the beginning of voting, no representative shall interrupt the voting except on a point of order in connexion with the actual conduct of the voting. The President may permit members to explain their votes, either before or after the voting, except when the vote is taken by secret ballot. The President may limit the time to be allowed for such explanations. The President shall not permit the proposer of a proposal or of an amendment to explain his vote on his own proposal or amendment.

Division of proposals and amendments

Rule 89[43] [129]

A representative may move that parts of a proposal or of an amendment should be voted on separately. If objection is made to the request for division, the motion for division shall be voted upon. Permission to speak on the motion for division shall be given only to two speakers in favour and two speaker against. If the motion for division is carried, those parts of the proposal or of the amendment which are approved shall then be put to the vote as whole. If all operative parts of the proposal or of the amendment have been rejected, the proposal or the amendment shall be considered to have been rejected, the proposal or the amendment shall be considered to have been rejected as whole.

---

[42]See introduction, para. 7; see also annex V, paras. 74-76, and annex VI, paras. 6, 7 and 11.
[43]See introduction, para. 7.

Voting on amendments

Rule 90[43] [130]

When an amendment is moved to a a proposal, the amendment shall be voted on first. When two or more amendments are moved to a proposal, the General Assembly shall first vote on the amendment furthest removed in substance from the original proposal and then on the amendment next furthest removed therefrom, and so on until all the amendments have been put to the vote. Where, however, the adoption of one amendment necessarily implies the rejection of another amendment, the latter amendment shall not put to the vote. If one or more amendments are adopted, the amended proposal shall then be voted upon. A motion is considered an amendment to a proposal if it merely adds to, deletes from or revised part of the proposal.

Voting on proposals

Rule 91 [131]

If two or more proposals related to the same question, the General Assembly shall, unless it decides otherwise, vote on the proposals in the order in which they have been submitted. The General Assembly may, after each vote on a proposal, decide whether to vote on the next proposal.

Elections

Rule 92[44] [103]

All election shall be held b secret ballot. There shall be no nominations.

Rule 93 [132]

When only one person or Member is to be elected and no candidate obtains in the first ballot the majority required, a second ballot shall be taken, which shall be restricted to the two candidates obtaining the largest number of votes. If in the second ballot the votes are equally divided, and a majority is required, the President shall decide between the candidates by drawing lots, if a two-thirds majority is required, the balloting shall be continued until one candidate secures two thirds of the votes cast; provided that, after the third inconclusive ballot, votes may be cast for any eligible person or Member. If there such unrestricted ballots are inconclusive, the three ballots shall be restricted to the two

---

[44]See annex VI, para. 16.

candidates who obtained the greatest number of votes in the third of the unrestricted ballots, and the following three ballots thereafter shall be unrestricted, and so on until a person or Member is elected. These provisions shall not prejudice the application of rules 143, 146 and 148.

Rule 94

When two or more elective places are to be filled at one time under the same conditions, those candidates obtaining the first ballot the majority required shall be elected. If the number of candidates obtaining such majority is less than the number of persons or members to be elected, there shall be additional ballots to fill the remaining places, the voting being restricted to the candidates obtaining the greasiest number of votes in the previous ballot to a number not more than twice the places remaining to be filled; provided that, after the third inconclusive ballot, votes may be cast for any eligible person or Member. If three such unrestricted ballots are inconclusive, the next three ballots shall be restricted to the candidates who obtained the greatest number of votes in the third unrestricted ballots, to a number not more than twice the places remaining to be filled, and the following three ballots thereafter shall be unrestricted, and so on until all the places have been filled. These provisions shall not prejudice the application of rules 143, 144, 146 and 148.

Equally divided votes

Rule 95 [133]

If a vote is equally divided on matters other than elections, a second vote shall be taken at a subsequent meeting which shall be held within forty-eight hours of the first vote, and it shall be expressly mentioned in the agenda that a second vote will be taken on the matter in question. If this votes also results in equality, the proposal shall be regarded as rejected.

XIII. COMMITTEES
ESTABLISHMENT, OFFICERS, ORGANIZATION OF WORK
Establishment of committees

Rule 96

The General Assembly may establish such committees as it deems necessary for the performance of its functions.

Categories of subjects

Rule 97[45]

Items relating to the same category of subjects shall be refereed to the committee or committees dealing with that category of subjects. Committees shall not introduce new items on their own initiative.

Main Committees

Rule 98[46]

The Main Committees of the General Assembly are the following:

(a) Political and Security Committee (including the regulation of armaments) (First Committee);

(b) Special Political Committee;

(c) Economic and Financial Committee (Second Committee);

(d) Social, Humanitarian and Cultural Committee (Third Committee);

(e) Trusteeship Committee (including Non-Self-Governing Territories) (Fourth Committee)

(f) Administrative and Budgetary Committee (Fifth Committee);

(g) Legal Committee (Sixth Committee).

Organization of work

Rule 99[47]

(a) All the Main Committees shall, during the first week of the session, hold the elections provided for in rule 103.

(b) Each Main Committee, taking into account the closing date for the session fixed by the General Assembly on the recommendation of the General Committee, shall adopt its own priorities and meet as may be necessary to complete the consideration of the items referred to it. It shall at the beginning of the session adopt a programme of work in indicating, if possible, a target date for the conclusion of its work, the approximate dates of consideration of items and the number of meetings to be allocated to each item.

---

[45]See annex I, paras. 22 and 23, annex II, paras. 1, 19 and 20, and annex V, paras. 25-28, annex VI, para. 4, and annex VII, para. 3.

[46]See introduction, paras. 17 and 30; see also annex V, paras. 29-38.

[47]See introduction, paras. 7, 15 and 30; see also annex VI, paras. 21 and 23.

Representation of Members

Rule 100

Each Member may be represented by one person on each Main Committee and on any other committee that may be established upon which all Members have the right to be represented. It may also assign to these committees advisers, technical advisers, experts or persons of similar status.

Rule 101

Upon designation by the chairman of the delegation, advisers, technical advisers, experts or persons similar status may act as members of committees. Persons of similar status may act as members of committees. Persons of this status shall not, however, unless designated as alternate representatives, be eligible for reelection as Chairmen, Vice-Chairmen or Rapporteurs of committees or for seats in the General Assembly.

Subcommittees

Rule 102[48]

Each committee may set up subcommittees, which shall elect their own officers.

Election of officers

Rule 103[49] [92]

Each Main Committee shall elect a Chairman, two Vice-Chairmen and a Rapporteur. In the case of other committees, each shall elect a Chairman, one or more Vice-Chairmen and a Rapporteur. These officer shall be elected on the basis of equitable geographical distribution, experience and personal competence. The elections shall be held by secret ballot unless the committee decides otherwise in an election where only one candidate is standing. The nomination of each candidate shall be limited to one speaker, after which the committee shall immediately proceed to the election.

---

[48]See annex I, para. 14, annex II, para. 29, annex IV, para. (e), and annex V, para. 66.
[49]See introduction, para. 30; see also annex V, paras. 40 and 54-57, and annex VI, para. 18-20.

The Chairman of a Main Committee shall not vote
Rule 104 [37]

The Chairman of a Main Committee shall not vote, but another member of his delegation may vote in his place.

Absence of officers
Rule 105⁵⁰ [32-34]

If the Chairman finds it necessary to be absent during a meeting or any part thereof, he shall designate one of the Vice-Chairmen to take his place. A Vice-Chairmen acting as Chairman shall have the same powers and duties as the Chairman. If any officer of the committee is unable to perform his functions, a new officer shall be elected for the unexpired term.

Functions of the Chairman
Rule 106⁵¹ [35]

The Chairman shall declare the opening and closing of each meeting of the committee, direct its discussions, ensure observance of these rules, accord the right to speak, put questions and announce decisions. He shall rule on points of order and subject to these rules, shall have complete control of the proceedings at any meeting and over the maintenance of order thereat. The Chairman may, in the course of the discussion of an item, propose to the committee the limitation of the time to be allowed to speakers, the limitation of the number of times each representative may speak, the closure of the list of speakers or the closure of the debate. He may also propose the suspension or the adjournment of the meeting or the adjournment of the debate on the item under discussion.

Rule 107⁵¹ [36]

The Chairman, in the exercise of his functions, remains under the authority of the committee.

---

[50]See introduction, para. 30.
[51]See introduction, para.7: see also annex I, para. 39, annex IV, para. (g), annex V, paras. 39 and 67, annex VI, paras. 3 and 22, and annex VII, paras. 6 and 7.

CONDUCT OF BUSINESS

Quorum

Rule 108[52] [67]

The Chairman may declare a meeting open and permit the debate to proceed when at least one quarter of the members of the committee are present. The presence of a majority of the members shall be required for any decision to be taken.

Speeches

Rule 109[53] [68]

No representative may address the committee without having previously obtained the permission of the Chairman. The Chairman shall call upon speakers in the order in which they signify their desire to speak. The Chairman may call a speaker to order if his remarks are not relevant to the subject under discussion.

Congratulations

Rule 110[54]

Congratulations to the officers of a Main Committee shall not be expressed by the Chairman of the previous session - or, in his absence, by a member of his delegation - after all the officers of the Committee have been elected.

Precedence

Rule 111 [69]

The Chairman and the Rapporteur of a committee or subcommittee may be accorded precedence for the purpose of explaining the conclusions arrived at by their committee or subcommittee.

---

[52]See introduction, paras. 7 and 30.
[53]See annex IV, para. (g), (ii), annex V, paras. 69-71 and annex VII, para. 6.
[54]See introduction, para. 30.

Statements by the Secretariat

Rule 112 [70]

The Secretary-General, or a member of the Secretariat designated by him as his representative, may at any time make either oral or written statements to any committee or subcommittee concerning any question under consideration by it.

Points of order

Rule 113[55] [71]

During the discussion of any matter, a representative may rise to a point of order, and the point of order shall be immediately decided by the Chairman in accordance with the rules of procedure. A representative may appeal against the ruling of the Chairman. The appeal shall be immediately put to the vote, and the Chairman's ruling shall stand unless overruled by a majority of the members present and voting. A representative rising to a point of order may not speak on the substance of the matter under discussion.

Time-limit on speeches

Rule 114[56] [72]

The committee may limit the time to be allowed to each speaker and the number of times each representative may speak on any question. Before a decision is taken, two representative may speak in favour of, and two against, a proposal to set such limits. When the debate is limited and a representative exceeds his allotted time, the Chairman shall call him to order without delay.

Closing of list of speaker, right of reply

Rule 115[57] [73]

During the course of a debate, the Chairman may announce the list of speakers and, with the consent of the committee, declare the list closed. He may, however, accord the right of reply to any member if a speech delivered after he has declared the list closed makes this desirable.

---

[55]See introduction, para. 7; see also annex V, para. 79.
[56]See introduction, paras. 7 and 30.
[57]See annex V, paras. 69, 77 and 78, annex VI, paras. 8-10, and annex VII, para. 6.

Adjournment of debate

Rule 116[58] [74]

During the discussion of any matter, a representative may move the adjournment of the debate on the item under discussion. In addition to the proposer of the motion, two representatives may speak in favour of, and two against, the motion, after which the motion shall be immediately put to the vote. The Chairman may limit the time to be allowed to speaker under this rule.

Closure of debate

Rule 117[58] [75]

A representative may at any time move the closure of the debate on the item under discussion, whether or not any other representative has signified his wish to speak. permission to speak on the closure of the debate shall be accorded only to two speakers opposing the closure, after which the motion shall be immediately put to the vote. If the committee is in favour of the closure, the Chairman shall declare the closure of the debate. The Chairman may limit the time to be allowed to speaker under this rule.

Suspension or adjournment of the meeting.

Rule 118[58] [76]

During the discussion of any matter, a representative may move the suspension or the adjournment of the meeting. Such motions shall not be debated but shall be immediately put to the vote. The Chairman may limit the time to be allowed to the speaker moving the suspension or adjournment of the meeting.

Order of procedural motions

Rule 119 [77]

Subject to rule 113, the motions indicated below shall have precedence in the following order over all other proposals or motions before the meeting:
   (a) To suspend the meeting;
   (b) To adjourn the meeting;
   (c) To adjourn the debate on the item under discussion;
   (d) To close the debate on the item under discussion.

---

[58]See introduction, para. 7.

Proposals and amendments

Rule 120[59] [78]

Proposals and amendments shall normally be submitted in writing to the Secretary-General, who shall circulate copies to the delegations. As a general rule, no proposal shall be discussed or put to the vote at any meeting of the committee unless copies of it have been circulated to all delegations not later than the day preceding the meeting. The Chairman may, however, permit the discussion and consideration of amendments, or of motions as to procedure, even though such amendments and motions have not been circulated or have only been circulated the same day.

Decision on competence

Rule 121[60] [79]

Subject to rule 119, any motion calling for a decision on the competence of the General Assembly or the committee to adopt a proposal submitted to it shall be put to the vote before a vote is taken on the proposal in question.

Withdrawal of motions

Rule 122 [80]

A motion may be withdrawn by its proposer at any time before voting on it has commence, provided that the motion has not been amended. A motion thus withdrawn may be reintroduced by any member.

Reconsideration of proposals

Rule 123 [81]

When a proposal has been adopted or rejected, it may not be reconsidered at the same session unless the committee, by a two-thirds majority of the members present and voting, so decides. Permission to speak on a motion to reconsider shall be accorded only to two speaker opposing the motion, after which it shall be immediately put to the vote.

---

[59]See annex V, paras. 87 and 88.
[60]See annex V, para. 96.

VOTING

Voting rights

Rule 124 [82]

Each member of the committee shall have one vote.

Majority required

Rule 125 [85]

Decisions of committees shall be made by a majority of the members present and voting.

Meaning of the phrase "members present and voting"
Rule 126 [86]

For the purposes of these rules, the phrase "members present and voting" means members casting an affirmative or negative vote. Members which abstain from voting are considered as not voting.

Method of voting

Rule 127[61] [87]

(a) The committee shall normally vote by show of hands or by standing, but any representative may request a roll-call. The roll-call shall be taken in the English alphabetical order of the names of the members, beginning with the member whose name is drawn by lot by the Chairman. The name of each member shall be called in any roll-call, and its representatives shall reply "yes", "no" or "abstention". The result of the voting shall be inserted in the record in the English alphabetical order of the names of the members.

(b) When the committee votes by mechanical means, a non-recorded vote shall replace a vote by show of hands or by standing and a recorded vote shall replace a roll-call vote. In the case of a recorded vote, the committee shall, unless a representative requests otherwise, dispense with the procedure of calling out the names of the members;

---

[61]See introduction, para. 24; see also annex V, para. 84.

nevertheless, the result of the voting shall be inserted in the record in the same manner as that of a roll-call vote.

Conduct during voting
Rule 128[62] [88]

After the Chairman has announced the beginning of voting, no representative shall interrupt the voting except on a point of order in connexion with the actual conduct of the voting. The Chairman may permit members to explain their votes, either or after the voting, except when the vote is taken by secret ballot. The Chairman may limit the time to be allowed for such explanations. The Chairman shall not permit the proposer of a proposal or of an amendment to explain his vote on his own proposal or amendment.

Division of proposals and amendments
Rule 129[63] [89]

A representative may vote that parts of a proposal or of an amendment should be voted on separately. If objection is made to the request for division shall be voted upon. Permission to speak on the motion for division shall be given only to two speakers in favour and two speakers against. If the motion for division is carried, those parts of the proposal or of the amendment which are approved shall then be put to the vote as whole. If all operative parts of the proposals or of the amendment have been rejected, the proposal of the proposal or of the amendment have been rejected, the proposal or the amendment shall be considered to have been rejected as whole.

Voting on amendments
Rule 130[63] [90]

When an amendment is moved to a proposal, the amendment shall be voted on first. When two or more amendments are moved to a proposal, the committee shall first vote on the amendment furthest removed in substance from the original proposal and then on the amendment next furthest removed therefrom, and so on until all the amendments have been put to the vote. Where, however, the adoption of one amendment necessarily implies the rejection of another amendment, the latter amendment shall not put to the vote. If one or more amendments are adopted, the amended proposal shall then be voted

---

[62]See introduction, para. 7; see also annex V, paras. 74-76, and annex VI, paras. 6 and 7.
[63]See introduction, para. 7.

upon. A motion is considered and amendment to a proposal if it merely adds to, deletes from or revises part of the proposal.

Voting on proposals

Rule 131 [91]

If two or more proposals relate to the same question, the committee shall, unless it decides otherwise, vote on the proposals in the order in which they have been submitted. The committee may, after each vote on a proposal, decide whether to vote on the next proposal.

Elections

Rule 132 [93]

When only one person or Member is to be elected and no candidate obtains in the first ballot the majority required, a second ballot shall be taken, which shall be restricted to the two candidates obtaining the largest number of votes. If in the second ballot the votes are equally divided, and a majority is required, the Chairman shall decide between the candidates by drawing lots.

Equally divided votes

Rule 133 [95]

If a vote is equally divided on matters other than elections, the proposal shall be regraded as rejected.

XIV. ADMISSION OF NEW MEMBERS TO THE UNITED NATIONS

Applications

Rule 134[64]

Any State which desires to become a Member of the United Nations shall submit an application to the Secretary-General. Such application shall contain a declaration, made in a formal instrument, that the State in question accepts the obligations contained in the Charter.

---

[64]See introduction, para. 4.

Notification of applications

Rule 135[64]

The Secretary-General shall, for information, send a copy of the application to the General Assembly, or to the Members of the United Nations if the Assembly is not in session.

Consideration of applications and decision thereon.

Rule 136[64]

If the Security Council recommends the applicant State for membership, the General Assembly shall consider whether the application is a peace-loving State and is able and willing to carry out the obligations contained in the charter and shall decide, by a two-thirds majority of the members present and voting, upon its application for membership.

Rule 137[64]

If the Security Council does not recommend the applicant State for membership or postpones the consideration of the application, the General Assembly may, after full consideration of the special report of the Security Council, send the application back to the Council, together with a full record of the discussion in the Assembly, for further consideration and recommendation or report.

Notification of decision and effective date of membership.

Rule 138[64]

The Secretary-General shall inform the applicant State of the decision of the General Assembly. If the application is approved, membership shall become effective on the date on which the General Assembly takes its decision on the application.

XV. ELECTIONS TO PRINCIPAL ORGANS
GENERAL PROVISIONS

Terms of office

Rule 139

Except as provided in rule 147, the term of office of members of Council shall begin on 1 January following their election by the General Assembly and shall end on 31 December following the election of their successors.

By-elections

Rule 140

Should a member cease to belong to a Council before its term of officer expires, a by-election shall be held separately at the next session of the General Assembly to elect a member for the unexpired term.

SECRETARY-GENERAL

Appointment of the Secretary-General

Rule 141

When the Security Council has submitted its recommendations on the appointment of the Secretary-General, the General Assembly shall consider the recommendation and vote upon it by secret ballot in private meeting.

SECURITY COUNCIL

Annual elections

Rule 142[65]

The General Assembly shall each year, in the course of its regular session, elect five non-permanent members of the Security Council for a term of two years.[66]

Qualifications for membership

Rule 143[67]

In the election of non-permanent members of the Security Council due regard shall, in accordance with Article 23, paragraph 1, of the Charter, be specially paid, in the first instance, to the contribution of Members of the United Nations to the maintenance of international peace and security and to the other purposes of the organization, and also to equitable geographical distribution.[66]

---

[65]Rule based directly on a provision of the Charter (Art. 23 para. 2 as amended under General Assembly resolution 1991 A (XVIII)). See introduction, para. 23.

[66]Under paragraph 3 of resolution 1991 A (XVIII) of 17 December 1963, the General Assembly decided that "the ten non-permanent members of the Security Council shall be elected according to the following pattern:

"(a) Five from African and Asian States;

"(b) One from Eastern European States;

"(c) Two from Latin American States;

"(d) Two from Western European and other States".

[67]Rule based directly on a provision of the Charter (Art. 23, para. 1).

Re-eligibility

Rule 144[68]

A retiring member of the Security Council shall not be eligible for immediate re-election.

ECONOMIC AND SOCIAL COUNCIL

Annual elections

Rule 145[69]

The General Assembly shall each year, in the course of its regular session, elect eighteen members of the Economic and Social Council for a term of three years.[70]

Re-eligibility

Rule 146[71]

A retiring member of the Economic and Social Council shall be eligible for immediate re-election.

TRUSTEESHIP COUNCIL

Occasions for elections

Rule 147

When a Trusteeship Agreement has been approved and a Member of the United Nations has become an Administering Authority of a Trust Territory in accordance with Article 83 or Article 85 of the Charter, the General Assembly shall hold such election or elections to the Trusteeship Council as may be necessary, in accordance with Article 86. A Member or Members elected at any such election at a regular session shall take

---

[68]Rule reproducing textually a provision of the Charter (Art. 23, para. 2, last sentence).

[69]Rule based directly on a provision of the Charter (Art. 61, para. 2. as amended under General Assembly resolution 2847 (XXVI)). See introduction, paras. 23 and 32.

[70]Under paragraph 4 of resolution 2847 (XXVI) of 20 December 1971, the General Assembly decided that "the members of the Economic and Social Council shall be elected according to the following pattern:

"(a) Fourteen members from African States;

"(b) Eleven members from Asian States;

"(c) Ten members from Latin American States;

"(d) Thirteen members from Western European and other States;

"(e) Six members from socialist States of Eastern Europe".

[71]Rule reproducing textually a provision of the Charter (Art. 61, para. 2, last sentence).

office immediately upon their election and shall complete their terms in accordance with the provisions of rule 139 as if they had begun their terms of office on 1 January following their election.

Terms of office and re-eligibility

Rule 148[72]

A non-administering member of the Trusteeship Council shall be elected for a term of three years and shall be eligible for immediate re-election.

Vacancies

Rule 149

At each session the General Assembly shall, in accordance with Article 86 of the Charter, elect members to fill any vacancies.

INTERNATIONAL COURT OF JUSTICE

Method of election

Rule 150

The election of the members of the International Court of Justice shall take place in accordance with the Statute of the Court.

Rule 151

Any meeting of the General Assembly held in pursuance of the Statute of the International Court of Justice for the purpose of electing members of the Court shall continue until as many candidates as are required for all the seats to be filled have obtained in one or more ballots an absolute majority of votes.

---

[72]Rule based directly on a provision of the Charter (Art. 86, para. 1c).

XVI. ADMINISTRATIVE AND BUDGETARY QUESTIONS
GENERAL PROVISIONS

Regulations for financial administration

Rule 152

The General Assembly shall establish regulations for the financial administration of the United Nations.[73]

Financial implication of resolutions

Rule 153[74]

No resolution involving expenditure shall be recommended by a committee for approval by the General Assembly unless it is accompanied by an estimate of expenditures prepared by the Secretary-General. No resolution in respect of which expenditures are anticipated by the Secretary-General shall be voted by the General Assembly until the Administrative and Budgetary Committee (Fifth Committee) has had an opportunity of stating the effect of the proposal upon the budget estimates of the United Nations.

Rule 154[74]

The Secretary-General shall keep all committees informed of the detailed estimated cost of all resolution which have been recommended by the committees for approval by the General Assembly.

ADVISORY COMMITTEE ON ADMINISTRATIVE AND BUDGETARY QUESTIONS

Appointment

Rule 155[75]

The General Assembly shall appoint an Advisory Committee on Administrative and Budgetary Questions consisting of sixteen members, including at least three financial experts of recognized standing.

---

[73]For the Financial Regulations of the United Nations, see ST/SGB/Financial Rule/1/Rev.3.
[74]See annex V, paras. 97 and 98, and annex VI, paras. 12 and 13.
[75]See introduction, paras. 19, 31, and 36.

Compositions

Rule 156[76]

The members of the Advisory Committee on Administrative and Budgetary Questions, no two of whom shall be nationals of the same State, shall be selected on the basis of broad geographical representation, personal qualification and experience and shall serve for a period of three years corresponding to three calendar years. Member shall retire by rotation and shall be eligible for reappointment. The three financial experts shall not retire simultaneously. The General Assembly shall appoint members of the Advisory Committee at the regular session immediately preceding the expiration of the term of office of the members or, in the case of vacancies, at the next session.

Functions

Rule 157[77]

The Advisory Committee on Administrative and Budgetary Questions shall be responsible for expert examination of the programme budget of the United Nations and shall assist the Administrative and Budgetary Committee (Fifth Committee). At the beginning of each regular session at which the proposed programme budget for the following biennium is to be considered. It shall submit to the General Assembly a detailed report on the proposed programme budget for that biennium. It shall also submit, at such times as may be specified in the applicable provisions of the Financial Regulations and Rules of the United Nations,[78] a report on the accounts of the United Nations and all United Nations entities for which the Secretary-General has administrative responsibility. It shall examine on behalf of the General Assembly the administrative budgets of specialized agencies and proposals for financial and budgetary arrangements with such agencies. It shall perform such other duties as may be assigned to it under the Financial Regulations of the United Nations.

---

[76]See introduction, paras. 19 and 36.
[77]See introduction, para. 36.
[78]ST/SGB/Financial Rules/1/Rev. 3.

COMMITTEE ON CONTRIBUTIONS

Appointment

Rule 158[79]

The General Assembly shall appoint an expert Committee on Contributions consisting of eighteen members.

Composition

Rule 159[80]

The members of the committee on Contributions, no two of who, shall be nationals of the same State, shall be selected on the basis of broad geographical representation, personal qualifications and experience and shall serve for a period of three years corresponding to three calendar years. Members shall retire by rotation and shall be eligible for appointment. The General Assembly shall appoint the members of the Committee on Contributions at the regular session immediately preceding the expiration of the term of office of the members or, in case of vacancies, at the next session.

Functions

Rule 160

The Committee on Contributions shall advise the General Assembly concerning the appointment, under Article 17, paragraph 2, of the Charter, of the expenses of the Organization among members, broadly according to capacity to pay. The scale of assessments, when once fixed by the General Assembly, shall not be subject to a general revision for at least three years unless it is clear that there have been substantial changes in relative capacity to pay. The Committee shall also advise the General Assembly on the assessments to the fixed for new Members, on appeals by Members for a change of assessments and on the action to be taken with regard to the application of Article 19 of the Charter.

---

[79]See introduction, para. 26, 33 and 35.
[80]See introduction, para. 37.

XVII. SUBSIDIARY ORGANS OF THE GENERAL ASSEMBLY

Establishment and rules of procedure

Rules 161[81]

The General Assembly may establish such subsidiary organs as it deems necessary for the performance of its functions.[82] The rules relating to the procedure of committees of the General Assembly, as well as rules 45 and 60, shall apply to the procedure of any subsidiary organ unless the Assembly or the subsidiary organ decides otherwise.

XVIII. INTERPRETATION AND AMENDMENTS

Italicized headings

Rule 162

The italicized headings of these rules, which were inserted for reference only, shall be disregarded in the interpretation of the rules.

Method of amendment

Rule 163[83]

These rules of procedure may be amended by a decision of the General Assembly, taken by a majority of the members present and voting, after a committee has reported on the proposed amendments.

---

[81]See annex VII, para. 11.
[82]Sentence reproducing textually a provision of the Charter (Art.22).
[83]See annex II, para. 1 (c).

ANNEX I[a]

Recommendations and suggestions of the Special Committee on Methods and Procedures of the General Assembly approved by the Assembly[b]

CONSIDERATION BY THE GENERAL ASSEMBLY OF INTERNATIONAL CONVENTIONS NEGOTIATED BY CONFERENCES OF GOVERNMENT REPRESENTATIVES OF ALL MEMBERS STATES

13. The Special Committee found that in the past some of the Main Committees of the General Assembly had devoted a particularly large number of meetings to the detailed consideration, article by article, of texts of international conventions. This was even the case where the text of a convention had been drawn up by an international conference on which all Member States had been represented. It was pointed out in this connexion that experience had shown that a Main Committee, by the very fact of its size, was not particularly fitted to draft conventions, and that when it was entrusted with the detailed study of conventions, it often did not have time to deal satisfactorily with the other questions for which it was responsible.

The Special Committee recognizes the importance of the sponsorship of conventions by the General Assembly. It believes that the authority of the General Assembly and the powerful influence its debates have on public opinion should, in many cases, be used for the benefit of international co-operation. It therefore favours the retention by the General Assembly of the necessary freedom of action.

The Special Committee therefore confines itself to recommending that when conventions have been negotiated by international conferences in which all the Members of the United Nations have been invited to take part, and on which they have been represented, not only by experts acting in a personal capacity but by representatives of

---

[a]By resolution 362 (IV) of 22 October 1949, the General Assembly approved various recommendations and suggestions of the Special Committee on Methods and Procedures of the General Assembly which had been established under resolution 271 (III) of 29 April 1949. The General Assembly considered these recommendations and suggestions "worthy of consideration by the General Assembly and its committees" and requested the Secretary-General "to prepare a document embodying the above-mentioned recommendations and suggestions in convenient form for use by the General Committee and the delegations of Member States in the General Assembly". In pursuance of this request, the recommendations and suggestions of the Special Committee, as set forth in annex II to resolution 362 (IV), have been reproduced in the present annex.

[b]The paragraph numbers refer to paragraphs of the report of the Special Committee. The full text of the report may be found in the *Official Records of the General Assembly, Fourth Session, Supplement No. 12* (A/937). Subtitles and footnotes have been inserted by the Secretariat for convenience of reference.

Governments, and when these conventions are subsequently submitted to the General Assembly for consideration, the Assembly should not undertake a further detailed examination, but should limit itself to discussing them in a broad manner and to giving its general views on the instruments submitted to it. After such a debate, the General Assembly could, if desirable, adopt the conclusions reached by the conferences and recommend to Members the acceptance of ratification of such conventions.

This procedure might be applied in particular to conventions submitted to the General Assembly as a result of conferences of all Member States convened by the Economic and Social Council under Article 62, paragraph 4, of the Charter.

CONSIDERATION BY THE GENERAL ASSEMBLY OF INTERNATIONAL CONVENTIONS PREPARED BY EXPERTS OR BY CONFERENCES IN WHICH NOT ALL MEMBER STATES TAKE PART--DRAFTING OF LEGAL TEXTS

14. Furthermore, when it is proposed that the General Assembly should consider conventions prepared by groups of experts not acting as governmental representatives, or by conferences in which not all Members of the United Nations have been invited to take part, it would be advisable for the General Committee and the General Assembly to determine whether one of the Main Committees, especially the Legal Committee, would have enough time during the session to examine these conventions in detail, or whether it would be possible to set up an *ad hoc* committee to undertake this study during the session.

If this is not possible, the Special Committee recommends that the General Assembly should decide, after or without a general debate on the fundamental principles of the proposed convention, that an *ad hoc* committee should be established to meet between sessions. Alternatively, the General Assembly might decide to convene a conference of plenipotentiaries, between two of its own sessions, to study, negotiate, draft, and possibly sign, the convention. The conference of plenipotentiaries might be empowered by the General Assembly to transmit the instruments directly to Governments for acceptance or ratification. In this case too, the General Assembly might, at a subsequent session, express its general opinion on the convention resulting from the conference, and might recommend to Members its acceptance or ratification.

With regard to the drafting of legal texts, the Special Committee strongly recommends that small drafting committees should be resorted to whenever possible.

MEETINGS OF THE GENERAL COMMITTEE AND OF THE MAIN COMMITTEES

20. In order that more frequent meetings of the General Committee should not delay the work of plenary and committee meetings, the Special Committee wishes to mention

that it would be desirable for the General Committee to be enabled to meet, whenever necessary, at the same time as the plenary or the Main Committees. (In such cases, one of the Vice-Presidents could take the chair at plenary meetings and the Vice-Chairman could replace the Chairman at Main Committee meetings.)

The Special Committee also considers that, in order to save time at the beginning of the session, some of the Main Committees should not wait until the end of the general debate before starting their work.

ALLOCATION OF AGENDA ITEMS TO THE MAIN COMMITTEES

22. In the past, some of the Main Committees have been allocated more items requiring prolonged consideration than have others. This has especially been the case for the First Committee. The Special Committee noted, however, that, during the third session of the General Assembly, exception had been made to the principle laid down in rule 89,[c] that "items relating to the same category of subjects shall be referred to the committee or committees dealing with that category of subjects".

The Special Committee feels that the allocation of items to committees might be effected in a less rigid manner and that questions which may be considered as falling within the competence of two or more committees should preferably be referred to the committee with the lightest agenda.

CONSIDERATION OF AGENDA ITEMS IN PLENARY MEETINGS WITHOUT PRIOR REFERENCE TO A MAIN COMMITTEE

23. Another means of lightening the task of any given Main Committee would be to consider directly in plenary meeting, without preliminary reference to committee, certain questions which fall within the terms of reference of the Main Committee. This procedure would, moreover, have the great advantage of reducing to a notable extent repetition of debate.

It is felt that the amount of time saved by this method would be considerable, especially if the Main Committee and plenary meetings could be held concurrently.

If the Main Committee could not meet at the same time as the plenary meeting, the fact that the Committee was not meeting would enable another Main Committee to meet in its place.

The consideration of questions in plenary meetings would have the benefit of the attendance of leaders of delegations and of greater solemnity and publicity. The slightly

---

[c]Rule 97 of the present rules of procedure.

higher cost to the United Nations of plenary meetings, due in particular to the distribution of verbatim records of the meetings, would undoubtedly be compensated by the shorter duration of the session.

The General Committee would be responsible for suggesting to the General Assembly which items on the agenda might be dealt with in this manner. The Special Committee recommends that this method should be introduced on an experimental basis at future sessions.

The Special Committee is of the opinion that this procedure would be especially appropriate for certain questions the essential aspects of which are already familiar to Members, such as items which have been considered by the General Assembly at previous sessions and which do not require either the presence of representatives of non-member States or the hearing of testimony.

THE ROLE OF THE PRESIDENT OF THE GENERAL ASSEMBLY, OF THE CHAIRMEN OF COMMITTEES AND OF THE SECRETARIAT

39. At this point the Special Committee desires to stress once more the importance of the role of the President of the General Assembly and of the Chairmen of committees. The satisfactory progress of the proceedings depends essentially on their competence, authority, tact and impartiality, their respect for the rights both of minorities as well as majorities, and their familiarity with the rules of procedure. The General Assembly, or the committee, as the case may be, is the master of the conduct of its own proceedings. It is, however, the special task of the Chairmen to guide the proceedings of these bodies in the best interests of all the Members.

The Special Committee considers that everything possible should be done to help Chairmen in the discharge of these important functions. The President of the General Assembly and the General Committee should assist the Chairmen of committees with their advice. The Secretary-General should place his experience and all his authority at their disposal.

The Special Committee is happy to note the Secretariat's valuable practice of holding daily meetings of the committee secretaries, under the chairmanship of the Executive Assistant to the Secretary-General, where the procedural questions arising from day to day in the General Assembly and committees are thoroughly examined. Furthermore, the Special Committee stresses the value of having, as in the past, a legal adviser from the Secretariat in attendance at meetings to give the Chairmen or the committees such advice as they need for the conduct of their business and the interpretation of the rules of procedure.

ANNEX II[a]

Methods and procedures of the General Assembly for dealing with legal and drafting questions[b]

Part 1
RECOMMENDATIONS OF THE GENERAL ASSEMBLY

The General Assembly,

...

1. *Recommends*:

(a) That, whenever any Committee contemplates making a recommendation to the General Assembly to request an advisory opinion from the International Court of Justice, the matter may, at some appropriate stage of its consideration by that Committee, be referred to the Sixth Committee for advice on the legal aspects and on the drafting of the request, or the Committee concerned may propose that the matter should be considered by a joint Committee of itself and the Sixth Committee;

(b) That, whenever any Committee contemplates making a recommendation to the General Assembly to refer a matter to the International Law Commission, the Committee may, at some appropriate stage of its consideration, consult the Sixth Committee as to the advisability of such a reference and on its drafting;

(c) That, whenever any Committee contemplates making a recommendation for the adoption by the General Assembly of any amendment to the rules of procedure of the General Assembly, the matter shall, at some appropriate stage of its consideration by that Committee, be referred to the Sixth Committee for advice on the drafting of such amendment and of any consequential amendment;

---

[a]By resolution 684 (VII) of 6 November 1952, the General Assembly, having examined the report of the Special Committee for the Consideration of the Methods and Procedures of the General Assembly for Dealing with Legal and Drafting Questions, established under resolution 597 (VI) of 20 December 1951, adopted certain recommendations on this subject and directed that the terms of these recommendations "shall be embodied as an annex to the rules of procedure of the General Assembly". The resolution further provided that "the said annex shall also set out, verbatim, paragraphs 19, 20, 29, 30, 35, 36, 37, 38 and 39 of the report of the Special Committee" (*Official Records of the General Assembly, Seventh Session, Annexes,* agenda item 53, document A/2174). The text of the aforementioned recommendations of the General Assembly is accordingly reproduced in part 1, and that of the specified paragraphs of the report of the Special Committee in part 2, of the present annex.

[b]The paragraph numbers refer to paragraphs of the report of the Special Committee. Subtitles as well as words in square brackets and foot-notes have been inserted by the Secretariat for convenience of reference.

(d) That, when a Committee considers the legal aspects of a question important, the Committee should refer it for legal advice to the Sixth Committee or propose that the question should be considered by a joint Committee of itself and the Sixth Committee.

Part 2

EXCERPTS FROM THE REPORT OF THE SPECIAL COMMITTEE FOR THE CONSIDERATION OF THE METHODS AND PROCEDURES OF THE GENERAL ASSEMBLY FOR DEALING WITH LEGAL AND DRAFTING QUESTIONS

Allocation of agenda items to the Main Committee

19. As to the first of those problems [namely, the allocation of agenda items to the Main Committees by the General Assembly at the outset of each session], the Special Committee recalled that rule 97 of the rules of procedure of the General Assembly provided that "Items relating to the same category of subjects shall be referred to the committee or committees dealing with that category of subjects . . . ". It also noted that a recommendation of the Special Committee on Methods and Procedures, approved by the General Assembly in resolution 362 (IV) of 22 October 1949 and annexed to the rules of procedure, provided that ". . . questions which may be considered as falling within the competence of two or more committees should preferably be referred to the committee with the lightest agenda".

20. In view of those provisions, the present Special Committee did not find it necessary to make any formal recommendation on the allocation of agenda items at the opening of each session. It was confident that the General Committee, in making recommendations to the General Assembly on the distribution of agenda items, would continue to bear in mind the Sixth Committee's function, laid down in rule 99[c] of the rules of procedure, as the Legal Committee.

Drafting of complex legal instruments

29. During the course of the discussion [on the question of the drafting of complex legal instruments such as international agreements, statutes of tribunals, etc.] it was pointed out that the Special Committee on Methods and Procedures, in paragraphs 13 and 14 of its report, approved by General Assembly resolution 362 (IV) of 22 October 1949

---

[c]Rule 98 of the present rules of procedure.

and annexed to the rules of procedure,[d] made certain recommendations concerning the drafting of conventions, and concluded: "With regard to the drafting of legal texts, the Special Committee strongly recommends that small drafting committees should be resorted to whenever possible".

30. The Special Committee was incomplete agreement with those recommendations and, in view of their previous approval by the General Assembly, did not find it necessary to adopt a new provision on the subject. However, the Special Committee considered it desirable that point should be reaffirmed in its report. On that understanding, the United Kingdom withdrew its draft proposal.[e]

Drafting of General Assembly resolutions

35. In addition to the above proposals,[f] the United Kingdom submitted a draft (A/AC.60/L.22) which provided for periodic meetings of the rapporteurs of Committees with the competent official, of the Secretariat to establish, in so far as practicable, common methods of drafting and to ensure that in general the drafting of resolutions was satisfactory from the point of view of style, form and the use of technical terms.

36. It was pointed out that there might be certain practical difficulties in arranging for periodic meetings of rapporteurs. The Special Committee decided to make no formal recommendation on the subject: nevertheless, the Committee believes that it is desirable that informal consultation should take place from time to time between the various

---

[d]See annex I.

[e]This proposal (A/AC.60/L.18) provided:

"That, in principle, the drafting of all clauses, texts or instruments of the following kinds should be either carried out, or, at some appropriate stage, reviewed, by a body of experts legally qualified to do so:

"(a) Any regulation for adoption by the General Assembly;

"(b) The terms of reference, functions and powers of subsidiary organs or tribunals hereafter set up by the General Assembly;

"(c) Any convention, declaration, agreement or other similar international instrument drawn up under the auspices of the General Assembly, and the drafting of which is to be effected by the Assembly itself, including agreements or instruments to which the United Nations as an Organization is to be a party."

[f]Proposal by El Salvador (A/AC.60/L.20) which was withdrawn in favour of a revised text (A/AC.60/L.20/Rev.1) incorporating amendments by the United Kingdom (A/AC.60/L.21), Belgium and Egypt. This revised text, which was worded as follows, was included in the recommendations of the Special Committee to the General Assembly:

"(c) That, normally, the Chairman of a Committee shall, at the appropriate time, call upon the Vice-Chairman and the Rapporteur to join him for the purpose of proceeding, in consultation with the competent officials of the Secretariat, to examine the draft resolutions from the point of view of style, form and the use of technical terms, and, when appropriate, to suggest to the Committee such changes as they deem necessary."

rapporteurs and officials of the Secretariat for the purpose described in the United Kingdom proposal.

Reports of the Secretary-General under General Assembly resolution 362 (IV)

37. The United Kingdom submitted a draft proposal (A/AC.60/L.23) suggesting that the Secretary-General should be requested to furnish to the General Assembly an annual report on the matters dealt with by the Special Committee, indicating to what extent the Assembly or its Committees had succeeded during the year in realizing the objectives aimed at and suggesting any appropriate adjustments or improvements in the methods and procedures involved.

38. During the discussion, the representative of the Secretary-General recalled that the General Assembly, in paragraph 6 of resolution 362 (IV) of 22 October 1949, had requested the Secretary-General "to carry out appropriate studies and to submit, at such times as the may consider appropriate, suitable proposals for the improvement of the methods and procedures of the General Assembly and its committees . . .". It was pointed out that the Secretary-General was much concerned with improving the procedures and methods of the Assembly and that there was no need for a new resolution requesting reports on that subject.

39. The Special Committee agreed that the points covered by the United Kingdom draft could be included when advisable in reports of the Secretary-General under resolution 362 (IV); such reports should be submitted at the appropriate times, and at reasonably frequent intervals. Consequently, the United Kingdom draft was withdrawn, and the Committee made no formal recommendation on the subject.

ANNEX III[a]

Procedure for the examination of reports and petitions relating to the Territory of South West Africa[b]

SPECIAL RULES ADOPTED BY THE GENERAL ASSEMBLY AT ITS NINTH SESSION

Procedure will regard to reports

Special rule A: The General Assembly shall receive annually from the Committee on South West Africa the report on South West Africa submitted to the Committee by the Union of South Africa (or a report on conditions in the Territory of South West Africa prepared by the Committee in accordance with paragraph 12 (c) of General Assembly resolution 749 A (VIII), together with the observations of the Committee on the report as well as the comments of the duly authorized representative of the Union of South Africa, should that Government decide to follow the General Assembly's recommendation and appoint such a representative.

Special rule B: The General Assembly shall, as a rule, be guided by the observations of the Committee on South West Africa and shall base its conclusions, as far as possible, on the Committee's observations.

Procedure with regard to petitions

Special rule C: The General Assembly shall receive annually from the Committee on South West Africa a report with regard to petitions submitted to it. The summary records of the meetings at which the petitions were discussed shall be attached.

Special rule D: The General Assembly shall, as a rule, be guided by the conclusions of the Committee on South West Africa and shall base its own conclusions, as far as possible, on the conclusions of the Committee.

---

[a]By resolution 844 (IX) of 11 October 1954, the General Assembly, having considered the report of the Committee on South West Africa (*Official Records of the General Assembly, Ninth Session, Supplement No. 14* (A/2666 and Corr.1 and Add.1)), adopted six special rules for the examination by the Assembly of reports and petitions relating to the Territory of South West Africa. These special rules are reproduced in the present annex.

[b]By resolution 2372 (XXII) of 12 June 1968, the General Assembly decided that "South West Africa" would be known as "Namibia".

Private meetings

Special rule E: Having regard to rule 62ᶜ of the rules of procedure of the General Assembly, meetings at which decisions concerning persons are considered shall be held in private.

Voting procedure

Special rule F: Decisions of the General Assembly on questions relating to reports and petitions concerning the Territory of South West Africa shall be regarded as important questions within the meaning of Article 18, paragraph 2, of the Charter of the United Nations.

ᶜRule 60 of the present rules of procedure.

ANNEX IV

Resolution 1898 (XVIII) adopted on the recommendation of the *Ad Hoc* Committee on the Improvement of the Methods of Work of the General Assembly[a]

The General Assembly,

Recalling with appreciation the initiative taken by the President of the sixteenth session of the General Assembly in his memorandum of 26 April 1962 on the methods of work of the Assembly,[b]

Recalling its decision of 30 October 1962 establishing the *Ad Hoc* Committee on the Improvement of the Methods of Work of the General Assembly and its resolution 1845 (XVII) of 19 December 1962, by which it decided to continue the Committee,

Having considered the report submitted by the *Ad Hoc* Committee in pursuance of the above-mentioned resolution,[c]

Conscious of the need to adapt its methods of work to the changed circumstances in the General Assembly, in particular those resulting from the recent increase in the number of Member States,

Concerned however to avoid reducing in any way the possibilities for action available to the General Assembly under the Charter of the United Nations and the rules of procedure of the Assembly,

Convinced that it is in the interests of the Organization and of Member States that the work of the General Assembly should be carried out as efficiently and expeditiously as possible and that, save in quite exceptional cases, the duration of regular sessions should not exceed thirteen weeks,

Takes note of the observations contained in the report of the *Ad Hoc* Committee on the Improvement of the Methods of Work of the General Assembly and approves the recommendations submitted by the Committee, in particular those which provide that:

(a) The President of the General Assembly should make every effort to ensure that the general debate proceeds in a methodical and regular manner, and should close the list of speakers, with the consent of the Assembly, as soon as he considers it feasible;

(b) All the Main Committees, except the First Committee, should begin their work not later than two working days after they have received the list of agenda items referred to them by the General Assembly;

---

[a]Adopted by the General Assembly at its 1256th plenary meeting, on 11 November 1963.
[b]*Official Records of the General Assembly, Seventeenth Session, Annexes,* agenda item 86, document A/5123.
[c]*Ibid, Eighteenth Session, Annexes,* agenda item 25, document A/5423.

(c) The First Committee should meet as soon as possible to organize its work, determine the order of discussion of the items allocated to it and start the systematic consideration of its agenda; at the beginning of the session, such meetings might be held when there is an interruption in the general debate; later, plenary meetings might be held during one part of the day, the other part being reserved for the First Committee, thus enabling the Committee to proceed with its regular work as soon as possible after the opening of the session;

(d) Each of the Main Committees should establish its programme of work as soon as possible, including the approximate dates on which it will consider the various items referred to it and the date on which it proposes to conclude its work, on the understanding that this programme will be transmitted to the General Committee to enable it to make such recommendations as it may deem relevant, including, when the General Committee consider it appropriate, recommendations as to the dates by which Main Committees should conclude their work;

(e) Each of the Main Committees should consider the establishment, in the circumstances referred to in paragraphs 29 to 32 of the report of the *Ad Hoc* Committee,[d] of subcommittees or working groups of limited size but representative of

---

[d]These paragraphs read as follows:

"29. The increase in the number of Members of the United Nations has created a situation in which it frequently happens that more than 100 delegations are present and most of them participate in the debates in the Main Committees. Although the presence of such a large number of delegations involves no practical difficulties when statements of the positions of Governments are being made, it makes it more difficult to discuss concrete points, to have a rapid exchange of views on subjects where ideas differ or to draft and modify texts. The Committee is of the opinion that in many cases the examination of agenda items by the committees would be greatly facilitated if, as soon as possible and especially when the main points of view have been expressed, the committee decided, on the initiative of its Chairman or of one or more of its members, to set up a subcommittee or working group, in conformity with rule 104 [now 102] of the rules of procedure (98 [now 96] in the case of the plenary Assembly). This procedure might be particularly helpful when there is general agreement on the question under discussion but disagreement on points of detail.

"30. The Ad Hoc Committee would recall in this connexion that in the course of the first sessions of the General Assembly frequent use was made of subcommittees and working groups and that they were of great assistance to the General Assembly in the preparation of texts which to this day govern the structures of the United Nations in the formulation of important international instruments and in the solution of difficult political problems (one example is the sub-committee which dealt with the future status of the former Italian colonies). As far back as 1947, the report of the Committee on Procedures and Organization expressed itself on this subject as follows:

"'The Main Committees should consider carefully at an early stage in their work how their programmes might be expedited by the establishment of sub-committees. It is, of course, impossible to adopt fixed rules on this matter. If the debate in full committee showed that there was general agreement on the question under discussion but disagreement on points of detail, it would clearly be desirable to set up a small drafting committee to prepare a resolution for submission to the Main Committee. Technical questions on which there is no

its membership, for the purpose of facilitating its work;

(f) The General Committee should fulfil its functions under rules 40, 41 and 42 of the rules or procedure and, in particular, make appropriate recommendations for furthering the progress of the Assembly and its Committees, in such a way as to facilitate the closing of the session by the date fixed; to this end, the General Committee should meet at least once every three weeks;

(g) Presiding officers should make use of the resources provided by the rules of procedure and exercise their prerogatives under rules 35 and 108,[e] in order to accelerate the work of the General Assembly; to that effect they should, *inter alia*:

(i) Open meetings at the scheduled time;

(ii) Urge representatives to take the floor in the order in which they were inscribed on the list of speakers, it being understood that representatives prevented from so doing will normally be placed at the end of the list, unless they have arranged to change places with other representatives;

(iii) Apply the rules of procedure in such a way as to ensure the proper exercise of the right of reply, explanation of votes and points of order.

---

substantial disagreement should be referred to sub-committees as quickly as possible. In some cases the work of sub-committees would be facilitated by working informally, and on occasion, in private.' (A/388, para. 21.)

"31. The subcommittees or working groups could, in most cases, consist of representatives of the delegations with the closest interest in the agenda item, representatives who are especially competent to deal with the problem under discussion and others chosen in such a way as to ensure that the sub-committee or working group will be broadly representative, geographically and politically.

"32. These bodies could meet either in public or in private, according to the circumstances, and could either follow formal procedures or discuss matters informally. Their function would be to make it possible for those primarily interested in an item to exchange views, thus facilitating subsequent agreement and compromise solutions; they could prepare draft resolutions or at least formulate alternative solutions; they could appoint rapporteurs to present their conclusions and to give the necessary explanations to the committee which established them. The committee itself would be entirely free to take final decisions but, since all aspects of the problem would have been given minute examination, it would undoubtedly find its own work greatly facilitated both with regard to substance and to the time thus saved. It would also often be possible for the committee to consider other items on its agenda while the sub-committee or working group was carrying out its assignment."

[e]Rule 106 of the present rules of procedure.

ANNEX Vᵃ

Conclusions of the Special Committee on the Rationalization of the Procedures and Organization of the General Assembly

CONTENTS

ᵃBy resolution 2837 (XXVI) of 17 December 1971, the General Assembly approved the conclusions of the Special Committee on the Rationalization of the Procedures and Organization of the General Assembly established under resolution 2632 (XXV) of 9 November 1970, declared those conclusions to be useful and worthy of consideration by the Assembly, its committees and other relevant organs and decided that they should be annexed to the rules of procedure; the conclusions of the Special Committee are reproduced in the present annex. By the same resolution, the General Assembly, on the recommendation of the Special Committee, decided to amend rules 39, 60 (now rule 58), 69 (now rule 67), 74 (now rule 72), 101 (now rule 98), 105 (now rule 103), 107 (now rule 105), 110 (now rule 108) and 115 (now rule 114) of its rules of procedure and to adopt a new rule 112 (now rule 110) (see introduction, para. 30). For the report of the Special Committee, see *Official Records of the General Assembly, Twenty-sixth Session, Supplement No. 26* (A/8426).

I. MANDATE OF THE SPECIAL COMMITTEE

1. The members of the Special Committee agreed that the existing rules of procedure were generally satisfactory and that most improvements would be achieved not through changes in the rules of procedure but through better application of the existing rules, due account being taken of the conclusions of, the Special Committee and of the various committees responsible for reviewing the procedures and organization of the General Assembly [*para. 12 of the report of the Special Committee*[b]].

2. The Special Committee considered, moreover, that it would be desirable to review from time to time the procedures and organization of the General Assembly [*para. 13*].

II. GENERAL ORGANIZATION OF SESSIONS
A. OPENING DATE

3. The Special Committee is of the opinion that it would not be desirable to change the date fixed for the opening of sessions [*para. 18*].

B. DURATION OF SESSIONS

4. The Special Committee, noting that, despite the appreciable increase in the number of Member States, it has been possible to maintain an average duration of thirteen weeks for regular sessions, is of the view that this period should not be changed and that, in any case, the session should end before Christmas [*para. 22*].

5. The Special Committee did not endorse the suggestion that the session should be divided into two parts. The Committee likewise did not endorse the suggestion that the session should theoretically last a whole year and should merely be adjourned after a two-month main session [*para. 23*].

C. RESIDUARY SESSIONS

6. The Special Committee did not endorse the suggestion that a brief meeting of the General Assembly, to be called a "residuary session", might be held at head-of-mission level about the end of April for the discussion of certain administrative and routine questions [*para. 24*].

---

[b]*Official Records of the General Assembly, Twenty-sixth Session, Supplement No. 26* (A/8426).

III. GENERAL COMMITTEE
A. COMPOSITION OF THE GENERAL COMMITTEE
1. *Increase in membership*

7. The Special Committee decided not to take any action on the question of either maintaining or increasing the present membership of the General Committee [*para. 31*].

8. Furthermore, the Special Committee did not retain the suggestion that the Chairman of the Credentials Committee should be authorized to participate in the work of the General Committee [*para. 32*].

2. *Absence of members of the General Committee elected in their personal capacity*

9. The Special Committee considers that the problems which arise when the Chairman or Vice-Chairman of a Main Committee cannot attend a meeting of the General Committee would be settled for the most part if the General Assembly decided to increase the number of Vice-Chairman of the Main Committees [*para. 36*].

10. The Special Committee also considers that, if the General Assembly took such a decision, the Chairman of a Main Committee, in designating a Vice-Chairman as his substitute, should take into account the representative character of the General Committee [*para. 37*].

B. FUNCTIONS OF THE GENERAL COMMITTEE
1. *Importance of the role of the General Committee*

11. The Special Committee considers that the General Committee, in view of the functions conferred on it by the rules of procedure, should play a major role in advancing the rational organization and general conduct of the proceedings of the General Assembly. The Committee is of the opinion that the General Committee should discharge completely and effectively the functions assigned to it under rules 40, 41 and 42 of the rules of procedure, the purpose of which is to assist the Assembly in the general conduct of its work [*para. 41*].

2. *Adoption of the agenda and allocation of items*

12. The Special Committee recommends that, within the framework of the functions conferred on it by the rules of procedure, and subject to the limitation prescribed in rule 40 as regards the discussion of the substance of an item, the General Committee should examine the provisional agenda, together with the supplementary list and requests for the inclusion of additional items, more attentively and carry out more fully and consistently

its functions of recommending with regard to each item its inclusion in the agenda, the rejection of the request for inclusion or its inclusion in the provisional agenda of a future session, as well as of allocating items to the Main Committees, regard being had to rules 99 and 101° of the rules or procedure, with a view to ensuring that all items inscribed on the agenda can be taken up by the end of the session [*para. 45*].

3. *Organization of the work of the General Assembly*

13. The Special Committee recalls the recommendation, in subparagraph (f) of General Assembly resolution 1898 (XVIII),[d] that the General Committee should meet at least once every three weeks. The Special Committee notes that the recommendation has not been complied with and expresses the hope that the General Committee will be able to hold more frequent meetings, in conformity with rule 42 of the rules of procedure, without thereby interfering with the normal meeting schedule of the plenary and the Main Committees [*para. 49*].

14. The Special Committee also considers that, in the discharge of the functions conferred by rules 41 and 42 of the rules of procedure and subject to the limitation prescribed in rule 41 regarding the decision of any political question, the General Committee should review the progress of the General Assembly and the Main Committees and should, as required, assist and make recommendations to the President and the Assembly for the co-ordination of the proceedings of the Main Committees and for expediting the general conduct of business [*para. 50*].

C. WAYS OF FACILITATING THE WORK OF THE GENERAL COMMITTEE
1. *Preparatory meetings*

15. The Special Committee does not consider that it is in a position to make any recommendation with regard to the holding of preparatory meetings of the General Committee [*para. 54*].

2. *Subsidiary organs*

16. The Special Committee does not consider that it is in a position to make any recommendation with regard to the establishment of subsidiary organs of the General Committee [*para. 58*].

---

[c]Rules 97 and 98 of the present rules of procedure.
[d]See annex IV.

IV. AGENDA
A. PRESENTATION AND PRELIMINARY CONSIDERATION
OF THE PROVISIONAL AGENDA

17. The Special Committee, aware of the need to assist delegations, to the greatest extent possible, to prepare for the work of the General Assembly, recommends to the Assembly that the Secretary-General should be requested:

(a) To communicate to Member States, not later than 15 February, the unofficial list of items proposed for inclusion in the provisional agenda of the Assembly;

(b) To communicate to Member States, not later than 15 June, an annotated list of items which would indicate briefly the history of each item, the available documentation, the substance of the matter to be discussed and earlier decisions by United Nations organs;

(c) To communicate to Member States before the opening of the session an addendum to the annotated list [*para. 64*].

18. Furthermore, the Special Committee recommends that member States requesting the inclusion of an item should, if they deem it advisable, make a suggestion concerning its referral to a Main Committee or to the plenary Assembly [*para. 65*].

B. REDUCTION IN THE NUMBER OF AGENDA ITEMS
1. *Non-inclusion of certain items*

19. The Special Committee, considering that the General Assembly should take into account the relative importance of agenda items in the light of the purposes and principles of the Charter of the United Nations, recommends to the Assembly that, in the context of rules 22 and 40 of the rules of procedure, Member States should take special interest in the contents of the Assembly's agenda and, in particular, in deciding on the appropriate solution of questions or on the elimination of items which have lost their urgency or relevance, are not ripe for consideration or could be dealt with and even disposed of equally well by subsidiary organs of the General Assembly [*para. 70*].

2. *Staggering of items over two or more years and grouping of related items*

20. The Special Committee considers that the staggering of items over two or more years constitutes one means of rationalizing the procedures of the General Assembly [*para. 74*].

21. Moreover, the Special Committee recommends to the General Assembly that, as far as possible and appropriate, related items should be grouped under the same title [*para. 75*].

3. *Referral to other organs*

22. The Special Committee recommends that the General Assembly should, where relevant, refer specific items to other United Nations organs or to specialized agencies, taking into account the nature of the question [*para. 79*].

23. The Special Committee also recommends that the General Assembly should give due weight to the debates that have taken place in other organs [*para. 80*].

4. *Non-receivability of certain additional items*

24. The Special Committee recommends to the General Assembly that additional items, which are proposed for inclusion in the agenda less than thirty days before the opening of a session, should be included only if the conditions prescribed by rule 15 of the rules of procedure are fully satisfied [*para. 84*].

C. ALLOCATION OF AGENDA ITEMS
1. *Division of work among the Main Committees*

25. The Special Committee wishes to draw attention to the importance of a rational distribution of agenda items among the Main Committees. In this connexion, the Committee, recognizing that the structure of the Main Committees gives them specialization and experience, recommends that the allocation of agenda items should be based not only on the workload of the Committees but also on the nature of the item, regard being had to rules 99 and 101c of the rules of procedure [*para. 89*].

26. The Special Committee also considers that it would be helpful if suggestions concerning the allocation of items were made much earlier so that Member States might have more time to study them [*para. 90*].

27. Lastly, the Special Committee recommends that the General Committee and the General Assembly should consider, in some cases, the possibility of referring more items directly to the plenary [*para. 91*].

2. *Non-referral of certain items to two or more Committees*

28. The Special Committee recommends to the General Assembly that agenda items should be so allocated as to ensure, as far as possible, that the same questions or the same aspects of a question are not considered by more than one Committee [*para. 95*].

V. ORGANIZATION OF THE WORK OF THE MAIN COMMITTEES
A. Functions OF THE INDIVIDUAL COMMITTEES

29. There was general agreement among the members of the Special Committee that a flexible approach should be adopted towards the whole question of the division of work among the Main Committees and that the Committee should not make any recommendation concerning the referral of specific items, in order not to go beyond its field of competence [*para. 97*].

30. The Special Committee, considering that the potential of the seven Main Committees should be utilized to the full, recommends that the General Assembly should ensure a more balanced division of work among the Committees, giving due account to the nature of items. The Committee does not, however, feel that it should specify which items might be transferred from one Committee to another [*para. 98*]

31. The Special Committee, recognizing that the workload of a number of Committees is extremely heavy, is of the opinion that the General Assembly should advise those Committees so to organize their work as to enable them to consider their agenda in the most effective way [*para. 99*].

1. *First Committee*

32. The Special Committee, recognizing that the role of the First Committee is essentially political, recommends that this Committee devote itself primarily to problems of peace, security and disarmament [*para. 103*].

33. The Special Committee, not wishing to make any specific recommendation concerning the allocation of agenda items, did not feel that it should take any decision on the proposal that the reports of the International Atomic Energy Agency and the United Nations Scientific Committee on the Effects of Atomic Radiation should be submitted to the First Committee [*para. 104*].

2. *Special Political Committee*

34. The Special Committee, reaffirming the major role which must be played by the Special Political Committee and recognizing further that the agenda of that Committee is relatively light, recommends that the General Assembly should consider transferring to the Special Political Committee one or two items usually considered by other Committees with a view to ensuring a better division of work among the Main Committees [*para. 108*].

35. The Special Committee did not endorse the suggestions concerning the renaming of the Special Political Committee [*para. 109*].

3. *Second Committee*

36. The Special Committee did not feel that it should take any decision on the proposals that all the social aspects of development should be dealt with by the Second Committee. Accordingly, it did not endorse the suggestion to change the name of that Committee [*para. 113*].

4. *Third Committee*

37. The Special Committee did not feel it should take a decision on the proposal that some of the items on the agenda of the Third Committee should be transferred to other Main Committees [*para. 117*].

5. *Conflicts of competence among Committees*

38. The Special Committee considers that conflicts of competence among the Main Committees should be avoided whenever possible. Without prejudging the decision to be taken in each individual case, the Committee wishes to draw attention to the existence of this problem and to the advisability for the General Committee and the General Assembly to consider the most effective ways of remedying it [*para. 119*].

B. ROLE OF THE PRESIDING OFFICERS

39. The Special Committee recommends to the General Assembly that the Chairmen of the Main Committees should fully exercise the functions assigned to them in the rules of procedure and, in particular, make use of the prerogatives given them in rule 108[e] [*para. 123*].

40. The Special Committee also reaffirms that the Chairman of the Main Committees should be elected on the basis of equitable geographical distribution as well as on that of experience and competence, as provided for in rule 105[f] of the rules of procedure [*para. 124*].

41. The Special Committee did not endorse the suggestion that candidates should have had at least one year's experience in one of the Main Committees or the suggestion that Chairmen should be elected at the end of the previous session [*para. 125*].

---

[e]Rule 106 of the present rules of procedure.
[f]Rule 103 of the present rules of procedure.

C. NUMBER OF VICE-CHAIRMAN

42. From its own experience, the Special Committee recommends to the General Assembly that its subsidiary organs should consider, as far as possible, the designation of three Vice-Chairmen in order to ensure the representative character of their officers [*para. 131*].

D. REPORTS OF THE COMMITTEE

43. The Special Committee, recalling General Assembly resolution 2292 (XXII), recommends to the Assembly that the reports of the Main Committees should be as concise as possible and, save in exceptional cases, should not contain a summary of the debates [*para. 133*].[8]

VI. MAXIMUM UTILIZATION OF AVAILABLE TIME
A. Plenary Assembly
1. *General debate*

(a) *Frequency*

44. The Special Committee, recognizing the unquestionable value of the general debate, considers that it should continue to be held every year and that the time devoted to it should be utilized to the maximum. It wishes to stress also the importance of participation by Heads of State or Government, Ministers for Foreign Affairs and other high officials as a means of enhancing the significance of the general debate [*para. 137*].

(b) *Organization of meetings*

(i) *Length of the general debate*

45. The Special Committee feels that the general debate would be more meaningful, as far as organization was concerned, if it took place intensively and without interruption. Its length should not normally exceed two and a half weeks if the time available were utilized to the maximum [*para. 142*].

(ii) *Closure of the list of speakers*

46. Considering that the organization of the general debate would be improved if delegations were required to decide more quickly when to speak, the Special Committee recommends to the General Assembly that the list of speakers wishing to take part in the general debate should be closed at the end of the third day after the opening of the debate [*para. 144*].

---

[8]For the recommendations concerning the reports of subsidiary organs, see para. 107 below.

(c) *Length of statements*

47. The Special Committee, noting that during the session commemorating the twenty-fifth anniversary of the United Nations it had been possible to hear a large number of speakers during a relatively short period without limiting the duration of statements, considers that this result was due to a better utilization of the time available and not to the imposition of a limitation on the length of speeches [*para. 147*].

48. The Committee notes that during recent sessions of the General Assembly the average length of speeches has been thirty-five minutes and expresses the hope that delegations will ensure that their statements will not be excessively long [*para. 148*].

(d) *Submission of written statements*

49. The Special Committee considers that the submission of written statements should not be formally instituted with regard to the general debate [para. 152].

2. *Debate on items already considered in Committee*

50. The Special Committee is of the opinion that rule 68[h] of the rules of procedure has been applied judiciously and with satisfactory results [*para. 155*].

3. *Non-utilization of the rostrum*

51. The Special Committee thinks that it would be useful to draw the attention of representatives to the possibility of speaking without going to the rostrum. It considers, however, that in all cases it is for representatives to decide whether they prefer to speak from their seats or from the rostrum, whether on a point of order, for an explanation of vote or in exercise of their right of reply [*para. 157*].

4. *Presentation of the reports of the Main Committees*

52. The Special Committee wishes to recall the recommendation made in 1947 by the Committee on Procedures and Organization of the General Assembly that Rapporteurs should not read out their reports in plenary meetings.[i] It wishes to stress that the presentation of reports in plenary meetings should be limited to brief introductory statements [*para. 158*].

---

[h]Rule 66 of the present rules of procedure.

[i]*Official Records of the General Assembly, Second Session, Plenary Meetings,* vol. II, annex IV, document A/388, para. 26.

53. The Special Committee recommends also that the General Assembly should confirm the practice whereby certain related reports of a non-controversial nature may be introduced simultaneously to the plenary Assembly by the Rapporteur [*para. 159*].

B. Main Committees
1. *Nomination of officers*

54. The members of the Special Committee agreed that the nomination of candidates involved a significant loss of time. They also recognized that the terms of rule 105 of the rules of procedure, which provided that elections should be held by secret ballot, no longer corresponded to the present practice, since in most cases, as a result of prior consultations, there was only one candidate for each post and voting by secret ballot was therefore superfluous [*para. 161*].[j]

55. The Special Committee, bearing in mind particularly the financial implications of such a procedure, did not retain the suggestion that nominations should be made in writing [*para. 162*].

56. Furthermore, in view of the dictates of courtesy and the possibility that cases might arise in which nominees would not be known until the last moment, the Special Committee did not deem it advisable to dispense completely with the oral nomination of candidates [*para. 163*].

57. The Special Committee considers that the nomination of candidates should be limited to one statement for each candidate, after which the Committee would proceed to the election immediately. The Special Committee considers, however, that the general principle that elections are held by secret ballot should be retained [*para. 164*].

2. *Commencement of work*

58. The Special Committee recommends that all the Main Committees, with the possible exception of the First Committee, should begin their work on the working day following the receipt of the list of items referred to them by the General Assembly [*para. 170*].

59. The Special Committee also recommends that the First Committee should be ready to meet whenever no plenary meeting of the Assembly is being held [*para. 171*].

---

[j]Rule 105 (now rule 103) was subsequently amended (see introduction, para. 30(e)).

3. *Progress of work*

60. The Special Committee recommends that the Main Committees should from time to time review the progress of their work [*para. 176*].

4. *General debate in Committee*

61. The Special Committee, while recognizing the unquestionable usefulness and importance of the general debate, considers that Chairmen should encourage the Main Committees:

(a) To recognize the advisability of shortening the general debate, whenever that is possible without detriment to the work of the Committees;

(b) To extend, whenever appropriate, the practice of holding a single debate on related and logically linked agenda items [*para. 180*].

62. The Special Committee recognizes that a general debate on questions previously considered by a United Nations organ and covered by a report of the organ concerned should be retained. The Committee, however, draws the attention of the Chairmen of the Main Committees to the possibility of consulting their Committees in every case when a general debate on a certain item does not seem to be needed. The Chairmen may resort to this practice to ascertain in particular whether the Committees desire to hold a general debate on every question referred to them by other organs [*para. 181*].

63. At the same time, the Special Committee wishes to reaffirm that the general debate serves a necessary and very useful purpose in the work of the Main Committees and that its organization should in no circumstances be changed without the consent of the Committees concerned, which therefore should decide on the applicability of the above-mentioned suggestions [*para. 182*].

64. The Special Committee did not deem it appropriate to make a recommendation concerning the suggestion that delegations sharing the same point of view could use a spokesman who would express those views in a single statement. Nor did the Committee retain the suggestion that the consideration of certain items already debated in previous sessions might be introduced by specially appointed rapporteurs who would summarize the main issues emerging from previous debates [*para. 183*].

5. *Concurrent consideration of several agenda items*

65. The Special Committee considers that in certain cases, when a Main Committee cannot proceed with its discussion of one item, it should be prepared to begin considering the next item on its agenda [*para. 187*].

6. Establishment of subcommittees or working groups

66. The Special Committee wishes to remind the General Assembly of the desirability of the Main Committees' making use of subcommittees or working groups [*para. 188*].

C. MEASURES APPLICABLE BOTH TO THE PLENARY ASSEMBLY AND TO THE MAIN COMMITTEES

1. *Opening of meetings at the scheduled time*

67. The members of the Special Committee agreed that the General Assembly would operate much more efficiently if the presiding officers made a special effort to open meetings at the scheduled time [*para. 190*].

68. The Special Committee did not endorse the suggestion to have meetings begin at 9.30 a.m. and 2.30 p.m. in view of the practical difficulties that such a measure would entail [*para. 192*].

2. *List of speakers*

69. The Special Committee recommends to the General Assembly that the President of the Assembly or the Chairman of a Main Committee should, soon after the beginning of the debate on an item, indicate a date for the closing of the list of speakers. He should endeavour to have the list of speakers closed at the latest after one third of the meetings allocated to the item have been held [*para. 202*].

70. Moreover, the Special Committee considers that speakers should, as far as possible, avoid putting down their names to speak on a given item and at the same time indicating an alternative meeting if they are unable to keep to their original schedule [*para. 203*].

71. Finally, the Special Committee wishes to reaffirm the practice whereby presiding officers should invite representatives to speak in the order of their inscription on the list of speakers, on the understanding that those prevented from doing so should normally be moved to the end of the list, unless they have arranged to change places with other representatives [*para. 204*].

3. *Limiting the length of speeches or number of speakers*

72. The Committee wishes to stress that the amendment on this subject[k] is of a purely technical nature, its only purpose being to limit the number of representatives who could speak on a proposal submitted under rules 74 and 115[l] of the rules of procedure [*para. 210*].

73. With regard to the general question of setting a time-limit on interventions, the Special Committee, while recognizing that, in so far as possible, statements should be kept brief so as to allow all delegations to present the views of their Governments, considers that no rigid rule on the question could be applied [*para. 211*].

4. *Explanations of vote*

74. The Special Committee considers that, in explaining their votes, delegations should limit their statements to an explanation, as brief as possible, of their own votes and should not use the occasion to reopen the debate [*para. 216*].

75. The Special Committee also considers that presiding officers should be encouraged to use, whenever they deem it appropriate, their powers under rules 90 and 129[m] of the rules of procedure [*para. 217*].

76. Finally, the Special Committee recommends to the General Assembly that a delegation should explain its vote only once on the same proposal, in either a Main Committee or a plenary meeting, unless the delegation considers it essential to explain it in both meetings. It recommends further that the sponsor of a draft resolution adopted by a Main Committee should refrain from explaining its vote during the consideration of that draft resolution in the plenary unless it deems it essential to do so [*para. 218*].

5. *Right of reply*

77. The Special Committee recommends to the General Assembly that delegations should use restraint in the exercise of their right of reply, both in plenary meetings and in the Main Committees, and that their statements in exercise of that right should be as brief as possible [*para. 223*].

78. The Special Committee recommends, furthermore, that statements made in the exercise of the right of reply should be delivered, as a general rule, at the end of meetings [*para. 224*].

---

[k]See introduction, para. 30(c).
[l]Rules 72 and 114 of the present rules of procedure.
[m]Rules 88 and 128 of the present rules of procedure.

6. *Points of order*

79. The Special Committee recommends to the General Assembly the adoption of the following text as a description of the concept of a point of order [*para. 229*]:

"(a) A point of order is basically an intervention directed to the presiding officer, requesting him to make use of some power inherent in his office or specifically given him under the rules of procedure. It may, for example, relate to the manner in which the debate is conducted, to the maintenance of order, to the observance of the rules of procedure or to the way in which presiding officers exercise the powers conferred upon them by the rules. Under a point of order, a representative may request the presiding officer to apply a certain rule of procedure or he may question the way in which the officer applies the rule. Thus, within the scope of the rules of procedure, representatives are enabled to direct the attention of the presiding officer to violations or misapplications of the rules by other representatives or by the presiding officer himself. A point of order has precedence over any other matter, including procedural motions (rules 73 [114][p] and 79 [120][o]).

"(b) Points of order raised under rule 73 [114][p] involve questions necessitating a ruling by the presiding officer, subject to possible appeal. They are therefore distinct from the procedural motions provided for in rules 76 [117][p] to 79 [120][o] which can be decided only by a vote and on which more than one motion may be entertained at the same time, rule 79 [120] laying down the precedence of such motions. They are also distinct from request for information or clarification, or from remarks relating to material arrangements (seating, interpretation system, temperature of the room), documents, translations etc., which -- while they may have to be dealt with by the presiding officer -- do not require rulings from him. However, in established United Nations practice, a representative intending to submit a procedural motion or to seek information or clarification often rises to 'a point of order' as a means of obtaining the floor. The latter usage, which is based on practical grounds, should not be confused with the raising of points of order under rule 73 [114].[n]

"(c) Under rule 73 [114],[n] a point of order must be immediately decided by the presiding officer in accordance with the rules of procedure; any appeal arising therefrom must also be put immediately to the vote. It follows that as a general rule:

"(i)   A point of order and any appeal arising from a ruling thereon is not debatable;

---

[n]Rule 71 [113] of the present rules of procedure.
[o]Rule 77 [119] of the present rules of procedure.
[p]Rule 74 [116] of the present rules of procedure.

"(ii)   No point of order on the same or a different subject can be permitted until the initial point of order and any appeal arising therefrom have been disposed of.

"Nevertheless, both the presiding officer and delegations may request information or clarification regarding a point of order. In addition, the presiding officer may, if he considers it necessary, request an expression of views from delegations on a point of order before giving his ruling; in the exceptional cases in which this practice is resorted to, the presiding officer should terminate the exchange of views and give his ruling as soon as he is ready to announce that ruling.

"(d) Rule 73 [114]" provides that a representative rising to a point of order may not speak on the substance of the matter under discussion. Consequently, the purely procedural nature of points of order calls for brevity. The presiding officer is responsible for ensuring that statements made on a point of order are in conformity with the present description."

7. *Congratulations*

80. The Special Committee is of the opinion that it would be better to retain the current practice of the plenary Assembly whereby congratulations to the President are confined to brief remarks included in the speeches made during the general debate [*para. 235*].

81. With regard to subsidiary organs of the General Assembly, the Special Committee recommends that, in the case of a newly established organ or of the rotation of officers on an existing one, congratulations to the Chairman should be expressed only by the temporary Chairman and congratulations to other officers should be expressed only by the Chairman [*para. 237*].[q]

8. *Condolences*

82. The Special Committee recommends to the General Assembly that condolences addressed to a delegation on the death of a prominent person or in the event of a disaster should be expressed solely by the President of the General Assembly, by the Chairman of a Main Committee or by the Chairman of a subsidiary organ on behalf of all members. Where circumstances warrant it, the President of the General Assembly might call a special plenary meeting for that purpose [*para. 242*].

---

[q]For congratulations in the Main Committees, see rule 110, adopted on the recommendation of the Special Committee.

83. The Special Committee moreover takes note of the practice whereby the President of the General Assembly, on behalf of all members, dispatches a cable to the country concerned [*para. 243*].

9. *Roll-call votes*

84. The Special Committee, while believing that there is no need to change the rules of procedure relating to roll-call votes, recommends that delegations should endeavour not to request such a vote except when there are good and sound reasons for doing so [*para. 247*].

10. *Electronic devices*

85. The Special Committee did not believe that it should express any views on the possible use of an electronic voting system by all Committees, since the question of the installation of mechanical means of voting was included in the draft agenda of the twenty-sixth session of the General Assembly [*para. 249*].

86. The Special Committee did not retain the suggestion that a mechanical or electronic timing device might be installed in the General Assembly Hall and the Main Committee rooms [*para. 250*].

VII. RESOLUTIONS
A. Submission of draft resolutions
1. *Date of submission of draft resolutions*

87. The Special Committee recommends to the General Assembly that draft resolutions should be submitted as early as possible so as to give debates a more concrete character. It considers, however, that no rigid rule should be established in the matter, since it is for delegations to determine, in each case, the most appropriate moment for submitting draft resolutions [*para. 254*].

88. So as to ensure that debates take shape as quickly as possible without making it mandatory for delegations to submit a formal draft resolution, the Special Committee also considers that delegations might resort more often to the possibility of circulating draft resolutions as informal working papers which would provide a basis for the discussion but whose contents would be strictly provisional [*para. 255*].

2. *Submission of draft resolutions in writing*

89. Because of the appreciable loss of time that such a procedure could entail, the Special Committee decided not to endorse the suggestion that proposals and amendments should be submitted in writing only [*para. 256*].

3. *Consultations*

90. The Special Committee, recognizing the indisputable value of consultations, believes that delegations should explore every avenue for arriving at negotiated texts. It considers, however, that the initiative for such consultations must rest solely with the delegations concerned and can, under no circumstances, be dictated in mandatory provisions [*para. 258*].

91. The Special Committee also believes that the Chairman of the Main Committees should be invited to bear in mind the possibility of establishing, where necessary, working groups for the purpose of facilitating the adoption of agreed texts. Such groups may be open, as appropriate, to interested delegations. It does not, however, consider it advisable to contemplate the establishment of such working groups whenever two or more draft resolutions have been introduced on the same matter [*para. 259*].

4. *Number of sponsors*

92. The Special Committee did not endorse the suggestion that the number of sponsors of a draft resolution should be limited [*para. 260*].

93. The Special Committee does, however, wish to draw attention to the practice whereby the sponsors of a proposal decide whether other delegations can become co-sponsors [*para. 261*].

5. *Time-lapse between the submission and the consideration of draft resolutions*

94. The Special Committee, while recognizing the difficulties experienced by some delegations in consulting their Governments within the time laid down by rules 80 and 121ʳ of the rules of procedure, does not deem it advisable to propose an amendment to those rules [*para. 265*].

ʳRules 78 and 120 of the present rules of procedure.

B. Content of Resolutions

95. The Special Committee is of the opinion that the wording of resolutions, to be effective, must be as clear and succinct as possible. It recognizes, however, that only the delegations concerned can decide upon the content of the proposals which they are sponsoring [*para. 267*].

96. The Special Committee also wishes to emphasize that the text of a draft resolution should not go beyond the competence of the Committee in which it is submitted. Where, however, it is suggested that a draft resolution does so, the Special Committee feels that it is up to the Committee concerned to take a decision in the matter [*para. 268*].

C. Financial Implications
1. *Financial controls*

97. The Special Committee feels that the provisions of rules 154 and 155[s] of the rules of procedure are satisfactory and should be strictly applied [*para. 272*].

98. The Special Committee is also of the opinion that the financial implications of draft resolutions should be viewed in terms of an over-all assessment of priorities and that the principal organs should give careful consideration to the draft resolutions adopted by their subsidiary organs where such drafts call for the appropriation of funds [*para. 273*].

2. *Work of the Advisory Committee on Administrative and Budgetary Questions*

99. The Special Committee recognizes that the Advisory Committee on Administrative and Budgetary Questions should meet more frequently, but does not consider itself qualified to make detailed recommendations on the matter [*para. 275*].

3. *Resolutions setting up new organs*

100. While acknowledging that new organs should be set up only after mature consideration, the Special Committee believes that it would be inadvisable to amend the rules of procedure and lay down hard and fast rules in the matter [*para. 277*].

---

[s]Rules 153 and 154 of the present rules of procedure.

D. Voting Procedure
1. *Required majority*

101. The Special Committee considers that rules RR and 127[t] of the rules of procedure should be left unchanged [*para. 282*].

102. The Special Committee also considers that the suggestion referred to in paragraph 279 of the report is unacceptable and, moreover, goes beyond its mandate [*para. 283*].

2. *Measures to accelerate procedures*

103. The Special Committee, recalling the recommendations which it has made elsewhere concerning debate on items already considered in Committee (see para. 50 above) and roll-call votes (see para. 84 above), feels that it is inadvisable to make any changes in the relevant provisions of the rules of procedure [*para. 287*].

3. *Consensus*

104. The Special Committee considers that the adoption of decisions and resolutions by consensus is desirable when it contributes to the effective and lasting settlement of differences, thus strengthening the authority of the United Nations. It wishes, however, to emphasize that the right of every Member State to set forth its views in full must not be prejudiced by this procedure [*para. 289*].

E. Reduction in the number of resolutions

105. The Special Committee did not endorse the suggestions aimed at reducing the number of resolutions adopted by the General Assembly [*para. 293*].

VIII. DOCUMENTATION[u]
A. Reduction in the volume of documentation

106. The Special Committee recommends that the General Assembly should:

---

[t]Rules 86 and 126 of the present rules of procedure.
[u]See also resolution 2836 (XXVI).

(a) Draw attention to the provisions of its resolutions 2292 (XXII) and 2538 (XXIV) summarized in document A/INF/136, and stress the need for strict adherence to them, not only in letter, but also in spirit, by Member States and also, in the light of its internal rules, by the Secretariat;

(b) Instruct its subsidiary organs to include in the agenda of each session an item on the control and limitation of the documentation of the organ itself in the spirit of paragraph 3 of General Assembly resolution 1272 (XIII) [*para. 300*].

B. Preparation and distribution of documents

107. The Special Committee recommends to the General Assembly that:

(a) Timely distribution of documents in all working languages should be scrupulously observed;

(b) All the subsidiary organs of the General Assembly should be required to complete their work and submit their reports before the opening of each regular session of the Assembly;

(c) Reports to be considered by the General Assembly should be as brief as possible and contain precise information confined to a description of the work done by the organ concerned, to the conclusions it has reached, to its decisions and to the recommendations made to the Assembly; the reports should include, where appropriate, a summary of proposals, conclusions and recommendations. As a rule, no previously issued material (working papers and other basic documents) should be incorporated in or appended to such reports, but, where necessary, referred to;

(d) Taking into account the needs of Member States, the number of copies of reports and other United Nations documents should, whenever appropriate, be limited, i.e., they should be issued in the /L. series [*para. 304*].[v]

C. RECORDS OF MEETINGS AND SOUND RECORDINGS

108. The Special Committee recommends that rule 60, as revised,[w] should be applied in accordance with the following observations:

(a) Summary records should continue to be provided for the General Committee and for all Main Committees other than the First Committee;

(b) The General Assembly, on the recommendation of the General Committee, should decide annually whether the option that has traditionally been approved for the Special

---

[v]For the recommendations concerning the reports of the Main Committees, see para. 43 above.
[w]Rule 58 of the present rules of procedure (see introduction, para. 30 (a)).

Political Committee to have, on specific request, transcriptions of the debates of some of its meetings, or portions thereof, should be maintained;

(c) The provision of summary records to subsidiary organs should be reviewed periodically by the General Assembly in the light of the report of the Joint Inspection Unit on the use of minutes instead of summary records, and of the comments of the Secretary-General and the Advisory Committee on Administrative and Budgetary Questions thereon;[x]

(d) Sound recordings should be kept by the Secretariat in accordance with its practice [*para. 309*].

IX. SUBSIDIARY ORGANS OF THE GENERAL ASSEMBLY
A. REDUCTION OF THE NUMBER OF ORGANS

109. The Special Committee recommends that the General Assembly should review, either periodically or when considering their reports, the usefulness of its various subsidiary organs [*para. 313*].

110. The Special Committee also recommends that the General Assembly should consider the possibility of merging some of these organs [*para. 314*].

B. COMPOSITION OF ORGANS

111. The Special Committee considers that membership of a body depends on the nature and function of that body and that it cannot, therefore, be subject to any general rule [*para. 318*].

112. The Special Committee is of the opinion that subsidiary organs of the General Assembly should, where appropriate, have the authority to invite a Member State which is not a member of the organ concerned to participate without vote in the discussion of a matter which the organ considers to be of particular interest to that Member State [*para. 319*].

113. The Special Committee is also of the opinion that the composition of subsidiary organs should be subject to periodic change [*para. 320*].

114. Finally, the Special Committee considers that visits of subsidiary organs away from their normal meeting places should be authorized by the General Assembly only when the nature of the work renders such visits essential [*para. 321*].

---

[x]E/4802 and Add. 1 and 2.

C. CALENDAR OF MEETINGS

115. The Special Committee recommends to the General Assembly that the Secretary-General should play a greater role in drawing up the calendar of meetings, it being understood that in every case the final decision rests with the organ concerned [*para. 323*].

X. OTHER QUESTIONS
A. CREDENTIALS OF DELEGATIONS

116. The Special Committee, while aware of the problems posed by the non-recognition by the General Assembly of a delegation's credentials, feels that it is not in a position to make any proposal on the matter [*para. 327*].

B. ROLE OF THE SECRETARY-GENERAL

117. The Special Committee is of the opinion that the Secretary-General should play an active role in making suggestions with regard to the organization of sessions, it being understood that the final decision on the recommendations he makes lies with the General Assembly [*para. 331*].

C. SECRETARIAT

118. The Special Committee considers that the question of the reorganization of the Secretariat, however valid it might be, does not come within its terms of reference. It is of the opinion, therefore, that it should not make any recommendation on the matter [*para. 333*].

D. GUIDANCE REGARDING GENERAL ASSEMBLY PROCEDURE AND ASSISTANCE TO PRESIDING OFFICERS
1. *Preparation of a manual on procedure*

119. The Special Committee recommends that the General Assembly should consider requesting the Secretary-General to prepare a systematic and comprehensive compilation of the conclusions which the Assembly may adopt on the basis of the reports of the Special Committee and of the Joint Inspection Unit, this compilation to form an annex to the rules of procedure of the General Assembly [para. 339].

2. *Repertory of Practice of United Nations Organs*

120. The Special Committee, recognizing the usefulness of the Repertory of Practice of United Nations Organs, expresses the hope that it will be brought up to date as quickly as possible [*para. 341*].

3. *Preparation of a repertory of practice on the rules of procedure of the General Assembly*

121. The Special Committee did not consider that it should endorse the proposal to issue a repertory of practice on the rules of procedure of the General Assembly [*para. 344*].

4. *Reminders of previous recommendations*

122. It was suggested that at the beginning of the session the President of the General Assembly should remind the Assembly of, and particularly invite the attention of the Chairmen of Main Committees to, the recommendations for improving the methods of work which were specifically approved in General Assembly resolution 1898 (XVIII).[y] While there was general agreement on the principle underlying that suggestion, the Special Committee did not feel that it need make any specific recommendation in that regard [*paras. 345 and 346*].

123. The Special Committee did not retain the suggestion that the report of the *Ad Hoc* Committee on the Improvement of the Methods of Work of the General Assembly[z] should be reissued on account of the financial implications that such a measure would entail [*paras. 345 and 346*].

5. *Assistance in procedural matters*

124. The Special Committee noted that it was not possible to assign a member of the Office of Legal Affairs continuously to each of the Main Committees but that legal advice was always furnished, either orally or in writing when requested [*para. 348*].

125. The Special Committee did not consider that it should make any recommendation on the proposal that the President of the General Assembly and the Chairmen of Main Committees should enlist several assistants under them, both from the

---

[y]See annex IV.

[z]*Official Records of the General Assembly, Eighteen Session, Annexes,* agenda item 25, document A/5423.

Secretariat and, wherever possible, from the delegations themselves, to whom they would allocate items on the agenda for the purpose of closely following them up with the delegations directly concerned and expediting the progress of the General Assembly [*paras. 347 and 348*].

E. STUDIES OF THÉ RULES OF PROCEDURE

126. The Special Committee did not consider that it should retain the suggestions concerning the insertion in the rules of procedure of the Economic and Social Council [*para. 352*].

127. The Special Committee took note of the proposal concerning a comparative study of the rules of procedure of the General Assembly and those of the governing bodies of the specialized agencies and suggests that the United Nations Institute for Training and Research should consider undertaking such a project [*para. 353*].

128. Lastly, the Special Committee recommends to the General Assembly that the Secretariat should be instructed to undertake a comparative study of the versions of the General Assembly's rules of procedure in the various official languages in order to ensure their concordance [*para. 354*].

F. SPECIAL TRAINING PROGRAMME

129. The Special Committee, aware of the training problems facing delegations, particularly as regards newly arrived representatives, suggests that the United Nations Institute for Training and Research should consider ways of helping to solve these problems [*para. 356*].

G. REGIONAL GROUPS

130. The Special Committee endorses the suggestion that the names of chairmen of the regional groups for the month should be published in the Journal of the United Nations and recommends that it should be left to the Secretariat to decide how often it should be applied [*para. 357 and 358*].

ANNEX VI

Decision 34/401 on the rationalization of the procedures and organization of the General Assembly[a]

I. ORGANIZATION OF THE SESSION
A. *General Committee*

1. The General Committee should, at the outset of each session, consider how the work of the session can best be rationalized.

2. The General Committee should also meet periodically throughout the session to review the progress of work and to make recommendations to the General Assembly on the general programme of the session and on measures aimed at improving its work.

B. *Schedule of meetings*

3. Both plenary and committee meetings should begin at 10.30 a.m. and 3 p.m. and, in order to expedite the work of the General Assembly, all meetings should begin promptly at the scheduled time.

C. *Allocation of items*

4. Substantive items should normally be discussed initially in a Main Committee and, therefore, items previously allocated to plenary meetings should henceforth be referred to a Main Committee unless there are compelling circumstances requiring their continued consideration in plenary meeting.

D. *General debate*

5. Out of consideration for the other speakers and in order to preserve the dignity of the general debate, delegations should refrain from expressing their congratulations in the General Assembly Hall after a speech has been delivered.

---

[a]Adopted by the General Assembly at its 4th, 46th, 82nd and 99th plenary meetings, on 21 September, 25 October, 29 November and 12 December 1979, on the recommendations of the General Committee. Section VI of the decision, which related mostly to the establishment of the *Ad Hoc* Committee on Subsidiary Organs, has not been reproduced in the present annex.

E. *Explanations of vote*

6.   Explanations of vote should be limited to ten minutes.

7.   When the same draft resolution is considered in a Main Committee and in plenary meeting, a delegation should, as far as possible, explain its vote only once, i.e., either in the Committee or in plenary meeting, unless that delegation's vote in plenary meeting is different from its vote in the Committee.

F. *Right of reply*

8.   Delegations should exercise their right of reply at the end of the day whenever two meetings have been scheduled for that day and whenever such meetings are devoted to the consideration of the same item.

9.   The number of interventions in the exercise of the right of the reply for any delegation at a given meeting should be limited to two per item.

10. The first intervention in the exercise of the right of reply for any delegation on any item at a given meeting should be limited to ten minutes and the second intervention should be limited to five minutes.

G. *Non-utilization of the rostrum*

11. Explanations of vote, interventions in the exercise of the right of reply and procedural motions should be made by delegations from their seats.

H. *Budgetary and financial questions*

12. It is imperative that Main Committees should allow sufficient time for the preparation of the estimate of expenditures by the Secretariat and for its consideration by the Advisory Committee on Administrative and Budgetary Questions and the Fifth Committee and that they should take this requirement into account when they adopt their programme of work.

13. Furthermore:

(a) A mandatory deadline, not later than 1 December, should be established for the submission to the Fifth Committee of all draft resolutions with financial implications;

(b) The Fifth Committee should, as a general practice, consider accepting without debate the recommendations of the Advisory Committee on Administrative and Budgetary Questions on the financial implications of draft resolutions up to a prescribed limit, namely, $25,000 on any one item:

(c) Firm deadlines should be set for the early submission of the reports of subsidiary organs which require consideration by the Fifth committee;

(d) A minimum period of forty-eight hours should be allowed between the submission and the voting of a proposal involving expenditure in order to allow the Secretary-General to prepare and present the related statement of administrative and financial implications.

I. *Reports of the Main Committees*

14. Reports of the Main Committees should be as concise as possible and, save in exceptional cases, should not contain a summary of the debates.

15. The practice of dealing in plenary meeting with reports of the Second Committee, whereby it is stated that the positions of delegations regarding draft resolutions recommended by the Second Committee have been made clear in the Committee and are reflected in the relevant official records, should be extended to reports of other committees.

J. *Balloting procedure*

16. The practice of dispensing with the secret ballot for elections to subsidiary organs when the number of candidates corresponds to the number of seats to be filled should become standard and the same practice should apply to the election of the President and Vice-Presidents of the General Assembly, unless a delegation specifically requests a vote on a given election.

K. *Concluding statements*

17. To save time at the end of the session, the practice of making concluding statements in the General Assembly and its Main Committees should be dispensed with except for statements by the presiding officers.

II. WORK OF THE MAIN COMMITTEES

18. Before the conclusion of a session of the General Assembly, regional groups should agree on the distribution of chairmanships among them for the following session.

19. Candidates for the chairmanships of the Main Committees should be nominated as soon as possible.

20. It is strongly recommended that nominees for the chairmanships of the Main Committees should have experience in the work of the General Assembly.

21. During sessions, the Chairmen or other officers of the Main Committees should be entrusted by their Committees, whenever appropriate, with the conduct of informal negotiations aimed at reaching agreement on specific issues.

22. Chairmen of Main Committees should fully exercise their authority under rule 106 of the rules of procedure and, in particular, propose more frequently the limitation of the time to be allowed to speakers or of the number of times each representative may speak on any given item.

23. The Main Committees which require the largest number of meetings should be encouraged to hold more meetings early in the session in order to ensure a better distribution of meetings over the whole session.

III. DOCUMENTATION

24. Subsidiary organs should be required to complete their work at the latest by 1 September, so that their reports may be available in all the working languages in time for consideration by the opening of the session of the General Assembly, and the Committee on Conferences should take this provision fully into account.

25. No reports should contain a compilation of other previous documents.

26. Subsidiary organs should not annex to their reports summary records of their meetings or other material which were already distributed to all Member States.

27. The General Assembly should review periodically the need for summary records of its subsidiary organs.

28. The General Assembly, including its Main Committees, should merely take note of those reports of the Secretary-General or subsidiary organs which do not require a decision by the Assembly and should neither debate nor adopt resolutions on them, unless specifically requested to do so by the Secretary-General or the organ concerned.

29. The publication of reports of the principal organs and of subsidiary organs of the General Assembly and of draft resolutions and amendments should be given priority over that of any individual communications received from Member States.

30. Member States should refrain, to the extent possible, from requesting the circulation of any individual communications as documents of the General Assembly and in lieu thereof, where circulation of such documents is desired, should, as far as possible, request such circulation under the cover of a not verbale in the official languages in which they submit them.

IV. RESOLUTIONS

31. Subsidiary organs reporting to the General Assembly should make every effort to submit draft resolutions in order to facilitate the consideration of the items.

32. Whenever possible, resolutions requesting the discussion of a question at a subsequent session should not call for the inclusion of a separate new item and such discussion should be held under the item under which the resolution was adopted.

V. PLANNING OF MEETINGS

33. The Committee on Conferences should be authorized to play a more effective role in the planning of meetings and in the use of conference facilities.

34. No subsidiary organ of the General Assembly should be permitted to meet at United Nations Headquarters during a regular session of the Assembly, unless explicitly authorized by the Assembly.

VI. SUBSIDIARY ORGANS OF THE GENERAL ASSEMBLY[b]

...

---

[b]This section, which related mostly to the establishment of the Ad Hoc Committee on Subsidiary Organs, has not been reproduced in the present annex.

ANNEX VII[a]

Conclusions of the Special Committee on the Charter of the United Nations and on the Strengthening of the Role of the Organization concerning the rationalization of the procedures of the General Assembly

1.   The agenda of the sessions of the General Assembly should be simplified as much as possible by grouping or merging related items, after consultation and with the agreement of the delegations concerned.[*]

2.   Specific items should be referred, where relevant, to other United Nations organs or to specialized agencies.   The right of States to request that specific items be discussed in the General Assembly should remain unimpaired.

3.   The recommendation in paragraph 28 of annex V to the rules of procedure of the General Assembly, according to which the Assembly should ensure, as far as possible, that the same questions, or the same aspects of a question, are not considered by more than one Main Committee, should be more fully implemented, except when it would be helpful for the Sixth Committee to be consulted on the legal aspects of questions under consideration by other Main Committees.

4.   The General Assembly should play more fully its role under rule 42 of the rules of procedure and paragraphs 1 and 2 of General Assembly decision 34/401, reviewing periodically the work of the Assembly and making the necessary recommendations.

5.   The Chairmen of the Main Committees should take the initiative, in the light of past experience, to propose the grouping of similar or related items and the holding of a single general debate on them.

6.   The Chairmen of the Main Committees should propose to the Committee the closing of the list of speakers on each item at a suitable early stage.

7.   Agreed programmes of work should be respected.   To this end, meetings should start at the scheduled time and the time allotted for meetings should be fully utilized.

8.   The officers of each Main Committee should review periodically the progress of work.   In the case of need, they should propose appropriate measures to ensure that the work remains on schedule.

---

[a]By resolution 39/88 B of 13 December 1984, the General Assembly approved the conclusions of the Special Committee on the Charter of the United Nations and on the Strengthening of the Role of the Organization concerning the rationalization of the procedures of the General Assembly and decided that they should be annexed to the rules of procedure; these conclusions are reproduced in the present annex.

[*]The view was expressed that the agreement of the delegations concerned was not an essential condition.

9. Negotiation procedures should be carefully selected to suit the particular subject-matter.

10. The Secretariat should facilitate informal considerations by providing adequate conference services.^{**}

11. The mandate of subsidiary organs should be carefully defined in order to avoid overlapping and duplication of work. The General Assembly should also review periodically the usefulness of its subsidiary organs.

12. Resolutions should be as clear and succinct as possible.

**The view was expressed that this recommendation was not intended to have any financial implications whatsoever and was approved subject to that condition.

4. INDEX TO THE RULES OF PROCEDURE OF THE GENERAL ASSEMBLY[1]

This index provides a reference to the rules of procedure and to the recommendations contained in the annexes to the rules. It should be noted that:

(a) In the first column, entitled "Rules", numbers in italics refer to the rules applicable to committees;

(b) In the second column, entitled "Annexes", Roman numerals I to V refer to the respective annexes and Arabic numerals indicate the relevant paragraphs in each annex.

---

[1] *Rules of Procedure of the General Assembly*, United Nations, New York, 1985, pp. 71-86.

	Rules	*Annexes*

C

E

N

5. PROVISIONAL RULES OF PROCEDURE OF THE SECURITY COUNCIL[1]

Contents

---

[1]*Provisional Rules of Procedure of the Security Council* (S/96/Rev.7), United Nations, New York, 1983. Adopted by the Security Council at its 1st meeting and amended at its 31st, 41st, 42nd, 44th and 48th meetings, on 9 April, 16 and 17 May, 6 and 24 June 1946; 138th and 222nd meetings, on 4 June and 9 December 1947; 468th meeting, on 28 February 1950; 1463rd meeting, on 24 January 1969; 1761st meeting, on 17 January 1974; and 2410th meeting, on 21 December 1982. Previous versions of the provisional rules of procedure were issued under the symbols S/96 and Rev. 1-6.

CHAPTER 1. MEETINGS
Rule 1

Meetings of the Security Council shall, with the exception of the periodic meetings referred to in rule 4, be held at the call of the President at any time he deems necessary, but the interval between meetings shall not exceed fourteen days.

Rule 2

The President shall call a meeting of the Security Council at the request of any member of the Security Council.

Rule 3

The President shall call a meeting of the Security Council if a dispute or situation is brought to the attention of the Security Council under Article 35 or under Article 11(3) of the Charter, or if the General Assembly makes recommendations or refers any question to the Security Council under Article 11(2), or if the Secretary-General brings to the attention of the Security Council any matter under Article 99.

Rule 4

Periodic meetings of the Security Council called for in Article 28(2) of the Charter shall be held twice a year, at such times as the Security Council may decide.

Rule 5

Meetings of the Security Council shall normally be held at the seat of the United Nations.

Any member of the Security Council or the Secretary-General may propose that the Security Council should meet at another place. Should the Security Council accept any such proposal, it shall decide upon the place and the period during which the Council shall meet at such place.

CHAPTER II. AGENDA
Rule 6

The Secretary-General shall immediately bring to the attention of all representatives on the Security Council all communications from States, organs of the United Nations, or the Secretary-General concerning any matter for the consideration of the Security Council in accordance with the provisions of the Charter.

Rule 7

The provisional agenda for each meeting of the Security Council shall be drawn up by the Secretary-General and approved by the President of the Security Council.

Only items which have been brought to the attention of the representatives on the Security Council in accordance with rule 6, items covered by rule 10, or matters which the Security Council had previously decided to defer, may be included in the provisional agenda.

Rule 8

The provisional agenda for a meeting shall be communicated by the Secretary-General to the representatives on the Security Council at least three days before the meeting, but in urgent circumstances it may be communicated simultaneously with the notice of the meeting.

Rule 9

The first item of the provisional agenda for each meeting of the Security Council shall be the adoption of the agenda.

Rule 10

Any item of the agenda of a meeting of the Security Council, consideration of which has not been completed at that meeting, shall, unless the Security Council otherwise decides, automatically be included in the agenda of the next meeting.

Rule 11

The Secretary-General shall communicate each week to the representatives on the Security Council a summary statement of matters of which the Security Council is seized and of the stage reached in their consideration.

Rule 12

The provisional agenda for each periodic meeting shall be circulated to the members of the Security Council at least twenty-one days before the opening of the meeting. Any subsequent change in or addition to the provisional agenda shall be brought to the notice of the members at least five days before the meeting. The Security Council may, however, in urgent circumstances, make additions to the agenda at any time during a periodic meeting.

The provisions of rule 7, paragraph 1, and of rule 9, shall apply also to periodic meetings.

CHAPTER III. REPRESENTATION AND CREDENTIALS
Rule 13

Each member of the Security Council shall be represented at the meetings of the Security Council by an accredited representative. The credentials of a representative on the Security Council shall be communicated to the Secretary-General not less than twenty-four hours before he takes his seat on the Security Council. The credentials shall be issued either by the Head of the State or of the Government concerned or by its Minister of Foreign Affairs. The Head of Government or Minister of Foreign Affairs of each member of the Security Council shall be entitled to sit on the Security Council without submitting credentials.

Rule 14

Any Member of the United Nations not a member of the Security Council and any State not a Member of the United Nations, if invited to participate in a meeting or meetings of the Security Council, shall submit credentials for the representative appoin ted by it for this purpose. The credentials of such a representative shall be communicated to the Secretary-General not less than twenty-four hours before the first meeting which he is invited to attend.

Rule 15

The credentials of representatives on the Security Council and of any representative appointed in accordance with rule 14 shall be examined by the Secretary-General who shall submit a report to the Security Council for approval.

Rule 16

Pending the approval of the credentials of a representative on the Security Council in accordance with rule 15, such representative shall be seated provisionally with the same rights as other representatives.

Rule 17

Any representative on the Security Council, to whose credentials objection has been made within the Security Council, shall continue to sit with the same rights as other representatives until the Security Council has decided the matter.

CHAPTER IV. PRESIDENCY
Rule 18

The presidency of the Security Council shall be held in turn by the members of the Security Council in the English alphabetical order of their names. Each President shall hold office for one calendar month.

Rule 19

The President shall preside over the meetings of the Security Council and, under the authority of the Security Council, shall represent it in its capacity as an organ of the United Nations.

Rule 20

Whenever the President of the Security Council deems that for the proper fulfilment of the responsibilities of the presidency he should not preside over the Council during the consideration of a particular question with which the member he represents is directly connected, he shall indicate his decision to the Council. The presidential chair shall then devolve, for the purpose of the consideration of that question, on the representative of the member next in English alphabetical order, it being understood that the provisions of this rule shall apply to the representatives on the Security Council called upon successively to preside. This rule shall not affect the representative capacity of the President as stated in rule 19, or his duties under rule 7.

CHAPTER V. SECRETARIAT
Rule 21

The Secretary-General shall act in that capacity in all meetings of the Security Council. The Secretary-General may authorize a deputy to act in his place at meetings of the Security Council.

Rule 22

The Secretary-General, or his deputy acting on his behalf, may make either oral or written statements to the Security Council concerning any question under consideration by it.

Rule 23

The Secretary-General may be appointed by the Security Council, in accordance with rule 28, as rapporteur for a specified question.

Rule 24

The Secretary-General shall provide the staff required by the Security Council. This staff shall form a part of the Secretariat.

Rule 25

The Secretary-General shall give to representatives on the Security Council notice of meetings of the Security Council and of its commissions and committees.

Rule 26

The Secretary-General shall be responsible for the preparation of documents required by the Security Council and shall, except in urgent circumstances, distribute them at least forty-eight hours in advance of the meeting at which they are to be considered.

CHAPTER VI. CONDUCT OF BUSINESS
Rule 27

The President shall call upon representatives in the order in which they signify their desire to speak.

Rule 28

The Security Council may appoint a commission or committee or a rapporteur for a specified question.

Rule 29

The President may accord precedence to any rapporteur appointed by the Security Council.

The Chairman of a commission or committee, or the rapporteur appointed by the commission or committee to present its report, may be accorded precedence for the purpose of explaining the report.

Rule 30

If a representative raises a point of order, the President shall immediately state his ruling. If it is challenged, the President shall submit his ruling to the Security Council for immediate decision and it shall stand unless overruled.

Rule 31

Proposed resolutions, amendments and substantive motions shall normally be placed before the representatives in writing.

Rule 32

Principal motions and draft resolutions shall have precedence in the order of their submission.

Parts of a motion or of a draft resolution shall be voted on separately at the request of any representative, unless the original mover objects.

Rule 33

The following motions shall have precedence in the order named over all principal motions and draft resolutions relative to the subject before the meeting:

1. To suspend the meeting;
2. To adjourn the meeting;
3. To adjourn the meeting to a certain day or hour;
4. To refer any matter to a committee, to the Secretary-General or to a rapporteur;

5. To postpone discussion of the question to a certain day or indefinitely; or

6. To introduce an amendment.

Any motion for the suspension or for the simple adjournment of the meeting shall be decided without debate.

Rule 34

It shall not be necessary for any motion or draft resolution proposed by a representative on the Security Council to be seconded before being put to a vote.

Rule 35

A motion or draft resolution can at any time be withdrawn so long as no vote has been taken with respect to it.

If the motion or draft resolution has been seconded, the representative on the Security Council who has seconded it may require that it be put to the vote as his motion or draft resolution with the same right of precedence as if the original mover had not withdrawn it.

Rule 36

If two or more amendments to a motion or draft resolution are proposed, the President shall rule on the order in which they are to be voted upon. Ordinarily, the Security Council shall first vote on the amendment furthest removed in substance from the original proposal and then on the amendment next furthest removed until all amendments have been put to the vote, but when an amendment adds to or deletes from the text of a motion or draft resolution, that amendment shall be voted on first.

Rule 37

Any Member of the United Nations which is not a member of the Security Council may be invited, as the result of a decision of the Security Council, to participate, without vote, in the discussion of any question brought before the Security Council when the Security Council considers that the interests of that Member are specially affected, or when a Member brings a matter to the attention of the Security Council in accordance with Article 35 (1) of the Charter.

Rule 38

Any Member of the United Nations invited in accordance with the preceding rule, or in application of Article 32 of the Charter, to participate in the discussions of the Security Council may submit proposals and draft resolutions. These proposals and draft resolutions may be put to a vote only at the request of a representative on the Security Council.

Rule 39

The Security Council may invite members of the Secretariat or other persons, whom it considers competent for the purpose, to supply it with information or to give other assistance in examining matters within its competence.

CHAPTER VII. VOTING
Rule 40

Voting in the Security Council shall be in accordance with the relevant Articles of the Charter and of the Statute of the International Court of Justice.

CHAPTER VIII. LANGUAGES
Rule 41

Arabic, Chinese, English, French, Russian and Spanish shall be both the official and the working languages of the Security Council.

Rule 42

Speeches made in any of the six languages of the Security Council shall be interpreted into the other five languages.

Rule 43

[Deleted]

Rule 44

Any representative may make a speech in a language other than the languages of the Security Council. In this case, he shall himself provide for interpretation into one of those languages. Interpretation into the other languages of the Security Council by the interpreters of the Secretariat may be based on the interpretation given in the first such language.

Rule 45

Verbatim records of meetings of the Security Council shall be drawn up in the languages of the Council.

Rule 46

All resolutions and other documents shall be published in the languages of the Security Council.

Rule 47

Documents of the Security Council shall, if the Security Council so decides, be published in any language other than the languages of the Council.

CHAPTER IX. PUBLICITY OF MEETINGS, RECORDS
Rule 48

Unless it decides otherwise, the Security Council shall meet in public. Any recommendation to the General Assembly regarding the appointment of the Secretary-General shall be discussed and decided at a private meeting.

Rule 49

Subject to the provisions of rule 51, the verbatim record of each meeting of the Security Council shall be made available to the representatives on the Security Council and to the representatives of any other States which have participated in the meeting not later than 10 a.m. of the first working day following the meeting.

Rule 50

The representatives of the States which have participated in the meeting shall, within two working days after the time indicated in rule 49, inform the Secretary-General of any corrections they wish to have made in the verbatim record.

Rule 51

The Security Council may decide that for a private meeting the record shall be made in a single copy alone. This record shall be kept by the Secretary-General. The representatives of the States which have participated in the meeting shall, within a period of ten days, inform the Secretary-General of any corrections they wish to have made in this record.

Rule 52

Corrections that have been requested shall be considered approved unless the President is of the opinion that they are sufficiently important to be submitted to the representatives on the Security Council shall submit within two working days any comments they may wish to make. In the absence of objections in this period of time, the record shall be corrected as requested.

Rule 53

The verbatim record referred to in rule 49 or the record referred to in rule 51, in which no corrections have been requested in the period of time required by rules 50 and 51, respectively, or which has been corrected in accordance with the provisions of rule 52, shall be considered as approved. It shall be signed by the President and shall become the official record of the Security Council.

Rule 54

The official record of public meetings of the Security Council, as well as the documents annexed thereto, shall be published in the official languages as soon as possible.

Rule 55

At the close of each private meeting the Security Council shall issue a communique through the Secretary-General.

Rule 56

The representatives of the Members of the United Nations which have taken part in a private meeting shall at all times have the right to consult the record of that meeting in the office of the Secretary-General. The Security Council may at any time grant access to this record to authorized representatives of other Members of the United Nations.

Rule 57

The Secretary-General shall, once each year, submit to the Security Council a list of the records and documents which up to that time have been considered confidential. The Security Council shall decide which of these shall be made available to other Members of the United Nations, which shall be made public, and which shall continue to remain confidential.

CHAPTER X. ADMISSION OF NEW MEMBERS
Rule 58

Any State which desires to become a Member of the United Nations shall submit an application to the Secretary-General. This application shall contain a declaration made in a formal instrument that it accepts the obligations contained in the Charter.

Rule 59

The Secretary-General shall immediately place the application for membership before the representatives on the Security Council. Unless the Security Council decides otherwise, the application shall be referred by the President to a committee of the Security Council upon which each member of the Security Council shall be represented. The committee shall examine any application referred to it and report its conclusions thereon to the Council not less than thirty-five days in advance of a regular session of the General Assembly or, if a special session of the General Assembly is called, not less than fourteen days in advance of such session.

Rule 60

The Security Council shall decide whether in its judgement the applicant is a peace-loving State and is able and willing to carry out the obligations contained in the Charter and, accordingly, whether to recommend the applicant State for membership.

If the Security Council recommends the applicant State for membership, it shall forward to the General Assembly the recommendation with a complete record of the discussion.

If the Security Council does not recommend the applicant State for membership or postpones the consideration of the application, it shall submit a special report to the General Assembly with a complete record of the discussion.

In order to ensure the consideration of its recommendation at the next session of the General Assembly following the receipt of the application, the Security Council shall make its recommendation not less than twenty-five days in advance of a regular session of the General Assembly, nor less than four days in advance of a special session.

In special circumstances, the Security Council may decide to make a recommendation to the General Assembly concerning an application for membership subsequent to the expiration of the time limits set forth in the preceding paragraph.

CHAPTER XI. RELATIONS WITH OTHER UNITED NATIONS ORGANS
Rule 61

Any meeting of the Security Council held in pursuance of the Statute of the International Court of Justice for the purpose of the election of members of the Court shall continue until as many candidates as are required for all the seats to be filled have obtained in one or more ballots an absolute majority of votes.

6. RULES OF PROCEDURE OF THE ECONOMIC AND SOCIAL COUNCIL[1]

CONTENTS

[1]United Nations Document: E/5715/Rev. 1, New York, 1983.

---

[1]The annex provides the relevant references with regard to the rules of procedure, including the decisions by which they were adopted.

I. SESSIONS
ORGANIZATIONAL AND REGULAR SESSIONS
Rule 1

The Council shall normally hold an organizational session and two regular sessions each year.

DATES OF CONVENING AND ADJOURNMENT
Rule 2

Subject to rule 3, the organizational session shall be convened on the first Tuesday in February, the first regular session on the first Tuesday in May and the second regular session on the first Wednesday in July. The second regular session shall be adjourned at least six weeks before the opening of the regular session of the General Assembly.

Rule 3

Any member of the Council or the Secretary-General may request an alteration of the date of a regular session. The President shall, through the Secretary-General, forthwith communicate the request to all members of the Council, together with such observation as the secretary-General may present. If a majority of the members of the Council concurs in the request within eight days of the communication, the Council shall be convened accordingly.

SPECIAL SESSIONS
Rule 4

1.   Special sessions of the Council shall be held:
(a) By decision of the Council;
(b) Upon the request or with the concurrence of a majority of the members of the Council;
(c) Upon the request of the General Assembly or the Security Council.
2.   The President, with the concurrence of the Vice-Presidents and, as appropriate, in consultation with members of the Council, may also call a special session of the Council.

3. Should a request for a special session be made by the Trusteeship Council, by any Member of the United Nations or by a specialized agency,[1] the President shall, through the Secretary-General, forthwith communicate the request to all members of the Council. Unless the President and the Vice-Presidents, as appropriate in consultation with members of the Council, have agreed to the request within four days of its receipt, the President shall, through the Secretary-General, inquire of all members of the Council whether or not they concur in the request; the replies to such an inquiry shall be communicated to the Secretary-General within eight days. If a majority of the members concurs in the request, the Council shall be convened accordingly.

4. Unless otherwise indicated in a decision or by a majority of the members of the Council, special sessions shall be convened within six weeks of a decision to hold such a session or of receipt by the President of a request for such a session, at a date fixed by the President.

PLACE OF SESSIONS
Rule 5

Sessions shall be held at the Headquarter of the United Nations unless, in pursuance of a previous decision of the Council or at the request of a majority of its members, another place is designated for the whole or part of a session.

NOTIFICATION OF OPENING DATE OF SESSIONS
Rule 6

The President shall, through the Secretary-General, notify the Members of the United Nations, the President of the Security Council, the President of the Trusteeship Council, the specialized agencies, the intergovernmental organizations referred to in rule 79 and the non-governmental organizations in category I or II or on the Roster of the date of the opening of each session. Such notification shall be sent at least six weeks in advance of the Organizational session or a regular session and at least twelve days in advance of a special session. If a special session is requested by the General Assembly or the Security Council, the President may reduce the period of notice to not less than eight days.

---

[1]When the term "specialized agency" is used in these rules, it refers to specialized agencies brought into relationship with the United Nations; it also includes the International Atomic Energy Agency.

ADJOURNMENT OF SESSIONS
Rule 7

The Council may decide at any session to adjourn temporarily and resume its meetings at a later date.

II. AGENDA
BASIC PROGRAMME OF WORK
Rule 8

In the course of the organizational session the Council shall draw up, with the assistance of the Secretary-General, the basic programme of its work for the year.

DRAWING UP OF THE PROVISIONAL AGENDA
Rule 9

1. The Secretary-General shall draw up the provisional agenda for each session of the Council. He shall submit to the Council;

(a) The provisional agenda for the organizational session at least three weeks in advance of the opening of that session;

(b) The provisional agenda for the first regular session at the organizational session;

(c) The provisional agenda for the second regular session at the first regular session.

2. The provisional agenda shall include all items required by these rules and by the basic programme of work, or proposed by:

(a) The Council;

(b) The General Assembly;

(c) The Security Council;

(d) The Trusteeship Council;

(e) A Member of the United Nations;

(f) The Secretary-General;

(g) A specialized agency, subject to rule 76.

3. A non-governmental organization in category I may request that the Committee on Non-Governmental Organizations recommended that items of special interest to the organization be included in the provisional agenda of the Council. In considering the request the Committee shall take into account:

(a) The adequacy of the documentation submitted by the organization;

(b) The extent to which the item may lend itself to early and constructive action by the Council;

(c) The possibility that the item might more appropriately be dealt with elsewhere than in the Council.

Any decision by the Committee not to grant a request submitted by a non-governmental organization to recommend that an item be placed on the provisional agenda of the Council shall be considered as final.

4. The agenda for the organizational session shall include the consideration of the provisional agenda for the first regular session of the Council. The agenda for the first regular session shall include the consideration of the provisional agenda for the second regular session.

5. Agenda items shall be arranged in an integrated manner, so that similar or connected issues can be discussed in one debate and under a single heading.

COMMUNICATION OF THE PROVISIONAL AGENDA
Rule 10

After the Council has considered the provisional agenda for a regular session as provided in paragraph 4 of rule 9, that agenda, incorporating any amendments made by the Council, shall be communicated by the Secretary-General to the Members of the United Nations, the President of the Security Council, the President of the Trusteeship Council, the specialized agencies, the intergovernmental organizations referred to in rule 79 and the non-governmental organizations in category I or II or on the Roster.

PROVISIONAL AGENDA FOR A SPECIAL SESSION
Rule 11

The provisional agenda for a special session shall consist only of those items proposed for consideration in the request for the holding of the session, subject, when appropriate, to rule 18. It shall be transmitted to the authorities listed in rule 10 at the same time as the notice convening the Council.

SUPPLEMENTARY ITEMS
Rule 12

1. The inclusion of supplementary items in a provisional agenda that has been considered by the Council under paragraph 4 of rule 9 may be proposed by the General Assembly, the Security Council, the Trusteeship Council, a Member of the United Nations, the Secretary-General or, subject to rule 76, a specialized agency, or by the Committee on Non-Governmental Organizations in accordance with the procedure provided in paragraph 3 of rule 9. The proposal shall, except if made by the General

Assembly, the Security Council or the Trusteeship Council, be accompanied by a supporting statement from the authority initiating it, indicating the urgency of the consideration of the item and the reasons that precluded its submission before the consideration of the provisional agenda by the Council.

2. The supplementary items shall be placed by the Secretary-General on a supplementary list and communicated to the Council together with the supporting statements and such observations as the Secretary-General may wish to offer.

ADOPTION OF THE AGENDA
Rule 13

1. The council shall at the beginning of each session, after the election of the Bureau when required under rule 18, adopt the agenda for that session on the basis of the provisional agenda and the supplementary list referred to in rule 12.

2. An organ of the United Nations, a Member of the United Nations or a specialized agency that has proposed the inclusion of an item in the provisional agenda or the supplementary list shall be entitled to be heard by the Council, or by the appropriate sessional committee designated by the Council, on the inclusion of the item in the agenda.

3. In the case of an item placed on the provisional agenda or on the supplementary list at the request of the Committee on Non-Governmental Organizations under paragraph 3 of rule 9 or under paragraph 1 rule of 12, the non-governmental organization that proposed the item to the Committee shall be entitled to be heard by the Council, or by the appropriate sessional committee designated by the Council, on the inclusion of the item in the agenda.

4. Unless the Council decides otherwise, if the documentation relating to an item of the agenda has not been circulated, in all working languages, six weeks before the opening of a regular session, the item shall be postponed to the following session, except in the case of reports of subsidiary and other bodies on meetings that have been concluded twelve weeks or less before the opening of the session of the Council.

ALLOCATION OF ITEMS
Rule 14

The Council shall allocate items between the plenary meetings and its sessional committees, and may refer items without preliminary debate:

(a) To a specialized agency, another organization or programme of the United Nations system, one or more of its commissions or standing committees, or the Secretary-General, for study and report to the Council at a subsequent session.

(b) To the proposer of the item, for further information or documentation.

REVISION OF THE AGENDA
Rule 15

During a session, the Council may revise the agenda by adding, deleting, deferring or amending items. Only important and urgent items shall be added to the agenda during a session. The Council may refer to a committee any request to add an item to the agenda.

III. REPRESENTATION, CREDENTIALS
REPRESENTATIVES, ALTERNATES AND ADVISERS
Rule 16

Each member of the Council shall be represented by an accredited representative, who may be accompanied by such alternate representatives and advisers as may be required.

CREDENTIALS
Rule 17

The credentials of representatives and the names of alternate representatives and advisers shall be submitted to the Secretary-General not less than three days before the first meeting they are to attend. the Bureau shall examine the credentials and submit a report thereon to the Council.

IV. BUREAU
ELECTION AND SPECIAL RESPONSIBILITIES
Rule 18

1. Each year, at the commencement of its first meeting, the Council shall elect a President and four Vice-Presidents[2] from among the representatives of its members. The President and the Vice-Presidents shall constitute the Bureau.

---

[2]In the election of the President of the Council, regard shall be had for the equitable geographical rotation of this office among the following regional groups: African States, Asian States, Eastern European States, Latin American States, and Western European and other States. The four Vice-Presidents of the Council shall be elected on the basis of equitable geographical distribution from the regional groups other than the one to which the President belongs.

2. The Council, upon the recommendation of the President, shall decide on the special responsibilities of each of the Vice-Presidents.

TERM OF OFFICE
Rule 19

The President and Vice-Presidents shall, subject to rule 22, hold office until their successors are elected. They shall be eligible for re-election.

ACTING PRESIDENT
Rule 20

1. If the President finds it necessary to be absent during a meeting or any part thereof, he shall designate one of the Vice-Presidents to take his place.

2. If the President ceases to hold office pursuant to rule 22, the remaining members of the Bureau shall designate one of the Vice-Presidents to take his place until the election of a new President.

POWERS OF THE ACTING PRESIDENT
Rule 21

A Vice-President acting as President shall have the powers and duties of the President.

REPLACEMENT OF THE PRESIDENT OR A VICE-PRESIDENT
Rule 22

If the President or any Vice-President ceases to be able to carry out his functions or ceases to be a representative of a member of the Council, or if the Member of the United Nations of which he is a representative ceases to be a member of the Council, he shall cease to hold such office and a new President or Vice-President shall be elected for the unexpired term.

VOTING RIGHTS OF THE PRESIDENT
Rule 23

The President, or a Vice-President acting as President, may delegate his right to vote to another member of his delegation.

V. SESSIONAL BODIES AND SUBSIDIARY ORGANS
ESTABLISHMENT
Rule 24

1. The Council may establish and define the composition and the terms of reference of:

(a) Functional commissions and regional commissions;

(b) Sessional committees of the whole and other sessional bodies;

(c) Standing and *ad hoc* committees.

2. Except for the regional commissions, the commissions and committees of the Council shall not create either standing or *ad hoc* intersessional subsidiary bodies without prior approval of the Council.

MEMBERSHIP
Rule 25

Unless the Council decides otherwise, the members of any body or organ of limited membership, other than those subsidiary to a regional commission, shall be elected by the Council.

OFFICERS
Rule 26

1. The Chairman of a sessional committee of the whole shall be one of the Vice-Presidents, designated by the Council upon the recommendation of the President. Each sessional committee of the whole shall elect two Vice-Chairmen.

2. Unless the Council decides otherwise, all other bodies and organs shall elect their own officers.

RULES OF PROCEDURE
Rule 27

1. The rules of procedure contained in chapters VI and VII to XII shall apply to the proceedings of the committees and sessional bodies of the Council and their subsidiary bodies, unless provided otherwise.

2. The rules of procedure of the commissions and their subsidiary bodies shall be drawn up by the Council, unless it decides otherwise.

VI. SECRETARIAT
DUTIES OF THE SECRETARY-GENERAL
Rule 28

1.   The Secretary-General shall act in that capacity in all meetings of the Council. He may designate a member of the Secretariat to act as his representative.

2.   He shall provide and direct the staff required by the Council and be responsible for all the arrangements that may be necessary for its meetings.

3.   He shall keep the members of the Council informed of any questions that may be brought before it for consideration.

DUTIES OF THE SECRETARIAT
Rule 29

The Secretariat shall:

(a) Interpret speeches made at meetings;

(b) Receive, translate and circulate documents;

(c) Print, publish and circulate the records of the sessions, the resolutions of the Council and the required documentation;

(d) Have custody of the documents in the archives;

(e) Generally perform all other work that may be required.

STATEMENTS BY THE SECRETARIAT
Rule 30

The Secretary-General, or his representative, may, subject to rule 44, make oral as well as written statements to the Council concerning any question under consideration.

ESTIMATES OF EXPENDITURE
Rule 31

1.   The Secretary-General shall circulate to the Council for its consideration every odd-numbered year a draft four-year medium-term plan and biennial programme budget covering activities in the economic, social and human rights fields, prepared on the basis of programme objectives approved and priorities established by the Council and other competent bodies.

2.   Programme budget proposals recommended by a committee or commission of the Council for its approval must be stated in terms of the objectives to be achieved. The Secretary-General shall have an opportunity to determine the most effective and

economical means of implementing those proposals and make appropriate recommendations to the Council thereon.

3. Before a proposal involving the expenditure of United Nations funds is approved by the Council, the Secretary-General shall prepare and provide to the Council an estimate of the programme budget implications of implementing the proposal. The President shall draw attention to that estimate and invite discussion on it when the proposal is considered by the Council. In accordance with the proposal approved by the Council, the Secretary-General shall make appropriate recommendations in the biennial programme budget and medium-term plan he subsequently presents to the General Assembly.

4. In cases of exceptional urgency, the Council may request the Secretary-General to implement a new programme decision, as a matter of priority, during the current biennium. Such a new programme shall be implemented either within the current programme budget or by additional appropriations to be approved by the General Assembly in accordance with the Financial Regulations and Rules of the United Nations.

VII. LANGUAGES
OFFICIAL AND WORKING LANGUAGES
Rule 32

Arabic, Chinese, English, French, Russian and Spanish shall be the official languages and English, French and Spanish the working languages of the Council.

INTERPRETATION
Rule 33

1. Speeches made in an official language shall be interpreted into the other official languages.

2. A speaker may make a speech in a language other than an official language if he provides for interpretation into one of the official languages. Interpretation into the other official languages by the interpreters of the Secretariat may be based on the interpretation given in the first such language.

LANGUAGES OF RECORDS
Rule 34

Records shall be drawn up in the working languages. A translation of the whole or part of any record into either of the other official languages shall be furnished if requested by a representative.

LANGUAGES OF RESOLUTIONS AND OTHER FORMAL DECISIONS
Rule 35

All resolutions and other formal decisions of the Council shall be published in the official languages.[3]

VIII. PUBLIC AND PRIVATE MEETINGS
GENERAL PRINCIPLES
Rule 36

The meetings of the Council shall be held in public unless it decides otherwise.

IX. RECORDS
SOUND RECORDINGS OF MEETINGS
Rule 37

Sound recordings of the meetings of the Council and of its sessional committees of the whole shall be made and kept by the Secretariat. Such recordings may also be made and kept of the meetings of other subsidiary organs if so decided by the Council.

RECORDS OF PUBLIC MEETINGS
Rule 38

1.   Summary records of public meetings of the Council, and its subsidiary organs where authorized, shall be prepared by the Secretariat in the working languages of the Council. They shall be distributed in provisional form as soon as possible to all members of the Council or of the organ concerned, and to any other participants in the meeting, who may, within three working days of their receipt, submit corrections to the Secretariat; at the end of sessions and in other special circumstances, the presiding officer may, in consultation with the Secretary-General, extend the time for submitting corrections. Any disagreement concerning such corrections shall be decided by the presiding officer of the body to which the records relates, after consulting, where necessary, the sound recordings of the proceedings. Separate corrigenda to provisional records shall not normally be issued.

---

[3]Such resolutions and decisions shall also be published in other languages as may be provided by the General Assembly.

2.   The summary records, with any corrections incorporated, shall be distributed promptly to the Members of the United Nations and to the specialized agencies. On publication, these records may be consulted by the public.

3.   Neither verbatim nor summary records shall be provided for newly established subsidiary organs of the Council unless they have been specifically authorized by the Council.

RECORDS OF PRIVATE MEETINGS
Rule 39

The records of private meetings of the Council shall be distributed promptly to all members of the Council and to any other participants in these meetings. They shall be made available to other Members of the United Nations upon decision of the Council. They may be made public at such time and under such conditions as the Council may decide.

RESOLUTIONS AND OTHER FORMAL DECISIONS
Rule 40

As soon as possible, the text of the resolutions and other formal decisions adopted by the Council shall be distributed to all members of the Council and to any other participants in the session. The printed text of such resolutions and other formal decisions shall be distributed as soon as possible after the close of the session to the Members of the United Nations, to the specialized agencies and to the intergovernmental organizations referred to in rule 79.

X. CONDUCT OF BUSINESS
QUORUM
Rule 41

The President may declare a meeting open and permit debate to proceed when representatives of at least one third of the members of the Council are present. The presence of representatives of a majority of the members of the body concerned shall be required for any decision to be taken.

GENERAL POWERS OF THE PRESIDENT
Rule 42

1. In addition to exercising the powers conferred upon him elsewhere by these rules, the President shall declare the opening and closing of each plenary meeting of the Council, direct the discussions, ensure observance of these rules, accord the right to speak, put questions to the vote and announce decisions. The President, subject to these rules, shall have complete control of the proceedings of the Council and over the maintenance of order at its meetings. He shall rule on points of order. He may propose to the Council the closure of the list of speakers, a limitation on the time to be allowed to speakers and on the number of times the representative of each member may speak on an item, the adjournment or closure of the debate, and the suspension or adjournment of a meeting.

2. The President, in the exercise of his functions, remains under the authority of the Council.

POINTS OF ORDER
Rule 43

1. During the discussion of any matter, a representative may at any time raise a point of order, which shall be decided immediately by the President in accordance with these rules. A representative may appeal against the ruling of the President. The appeal shall be immediately put to the vote, and the ruling of the President shall stand unless overruled by a majority of the members present and voting.

2. A representative may not, in raising a point of order, speak on the substance of the matter under discussion.

SPEECHES
Rule 44

1. No one may address the Council without having previously obtained the permission of the President. Subject to rules 43, 46 and 49 to 51, the President shall call upon speakers in the order in which they signify their desire to speak.

2. Debate shall be confined to the question before the Council, and the President may call a speaker to order if his remarks are not relevant to the subject under discussion.

3. The Council may limit the time allowed to speakers and the number of times the representative of each member may speak on any question; permission to speak on a motion to set such limits shall be accorded only to two representatives favouring and to

two opposing such limits, after which the motion shall be put to the vote immediately. Interventions on procedural questions shall not exceed five minutes unless the Council decides otherwise. When debate is limited and a speaker exceeds the allotted time,the President shall call him to order without delay.

CLOSING OF LIST OF SPEAKERS
Rule 45

During the course of a debate the President may announce the list of speakers and, with the consent of the Council, declare the list closed. When there are no more speakers, the President shall, with the consent of the Council, declare the debate closed. Such closure shall have the same effect as closure by decision of the Council.

RIGHT OF REPLY
Rule 46

The right of reply shall be accorded by the President to any member who requests it. Representatives should attempt, in exercising this right, to be as brief as possible and preferably to deliver their statements at the end of the meeting at which this right is requested.

CONGRATULATIONS
Rule 47

Congratulations to the newly elected members of the Bureau shall be expressed only by the outgoing President or a member of his delegation, or by a representative designated by the outgoing President.

CONDOLENCES
Rule 48

Condolences shall be expressed solely by the President on behalf of all members. The President, with the agreement of the Council, may dispatch a message on behalf of all members of the Council.

SUSPENSION OR ADJOURNMENT OF THE MEETING
Rule 49

During the discussion of any matter, a representative may at any time move the suspension or the adjournment of the meeting. No discussion on such motions shall be permitted, and they shall be put to the vote immediately.

ADJOURNMENT OF DEBATE
Rule 50

A representative may at any time move the adjournment of the debate on the item under discussion. Permission to speak on the motion shall be accorded only to two representatives favouring and to two opposing the adjournment, after which the motion shall be put to the vote immediately.

CLOSURE OF DEBATE
Rule 51

A representative may at any time move the closure of the debate on the item under discussion, whether or not any other representative has signified his wish to speak. Permission to speak on the motion shall be accorded only to two representatives opposing the closure, after which the motion shall be put to the vote immediately.

ORDER OF MOTIONS
Rule 52

Subject to rule 43, the motions indicated below shall have precedence in the following order over all proposals or other motions before the meeting:
(a) To suspend the meeting;
(b) To adjourn the meeting;
(c) To adjourn the debate on the item under discussion;
(d) To close the debate on the item under discussion.

DISCUSSION OF REPORTS OF SESSIONAL COMMITTEES OF THE WHOLE
Rule 53

Discussion of a report of a sessional committee of the whole in a plenary meeting of the Council shall take place if at least one third of the members present and voting at the plenary meeting consider such discussion to be necessary. A motion to this effect shall not be discussed but shall be put to the vote immediately.

SUBMISSION OF PROPOSALS AND SUBSTANTIVE AMENDMENTS
Rule 54

Proposals and substantive amendments shall normally be submitted in writing to the Secretary-General who shall circulate copies to the members of the Council in all the official languages. Unless the Council decides otherwise, proposals and substantive amendments shall be discussed or put to the vote no earlier than twenty-four hours after copies have been circulated to all members.

WITHDRAWAL OF PROPOSALS AND MOTIONS
Rule 55

A proposal or a motion may be withdrawn by its sponsor at any time before voting on it has commenced, provided that it has not been amended. A proposal or a motion thus withdrawn may be reintroduced by any representative.

DECISIONS ON COMPETENCE
Rule 56

A motion calling for a decision on the competence of the Council to adopt a proposal submitted to it shall be put to the vote before a vote is taken on the proposal in question.

RECONSIDERATION OF PROPOSALS
Rule 57

When a proposal has been adopted or rejected, it may not be reconsidered at the same session unless the Council so decides. Permission to speak on a motion to reconsider shall be accorded only to two representatives opposing the motion, after which it shall be put to the vote immediately.

XI. VOTING AND ELECTIONS
VOTING RIGHTS
Rule 58

Each member of the Council shall have one vote.

REQUEST FOR A VOTE
Rule 59

A proposal or motion before the Council for decision shall be voted upon if any member so requests. Where no member requests a vote, the Council may adopt proposals or motions without a vote.

MAJORITY REQUIRED
Rule 60

1.   Decisions of the Council shall be made by a majority of the members present and voting.

2.   For the purpose of these rules, the phrase "members present and voting" means members casting an affirmative or negative vote. Members which abstain from voting are considered as not voting.

METHOD OF VOTING
Rule 61

1.   Except as provided in rule 68, the Council shall normally vote by show of hands, except that a representative may request a roll-call, which shall then be taken in the English alphabetical order of the names of the members, beginning with the member whose name is drawn by lot by the President. The name of each member shall be called in all roll-calls, and its representative shall reply "yes", "no", or "abstention".

2.   When the Council votes by mechanical means, a non-recorded vote shall replace a vote by show of hands and recorded vote shall replace a roll-call. A representative may request a recorded vote. In the case of a recorded vote, the Council shall, unless a representative request otherwise, dispense with the procedure of calling out the names of the members.

3.   The vote of each member participating in a roll-call or a recorded vote shall be inserted in the record.

EXPLANATION OF VOTE
Rule 62

Representatives may make brief statements consisting solely of explanation of their votes, before the voting has commenced or after the voting has been completed. The representative of a member sponsoring a proposal or motion shall not speak in explanation of vote thereon, except if it has been amended.

CONDUCT DURING VOTING
Rule 63

After the President has announced the commencement of voting, no representative may interrupt the voting except on a point of order in connexion with the actual process of voting.

DIVISION OF PROPOSALS AND AMENDMENTS
Rule 64

Parts of a proposal or an amendment shall be voted on separately if a representative requests that the proposal be divided. Those parts of the proposal or the amendment which have been approved shall then be put to the vote as a whole; if all the operative parts of a proposal or amendment have been rejected, the proposal or amendment shall be considered to have been rejected as a whole.

AMENDMENTS
Rule 65

An amendment is a proposal that does no more than add to, delete from or revise part of another proposal.

ORDER OF VOTING ON AMENDMENTS
Rule 66

When an amendment is moved to a proposal, the amendment shall be voted on first. When two or more amendments are moved to a proposal, the amendment furthest removed in substance from the original proposal shall be voted on first and then the amendment next furthest removed therefrom, and so on until all the amendments have been put to the vote. Where, however, the adoption of one amendment necessarily implies the rejection of another amendment, the latter shall not be put to the vote. If one or more amendments are adopted, the amended proposal shall then be voted on.

ORDER OF VOTING ON PROPOSALS
Rule 67

1. If two or more proposals, other than amendments, relate to the same question, they shall, unless the Council decides otherwise, be voted on in the order in which they

were submitted. The Council may, after each vote on a proposal, decide whether to vote on the next proposal.

2.   A motion requiring that no decision be taken on a proposal shall have priority over that proposal.

ELECTIONS
Rule 68

All elections shall be held by secret ballot, unless, in the absence of any objection, the Council decides to proceed without taking a ballot on an agreed candidate or slate. When candidates are to be nominated, each nomination shall be made only by one representative, after which the Council shall immediately proceed to the election.

Rule 69

1.   If, when only one elective place is to be filled, no candidate obtains in the first ballot the majority required, a second ballot shall be taken, confined to the two candidates having obtained the largest number of votes. If in the second ballot the votes are equally divided, the President shall decide between the candidates by drawing lots.

2.   In the case of a tie in the first ballot among the candidates obtaining the second largest number of votes, a special ballot shall be held among such candidates for the purpose of reducing their number to two; similarly, in the case of a tie among three or more candidates obtaining the largest number of votes, a special ballot shall be held. If a tie again results in the special ballot, the President shall eliminate one candidate by drawing lots, and thereafter another ballot shall be taken among all the remaining candidates. The procedure prescribed by these rules shall, if necessary, be repeated until one candidate is duly elected.

Rule 70

1.   When two or more elective places are to be filled at one time under the same conditions, those candidates, in a number not exceeding the number of such places, obtaining in the first ballot the majority required and the largest number of votes shall be elected.

2.   If the number of candidates obtaining such majority is less than the number of places to be filled, additional ballots shall be held to fill the remaining places, provided that if only one place remains to be filled the procedures in rule 69 shall be applied. The ballot shall be restricted to the unsuccessful candidates having obtained the largest number of votes in the previous ballot, but not exceeding twice the number of places remaining

to be filled. However, in the case of a tie between a greater number of unsuccessful candidates, a special ballot shall be held for the purpose of reducing the number of candidates to the required number; if a tie again results among more than the required number of candidates, the President shall reduce their number to that required by drawing lots.

3.   If such a restricted ballot (not counting a special ballot held under the conditions specified in the last sentence of paragraph 2) is inconclusive, the President shall decide among the remaining candidates by drawing lots.

EQUALLY DIVIDED VOTES
Rule 71

If a vote is equally divided on a matter other than an election, the proposal or motion shall be regarded as rejected.

XII. PARTICIPATION OF NON-MEMBERS OF THE COUNCIL
PARTICIPATION OF NON-MEMBER STATES
Rule 72

1.   The Council shall invite any Member of the United Nations that is not a member of the Council, and any other state,[4] to participate in its deliberations on any matter of particular concern to that State.

2.   A committee or sessional body of the Council shall invite any State[4] that is not one of its own members to participate in its deliberations on any matter of particular concern to that State.

3.   A State thus invited shall not have the right to vote, but may submit proposals which may be put to the vote on request of any member of the body concerned.

PARTICIPATION OF NATIONAL LIBERATION MOVEMENTS
Rule 73

The Council may invite any national liberation movement recognized by or in accordance with resolutions of the General Assembly to participate, without the right to vote, in its deliberations on any matter of particular concern to that movement.

---

[4]It is the understanding of the Economic and Social Council that in discharging its functions under this rule it will follow the practice of the General Assembly in implementing an "all States" clause, and that in all cases where its is advisable it will request the opinion of the Assembly before taking decisions.

PARTICIPATION OF THE PRESIDENT OF THE TRUSTEESHIP COUNCIL
Rule 74

The President of the Trusteeship Council, or his representative, may participate, without the right to vote, in the deliberations of the Economic and Social Council on any matter of particular concern to the Trusteeship Council, including questions that have been proposed by the Trusteeship Council for inclusion in the provisional agenda of the Economic and Social Council.

PARTICIPATION OF AND CONSULTATION WITH SPECIALIZED AGENCIES[5]
Rule 75

In accordance with the agreements concluded between the United Nations and the specialized agencies, the specialized agencies shall be entitled:

(a) To be presented at meetings of the Council, its committees and sessional bodies;

(b) To participate, without the right to vote, through their representatives, in deliberations with respect to items of concern to them and to submit proposals regarding such items, which may be put to the vote at the request of any member of the Council or of the committee or sessional body concerned.

Rule 76

Before the Secretary-General places and item proposed by a specialized agency on the provisional agenda, he shall carry out with the agency concerned such preliminary consultation as may be necessary.

Rule 77

1. Where an item proposed for inclusion in the provisional agenda or the supplementary list contains a proposal for new activities to be undertaken by the United Nations relating to matters that are of direct concern to one or more specialized agencies, the Secretary-General shall enter into consultation with the agencies concerned and report to the Council on the means of achieving a co-ordinated use of the resources of the organizations concerned.

2. When in the course of a meeting of the Council a proposal for new activities to be undertaken by the United Nations relates to matters that are of direct concern to one

---

[5]See footnote 1.

or more specialized agencies, the Secretary-General shall, after such consultation as may be possible with the representatives of the agencies concerned, draw the attention of the Council to the implications of the proposal.

3. Before deciding on proposals referred to above, the Council shall satisfy itself that adequate consultations have taken place with the agencies concerned.

Rule 78

Whenever the Council is to consider a proposed international convention, the Secretary-General shall, at the same time that he requests Governments to comment on the proposed convention, consult the specialized agencies in respect of any provision of the proposed convention that may affect the activities of such agencies. The views of such agencies shall be brought before the Council together with the comments received from Governments.

PARTICIPATION OF OTHER INTERGOVERNMENTAL ORGANIZATIONS
Rule 79

Representatives of intergovernmental organizations accorded permanent observer status by the General Assembly and other intergovernmental organizations designated on an *ad hoc* or a continuing basis by the council on the recommendation of the Bureau, may participate, without the right to vote, in the deliberations of the Council on questions within the scope of the activities of the organizations.

XIII. CONSULTATION WITH NON-GOVERNMENTAL ORGANIZATIONS
COMMITTEE ON NON-GOVERNMENTAL ORGANIZATIONS
Rule 80

1. The Committee on Non-Governmental Organizations shall consist of nineteen Members of the United Nations elected for four years on the basis of equitable geographical representation. Accordingly, the membership of the Committee shall include:

(a) Five members from African States;

(b) Four members from Asian States;

(c) Four members from Latin American States;

(d) Four members from Western European and other States;

(e) Two members from East European States.

2.   The Committee shall carry out the functions assigned to it by the Council in connexion with the arrangements for consultations with non-governmental organizations adopted by the Council in accordance with Article 71 of the Charter.

3.   The Committee shall elect its own officers.

4.   When considering applications for granting consultative status to non-governmental organizations, the Committee shall be guided by the rules of procedure of the Council. Non-Governmental organizations applying for consultative status shall have an opportunity to submit written statements or be heard by the Committee, at the request of the latter, by means of an oral statement made by a duly authorized representative.

REPRESENTATION
Rule 81

Non-governmental organizations in category I or II may designate authorized representatives to sit as observers at public meetings of the Council, its committees and sessional bodies. Those on the Roster may have representatives present at such meetings when matters within their field of competence are being discussed.

GENERAL CONSULTATION OF THE COMMITTEE WITH ORGANIZATIONS IN CONSULTATIVE STATUS
Rule 82

The Committee on Non-Governmental Organizations may consult, in connexion with sessions of the Council or at such other times as it may decide, with organizations in categories I and II on matters within their competence, other than items on the agenda of the Council, on which the Council or the Committee or the organization requests consultation. The Committee shall report to the Council on such consultations.

CONSULTATION OF THE COMMITTEE WITH ORGANIZATIONS IN CATEGORIES I AND II ON ITEMS ON THE PROVISIONAL AGENDA OF THE COUNCIL
Rule 83

The Committee on Non-Governmental Organizations may consult, in connexion with any particular session of the council, with organizations in categories I and II on matters within the competence of the organizations concerning specific items already on the provisional agenda of the Council on which the Council or the Committee or the Organization requests consultation, and shall make recommendations as to which organizations, subject to the provisions of paragraph 1 of rule 84, should be heard by the

Council or the appropriate committee and regarding which subjects on which they should be heard. Organizations desiring such consultation shall apply in writing so that the request may reach the Secretary-General as soon as possible after the issue of the provisional agenda for the session, and in any case not later than five days after the adoption of the agenda. The Committee shall report to the Council on such consultations.

HEARING OF ORGANIZATIONS IN CATEGORY I BY THE COUNCIL OR ITS COMMITTEES
Rule 84

1. The Committee on Non-Governmental Organizations shall make recommendations to the Council as to which organizations in category I should be heard by the Council or by its sessional committees and on which items they should be heard. Such organizations shall be entitled to make one statement on each such item to the Council or the appropriate sessional committee, subject to the approval of the Council or of the sessional committee concerned. In the absence of the subsidiary body of the Council with jurisdiction in a major field of interest to the Council and to an organization in category II, the Committee may recommend that an organization in category II be heard by the Council on the subject in its field of interest.

2. Whenever the Council discusses the substance of an item proposed by a non-governmental organization in category I and included in the agenda of the Council, such an organization shall be entitled to present orally to the Council or a sessional committee of the Council, as appropriate, an introductory statement of an expository nature. Such an organization may be invited by the President of the Council or the Chairman of the committee, with the consent of the relevant body, to make, in the course of the discussion of the item before the Council or before the Committee, an additional statement for purposes of clarification.

XIV. AMENDMENT AND SUSPENSION OF RULES OF PROCEDURE
METHOD OF AMENDMENT
Rule 85

Any of these rules may be amended by the Council. These rules may, however, not be amended until the Council has received a report on the proposed amendment from a committee of the Council.

METHOD OF SUSPENSION
Rule 86

Any of these rules may be suspended by the Council provided that twenty-four hours notice of the proposal for the suspension has been given, which may be waived if no representative objects. Any such suspension shall be limited to a specific and stated purpose and to a period required to achieve that purpose.

ANNEX

1. The Preparatory Commission of the United Nations, at its second session in London in 1945, prepared draft rules of procedure for the Council (PC/20, chap.III, section 3). These provisional rules were approved, without change, at the first meeting of the Joint Sub-Committee of the Second and Third Committees during the first session of the General Assembly on 22 January 1946 (A/C.2/7 and A/C.3/3). The General Assembly adopted the conclusions of the reports of the Second and Third Committees at its 19th plenary meeting, on 29 January 1946 (A/16 and A/17). At its 12th meeting, during its first session, on 16 February 1946, the Council adopted these provisional rules of procedure, as contained in chapter III, section 3 (E/33).

2. The Council subsequently revised its rules of procedure at its second, fourth, fifth, seventh, eighth, tenth, fourteenth, fifteenth, fortieth, forty-first, forty-second, forty-sixth, resumed forty-seventh, organizational sessions for 1973, 1974 and 1975, and fifty-eighth session.

3. At the eighth session of the Council the revisions were of a comprehensive character (resolution 217 (VIII)(text of rules in E/33/Rev.5)). At the fourteenth session, the rules dealing with sessions and the agenda of the Council were revised by resolution 456 (XIV), as a consequence of the provisions of Council resolution 414 (XIII) on the organization and operation of the Council, and additional rules were adopted regarding inter-agency consultation, on the basis of the Council's recommendations contained in its resolution 402 B (XIII) (annex, para. 39) (text of rules in E/2336). At the fifteenth session, the rules concerning languages were amended by resolution 481 (XV) (text of rules in E/3063, rules 35-38). At the fortieth session, by resolution 1099 (XL), amendments were made in the rule regarding the Council Committee on Non-Governmental Organizations (text of rule in E/3063/Rev. 1, rule 82). Amendments made by resolution 1193 (XLI) at the resumed forty-first session related to rules 20, 22, and 23 (text of rules in E/3063/Rev. 1) and those made at the forty-second session to rules 4,19, 26 and 27 (text of rules in E/3063/Rev. 1). At the forty-sixth session, *pro forma* changes were made by resolution 1392 (XLVI) to rules 7, 10 and 12, and rules 83, 84, 85 and 86 were amended (text of amended rules in E/3063/Rev. 1). At the resumed forty-seventh session, as a result of the measures adopted by the Council during its forty-seventh session to improve the organization of its work and in consequence of its approval of the calendar of conferences and meetings for 1970 and 1971 (Council decisions taken at its 1637th meeting, on 8 August 1969; see also *Official Records of the Economic and Social Council, Forty-seventh Session, Supplement No. 1* (E/4735), pp. 18-20), the Council decided, *inter alia*, to adopt, on a provisional basis, the Secretary-General's proposals for the amendment of the relevant rules of procedure of the Council and other organizational changes (E/4757 and Corr. 1, paras 4-8) and to suspend rules

2, 9 and 14 of its rules of procedure which appear in E/3063/Rev.1 (Council decision taken at its 1647th' meeting, on 17 November 1969; see also *Official Records of the Economic and Social Council, Resumed Forty-seventh Session, Supplement No 1A* (E/4735/Add.1), p. 5). At its organizational session for 1973, the Council decided to suspend that part of rule 82 (text of rule in E/3063/Rev.1) which stipulates that the members of the Council Committee on Non-Governmental Organizations shall be members of the Council, in order to permit members of the sessional committees also to serve on that Committee (Council decision taken at its 1848th meeting on 8 January 1973; see also *Official Records of the Economic and Social Council, Fifty-fourth Session, Supplement No.1* (E/5367), p. 41). At its organizational session for 1974, the Council decided to suspend rule 20 in order to provide for the representation of all regional groups of countries among its officers and elected four Vice-Presidents instead of three as a consequence of paragraph 6 of Council resolution 1807 (LV) (Council decision taken at its 1887th meeting on 7 January 1974; see *Official Records of the Economic and Social Council, Organizational Session for 1974*, p. 2). At its organizational session for 1975, the Council decided to suspend that part of rule 82 (text of rule in E/3063/Rev.1) which stipulates that the members of the Council Committee on Non-Governmental Organizations shall serve for one year, in order to permit members of the Committee to serve for four years (Council decision taken at its 1939th meeting on 28 January 1975; see also *Official Records of the Economic and Social Council, Fifty-eighth Session, Supplement No.1* (E/5683), decision 70 (ORG-75)). At the fifty-eighth session of the Council the revisions were of a comprehensive character (Council resolution 1949 (LVIII)).

4.   The relevant references are as follows:

(a)   Decision of 4 June 1946 - See *Official Records of the Economic and Social Council, First Year, Second Session*, 7th meeting, page 49;

(b)   Decisions of 28 February and 11 March 1947 - See *Official Records of the Economic and Social Council, Second Year, Fourth Session*, 52nd and 65th meetings, pages 6-8; 91 and 292; text of the rules in E/33/Rev.3;

(c)   Resolution 99 (v) of 12 August 1947 - See *Official Records of the Economic and Social Council, Fifth Session* [Resolutions of the Council] (E/573 and Corr.1), page 91; text of the rules in E/33/Rev.4;

(d)   Resolution 138 (VI) of 8 March 1948 - See *Official Record of the Economic and Social Council, Sixth Session* [Resolutions of the Council], pages 46 and 47;

(e)   Resolution 176 (VII) of 28 August 1948 and decision of 28 August 1948 - See *Official Records of the Economic and Social Council, Seventh Session* [Resolutions of the Council] (E/1065 and Corr.1), pages 76, 77 and 78);

(f)   Resolution 217(VIII) of 18 March 1949 - See *Official Records of the Economic and Social Council, Eighth Session, Supplement No. 1* (E/1310), pages 26-40; text of the rules in E/33/Rev.5;

(g)   Decision of 6 March 1950, consequent on resolution 288 (X) of 27 February 1950 - See *Official Records of the Economic and Social Council, Tenth Session, Supplement No. 1* (E/1661), pages 33-37; text of the rules in E/1662;

(h)   Resolutions 456, A,B and C (XIV) of 22 and 29 July 1952 - See *Official Records of the Economic and Social Council, Fourteenth Session, Supplement No. 1* (E/2332), pages 61-67; text of rules in E/2336;

(i)   Resolution 481 (XV) of 1 April 1953 - See *Official Records of the Economic and Social Council, Fifteenth Session, Supplement No. 1* (E/2419), pages 25 and 26;

(j)   Decision of 5 August 1954 - See *Official Records of the Economic and Social Council, Eighteenth Session, Supplement No. 1* (E/2654), page 28;

(k)   Resolution 1099 (XL) of 4 March 1966 - See *Official Records of the Economic and Social Council, Fortieth Session, Supplement No. 1* (E/4176), page 7;

(l)   Resolution 1193 (XLI) of 20 December 1966 - See *Official Records of the Economic and Social Council, Resumed Forty-first Session, Supplement No. 1A* (E/4264/Add.1), page 3;

(m)   Decision of 29 May 1967 - See *Official Records of the Economic and Social Council, Forty-Second Session, Supplement No. 1* (E/4393), pages 30 and 31;

(n)   Resolution 1392(XLVI) of 3 June 1969 - See *Official Records of the Economic and Social Council, Forty-sixth Session, Supplement No. 1* (E/4715 and Corr.1), page 20;

(o)   Decision of 17 November 1969 - See *Official Records of the Economic and Social Council, Resumed Forty-seventh Session, Supplement No. 1A* (E/4735/Add.1), page 5; text of the rules in E/4757 and Corr.1, paragraphs 4-8;

(p)   Decision of 8 January 1973 - See *Official Records of the Economic and Social Council, Fifty-fourth Session, Supplement No.1* (E/5367), page 41;

(q)   Decision of 7 January 1974 - See *Official Records of the Economic and Social Council, Organizational Session for 1974*, 1887th meeting, page 2;

(r)   Decision of 28 January 1975 - See *Official Records of the Economic and Social Council, Fifty-eighth Session, Supplement No.1* (E/5683), decision 70 (ORG-75);

(s)   Resolution 1949 (LVIII) of 7 May 1975 - See *Official Records of the Economic and Social Council, Fifty-eighth Session, Supplement No.1* (E/5683).

5.   The previous versions of the rules of procedure have been issued under the following symbols:

February 1946 . . . .   E/33

June 1946 . . . .   E/33/Rev.1

March 1947   . . . .   E/33/Rev.2

March 1947   . . . .   E/33/Rev.3

August 1947   . . . .   E/33/Rev.4

March 1949   . . . .   E/33/Rev.5

April 1950   . . . .   E/1662

November 1952   . . . .   E/2336

March 1958   . . . .   E/3063

October 1967   . . . .   E/3063/Rev.1

6.   References to certain resolutions and decisions of the Council bearing on the present rules of procedure are given below:

Rule 1: Adopted on 16 February 1946, first session (E/33), amended by resolution 217 (VIII) (E/33/Rev. 5),amended by resolution 456 (XIV) (E/2336) as a consequence of resolution 414 (XIII), paragraph 8(a), and amended by resolution 1949 (LVIII) as a consequence of resolution 1623 (LI), paragraph 2;

Rule 2: Adopted on 16 February 1946, first session (E/33), amended by resolution 456 (XIV) (E/2336) as a consequence of resolution 414 (XIII), paragraph 8 (b), (c), (d) and (e), suspended and provisionally amended by decision of 17 November 1969, resumed forty-seventh session (E/4735/Add. 1, p. 5), amended by resolution 1949 (LVIII), and further amended by decision 1978/72 of 4 August 1978 and resolution 1982/50 of 28 July 1982;

Rule 3: Adopted by resolution 217 (VIII) (E/33/Rev. 5, rule 4) and amended by resolution 1949 (LVIII);

Rule 4: Adopted on 16 February 1946, first session (E/33, rule 3), and amended by resolution 217 (VIII) (E/33/Rev.5, rule 4) and resolution 456 (XIV) (E/2336, rule 4), decision of 29 May 1967, forty-second session (E/4393, p. 30), and resolution 1949 (LVIII). Former rule 5, adopted on 16 February 1946, first session (E/33, rule 5), and amended by resolution 217 (VIII) (E/33/Rev. 5, rule 5), was incorporated in paragraph 2 of present rule 4;

Rule 5: Adopted on 16 February 1946, first session (E/33, rule 6), and amended by resolution 456 (XIV) (E/2336, rule 6) and resolution 1949 (LVIII);

Rule 6: Adopted on 16 February 1946, first session (E/33, rule 7), and amended by resolution 217 (VIII) (E/33/Rev. 5, rule 7) and decision of 6 March 1950, tenth session (E/1661, p.34); *pro forma* changes were introduced pursuant to resolution 1392 (XLVI); amended and renumbered by resolution 1949 (LVIII);

Rule 7: Adopted on 16 February 1946, first session(E/33, rule 8), amended by resolution 217 (VIII) (E/33/Rev. 5, rule 8) and decision of 6 March 1950, tenth session (E/1661, p.34), and renumbered by resolution 1949 (LVIII);

Rules 8-15: Original rules relating to the agenda were adopted on 16 February 1946, first session (E/33, rules 9-13), and subsequently amended by decision of 11

March 1947, fourth session (65th meeting) (E/33/Rev. 3, rules 9-15), and resolutions 55 (IV), 57 (IV) and 99 (V), decision of 28 August 1948, seventh session (E/1065 and Corr. 1, p. 77), resolution 217 (VIII), decision of 6 March 1950, tenth session (E/1661, pp. 34-36), and by resolution 456 (XIV) (E/2336, rules 9-17) as consequence of resolution 414 (XIII), paragraph 8 (c), (d), (e), (f) and (g); *pro forma* changes were introduced in rules 10 and 12 by resolution 1392 (XLVI), and rules 9 and 14 were suspended and provisionally amended by decision of 17 November 1969, resumed forty-seventh session (E/4735/Add. 1, p. 5). Rules 9 to 17 (E/2336) were amended and restructured by resolution 1949 (LVIII);

Rule 16: Adopted on 16 February 1946, first session (E/33, rule 14), amended by resolution 217 (VIII) (E/33/Rev. 5, rule 17) and renumbered by resolution 456 (XIV) (E/2336, rule 18) and resolution 1949 (LVIII);

Rule 17: Adopted on 16 February 1946, first session (E/33, rule 15), amended by resolution 217 (VIII) (E/33/Rev. 5, rule 18), renumbered by resolution 456 (XIV) (E/2336, rule 19), amended by decision of 29 May 1967, forty-second session (E/4393, p. 30), and further amended and renumbered by resolution 1949 (LVIII);

Rule 18: Adopted on 16 February 1946, first session (E/33, rule 16), amended by resolution 217 (VIII) (E/33/Rev. 5, rule 19), renumbered by resolution 456 (XIV) (E/2336, rule 20), amended by resolution 1193 (XLI), suspended by decision of 7 January 1974, during the organizational session for 1974 (1887th meeting), and amended and renumbered by resolutions 1949 (LVIII);

Rule 19: Adopted on 16 February 1946, first session (E/33, rule 17), amended by resolution 217 (VIII) (E/33/Rev. 5, rule 20), renumbered by resolution 456 (XIV) (E/2336, rule 21), and amended and renumbered by resolution 1949 (LVIII);

Rule 20: Adopted on 16 February 1946, first session (E/33, rule 18), renumbered as a consequence of decision of 11 March 1947, fourth session (65th meeting) (E/33/Rev. 3, rule 20), renumbered by resolution 217 (VIII) (E/33/Rev. 5, rule 21), renumbered by resolution 456 (XIV) (E/2336, rule 22), amended and renumbered by resolution 456 (XIV) (E/2336, rule 22), amended and renumbered by resolution 1193 (XLI), and amended and renumbered by resolution 1949 (LVIII);

Rule 21: Adopted on 16 February 1946, first session (E/33, rule 20), renumbered as a consequence of decision 11 March 1947, fourth session (65th meeting) (E/33/Rev. 3, rule 22), and of resolution 217 (VIII) (E/33/Rev. 5, rule 23) and resolution 456 (XIV) (E/2336, rule 24), and amended and renumbered by resolution 1949 (LVIII);

Rule 22: Adopted on 16 February 1946, first session (E/33, rule 19) renumbered as a consequence of decision of 11 March 1947, fourth session (65th meeting) (E/33/Rev. 3, rule 21), amended by resolution 217 (VIII) (E/33/Rev. 5, rule 22), renumbered by resolution 456 (XIV) (E/2336, rule 23), amended by resolution 1193 (XLI), and amended and renumbered by resolution 1949 (LVIII);

Rule 23: Adopted on 4 June 1946, second session (E/33/Rev. 1, rule 21), renumbered as a consequence of decision of 11 March 1947, fourth session (65th meeting) (E/33/Rev. 3, rule 23), renumbered by resolution 217 (VIII) (E/33/Rev. 5, rule 24) and resolution 456 (XIV) (E/2336, rule 25), and amended and renumbered by resolution 1949 (LVIII);

Rules 24-27: Adopted by resolution 1949 (LVIII). The provisions of former rules 26 and 27 of chapter V and former rules 71 to 74 of chapter XII (E/3063/Rev. 1) were revised and combined into present chapter V.

Rule 26 (E/3063/Rev. 1): adopted on 16 February 1946, first session (E/33, rule 21), renumbered as a consequence of decision of 4 June 1946, second session(7th meeting) (E/33/Rev. 1, rule 22), and decision of 11 March 1947, fourth session (65th meeting) (E/33/Rev. 3, rule 24), amended and renumbered by resolution 217 (VIII) (E/33/Rev. 5, rule 25), renumbered by resolution 456 (XIV) (E/2336, rule 26) and amended by decision of 29 May 1957, forty-second session (E/4393, p.31).

Rule 27 (E/3063/Rev. 1): adopted by resolution 217 (VIII) (E/33/Rev. 5, rule 26), renumbered by resolution 456 (XIV) (E/2336, rule 27) and amended by decision of 29 May 1967, forty-second session (E/4393, p. 32).

Rule 71 (E/3063/Rev. 1): adopted on 16 February 1946 (E/33, rule 60), renumbered as a consequence of decision of 4 June 1946, second session (7th meeting) (E/33/Rev. 1, rule 61), and of decisions of 28 February and 11 March 1947, fourth session (52nd and 65th meetings) (E/33/Rev. 3, rule 64), amended and renumbered by resolution 217 (VIII) (E/33/Rev. 5, rule 70), and renumbered by resolution 456 (XIV) (E/2336, rule 71).

Rule 72 (E/3063/Rev. 1): adopted by resolution 217 (VIII) (E/33/Rev. 5, rule 71) and renumbered by resolution 456 (XIV) (E/2336, rule 72).

Rule 73 (E/3063/Rev. 1): adopted on 16 February 1946, first session (E/33, rule 61), renumbered as a consequence of decision 4 June 1946, second session (7th meeting) (E/33/Rev. 1, rule 62), and of decisions of 28 February and 11 March 1947, fourth session (52nd and 65th meetings) (E/33/Rev. 3, rule 65), amended by resolution 99 (V) (E/33/Rev. 4, rule 65), amended and renumbered by resolution 217 (VIII) (E/33/Rev. 5, rule 72) and renumbered by resolution 456 (XIV) (E/2336, rule 73).

Rule 74 (E/3063/Rev. 1): adopted on 16 February 1946, first session (E/33, rule 62), renumbered as a consequence of decision of 4 June 1946, second session (7th meeting) (E/33/Rev. 1, rule 63), and of decisions of 28 February and 11 March 1947, fourth session (52nd and 65th meetings) (E/33/Rev. 3, rule 66), amended by resolution 99(V) (E/33/Rev. 4, rule 66), and amended and renumbered by resolution 217 (VIII) (E/33/Rev. 5, rule 74);

Rules 28 and 30: Adopted by resolution 1949 (LVIII). The provisions of former rules 28 to 32 (E/3063/Rev. 1) were amended and restructured into present rules 28 and 30. Rules 28-32 (E/3063/Rev. 1): adopted on 16 February 1946, first session (E/33, rules 22-26), renumbered as a consequence of decision of 4 June 1946, second session (7th meeting) (E/33/Rev. 1, rules 23-27), and of decision of 11 March 1947, fourth session (65th meeting) (E/33/Rev. 3, rules 25-29), amended and renumbered by resolution 217 (VIII) (E/33/Rev.5, rules 27-31) and renumbered by resolution 456 (XIV) (E/2336, rules 28-32);

Rule 29: Adopted by resolution 217 (VIII) (E/33/Rev. 5, rule 32), renumbered by resolution 456 (XIV) (E/2336, rule 33), and amended and renumbered by resolution 1949 (LVIII);

Rule 30: See rules 28 and 30 above;

Rule 31: Original rule adopted by decision of 28 February 1947, fourth session (52nd meeting), in pursuance of regulation 25 of the Provisional Financial Regulations of the United Nations (E/33/Rev.3, rule 30). Amended by decision of 28 August 1948, seventh session (E/1065 and Corr. 1, p. 77), based on resolution 175 (VII), pursuant to General Assembly resolutions 125 (II) and 163 (II) and financial regulation 38 (E/33/Rev. 5, rule 33). Pursuant to General Assembly resolutions 413 (V) and 456 (V) (regulation 13.1 of the Financial Regulations of the United Nations) and Council resolution 402 (XIII), further amended and renumbered by resolution 456B (XIV) (E/2336, rule 34). Taking into account financial regulations 3.1 and 13.1 and 13.2 of the United Nations, the rule was further amended and renumbered by resolution 1949 (LVIII);

Rule 32: Adopted on 16 February 1946 (E/33, rule 27), renumbered as a consequence of decision of 4 June 1946, second session (7th meeting) (E/33/Rev. 1, rule 28), and of decisions of 28 February and 11 March 1947, fourth session (52nd and 65th meetings) (E/33/Rev. 3, rule 31), and by resolution 217 (VIII) (E/33/Rev. 5, rule 34) and resolution 456 (XIV) (E/2336, rule 35), amended by resolution 481 (XV) and renumbered by resolution 1949 (LVIII), and further amended by decision 1982/147 of 15 April 1982;

Rule 33: Adopted by resolution 1949 (LVIII). The provisions of rules 36 to 38 (E/3063/Rev. 1) were amended and restructured within the present rule 33. Rules 36-38 (E/3063/Rev. 1): adopted on 16 February 1946 (E/33, rules 28-30), renumbered as a consequence of decision of 4 June 1946, second session (7th meeting) (E/33/Rev. 1, rules 29-31), and decisions of 28 February and 11 March 1947, fourth session (52nd and 65th meetings) (E/33/Rev. 3, rules 32-34), and by resolution 217

(VIII) (E/33/Rev. 5, rules 35-37) and resolution 456 (XIV) (E/2336, rules 36-38); rules 36 to 37 were amended by resolution 481 (XV);

Rule 34: Adopted on 16 February 1946 (E/33, rule 31), renumbered as a consequence of decision of 4 June 1946, second session (7th meeting) (E/33/Rev. 1, rule 32), and of decisions of 28 February and 11 March 1947, fourth session (52nd and 65th meetings) (E/33/Rev. 3, rule 35), amended and renumbered by resolution 217 (VIII) (E/33/Rev. 5, rule 38), renumbered by resolution 456 (XIV) (E/2336, rule 39) and further renumbered by resolution 1949 (LVIII);

Rule 35: Adopted on 16 February 1946 (E/33, rule 34), renumbered as a consequence of decision of 4 June 1946, second session (7th meeting) (E/33/Rev. 1, rule 35), and decisions of 28 February and 11 March 1947, fourth session (52nd and 65th meetings) (E/33/Rev. 3, rule 38), and by resolution 217 (VIII) (E/33/Rev. 5, rule 39), resolution 456 (XIV) (E/2336, rule 40) and resolution 1949 (LVIII);

Rule 36: Adopted on 16 February 1946 (E/33, rule 43), renumbered as a consequence of decision of 4 June 1946, second session (7th meeting) (E/33/Rev. 1, rule 44), and decisions of 28 February and 11 March 1947, fourth session (52nd and 65th meetings) (E/33/Rev. 3, rule 47), and by resolution 217 (VIII) (E/33/Rev. 5, rule 40, resolution 456 (XIV) (E/2336, rule 41) and resolution 1949 (LVIII). Former rule 42 (E/3063/Rev. 1), providing that "at the close of each private meeting, the Council may issue a communique through the Secretary-General", originally adopted on 16 February 1946 (E/33, rule 44), was deleted during the consideration of the present rules;

Rule 37: Adopted on 16 February 1946 (E/33, rule 46), suspended by resolutions 138 (VI) and 176 (VII) and replaced by a new rule in accordance with resolution 456 (XIV) (E/2336, rule 46), and amended and renumbered by resolution 1949 (LVIII);

Rule 38: Adopted on 16 February 1946 (E/33, rule 45), renumbered as a consequence of decision of 4 June 1946, second session (7th meeting) (E/33/Rev. 1, rule 46), and decisions of 28 February and 11 March 1947, fourth session (52nd and 65th meetings) (E/33/Rev. 3, rule 49), and amended and renumbered by resolution 217 (VIII) (E/33/Rev. 5, rule 42), resolution 456 (XIV) (E/2336, rule 43) and resolution 1949 (LVIII);

Rule 39: Adopted on 16 February 1946 (E/33, rule 48), renumbered as a consequence of decision of 4 June 1946, second session (7th meeting) (E/33/Rev. 1, rule 49), and decisions of 28 February and 11 March 1947, fourth session (52nd and 65th meetings) (E/33/Rev. 3, rule 52), and amended and renumbered by resolution 217 (VIII) (E/33/Rev. 5, rule 44), resolution 456 (XIV) (E/2336, rule 44) and resolution 1949 (LVIII);

Rule 40: Adopted on 16 February 1946 (E/33, rule 47), renumbered as a consequence of decision of 4 June 1946, second session (7th Meeting) (E/33/Rev.

1, rule 48), and decisions of 28 February and 11 March 1947, fourth session (52nd and 65th meetings) (E/33/Rev. 3, rule 51), and amended and renumbered by resolution 217 (VIII) (E/33/Rev. 5, rule 45) and resolution 1949 (LVII);

Rules 41-71: The Original rules dealing with conduct of business and voting, adopted on 16 February 1946 (E/33, rules 49-59 and 35-42), were substantially restructured by resolution 217 (VIII), using as far as applicable the text employed in the corresponding rules of the General Assembly (E/33/Rev. 5, rules 46-69). Rule 60, first part, reproduced textually Article 67, paragraph 2, of the Charter, renumbered as a consequence of resolution 456 (XIV) (E/2336, rules 47-70) and substantially restructured by resolution 1949 (LVIII) (rules 41-71), using as far as applicable the text employed in the corresponding rules of the General Assembly (A/520/Rev. 12), as well as relevant resolutions and decisions taken by the Council (see comments listed in E/5450, opposite proposed rules 47-70). Under the present rules, separate rules are provided concerning "Right of reply" (rule 46), "Congratulations" (rule 47), "Condolences" (rule 48), "Discussion of reports of sessional committees of the whole" (rule 53), "Reconsideration of proposals" (rule 57), "Request for a Vote" (rule 59), "Explanation of vote" (rule 62) and "Amendments" (rule 65);

Rule 72: The rules concerning the participation of Members of the United Nations not members of the Council were originally adopted by resolution 217 (VIII) (E/33/Rev. 5, rules 74-75), based on Article 69 of the Charter, renumbered as a consequence of resolution 456 (XIV) (E/2336, rules 75-76), and amended and replaced by present rule 72 (resolution 1949 (LVIII));

Rule 73: Adopted by resolution 1949 (LVIII), taking into account, *inter alia,* General Assembly resolutions 3237 (XXIX) of 22 November 1974 and 3280 (XXIX) of 10 December 1974 (in particular para. 7) relating to national liberation movements, adopted by the Assembly at its twenty-ninth session;

Rule 74: For arrangements for co-operation between the Economic and Social Council and the Trusteeship Council in matters of common concern, see *Official Records of the Economic and Social Council, Second Year, Fifth Session,* annex 20, pp.477-486; pursuant to resolution 216 (VIII), a new rule was adopted by resolution 217 (VIII) (E/33/Rev. 5, rule 76); renumbered by resolution 456 (XIV) (E/2336, rule 77) and resolution 1949 (LVIII);

Rule 75: Based on Article 70 of the Charter, adopted by resolution 217 (VIII) (E/33/Rev. 5, rule 77) and renumbered as a consequence of resolution 456 (XIV) (E/2336, rule 78) and resolution 1949 (LVIII);

Rule 76: Adopted by decision of 11 March 1974, fourth session (65th meeting) (E/33/Rev. 3, rule 11), amended and renumbered by resolution 217 (VIII)

(E/33/Rev. 5, rule 12), amended and renumbered by resolution 456 (XIV) (E/2336, rule 79) and renumbered by resolution 1949 (LVIII);

Rules 77-78: Adopted by resolution 456 (XIV) (E/2336, rules 80 and 81) and renumbered as a consequence of resolution 1949 (LVIII);

Rule 79: Adopted by resolution 1949 (LVIII);

Rule 80: Arrangements for consultation with non-governmental organizations were originally based on resolution 2/3 (second session) adopted on 21 June 1946 (see *Official Records of the Economic and Social Council, First Year, Second Session*, pp.360-365). The original rule was adopted by resolution 217 (VIII) (E/33/Rev. 5, rule 78) as a consequence of resolution 288 B (X), amended by decision of 6 March 1950, tenth session (E/1661, p. 36), renumbered as a consequence of resolution 456(XIV) (E/2336, rule 82), amended by decision of 5 August 1954, eighteenth session (E/2654, p. 28) and further amended by resolution 1099 (XL) (E/3063, rule 82). By its decision of 8 January 1973, during the organizational session for 1973 (E/5367, p.41), the Council decided to suspend that part of the rule which stipulates that the members of the Council Committee on Non-Governmental Organizations shall be members of the Council, in order to permit the additional members of the sessional committees also to serve on the Committee; further, by decision 70 (ORG-75) of 28 January 1975, during the organizational session for 1975 (E/5683), the Council decided to suspend that part of the rule which stipulates that the members of the Council Committee on Non-Governmental Organizations shall serve for one year, in order to permit members of the Committee to serve for four years; amended and renumbered by resolution 1949 (LVIII). The Council decided to enlarge the membership of the Committee on Non-Governmental Organizations by its resolution 1981/50 of 20 July 1981;

Rules 81-84: Arrangements for consultation with non-governmental organizations were originally based on resolution 2/3 (second session) adopted on 21 June 1946 (see *Official Records of the Economic and Social Council, First Year, Second Session*, pp. 360-365). The original rules were adopted by resolution 217 (VIII) (E/33/Rev. 5, rules 79-81) consequent to resolution 288 B (X), amended by decision of 6 March 1950, tenth session (E/1661, pp. 36-37), renumbered as a consequence of resolutions 456 (XIV) (E/2336, rules 83-86), amended by resolution 1392 (XLVI) and renumbered as a consequence of resolution 1949 (LVIII);

Rules 85-86: Adopted by resolution 1949 (LVIII), restructured former rules 87 to 89 (E/3063/Rev. 1). Rule 87 (E/3063/Rev. 1) was adopted on 16 February 1946 (E/33, rule 64), renumbered as a consequence of decision of 6 June 1946, second session (7th meeting) (E/33/Rev. 1, rule 65), and decisions of 28 February and 11 March 1947, fourth session (52nd and 65th meetings) (E/33/Rev. 3, rule 68), amended and renumbered by resolution 217 (VIII) (E/33/Rev. 5 rule 82), and renumbered as a consequence of resolution 456 (XIV) (E/2336, rule 87). Rules 88 and 89 were adopted on 16 February 1946 (E/33, rules 65 and 66) and renumbered as a consequence of decision of 6 June 1946, second session (7th meeting) (E/33/Rev. 1, rules 66 and 67), and decisions of 28 February and 11 March 1947, fourth session (52nd and 65th meetings) (E/33/Rev. 3, rules 69 and 70), and resolution 456 (XIV) (E/2336, rules 88 and 89).

7. RULES OF PROCEDURE OF THE TRUSTEESHIP COUNCIL[1]

Contents

---

[1]*Rules of Procedure of the Trusteeship Council* (as amended up to and during its twenty-ninth session), United Nations, New York, 1962.

I. SESSIONS
Rule 1

The Trusteeship Council shall meet in one regular session each year. This session shall be convened during the month of May.

Rule 2

Special sessions shall be held as and where occasion may require, by decision of the Trusteeship Council, or at the request of a majority of its members, or at the request of the General Assembly, or at the request of the Security Council acting in pursuance of the relevant provisions of the Charter.

Rule 3

A request for a special session may be made by the Economic and Social Council or by any member of the Trusteeship Council, and shall be addressed to the Secretary-General of the United Nations, who without delay shall communicate the request to other members of the Trusteeship Council. On notification by the Secretary-General that the majority of the members have concurred, the President of the Trusteeship Council shall request the Secretary-General to call a special session.

Rule 4

The President of the Trusteeship Council shall notify the members of the Council of the date ad place of the first meeting of each session through the Secretary-General. Such notification, as a rule, shall be given at least thirty days in advance of the date of the session. Notifications shall also be addressed to the Security Council, to the Economic and Social Council, to such Members of the United Nations as have proposed an item for the agenda, and to such of the specialized agencies as may attend and participate in the meetings of the Trusteeship Council under the terms of the agreements with the United Nations.

Rule 5

A request for an alteration of the date of a regular session may be made by any member of the Trusteeship Council or the Secretary-General and shall be dealt with by a procedure similar to that provided in rule 3 for a request for a special session.

Rule 6

Each session shall be held at the seat of the United Nations, unless in pursuance of a previous decision of the Trusteeship Council or at the request of a majority of its members another place is designated. A request for a place of meeting other than the seat of the United Nations may be made by any member of the Trusteeship Council or by the Secretary-General and shall be dealt with by a procedure similar to that provided in rule 3 for a request for a special session.

Rule 7

The Trusteeship Council may decide at any session to adjourn temporarily and resume its meetings at a later date.

II. AGENDA
Rule 8

The provisional agenda for each session of the Trusteeship Council shall be drawn up by the Secretary-General in consultation with the President and shall be communicated together with the notice summoning the Council to the organs, Members and specialized agencies referred to in rule 4.

Rule 9

The provisional agenda shall include consideration of:

(a) Such annual reports and other documents as may have been submitted by the Administering Authorities;

(b) Such petitions as may have been presented, a list of which shall be attached;

(c) Arrangements for and reports on visits to Trust Territories;

(d) All items proposed by the Trusteeship Council at a previous session;

(e) All items proposed by any Member of the United Nations;

(f) All items proposed by the General Assembly, the Security Council, the Economic and Social Council, or a specialized agency under the terms of its agreement with the United Nations; and

(g) All items or reports which the President or the Secretary-General may deem necessary to put before the Trusteeship Council.

Rule 10

The first item on the provisional agenda of any meeting of the Trusteeship Council shall be the adoption of the agenda. The Trusteeship Council may revise the agenda and may, as appropriate, add, defer or delete items. During any special session priority shall be given to the consideration of those items for which the session has been called.

III. REPRESENTATION AND CREDENTIALS
Rule 11

Each member of the Trusteeship Council shall designate one specially qualified person to represent it therein.

Rule 12

Members of the United Nations which are not members of the Trusteeship Council but which have proposed items on the agenda of that Council shall be invited to have present, at the appropriate meetings of the Council, representatives who shall be entitled to participate, without vote, in the deliberations on those items.

Rule 13

Representatives of specialized agencies shall be invited to attend meetings of the Trusteeship Council and to participate, without vote, in its deliberations in the circumstances indicated in the respective agreements between the United Nations and the specialized agencies.

Rule 14

1. The credentials of representatives on the Trusteeship Council shall normally be communicated to the Secretary-General not less than twenty-four hours before the meeting at which the representatives will take their seats. The credentials shall be issued either by the Head of the State or by the Minister of Foreign Affairs of the respective member governments.

2. The credentials shall be examined by the Secretary-General, who shall submit a report thereon to the Trusteeship Council for approval.

Rule 15

1.   Any member of the United Nations not a member of the Trusteeship Council, when invited to participate in a meeting or meetings of the Council, shall submit credentials for the representative appointed by it for this purpose in the same manner as provided in rule 14. The credentials of such a representative shall be communicated to the Secretary-General not less than twenty-four hours before the first meeting which he is to attend.

2.   The credentials of representatives referred to in the paragraph immediately preceding and of any representatives appointed in accordance with rule 74 shall be examined by the Secretary-General, who shall submit a report to the Trusteeship Council for approval.

Rule 16

The credentials of representatives of specialized agencies which have been invited to attend meetings of the Trusteeship Council in pursuance of rule 13 shall be issued by the competent officer of each such specialized agency and shall be subject to the same procedure as defined in rule 14.

Rule 17

Pending the decision on the credentials of a representative on the Trusteeship Council, such representative shall be seated provisionally and shall enjoy the same rights as he would have if his credentials were found to be in good order.

Rule 18

Each representative on the Trusteeship Council may be accompanied by such alternates and advisers as he may require. An alternate or an adviser may act as a representative when so designated by the a representative.

IV.   PRESIDENT AND VICE-PRESIDENT
Rule 19

The Trusteeship Council shall elect, at the beginning of its regular session, a President and a Vice-President from among the representatives of the members of the Trusteeship Council.

Rule 20

The president and the Vice-President shall hold office until their respective successors are elected, and shall not be eligible for immediate re-election.

Rule 21

1. If the president should be temporarily absent, the Vice-President shall act as President in the same conditions.

2. In the event that the President for any reason is no longer able to act in that capacity, the Council shall elect a new President for the unexpired term. The same procedure shall be followed if the Vice-President for any reason is no longer able to act in that capacity.

Rule 22

The President may appoint one of his alternates or advisers to participate in the proceedings and to vote in the Trusteeship Council. In such a case the President shall not exercise his right to vote.

V. SECRETARIAT
Rule 23

The Secretary-General shall act in that capacity at the meetings of the Trusteeship Council and of its committees, sub-committees and such subsidiary bodies as may be established by it. The Secretary-General may authorize a deputy to act in his place.

Rule 24

The Secretary-General shall transmit promptly to the members of the Trusteeship Council all communications which may be addressed to the Council from Members and organs of the United Nations and from specialized agencies. The Secretary-General shall also circulate promptly to the members of the Council communications from other sources, except those which are manifestly inconsequential, if they relate to the activities of the Trusteeship Council. Such communications shall be transmitted in full, unless their length precludes this, in which case the procedure set forth in paragraph 3 of rule 85 shall apply.

Rule 25

The Secretary-General shall provide and direct the staff required by the Trusteeship Council and such committees, sub-committees and other subsidiary bodies as it may establish.

Rule 26

The Secretary-General or his representative may, subject to the provisions of rule 53, make oral as well as written statements to the Council, its committees or subsidiary bodies concerning any question under consideration.

Rule 27

The Secretary-General shall be responsible for all the necessary arrangements for meetings and other activities of the Trusteeship Council, its committees, sub-committees and subsidiary bodies.

VI. LANGUAGES
Rule 28

Chinese, English, French, Russian and Spanish shall be the official languages. English and French shall be the working languages of the Trusteeship Council.

Rule 29

Speeches made in one of the working languages shall be interpreted into the other working language.

Rule 30

Speeches made in any of the other three official languages shall be interpreted into both working languages.

Rule 31

Any representative may speak in a language other than the official languages. In such case, he shall himself provide for interpretation into one of the working languages.

Interpretation into the other working language by an interpreter of the Secretariat may be based on the interpretation given in the first working language.

Rule 32

Records of meetings of the Trusteeship Council shall be drawn up in the working languages. A translation of the whole or part of any record into any of the other official languages shall be furnished if requested by any representative in the Trusteeship Council.

Rule 33

The official records of the Trusteeship Council shall be issued in the working languages.

Rule 34

All resolutions of the Trusteeship Council shall be made available in the official languages. Other documents originating with the Council shall be made available in any of the official languages at the request of representatives of members of the Council.

Rule 35

Documents of the Trusteeship Council shall, if the Trusteeship Council so decides, be published in any language other than the official languages.

VII. VOTING
Rule 36

Each member of the Trusteeship Council shall have one vote.

Rule 37

Decisions or recommendations of the Trusteeship Council shall be made by a majority of the members present and voting. Members who abstain in particular votes shall not in those instances be counted as voting.

Rule 38

If a vote other than for an election is equally divided, a second vote shall be taken at the next meeting or, by decision of the Trusteeship Council, following a brief recess. Unless at the second vote there is a majority in favour of the proposal, it shall be deemed to be lost.

Rule 39

The Trusteeship Council shall vote by show of hands except that, before a vote is taken, any representative of a member may request a roll-call, which shall then be taken in the English alphabetical order of the names of the members of the Trusteeship Council, beginning with the member of the Trusteeship Council whose name is drawn by lot by the President. The name of each member shall be called and the representative shall reply "Yes", "No" or "Abstain". The result of the voting shall be inserted in the record in the English alphabetical order of the names of the members.

Rule 40

The vote of each member participating in any roll-call shall be inserted in the record.

Rule 41

The election of the President and the Vice-President of the Trusteeship Council shall be taken by secret and separate ballot. The Council may decide that the election to any other office or function established by the Council shall also be taken by secret ballot.

Rule 42

When only one person or member is to be elected and no candidate obtains in the first ballot the majority required, a second ballot shall be taken, which shall be confined to the two candidates obtaining the largest number of votes. If in the second ballot the votes are equally divided, the President shall decide between the candidates by drawing lots.

Rule 43

When two or more elective places are to be filled at one time under the same conditions, those candidates obtaining in the first ballot the majority required shall be elected. If the number of candidates obtaining such majority is less than the number of persons or members to be elected, there shall be additional ballots to fill the remaining places, the voting being restricted to the candidates obtaining the greatest number of votes in the previous ballot, the number of candidates being not more than twice as many as the places remaining to be filled.

VIII. PUBLICITY OF MEETINGS
Rule 44

The meetings of the Trusteeship Council and of all of its subsidiary bodies shall be held in public, unless the Council or subsidiary body concerned decides that circumstances require that meetings be held in private.

Rule 45

At the close of private meetings, as may be appropriate, the Trusteeship Council shall issue a communique through the Secretary-General.

IX. RECORDS
Rule 46

The records of all public and private meetings shall be prepared by the Secretariat. They shall be made available in so far as possible within twenty-four hours of the end of the meetings to the representatives who have participated in the meetings.

Rule 47

The representatives who have participated in the meetings shall, within two working days after the distribution of the records, inform the Secretary-General of any corrections they wish to have made. Corrections that have been requested shall be considered approved, unless the President is of the opinion that they are sufficiently important to be submitted to the Trusteeship Council for approval.

Rule 48

The records of public and private meetings in which no corrections have been requested or which have been corrected in accordance with rule 47 shall be considered as the official records of the Trusteeship Council. The official records of public meetings shall be published by the Secretariat as promptly as possible and communicated to the members of the United Nations and to the specialized agencies referred to in rule 4.

Rule 49

The official records of private meetings shall be accessible only to the Members of the United Nations, except that the Trusteeship Council may make public the records of any private meeting at such time and under such conditions as it may decide. When such records relate to strategic areas the Administering Authority concerned may request the Trusteeship Council to confine their availability to the Trusteeship and Security Councils.

X. CONDUCT OF BUSINESS
Rule 50

At any meeting of the Trusteeship Council two-thirds of the members shall constitute a quorum.

Rule 51

In addition to exercising the powers which are conferred upon him elsewhere by these rules, the President shall declare the opening and closing of each meeting, direct the discussions, ensure observance of the rules of procedure, accord the right to speak, put questions and announce decisions. Subject to the rules of procedure, he shall have complete control of the proceedings of any meeting. The President, acting under the authority of the Trusteeship Council, shall represent it as an organ of the United Nations.

Rule 52

Whenever the President of the Trusteeship Council deems that for the proper fulfillment of the responsibilities of the presidency he should not preside over the Trusteeship Council during the consideration of a question with which the member he represents is directly connected, and in particular when annual reports and petitions relating to a Trust Territory of which the member he represents is the Administering Authority are under consideration, he shall indicate his decision to the Trusteeship Council. The presidency shall then devolve for the purpose of the consideration of that question upon the Vice-President.

Rule 53

No one may address the Trusteeship Council without having previously obtained the permission of the President. The President shall call upon speakers in the order in which they signify their desire to speak. The chairman of a subsidiary body, or a rapporteur, or the Secretary-General, however, may be accorded precedence. The President may call a speaker to order if his remarks are not relevant to the subject under discussion.

Rule 54

During the discussion of any matter, a representative may rise to a point of order and the point of order shall be immediately decided by the President, in accordance with the rules of procedure.

Rule 55

A representative may appeal from any ruling of the President. The appeal shall be put to the vote without discussion.

Rule 56

1. The following motions shall have precedence in the order named over all draft resolutions or other motions relative to the subject before the meeting:

(a) To suspend the meeting;

(b) To adjourn the meeting;

(c) To adjourn the meeting to a certain day or hour;

(d) For the closure of the debate on any motion or draft resolution, including amendments thereto, or on any amendment or amendments to a motion or draft resolution;

(e) To limit the time allowed to each speaker;

(f) To refer any matter to a committee, to the Secretary-General or to a rapporteur;

(g) To postpone discussion of the question to a certain day or indefinitely; or

(h) To amend.

2. Any motion for the suspension or for the simple adjournment of a meeting shall be decided without debate.

3. A motion for closure of debate on a draft resolution or other motion shall not be considered by the Trusteeship Council until each representative shall have had the opportunity to speak on that draft resolution or other motion. Debate on a motion for closure of debate shall be limited to one speaker for each side.

Rule 57

Reports, draft resolutions and other substantive motions or amendments shall be introduced in writing and handed to the Secretary-General. The Secretary-General shall, to the extent possible, circulate copies to the representatives twenty-four hours in advance of the meeting at which they are to be considered. The Trusteeship Council may decide to postpone the consideration of draft resolutions and other substantive motions or amendments, copies of which have not been circulated twenty-four hours in advance.

Rule 58

Draft resolutions and other motions or amendments proposed by representatives of members on the Trusteeship Council may be put to the vote without having been seconded.

Rule 59

1. Draft resolutions, motions or amendments may be withdrawn by the representative who introduced them at any time prior to the vote.

2. In a case where a representative withdraws a draft resolution, motion or amendment prior to the vote, any other representative on the Trusteeship Council may require that it be put to the vote as his draft resolution, motion or amendment under the same conditions as if the original mover had not withdrawn it.

Rule 60

Parts of a report, draft resolution, other motion or amendment may be voted on separately at the request of a representative and subject to the will of the Trusteeship Council. The proposal shall then be voted on as a whole.

Rule 61

A proposal to add to or delete from or otherwise revise a part of a draft resolution or a motion shall be considered as an amendment. An amendment shall be voted on first and if it is adopted, the amended resolution or motion shall then be voted on.

Rule 62

If two or more amendments are moved to a draft resolution another motion, the President shall first put to the vote the amendment furthest removed in substance from the draft resolution or motion and then the amendment next furthest removed, and so on, until all the amendments have been voted upon or and amendment has been approved which, in the opinion of the Trusteeship Council, makes voting on the remaining amendments unnecessary.

Rule 63

If two or more draft resolutions or other motions relating to an original proposal are introduced, the President shall first put to the vote the resolution or motion furthest removed in substance from the original proposal. If that draft resolution or motion is rejected, the President shall put to the vote the draft resolution or motion next furthest removed, and so on, until either all the draft resolutions or motions have been put to a vote or one or more of them has been adopted which, in the opinion of the Trusteeship Council, makes voting on the remaining proposals unnecessary.

Rule 64

A statement of minority views may be appended to a report or recommendation of the Trusteeship Council at the request of any member.

Rule 65

No resolution involving expenditure from United Nations funds shall be approved by the Trusteeship Council unless the Trusteeship Council has before it a report from the Secretary-General on the financial implications of the proposal, together with an estimate of the costs involved in the specific proposal.

XI. COMMITTEES AND RAPPORTEURS
Rule 66

The Trusteeship Council may set up such committees as it deems necessary, define their composition and their terms of reference, and refer to them any questions on the agenda for study and report. The committees may be authorized to sit while the Trusteeship Council is not in session.

Rule 67

The procedure set forth in rules 28 to 31, 36 to 38, and 51 to 63 inclusive shall apply to proceedings of committees of the Trusteeship Council. The committees may decide upon the form of the records and adopt such other rules of procedure as may be necessary.

XII. QUESTIONNAIRES
Rule 68

Upon the coming into effect of each Trusteeship Agreement, the Trusteeship Council shall transmit to the Administering Authority concerned, through the Secretary-General, such questionnaire as it shall have formulated, in accordance with Article 88 of the Charter, on the political, economic, social and educational advancement of the inhabitants of the Trust Territory involved.

Rule 69

The Trusteeship Council may modify the questionnaires at its discretion.

Rule 70

When, in accordance with Article 91 of the Charter, the Trusteeship Council considers it appropriate to avail itself of the assistance of the Economic and Social Council or of any specialized agency in the preparation of questionnaires, the President of the Trusteeship Council shall transmit through the Secretary-General to the Economic and Social Council or to the specialized agency concerned those sections of the questionnaires with regard to which its advice may be desired.

Rule 71

1. The questionnaire shall be communicated to each Administering Authority at least six months before the expiration of the year covered by the first annual report, and shall remain in force, without specific renewal, from year to year.

2. Any subsequent modifications shall be communicated to the Administering Authority concerned at least six months before the date fixed for the presentation of the first annual report which is to be based on the modified questionnaire.

XIII. ANNUAL REPORTS OF ADMINISTERING AUTHORITIES
Rule 72

1. The annual report of an Administering Authority prepared on the basis of the questionnaire formulated by the Trusteeship Council shall be submitted to the Secretary-General within six months from the termination of the year to which it refers.

2. Each report of an Administering Authority shall be considered by the Trusteeship Council at the regular session following the expiration of six weeks from the receipt of the report by the Secretary-General, unless the Administering Authority concerned shall agree to an earlier examination of the report.

3. The Secretary-General shall transmit these reports without delay to the members of the Trusteeship Council.

Rule 73

The Administering Authority shall furnish to the Secretary-General 400 copies of each report for a Trust Territory. Copies of each such report shall at the same time be sent directly by the Administering Authority to the members of the Trusteeship Council as a means of expediting the work of the Council.

XIV. EXAMINATION OF ANNUAL REPORTS
Rule 74

In the examination of all annual reports the Administering Authority concerned shall be entitled to designate and to have present a special representative who should be well informed on the Territory involved.

Rule 75

The special representative of the Administering Authority may participate without vote in the examination and discussion of a report, except in a discussion directed to specific conclusions concerning it.

XV. PETITIONS
Rule 76

Petitions may be accepted and examined by the Trusteeship Council if they concern the affairs of one or more Trust Territories or the operation of the International Trusteeship System as laid down in the Charter, except that with respect to petitions relating to a strategic area the functions of the Trusteeship Council shall be governed by Article 83 of the Charter and the terms of the relevant Trusteeship Agreements.

Rule 77

Petitioners may be inhabitants of Trust Territories, or other parties.

Rule 78

Petitions may be presented in writing in accordance with rules 79 to 86, or orally in accordance with rules 87 to 90.

Rule 79

A written petition may be in the form of a letter, telegram, memorandum or other document concerning the affairs of one or more Trust Territories or the operation of the International Trusteeship System as laid down in the Charter.

Rule 80

1.   The Trusteeship Council may hear oral presentations in support or elaboration of a previously submitted written petition. Oral presentations shall be confined to the subject-matter of the petition as stated in writing by the petitioners. The Trusteeship Council, in exceptional cases, may also hear orally petitions which have not been previously submitted in writing, provided that the Trusteeship Council and the Administering Authority concerned have been previously informed with regard to their subject-matter.

2.   The President of the Council shall be authorized between sessions of the Council, through the Secretary-General, to inform any petitioner who requests an opportunity for an oral presentation or petition under this rule, that the Council will grant him a hearing at such a time and place as the President may name. Before communicating such information to the petitioner, the President shall inquire of the Administering Authority or Authorities concerned as to whether there are substantial reasons why the matter should first be discussed in the Council. If the Administering Authority is of the opinion that such substantial reasons exist, the President shall defer action until the matter has been decided by the Council.

Rule 81

Normally, petitions shall be considered inadmissible if they are directed against judgements of competent courts of the Administering Authority or if they lay before the Council a dispute with which the courts have competence to deal. This rule shall not be interpreted so as to prevent consideration by the Trusteeship Council of petitions against legislation on the grounds of its incompatibility with the provisions of the Charter of the United Nations or of the Trusteeship Agreement, irrespective of whether decisions on cases arising under such legislation have previously been given by the courts of the Administering Authority.

Rule 82

Written petitions may be addressed directly to the Secretary-General or may be transmitted to him through the Administering Authority.

Rule 83

Written petitions submitted to the Administering Authority for transmission shall be communicated promptly to the Secretary-General, with or without comments by the Administering Authority, at its discretion, or with an indication that such comments will follow in due course.

Rule 84

1. Representatives of the Trusteeship Council engaged in periodic visits to Trust Territories or on other official missions authorized by the Council may accept written petitions, subject to such instructions as may have been received from the Trusteeship Council. Petitions of this kind shall be transmitted promptly to the Secretary-General for circulation to the members of the Council. A copy of each such petition shall be communicated to the competent local authority. Any observations which the visiting representatives may wish to make on the petitions, after consultation with the local representative of the Administering Authority, shall be submitted to the Trusteeship Council.

2. The visiting mission shall decide which of the communications it receives are intended for its own information and which of these are petitions to be transformed to the Secretary-General, pursuant to paragraph 1 of this rule, to be dealt with in accordance with rules 85 and 86.

Rule 85

1. The Secretary-General shall circulate promptly to the members of the Trusteeship Council all written petitions received by him which contain requests, complaints and grievances seeking action by the Trusteeship Council.

2. Petitions concerning general problems to which the attention of the Trusteeship Council has already been called and on which the Council has taken decisions or has made recommendations, as well as anonymous communications, shall be circulated by the Secretary-General in the manner provided for in rule 24.

3. In the case of lengthy petitions, the Secretary-General will first circulate a summary of the petition, the original petition being made available to the Trusteeship Council. The original petition, however, will be circulated if the President of the Trusteeship Council, during the recess of the Council, or the Council, if it is in session, so decides.

4. The Secretary-General shall not circulate petitions which are manifestly inconsequential, a list of which, with a summary of their contents, shall be communicated to the members of the Trusteeship Council.

5. With respect to petitions relating to a strategic area, the functions of the Trusteeship Council shall be governed by Article 83 of the Charter and the terms of the relevant Trusteeship Agreement.

Rule 86

1. Written petitions will normally be placed on the agenda of a regular session provided that they shall have been received by the Administering Authority concerned either directly or through the Secretary-General at least two months before the date of the next following regular session.

2. The date of receipt of a petition shall be considered as being:

(a) In respect of a petition which is presented through the Administering Authority, the date on which the petition is received by the competent local authority in the Territory or the metropolitan government of the Administering Authority, as the case may be;

(b) In respect of a petition received by a visiting mission, the date on which the copy of the petition is communicated to the local authority in accordance with rule 84;

(c) In respect of a petition not presented through the Administering Authority, the date on which the petition is received by the Administering Authority through the Secretary-General. The Administering Authority concerned shall immediately notify the Secretary-General of the date of receipt of all such petitions.

3. In cases where the Administering Authority may be prepared to consider a written petition at shorter notice than is prescribed by the foregoing rules, or where, in

exceptional cases, as a matter of urgency, it may be so decided by the Trusteeship Council in consultation with the Administering Authority concerned, such written petition may be placed on the agenda of a regular session notwithstanding that it has been presented after the due date, or it may be placed on the agenda of a special session.

4. Complete and precise written observations by the Administering Authority concerned on the petitions to which the established procedure is to be applied shall be transmitted within three months of date of their receipt by the Administering Authority.

Rule 87

Requests to present petitions orally or to make oral presentations in support or elaboration of written petitions, in accordance with rule 80, may be addressed directly to the Secretary-General or may be transmitted to him through the Administering Authority. In the latter case the Administering Authority concerned shall communicate such requests promptly to the Secretary-General.

Rule 88

The Secretary-General shall promptly notify the members of the Trusteeship Council of all requests for oral petitions or oral presentations received by him, except for petitions relating to a strategic area with respect to which the functions of the Trusteeship Council shall be governed by Article 83 of the Charter and the terms of the relevant trusteeship Agreement.

Rule 89

Representatives of the Trusteeship Council engaged in periodic visits to Trust Territories or on other official missions authorized by the Council may receive oral presentations or petitions, subject to such instructions as may have been received from the Trusteeship Council. Such oral presentations or petitions shall be recorded by the visiting mission, and the record shall be transmitted promptly to the Secretary-General for circulation to the members of the Council and to the Administering Authority for comment. A copy of each such record shall be communicated to the competent local authority. Any observations which the visiting representatives may wish to make on the oral presentations or petitions, after consultation with the local representative of the Administering Authority, shall be submitted to the Trusteeship Council.

Rule 90

The Trusteeship Council may designate one or more of its representatives to accept oral petitions the subject-matter of which has been previously communicated to the Trusteeship Council and to the Administering Authority concerned. Oral petitions and oral presentations may be examined either in public or in private, as may be determined, in accordance with rule 44.

Rule 91

In the examination of all petitions the Administering Authority concerned shall be entitled to designate and to have present a special representative who should be well informed on the Territory involved.

Rule 92

The Secretary-General shall inform the Administering Authorities and the petitioners concerned of the actions taken by the Trusteeship Council on each petition, and shall transmit to them the official records of the public meetings at which the petitions were examined.

XVI. VISITS TO TRUST TERRITORIES
Rule 93

The Trusteeship Council, in accordance with the provisions of Article 87 c and Article 83, paragraph 3, of the Charter, as the case may be, and with the terms of the respective Trusteeship Agreements, shall make provision for periodic visits to each Trust Territory with a view to achieving the basic objectives of the International Trusteeship System.

Rule 94

The Trusteeship Council, acting in conformity with the terms of the respective Trusteeship Agreements, shall define the terms of reference of each visiting mission and shall issue to each mission such special instructions as it may consider appropriate.

Rule 95

The Trusteeship Council shall select the members of each visiting mission, who shall preferably be one or more of the representatives on the Council. Each mission may be assisted by experts and by representatives of the local administration. A mission and the individual members thereof shall, while engaged in a visit, act only on the basis of the instructions of the Council and shall be responsible exclusively to it.

Rule 96

The Trusteeship Council may, in agreement with the Administering Authority, conduct special investigations or inquiries when it considers that conditions in a Trust Territory make such action desirable.

Rule 97

All expenses of periodic visits, special investigations and inquiries, including the travel expenses of the visiting missions, shall be borne by the United Nations.

Rule 98

Each visiting mission shall transmit to the Trusteeship Council a report on its visit, a copy of which shall be promptly and, as a general rule, simultaneously transmitted to the Administering Authority and to each other member of the Trusteeship Council by the Secretary-General. The mission may authorize the Secretary-General to release its report in such form and at such date as it may deem appropriate. The report and the decisions or observations of the Council with respect to each such report, as well as the comments made by the Administering Authority concerned, may be published in such form and at such date as the Council may determine.

XVII. REPORTS OF THE TRUSTEESHIP COUNCIL
Rule 99

The Trusteeship Council shall present annually to the General Assembly a general report on its activities and on the discharge of its responsibilities under the International Trusteeship System. Each such report shall include an annual review of the conditions in each Trust Territory.

Rule 100

1. The sections of the general reports of the Trusteeship Council to the General Assembly relating to conditions in specific Trust Territories, referred to in rule 99, shall take into account the annual reports of the Administering Authorities, and such other sources of information as may be available, including petitions, reports of visiting missions, and any special investigations or inquiries, as provided for in rule 96.

2. The general reports shall include, as appropriate, the conclusions of the Trusteeship Council regarding the execution and interpretation of the provisions of Chapters XII and XIII of the Charter and of the Trusteeship Agreements, and such suggestions and recommendations concerning each Trust Territory as the Council may decide.

Rule 101

The reports of the Trusteeship Council to the General Assembly provided for in rules 99 and 100 shall be transmitted through the Secretary-General at least thirty days before the opening of the regular session of the General Assembly.

Rule 102

The Trusteeship Council may designate the President, the Vice-President or another of its members to represent it during the consideration of its reports by the General Assembly.

XVIII. OTHER FUNCTIONS
Rule 103

The Trusteeship Council shall perform such other functions as may be provided for in the Trusteeship Agreements, and, in pursuance of the duty imposed upon it by Article 85 of the Charter, may submit to the General Assembly recommendations concerning the functions of the United Nations with regard to Trusteeship Agreements, including the approval of the terms of the Trusteeship Agreements and of their alteration or amendment. With regard to strategic areas, the Trusteeship Council may similarly perform such functions in so far as it may be requested to do so by the Security Council.

XIX. RELATIONSHIP WITH OTHER BODIES
Rule 104

1.   The Trusteeship Council shall, when appropriate, avail itself of the assistance of the Economic and Social Council, of the specialized agencies and of appropriate intergovernmental regional bodies which may be separately established, relating to matters with which they may be concerned.

2.   The Secretary-General shall promptly communicate to these bodies the annual reports of the Administering Authorities and such reports and other documents of the Trusteeship Council as may be of special concern to them.

XX. SUSPENSION OF RULES
Rule 105

When the Trusteeship Council is in session, a rule of procedure may be suspended by decision of the Council.

XXI. AMENDMENT
Rule 106

These rules of procedure may be amended by the Trusteeship Council. Normally, a vote shall not be taken until four days after a proposal for amendment has been submitted.

8. RULES OF THE INTERNATIONAL COURT OF JUSTICE[1]

Contents

[1]Adopted on 14 April 1978.

PREAMBLE

The Court,

Having regard to chapter XIV of the Charter of the United Nations;

Having regard to the Statute of the Court annexed thereto;

Acting in pursuance of Article 30 of the Statute;

Adopts the following revised Rules of the Court, approved on 14 April 1978, which shall come into force on 1 July 1978, and shall as from that date replace the Rules adopted by the Court on 6 May 1946 and amended on 10 May 1972, save in respect of any case submitted to the Court before 1 July 1978, or any phase of such a case, which shall continue to be governed by the Rules in force before that date.

PART I
THE COURT
SECTION A. JUDGES AND ASSESSORS
Subsection 1. The Members of the Court
Article 1

1.   The Members of the Court are the judges elected in accordance with Articles 2 to 15 of the Statute.

2.   For the purposes of a particular case, the Court may also include upon the Bench one or more persons chosen under Article 31 of the Statute to sit as judges *ad hoc*.

3.   In the following Rules, the term "Members of the Court" denotes any elected judge; the term "judge" denotes any Member of the Court and any judge *ad hoc*.

Article 2

1.   The term of office of Members of the Court elected at a triennial election shall begin to run from the sixth of February[1] in the year in which the vacancies to which they are elected occur.

2.   The term of office of a Member of the Court elected to replace a Member whose term of office has not expired shall begin to run from the date of the election.

---

[1]This is the date on which the terms of office of the Members of the Court elected at the first election began in 1946.

Article 3

1. The Members of the Court, in the exercise of their functions, are of equal status, irrespective of age, priority of election or length of service.

2. The Members of the Court shall, except as provided in paragraphs 4 and 5 of this Article, take precedence according to the date on which their terms of office respectively began, as provided for by Article 2 of these Rules.

3. Members of the Court whose terms of office began on the same date shall take precedence in relation to one another according to seniority of age.

4. A Member of the Court who is re-elected to a new term of office which is continuous with his previous term shall retain his precedence.

5. The President and the Vice-President of the Court, while holding these offices, shall take precedence before all other Members of the Court.

6. The Member of the Court who, in accordance with the foregoing paragraphs, takes precedence next after the President and the Vice-President is in these Rules designated the "senior judge". If that Member is unable to act, the Member of the Court who is next after him in precedence and able to act is considered as senior judge.

Article 4

1. The declaration to be made by every Member of the Court in accordance with Article 20 of the Statute shall be as follows:

"I solemnly declare that I will perform my duties and exercise my powers as judge honourably, faithfully, impartially and conscientiously."

2. This declaration shall be made at the first public sitting at which the Member of the Court is present. Such sitting shall be held as soon as practicable after his term of office begins and, if necessary, a special sitting shall be held for the purpose.

3. A Member of the Court who is re-elected shall make a new declaration only if his new term is not continuous with his previous one.

Article 5

1. A Member of the Court deciding to resign shall communicate his decision to the President, and the resignation shall take effect as provided in Article 13, paragraph 4, of the Statute.

2. If the Member of the Court deciding to resign from the Court is the President, he shall communicate his decision to the Court, and the resignation shall take effect as provided in Article 13, paragraph 4, of the Statute.

Article 6

In any case in which the application of Article 18 of the Statute is under consideration, the member of the Court concerned shall be so informed by the President or, if the circumstances so require, by the Vice-President, in a written statement which shall include the grounds therefor and any relevant evidence. He shall subsequently, at a private meeting of the Court specially convened for the purpose, be afforded an opportunity of making a statement, of furnishing any information or explanations he wishes to give, and of supplying answers, orally or in writing, to any questions put to him. At a further private meeting, at which the Member of the Court concerned shall not be present, the matter shall be discussed; each Member of the Court shall state his opinion, and if requested a vote shall be taken.

Subsection 2. *Judges* ad hoc
Article 7

1.   Judges *ad hoc,* chosen under Article 31 of the Statute for the purposes of particular cases, shall be admitted to sit on the Bench of the Court in the Circumstances and according to the procedure indicated in Article 17, paragraph 2, Articles 35, 36, 37, Article 91, paragraph 2, and Article 102, paragraph 3, of these Rules.

2.   They shall participate in the case in which they sit on terms of complete equality with the other judges on the Bench.

3.   Judges *ad hoc* shall take precedence after the Members of the Court and in order of seniority of age.

Article 8

1.   The solemn declaration to be made by every judge *ad hoc* in accordance with Articles 20 and 31, paragraph 6, of the Statute shall be as set out in Article 4, paragraph 1, of these Rules.

2.   This declaration shall be made at a public sitting in the case in which the judge *ad hoc* is participating. If the case is being dealt with by a chamber of the Court, the declaration shall be made in the same manner in that chamber.

3.   Judges *ad hoc* shall make the declaration in relation to any case in which they are participating, even if they have already done so in a previous case, but shall not make a new declaration for a later phase of the same case.

Subsection 3.   Assessors
Article 9

1.   The Court may, either *proprio motu* or upon a request made not later than the closure of the written proceedings, decide, for the purpose of a contentious case or request for advisory opinion, to appoint assessors to sit with it without the right to vote.

2.   When the Court so decides, the President shall take steps to obtain all the information relevant to the choice of the assessors.

3.   The assessors shall be appointed by secret ballot and by a majority of the votes of the judges composing the Court for the case.

4.   The same powers shall belong to the Chambers provided for by Articles 26 and 29 of the Statute and to the presidents thereof, and may be exercised in the same manner.

5.   Before entering upon their duties, assessors shall make the following declaration at a public sitting:

"I solemnly declare that I will perform my duties as an assessor honourably, impartially and conscientiously, and that I will faithfully observe all the provisions of the Statute and of the Rules of the Court."

SECTION B. THE PRESIDENCY
Article 10

1.   The term of office of the President and that of the Vice-President shall begin to run from the date on which the terms of office of the Members of the Court elected at a triennial election begin in accordance with Article 2 of these Rules.

2.   The elections to the presidency and vice-presidency shall be held on that date or shortly thereafter. The former President, if still a Member of the Court, shall continue to exercise his functions until the election to the presidency has taken place.

Article 11

1.   If, on the date of the election to the presidency, the former President is still a Member of the Court, he shall conduct the election. If he has ceased to be a Member of the Court, or is unable to act, the election shall be conducted by the Member of the Court exercising the functions of the presidency by virtue of Article 13, paragraph 1, of these Rules.

2.   The election shall take place by secret ballot, after the presiding Member of the Court has declared the number of affirmative votes necessary for election; there shall be no nominations. The Member of the Court obtaining the votes of a majority of the

Members composing it at the time of the election shall be declared elected, and shall enter forthwith upon his functions.

3.   The new President shall conduct the election of the Vice-President either at the same or at the following meeting. The provisions of paragraph 2 of this Article shall apply equally to this election.

Article 12

The President shall preside at all meetings of the Court; he shall direct the work and supervise the administration of the Court.

Article 13

1.   In the event of a vacancy in the presidency or of the inability of the president to exercise the functions of the presidency, these shall be exercised by the Vice-President, or failing him, by the senior judge.

2.   When the President is precluded by a provision of the Statute or of these Rules either from sitting or from presiding in a particular case, he shall continue to exercise the functions of the presidency for all purposes save in respect of that case.

3.   The President shall take measures necessary in order to ensure the continuous exercise of the functions of the presidency at the seat of the Court. In the event of his absence, he may, so far as is compatible with the Statute and these Rules, arrange for these functions to be exercised by the Vice-President, or failing him, by the senior judge.

4.   If the President decides to resign the presidency, he shall communicate his decision in writing to the Court through the Vice-President, or failing him, the senior judge. If the Vice-President decides to resign his Office, he shall communicate his decision to the President.

Article 14

If a vacancy in the presidency or the vice-presidency occurs before the date when the current term is due to expire under Article 21, paragraph 1, of the Statute and Article 10, paragraph 1, of these Rules, the Court shall decide whether or not the vacancy shall be filled during the remainder of the term.

SECTION C. THE CHAMBERS
Article 15

1.   The Chamber of Summary Procedure to be formed annually under Article 29 of the Statute shall be composed of five Members of the Court, comprising the President and Vice-President of the Court, acting ex officio, and three other members elected in accordance with Article 18, paragraph 1, of these Rules. In addition, two Members of the Court shall be elected annually to act as substitutes.

2.   The election referred to in paragraph 1 of this Article shall be held as soon as possible after the sixth of February in each year. The members of the Chamber shall enter upon their functions on election and continue to serve until the next election; they may be re-elected.

3.   If a member of the Chamber is unable, for whatever reason, to sit in a given case, he shall be replaced for the purposes of that case by the senior in precedence of the two substitutes.

4.   If a member of the Chamber resigns or otherwise ceases to be a member, his place shall be taken by the senior in precedence of the two substitutes, who shall thereupon become a full member of the Chamber and be replaced by the election of another substitute. Should vacancies exceed the number of available substitutes, election shall be held as soon as possible in respect of the vacancies still existing after the substitutes have assumed full membership and in respect of the vacancies in the substitutes.

Article 16

1.   When the Court decides to form one or more of the Chambers provided for in Article 26, paragraph 1, of the Statute, it shall determine the particular category of cases for which each Chamber is formed, the number of its members, the period for which they will serve, and the date at which they will enter upon their duties.

2.   The members of the Chamber shall be elected in accordance with Article 18, paragraph 1, of these Rules from among the Members of the Court, having regard to any special knowledge, expertise or previous experience which any of the Members of the Court may have in relation to the category of case the Chamber is being formed to deal with.

3.   The Court may decide upon the dissolution of a Chamber, but without prejudice to the duty of the Chamber concerned to finish any cases pending before it.

Article 17

1.   A request for the formulation of a Chamber to deal with particular case, as provided for in Article 26, paragraph 2, of the Statute, may be filed at any time until the closure of the written proceedings. Upon receipt of a request made by one party, the president shall ascertain whether the other party assents.

2.   When the parties have agreed, the President shall ascertain their views regarding the composition of the Chamber, and shall report to the Court accordingly. He shall also take such steps as may be necessary to give effect to the provisions of Article 31, paragraph 4, of the Statute.

3.   When the Court has determined, with the approval of the parties, the number of its Members who are to constitute the Chamber, it shall proceed to their election, in accordance with the provisions of Article 18, paragraph 1, of these Rules. The same procedure shall be followed as regards the filling of any vacancy that may occur on the Chamber.

4.   Members of a Chamber formed under this Article who have been replaced, in accordance with Article 13 of the Statute following the expiration of their terms of office, shall continue to sit in all phases of the case, whatever the stage it has then reached.

Article 18

1.   Elections to all Chambers shall take place by secret ballot. The Members of the Court obtaining the largest number of votes constituting a majority of the Members of the Court composing it at the time of the election shall be declared elected. If necessary to fill vacancies, more than one ballot shall take place, such ballot being limited to the number of vacancies that remain to be filled.

2.   If a Chamber when formed includes the President or Vice-President of the Court, or both of them, the President or Vice-President, as the case maybe, shall preside over that Chamber. In any other event, the Chamber shall elect its own president by secret ballot and by a majority of votes of its members. The Member of the Court who, under this paragraph, presides over the Chamber at the time of its formation shall continue to preside so long as he remains a member of that Chamber.

3.   The president of a Chamber shall exercise, in relation to cases being dealt with by that Chamber, all the functions of the President of the Court in relation to cases before the Court.

4.   If the president of a Chamber is prevented from sitting or from acting as president, the functions of the presidency shall be assumed by the member of the Chamber who is the senior in precedence and able to act.

SECTION D. INTERNAL FUNCTIONING OF THE COURT
Article 19

The internal judicial practice of the Court shall, subject to the provisions of the Statute and these Rules, be governed by any resolutions on the subject adopted by the Court[1].

Article 20

1. The quorum specified by Article 25, paragraph 3, of the Statute applies to all meetings of the Court.

2. The obligation of Members of the Court under Article 23, paragraph 3, of the Statute, to hold themselves permanently at the disposal of the Court, entails attendance at all such meetings, unless they are prevented from attending by illness or for other serious reasons duly explained to the President, who shall inform the Court.

3. Judges *ad hoc* are likewise bound to hold themselves at the disposal of the Court and to attend all meetings held in the case in which they are participating. They shall not be taken into account for the calculation of the quorum.

4. The Court shall fix the dates and duration of the judicial vacations and the periods and conditions of leave to be accorded to individual Members of the Court under Article 23, paragraph 2, of the Statute, having regard in both cases to the state of its General List and to the requirements of its current work.

5. Subject to the same considerations, the Court shall observe the public holidays customary at the place where the Court is sitting.

6. In case of urgency the President may convene the Court at any time.

Article 21

1. The deliberations of the Court shall take place in private and remain secret. The Court may however at any time decide in respect of its deliberations on other than judicial matters to publish or allow publication of any part of them.

2. Only judges, and the assessors, if any, take part in the Court's judicial deliberations. The Registrar, or his deputy, and other members of the staff of the Registry as may be required shall be present. No other person shall be present except by permission of the Court.

---

[1] The resolution now in force was adopted on 12 April 1976.

3.   The minutes of the Court's judicial deliberations shall record only the title or nature of the subjects or matters discussed, and the results of any vote taken. They shall not record any details of the discussions nor the views expressed, provided however that any judge is entitled to require that a statement made by him be inserted in the minutes.

PART II
THE REGISTRY
Article 22

1.   The Court shall elect its Registrar by secret ballot from amongst candidates proposed by Members of the Court. The Registrar shall be elected for a term of seven years. He may be re-elected.

2.   The President shall give notice of a vacancy or impending vacancy to Members of the Court, either forthwith upon the vacancy arising, or, where the vacancy will arise on the expiration of the term of office of the Registrar, not less than three months prior thereto. The President shall fix a date for the closure of the list of candidates so as to enable nominations and information concerning the candidates to be received in sufficient time.

3.   Nominations shall indicate the relevant information concerning the candidate, and in particular as to his age, nationality, and present occupation, university qualifications, knowledge of languages, and any previous experience in law, diplomacy or the work of international organizations.

4.   The candidate obtaining the votes of the majority of the Members of the Court composing it at the time of the election shall be declared elected.

Article 23

The Court shall elect a Deputy-Registrar: the provisions of Article 22 of these Rules shall apply to his election and term of office.

Article 24

1.   Before taking up his duties, the Registrar shall make the following declaration at a meeting of the Court:

"I solemnly declare that I will perform the duties incumbent upon me as Registrar of the International Court of Justice in all loyalty, discretion and good conscience, and that I will faithfully observe all the provisions of the Statute and of the Rules of the Court."

2. The Deputy-Registrar shall make a similar declaration at a meeting of the Court before taking up his duties.

Article 25

1. The staff-members of the Registry shall be appointed by the Court on proposals submitted by the Registrar. Appointments to such posts as the Court shall determine may however be made by the Registrar with the approval of the President.

2. Before taking up his duties, every staff-member shall make the following declaration before the President, the Registrar being present:

> "I solemnly declare that I will perform the duties incumbent upon me as an official of the International Court of Justice in all loyalty, discretion and good conscience, and that I will faithfully observe all the provisions of the Statute and of the Rules of the Court."

Article 26

1. The Registrar, in the discharge of his functions, shall:

(a) be the regular channel of communications to and from the Court, and in particular shall effect all communications, notifications and transmission of documents required by the Statute or by these Rules and ensure that the date of despatch and receipt thereof may be readily verified;

(b) keep, under the supervision of the President, and in such form as may be laid down by the Court, a General List of all cases, entered and numbered in the order in which the documents instituting proceedings or requesting an advisory opinion are received in the Registry;

(c) have the custody of the declarations accepting the jurisdiction of the Court made by States not parties to the Statute in accordance with any resolution adopted by the Security Council under Article 35, paragraph 2, of the Statute, and transmit certified copied thereof to all States parties to the Statute, to such other States as shall have deposited declarations, and to the Secretary-General of the United Nations;

(d) transmit to the parties copies of all pleadings and documents annexed upon receipt thereof in the Registry;

(e) communicate to the government of the country in which the Court or a Chamber is sitting, and any other governments which may be concerned, the necessary information as to the persons from time to time entitled, under the Statute and relevant agreements, to privileges, immunities, or facilities;

(f)   be present, in person or by his deputy, at meeting of the Court, and of the Chambers, and be responsible for the preparation of minutes of such meetings;

(g)   make arrangements for such provision or verification of translations and interpretations into the Court's official languages as the Court may require;

(h)   sign all judgements, advisory opinions and orders of the Court, and the minutes referred to in subparagraph (f);

(i)   be responsible for the printing and publication of the Court's judgements, advisory opinions and orders, the pleadings and statements, and minutes of public sittings in cases, and of such other documents as the Court may direct to be published;

(j)   be responsible for all administrative work and in particular for the accounts and financial administration in accordance with the financial procedures of the United Nations;

(k)   deal with enquiries concerning the Court and its work;

(l)   assist in maintaining relations between the Court and other organs of the United Nations, the specialized agencies, and international bodies and conferences concerned with the codification and progressive development of international law;

(m)   ensure that information concerning the Court and its activities is made accessible to governments, the highest national courts of justice, professional and learned societies, legal faculties and schools of law, and public information media;

(n)   have custody of seals and stamps of the Court, of the archives of the Court, and such other archives as may be entrusted to the Court[1].

2.   The Court may at any time entrust additional functions to the Registrar.

3.   In the discharge of his functions the Registrar shall be responsible to the Court.

Article 27

1.   The Deputy-Registrar shall assist the Registrar, act as Registrar in the latter's absence and, in the event of the office becoming vacant, exercise the functions of the Registrar until the office has been filled.

2.   If both the Registrar and the Deputy-Registrar are unable to carry out the duties of Registrar, the President shall appoint an official of the Registry to discharge those duties for such time as may be necessary. If both offices are vacant at the same time, the

---

[1]The Registrar also keeps the Archives of the Permanent Court of International Justice, entrusted to the present Court by decision of the Permanent Court of October 1945 (*I.C.J. Yearbook 1946-47, p.26*), and the Archives of the Trial of the Major War Criminals before the International Military Tribunal at Nürnberg (1945-1946), entrusted to the Court by decision of that Tribunal of 1 October 1946; the Court authorized the Registrar to accept the latter Archives by decision of 19 November 1949.

President, after consulting the Members of the Court, shall appoint an official of the Registry to discharge the duties of Registrar pending an election to that office.

Article 28

1.   The Registry shall comprise of Registrar, the Deputy-Registrar, and such other staff as the Registrar shall require for the efficient discharge of his functions.

2.   The Court shall prescribe the organization of the Registry, and shall for this purpose request the Registrar to make proposals.

3.   Instructions for the Registry shall be drawn up by the Registrar and approved by the Court.

4.   The staff of the Registry shall be subject to Staff Regulations drawn up by the Registrar, so far as possible in conformity with the United Nations Staff Regulations and Staff Rules, and approved by the Court.

Article 29

1.   The Registrar may be removed from office only if, in the opinion of two-thirds of the Members of the Court, he has either become permanently incapacitated from exercising his functions, or has committed a serious breach of his duties.

2.   Before a decision is taken under this Article, the Registrar shall be informed by the President of the action contemplated, in a written statement which shall include the grounds therefor and any relevant evidence. He shall subsequently, at a private meeting of the Court, be afforded an opportunity of making a statement, of furnishing any information or explanations he wishes to give, and of supplying answers, orally or in writing, to any questions put to him.

3.   The Deputy-Registrar may be removed from office only on the same grounds and by the same procedure.

PART III
PROCEEDINGS IN CONTENTIOUS CASES
SECTION A.   COMMUNICATIONS TO THE COURT AND CONSULTATIONS
Article 30

All communications to the Court under these Rules shall be addressed to the Registrar unless otherwise stated. Any request made by a party shall likewise be addressed to the Registrar unless made in open court in the course of the oral proceedings.

Article 31

In every case submitted to the Court, the President shall ascertain the views of the parties with regard to questions of procedure. For this purpose he shall summon the agents of the parties to meet him as soon as possible after their appointment, and whenever necessary thereafter.

SECTION B. THE COMPOSITION OF THE COURT
FOR PARTICULAR CASES
Article 32

1.   If the President of the Court is a national of one of the parties in a case he shall not exercise the functions of the presidency in respect of that case. The same rule applies to the Vice-President, or to the senior judge, when called on to act as President.

2.   The Member of the Court who is presiding in a case on the date on which the Court convenes for the oral proceedings shall continue to preside in that case until completion of the current phase of the case, notwithstanding the election in the meantime of a new President or Vice-President. If he should become unable to act, the presidency for the case shall be determined in accordance with Article 13 of these Rules, and on the basis of the composition of the Court on the date on which it convened for the oral proceedings.

Article 33

Except as provided in Article 17 of these Rules, Members of the Court who have been replaced, in accordance with Article 13, paragraph 3, of the Statute following the expiration of their terms of office, shall discharge the duty imposed upon them by that paragraph by continuing to sit until the completion of any phase of a case in respect of which the Court convenes for the oral proceedings prior to the date of such replacement.

Article 34

1.   In case of any doubt arising as to the application of Article 17, paragraph 2, of the Statute or in case of a disagreement as to the application of Article 24 of the Statute, the President shall inform the Members of the Court, with whom the decision lies.

2.   If a party desires to bring to the attention of the Court facts which it considers to be of possible relevance to the application of the provisions of the Statute mentioned in the previous paragraph, but which it believes may not be known to the Court, that party shall communicate confidentially such facts to the President in writing.

Article 35

1.   If a party proposes to exercise the power conferred by Article 31 of the Statute to choose a judge *ad hoc* in a case, it shall notify the Court of its intention as soon as possible. If the name and nationality of the judge selected are not indicated at the same time, the party shall, not later than two months before the time-limit fixed for the filing of the Counter-Memorial, inform the Court of the name and nationality of the person chosen and supply brief biographical details. The judge *ad hoc* may be of a nationality other than that of the party which chooses him.

2.   If a party proposes to abstain from choosing a judge *ad hoc*, on condition of a like abstention by the other party, it shall so notify the Court which shall inform the other party. If the other party thereafter gives notice of its intention to choose, or chooses, a judge *ad hoc*, the time-limit for the party which has previously abstained from choosing a judge may be extended by the President.

3.   A copy of any notification relating to the choice of a judge *ad hoc* shall be communicated by the Registrar to the other party, which shall be requested to furnish, within a time-limit to be fixed by the President, such observations as it may wish to make. If within the said time-limit no objection is raised by the other party, and if none appears to the Court itself, the parties shall be so informed.

4.   In the event of any objection or doubt, the matter shall be decided by the Court, if necessary after hearing the parties.

5.   A judge *ad hoc* who has accepted appointment but who becomes unable to sit may be replaced.

6.   If and when the reasons for the participation of a judge *ad hoc* are found no longer to exist, he shall cease to sit on the Bench.

Article 36

1.   If the Court finds that two or more parties are in the same interest, and therefore are to be reckoned as one party only, and that there is no Member of the Court of the nationality of any one of those parties upon the Bench, the Court shall fix a time-limit within which they may jointly choose a judge *ad hoc*.

2.   Should any party amongst those found by the Court to be in the same interest allege the existence of a separate interest of its own, or put forward any another objection, the matter shall be decided by the Court, if necessary after hearing the parties.

Article 37

1.   If a Member of the Court having the nationality of one of the parties is or becomes unable to sit in any phase of a case, that party shall thereupon become entitled to choose a judge *ad hoc* within a time-limit to be fixed by the Court, or by the President if the Court if not sitting.

2.   Parties in the same interest shall be deemed not to have a judge of one of their nationalities upon the Bench if the Member of the Court having one of their nationalities is or becomes unable to sit in any phase of the case.

3.   If the Member of the Court having the nationality of a party becomes able to sit not later than the closure of the written proceedings in that phase of the case, that Member of the Court shall resume his seat on the Bench in the case.

SECTION C. PROCEEDINGS BEFORE THE COURT
Subsection 1. Institution of Proceedings
Article 38

1.   When proceedings before the Court are instituted by means of an application addressed as specified in Article 40, paragraph 1, of the Statute, the application shall indicate the party making it, the State against which the claim is brought, and the subject of the dispute.

2.   The application shall specify as far as possible the legal grounds upon which the jurisdiction of the Court is said to be based; it shall also specify the precise nature of the claim, together with a succinct statement of the facts and grounds on which the claim is based.

3.   The original of the application shall be signed either by the agent of the party submitting it, or by the diplomatic representative of that party in the country in which the Court has its seat, or by some other duly authorized person. If the application bears the signature of someone other than such diplomatic representative, the signature must be authenticated by the latter or by the competent authority of the applicant's foreign ministry.

4.   The Registrar shall forthwith transmit to the respondent a certified copy of the application.

5.   When the applicant State proposes to found the jurisdiction of the Court upon a consent thereto yet to be given or manifested by the State against which such application is made, the application shall be transmitted to that State. It shall not however be entered in the General List, nor any action be taken in the proceedings, unless and until the State against which such application is made consents to the Court's jurisdiction for the purposes of the case.

Article 39

1. When proceedings are brought before the Court by the notification of a special agreement, in conformity with Article 40, paragraph 1, of the Statute, the notification may be effected by the parties jointly or by any one or more of them. If the notification is not a joint one, a certified copy of it shall forthwith be communicated by the Registrar to the other party.

2. In each case the notification shall be accompanied by an original or certified copy of the special agreement. The notification shall also, in so far as this is not already apparent from the agreement, indicate the precise subject of the dispute and identify the parties to it.

Article 40

1. Except in the circumstances contemplated by Article 38, paragraph 5, of these Rules, all steps on behalf of the parties after proceedings have been instituted shall be taken by agents. Agents shall have an address for service at the seat of the Court to which all communications concerning the case are to be sent. Communications addressed to the agents of the parties shall be considered as having been addressed to the parties themselves.

2. When proceedings are instituted by means of an application, the name of the agent for the applicant shall be stated. The respondent, upon receipt of the certified copy of the application, or as soon as possible thereafter, shall inform the Court of the name of its agent.

3. When proceedings are brought by notification of a special agreement, the party making the notification shall state the name of its agent. Any other party to the special agreement, upon receiving from the Registrar a certified copy of such notification, or as soon as possible thereafter, shall inform the Court of the name of its agent if it has not already done so.

Article 41

The institution of proceedings by a State which is not a party to the Statute but which, under Article 35, paragraph 2, thereof, has accepted the jurisdiction of the Court by a declaration made in accordance with any resolution adopted by the Security Council under that Article[1], shall be accompanied by a deposit of the declaration in question,

---

[1]The resolution now in force was adopted on 15 October 1946.

unless the latter has previously been deposited with the Registrar. If any question of the validity or effect of such declaration arises, the Court shall decide.

Article 42

The Registrar shall transmit copies of any application or notification of a special agreement instituting proceedings before the Court to: (a) the Secretary-General of the United Nations; (b) the Members of the United Nations; (c) other States entitled to appear before the Court.

Article 43

Whenever the construction of a convention to which States other than those concerned in the case are parties may be in question within the meaning of Article 63, paragraph 1, of the Statute, the Court shall consider what directions shall be given to the Registrar in the matter.

Subsection 2. The Written Proceedings
Article 44

1.   In the light of the information obtained by the president under Article 31 of these Rules, the Court shall make the necessary orders to determine, *inter alia*, the number and the order of filing of the pleadings and the time-limits within which they must be filed.

2.   In making an order under paragraph 1 of this Article, any agreement between the parties which does not cause unjustified delay shall be taken into account.

3.   The Court may, at the request of the party concerned, extend any time-limit, or decide that any step taken after the expiration of the time-limit fixed therefor shall be considered as valid, if it is satisfied that there is adequate justification for the request. In either case the other party shall be given an opportunity to state its views.

4.   If the Court is not sitting, its powers under this Article shall be exercised by the President, but without prejudice to any subsequent decision of the Court. If the consultation refereed to in Article 31 reveals persistent disagreement between the parties as to the application of Article 45, paragraph 2, or Article 46, paragraph 2, of these Rules, the Court shall be convened to decide the matter.

Article 45

1.   The pleadings in a case begun by means of an application shall consist, in the following order, of: a Memorial by the applicant; a Counter-Memorial by the respondent.

2.   The Court may authorize or direct that there shall be a Reply by the applicant and a Rejoinder by the respondent if the parties are so agreed, or if the Court decides, *proprio motu* or at the request of one of the parties, that these pleadings are necessary.

Article 46

1.   In a case begun by the notification of a special agreement, the number and order of the pleadings shall be governed by the provisions of the agreement, unless the Court, after ascertaining the views of the parties, decides otherwise.

2.   If the special agreement contains no such provision, and if the parties have not subsequently agreed on the number and order of pleadings, they shall each file a Memorial and Counter-Memorial, within the same time-limits. The Court shall not authorize the presentation of Replies unless it finds them to be necessary.

Article 47

The Court may at any time direct that the proceedings in two or more cases be joined. It may also direct that the written or oral proceedings, including the calling of witnesses, be in common; or the Court may, without effecting any formal joinder, direct common action in any of these respects.

Article 48

Time-limits for the completion of steps in the proceedings may be fixed by assigning a specified period but shall always indicate definite dates. Such time-limits shall be as short as the charter of the case permits.

Article 49

1.   A Memorial shall contain a statement of the relevant facts, a statement of law, and the submissions.

2.   A Counter-Memorial shall contain: and admission or denial of the facts stated in the Memorial; any additional facts, if necessary; observations concerning the statement of law in the Memorial; a statement of law in answer thereto; and the submissions.

3.   The Reply and Rejoinder, whenever authorized by the Court, shall not merely repeat the parties' contentions, but shall be directed to bringing out the issues that still divide them.

4.   Every pleading shall set out the party's submissions at the relevant stage of the case, distinctly from the arguments presented, or shall confirm the submissions previously made.

Article 50

1.   There shall be annexed to the original of every pleading certified copies of any relevant documents adduced in support of the contentions contained in the pleading.

2.   If only parts of a document are relevant, only such extracts as are necessary for the purpose of the pleading in question need be annexed. A copy of the whole document shall be deposited in the Registry, unless it has been published and is readily available.

3.   A list of all documents annexed to a pleading shall be furnished at the time the pleading is filed.

Article 51

1.   If the parties are agreed that the written proceedings shall be conducted wholly in one of the two official languages of the Court, the pleadings shall be submitted only in that language. If the parties are not so agreed, any pleading or any part of a pleading shall be submitted in one or other of the official languages.

2.   If in pursuance of Article 39, paragraph 3, of the Statute a language other than French or English is used, a translation into French or English certified as accurate by the party submitting it, shall be attached to the original of each pleading.

3.   When a document annexed to a pleading is not in one of the official languages of the Court, it shall be accompanied by a translation into one of these languages certified by the party submitting it as accurate. The translation may be confined to part of an annex, or to extracts therefrom, but in this case it must be accompanied by an explanatory note indicating what passages are translated. The Court may however require a more extensive or a complete translation to be furnished.

Article 52[1]

1.   The original of every pleading shall be signed by the agent and filed in the Registry. It shall be accompanied by a certified copy of the pleading, documents annexed, and any translations, for communication to the other party in accordance with Article 43,

---

[1]The agents of the parties are requested to ascertain from the Registry the usual format of the pleadings, and the conditions on which the Court may bear part of the cost of printing.

paragraph 4, of the Statute, and by the number of additional copies required by the Registry, but without prejudice to an increase in that number should the need arise later.

2. All pleadings shall be dated. When a pleading has to be filed by a certain date, it is the date of the receipt of the pleading in the Registry which will be regarded by the Court as the material date.

3. If the Registrar arranges for the printing of a pleading at the request of a party, the text must be supplied in sufficient time to enable the printed pleading to be filed in the Registry before the expiration of any time-limit which may apply to it. The printing is done under the responsibility of the party in question.

4. The correction of a slip or error in any document which has been filed may be made at any time with the consent of the other party or by leave of the President. Any correction so effected shall be notified to the other party in the same manner as the pleading to which it relates.

Article 53

1. The Court, or the President if the Court is not sitting, may at any time decide, after ascertaining the views of the parties, that copies of the pleadings and documents annexed shall be made available to a State entitled to appear before it which has asked to be furnished with such copies.

2. The Court may, after ascertaining the views of the parties, decide that copies of the pleadings and documents annexed shall be made accessible to the public or after the opening of the oral proceedings.

Subsection 3. The Oral Proceedings
Article 54

1. Upon the closure of the written proceedings, the case is ready for hearing. The date of the opening of the oral proceedings shall be fixed by the Court, which may also decide, if occasion should arise, that the opening or the continuance of the oral proceedings be postponed.

2. When fixing the date for, or postponing, the opening of the oral proceedings the Court shall have regard to the priority required by Article 74 of these Rules and to any other special circumstances, including the urgency of a particular case.

3. When the Court is not sitting, its powers under this Article shall be exercised by the President.

Article 55

The Court may, if it considers it desirable, decide pursuant to Article 22, paragraph 1, of the Statute that all or part of the further proceedings in a case shall be held at a place other than the seat of the Court. Before so deciding, it shall ascertain the views of the parties.

Article 56

1. After the closure of the written proceedings, no further documents may be submitted to the Court by either party except with the consent of the other party or as provided in paragraph 2 of this Article. The party desiring to produce a new document shall file the original or a certified copy thereof, together with the number of copies required by the Registry, which shall be responsible for communicating it to the other party and shall inform the Court. The other party shall be held to have given its consent if it does not lodge an objection to the production of the document.

2. In the absence of consent, the Court, after hearing the parties, may, if it considers the document necessary, authorize its production.

3. If a new document is produced under paragraph 1 or paragraph 2 of this Article, the other party shall have an opportunity of commenting upon it and of submitting documents in support of its comments.

4. No reference may be made during the oral proceedings to the contents of any document which has not been produced in accordance with Article 43 of the Statute or this Article, unless the document if part of a publication readily available.

5. The application of the provisions of this Article shall not in itself constitute a ground for delaying the opening or the course of the oral proceedings.

Article 57

Without prejudice to the provisions of the Rules Concerning the production of documents, each party shall communicate to the Registrar, in sufficient time before the opening of the oral proceedings, information regarding any evidence which it intends to produce or which it intends to request the Court to obtain. This communication shall contain a list of the surnames, first names, nationalities, descriptions and places of residence of the witnesses and experts whom the party intends to call, with indications in general terms of the point or points to which their evidence will be directed. A copy of the communication shall also be furnished for transmission to the other party.

Article 58

1. The Court shall determine whether the parties should present their arguments before or after the production of the evidence; the parties shall, however, retain the right to comment on the evidence given.

2. The order in which the parties will be heard, the method of handling the evidence and of examining any witnesses and experts, and the number of counsel and advocates to be heard on behalf of each party, shall be settled by the Court after the views of the parties have been ascertained in accordance with Article 31 of these Rules.

Article 59

The hearing in Court shall be public, unless the Court shall decide otherwise, or unless the parties demand that the public be not admitted. Such a decision or demand may concern either the whole or part of the hearing, and may made at any time.

Article 60

1. The oral statements made on behalf of each party shall be succinct as possible within the limits of what is requisite for the adequate presentation of that party's contentions at the hearing. Accordingly, they shall be directed to the issues that still divide the parties, and shall not go over the whole ground covered by the pleadings, or merely repeat the facts and arguments these contain.

2. At the conclusion of the last statement made by a party at the hearing, its agent, without recapitulation of the arguments, shall read that party's final submissions. A copy of the written text of these, signed by the agent, shall be communicated to the Court and transmitted to the other party.

Article 61

1. The Court may at any time prior to or during the hearing indicate any points or issues to which it would like the parties specially to address themselves, or on which it considers that there has been sufficient argument.

2. The Court may, during the hearing, put questions to the agents, counsel and advocates, and may ask them for explanations.

3. Each judge has a similar right to put questions, but before exercising it should make his intention known to the President, who is made responsible by Article 45 of the Statute for the control of the hearing.

4.   The agents, counsel and advocates may answer either immediately or within a time-limit fixed by the President.

Article 62

1.   The Court may at any time call upon the parties to produce such evidence or to give such explanations as the Court may consider to be necessary for the elucidation of any aspect of the matters in issue, or may itself seek other information for this purpose.

2.   The Court may, if necessary, arrange for the attendance of a witness or expert to give evidence in the proceedings.

Article 63

1.   The parties may call any witnesses or experts appearing on the list communicated to the Court pursuant to Article 57 of these Rules. If at any time during the hearing a party wishes to call a witness or expert whose name was not included in that list, it shall so inform the Court and the other party, and shall supply the information required by Article 57. The witness or expert may be called either if the other party makes no objection or if the Court is satisfied that his evidence seems like to prove relevant.

2.   The Court, or the President if the Court is not sitting, shall, at the request of one of the parties or *proprio motu*, take necessary steps for the examination of witnesses other wise than before the Court itself.

Article 64

Unless on account of special circumstances the Court decides on a different form of words,

(a) every witness shall make the following declaration before giving any evidence:

"I solemnly declare upon my honour and conscience that I will speak the truth, the whole truth and nothing but the truth";

(b) every expert shall make the following declaration before making any statement:

"I solemnly declare upon my honour and conscience that I will speak the truth, the whole truth and nothing but the truth, and that my statement will be in accordance with my sincere belief."

Article 65

Witnesses and experts shall be examined by the agents, counsel or advocates of the parties under the control of the President. Questions may be put to them by the President and by the judges. Before testifying, witnesses shall remain out of court.

Article 66

The Court amy at any time decide, either *proprio motu* or at the request of a party, to exercise its functions with regard to the obtaining of evidence at a place or locality to which the case relates, subject to such conditions as the Court may decide upon after ascertaining the views of the parties. The necessary arrangements shall be made in accordance with Article 44 of the Statute.

Article 67

1. If the Court considers it necessary to arrange for an enquiry or an expert opinion, it shall, after hearing the parties, issue an order to this effect, defining the subject of the enquiry or expert opinion, stating the number and mode of appointment of the persons to hold the enquiry or of the experts, and laying down the procedure to be followed. Where appropriate, the Court shall require persons appointed to carry out an enquiry, or to give an expert opinion, to make a solemn declaration.

2. Every report or record of an enquiry and every expert opinion shall be communicated to the parties, which shall be given the opportunity of commenting upon it.

Article 68

Witnesses and experts who appear at the instance of the Court under Article 62, paragraph 2, and persons appointed under Article 67, paragraph 1, of these Rules, to carry out an enquiry or to give an expert opinion, shall, where appropriate, be paid out of the funds of the Court.

Article 69

1. The Court may, at any time prior to the closure of the oral proceedings, either *proprio motu* or at the request of one of the parties communicated as provided in Article 57 of these Rules, request a public international organization, pursuant to Article 34 of the Statute, to furnish information relevant to a case before it. The Court, after consulting

the chief administrative officer of the organization concerned, shall decide whether such information shall be presented to it orally or in writing, and the time-limits for its presentation.

2. When a public international organization sees fit to furnish, on its own initiative, information relevant to a case before the Court, it shall do so in the form of a Memorial to be filled in the Registry before the closure of the written proceedings. The Court shall retain the right to require such information to be supplemented, either orally or in writing, in the form of answers to any questions which it may see fit to formulate, and also to authorize the parties to comment, either orally or in writing, on the information thus furnished.

3. In the circumstances contemplated by Article 34, paragraph 3, of the Statute, the Registrar, on the instructions of the Court, or of the President if the Court is not sitting, shall proceed as prescribed in that paragraph. The Court, or the President if the Court is not sitting, may, as from the date on which the Registrar has communicated copies of the written proceedings and after consulting the chief administrative officer of the public international organization concerned, fix a time-limit within which the organization may submit to the Court its observations in writing. These observations shall be communicated to the parties and may be discussed by them and by the representative of the said organization during the oral proceedings.

4. In the foregoing paragraphs, the term "public international organization" denotes an international organization of states.

Article 70

1. In the absence of any decision to the contrary by the Court, all speeches and statements made and evidence given at the hearing in one of the official languages of the Court shall be interpreted into other official language. If they are made or given in any other language, they shall be interpreted into the two official languages of the Court.

2. Whenever, in accordance with Article 39, paragraph 3, of the Statute, a language other than French or English is used, the necessary arrangements for interpretation into one of the two official languages shall be made by the party concerned; however, the Registrar shall make arrangements for the verification of the interpretation provided by a party of evidence given on the party's behalf. In the case of witnesses or experts who appear at the instance of the Court, arrangements for interpretation shall be made by the Registry.

3. A party on behalf of which speeches or statements are to be made, or evidence given, in a language which is not one of the official languages of the Court, shall so notify the Registrar in sufficient time for him to make the necessary arrangements.

4.   Before first interpreting in the case, interpreters provided by a party shall make the following declaration in open court:

"I solemnly declare upon my honour and conscience that my interpretation will be faithful and complete."

Article 71

1.   A verbatim record shall be made by the Registrar of every hearing, in the official language of the Court which has been used. When the language used is not one of the two official languages of the Court, the verbatim record shall be prepared in one of the Court's official languages.

2.   When speeches or statements are made in a language which is not one of the official languages of the Court, the party on behalf of which they are made shall supply to the Registry in advance a text thereof in one of the official languages, and this text constitute the relevant part of the verbatim record.

3.   The transcript of the verbatim record shall be preceded by the names of the judges present, and those of the agents, counsel and advocates of the parties.

4.   Copies of the transcript shall be circulated to the judges sitting in the case, and to the parties. The latter may, under the supervision of the Court, correct the transcripts of speeches and statements made on their behalf, but in no case may such corrections affect the sense and bearing thereof. The judges may likewise make corrections in the transcript of anything they may have said.

5.   Witnesses and experts shall be shown that part of the transcript which relates to the evidence given, or the statements made by them, and may correct it in like manner as the parties.

6.   One certified true copy of the eventual corrected transcript, signed by the President and the Registrar, shall constitute the authentic minutes of the sitting for the purposes of Article 47 of the Statute. The minutes of public hearings shall be printed and published by the Court.

Article 72

Any written reply by a party to a question put under Article 61, or any evidence or explanation supplied by a party under Article 62 of these Rules, received by the Court after the closure of the oral proceedings, shall be communicated to the other party, which shall be given the opportunity of commenting upon it. If necessary the oral proceedings may be reopened for that purpose.

SECTION D. INCIDENTAL PROCEEDINGS
Subsection 1. Interim Protection
Article 73

1. A written request for the indication of provisional measures may be made by a party at any time during the course of the proceedings in the case in connection with which the request is made.

2. The request shall specify the reasons therefor, the possible consequences if it is not granted, and the measures requested. A certified copy shall forthwith be transmitted by the Registrar to the other party.

Article 74

1. A request for the indication of provisional measures shall have priority over all other cases.

2. The Court, if it is not sitting when the request is made, shall be convened forthwith for the purpose of proceeding to a decision on the request as a matter of urgency.

3. The Court, or the President if the Court is not sitting, shall fix a date for a hearing which will afford the parties an opportunity of being represented at it. The Court shall receive and take into account any observations that may be presented to it before the closure of the oral proceedings.

4. Pending the meeting of the Court, the President may call upon the parties to act in such a way as will enable any order the Court may make on the request for provisional measures to have its appropriate effects.

Article 75

1. The Court may at any time decide to examine *proprio motu* whether the circumstances of the case require the indication of provisional measures which ought to be taken or complied with by any or all of the parties.

2. When a request for provisional measures has been made, the Court may indicate measures that are in whole or in part other than those requested, or that ought to be taken or complied with by the party which has itself made the request.

3. The rejection of a request for the indication of provisional measures shall not prevent the party which made it from making a fresh request in the same case based on new facts.

Article 76

1. At the request of a party the Court may, at any time before the final judgement in the case, revoke or modify any decision concerning provisional measures if, in its opinion, some change in the situation justifies such revocation or modification.

2. Any application by a party proposing such a revocation or modification shall specify the change in the situation considered to be relevant.

3. Before taking any decision under paragraph 1 of this Article the Court shall afford the parties an opportunity of presenting their observations on the subject.

Article 77

Any measures indicated by the Court under Articles 73 and 75 of these Rules, and any decision taken by the Court under Article 76, paragraph 1, of these Rules, shall forthwith be communicated to the Secretary-General of the United Nations for transmission to the Security Council in pursuance of Article 41, paragraph 2, of the Statute.

Article 78

The Court may request information from the parties on any matter connected with the implementation of any provisional measures it has indicated.

Subsection 2. Preliminary Objections
Article 79

1. Any objection by the respondent to the jurisdiction of the Court or to the admissibility of the application, or other objection the decision upon which is requested before any further proceedings on the merits, shall be made in writing within the time-limit fixed for the delivery of the Counter-Memorial. Any such objection made by a party other than the respondent shall be filed within the time-limit fixed for the delivery of that party's first pleading.

2. The preliminary objection shall set out the facts and the law on which the objection is based, the submissions and a list of the documents in support; it shall mention any evidence which the party may desire to produce. Copies of the supporting documents shall be attached.

3. Upon receipt by the Registry of a preliminary objection, the proceedings on the merits shall be suspended and the Court, or the President if the Court is not sitting, shall fix the time-limit within which the other party may present a written statement of its

observations and submissions; documents in support shall be attached and evidence which it is proposed to produce shall be mentioned.

4.   Unless otherwise decided by the Court, the further proceedings shall be oral.

5.   The statements of fact and law in the pleadings referred to in paragraphs 2 and 3 of this Article, and the statements and evidence presented at the hearings contemplated by paragraph 4, shall be confined to those matters that are relevant to the objection.

6.   In order to enable the Court to determine its jurisdiction at the preliminary stage of proceedings, the Court, whenever necessary, may request the parties to argue all questions of law and fact, and to adduce all evidence, which bear on the issue.

7.   After hearing the parties, the Court shall give its decision in the form of a judgement, by which it shall either uphold the objection, reject it, or declare that the objection does not possess, in the circumstances of the case, an exclusively preliminary character. If the Court rejects the objection or declares that it does not possess an exclusively preliminary character, it shall fix time-limits for the further proceedings.

8.   Any agreement between the parties that an objection submitted under paragraph 1 of this Article be heard and determined within the framework of the merits shall be given effect by the Court.

Subsection 3.   Counter-Claims
Article 80

1.   A counter-claim may be presented provided that it is directly connected with the subject-matter of the claim of the other party and that it comes within the jurisdiction of the Court.

2.   A counter-claim shall be made in the Counter-Memorial of the party presenting it, and shall appear as part of the submissions of that party.

3.   In the event of doubt as to the connection between the question presented by way of counter-claim and the subject-matter of the claim of the other party the Court shall, after hearing the parties, decide whether or not the question thus presented shall be joined to the original proceedings.

Subsection 4.   Intervention
Article 81

1.   An application for permission to intervene under the terms of Article 62 of the Statute, signed in the manner provided for in Article 38, paragraph 3, of these Rules, shall be filed as soon as possible, and not later than the closure of the written proceedings. In exceptional circumstances, an application submitted at a later stage may however be admitted.

2.   The application shall state the name of an agent. It shall specify the case to which it relates, and shall set out:

(a) the interest of a legal nature which the State applying to intervene considers may be affected by the decision in that case;

(b) the precise object of the intervention;

(c) any basis of jurisdiction which is claimed to exist as between the State applying to intervene and the parties to the case.

3.   The application shall contain a list of the documents in support, which documents shall be attached.

Article 82

1.   A State which desires to avail itself of the right of intervention conferred upon it by Article 63 of the Statute shall file a declaration to that effect, signed in the manner provided for in Article 38, paragraph 3, of these Rules. Such a declaration shall be filed as soon as possible, and not later than the date fixed for the opening of the oral proceedings. In exceptional circumstances a declaration submitted at a later stage may however be admitted.

2.   The declaration shall state the name of an agent. It shall specify the case and the convention to which it relates and shall contain:

(a) particulars of the basis on which the declarant State considers itself a party to the convention;

(b) identification of the particular provisions of the convention the construction of which it considers to be in question;

(c) a statement of the construction of those provisions for which it contends;

(d) a list of the documents in support, which documents shall be attached.

3.   Such a declaration may be filed by a State that considers itself a party to the convention the construction of which is in question but has not received the notification referred to in Article 63 of the Statute.

Article 83

1.   Certified copies of the application for permission to intervene under Article 62 of the Statute, or of the declaration of intervention under Article 63 of the Statute, shall be communicated forthwith to the parties to the case, which shall be invited to furnish their written observations within a time-limit to be fixed by the Court or by the President if the Court is not sitting.

2.   The Registrar shall also transmit copies to: (a) the Secretary-General of the United Nations; (b) the Members of the United Nations; (c) other States entitled to appear

before the Court; (d) any other States which have been notified under Article 63 of the Statute.

Article 84

1.   The Court shall decide whether an application for permission to intervene under Article 62 of the Statute should be granted, and whether and intervention under Article 63 of the Statute is admissible, as a matter of priority unless in view of the circumstances of the case the Court shall otherwise determine.

2.   If, within the time-limit fixed under Article 83 of these Rules, an objection is filed to an application for permission to intervene, or to the admissibility of a declaration of intervention, the Court shall hear the State seeking to intervene and the parties before deciding.

Article 85

1.   If an application for permission to intervene under Article 62 of the Statute is granted, the intervening State shall be supplied with copied of the pleadings and documents annexed and shall be entitled to submit a written statement within a time-limit to be fixed by the Court. A further time-limit shall be fixed within which the parties may, if they so desire, furnish their written observations on that statement prior to the oral proceedings. If the Court is not sitting, these time-limits shall be fixed by the President.

2.   The time-limits fixed according to the preceding paragraph shall, so far as possible, coincide with those already fixed for the pleadings in the case.

3.   The intervening State shall be entitled, in the course of the oral proceedings, to submit its observations with respect to the subject-matter of the intervention.

Article 86

1.   If an intervention under Article 63 of the Statute is admitted, the intervening States shall be furnished with copies of the pleadings and documents annexed, and shall be entitled, within a time-limit to be fixed by the Court, or by the President if the Court is not sitting, to submit its written observations on the subject-matter of the intervention.

2.   These observations shall be communicated to the parties and to any other State admitted to intervene. The intervening State shall be entitled, in the course of the oral proceedings, to submit its observations with respect to the subject-matter of the intervention.

Subsection 5.   Special Reference to the Court
Article 87

1.   When in accordance with a treaty or convention in force a contentious case is brought before the Court concerning a matter which has been the subject of proceedings before some other international body, the provisions of the Statute and of the Rules governing contentious cases shall apply.

2.   The application instituting proceedings shall identify the decision or other act of the international body concerned and a copy thereof shall be annexed; it shall contain a precise statement of the questions raised in regard to that decision or act, which constitute the subject of the dispute referred to the Court.

Subsection 6.   Discontinuance
Article 88

1.   If at any time before the final judgement on the merits has been delivered the parties, either jointly or separately, notify the Court in writing that they have agreed to discontinue the proceedings, the Court shall make an order recording the discontinuance and directing that the case be removed from the list.

2.   If the parties have agreed to discontinue the proceedings in consequence of having reached a settlement of the dispute and if they so desire, the Court may record this fact in the order for removal of the case from the list, or indicate in, or annex to, the order, the terms of the settlement.

3.   If the Court is not sitting, any order under this Article may be made by the President.

Article 89

1.   If in the course of proceedings instituted by means of an application, the applicant informs the Court in writing that it is not going on with the proceedings, and if, at the date on which this communication is received by the Registry, the respondent has not yet taken any step in the proceedings, the Court shall make an order officially recording the discontinuance of the proceedings and directing the removal of the case from the list. A copy of this order shall be sent by the Registrar to the respondent.

2.   If, at the time when the notice of discontinuance is received, the respondent has already taken some step in the proceedings, the Court shall fix a time-limit within which the respondent may state whether it opposes the discontinuance of the proceedings. If no objection is made to the discontinuance before the expiration of the time-limit, acquiescence will be presumed and the Court shall make an order officially recording the

discontinuance of the proceedings and directing the removal of the case from the list. If objection is made, the proceedings shall continue.

3. If the Court, is not sitting, its powers under this Article may be exercised by the President.

SECTION E. PROCEEDINGS BEFORE THE CHAMBERS
Article 90

Proceedings before the Chambers mentioned in Articles 26 and 29 of the Statute shall, subject to the provisions of the Statute and of these Rules relating specifically to the Chambers, be governed by the provisions of Parts I to III of these Rules applicable in contentious cases before the Court.

Article 91

1. When it is desired that a case should be dealt with by one of the Chambers which has been formed in pursuance of Article 26, paragraph 1, or Article 29 of the Statute, a request to this effect shall either be made in the document instituting the proceedings or accompany it. Effect will be given to the request if the parties are in agreement.

2. Upon receipt by the Registry of this request, the President of the Court shall communicate it to the members of the Chamber concerned. He shall take such steps as may be necessary to give effect to the provisions of Article 31, paragraph 4, of the Statute.

3. The President of the Court shall convene the Chamber at the earliest date compatible with the requirements of the procedure.

Article 92

1. Written proceedings in a case before a Chamber shall consist of a single pleading by each side. In proceedings begun by means of an application, the pleadings shall be delivered within successive time-limits. In proceedings begun by the notification of a special agreement, the pleadings shall be delivered within the same time-limits, unless the parties have agreed on successive delivery of their pleadings. The time-limits referred to in this paragraph shall be fixed by the Court, or by the President if the Court is not sitting, in consultation with the Chamber concerned if it is already constituted.

2. The Chamber may authorize or direct that further pleadings be filed if the parties are so agreed, or if the Chamber decides, *proprio motu* or at the request of one of the parties, that such pleadings are necessary.

3. Oral proceedings shall take place unless the parties agree to dispense with them, and the Chamber consents. Even when no oral proceedings take place, the Chamber may call upon the parties to supply information or furnish explanations orally.

Article 93

Judgements given by a Chamber shall be read at a public sitting of that Chamber.

SECTION F. JUDGEMENTS, INTERPRETATION AND REVISION
Subsection 1. Judgements
Article 94

1. When the Court has completed its deliberations and adopted its judgement, the parties shall be notified of the date on which it will be read.

2. The judgement shall be read at a public sitting of the Court and shall become binding on the parties on the day of the reading.

Article 95

1. The judgement, which shall state whether it is given by the Court or by a Chamber, shall contain:

the date on which it is read;

the names of the judges participating in it;

the names of the parties;

the names of the agents, counsel and advocates of the parties;

a summary of the proceedings;

the submissions of the parties;

a statement of the facts;

the reasons in point of law;

the operative provisions of the judgement;

the decision, if any, in regard to costs;

the number and names of the judges constituting the majority;

a statement as to the text of the judgement which is authoritative.

2. Any judge may, if he so desires, attach his individual opinion to the judgement, whether he dissents from the majority or not; a judge who wishes to record his concurrence or dissent without stating his reasons may do so in the form of a declaration. The shame shall also apply to orders made by the Court.

3. One copy of the judgement duly signed and sealed, shall be placed in the archives of the Court and another shall be transmitted to each of the parties. Copies shall

be sent by the Registrar to: (a) the Secretary-General of the United Nations; (b) the Members of the United Nations; (c) other States entitled to appear before the Court.

Article 96

When by reason of an agreement reached between the parties, the written and oral proceedings have been conducted in one of the Court's two official languages, and pursuant to Article 39, paragraph 1, of the Statute the judgement is to be delivered in that language, the text of the judgement in that language shall be the authoritative text.

Article 97

If the Court, under Article 64 of the Statute, decides that all or part of a party's costs shall be paid by the other party, it may make and order for the purpose of giving to that decision.

Subsection 2. *Requests for the Interpretation or Revision of a Judgement*
Article 98

1.   In the event of dispute as to the meaning or scope of a judgement any party may make a request for its interpretation, whether the original proceedings were begun by an application or by the notification of a special agreement.

2.   A request for the interpretation of a judgement may be made either by an application or by the notification of a special agreement to that effect between the parties; the precise point or points in dispute as to the meaning or scope of the judgement shall be indicated.

3.   If the request for interpretation is made by an application, the requesting party's contentions shall be set out therein, and the other party shall be entitled to file written observations thereon within a time-limit fixed by the Court, or by the President if the Court is not sitting.

4.   Whether the request is made by an application or by notification of a special agreement, the Court may, if necessary, afford the parties the opportunity of furnishing further written or oral explanations.

Article 99

1.   A request for the revision of a judgement shall be made by an application containing the particulars necessary to show that the conditions specified in Article 61 of

the Statute are fulfilled. Any documents in support of the application shall be annexed to it.

2. The other party shall be entitled to file written observations on the admissibility of the application within a time-limit fixed by the Court, or by the President if the Court is not sitting. These observations shall be communicated to the party making the application.

3. The Court, before giving its judgement on the admissibility of the application may afford the parties a further opportunity of presenting their views thereon.

4. If the Court finds that the application is admissible it shall fix time-limits for such further proceedings on the merits of the application as, after ascertaining the views of the parties, it considers necessary.

5. If the Court decides to make the admission of the proceedings in revision conditional on previous compliance with the judgement, it shall make an order accordingly.

Article 100

1. If the judgement to be revised or to be interpreted was given by the Court, the request for its revision or interpretation shall be dealt with by the Court. If the judgement was given by a Chamber, the request for its revision or interpretation shall be dealt with by that Chamber.

2. The decision of the Court, or of the Chamber, on a request for interpretation or revision of a judgement shall itself be given in the form of a judgement.

SECTION G. MODIFICATIONS PROPOSED BY THE PARTIES
Article 101

The parties to a case may jointly propose particular modifications or additions to the rules contained in the present Part (with the exception of Articles 93 to 97 inclusive), which may be applied by the Court or by a Chamber if the Court or Chamber considers them appropriate in the circumstances of the case.

PART IV
ADVISORY PROCEEDINGS
Article 102

1. In the exercise of its advisory functions under Article 65 of the Statute, the Court shall apply, in addition to the provisions of Article 96 of the Charter and Chapter IV of the Statute, the provisions of the present Part of the Rules.

2.   The Court shall also be guided by the provisions of the Statute and of these Rules which apply in contentious cases to the extent to which it recognizes them to be applicable. For this purpose, it shall above all consider whether the request for the advisory opinion relates to a legal question actually pending between two or more States.

3.   When an advisory opinion is requested upon a legal question actually pending between two or more states, Article 31 of the Statute shall apply, as also the provisions of these Rules concerning the application of that Article.

Article 103

When the body authorized by or in accordance with the Charter of the United Nations to request an advisory opinion informs the Court that its request necessitates an urgent answer, or the Court finds that an early answer would be desirable, the Court shall take all necessary steps to accelerate the procedure, and it shall convene as early as possible for the purpose of proceeding to a hearing and deliberation on the request.

Article 104

All requests for advisory opinions shall be transmitted to the Court by the Secretary-General of the United Nations or, as the case may be, the chief administrative officer of the body authorized to make the request. The documents referred to in Article 65, paragraph 2, of the Statute shall be transmitted to the Court at the same time as the request or as soon as possible thereafter, in the number of copies required by the Registry.

Article 105

1.   Written statements submitted to the Court shall be communicated by the Registrar to any states and organizations which have submitted such statements.

2.   The Court, or the President if the Court is not sitting, shall:

(a) determine the form in which, and the extent to which, comments permitted under Article 66, paragraph 4, of the Statute shall be received, and fix the time-limit for the submission of any such comments in writing;

(b) decide whether oral proceedings shall take place at which statements and comments may be submitted to the Court under the provisions of Article 66 of the Statute, and fix the date for the opening of such oral proceedings.

Article 106

The Court, or the president if the Court is not sitting, may decide that the written statements and annexed documents shall be made accessible to the public on or after the opening of the oral proceedings. If the request for advisory opinion relates to a legal question actually pending between two or more States, the views of those States shall first be ascertained.

Article 107

1.   When the Court has completed its deliberations and adopted its advisory opinion, the opinion shall be read at a public sitting of the Court.

2.   The advisory opinion shall contain:

the date on which it is delivered;

the names of the judges participating;

a summary of proceedings;

a statement of the facts;

the reasons in point of law;

the reply to the question put to the Court;

the number and names of the judges constituting the majority;

a statement as to the text of the opinion which is authoritative.

3.   Any judge may, if he so desires, attach his individual opinion to the advisory opinion of the Court, whether he dissents from the majority or not; a judge who wishes to record his concurrence or dissent without stating his reasons may do so in the form of a declaration.

Article 108

The Registrar shall inform the Secretary-General of the United Nations, and, where appropriate, the chief administrative officer of the body which requested the advisory opinion, as to the date and the hour fixed for the public sitting to be held for the reading of the opinion. He shall also inform the representatives of the Members of the United Nations and other States, specialized agencies and public international organizations immediately concerned.

Article 109

One copy of the advisory opinion, duly signed and sealed, shall be placed in the archives of the Court, another shall be sent to the Secretary-General of the United

Nations and, where appropriate, a third to the chief administrative officer of the body which requested the opinion of the Court. Copies shall be sent by the Registrar to the Members of the United Nations and to any other States, specialized agencies and public international organizations immediately concerned.

(Signed) E. JIMÉNEZ DE ARÉCHAGA,
President.

(Signed) S. AQUARONE,
Registrar.

9. STAFF REGULATIONS OF THE UNITED NATIONS[1]

CONTENTS

---

[1]United Nations Document: ST/SGB/Staff Regulations/Rev. 21/Amend. 1, New York, 1992.

Scope and purpose

The Staff Regulations embody the fundamental conditions of service and the basic rights, duties and obligations of the United Nations Secretariat. They represent the broad principles of personnel policy for the staffing and administration of the Secretariat. The Secretary-General, as the chief administrative officer, shall provide and enforce such staff rules consistent with these principles as he considers necessary.

Article I
Duties, obligations and privileges

Regulation 1.1: Members of the Secretariat are international civil servants. Their responsibilities are not national but exclusively international. By accepting appointment, they pledge themselves to discharge their functions and to regulate their conduct with the interests of the United Nations only in view.

Regulation 1.2: Staff members are subject to the authority of the Secretary-General and to assignment by him to any of the activities or offices of the United Nations. They are responsible to him in the exercise of their functions. The whole time of Staff members shall be at the disposal of the Secretary-General. The Secretary-General shall establish a normal working week.

Regulation 1.3: In the performance of their duties members of the Secretariat shall neither seek nor accept instructions from any Government or from any other authority external to the Organization.

Regulation 1.4: Members of the Secretariat shall conduct themselves at all times in a manner befitting their status as international civil servants. They shall not engage in any activity that is incompatible with the proper discharge of their duties with the united Nations. They shall avoid any action and in particular any kind of public pronouncement that may adversely reflect on their status, or on the integrity, independence and impartiality that are required by that status. While they are not expected to give up their national sentiments or their political and religious convictions, they shall at all times bear in mind the reserve and tact incumbent upon them by reason of their international status.

Regulation 1.5: Staff members shall exercise the utmost discretion in regard to all matters of official business. They shall not communicate to any person any information known to them by reason of their official position that has not been made public, except in the course of their duties or by authorization of the Secretary-General. Nor shall they at any time use such information to private advantage. These obligations do not cease upon separation from the Secretariat.

Regulation 1.6: No staff member shall accept any honor, decoration, favor, gift or remuneration from any Government excepting for war service; nor shall a staff member accept any honor, decoration, favor, gift or remuneration from any source external to the Organization without first obtaining the approval of the Secretary-General. Approval shall be granted only in exceptional cases and where such acceptance is not incompatible with the terms of staff regulation 1.2 and with the individual's status as an international civil servant.

Regulation 1.7: Staff members may exercise the right to vote but shall not engage in any political activity that is inconsistent with or might reflect upon the independence and impartiality required by their status as international civil servants.

Regulation 1.8: The immunities and privileges attached to the United Nations by virtue of Article 105 of the Charter are conferred in the interests of the Organization. These privileges and immunities furnish no excuse to the staff members who enjoy them for non-performance of their private obligations or failure to observe laws and police regulations. In any case where these privileges and immunities arise, the staff member shall immediately report to the Secretary-General, with whom alone it rests to decide whether they shall be waived.

Regulation 1.9: Members of the Secretariat shall subscribe to the following oath or declaration:

"I solemnly swear (undertake, affirm, promise) to exercise in all loyalty, discretion and conscience the functions entrusted to me as an international civil servant of the United Nations, to discharge these functions and regulate my conduct with the interests of the United Nations only in view, and not to seek or accept instructions in regard to the performance of my duties from any Government or other authority external to the Organization."

Regulation 1.10: The oath or declaration shall be made orally by the Secretary-General at a public meeting of the General Assembly. All other members of the Secretariat shall make the oath or declaration before the Secretary-General or his authorized representative.

Article II
Classification of posts and staff

Regulation 2.1: In conformity with principles laid down by the General Assembly, the Secretary-General shall make appropriate provision for the classification of posts and staff according to the nature of the duties and responsibilities required.

Article III
Salaries and related allowances

Regulation 3.1: Salaries of staff members shall be fixed by the Secretary-General in accordance with the provisions of annex I to the present Regulations.

Regulation 3.2: (a) The Secretary-General shall establish terms and conditions under which an education grant shall be available to a staff member serving outside his or her recognized home country whose dependent child is in full-time attendance at a school, university, or similar educational institution of a type that will, in the opinion of the Secretary-General, facilitate the child's reassimilation in the staff member's recognized home country. The grant shall be payable in respect of the child up to the end of the fourth year of post-secondary studies or the award of the first recognized degree, whichever is the earlier. The amount of the grant per scholastic year for each child shall be 75 percent of the first $11,000 of admissible educational expenses, up to a maximum grant of $8,250. Travel costs of the child may also be paid for an outward and return journey once in each scholastic year between the educational institution and the duty station, except that in the case of staff members serving at designated duty stations where schools do not exist that provide schooling in the language or in the cultural tradition desired by staff members for their children, such travel costs may be paid twice in the year in which the staff member is not entitled to home leave. Such travel shall be by a route approved by the Secretary-General but not in an amount exceeding the cost of such a journey between the home country and the duty station.

(b) The Secretary-General shall also establish the terms and conditions under which, at designated duty stations, an additional amount of 100 per cent of boarding costs up to $3,000 a year may be paid in respect of children in school attendance at the primary and secondary levels.

(c) The Secretary-General shall also establish terms and conditions under which an education grant shall be available to a staff member serving in a country whose language is different from his or her own and who is obliged to pay tuition for the teaching of the mother tongue to a dependent child attending a local school in which the instruction is given in a language other than his or her own.

(d)   The Secretary-General shall also establish terms and conditions under which and education grant shall be available to a staff member whose child is unable, by reason of physical or mental disability, to attend a normal educational institution and therefore requires special teaching or training to prepare him or her for full integration into society or, while attending a normal educational institution, requires special teaching or training to assist him or her in overcoming the disability. The amount of this grant per year for each disabled child shall be equal to 100 per cent of the educational expenses actually incurred, up to a maximum of $11,000.

(e)   The Secretary-General may decide in each case whether the education grant shall extend to adopted children or stepchildren.

Regulation 3.3:   (a) An assessment at the rates and under the conditions specified below shall be applied to the salaries and such other emoluments of staff members as are computed on the basis of salary, excluding post adjustments, provided that the Secretary-General may, where he deems it advisable, exempt from the assessment the salaries and emoluments of staff members engaged at locality rates;

(b)   (i)   The assessment shall be calculated at the following rates for staff members whose salary rates are set forth in paragraphs 1 and 3 of annex I to the present Regulations:

Assessment

(In percentages)

Total assessable payments (United States dollars)	Staff assessment rates for purposes of pensionable remuneration and pensions
First $15 000 per year	4
Next $10 000 per year	20
Next $10 000 per year	25
Next $20 000 per year	29
Next $20 000 per year	32
Next $20 000 per year	35
Next $30 000 per year	37
Remaining assessable payments	39

Total assessable payments (United States dollars)	Staff assessment rates used in conjunction with gross base salaries	
	Staff member with a dependent spouse or a dependent child	Staff member with neither a dependent spouse nor a dependent child
First $15 000 per year	13.0	17.3
Next $5 000 per year	31.0	34.3
Next $5 000 per year	34.0	38.5
Next $5 000 per year	37.0	41.8
Next $5 000 per year	39.0	43.8
Next $10 000 per year	41.0	45.9
Next $10 000 per year	43.0	48.1
Next $10 000 per year	45.0	50.4
Next $15 000 per year	46.0	51.0
Next $20 000 per year	47.0	52.6
Remaining assessable payments	48.0	57.0

(ii) The assessment shall be calculated at the following rates for staff members whose salary rates are established under paragraph 7 of annex I to the present Regulations:

(See table on the following page)

(iii)   The Secretary-General shall determine which of the scales of assessment set out in subparagraphs (i) and (ii) above shall apply to each of the groups of personnel whose salary rates are established under paragraph 6 of annex I to the present Regulations;

(iv)   In the case of staff members whose salary scales are established in currencies other than United States dollars, the relevant amounts to which the assessment applies shall be fixed at the local currency equivalent of the above-mentioned dollar amounts at the time the salary scales of the staff member concerned are approved;

Total assessable payments (United States dollars)	*Assessment* (percentage)
First $2 000 per year	15
Next $2 000 per year	18
Next $2 000 per year	20
Next $2 000 per year	21
Next $4 000 per year	22
Next $4 000 per year	23
Next $4 000 per year	24
Next $6 000 per year	25
Next $6 000 per year	25.5
Next $6 000 per year	26
Next $8 000 per year	26.5
Next $8 000 per year	27
Next $8 000 per year	27.5
Next $8 000 per year	28
Remaining assessable payments	29

(c) In the case of a person who is not employed by the United Nations for the whole of a calendar year or in cases where there is a change in the annual rate of payments made to a staff member, the rate of assessment shall be governed by the annual rate of each such payment made to him or her;

(d) The assessment computed under the foregoing provisions of the present regulation shall be collected by the United Nations by withholding it from payments. No part of the assessment so collected shall be refunded because of cessation of employment during the calendar year;

(e) Revenue derived from staff assessment not otherwise disposed of by specific resolution of the General Assembly shall be credited to the Tax Equalization Fund established by General Assembly resolution 973 A (X);

(f) Where a staff member is subject both to staff assessment under this plan and to national income taxation in respect of the salaries and emoluments paid to him or her by the United Nations, the Secretary-General is authorized to refund to him or her the amount of staff assessment collected from him or her provided that:

(i)   The amount of such refund shall in no case exceed the amount of his or her income taxes paid and payable in respect of his or her United Nations income;

(ii)   If the amount of such income taxes exceeds the amount of staff assessment, the Secretary-General may also pay to the staff member the amount of such excess;

(iii)   Payments made in accordance with the provisions of the present regulation shall be charged to the Tax Equalization Fund;

(iv)   A payment under the conditions prescribed in the three preceding subparagraphs is authorized in respect of dependency benefits and post adjustments, which are not subject to staff assessment but may be subject to national income taxation.

Regulation 3.4: (a) Staff members whose salary rates are set forth in paragraph 1 and 3 of annex I to the present Regulations shall be entitled to receive dependency allowances as follows:

(i)   At $1,050 a year for each dependent child, except that the allowance shall not be paid in respect of the first dependent child if the staff member has no dependent spouse, in which case the staff member shall be entitled to the dependency rate of staff assessment under subparagraph (b) (i) of regulation 3.3;

(ii)   At $2,100 for each disabled child. However, if the staff member has no dependent spouse and is entitled to the dependency rate of staff assessment under subparagraph (b) (i) of regulation 3.3 in respect of a disabled child, the allowance will be $1,050 for that child;

(iii)   Where there is no dependent spouse, a single annual allowance of $300 a year for either a dependent parent, a dependent brother or a dependent sister;

(b) If both husband and wife are staff members, one may claim, for dependent children, under subparagraph (a) (i) and (ii) above, in which case the other may claim only under subparagraph (a) (iii) above, if otherwise entitled;

(c) With a view to avoiding duplication of benefits and in order to achieve equality between staff members who receive dependency benefits under applicable laws in the form of governmental grants and staff members who do not receive such dependency benefits, the Secretary-General shall prescribe conditions under which the dependency allowance for a child specified in subparagraph (a) (i) above shall be payable only to the extent that the dependency benefits enjoyed by the staff member or his or her spouse under applicable laws amount to less than such a dependency allowance;

(d) Staff members whose salary rates are set by the Secretary-General under paragraph 6 or 7 of annex I to the present Regulations shall be entitled to receive dependency allowances at rates and under conditions determined by the Secretary-General, due regard being given to the circumstances in the locality in which the office is located;

(e) Claims for dependency allowances shall be submitted in writing and supported by evidence satisfactory to the Secretary-General. A separate claim for dependency allowance shall be made each year.

Article IV
Appointment and promotion

Regulation 4.1: As stated in Article 101 of the charter, the power of appointment of staff members rests with the Secretary-General. Upon appointment each staff member shall receive a letter of appointment in accordance with the provisions of annex II to the present Regulations and signed by the Secretary-General or by an official in the name of the Secretary-General.

Regulation 4.2: The paramount consideration in the appointment, transfer or promotion of the staff shall be the necessity for securing the highest standards of efficiency, competence and integrity. Due regard shall be paid to the importance of recruiting the staff on as wide a geographical basis as possible.

Regulation 4.3: In accordance with the principles of the Charter, selection of staff members shall be made without distinction as to race, sex or religion. So far as practicable, selection shall be made on a competitive basis.

Regulation 4.4: Subject to the provisions of Article 101, paragraph 3, of the Charter, and without prejudice to the recruitment of fresh talent at all levels, the fullest regard shall be had, in filling vacancies, to the requisite qualifications and experience of persons already in the service of the United Nations. This consideration shall also apply, on a reciprocal basis, to the specialized agencies brought into relationship with the United Nations.

Regulation 4.5: (a) Appointment of Under-Secretaries-General and of Assistant Secretaries-General shall normally be for a period of five years, subject to prolongation or renewal. Other staff members shall be granted either permanent or temporary appointments under such terms and conditions consistent with the present Regulations as the Secretary-General may prescribe;

(b) The Sectary-General shall prescribe which staff members are eligible for permanent appointments. The probationary period for granting or confirming a permanent appointment shall normally not exceed two years, provided that in individual cases the Secretary-General may extend the probationary period for not more than one additional year.

Regulation 4.6: The Secretary-General shall establish appropriate medical standards that staff members shall be required to meet before appointment.

Article V
Annual and special leave

Regulation 5.1: Staff members shall be allowed appropriate annual leave.

Regulation 5.2: Special leave may be authorized by the Secretary-General in exceptional cases.

Regulation 5.3: Eligible staff members shall be granted home leave once in every two years. However, in the case of service at designated duty stations having very difficult conditions of life and work, eligible staff members shall be granted home leave once in every twelve months. A staff member whose home country is the country of his her official duty station or who continues to reside in his or her home country while performing his or her official duties shall not be eligible for home leave.

Article VI
Social Security

Regulation 6.1: Provision shall be made for the participation of staff members in the United Nations Joint Staff Pension Fund in accordance with the regulations of that Fund.

Regulation 6.2: The Secretary-General shall establish a scheme of social security for the staff, including provisions for health protection, sick leave and maternity leave, and reasonable compensation in the event of illness, accident or death attributable to the performance of official duties on behalf of the United Nations.

Article VII

Travel and removal expenses

Regulation 7.1: Subject to conditions and definitions prescribed by the Secretary-General, the United Nations shall in appropriate cases pay the travel expenses of staff members, their spouses and dependent children.

Regulation 7.2: Subject to conditions and definitions prescribed by the Secretary-General, the United Nations shall pay removal costs for staff members.

Article VIII

Staff relations

Regulation 8.1: (a) The Secretary-General shall establish and maintain continuous contact and communication with the staff in order to ensure the effective participation of the staff in identifying, examining and resolving issues relating to staff welfare, including conditions of work, general conditions of life and other personnel policies;

(b) Staff representative bodies shall be established and shall be entitled to initiate proposals to the Secretary-General for the purpose set forth in subparagraph (a) above. They shall be organized in such way as to afford equitable representation to all staff members, by means of elections that shall take place at least biennially under electoral regulations drawn up by the respective staff representative body and agreed to by the Secretary-General;

(c) Cancelled.

Regulation 8.2: The Secretary-General shall establish joint staff/management machinery at both local and Secretariat-wide levels to advise him regarding personnel policies and general questions of staff welfare as provided in regulation 8.1.

Article IX

Separation from service

Regulation 9.1: (a) The Secretary-General may terminate the appointment of a staff member who holds a permanent appointment and whose probationary period has been completed, if the necessities of the service require abolition of the post or reduction of the staff, if the services of the individual concerned prove unsatisfactory, or if he or she is, for reasons of health, incapacitated for further service;

The Secretary-General may also, giving his reasons therefor, terminate the appointment of a staff member who holds a permanent appointment:

(i) If the conduct of the staff member indicates that the staff member does not meet the highest standards of integrity required by Article 101, paragraph 3, of the Charter;

(ii) If facts anterior to the appointment of the staff member and relevant to his suitability come to light that, if they had been known at the time of his appointment, should, under the standards established in the Charter, have precluded his appointment;

No termination under subparagraphs (i) and (ii) shall take place until the matter has been considered and reported on by a special advisory board appointed for that purpose by the Secretary-General;

Finally, the Secretary-General may terminate the appointment of a staff member who holds a permanent appointment if such action would be in the interest of the good administration of the Organization and in accordance with the standards of the Charter, provided that the action is not contested by the staff member concerned;

(b) The Secretary-General may terminate the appointment of a staff member with a fixed-term appointment prior to the expiration date for any of the reasons specified in subparagraph (a) above, or for such other reason as may be specified in the letter of appointment;

(c) In the case of all other staff members, including staff members serving a probationary period for a permanent appointment, the Secretary-General may at any time terminate the appointment if, in his opinion, such action would be in the interest of United Nations.

Regulation 9.2: Staff members may resign from the Secretariat upon giving the Secretary-General the notice required under the terms of their appointment.

Regulation 9.3: (a) If the Secretary-General terminates an appointment the staff member shall be given such notice and such indemnity payment as may be applicable under the Staff Regulations and Staff Rules. Payments of termination indemnity shall be made by the Secretary-General in accordance with the rates and conditions specified in annex III to the present Regulations;

(b) The Secretary-General may, where the circumstances warrant and he considers it justified, pay to a staff member terminated under the final paragraph of staff regulation 9.1 (a) a termination indemnity payment not more than 50 per cent higher than that which would otherwise be payable under the Staff Regulations.

Regulation 9.4: The Secretary-General shall establish a scheme for the payment of repatriation grants within the maximum rates and under the conditions specified in annex IV to the present Regulations.

Regulation 9.5: Staff members shall not be retained in active service beyond the age of sixty years or, if appointed on or after 1 January 1990, beyond the age of sixty-two years. The Secretary-General may, in the interest of the Organization, extend this age limit in exceptional cases.

Article X
Disciplinary measures

Regulation 10.1: The Secretary-General may establish administrative machinery with staff participation which will be available to advise him in disciplinary cases.

Regulation 10.2: The Secretary-General may impose disciplinary measures on staff members whose conduct is unsatisfactory.

He may summarily dismiss a member of the staff for serious misconduct.

Article XI
Appeals

Regulation 11.1: The Secretary-General shall establish administrative machinery with staff participation to advise him in case of any appeal by staff members against an administrative decision alleging the non-observance of their terms of appointment, including all pertinent regulations and rules, or against disciplinary action.

Regulation 11.2: The United Nations Administrative Tribunal shall, under conditions prescribed in its statute, hear and pass judgement upon applications from staff members alleging non-observance of their terms of appointment, including all pertinent regulations and rules.

Article XII
General provisions

Regulation 12.1: The present Regulations may be supplemented or amended by the General Assembly, without prejudice to the acquired rights of staff members.

Regulation 12.2: Such staff rules and amendments as the Secretary-General may make to implement the present Regulations shall be provisional until the requirements of the regulations 12.3 and 12.4 below have been met.

Regulation 12.3: The full text of provisional staff rules and amendments shall be reported annually to the General Assembly. Should the Assembly find that a provisional rule and/or amendment is inconsistent with the intent and purpose of the Regulations, it may direct that the rule and/or amendment be withdrawn or modified.

Regulation 12.4: The provisional rules and amendments reported by the Secretary-General, taking into account such modifications and/or deletions that may be directed by the General Assembly, shall enter into full force and effect on 1 January following the year in which the report is made to the Assembly.

Regulation 12.5: Staff rules shall not give rise to acquired rights within the meaning of regulation 12.1 while they are provisional.

Annex I
SALARY SCALES AND RELATED PROVISIONS

1. The Administrator of the United Nations Development Program, having the status equivalent to that of the executive head of a major specialized agency, shall receive a salary of $US 151,233 a year; the Director-General for Development and International Economic Cooperation shall receive a salary of $US 151,233 a year; an Under-Secretary-General shall receive a salary of $US 121,635 a year; and an Assistant Secretary-General shall receive a salary of $US 110,000 a year, subject to the Staff assessment plan provided in staff regulation 3.3 and to post adjustments wherever applied. If otherwise eligible, they shall receive the allowances that are available to staff members generally.

2. The Secretary-General is authorized, on the basis of appropriate justification and/or reporting to make additional payments to the Director-General for Development and International Economic Cooperation, to Under-Secretaries-General and to Assistant Secretaries-General to compensate for such special costs as may be reasonably incurred, in the interests of the Organization, in the performance of duties assigned to them by the Secretary-General. The maximum total amount of such payments is to be determined in the program budget by the General Assembly.

3. Except as provided in paragraph 6 of the present annex, the salary scales for staff members in the Director and Principal Officer category and in the Professional category shall be as shown in the present annex.

4. Subject to satisfactory service, salary increments within the levels set forth in paragraph 3 of the present annex shall be awarded annually, except that any increments to step XII of the Associate Officer level, steps XIV and XV of the Second Officer level, steps XIII, XIV and XV of the First Officer level, steps XI, XII and XIII of the Senior Officer level and above step IV of the Principal Officer level shall be preceded by two years at the previous step. The Secretary-General is authorized to reduce the interval between salary increments to ten months and twenty months, respectively, in the case of staff subject to geographical distribution who have an adequate and confirmed knowledge of a second official language of the United Nations.

5. The Secretary-General is authorized, on the basis of appropriate justification and/or reporting, to make additional payments to Directors and, where offices are away from Headquarters, to their heads, to compensate for such special costs as may be reasonably incurred in the interest of the Organization in the performance of duties assigned to them by the Secretary-General. The maximum total amount of such payments is to be determined in the program budget by the General Assembly.

6. The Secretary-General shall determine the salary rates to be paid to personnel specifically engaged for conferences and other short-term service, to consultants, to Field Service personnel, and to technical assistance experts.

7.   The Secretary-General shall fix the salary scales for staff members in   the General Service category and the salary or wage rates for manual workers, normally on the basis of the best prevailing conditions of employment in the locality of the United Nations office concerned, provided that the Secretary-General may, where he deems it appropriate, establish rules and salary limits for payment of a non-resident's allowance to General Service staff members recruited from outside the local area.

8.   The Secretary-General shall establish rules under which a language allowance may be paid to staff members in the General Service category who pass an appropriate test and demonstrate continued proficiency in the use of two or more official languages.

9.   In order to preserve equivalent standards of living at different offices, the Secretary-General may adjust the basic salaries set forth in paragraphs 1 and 3 of the present annex by the application of non-pensionable post adjustments based on relative costs of living, standards of living and related factors at the office concerned as compared to New York. Such post adjustments shall not be subject to staff assessment.

10. No salary shall be paid to staff members in respect of periods of unauthorized absence from work unless such absence was caused by reasons beyond their control or duly certified medical reasons.

SALARY SCALE FOR STAFF IN THE PROFESSIONAL AND HIGHER CATEGORIES*

Annual gross salaries and net equivalents after application of staff assessment

Effective 1 March 1992

(In United states dollars)

Level	I	II	III	IV	V	VI	VII	VIII	IX	X	XI	XII	XIII	XIV	XV
Under-Secretary-General															
USG Gross	137 508														
Net D	81 304														
Net S	73 003														
Assistant Secretary-General															
ASG Gross	124 560														
Net D	74 571														
Net S	67 436														
Director															
D-2 Gross	101 163	103 504	105 844	108 183	110 523	112 863									
Net D	62 405	63 622	64 839	66 055	67 272	68 489									
Net S	57 375	58 382	59 388	60 394	61 400	62 406									
Principal Officer															
D-1 Gross	89 026	90 992	92 958	94 923	96 889	98 855	100 837	102 840	104 842						
Net D	55 984	57 026	58 068	59 109	60 151	61 193	62 235	63 277	64 318						
Net S	51 673	52 605	53 537	54 469	55 400	56 332	57 235	58 096	58 957						
Senior Officer															
P-5 Gross	78 037	79 783	81 558	83 338	85 117	86 894	88 674	90 453	92 230	94 009	95 789	97 566	99 345		
Net D	50 140	51 083	52 026	52 969	53 912	54 854	55 797	56 740	57 682	58 625	59 568	60 510	61 453		
Net S	46 433	47 289	48 133	48 977	49 820	50 663	51 506	52 350	53 192	54 035	54 879	55 721	56 565		
First Officer															
P-4 Gross	63 635	65 313	67 015	68 717	70 420	72 122	73 824	75 528	77 230	78 931	80 645	82 383	84 117	85 851	87 587
Net D	42 349	43 269	44 188	45 107	46 027	46 946	47 865	48 785	49 704	50 623	51 542	52 463	53 382	54 301	55 221
Net S	39 368	40 198	41 032	41 866	42 701	43 535	44 369	45 204	46 038	46 871	47 701	48 525	49 346	50 168	50 991
Second Officer															
P-3 Gross	51 421	52 937	54 453	56 002	57 573	59 142	60 713	62 284	63 855	65 433	67 031	68 631	70 230	71 830	73 430
Net D	35 560	36 424	37 288	38 151	39 015	39 878	40 742	41 606	42 470	43 334	44 197	45 061	45 924	46 788	47 652
Net S	33 227	34 014	34 801	35 582	36 361	37 139	37 919	38 698	39 477	40 257	41 040	41 824	42 608	43 392	44 176
Associate Officer															
P-2 Gross	40 903	42 214	43 522	44 832	46 181	47 535	48 891	50 246	51 602	52 956	54 311	55 691			
Net D	29 483	30 256	31 028	31 801	32 573	33 345	34 118	34 890	35 663	36 435	37 207	37 980			
Net S	27 679	28 388	29 095	29 804	30 508	31 211	31 914	32 618	33 321	34 024	34 727	35 428			
Assistant Officer															
P-1 Gross	30 638	31 856	33 072	34 290	35 524	36 781	38 041	39 298	40 556	41 815					
Net D	23 339	24 082	24 824	25 567	26 309	27 051	27 794	28 536	29 278	30 021					
Net S	22 034	22 718	23 401	24 086	24 768	25 449	26 130	26 810	27 491	28 172					

STEPS

D = Rate applicable to staff members with a dependent spouse or child; S = Rate applicable to staff members with no dependent spouse or child.

* This scale represents the result of a consolidation of six multiplier points of post adjustment into net base salary. There will be consequential adjustments in the post adjustment indices and multipliers effective 1 March 1992. Thereafter changes in post adjustment classifications will be effected on the basis of the movements of the newly consolidated post adjustment indices.

Annex II

LETTERS OF APPOINTMENT

(a) The letter of appointment shall state:

(i)   That the appointment is subject to the provisions of the Staff Regulations and of the Staff Rules applicable to the category of appointment in question, and to changes that may be duly made in such regulations and rules from time to time;

(ii)   The nature of the appointment;

(iii)   The date at which the staff member is required to enter upon his or her duties;

(iv)   The period of appointment, the notice required to terminate it and period of probation, if any;

(v)   The category, level, commencing rate of salary and, if increments are allowable, the scale of increments, and the maximum attainable;

(vi)   Any special conditions that may be applicable.

(b) A copy of the Staff Regulations and the Staff Rules shall be transmitted to the staff member with the letter of appointment. In accepting appointment the staff member shall state that he or she has been made acquainted with and accepts the conditions laid down in the Staff Regulations and in the Staff Rules.

Annex III

TERMINATION INDEMNITY

Staff members whose appointments are terminated shall be paid an indemnity in accordance with the following provisions:

(a) Except as provided in paragraphs (b), (c) and (e) below and in regulation 9.3 (b), the termination indemnity shall be paid in accordance with the following schedule:

(See table on the following page)

(b) A staff member whose appointment is terminated for reasons of health shall receive an indemnity equal to the indemnity provided under paragraph (a) of the present annex reduced by the amount of any disability benefit that the staff member may receive under the Regulations of the United Nations Joint Staff Pension Fund for the number of months to which the indemnity rate corresponds;

(c) A staff member whose appointment is terminated for unsatisfactory services or who for disciplinary reasons is dismissed for misconduct other than by summary dismissal may be paid, at the discretion of the Secretary-General, an indemnity not exceeding one half of the indemnity provided under paragraph (a) of the present annex;

(d) No indemnity payments shall be made to:

A staff member who resigns, except where termination notice has been given and the termination date agreed upon;

A staff member who has a temporary appointment that is not for a fixed term and that is terminated during the first year of service;

A staff member who has a temporary appointment for a fixed term that is completed on the expiration date specified in the letter of appointment;

A staff member who is summarily dismissed;

A staff member who abandons his her post;

A staff member who is retired under the Regulations of the United Nations Joint Staff Pension Fund;

(e) Staff members specifically engaged for conference and other short-term service or for service with a mission as consultants or as experts, and staff members who are locally recruited for service in established offices away from Headquarters may be paid termination indemnity if and as provided in their letters of appointment.

Months of gross salary, less staff assessment, where
applicable a/ or

Months of pensionable remuneration less staff assessment,
where applicable b/

Completed years of service	Permanent appointments	Temporary appointments which are not for a fixed term	Temporary appointments for a fixed term exceeding six months
Less than 1	Not applicable	Nil)	One week for each month
1	Not applicable	1)	of uncompleted service
2	3	1)	subject to a minimum of
3	3	2)	six weeks' and a
4	4	3)	maximum of three months'
5	5	4)	indemnity pay
6	6	5	3
7	7	6	5
8	8	7	7
9	9	9	9
10	9.5	9.5	9.5
11	10	10	10
12	10.5	10.5	10.5
13	11	11	11
14	11.5	11.5	11.5
15 or more	12	12	12

a/ For staff in the Professional and higher categories and in the Field Service category.

b/ For staff in the General Service and related categories.

Annex IV
REPATRIATION GRANT

In principle, the repatriation grant shall be payable to staff members whom the Organization is obligated to repatriate. The repatriation grant shall not, however, be paid to a staff member who is summarily dismissed. Staff members shall be entitled to a repatriation grant only upon relocation outside the country of the duty station. Detailed conditions and definitions relating to eligibility and requisite evidence of relocation shall be determined by the Secretary-General. The amount of grant shall be proportional to the length of service with the United Nations, as follows:

(See table on the following page)

Years of continuous service away from home country	Staff member with a spouse or dependent child at time of separation	Staff member with neither a spouse nor dependent child at time of separation	
		Professional and higher categories	General Service category
	Weeks of gross salary, less staff assessment, where applicable a/ or Weeks of pensionable remuneration less staff assessment, where applicable b/		
1	4	3	2
2	8	5	4
3	10	6	5
4	12	7	6
5	14	8	7
6	16	9	8
7	18	10	9
8	20	11	10
9	22	13	11
10	24	14	12
11	26	15	13
12 or more	28	16	14

a/ For staff in the Professional and higher categories and in the Field Service category.

b/ For staff in the General Service and related categories.